The Dynamics
of
Mass Communication

THIRD EDITION

The Dynamics

of

Mass Communication

JOSEPH R. DOMINICK
University of Georgia, Athens

McGraw-Hill Publishing Company

New York   St. Louis   San Francisco   Auckland   Bogotá   Caracas   Hamburg
Lisbon   London   Madrid   Mexico   Milan   Montreal   New Delhi   Oklahoma City
Paris   San Juan   São Paulo   Singapore   Sydney   Tokyo   Toronto

The Dynamics of Mass Communication

Copyright © 1990, 1987 by McGraw-Hill, Inc. All rights reserved.
Printed in the United States of America. Except as permitted under the
United States Copyright Act of 1976, no part of this publication may be
reproduced or distributed in any form or by any means, or stored in a
data base or retrieval system, without the prior written permission of the
publisher.

234567890 VNH   VNH   943210

ISBN 0-07-017559-4

This book was set in Times Roman by Ruttle Shaw & Wetherill, Inc.
The editors were Hilary Jackson and Elaine Rosenberg;
the designer was Jack Ehn;
the production supervisor was Stacey B. Alexander.
Von Hoffmann Press, Inc., was printer and binder.

Library of Congress Cataloging-in-Publication Data

Dominick, Joseph R.
    The dynamics of mass communication / Joseph R. Dominick.—3rd
ed.
        p.   cm.
    Includes index.
    1. Mass media.   I. Title.
P90.D59   1990
302.23—dc20
                                            89-12564

Contents

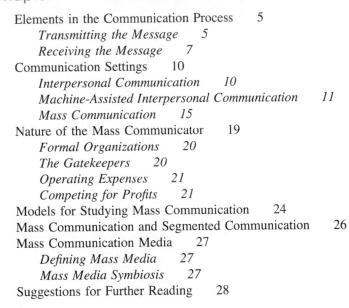

Chapter 18   Informal Controls: Ethics, Codes, Self-Regulations, and External Pressures   418

PART 6   MASS MEDIA AUDIENCES   447

Chapter 19   Audience Characteristics and Patterns of Use   448

Chapter 20   Mass Media Feedback Systems   471

PART 7   THE SOCIAL IMPACT OF MASS COMMUNICATION   501

Chapter 21   Effects of Mass Communication on Knowledge and Attitudes   502

Chapter 22   The Effects of Mass Communication on Behavior   529

PART 8   MASS COMMUNICATION AND THE FUTURE   557

Chapter 23   Mass Media in the Future: Progress Report on the Communication Revolution   558

Preface

In discussing textbooks, American Federation of Teachers president Albert Shanker wrote that too many of them are plagued by the "Rubicon factor." Somewhere, in some chapter, there's a line students dare not cross. Their eyes glaze over, their minds wander, and they read no further. In short, the textbook author has lost them. As Shanker notes, one easy way to solve this problem is to "dumb down the book": to sacrifice academic content for ease of reading. A better solution, says Shanker, is for authors to write books that are lively, interesting, and readable but still intellectually substantial and challenging.

As most authors will attest, Shanker's advice is not easy to follow. Nonetheless, the original objective of *Dynamics* was to produce a book with academic depth that students would not dread to pick up. This third edition continues to strive to achieve this goal.

To do this, I have emphasized, as in previous editions of this book, the growing interdependence and symbiosis that exist between and among the various media. The film and television industries are becoming increasingly difficult to separate. Radio and the recording business are closer than ever. Best-selling books become motion pictures; contemporary news events are turned into made-for-TV movies. Newspapers and magazines use similar production methods and audience research techniques. These and other interrelationships are important for beginning students to understand.

Second, this edition continues its predecessors' emphasis on mass media economics. Corporate mergers, media conglomerates, and growing foreign ownership of the American mass communication system all have great impact on what we see and hear. Never before in the seven years or so of this book's existence has the bottom line played such an important part in mass communication.

Third, the book continues to underscore the importance of the social effects of the media. Some introductory texts give the impression that the effects of the media are unknown or mainly matters of opinion. In fact, thanks to an increasing amount of research in the field, there is much that we do know. Consequently, the two chapters in the text devoted to this area are based on the latest empirical findings and try to present a consensus view on the major research topics. Given the continuing debate over the effects of the media on antisocial behavior, politics, and intellectual skills, this material is crucial for students.

This book also contains several features that I hope will make the book easier for teachers to use and for students to read. I have tried to keep the writing style informal and conversational. Technical terms appear in boldface type and are defined in the glossary. Every chapter contains a number of boxed readings that give examples and extended illustrations of points in the text. I have tried to make the descriptions of the various media industries as contemporary as possible. The book also contains numerous charts, tables, photographs, and other illustrations that explain and amplify the text.

Users of the second edition will note some improvements. The organization has been slightly modified. Many who adopted the book suggested that it would be easier to use if the appropriate history chapters were repositioned to precede the chapters on media structure and economics, and I am happy to report that this edition accommodates their wishes.

Further, significant new information has been added. Chapter 3, "International and Comparative Mass Media Systems," contains a discussion of global print and electronic media. Chapter 12, "Structure of the Motion Picture Industry," contains an expanded treatment of the home video industry and Chapter 13, "Structure of the Television Industry," includes more material on cable TV. Chapter 14, "News Gathering and Reporting," describes the significant impact that technology is having on TV news, and Chapter 16, "The Structure of the Advertising Industry," has a new section on business-to-business advertising, one of the fastest growing segments of the industry. Chapter 20, "Mass Media Feedback Systems," discusses the new Peoplemeter TV measurement device. Chapter 21, "Effects of Mass Communication on Knowledge and Attitudes," examines the impact of TV on cognitive skills. Finally, Chapter 22, "Effects of Mass Communication on Behavior," presents the latest conclusions drawn from research about the impact of TV violence on antisocial behavior.

In addition, every chapter has been updated and revised to reflect the tremendous changes that have occurred in the mass communication industries in the last three years. More than forty new boxed inserts have been added to this edition to illustrate the dynamic media environment. All tables have been updated to reflect the latest available data.

Finally, I wish to thank all of the faculty and students who have used the first two editions and were kind enough to provide me with suggestions for improvement. As noted in the text, feedback in mass communication is difficult and these comments were greatly appreciated.

All in all, I hope there are no Rubicons in this edition.

ACKNOWLEDGEMENTS

Once more I wish to thank all those people who helped make the first two editions successful. Several people in particular deserve special mention for their help with the third edition. Colleagues Barry Sherman, Don Davis, Jim Fletcher, Tom Russell, Len Reid, James Weaver, Bill Lee, and Dean Krugman were valuable sources of information. Terry Frye and Youyi Shi helpd me track down a good deal of arcane information.

I would also like to acknowledge the reviewers and questionnaire respondents who provided me with valuable guidance throughout the course of another revision: David G. Clark, Colorado State University; James Ellis, University of Nevada—Reno; A. Gibbons, Fashion Institute of Technology; J. Gula, University of Houston; Alan Hantz, University of North Carolina; Joseph Howland, University of Nevada—Reno; T. G. Kim, North Texas State University; Ed Kumbrell, Middle Tennessee State University; John Lee, Memphis State University; Larry Leslie, University of South Florida; Kate Matichek, Normandale Community College; Robert McGaughey III, Murray State University; Robert M. Ogles, Purdue University; Jerry Pinkham, College of Lake County; Mark Poindexter, Central Michigan University; Charles Rainey, Grossmont College; Rhoda Roth, Fashion Institute of Technology; Leonard Sellers, San Francisco State University; Robert O. Shipman, Mankato State University; Todd Simon, Michigan State University; William J. Stone, Jr., University of

Texas—Arlington; Gordon C. Whiting, Brigham Young University; Bonnie Wiley, University of Hawaii; K. Tim Wulfemeyer, San Diego State University; and Robert Wyatt, Middle Tennessee State University.

And of course I want to thank Kathleen Domenig, Peter Labella, Hilary Jackson, and the editorial staffs at Random House and McGraw-Hill for their sedulous (a word I learned from Peter) efforts.

Once again, since it's still appropriate, I'll close with a slightly revised final paragraph from the preface to the first edition: The mass media are an influential, ubiquitous, and vital force in our lives. Unfortunately, their inner workings and impact on both individuals and society as a whole are not well understood. It is my hope that this book has been and will continue to be a step in the direction of better understanding.

JOSEPH R. DOMINICK

The Dynamics
of
Mass Communication

Part One

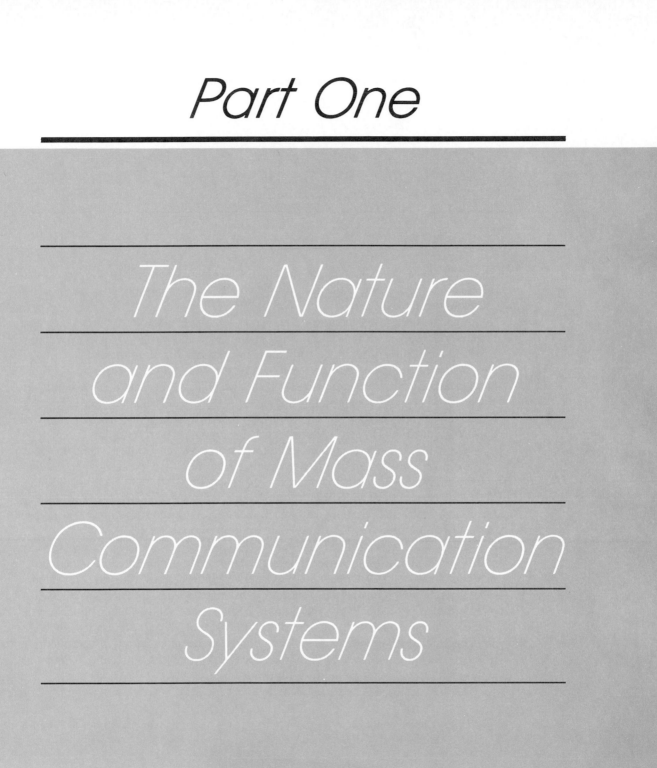

The Nature and Function of Mass Communication Systems

Chapter 1

Communication:
Mass and Other Forms

Human beings are constantly involved in the communication process—a process that is sometimes effective but that at other times leads to unexpected results, as the following examples illustrate.

At first, everybody thought it was Ernie's fault. Ernie was the nickname of a computer at the University of California at Berkeley and on the night of November 2, 1988, scientists all over the country were afraid Ernie had gone wacko.

It started around 10 P.M. Researchers at the Massachusetts Institute of Technology noticed that their computers were acting oddly. Programs that normally ran in the blink of an eye were taking minutes. Scientists at the Lawrence Livermore Laboratory (which designs nuclear weapons), NASA, Stanford University, and the University of Michigan also noticed that their computers were grinding to a halt. It didn't take experts long to figure out the problem: a virus was on the loose.

Computer viruses are tiny programs that jokesters—or vandals—enter in computers. Viruses take over the computer's operations and give their own instructions. They can be harmless and simply tie up computer space or malicious and destroy records and information. They can attach themselves to other programs and spread like a communicable disease through software or computer networks.

It was quickly determined that this particular virus was spreading via electronic mail through an unclassified research and defense computer network called Internet that linked about 50,000 machines. Once inside a machine, the virus repeatedly cloned itself and took up the computer's memory space. In addition, the virus detected other computers that could be reached and sent itself to them, thus starting an electronic chain reaction. On computer in Maryland logged 2000 failed infection attempts by the persistent bug. Ingeniously, in an apparent attempt to divert attention from its real origin, whenever the virus successfully infected a machine it immediately made contact with Ernie in California.

At 2:30 A.M. a researcher at Berkeley sent the following warning:

> We are currently under attack from an Internet virus. . . . The program appears as files that start with the letter x. Removing them is not enough, as they will come back in the next wave of attacks.

Computer experts all over the country worked feverishly to find an antidote. The first thing they did was to shut down the electronic mail system. This stopped the virus from spreading, but it also hampered communications. The researchers were so used to communicating by the computer network that they didn't have one another's phone numbers.

Twenty-four hours later the virus was contained and the crisis over. Investigators were relieved to find the virus was benign and no data were lost. Eventually the whole thing was traced to a twenty-three-year-old graduate student and computer whiz who apparently created the virus as an experiment, intending only for the virus to copy itself slowly and harmlessly across Internet. Unfortunately, the grad student, after a long and exhausting night of working on the program, hit a wrong key, causing the virus to spread far more rapidly than planned.

A computer industry association figured out how much it cost to clean up the virus. Total tab: $96 million. On the brighter side, Ernie was resolved of all blame.

During early November 1982, in Springfield, Illinois, listeners to WSSR, the student-run radio station at nearby Sangamon State University, were surprised to hear a loud civil-defense-like "Beep" and a message to stay tuned for an important announcement. An announcer breathlessly reported that a nuclear reactor in a power plant in Clinton, Illinois, about twenty-five miles away, had suffered a critical meltdown and that a large cloud of lethal radioactive material was drifting quickly toward Springfield. The news report ended and a disc jockey came on the air. "I don't really know what to do," said the DJ. "I guess I'll play a record."

At this point, the state's Emergency Services and Disaster Agency began receiving numerous phone calls from people asking if what they had heard on the radio was true—would a nuclear cloud wipe out Springfield? Somewhat perplexed and surprised, agency personnel called the plant at Clinton and determined that nothing unusual had occurred. There had been no accident.

The agency next called the radio station. It was a false alarm. The radio station was broadcasting a dramatic portrayal of what *might* happen if such a meltdown occurred. Some listeners had obviously tuned in late and had missed an opening announcement that the show was fictional. But, fearing that the show might cause a panic, the school's director of communications cut the program after only three minutes on the air. Despite this, the station continued to receive calls from frightened listeners for another hour. (For another famous false alarm, see Chapter 22.)

During the 1985 Christmas season, an 800 number was set up so that young children could call Santa Claus and tell him what they wanted for Christmas. Unfortunately, the phone lines got crossed and the little toddlers were connected to a Las Vegas bookie who dutifully informed them about the betting line on that Sunday's pro football games.

A Midwestern travel agency was besieged by calls from consumers asking about the new specialty tours mentioned in the agency's ad in the Yellow Pages. Bewildered, staffers at the agency checked their ad. A typographical error had changed "Specialists in Exotic Travel" to "Specialists in Erotic Travel."

In the summer of 1986, "ABC World News Tonight" introduced footage of what anchor Peter Jennings described as the damaged Soviet nuclear reactor at Chernobyl. In fact, ABC had been duped into buying footage of an old cement factory in Trieste, Italy. ABC admitted its error and apologized.

A Seattle newspaper published a "Dear Abby" column in which Diana, Princess of Wales, was referred to as the "Princess of Whales."

Thanks to a foul-up at the factory, a new compact disc package, labeled Lawrence Welk's "Polka Party" and issued by Welk Enterprises, accidentally contained the punk rock soundtrack from *Sid and Nancy*, the sordid movie biography of Sex Pistol Sid Vicious.

The Milwaukee branch of the National Association of Theater Owners was raffling off five autographed posters for the Chuck Norris film *Missing in Action III*. However, an ad for the promotion was garbled so the headline read "Register to Win a Toaster Autographed by Chuck Norris." Before the paper could correct the ad, thousands of people had entered. A representative of the theater association sheepishly called Norris and explained what had happened. Luckily, Norris was a good sport and sent back a pop-up toaster with his name engraved on the side. The winner of the raffle was a young woman who, as luck would have it, hadn't owned a toaster.

In 1984, the Coca-Cola Company introduced a new advertising campaign to promote a diet soft drink, Tab. The theme of the campaign was "Let's taste new Tab." TV spots, billboards, print ads, and radio commercials were duly prepared, all stressing the theme. Pretty soon, however, a problem developed. The print ads, billboards, and TV spots were doing fine but the radio spots seemed to be causing confusion. The radio spot consisted of people singing the theme with a music background. People who could only hear the commercial thought they said "*Less* taste, new Tab." They couldn't see the message spelled out. Embarrassed, the Coca-Cola Company pulled the ads from the air, at a considerable loss in money, and designed a new campaign.

February 20, 1971, was a fairly uneventful day. Had it not been for World War III, which apparently started early that morning, almost no one would remember it.

One of those who will not forget it is Flawn Williams. Working at Channel 44 in Chicago that morning, Williams was looking forward to an uneventful Saturday when the bell on the station's Associated Press wire machine began to clang. Williams walked over to the machine and discovered to his great surprise that World War III was beginning.

The keys on the machine were clattering out the following message:

> Message authenticator: hatefulness, hatefulness. This is an emergency action notification (EAN) directed by the President. Normal broadcasting will cease immediately. Stations will broadcast EAN Message One preceded by the attention signal per FCC rules.

An EAN was to be transmitted only in the case of a nuclear war, an invasion from outer space, or some other cataclysmic event. Obviously, something serious was happening. Somewhat incredulously, Williams hurried over to the master switcher, where a rather dusty EAN folder was posted, to get further instructions on exactly what "Message One" was. With shaking hands, he ripped open the envelope and looked quickly for the secret code word, the authenticator, which would verify the message. There in front of him in black and white was the following:

> Message authenticator: hatefulness

Evidently it was the real thing. But to add to the confusion, a quick spin around the dial disclosed that every other TV station in Chicago was broadcasting its usual Saturday morning schedule. Perhaps Channel 44 was the first to notice? And to further obscure an already muddy situation, the EAN envelope did not contain Message One.

Williams was in an unenviable position. Seemingly, the president himself had declared a national emergency and ordered all the stations in Chicago off the air, except for WGN (which was to broadcast emergency messages). The nation was in desperate straits, but nobody seemed to care. Williams decided to follow procedure as best he could. In just thirty seconds, the station went dark. Throughout the country, fewer than 10 percent of broadcast stations followed orders and did the same. The other 90 percent evidently decided the whole thing was a mistake and kept on broadcasting their usual cartoons and kiddie programs. Fortunately, they were right. An Air Force technician at the National Warning Center in Colorado had loaded the wrong tape into the communication network.

These seemingly unrelated examples illustrate different types of human communication. They range from the relatively simple—dialing a phone number—to the relatively complicated—publishing a newspaper. Despite their apparent lack of similarity, these illustrations share certain elements common to communication. A glance at these elements will serve as a starting point for our examination of the differences between mass and other forms of communication.

ELEMENTS IN THE COMMUNICATION PROCESS

At a general level, communication events involve the following:

1. a source

2. a process of encoding

3. a message

4. a channel

5. a process of decoding

6. a receiver

7. the potential for feedback

8. the chance of noise

Figure 1.1 on page 6 is a rough sketch of this process. We will refer back to this figure as we examine the process more fully.

Transmitting the Message

To begin with, the **source** initiates the process by having a thought or an idea that he or she wishes to transmit to some other entity. Naturally, sources differ in their communication skills ("Garçon . . . I will have du Boeuf Haché Grillé au Charbon de Bois" versus "Gimmeahamburger"). The source may or may not have knowledge about the receiver of the message. If you are in a conversation with your roommate, you probably know there are some topics that might send him or her up the wall. So you avoid bringing them up (most of the time). Conversely, as I write these lines

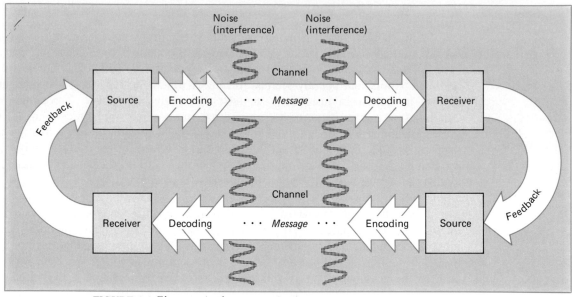

FIGURE 1.1 *Elements in the communication process.*

I have only a general notion about the kind of people who will read them, and I have absolutely no idea of what you'll be doing while you're reading them (that's probably for the best). Sources can be single individuals, groups, or even organizations. For example, in the illustration dealing with Chernobyl, ABC was the source. In the EAN example, the source is harder to pin down. At first glance, it appears that the machine was the source of the errant message. Upon closer examination, however, it turns out that the machine was operated by a human being, so perhaps that person is the ultimate source.

Encoding refers to the activities that a source goes through to translate thoughts and ideas into a form that may be perceived by the senses. When you have something to say, your brain and your tongue work together (usually) to form words and spoken sentences. When you write a letter, your brain and your fingers cooperate to produce patterns of ink or some other substance on paper that can be seen. If you were trying to communicate with someone who has impaired vision, you might produce a series of pinholes in a piece of paper that can be experienced by touch. If you were a Hollywood director, you would point your camera at a scene that recreates the image you had in your mind, and you would capture light rays with photosensitive chemicals. Encoding in a communication setting can take place one or more times. In a face-to-face conversation, the speaker encodes thoughts into words. Over the telephone, this phase is repeated, but the mechanism in the phone subsequently takes sound waves and encodes them into electrical energy. Some people are better encoders than others; in like manner, some machines are better encoders than others as well. Music recorded on a $40,000 audio console in a sound studio will probably sound better than that recorded on a pocket cassette recorder.

The **message** is the actual physical product that the source encodes. When we talk, our speech is the message. When we write a letter home, what we put on the paper is the message. When a television network presents ''The Cosby Show'' or ''Roseanne,'' the programs are the message. Human beings usually have a large number of messages at their disposal from which they can choose to send, ranging from the simple but effective "No!" to something as complicated as Darwin's *On the Origin of Species*. Messages can be directed at one specific individual ("You turkey!") or at millions (*People* magazine). Messages can be cheap to produce (the spoken word) or very expensive (this book). Some messages are more under the control of the receiver than others. For example, think about how hard or easy it is for you to break off communication in (1) a face-to-face conversation with another person, (2) a telephone call, and (3) a TV commercial.

Channels refer to the ways in which the message travels to the receiver. Sound waves carry spoken words; light waves carry visual messages. Air currents can also serve as an olfactory channel carrying messages to our noses—messages that are subtle but nonetheless significant. What kind of message do you get from someone who reeks of Chanel No. 5? Of Brut? Of garlic? Touch is also a channel (e.g., braille). Some messages use more than one channel to travel to the receiver. Radio signals travel by electromagnetic radiation until they are transformed by receiving sets into sound waves that travel through the air to our ears. A rock song starts out using sound waves and is then transformed into patterns of ferrous oxide particles that are sealed in a plastic tape. A cassette player then transforms these patterns back into sound waves that use the air as their channel.

Receiving the Message

The **decoding** process is the opposite of the encoding process. It consists of activities that translate or interpret physical messages into a form that has eventual meaning for a receiver. As you read these lines, you are decoding a message. If you are playing the radio while you are reading these lines, you are decoding two messages simultaneously—one aural, one visual. If you are listening to a friend while you are playing the radio while you are reading this, you are probably doing too much. Both humans and machines can be thought of as decoders. The radio is a decoder; so is a videotape playback unit; so is the telephone (one end encodes and the other end decodes); so is a film projector. A single communication event can involve many stages of decoding. A reporter sits in on a city council meeting and takes notes (decoding); he or she phones in a story to the rewrite desk where another reporter types the story as it is read (decoding). The story is read by an editor (decoding). Eventually it is printed and read by the audience (decoding). What we said earlier about encoding also applies to decoding: Some people are better at it than others. Many of you will not be able to decode "¿Dónde está el baño?"; others will. Some people are able to read 1500 words a minute; other struggle along at 200. There are some messages that may never be decoded because the encoder put the message in the wrong channel. A letter will have no meaning if the receiver lacks the ability to read. A telephone call may not be decoded by someone with impaired hearing.

The **receiver** is the target of the message—its ultimate goal. The receiver can be a single person, a group, an institution, or even a large, anonymous collection of people. In today's environment, people are more often the receivers of communication messages than the sources. Most of us see more billboards than we put up and listen to more radio programs than we broadcast. In addition, most college students receive more mail than they send—thanks in part to subscription offers from magazines and special deals from insurance agents. The receivers of the message can be determined by the source, as in a telephone call, or they can self-select themselves into the audience, as would be the case with the audience for a TV show. It should also be clear that in some situations the source and receiver can be in each

Music in My Bones

Light waves, sound waves, electromagnetic waves . . . these are some of the more common channels through which messages travel. But these are not the only channels, as illustrated by a 1979 invention—the BoneFone.

Here are some excerpts taken from the ad copy for this invention:

> You're standing in an open field. Suddenly there's music from all directions. Your bones resonate as if you're listening to beautiful stereo music in front of a powerful home stereo system. . . .
>
> The BoneFone is . . . an AM/FM stereo . . .

radio with its speakers located near your ears. . . .

The sound will also resonate through your bones—all the way to the sensitive bones of your inner ear.

The BoneFone looks like a scarf that is worn around your neck. One of its advantages is that you are the only one who can hear the radio; no one else knows what you listening to. It would appear that the BoneFone could easily be adapted to receive television signals, in which case the expression ''TV gets under my skin'' would have a whole new meaning.

other's immediate presence while in other situations they can be separated by both space and time.

Now let us examine the bottom half of Fig. 1.1. This portion of the figure represents the potential for **feedback** to occur. Feedback refers to those responses of the receiver that shape and alter the subsequent messages of the source. Feedback represents a reversal of the flow of communication. The original source becomes the receiver; the original receiver becomes the new source. Feedback is useful to the source because it allows the source to answer the question, ''How am I doing?'' Feedback is important to the receiver because it allows the receiver to attempt to change some element in the communication process. Communication scholars have traditionally identified two different kinds of feedback—positive and negative. In general terms, positive feedback from the receiver usually encourages the communication behavior in progress; negative feedback usually attempts to change the communication or even to terminate it.

Consider the following telephone call:

''Bambi?''

''Yes.''

''This is Harold. I sit in front of you in econ class.''

''Are you the one who keeps scratching your head with a pencil?''

''. . . Gee, I never noticed it. I guess I do it unconsciously. Say, I was wondering if you would like to have coffee with me sometime after class?''

''Are you kidding?''

Click.

Negative feedback. The original receiver terminated the message. Another conversation:

"Bambi, this is Rod."

"Oh hi Rod. Has your leg healed up from the last game yet?"

"Yeh."

"How are your classes going?"

"I can't get econ."

"I'll be over in 20 minutes to give you some help. OK?"

"OK."

Click.

Positive feedback. The original receiver encouraged the communication.

Feedback can be immediate or delayed. Immediate feedback occurs when the reactions of the receiver are directly perceived by the source. A speechmaker who hears the audience boo and hiss while he or she is talking is getting immediate feedback. On the other hand, if after reading this chapter you decide it was the silliest thing you've ever read, it would take a while for you to communicate that evaluation to me. You would first have to double-check my name, find an address or a phone number, and write or call. By the time your letter or call got to me, at least several hours, more probably several days, would have passed.

The receiver of a message in mass communication is an audience, like this group of fans at a rock concert. The audience provides feedback, which then reverses the flow of communication, sending a message back to the original source. Positive feedback—the cheering portrayed in this photo, for example—encourages the original sender, in this case the musicians. (Martin Benjamin/The Image Works)

The last factor we will consider is **noise**. Communication scholars define noise as anything that interferes with the delivery of the message. A little noise might pass unnoticed, while too much noise might prevent the message from reaching its destination in the first place. There are at least three different types of noise: semantic, mechanical, and environmental.

Semantic noise occurs when different people have different meanings for different words and phrases. If you ask a New Yorker for a ''soda'' and expect to receive something that has ice cream in it, you'll be disappointed. The New Yorker will give you a bottle of what is called ''pop'' in the Midwest. A leading national shoe company premiered this slogan in 1987: ''We'll only sell you the right shoe.'' Semantic noise again. A colleague reported that on the first day of his class he asked his students to sit in alphabetical order because then, as he put it, ''I'll be able to get to know you by looking at your seats.'' More semantic noise.

Noise can also be mechanical. This type of noise occurs when there is a problem with a machine that is being used to assist communication. A TV set with a broken focus knob, a pen running out of ink, a static-filled radio, atypewriterwithabrokenspacebar are all examples of mechanical noise. In addition, problems that are caused by people encoding messages to machines can also be thought of as a type of mechanical noise. Thus the typographical errors in the Princess Diana and travel agency examples and the technician feeding the wrong tape into the communication network at the National Warning Center are examples of mechanical noise.

A third form of noise can be called environmental. This type refers to sources of noise that are external to the communication process but that nonetheless interfere with it. Some environmental noise might be out of the communicator's control; a noisy restaurant, for example, where the communicator is trying to hold a conversation. Some environmental noise might be introduced by the source or the receiver; for example, you might try to talk to somebody who keeps drumming his or her fingers on the table. A reporter not getting a story right because of a noisy room is an example of someone subjected to environmental noise.

As noise increases, message fidelity (how closely the message that is sent resembles the message that is received) goes down. As noise is eliminated, message fidelity goes up. Clearly, feedback is important in reducing the effects of noise. The greater the potential for immediate feedback—that is, the more interplay between source and receiver—the greater the chance that semantic noise will be overcome (''What do you mean by 'the right shoe'?''), that mechanical noise will be corrected (''Is Norris really going to autograph a toaster?''), and that environmental noise will be brought under control (''Turn down that stereo. I'm trying to talk.'').

COMMUNICATION SETTINGS

Interpersonal Communication

Having looked at the key elements in the communication process, we next examine three common communication settings or situations and explore how these elements vary from setting to setting. The first and perhaps the most common setting is called **interpersonal communication**. In this situation, one person (or group) is interacting with another person (or group) without the aid of a mechanical device. The source and receiver in this form of communication are within one another's physical presence. Talking to your roommate, participating in a class discussion, and conversing with your professor after class are all examples of interpersonal communication. The

Stumbling Across The Language Barrier

Semantic noise is bad enough in a person's own language, but imagine some of the problems that crop up when messages are translated into a foreign tongue.

During President Jimmy Carter's visit to Poland, the English sentence "I have a deep affection for the Polish people" was somehow translated into Polish as "I lust after the Polish people."

When Chevrolet introduced its Nova model to South America it was puzzled by sluggish sales. Someone then pointed out that "no va" was Spanish for "it doesn't go."

In 1987, Braniff introduced a Spanish-language advertising campaign touting its new comfy leather airline seats. Braniff used the headline "Sentado en cuero," thinking it meant "seats of leather." Unknown to Braniff, the words "Sentado en cuero" constituted a slang phrase translated by most Hispanics as "sit naked"—not exactly what Braniff had intended.

source in this communication setting can be one or more individuals, as can the receiver. Encoding is usually a one-step process as the source transforms thoughts into speech and/or gestures. A variety of channels are available for use. The receiver can see, hear, and perhaps even smell and touch the source. Messages are relatively difficult for the receiver to terminate and are produced at little expense. In addition, interpersonal messages can be private (a letter to your probation officer) or public (a proclamation that the end of the world is near from a person standing on a street corner). Messages can also be pinpointed to their specific targets. For example, you might ask the following of your English professor: "Excuse me, Dr. Iamb, but I was wondering if you had finished perusing my term paper?" The very same message directed at your roommate might be put another way: "Hey Space Cadet! Aren't you done with my paper yet?" Decoding is also a one-step process performed by those receivers who can perceive the message. Feedback is immediate and makes use of visual and auditory channels. Noise can be either semantic or environmental. Interpersonal communication is far from simple, but in this classification it represents the least complicated situation.

Machine-Assisted Interpersonal Communication

Machine-assisted interpersonal communication combines characteristics of both the interpersonal and mass communication situations. In this setting, one or more people are communicating by means of a mechanical device (or devices) with one or more receivers. The source and receiver may or may not be in each other's immediate physical presence. In fact, one of the important characteristics of machine-assisted interpersonal communication is that it allows the source and receiver to be separated by both time and space. The machine can give a message permanence by storing it on paper, magnetic tape, or some other material. The machine can also extend the range of the message by amplifying it and/or transmitting it over large distances. Without a microphone, one person can talk only to those who can hear the unaided human voice; with a public address system, assembled thousands can

This conversation conveys the essence of interpersonal communication: an often informal, face-to-face situation in which verbal and nonverbal communication take place. (Richard Wood/The Picture Cube)

hear. The telephone allows two people to converse even though they are hundreds, even thousands of miles apart (Richard Nixon placed a person-to-person call to the Apollo 11 astronauts while they were on the moon). A pen and a piece of paper, which make up what we might consider a very simple machine, allow us to send a message over great distances and across time. A letter can be reread several years after it was written and communicate anew.

There are certain examples of machine-assisted interpersonal communication that closely resemble mass communication; at the same time, there are other examples that are quite similar to normal interpersonal communication. A tremendous variety of human communication falls into this category. This fact should become clear as we examine briefly how each of the eight major elements of communication functions in the machine-assisted interpersonal situation.

The source in the machine-assisted situation is easy to identify in some instances, harder in others. The person on the other end of the telephone, the person who wrote the letter, the person behind the microphone—all of these are fairly clear examples. But consider the following situations.

1. Banks now have an automated ''teller,'' which (who?) allows a customer to make withdrawals and deposits and to conduct other transactions by inserting a magnetically striped card and then punching an access code and a few buttons on a machine.

2. In Las Vegas, computerized slot machines flash the following electronic message to gamblers as they pull the handles: ''Too bad. Better luck next time.''

3. There are machines that play chess by displaying their moves electronically. Some even have a built-in voice, which (who?) talks to you while you play: "I was expecting that."

4. For those people who don't like to go to psychiatrists, there are computer programs available that do psychoanalysis.

5. In New York, people who feel guilty can call the Apology Line and hear a taped message of various people saying they're sorry. At the tone, the caller gets a chance to apologize for something he or she has done.

6. Dilk's Creative Tombstones, Inc., sells a solar-powered headstone with a video display screen so that a person can tape messages to loved ones left behind. (For a few dollars more, Dilk's will add such options as sensors to detect when visitors are present or when the flowers need watering and a mechanical arm to cut the grass.)

These examples show that some machine-assisted interpersonal transactions are very similar to mass communication transactions. In the preceding examples, the source of the message is actually a human being (or perhaps a group of humans) who programmed these devices in the first place. The machine serves as the channel that links an anonymous source with one or more anonymous receivers. It appears that with the coming of two-way cable TV, home computers, and teaching machines, machine-assisted communication might become more important. To sum up, the source in the machine-assisted setting can be a single person or persons. The source may or may not have firsthand knowledge of the receiver.

In machine-assisted communication, a machine links the source and receiver of a message; they are not in each other's physical presence. Here a French family uses a videophone to communicate with a friend. (Gilles Peress/Magnum)

Encoding can also take several forms in this setting. It might be as complicated as writing a computer program or as simple as speaking into a CB microphone. There are at least two separate stages of encoding in machine-assisted communication. The first involves the source translating his or her thoughts into words or other appropriate symbols, while the second occurs when the machine encodes the message for transmission or storage. Thus when you are typing a term paper, the first encoding stage occurs when you form your thoughts into words and sentences ("It will be the purpose of this paper to examine the pros and cons of fraternity and sorority membership in today's college world."). The second stage occurs as your fingers fly over the typewriter keys to produce a permanent message ("It will be the purpose of thispaper to examin the pros and cons of fraternity and sorrity membership in today's college world . . . "). As you can see, some noise might get into the message. In other forms of machine-assisted communication, there may be several stages (e.g., writing a computer program on paper, keying it in, debugging it, testing it, and loading the finished program into a teaching machine).

Channels are more restricted in machine-assisted communication. Whereas interpersonal communication can make use of several channels, machine-assisted settings generally restrict the message to one or two. The telephone relies on sound waves and electrical energy. CB radio does the same. A written document uses light rays to convey the message. A closed-circuit TV system makes use of light waves, electromagnetic energy, and sound waves. Furthermore, as is implied by the definition, machine-assisted interpersonal communication has at least one machine interposed between source and receiver.

Messages vary widely in machine-assisted communication. They can range from messages that can be altered and tailor-made for the receiver, as is the case with a telephone call, to a small number of predetermined messages that cannot be altered once they are encoded. An automatic bank teller, for example, can send no more than two dozen or so messages. If you accidentally got your necktie or scarf caught in the machinery, the machine could only print: "Ineligible transaction. Please contact customer service." Messages are relatively cheap to send in most forms of machine-assisted communication. A telephone call costs a small amount (unless you're talking to your sweetheart who happens to live in Brazil) and, of course, there is also the cost of installing the phone. Writing a letter is a fairly cheap way to send a message, even when the postage is included. On the other hand, using a computer-assisted instruction machine might be quite costly if you figured in the cost of the machine and the labor that went into programming. Talking over CB radio is fairly cheap once the necessary equipment is purchased. Showing home videos is a little more expensive. Using closed-circuit TV is quite costly.

Messages can be both private and public, depending on the circumstances. A letter, a phone call, a telegram are examples of private machine-assisted messages. A sound truck broadcasting an election-day message, a person handing out pamphlets, a poster nailed to a telephone pole are all examples of public messages. The ease with which the message can be terminated is also variable but, by and large, people need little effort to end communication. Throwing away the pamphlet, hanging up the phone, closing your window to avoid the sound truck are all accomplished with ease. Walking out on a speaker while he or she is at the microphone is a little harder, but the interposition of a machine between source and receiver tends to increase what we might call the psychological distance between these two elements. Consequently, the transaction can be terminated by the receiver much more easily than in interpersonal communication settings, where the source has a bit more control over the situation.

Decoding in machine-assisted communication can go through one or more stages, similar to the encoding process. Reading a letter requires a single phase of decoding. Hearing a hit song on the radio requires two phases: one for the machine to decode the electrical energy into sound waves and another for your ear to decode the sound waves into words or symbols that have meaning.

The receiver in the machine-assisted setting can be a single person or it can be a small or large group. The receivers can be in the physical presence of the source, as would be the case if you were attending a political convention and were listening to the amplified speeches of the people on the podium. Or the receivers can be out of physical view (as was the case with Nixon's call to the moon). The receivers can be selected by the source, as would be the case for a letter or a telephone call, or they can self-select themselves into the audience, as would happen if you took a pamphlet from a person on a street corner.

Feedback can be immediate or delayed. When the source and receiver are in close proximity, then feedback will be immediate. The speaker at a political convention will hear the applause immediately. If the source and receiver are separated by geography, then feedback may or may not be immediate. A telephone call is a situation in which feedback would be nearly instantaneous. Answering a letter, leaving a message with an automatic phone-answering device, and inserting your plastic card into an automated machine and having it disappear without a sound would be examples of situations in which feedback would be delayed, if it occurred at all. The person who plays back the tape on the automatic phone-answering machine may not want to call back, the letter might not be answered, and so on. The extent of possible feedback is dependent on the actual circumstances surrounding the machine-assisted setting. Although some circumstances allow for a great deal of feedback (the speaker at the political rally can see and hear the audience react), it is never as abundant as it is in the interpersonal setting. To return to our example of the somewhat long-winded speaker at the political rally (he or she has been talking for several pages now), in an interpersonal setting it might be possible for the speaker to seek out reactions from some or perhaps all of the audience. The speaker in front of an audience of thousands may not have that opportunity. In other situations, feedback is limited. In a telephone conversation feedback is limited to the audio channel. Feedback in the form of written communication is limited to the visual channel. In some situations, as we have mentioned before, feedback may be virtually impossible. When the Las Vegas slot machine smugly flashes ''Too bad,'' there is little the unlucky gambler can do to show the machine (or whoever programmed it) exactly what he or she thinks of that message, short of physical violence. If the automatic teller gives you a coded message that says ''Insufficient funds,'' you cannot tell it ''Well, I just made a deposit this morning. Look it up.''

Noise in machine-assisted communication can be semantic and environmental, as in interpersonal communication, but it can also be mechanical, since interference with the message might be due in part to difficulties with the machine involved.

Mass Communication

The third major communication setting is the one that we will be most interested in. Although the differences between machine-assisted communication and unaided interpersonal communication are fairly easily seen, the differences between machine-assisted interpersonal communication and mass communication are not that clear. A working definition of what we mean by **mass communication** may be appropriate at this point. Mass communication refers to the process by which a complex orga-

In mass communication, messages are intended to reach a large, heterogeneous, and often geographically scattered audience. The source of the message expends considerable time and effort to attract the receiver's attention, as this radio promotion demonstrates. Known in the radio industry as ''Birthday Bucks,'' this television ad offers money to encourage listeners to tune in the local radio station. This also illustrates the symbiosis between television and radio. (Film House, Inc.)

nization with the aid of one or more machines produces and transmits public messages that are directed at large, heterogeneous, and scattered audiences. This definition, while slightly cumbersome, will serve us adequately in most instances. There are, of course, situations that will fall into a gray area. How large does the audience have to be before we call it mass communication? How scattered? How heterogeneous? How complex must the organization be? The boundaries are a little blurry. For example, a billboard is constructed on a busy street in a small town. Obviously, this would qualify as machine-assisted communication (a machine was used to print the billboard), but is this example better defined as mass communication? An automatic letter-writing device can write thousands of similar letters. Is this mass communication? There are no ''correct'' answers to these questions. The dividing line between what we have labeled machine-assisted interpersonal communication and mass communication is not a distinct one. The degree of ''massness'' involved in any particular situation should be viewed as a continuum where one setting shades into another. True, there are some clear examples at both extremes, but the middle contains a large gray area. Perhaps if we examine our eight communication elements as they occur in settings that should obviously be labeled mass communication, our definition will become clearer.

The source in the mass communication situation is a group of individuals who usually act within predetermined roles in an organizational setting. That sentence is a rather complicated observation of a simple fact: Mass communication is the end product of more than one person. Think about how a newspaper is put together. Reporters gather news; writers draft editorials; a cartoonist may draw an editorial cartoon; the advertising department lays out ads; editors paste all of these things together on a sample page; technicians transfer this page to a master, which is taken to a press where other technicians produce the final paper; the finished copies are given to the delivery staff who distribute them; and, of course, behind all of this is a publisher who has the money to pay for a building, presses, staff, trucks, paper, ink, and so on. As you can see, this particular newspaper is not the product of a single individual but of an organization. This institutional nature of mass communication has several consequences that we will consider later in this book.

Mass communication sources have little detailed information about their particular audience. They may have collective data, but these will be expressed as gross audience characteristics. The newspaper editor, for example, may know that 40 percent of the readers are between twenty-five and forty years old and that 30 percent earn between $20,000 and $50,000, but the editor has no idea about the individual tastes, preferences, quirks, or individual identities of these people. They are an anonymous group, known only by summary statistics.

Encoding in mass communication is always a multistage process. A film producer has an idea. He or she explains it to a screenwriter. The writer goes off and produces a script. The script goes to a director, who translates it for the camera. Cinematographers capture the scenes on film. The raw film goes to an editor, who splices together the final version. The film is copied and sent to motion picture theaters, where a projector displays it on the screen, where the audience watches it. How many examples of encoding can you find in that oversimplified version of movie-making?

Mass communication channels are characterized by the imposition of at least one and usually more than one machine in the process of sending the message. These machines translate the message from one channel to another. Television makes use of complicated devices that transform light energy into electrical energy and back again. Radio does the same with sound energy. Unlike interpersonal communication, in which many channels are available, mass communication is usually restricted to one or two.

Messages in mass communication are public. Anyone who can afford the cost of a newspaper or a tape deck or a TV set (or who can borrow them from a friend) can receive the message. Additionally, the same message is sent to all receivers. In a sense, mass communication is addressed "to whom it may concern." These messages are also expensive. A typical half-hour TV show might cost $600,000 or more; a film might run into the tens of millions. Of all the various settings, message termination is easiest in mass communication. The TV set goes dark at the flick of a switch, an automatic timer can turn off the radio, the newspaper is quickly put aside, and so forth. There is little the source can do to prevent these sudden terminations, other than bullying the audience ("Don't touch that dial!") or trying to stay interesting at all times ("We'll be back after these important messages.").

Mass communication typically involves multiple decoding before the message is received. The tape deck decodes patterns of magnetic particles into sound waves for our hearing mechanism. The TV receiver decodes both sight and sound transmissions.

One of the prime distinguishing characteristics of mass communication is the audience. In the first place, the mass communication audience is a large one, sometimes numbering in the millions of people. Second, the audience is also heterogeneous; that is, it is made up of several dissimilar groups who may differ in age, intelligence, political beliefs, ethnic backgrounds, and so on. Even in situations where the mass communication audience is somewhat well defined, heterogeneity is still present. (For example, consider the publication *Turkey Grower's Monthly*. At first glance, the audience for this publication might appear to be pretty much the same, but upon closer examination we might discover that it differs in intelligence, social class, income, age, political party, education, place of residence, and so on. The only thing we know that the audience has in common is an interest in growing turkeys.) Third, the audience is spread out over a wide geographic area; source and receiver are not in each other's immediate physical presence. The large size of the audience and its geographic separation both contribute to a fourth distinguishing factor: The audience is anonymous to one another. The person watching the "CBS Evening News" is unaware of the several million others who might also be in the audience. Lastly, in keeping with the idea of a public message, the audience in mass communication is self-defined. The receiver chooses what film to see, what paper to read, and what program to watch. In the interpersonal and machine-assisted settings, sources may search you out and select you as the receiver of the message ("Hey you! What's in that bag?"), but in mass communication, the receiver is the key to the process. If the receiver chooses not to attend to the message, the message is not received. Consequently, the various mass communication sources spend a great deal of time and effort to get your attention so that you will include yourself in the audience.

Feedback is another area where mass communication contrasts greatly with interpersonal communication. The message flow in mass communication is generally in one direction only, from source to receiver, and feedback is minimal. In fact, in many mass communication settings, feedback between receiver and source is quite difficult to achieve. If, for example, you were offended by the content of a TV program, you might call the station immediately after viewing. If you got through, you would probably be instructed to call back during business hours when the manager was in. The next day, assuming you got in touch with the manager, he or she might refer you to the network, since what you saw was probably a network show. If you chose to call the network (a long-distance call for most people), you might be connected to a receptionist, who might graciously suggest that if you put your complaint in writing, "someone will get back to you." Eventually, someone probably will respond with a form letter. This hypothetical example illustrates the difficulty in achieving feedback and the fact that feedback is typically delayed. It might be hours or even days before the source of the message is aware of the receiver's response. The delayed nature of feedback in mass communication is further pronounced because, as we shall see in a later chapter, much of it is indirect and travel through a third party before it returns to the source.

Finally, noise in the mass communication setting can be semantic, environmental, or mechanical. In fact, since there may be more than one machine involved in the process, mechanical noise can be compounded (watching a scratchy copy of an old film on a snowy TV set).

As a review, Fig. 1.2 summarizes some of the differences among the three communication settings that we have talked about.

ELEMENT		SETTING		
		Interpersonal	Machine–assisted interpersonal	Mass
	Source	Single person; has knowledge of receiver	Single person or group; great deal of knowledge or no knowledge of receiver	Organizations; little knowledge of receivers
	Encoding	Single stage	Single or multiple stage	Multiple stages
	Message	Private or public; cheap; hard to terminate; altered to fit receivers	Private or public; low to moderate expense; relatively easy to terminate; can be altered to fit receivers in some situations	Public; expensive; easily terminated; same message to everybody
	Channel	Potential for many; no machines interposed	Restricted to one or two; at least one machine interposed	Restricted to one or two; usually more than one machine interposed
	Decoding	Single stage	Single or multiple stage	Multiple stages
	Receiver	One or a relatively small number; in physical presence of source; selected by source	One person or a small or large group; within or outside of physical presence of source; selected by source or self-defined	Large numbers; out of physical presence of source; self-selected
	Feedback	Plentiful; immediate	Somewhat limited; immediate or delayed	Highly limited; delayed
	Noise	Semantic; environmental	Semantic; environmental; mechanical	Semantic; environmental; mechanical

FIGURE 1.2 *Differences in communication settings.*

NATURE OF THE MASS COMMUNICATOR

Since a large portion of this book will examine the institutions that are in the business of mass communication, it will be to our advantage to consider some common characteristics that typify "mass communicators." We will list them first and then elaborate.

1. Mass communication is produced by complex and formal organizations.

2. Mass communication organizations have multiple gatekeepers.

3. Mass communication organizations need a great deal of money to operate.

4. Mass communication organizations exist to make a profit.

5. Mass communication organizations are highly competitive.

Formal Organizations

Publishing a newspaper or operating a TV station requires control of money, management of personnel, coordination of activities, and application of authority. To accomplish all of these tasks, a well-defined organizational structure characterized by specialization, division of labor, and focused areas of responsibility is necessary. Consequently, this means that mass communication will be the product of a bureaucracy. As in most bureaucracies, decision making will take place at several different levels of management, and channels of communication within the organization will be formalized. Thus many of the decisions about what gets included in a newspaper or in a TV program will be the result of committee or group decisions. Further, this means that decisions will have to be made by several different individuals in ascending levels of the bureaucracy and that communication will follow predetermined and predictable patterns within the organization. On occasion, this leads to communication problems and misunderstandings (see the ''Heidi'' example in the accompanying boxed material). On other occasions, decisions will be made that have to satisfy various individuals at several different levels of the bureaucracy, and this results in end products that seldom resemble the original idea of the creator. For example, TV writer Merle Miller describes one such experience in his book *Only You Dick Daring or How to Write One Television Script and Make $50,000,000*. Miller's idea for a TV show about a Peace Corps worker had to be approved by the vice president of the production company, the vice president of CBS Program Development, the vice president of CBS Programming, the president of CBS, the producer, the director, and the research department. When everything had settled, the show was about a county agent working in the Southwest, and Miller, totally frustrated, quit the project.

The Gatekeepers

Another important factor that characterizes the mass communicator is the presence of multiple **gatekeepers.** A gatekeeper is any person (or group) who has control over what material eventually reaches the public. Gatekeepers exist in large numbers in all mass communication organizations. Some are more obvious than others, for example, the editor of a newspaper or the news director at a TV station. Some gatekeepers are less visible. To illustrate, let's imagine that you have the world's greatest idea for a TV series, an idea that will make ''M*A*S*H'' and ''The Cosby Show'' look like mediocre successes. You write the script, check possible production companies, and mail it off to Universal Studios in California. A clerk in the mailroom judges by the envelope that it is a script and sees by the return address that it has come from an amateur writer. The clerk has been instructed to return all such packages unopened with a note saying that Universal does not consider unsolicited material. Gate closed.

Frustrated, you decide to go to Los Angeles in person and hand deliver your work. You rush in from the airport to the office of Universal's vice president in charge of production, where a receptionist politely tells you that Universal never looks at scripts that were not submitted through an agent. Gate closed. You rush out to a phone booth and start calling agents. Fourteen secretaries tell you that their agencies are not accepting new writers. Fourteen closed gates. Finally, you find an agent who will see you (gate open!). You rush to the agent's office where he or she glances through your script and says "No thanks" (gate closed). By now the point is probably clear. Many people serve as gatekeepers. In our hypothetical example, even if an agent agreed to represent you, the agent would then have to sell your script to a producer who, in turn, might have to sell it to a production company which, in turn, might have to sell it to a network. There are many gates to pass through, and you can begin to appreciate some of Merle Miller's frustration.

In the newsroom, an assignment editor decides whether to send a reporter to cover a certain event. The reporter then decides if anything about the event is worth reporting. An editor may subsequently shorten the story, if submitted, or delete it altogether. Obviously, gatekeepers abound in mass communication. The more complex the organization, the more gatekeepers will be found.

Operating Expenses

It costs a large sum of money to start a mass communication organization and to keep it running. Recently, the *Houston Chronicle* was sold for more than $400 million. A dozen magazines formerly owned by CBS were sold to a French company for about $700 million. *U.S. News and World Report* brought $167 million. In Los Angeles an FM station was sold for nearly $80 million and a TV station was bought for $510 million.

Once the organization is in operation, expenses are also sizable. In the late 1980s, it cost approximately $4 million annually to run a small daily (one with a circulation of about 35,000 to 40,000). A radio station in a medium-sized urban market might spend $700,000 annually in operating expenses. A TV station in the top ten markets might need more than $10 million to keep it going. These economic facts mean that only those organizations that have the money necessary to institute and maintain these levels of support are able to enter into the production of mass communication.

Media economics have contributed to another trend that made itself evident at the end of the decade: consolidation of ownership. Companies that have strong financial resources are the likeliest to survive high operating expenses and are better able to compete in the marketplace. Consequently, by 1989 a number of global media giants had emerged that dominated the field. The biggest of these companies is Time Warner Inc., formed in 1989 by the merger of Time, Inc. with Warner Communications. If approved, this company would generate annual revenues of more than $10 billion. Table 1.1, p. 24, lists other "mega-media" companies. Note that the names listed in the table will frequently turn up in succeeding chapters.

Competing for Profits

Since we are talking about money, we should also note that most mass communication organizations exist to make a profit. Although there may be some exceptions to this generalization (the public broadcasting system, for example), most newspapers, magazines, record companies, TV and radio stations in the United States strive to

The Jets and the Raiders vs. Heidi

Mass communication organizations are complex bureaucracies with formal lines of communication and distinct layers of authority. Occasionally, this complexity causes problems, such as the one that occurred on Sunday evening, November 17, 1968.

Pregame

The National Broadcasting Company (NBC) was televising the Oakland Raiders–New York Jets pro football game from California. The game was crucial in determining who made the playoffs.

The Lineups

1. Julian Goodman, President of NBC.

2. Carl Lindemann, Vice President, NBC Sports.

3. Scotty Connal, Manager of NBC Sports Programs.

4. Don Ellis, Producer for NBC Sports in Oakland.

5. An assistant director at NBC studios in Burbank, California.

6. The head engineer at NBC Broadcast Operations Control in New York.

The Situation

It was the policy of NBC Sports to broadcast all sports events to their conclusion, but Broadcast Operations Control had to get approval from Julian Goodman to run overtime. At 7 P.M. this particular evening, NBC had scheduled "Heidi," a high-priced TV version of the classic story about the little Swiss girl and her grandfather. At 6:40 P.M., Scotty Connal was watching the game in his Connecticut home. Don Ellis was watching the game on his monitor in the NBC remote truck in Oakland. The Jets were ahead 32–29.

The Play by Play

6:41 P.M.   Lindemann phoned Connal and told him it looked as if the game wouldn't be finished by 7 P.M. Lindemann said he would call NBC president Goodman to get permission to run over.

6:55 P.M.   Lindemann phoned Connal and told him that Goodman said the game must stay on until it was over. The beginning of "Heidi" would be delayed.

6:56 P.M.   Connal called NBC Operations Control in New York. He could not reach them. (It turned out that hundreds of parents had tied up the NBC switchboard to ask whether the network would show "Heidi" or keep televising that dumb football game.) Connal momentarily panicked.

6:57 P.M.   Connal remembered that the NBC studios in Burbank had a direct open line to NBC in New York. He decided to call Don Ellis in the truck in Oakland. Ellis could pass the message to Burbank, which, in turn, could pass it on to New York.

6:58 P.M.   Connal told Ellis: "Don, call NBC in Burbank. Tell them to tell New York that Julian Goodman says to continue with the game until conclusion."

Ellis told Burbank: "Call NBC in New York and tell

them Goodman says to stay with the game."

An anonymous assistant director in Burbank told the head engineer at Broadcast Operations Control in New York: "The guys in the truck at Oakland say we should keep the game on the air."

6:59 P.M.   The head engineer in New York, unused to this irregular channel of communication, decided that he wasn't going to take orders from the guys in the truck at Oakland. There were still fifty seconds left to play and the Jets were still leading 32–29 as the image of Oakland stadium faded into shots of the Swiss Alps on TV screens all over America.

7:00 P.M.   Don Ellis in Oakland sat dumbfounded as New York took the game off the air. Scotty Connal shouted helplessly at his TV set.

7:01 P.M.   Don Ellis on the phone to Scotty Connal: "Scotty," gasped Ellis, "Oakland just scored!"

Postgame

The Oakland Raiders scored fourteen points in those final fifty seconds after the game went off the air to beat the Jets 43–32. The switchboard at NBC in New York was so deluged with calls from enraged fans that the entire CIrcle 7 telephone exchange in Manhattan broke down. Heidi, however, lived happily ever after.

Postgame Postscript

The ghost of Heidi is alive and well at NBC. In November of 1984, during a broadcast of "The Skins Game," a high-stakes golf match, NBC infuriated golf fans all over the country by cutting away from pro golfer Jack Nicklaus' attempt to win $240,000 by making a single putt. The network preempted Jack's putt and went instead to the beginning of a professional football pregame show, leaving golf fans in the dark. Somewhere, Heidi was smiling.

produce a profit for their owners and stockholders. Although it is true that radio and television stations are licensed to serve in the public interest and that newspapers commonly assume a "watchdog" role on behalf of their readers, if they do not make money, they go out of business. The consumer is the ultimate source of this profit. When you buy an album or a movie ticket, part of the price includes the profit. Newspapers, TV, magazines, and radio earn most of their profits by selling their audiences to advertisers. The cost of advertising, in turn, is passed on by the manufacturers to the consumer. Thus, although the process may be direct or indirect, the audience eventually pays the bills. The economics of mass communication is an important topic, and we will have more to say about it later in this book.

Since the audience is the source of profits, mass communication organizations compete with one another as they attempt to attract an audience. This should come as no surprise to anyone who has ever watched television or passed a magazine stand. The major TV networks compete with one another to get high ratings. Millions of dollars are spent each year in promoting the new fall season. Radio stations compete with other stations that have similar formats. Some even give away prizes for listening; others play more music. Record companies spend large sums promoting their records, hoping to outsell their competitors. Designing album covers has

TABLE 1.1 Global Media Giants

COMPANY (HOME COUNTRY)	1988 REVENUE (IN BILLIONS)
Time Warner Inc. (USA)	$10.0
Bertelsmann A. G. (W. Germany)	6.6
Fininvest (Italy)	6.4
Paramount Communications, Inc.	5.1
Capital Cities/ABC (USA)	4.8
Thomson Corp. (Canada)	4.7
News Corporation (Australia)	4.4
Hachette S.A. (France)	3.5
Walt Disney Co. (USA)	3.4
MCA Inc. (USA)	3.0

become a new art form. Daily newspapers compete with weeklies and radio and television. *Time* competes with *Newsweek*. Motion picture companies gamble millions on films in an effort to compete successfully. This fierce competition has several consequences, and this will be a topic that we will return to time and again.

MODELS FOR STUDYING MASS COMMUNICATION

Figure 1.1 outlined the elements present in the general process of communication. When we want to talk about mass communication, however, we need to construct a new model that adequately represents its distinctive features. But first a word about models. At a basic level models try to show the main elements of any structure or process and the relationship between these main elements. Models are helpful for several reasons:

1. They help us *organize* by ordering and relating various elements and concepts to one another.

2. They help us *explain* things by illustrating in simplified form information that might otherwise be complicated or ambiguous.

3. They help us *predict* outcomes or the end processes of events.

At the same time, there are some risks in using models. Inevitabily, models are incomplete and oversimplified. There is no single model that is appropriate for all purposes and situations. Models are aids to help us understand the mass communication process. We need to be careful to choose the proper model for the purpose we have in mind.

Now let's examine a model that seems useful in our study of the dynamics of communication. This is the Westley–MacLean model and is presented in Fig. 1.3. At first glance the model seems complicated, but closer examination shows that it is straightforward.

Let's begin our discussion by starting at the left side and working to the right. The X's in the model (X_1, X_2, X_3) stand for events or objects in the social environ-

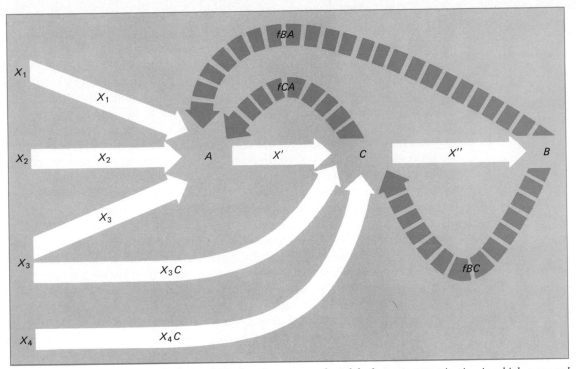

FIGURE 1.3 *Westley and MacLean's conceptual model of mass communication in which a second type of communicator, C (channel role), is introduced. (From Westley and MacLean, "A Conceptual Model for Mass Communication Research,"* Journalism Quarterly, *34: 31–38, 1957. Reprinted by permission of* Journalism Quarterly.*)*

ment. They may be election results, earthquakes, a new album by Bruce Springsteen, baseball scores, or another Rocky movie. The *A* in the model refers to *advocates*. These are individuals or organizations that have something to say about the *X*'s to the general public. The *A*'s might be politicians ("Vote for me"), public relations agencies ("We'd like to tell you what our company is doing to clean up pollution"), advertisers ("Buy our jeans"), news sources ("I'm announcing my resignation"), or special-interest groups ("We must save the sparrows"). In short, they are purposive communicators.

The *C* in the model stands for the channel. More precisely, the *C* stands for the individual or individuals within a media organization who select from the messages offered by the *A*'s those that they (the *C*'s) think are of interest to the audience ("We'd better cover the resignation, but let's ignore the save the sparrows people"). Also note that the *C*'s can select directly from the *X*'s in the environment and communicate information about them to the audience as well ("The earthquake is our lead story"). The *C*'s are seen as neutral; they are nonpurposive communicators. Turning back to the model, *X'* represents a message coming from *A* that is selected by the media organization to be communicated to the audience (for example, a resignation speech). X_3C represents the observation of an event made directly by the media without the intervention of an *A* (for example, a reporter covering a traffic accident). The *X''* represents the message as modified by the media organization for transmission. The resignation speech, for example, might have lasted fifteen minutes, but the evening TV news might contain only a ninety-second summary.

The B in the model stands for a behavioral role, an individual or group or even a social system. In other words, the B's are the audience, people like you and me, at whom the messages from media organizations are aimed. The arrows going from right to left in the model represent the channels of feedback. For example, fBC is the feedback from audience member to the communication organization, either by way of direct contact, such as a letter to the editor, or indirectly, through audience research. The notation fBA represents the feedback from a member of the audience (B) to the original source (A). For example, this might be a vote for a candidate or the purchase (or nonpurchase) of some product. The feedback from communicator to advocate is fCA. This might take the form of additional coverage in the future or other attempts to somehow change or modify A's purposive communications.

In addition, the model helps us predict certain things about the process. For example, let's say that the unemployment rate in a certain state has fallen dramatically in the last six months (an example of X, an event in the environment), and a local politican (an A role) holds a news conference to take credit for it. The news conference is covered by the local TV news crew (a C role) and from a thirty-minute press conference (X') a sixty-second story (X'') is carried on the evening news. The model suggests that the news story (X'') may be significantly different from the original event (X) and the interpretation offered by the politician (X'). The news story might point out that the drop in unemployment is really just a statistical quirk or that the politician had little to do with the decline. In short, the model alerts us to the fact that messages will be altered as they pass through the various communication stages.

This model is useful in drawing our attention to several distinctive features of mass communication:

1. the several stages at which selection (gatekeeping) takes place

2. the self-regulating nature of the system since a large number of C roles compete for B's

3. the importance of feedback in the total process

Of course, the model is not perfect. One of the things it does not portray is the relationship of the communicators and audience members to society. A and C are influenced by the political and economic climate as well as their own organizational arrangements. Audience members (B) are also part of the larger social environment. They belong to families, have friends, classmates, or co-workers, belong to political parties, and are part of the social fabric. In sum, the impact of social processes should not be overlooked.

The remainder of this book can be organized according to the Westley–MacLean model. Parts Two and Three concentrate on the C roles in the model. Part Four includes a look at the A's, as exemplified by advertising and public relations, and the X's, as seen in news gathering and reporting. Part Five looks at the social implications of the media as illustrated by controls, rules, and regulations. Parts Six and Seven look at the audience, the B roles, and the various feedback channels used by the audience.

MASS COMMUNICATION AND SEGMENTED COMMUNICATION

In the 1930s, a top-rated network radio show might attract about 40 percent of all the people in the United States. Today, the top-rated network radio show gets about

2 or 3 percent of the audience. In the 1950s, the top-rated TV shows would attract about 45 percent of all the TV households in the country. This figure dropped to 33 percent in the 1960s and to 31 percent in the 1970s. Currently, the top-rated shows get about 26–28 percent of the audience (with the exception of ''The Cosby Show''). The three TV networks' share of the audience was above 90 percent in the 1960s. Now, thanks to competition from cable, VCRs, and independent stations, the three nets get around 70 percent. In the 1940s and 1950s, general-interest magazines such as *Life*, *Look*, and *Collier's* were popular. All of these have ceased publication. (*Life* has since reappeared in a different format.) In 1960, about 75 percent of the adult population read a newspaper. In 1988, that figure was down to about 55 percent. What we are seeing is the ''fractionalization'' of the mass communication audience. Some scholars have asked if the term ''mass communication'' is as descriptive as it was forty or fifty years ago. The mass audiences of today are relatively smaller (at least in terms of percentage of audience reached) than they were in the past. Perhaps a better name might be ''segmented communication'' since each particular medium seems to be concentrating on attracting a well-defined portion of the mass audience. The only time a mass audience, in its broadest sense, is now assembled is for a special event on TV, such as the Olympics, the ''M*A*S*H'' farewell episode, or for ''The Winds of War.'' In any case, the size of the audience for any particular media vehicle seems to be declining in the wake of increased availability of choices. As will be discussed more in Chapter 19, this trend should be kept in mind when we talk about the concept of mass communication.

MASS COMMUNICATION MEDIA

Defining Mass Media

In the broadest sense of the word, a medium is the channel through which a message travels from the source to the receiver (''medium'' is singular; ''media'' is plural). Thus in our discussion, we have pointed to sound and light waves as media of communication. When we talk about mass communication, we also need channels to carry the message. We will refer to these channels as the **mass media**. Our definition of a mass medium will include not only the mechanical devices that transmit and sometimes store the message (TV cameras, radio microphones, printing presses), but also the institutions that use these machines to transmit messages. When we talk about the mass media of television, radio, newspapers, magazines, sound recording, and film, we will be referring to the people, the policies, the organizations, and the technology that go into producing mass communication.

In this book we will examine seven different mass media: radio, television, film, book publishing, sound recording, newspapers, and magazines. Of course, these seven are not the only mass media that exist. If we choose, we might also include billboards, comic books, posters, direct mail, matchbooks, and buttons in our discussion. To do that, however, would require a volume much larger than this. In an effort to conserve space (and to make the book easier to carry), we will limit ourselves to the seven we have mentioned. These seven tend to be the ones that have the largest audiences, employ the most people, and have the greatest impact. They are also the ones with which most of us are familiar.

Mass Media Symbiosis

If we can borrow a term from biology, we can easily see that the mass media have evolved a system of **symbiotic relationships**. In biology, symbiosis is defined as

Media symbiosis: A film about TV. In Broadcast News, *William Hurt plays a glamorous anchorman for a television network.* (Sygma)

the association of two organisms for mutual benefit. To draw an analogy, in mass media, the television and film industries demonstrate what we might call a form of symbiosis. The same companies produce works for both media; films that originally played in the theaters find their way to television in videocassettes, over cable, and over network and local stations. Film actors and actresses make TV shows and vice versa; executives from one industry sometime cross over into the other. The sound recording and radio industries demonstrate another symbiotic relationship. Most radio stations depend on recordings to fill their air time; most records need air play to sell. MTV demonstrates a three-way symbiosis: Record companies use it as a promotional tool; MTV uses videos supplied by the record companies as their programming source, and radio stations use MTV as a sounding board for new releases. Similar relationships exist between newspapers and magazines. Most Sunday editions carry a magazine insert; the same writers contribute to both media and both employ the same audience measurement and marketing techniques. Some intermedia relationships have crossed traditional boundaries. Many local newspapers also operate a local cable TV channel. Best-selling books are made into theatrical and TV movies, while movie scripts are transformed into books. There are TV shows that review films. *USA Today*, the newspaper, spawned *USA Today*, the syndicated TV show. The Macmillan Publishing Company recently released ''The Macmillan Video Almanac for Kids,'' an example of a video book. Although the following chapters discuss the various media individually, it should be kept in mind that they do not exist in a vacuum. In the future, we are likely to see more examples of the synergy that exists among all communication media.

SUGGESTIONS FOR FURTHER READING

The books listed below are good sources to consult for further information about the concepts discussed in this chapter.

BERLO, DAVID K., *The Process of Communication*, New York: Holt, Rinehart and Winston, 1960.

DEFLEUR, MELVIN, AND SANDRA BALL-ROKEACH, *Theories of Mass Communication,* New York: David McKay, 1975.

GUMPERT, GARY, *Talking, Tombstones and Other Tales of the Media Age*, New York: Oxford University Press, 1987.

HARMS, L.S., *Human Communication: The New Fundamentals*, New York: Harper & Row, 1974.

LEDERMAN, LINDA COSTIGAN, *New Dimensions: An Introduction to Human Communication,* Dubuque, Iowa: William C. Brown, 1977.

McQUAIL, DENIS, AND SVEN WINDAHL, *Communication Models,* New York: Longman, 1981.

MEYROWITZ, JOSHUA, *No Sense of Place,* New York: Oxford University Press, 1985.

SCHRAMM, WILBUR, *Men, Women, Messages, and Media,* New York: Harper & Row, 1982.

Chapter 2

Uses and Functions of Mass Communication

There are several methods that we can use to describe the relationship among media, society, and individuals. We might, for example, look at the persuasive aspect of mass communication or the sociological environment of the media. (For more information on these approaches, see the books by Tan and McQuail listed at the end of this chapter.) Of the many that we might discuss, the **functional approach** seems the most advantageous. Specifically, this technique:

- provides us with a perspective from which to examine mass communication

- generates concepts that are helpful in understanding media behavior

- makes us aware of the diversity of gratifications provided by the media.

In its simplest form, the functional approach holds that something is best understood by examining how it is used. In mass communication, this means examining the use that audiences make of their interactions with the media.

By way of introduction, below are some more or less typical responses that were given by college students to the following questions:

1. Why do you watch TV?
   "I like to vegetate sometimes."
   "I like to watch when there's nothing else to do."

2. Why do you go to movies?
   "I enjoy going to the theater with someone I like. I also enjoy the buttered popcorn."
   "I like to go to movies because they afford an opportunity to lose two hours in someone else's life."

3. Why do you listen to records and tapes?
   "I listen because music can make a room more comfortable."
   "I like music and it takes my mind off what I'm doing (work, driving, etc.)."

4. Why do you watch TV soap operas?
   "I watch them because I like to see just how bizarre they can get in terms of smut."
   "I watch them because I feel as if I know the characters personally and as if I'm actually involved in their lives."

Responses like these have led to several generalizations about the functions that media have for a society and for its individual members. This chapter will focus on cataloguing and describing those functions.

THE ROLE OF MASS COMMUNICATION

Maybe the best way to appreciate the role that mass communication plays in our society would be to imagine what it would be like if, all of a sudden, the whole system never existed. How would we find out what was on sale at the local supermarket? How would we know what songs were most popular? How would we know Cher's current love interest? (Would there *be* a Cher?) How could we find out what was happening in the Middle East? How would we find out the real story behind the resignation of a prominent cabinet member? How could we avoid the traffic jams during rush hour? How would we spend our evenings? Obviously, the mass media are a pervasive part of our life. Just how pervasive might become clear if we charted the various functions the media perform for us. Before we do this, however, we need to realize that different media have different primary uses. Not many people, for example, listen to records to find out the latest news. Even fewer people read the newspaper while driving their cars. Moreover, different groups of people make use of the same mass media content for different reasons. History professors, for example, might read articles in scholarly journals in order to keep up with their profession. Others who pursue history as a hobby might read the same journals in order to relax and be diverted from their normal routine.

One more qualification needs to be mentioned before we begin examining the functions and uses of mass communication. It is possible to conduct this analysis on at least two different levels. On the one hand, we could take the perspective of a sociologist and look through a wide-angle lens and consider the functions performed by the mass media for the entire society (this approach is sometimes called **macroanalysis**).

This viewpoint focuses on the apparent intention of the mass communicator and emphasizes the manifest purpose inherent in the media content. On the other hand, we could look through a close-up lens at the individual receivers of the content, the audience, and ask them to report how they use mass media (this approach is called **microanalysis**). Sometimes the end results of these two methods are similar in that the consumer uses the content in the way that the source intended. Sometimes they are not similar, and the consumer uses the media in a way not anticipated by the mass communicator. Let's begin our analysis by using the wide-angle lens.

FUNCTIONS OF MASS COMMUNICATION FOR SOCIETY

For a society to exist, certain communication needs must be met. These needs existed long before Gutenberg bolted together his printing press and Morse started sending dots and dashes. Primitive tribes had sentinels that scanned the environment and reported dangers. Councils of elders interpreted facts and made decisions. Tribal meetings were used to transmit these decisions to the rest of the group. Other members of the tribe may have been storytellers and jesters who functioned to entertain the group. As society became larger and more complex, these jobs grew too big to be handled by single individuals. With the advent of a technology that allowed the development of mass communication, these jobs were taken over by the mass media. This change was an important one, and throughout the following discussion we will examine the consequences of performing these communication functions by means of mass communication as opposed to interpersonal communication. Furthermore, there may be instances where these consequences are undesirable from the point of view of the welfare of the society. These harmful or negative consequences are called **dysfunctions.** We will mention some of these as well.

Lastly, these functions are not mutually exclusive. A given example might illustrate several different categories.

Surveillance

Of all the media functions, this one is probably the most obvious. **Surveillance** refers to what we popularly call the news and information role of the media. The media have taken the place of sentinels and lookouts. Correspondents for wire services, TV networks, and newspapers are located across the globe. These individuals gather information for us that we couldn't get for ourselves. Their reports are funneled back to mass media organizations that, in turn, produce a radio or TV newscast or print a paper or magazine. The size of this surveillance apparatus is impressive; in the 1980s, more than 90,000 people were employed in news-gathering jobs in radio, television, newspapers, news magazines, and wire services. Some 15,000 reporters covered the 1988 Democratic convention in Atlanta. The output is also substantial. The three national television networks provide approximately 600 hours of regularly scheduled news programs. In 1980, a cable news network was instituted that provided a twenty-four–hour news service to cable subscribers. Many radio stations, of course, have been broadcasting solid news for several years. News magazines reach nearly 10 million people. There are approximately 1650 daily newspapers and around 7500 weeklies that also spread the news. Surveillance is apparently an important function, and the degree of audience dependence on the media for news supports this observation. In any given day, approximately 50 million to 60 million Americans are exposed to mass-communicated news. About 90 percent of the American public report that they receive most of their news from either the electronic media or newspapers.

The surveillance function can be divided further into two main types. **Warning** or **beware surveillance** occurs when the media inform us about threats from hurricanes, erupting volcanoes, depressed economic conditions, increasing inflation, or military attack. These warnings can be about immediate threats (a television station interrupts programming to broadcast a tornado warning), or they can be about long-term or chronic threats (a newspaper series about air pollution or unemployment). There is, however, much information that is not particularly threatening to society that people might like to know about. The second type, called **instrumental surveillance,** has to do with the transmission of information that is useful and helpful in everyday life. News about what films are playing at the local theaters, stock market prices, new products, fashion ideas, recipes, teen fads, and so on, are examples of instrumental surveillance. Note also that not all examples of surveillance occur in what we traditionally label the news media. *People* magazine and *Reader's Digest* perform a surveillance function (most of it instrumental); so does *Modern Screen* ("Find Out Sting's New Love!!!!!"). Smaller, more specialized publications such as technical journals also perform the job of surveillance. In fact, the surveillance function can be found in content that is primarily meant to entertain. A soap opera might perform an instrumental surveillance function by portraying new hair styles and furniture arrangements.

What are some of the consequences of relying on the mass media to perform this surveillance function? In the first place, news travels much faster, especially since the advent of the electronic media. It took months for the news of the end of the War of 1812 to travel across the Atlantic. The famous Battle of New Orleans was actually fought after peace had been declared. It took weeks for news of Lincoln's assassination to spread to the rural Midwest. In contrast, when John

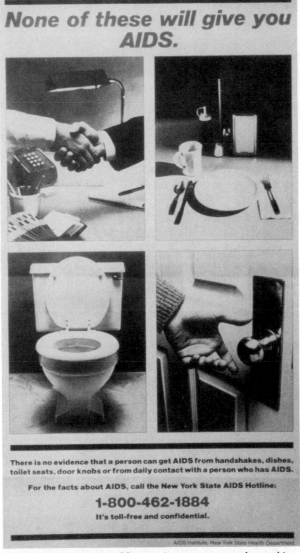

Beware function: *a public service message such as this AIDS poster warns the public not to believe unsubstantiated rumors but to get the facts about AIDS.* (*Doug Menuez/Picture Group*)

Kennedy was assassinated, 90 percent of the U.S. population knew about it within one hour. This speed sometimes leads to problems. Inaccuracies and distortions travel just as fast as truthful statements. In 1961, an airplane was hijacked en route to El Paso, Texas. The first wire service reports identified the hijackers as four Cuban supporters of Fidel Castro. Within minutes, this report was received on the wire service machines in the U.S. Congress. When the legislators heard the news, there was serious talk about instituting a blockade of Cuba and even some sentiment for a declaration of war. It later turned out that the "Cuban" hijackers were a used-car salesman from Arizona and his sixteen-year-old son. The first reports were inaccurate. During the 1980 Republican convention in Detroit, the anchorman for one TV network reported that former President Gerald Ford would be the vice-presidential nominee. The *Chicago Sun Times* carried a front-page banner headline: ''It's Reagan–Ford.'' These reports were somewhat premature.

The second consequence is a bit more subtle. In prehistoric times, if war broke out, it was fairly simple for people to find out about it. A stranger would appear at the mouth of a cave and belt the inhabitant with a club. There was little doubt about the validity of this information; it was directly observable. The world of early men and women was small and easily surveyed. All of it was within the range of their eyesight, and seldom did it extend over the next hill. Today, thanks to the mass media, there aren't any more hills. Our world now extends well beyond our eyesight, and we can no longer observe all of it directly. The media relay to us news from environments beyond our immediate senses that we cannot easily verify. Much of what we know about the world is machine-processed, hand-me-down information. News is prescreened for us by a complex arrangement of reporters and editors, and our conception of reality is based on this second-generation information, whose authenticity we do not usually question. For example, human beings have allegedly walked on the moon. Millions saw it—on TV. Not many saw it in person. Instead, we took the word of the TV networks that what we were seeing was fact, not fiction. The creative people in TV and movies, however, were perfectly capable of fabricating the whole event. In fact (interesting expression), many of the networks' simulations looked more convincing than the ''real thing.'' (Some people feel that television staged the whole thing somewhere in Arizona as part of a massive, government-inspired publicity stunt.) The point is this: In today's world, with its sophisticated system of mass communication, we are highly dependent on others for news. Much of this news is difficult to verify firsthand, so we must rely on what others tell us. Consequently, we have to put a certain amount of trust in the media that do our

Surveillance function: *as news and information providers, the mass media broad-cast the confirmation hearings of Senator John Tower for Secretary of Defense. The extensive media coverage kept the public informed of the issues surrounding Tower's nomination and his ultimate defeat. (UPI/Bettmann Newsphotos)*

Johnny Carson and the Great Toilet-Paper Dysfunction

Even entertainment programs can perform the surveillance function, sometimes with unforeseen results. For example, on December 19, 1973, the writers for NBC's "Tonight Show starring Johnny Carson" noticed a short newspaper item that quoted a Wisconsin congressman as saying that the federal government had fallen behind in getting bids from its toilet-paper suppliers. Immediately sensing the humor in such a situation, the writers put together a couple of gags for Carson's opening monologue. Later that night Johnny Carson jokingly informed his millions of viewers that the United States was facing an acute toilet-paper shortage.

Unfortunately, some people confused the "Tonight" show with the "NBC Nightly News," and when the supermarkets opened the next morning the rush was on. People didn't want to be caught empty-handed, and roll after roll was snatched from the shelves. Some people appeared at check out counters with as much as twenty dollars' worth of the stuff. In Flushing, New York, one woman bought a case of sixty-four rolls. The hoarding got so bad that some grocery stores started rationing toilet paper, four rolls to a customer. The paper companies that produce toilet tissue were caught off guard; they never anticipated such a run on their product. They geared up to meet the abnormal demand, but it would take time to get their shipments to the stores. Meanwhile, customers, in their eagerness to stockpile, had wiped out the supermarkets' supply. Other consumers, seeing the empty shelves, were convinced that Carson was right about the shortage and scrambled quickly to other stores.

Carson tried to stem the tide. He announced that he was only joking. The news item referred to the production of low-grade, government-issued paper. There was no shortage of the squeezably soft, high-grade consumer type. This helped a little, but since panic feeds on itself, it took another three weeks before the shelves were back to normal.

surveillance. This trust, called **credibility**, is an important factor in determining which news medium people find the most believable. We will discuss this concept at length in Chapter 14.

Media surveillance might also cause needless anxiety. In 1988, the media devoted a lot of publicity to a vague prediction made hundreds of years ago by Nostradamus. The prophecy apparently stated that a devastating earthquake would destroy the "new city" in May of 1988. Many interpreted this to mean that Los Angeles was going to be wiped out. Had the media not publicized this rather obscure prediction, nothing much would have happened. As it was, several thousand Angelinos arranged to be out of town that particular week and many others spent the appointed day glued to their radios and TVs in case something did happen.

On a more serious note, a great deal of media publicity was given to the AIDS epidemic. Most of it was factual and informative. The media, however, played up the fact that several scientists were predicting that the disease would spread at epidemic rates among nondrug-using heterosexuals, a part of the population thought to be at minimum risk. What the news coverage failed to point out was that these forecasts were based on questionable data, but the reports undoubtedly caused anxiety to many.

Lastly, the very fact that certain individuals or issues receive media attention means that they achieve a certain amount of prominence. Sociologists call this process **status conferral.** At the basis of this phenomenon is a rather circular belief that audiences seem to endorse. The audience evidently believes that if you *really* matter, you will be at the focus of mass media attention, and if you are the focus of media attention, then you *really* matter. Knowing this fact, many individuals and groups go to extreme measures to get media coverage for themselves and their causes so that this status-conferral effect will occur. Parades, demonstrations, publicity stunts, and outlandish behavior are commonly employed to capture air time or column inches. In the late 1980s, a disabled veteran stopped traffic by riding his wheelchair to the middle of the Brooklyn Bridge. Some political candidates walked from one end of their state to the other in an attempt to generate media coverage. Those concerned about nuclear war stage ''die-ins'' to capture attention. Those who favor the legalization of marijuana sponsor ''smoke-ins'' to attract media attention. In mid-1986, ''Hands Across America'' generated media coverage for the plight of the homeless. Other groups have resorted to violence and terrorism. The Symbionese Liberation Army, which probably never had more than a dozen active members, was able to win large amounts of media coverage in the late 1970s by carrying out kidnapings and robberies. In 1977, a group of Hanafi Muslims took 134 persons hostage in Washington, D.C. The leader of this group, extremely conscious of media attention, called up the anchorman of the six o'clock newscast at a local D.C. television station and read his list of demands over the air. The 1985 hijacking of a TWA airplane and subsequent hostage taking is another example. In a similar vein, Mideast terrorists released to the media videotaped messages from their hostages. As long as the media perform a surveillance function, this type of activity, unfortunately, will probably continue.

Interpretation

Closely allied with the surveillance function is the interpretation function. The mass media do not supply just facts and data. They also provide information on the ultimate meaning and significance of those events. One form of interpretation is so obvious that many people overlook it. Not everything that happens in the world on any given day can be included in the newspaper or in a TV or radio newscast. Media organizations select those events that are to be given time or space and decide how much prominence they are to be given. Those stories that are given page-one space and eight-column headlines are obviously judged to be more important than those items that are given two paragraphs on page twelve. In a TV newscast, those stories that are given two minutes at the beginning of the show are deemed more newsworthy than the item that gets two minutes toward the end. Stories that ultimately make it into the paper or the newscast have been judged by the various gatekeepers involved to be more important than those that didn't make it.

The most obvious example of this function can be found on the editorial pages of a newspaper. Interpretation, comment, and opinion are provided for the reader so that he or she gains an added perspective on the news stories carried on other pages. Perhaps an elected official has committed some impropriety. An editorial might call for that person's resignation, thus demonstrating that the management of the newspaper considers this impropriety to be serious. A newspaper might endorse one candidate for public office over another, thereby indicating that at least in the paper's opinion, the available information indicates that this individual is more qualified than the other.

Interpretation is not confined to editorials. Articles devoted to an analysis of the causes behind a particular event or a discussion of implications of a new government policy are also examples of the interpretation function. Why is the price of gasoline going up? What impact will a prolonged dry spell have on food prices? Treatment of these topics may deal with more than the factual information that might be contained in a straight news story. Radio and television also carry programs or segments of programs that fall under this heading. An editorial by David Brinkley or by the manager of the local TV or radio station are two such examples. TV documentaries such as "Eyes on the Prize" or "The Selling of the Pentagon" are others. When the president broadcasts a major political address, network correspondents usually appear afterward to tell us what the president "really said." At special events such as political conventions, rocket launches, and elections, commentators are on hand to interpret for us the meaning behind what is going on.

Interpretation, as is probably obvious by now, can take various forms. Editorial cartoons, which originated in 1754, may be the most popular form. Other examples are less obvious but no less important. Critics are employed by the various media to rate motion pictures, plays, books, and records. Restaurants, cars, architecture, and even religious services are reviewed by some newspapers and magazines. One entire magazine, *Consumer Reports*, is devoted to analysis and evaluation of a wide range of general products.

The interpretation function can also be found in media content that at first glance might appear to be purely entertainment. The TV movie "The Day After" conveyed a certain opinion about nuclear war. *Red Dawn* and *Rambo III* offered their own political interpretations of communism and patriotism. Cheech and Chong movies convey a certain interpretation about the use of marijuana. Editorial statements about race relations can be found in episodes of "Amen" or "227." Viewpoints about the role of women in society are often included in "Cheers" and "Designing Women." The Billy Joel song "Second Wind" made a strong statement against teenage suicide.

What are the consequences of the mass media's performing this function? First, the individual is exposed to a large number of different points of view, probably far more than he or she could come in contact with through personal channels. Because of this, a person (with some effort) can evaluate all sides of an issue before arriving at an opinion. Additionally, the media make available to the individual a wide range of expertise that he or she might not have access to through interpersonal communication. Should we change the funding structure of Social Security? Thanks to the media, a person can read or hear the views of various economists, political scientists, politicians, and government workers.

There are, however, certain dysfunctions that might occur. Since media content is public, any criticism or praise of a certain individual or group is also public and might have positive or negative consequences for the medium involved. For example, when the television networks were carrying damaging news-analysis programs examining the Nixon administration's involvement in the Watergate affair, the White House threatened the networks with economic reprisals. Frank Stanton, then the president of CBS, claimed that a Nixon aide told him that the White House would bring CBS "to its knees in Wall Street and on Madison Avenue." A similar event occurred in 1986 when the Justice Department considered prosecuting five news organizations for publishing an analysis of the United States' code-breaking abilities. A newspaper that carries an interpretive piece critical of the insurance industry might prompt these companies to switch their advertising to a competitor. In 1976, when *The Atlantic Monthly* carried a cover story entitled "Rip-Off at the Supermarket," a number of store managers for a large supermarket chain pulled the copies of the

New Hampshire: The Media and Interpretation

Suppose you were running in an election in a state where your name wasn't even on the ballot and where you never made a single personal appearance. Suppose further that when the votes were counted, you had received 49.4 percent while your nearest opponent had tallied only 42.2 percent. You would probably consider it a clear-cut victory. Interestingly enough, that is exactly the situation that occurred when incumbent President Lyndon Johnson outpolled Eugene McCarthy in the 1968 New Hampshire Democratic Primary. Even more interesting is the way the mass media interpreted the results of the election. Despite what it seemed on the surface, the media called it a great victory for McCarthy. *Time* put him on the cover of its next issue. Inside, the magazine called his showing a victory in "all but the figures." "McCarthy Strong in N.H. Voting" said a headline in the *Washington Post*. "Senator Exceeds Top Primary Predictions. . . ." said a headline in the *New York Times*. The media interpreted the results in such a way that McCarthy came out on top. A few weeks later, Lyndon Johnson withdrew from the race.

In 1972, Senator Edmund Muskie received 48 percent of the New Hampshire Democratic vote while Senator George McGovern, his nearest challenger, got only 37 percent. A big victory for Muskie? The media did not interpret it that way. "Ed Muskie's Underwhelming Victory," read a headline in *Newsweek*; "Disappointing," wrote *Time* about Muskie's vote total. McGovern went on to win the nomination.

By now you probably are thinking that the front-runner in the New Hampshire election is always perceived to be the loser by the mass media. Not exactly. In 1976, Jimmy Carter got only 30 percent of the Democratic vote, just six percentage points ahead of his nearest rival, Representative Morris Udall. A great showing for Udall? No. NBC called Carter "the man to beat." *Time* said his campaign was the only one "with real possibilities of breaking far ahead of the pack." Both *Time* and *Newsweek* put Carter on the cover. *Time* gave Carter more than 2600 lines of coverage; all of the other candidates got only 300 lines total. Carter went on to win the nomination.

The room for interpretation was much narrower in 1980 as Ronald Reagan collected 50 percent of the Republican vote while his nearest pursuer collected only 23 percent. On the Democratic side incumbent Jimmy Carter collected 49 percent of the vote without even appearing in the state. His nearest rival, Senator Ted Kennedy, spent a great deal of time campaigning in New Hampshire but was able to garner only 38 percent of the vote. The news media labeled both Reagan and Carter the front-runners, and each went on to win his party's nomination.

In 1984, the media, now more conscious of their role as political interpreters, were more cautious. The Democratic primary saw Gary Hart upset preelection favorite Walter Mondale by nine percentage points. The media gave more coverage to Hart (the number of reporters following his campaign increased from six to about seventy-five), but Mondale was not counted out. "Now It's a Race" was the headline in *Time* and both candidates were featured on the cover. The two-man race theme was featured throughout the next few months until Mondale won enough delegates to become the clear front-runner.

In 1988, the New Hampshire primary was upstaged by the Iowa caucuses, where instead of voting, people merely stood up in a group to support their candidates. Nonetheless, according to the *Media Monitor,* Iowa—with a total of eighty-nine delegates at stake—was the focus of 105 network TV stories. New Hampshire, with forty total delegates, was the subject of eighty-four stories. (In contrast, the "Super Tuesday" primaries, where 2056 delegates were up for grabs, were the focus of only 53 stories. Obviously, as far as the electronic media are concerned, the first contest is the most important.) The dangers of placing too much faith in caucus results were vividly illustrated by the interpretation of the Iowa aftermath. On the Democratic side, Congressman Richard Gephardt won and was dubbed the front-runner. On the Republican side, Senator Bob Dole won but the media paid more attention to the surprising showing of TV preacher Pat Robertson, labeling him a strong and viable candidate, and the weak showing of Vice President George Bush. A week later, Bush and Massachusetts Governor Michael Dukakis won in New Hampshire and each went on to win his party's nomination. "Front-runner" Gephardt and "viable candidate" Robertson were out of the race shortly thereafter.

magazine from their shelves. The public nature of interpretation and its possible negative consequences might discourage critical evaluation of controversial topics.

On another level, there is also the danger that an individual may in the long run come to rely too heavily on the views carried in the media and lose his or her critical ability. Accepting without question the views of the *New York Times* or David Brinkley may be easier than forming individual opinions, but it might lead to the dysfunctional situation in which the individual becomes passive and allows others to think for him or her.

Linkage

The mass media are able to join together by interpersonal channels different elements of society that are not directly connected. For example, mass advertising attempts to link the needs of buyers with the products of sellers. Legislators in Washington may try to keep in touch with constituents' feelings by reading their hometown papers. Voters, in turn, learn about the doings of their elected officials through newspapers, TV, and radio. Telethons that attempt to raise money for the treatment of certain diseases are another example of this **linkage** function. The needs of those suffering from the disease are matched with the desires of others who wish to see the problem eliminated.

Another type of linkage occurs when geographically separated groups that share a common interest are linked by the media. In 1980, when registration for the draft was reinstituted, protests took place at many places across the country. These demonstrations were covered by the media, and young people in California saw what was happening in Massachusetts and vice versa. This coverage provided an informational as well as an emotional linkage among these various groups and helped to foster a general feeling that they were part of a nationwide movement. The same thing happened in 1985 during the Live Aid rock concert for famine relief. Probably more than a billion and a half people worldwide were linked via TV. To a lesser extent, the same thing occurred during the 1988 Freedomfest concert against apartheid.

Similarly, news coverage of those groups that favored or opposed the Equal Rights Amendment might have caused some people who ordinarily might not have gotten involved to become more active. This linkage function is present at other levels as well. People who wear "No Nukes" buttons and T-shirts are advertising their feelings so that others with similar concerns might "link up" with them. The magazine *Gambling Times* allows a person who is interested in games of chance to

Media link members of society by helping them to recognize that others share common interests or concerns. Demonstrations such as the huge pro-choice rally in Washington, D.C., are covered by the mass media; this coverage provides informational as well as emotional linkage between various groups and fosters a feeling of participation in a national movement. (UPI/Bettmann Newsphotos)

be linked to others with similar interests. *The General*, a publication devoted to those who play board war games, contains a classified ad section where readers advertise for opponents. If a partner is found, then the two people turn to another channel, the postal system, to solidify the linkage. *Swinger*, a publication for those with "emancipated" attitudes toward sex, also contains a section where readers advertise to meet other swingers. Some firms, with the help of the local phone company, are offering "party lines" or "gab lines." A person dials a number and is linked up with similarly minded folks. Most users of this service are looking for dates, and if two people hit it off, they can ask the operator to transfer them to a private line. One New York–based party line logged about 100,000 minutes in calls a day.

Of course, it is entirely possible that the media can create totally new social groups by linking members of society who have not previously recognized that others have similar interests. Some writers call this function the "public-making" ability of the mass media. In the movie *Network*, for example, newscaster/guru Howard Beal urges people to stand up for their rights by shouting, "I'm mad as hell and I'm not going to take it anymore!" The next scenes show people all over the country throwing open their windows and shouting this line into the night. Pretty soon, an organized I'm-Not-Going-To-Take-It-Any-More movement is born. A new group has been formed, with the media acting as linkage. This same phenomenon may account for the growth of the ecology movement in the 1970s and the antinuclear and antiapartheid movements in the mid-1980s.

When the media perform in this role, one obvious consequence is that societal groups can be mobilized quickly. For example, a plea by a TV performer to "Save the Whales" might result in many local organizations springing up in the next few weeks. In the early 1970s, several noncommercial TV stations covered the Bobby Fisher–Boris Spassky chess match. Over the next few months, the popularity of chess and membership in chess clubs skyrocketed. The same explanation might hold for the quick upsurge in the popularity of tennis during the 1970s. Media coverage of the recent wrestling craze also helped its rapidly growing popularity. In 1987, a rare "harmonic convergence" occurred—all the nine planets lined up in kind of a straight line. This event might have gone unnoticed by all but astronomers had not the media publicized the fact that some groups expected the harmonic convergence to cause disasters while some others thought it would convey mystical powers, insight, and a sense of general well-being to those who believed in its power. The publicity linked these believers, and thousands marked the occasion with "convergence parties" that took place across the country. (In case you missed it, the next convergence will take place in about 20,000 years.) On the other hand, this linkage function may have negative consequences. Persons with antisocial interests can be linked as easily as chess buffs and harmonic convergers. Thus media attention to terrorists and other extremist groups might prompt others in the same direction.

Transmission of Values

The transmission of values is a subtle but nonetheless important function of the mass media. It has also been called the **socialization** function. Socialization refers to the ways in which an individual comes to adopt the behavior and values of a group. The mass media present portrayals of our society, and by watching, listening, and reading, we learn how people are supposed to act and what values are important. To illustrate, let's consider the images of two totally different concepts as seen in the media: motherhood and pets. The next time you watch television or thumb through a magazine pay close attention to the way mothers and children are presented. Mass media mommies are usually clean, loving, pretty, and cheerful. Ivory Snow laundry detergent typically adorns the packages of their products with the equivalent of a modern madonna—a wholesome-looking mother and healthy child smile out across grocery aisles (the company was embarrassed a few years ago when one of their clean-scrubbed, all-American types went on to star in X-rated films). The Clairol company sponsored an ad campaign that featured the "Clairol mother," an attractive and glamorous female who never let raising a child interfere with maintaining her hair. Babies, as seen in the media, are usually happy, healthy, content, and cherubic. They seldom cry and never spit up. All of them seem to resemble the bouncing baby that graces the little jars of Gerber's baby food in the supermarket. When they interact with their children, media mothers tend to be positive, warm, and caring. Consider these media mommies drawn from TV. Mrs. Cleaver (Beaver's mother), Mrs. Cunningham ("Happy Days"), Mrs. Partridge, Mrs. Walton, Mrs. Keaton ("Family Ties"), or Mrs. Huxtable ("The Cosby Show"), even the sharp-tongued Roseanne (from the show of the same name), to name just a few, are all understanding, reasonable, friendly, and devoted to their children. Obviously, these examples show that these media portrayals picture motherhood and childrearing as

A more subtle function of the mass media is the transmission of values. Television viewers are often influenced by the behavior and values depicted on the screen. For example, parenthood and family life are generally portrayed as positive and beneficial. Cliff and Claire Huxtable, shown here with two of their children on the popular "Cosby Show," exemplify understanding parents, devoted to their children and successful in their careers. (© 1988 National Broadcasting Company, Inc.)

activities that have a positive value for society. Individuals who are exposed to these portrayals are likely to grow up and accept this value. Thus a social value is transmitted from one generation to another.

Pets provide another example in which this transmission of values is readily apparent. Think of some famous media pets: Sandy, Lassie, Rin Tin Tin, Gentle Ben, Flipper, Benji, Boomer, and so on. What do they have in common? They are all pets who are trusted companions, loyal pals, and protectors of the young. Media dogs seldom snarl at a baby sister and never soil the carpet. Not surprisingly, as each new generation is exposed to the portrayal of media pets, they are likely to come away with a positive value attached to the idea of owning a pet.

The mass media also teach us about people; they show us how they act and what is expected of them. In other words, the media present us with role models that we may observe and perhaps imitate. A study once indicated that many adolescents learned about dating behavior by watching films and television programs that featured this activity. To take another example, what do the media tell us about being fat? In the first place, it appears that fewer and fewer fat performers are visible in mass entertainment. In pop music, Mama Cass has given way to Cher. Few contemporary rock stars are overweight. (O.K., the Fat Boys are an obvious exception.) Even rock songs have placed a value on slimness ("Long Tall Sally," "Boney Maroney"). In motion pictures there are few current stars who are fat, and those who exist seem to be relegated to primarily comic roles (Dom DeLuise, John Candy). Fat TV stars are also rare, and the desirability of weight loss has been a central theme in some situation comedies. Jane Fonda's "Workout" and many other exercise tapes are best-selling videocassettes. Diets in books and magazines are read by millions. Evidently, the media are showing us that the ideal body type is a thin one.

Sometimes the media consciously try to instill values and behavior patterns in the audience. The producers of ''Cagney and Lacey'' purposely inserted a scene that showed their two stars buckling their safety belts before driving. In ''Happy Days,'' the Fonz was always shown wearing a crash helmet when on his motorcycle. More recently, many newspapers have begun reporting if accident victims were wearing seatbelts at the time of the mishap. In 1989, TV writers voluntarily agreed to portray alcohol usage more responsibly in their programs and to include references to ''designated drivers'' whenever possible.

There are probably countless other examples of values and behaviors that are, in part at least, socialized through the media. However, at this point let us examine some of the consequences of having the mass media serve as agents of socialization. At one level, value transmission via the mass media will aid the stability of society. Common values and experiences are passed down to all members, thereby creating common bonds between them. On the other hand, the kinds of values and cultural information that are included in mass media content are selected by large organizations that may select values and behaviors that encourage the status quo. For example, the ''baby industry'' in this country is a multimillion-dollar one. This industry advertises heavily in the media; it is not surprising, then, that motherhood and babyhood are depicted in such an attractive light. To show mothers as harried, exhausted, overworked, and frazzled and babies as colicky, cranky, and drooling would not help maintain this profitable arrangement.

Of all the mass media, it is probably television that has the greatest potential for the socialization of young children. By the time an individual has reached eighteen, he or she will have spent more time in watching television than any other single activity except sleep. A prime-time program that is popular with youngsters might draw an audience of 10 million six- to eleven-year-olds. Because of this wide exposure, several writers have warned of possible dysfunctions that might occur if television became the most important channel of socialization. For instance, since so many TV programs contain violence, it has been feared that youngsters who watch many violent programs might be socialized into accepting violence as a legitimate method of problem solving. In one survey among grade school youngsters, heavy TV viewers were more likely than light TV viewers to agree with the statement: ''It's almost always all right to hit someone if you are mad at them.'' Or another possibility might be that the pervasiveness of television violence might encourage attitudes about the ''real world'' that would reflect the jeopardy found in the television content. One study, for example, found that children who were heavy TV viewers were more fearful of going out at night than were light TV viewers.

Another area that has received detailed attention is the potential negative consequences of mass media presentation of women. To be more specific, surveys about television have indicated that this medium can function as a source of knowledge about occupations. Since TV portrays its own peculiar world, it might present a distorted image of the world of work to its younger viewers. For example, during the 1970s, the two most common occupations held by leading female characters in prime-time TV were those of housewife and law enforcement officer. No other occupation came close to these two in frequency of portrayal. If she had no other sources of countervailing information, a young girl growing up in this decade might have been socialized into believing she had two career choices when she grew up: to get married or to become a cop.

Socialization via the mass media is not necessarily confined to children. During the early 1970s, when "Marcus Welby, M.D." was a popular TV show, physicians began to worry that it was socializing both children and adults into a false expectation about their own family doctors. Welby was too caring, too dedicated, and too involved with his own patients to be real. In short, he was too perfect a role model. Having been socialized into expecting the Welby treatment, many people found that their own real-life doctors did not measure up to the TV model, thus creating some disappointment and frustration among patients and physicians. The same thing can be said about police. Television cops almost always solve the crime; real-life police are not always that effective.

Finally, it has been argued that for many years the image of minority groups transmitted from one generation to the next by the mass media reflected the stereotypes held by those who were in power: white, Anglo-Saxon, Protestant males. As a result, American Indians and black Americans endured many years during which Indians were seen as savages who murdered civilized whites and blacks were depicted in menial and subordinate roles. These stereotypes were slow to change, partly because it took a long time for members of these minority groups to influence the workings of large media organizations.

Entertainment

The most obvious of all media functions is that of entertainment. Two of the media examined in this book, motion pictures and sound recording, are devoted primarily to entertainment. Even though most of a newspaper is devoted to covering the events of the day, comics, puzzles, horoscopes, games, advice, gossip, humor, and general entertainment features usually account for around 12 percent of the typical content in an American daily paper. (If we considered sports news as entertainment, that would add another 14 percent to this figure.) Television is primarily devoted to entertainment, with about three-quarters of a typical broadcast day falling into this category. The entertainment content of radio varies widely according to station format. Some stations may program 100 percent news, while others may schedule less than 5 percent. In like manner, some magazines may have little entertainment content (*Forbes*), while others may be almost entirely devoted to it (*National Lampoon*). Even those magazines that are concerned primarily with news—*Time* and *Newsweek*, for example—usually mix in some entertaining features with their usual reporting.

The scope of mass media entertainment is awesome. By early 1988, approximately 25 million people had paid money to see *Fatal Attraction*. About 125 million people watched the last episode of "M*A*S*H." In a typical month, more than 5 million read (or at least look at) *Playboy*. Michael Jackson's *Bad* album had sold more than 6 million copies by 1988. The comic strip "Doonesbury" is read by 18 million people. The importance of this entertainment function has grown as Americans have accumulated more leisure time. The work week has decreased from about seventy-two hours at the turn of the century to the current forty hours. In the future, it appears that the work week will shrink even more, thereby giving Americans more free time, which they will probably fill with entertainment provided by the media.

In the past, this entertainment function had been filled by interpersonal communication. Troubadors, storytellers, court jesters, and magicians fulfilled this function in the centuries before the media. What are the consequences of having this task now taken over by mass communication? Clearly, the media can make entertainment available to a large number of people at relatively little cost. This helps make leisure and recreational time more enjoyable. On the other hand, entertainment

G'Day Mate

The power of the media to create role models was vividly illustrated in 1987–1988 when America was swept by Australia fever. Maybe it was caused by *Crocodile Dundee* and *Crocodile Dundee II*, or the televising of the America's Cup yacht races from Perth, or the new TV show "Dolphin Cove," or those ads with the cute little koala bear, or the rock groups INXS and Midnight Oil. Whatever the cause, Americans appeared to be imitating their counterparts down under. "Outback" bars, serving brews like Foster's, Cooper Ale, and Swan Lager, were popular, as were restaurants serving Australian dishes such as "boomers"—stuffed sausage—"hot Mimi Bird in the bush"—quail and mushroom sauce—and Sydney prawn soup. And more than one American took Aussie Paul Hogan's advice and "put another shrimp on the barbie." Australian fashions, such as akubra bush hats and drizabone overcoats, started showing up in trendy shops. In addition, many Americans wanted to see Australia firsthand. The number of U.S. visitors nearly tripled from 1984 to 1987.

that is carried by the mass media must, almost by definition, appeal to a mass audience. The ultimate result of this state of affairs is that media content is designed to appeal to the lowest common denominator of taste. More programs that resemble "Miami Vice" and "The Cosby Show" will find their way to TV than will opera performances. Newsstands are filled with more imitators of *Playboy* than imitators of *Saturday Review*. We are more apt to see sequels such as *Rocky II, III*, and *IV*, *Rambo II* and *III*, *Nightmare on Elm Street II* and *III*, and *Crocodile Dundee II* than we are to see *Romeo and Juliet II* and *More King Lear*. Rock stations outnumber classical stations thirteen to one. Many critics have argued that the media have lowered the level of American culture and have cheapened taste.

One other consequence of the widespread use of media for entertainment is that it is now quite easy to sit back and let others entertain you. Flicking on the TV set, picking up a magazine, and going to a movie require little effort on our part, and some fear that the media do such a good job of entertaining society that they encourage passivity. Instead of playing baseball, people might simply watch it on TV. Instead of learning to play the guitar, an adolescent might decide to listen to a record of someone else playing the guitar. On more than one occasion critics have charged that the mass media will turn Americans into a nation of watchers and listeners instead of doers.

HOW PEOPLE USE THE MASS MEDIA

It is probably clear by now that statements made about the functions of mass communication in society could be paralleled by statements about how the media function at the level of the individual. Consequently, we are going to shift from our wide-angle lens to a close-up lens and focus on how the individual uses mass communication (in other words, we are moving from macro to microanalysis). At the individual level, the functional approach is given the general name of the **uses-and-gratifications model.** In its simplest form, the uses-and-gratifications model posits that audience members have certain needs or drives that are satisfied by using both nonmedia and media sources. This discussion will be concerned more with media-related sources of satisfaction. The actual needs satisfied by the media are called media gratifications. Our knowledge of these uses and gratifications typically comes from surveys that have asked people a large number of questions about how they use the media (much like the questions at the beginning of this chapter). Several researchers have classified the various uses and gratifications into a fourfold category system:

1. cognition

2. diversion

3. social utility

4. withdrawal

We will examine each in turn.

Cognition

Cognition means the act of coming to know something. When a person uses a mass medium to obtain information about something, then he or she is using the medium in a cognitive way. Clearly, the individual's cognitive use of a medium is directly parallel to the surveillance function at the macroanalytical level. At the individual level, however, researchers have noted that there are two different types of cognitive functions that are performed. One has to do with using the media to keep up with information on current events, while the other has to do with using the media to learn about things in general or things that relate to a person's general curiosity. To illustrate, several surveys have found that many people give the following reasons for using the media:

I want to keep up with what the government is doing.

I want to understand what is going on in the world.

I want to know what political leaders are doing.

These reasons constitute the current-events type of cognitive gratification. At the same time, many people also report the following reasons for using mass media:

I want to learn how to do things I've never done before.

I want to satisfy my curiosity.

The media make me want to learn more about things.

The media give me ideas.

These statements illustrate the second type of cognition—using the media to satisfy a desire for general knowledge.

Psychologists and sociologists point out that using the media in this fashion seems to address a person's cognitive needs. These needs are related to strengthening our knowledge and understanding of the world we live in and are based to a certain extent on a desire to explore and master the surrounding environment. Thus the use of the media in this way is linked to the fulfillment of a basic human need.

a

b

c

The public uses the mass media to keep up with current events such as the tragic crash of Pan Am flight 103 over Lockerbie, Scotland. These photos illustrate (a) the physical evidence of the crash as displayed on television and in magazines following the disaster; (b) the reaction, as a relative of a victim collapses at New York's JFK Airport upon hearing of the crash; and (c) a press conference hastily called to explain to the public what was known about the event and broadcast on local and national television. (a and b, AP/Wide World Photos; c, UPI/Bettmann Newsphotos)

Diversion

Another basic need of human beings is for diversion. Diversion can take many forms. Some of these forms identified by researchers include (1) stimulation, or seeking relief from boredom or the routine activities of everyday life; (2) relaxation, or escape from the pressures and problems of day-to-day existence; and (3) emotional release of pent-up emotions and energy. Let's look at each of these gratifications in more detail.

Stimulation. One thing that human beings cannot seem to cope with is boredom. In fact, when individuals are deprived of all external stimulation—a situation created by psychologists in studies dealing with sensory deprivation—the mind begins to hallucinate in order to create its own amusement. In less drastic circumstances, seeking emotional or intellectual stimulation seems an inherent motivation in a human being. Psychologists, in fact, have labeled these activities "ludic behaviors"—play, recreation, and other forms of activity that seem to be performed to maintain a minimum level of intellectual activity. Several surveys have shown that many people report that they watch, read, or listen simply to pass the time. When there is nothing else to do, many individuals fill up their idle time with mass media content simply because it's better than being bored. For example, a good deal of listening to radio and record players occurs when people are alone and are seeking additional stimulation. At the same time, many parties with a lot of people present are characterized by loud music, which also represents an attempt to increase the level of stimulation normally present. TV sets are provided at airports to help make the wait less boring. Muzak and old magazines serve the same function at doctors' offices.

Relaxation. Too much stimulation, however, is undesirable. Psychological experiments have indicated that human beings are negatively affected by a condition called "sensory overload" in which too much information and stimulation are present in the environment. When faced with sensory overload, people tend to seek relief. The media are one source of this relief. To illustrate, people read magazines or newspapers or watch TV in an attempt to get away from the cares of the day. Watching "Leave It to Beaver" or reading *People* magazine represents a pleasant diversion from the frustrations of everyday life. The choice of material used for relaxation might not always be apparent from surface content. Some people might relax by reading articles about Civil War history; others might read about astronomy or electronics. Still others might relax by listening to serious classical music. The content is not the defining factor since virtually any media material might be used for relaxation by some audience members. Of all the media, radio or recordings seem to serve the relaxation function most frequently. Many people use clock radios with an automatic shut-off to help them get to sleep at night. "Beautiful music" stations play relaxing music all day long. Even television newscasts are structured in such a way as to help the audience relax. No matter how terrible the events of the day, the newscaster is there with a calm, confident manner, apparently reassuring us that things are under control.

Emotional Release. The last manifestation of the diversion function is the most complex. On the one hand, the use of the media for emotional release is fairly obvious. To illustrate, the horror movie has had a long history of popularity in America. Starting with *Dracula* and *Frankenstein* and continuing through *The Crea-*

Don't Worry. I'm Not Scared

Teens love to be terrorized—at least at the movies. Eighty percent of the audience for slice and dice films, like the *Nightmare on Elm Street* series, is under twenty-one. In addition, the terror audience is almost always split 50–50 between males and females. This even split is not coincidental; slasher and splatter films are popular date movies. Apparently they serve an important function for their young audience. As one teenager, quoted in a recent issue of *Seventeen*, put it: "Sometimes you feel weird or self-conscious holding onto a guy's hand on the first date but this way you can just grab him." Said another teenage girl: "Guys like to take you to horror movies, hoping you'll be real afraid and need them to comfort you." Said a third: "You can get all rowdy with boys and jump into their lap."

Scientific studies seem to confirm that horror films are performing this social function for teens. In one experiment done at the University of Indiana, female college students were paired with male confederates of the researchers. One male was instructed to remain silent while the couple watched a scene from a horror movie. A second male confederate acted wimpy, saying "Oh my God" at the gory scenes and generally acting afraid. The third male confederate acted macho, showing no

(Movie Star News)

signs of fear and shouting "All right!!" during the gory scenes. And males were paired with female confederates who acted the same way.

The results? Males enjoyed the horror film most when they were paired with the females who acted afraid. In contrast, females enjoyed the film most when paired with the macho males. The researchers concluded that horror movies encourage traditional gender-specific ways of behavior for both men and women, a conclusion supported by the preceding quotes from teen moviegoers.

---

ture from the *Black Lagoon*, *Them*, and *The Thing* right up to *Nightmare on Elm Street*, *Friday the 13th*, and *Aliens*, people have sat in dark theaters and screamed their lungs out. Tearjerkers have also drawn crowds. *Broken Blossoms*, *Since You Went Away*, *The Best Years of Our Lives*, *West Side Story*, *Brian's Song*, and *Beaches* have prompted thousands, perhaps millions, to cry their eyes out. Why do audiences cheer when Rocky goes the distance against the champ? Probably because people enjoy a certain amount of emotional release. People feel better after a good scream (especially when the monster and bad guys are on the screen where they can't get at you) or a good cry (especially when the troubles are happening to somebody else).

On the other hand, emotional release can take more subtle forms. One of the big attractions of soap operas, for example, seems to be that many people in the audiences are comforted by seeing that other people (even fictional people) have troubles greater than their own. Other people identify with media heroes and heroines and participate vicariously in their triumphs. Such a process evidently enables these people to vent some of the frustrations connected with their normal lives.

Before moving on to another topic, we should mention that the notion of emotional release was probably one of the first functions to be attributed to media content. Aristotle, in his *Poetics*, talked about the phenomenon of **catharsis** (a release of pent-up emotion or energy) occurring as a function of viewing tragic plays. In fact, the catharsis theory has surfaced many times since then, usually in connection with the portrayals of television violence. Chapter 22 contains a discussion of research that has dealt expressly with the catharsis notion.

Social Utility

Psychologists have also identified a set of social integrative needs, including our need to strengthen our contact with family, friends, and others in our society. The social integrative need seems to spring from an individual's need to affiliate with others. The media function that addresses this need is called **social utility,** and this usage can take several forms. First, have you ever talked about a TV program with a friend? Have you ever discussed a current movie or the latest record you've heard on the radio? If so, then you are using the media as **conversational currency.** The media provide a common ground for social conversations, and many people use things that they have read, seen, or heard as topics for discussion when talking with others. There is a certain social usefulness in having a large repository of things to talk about so that no matter where you are you can usually strike up a conversation and be fairly sure that the person you are talking to is familiar with the subject. ("What did you think of the Super Bowl?" "How did you like *Crocodile Dundee?*")

Social utility is apparent in other instances as well. Going to the movies is probably the most common dating behavior among adolescents. The motion picture theater represents a place where it is socially acceptable to sit next to your date in a dark room without parental supervision. In fact, many times the actual film is of secondary importance, and the social event of going out has the most appeal.

Other people report that they use the media, particularly TV and radio, as a means to overcome loneliness. The TV set represents a voice in the house for people who might otherwise be alone. Radio keeps people company in their cars. People who might otherwise be deprived of social relationships find companionship in media content and media personalities. In fact, some viewers might go so far as to develop feelings of kinship and friendship with media characters. Audience members might react to media performers and the characters they portray as if the performers were actual friends. This phenomenon is called a **parasocial relationship,** and there is some evidence that it actually occurs. For example, in one study done during the 1970s that examined parasocial relationships between the audience and TV newscasters, more than half the people surveyed agreed with the statement, "The newscasters are almost like friends you see every day." One person went on to explain, "I grew up watching Walter Cronkite. . . . We've been through a lot together. Men on the moon and things like that."

TV sometimes reinforces the confusion. Many of you have probably seen the ad that starts "I'm not a doctor but I play one on TV." The nondoctor then goes on to endorse a health-related product. Further, one local TV station tried to get closer to its audience by doing an entire newscast from the living room of one of its viewers.

Withdrawal

In our previous discussion we noted that humans occasionally need to escape from certain activities and that, in this connection, they use the media not only for relaxation but also for purposes that are best described as withdrawal uses. At times, people use the mass media to create a barrier between themselves and other people or other activities. For example, the media help people avoid certain chores that should be done. Perhaps many of you have put off your homework and class assignments until after you've finished watching a TV program or reading the newspaper. Children are quick to learn how to use the media in this fashion. This hypothetical exchange might be familiar:

"It's your turn to let the dog out."

"I can't. I want to finish watching this program. You do it."

Or:

"Answer the telephone."

"I can't. I'm reading. You get it."

In both instances, attending to mass media content was defined as a socially appropriate behavior that should not be interrupted. In this manner, other tasks might be put off or avoided entirely.

People also use the media to create a buffer zone between themselves and other people. When you are riding a bus or an airplane or sitting in a public place and don't want to be disturbed, you bury your head in a book, magazine, or newspaper. (The newspaper works best. If you fold it correctly, it can serve as an effective screen. Unfortunately, holding it in this manner makes your arms tired.) If you are on an airplane, you might insert a pair of stethoscopelike earphones in your ears and tune everybody out. Television can perform this same function at home by isolating adults from children ("Don't disturb Daddy. He's watching the game.") or children from adults ("Don't bother me now. Go into the other room and watch 'Sesame Street.' ").

CONTENT AND CONTEXT

In closing, we should emphasize that it is not only media content that determines audience usage, but also the social context within which the media exposure occurs. For example, soap operas, situation comedies, and movie magazines all contain material that audiences can use for escape purposes. People going to a movie, however, might value the opportunity to socialize more than they value any aspect of the film itself. Here the social context is the deciding factor.

It is also important to note that the functional approach makes several assumptions:

1. Audiences take an active role in their interaction with various media. That is, the needs of each individual provide motivation that channels that individual's media use.

2. The mass media compete with other sources of satisfaction. Relaxation, for example, can also be achieved by taking a nap or having a couple of drinks, and social utility needs can be satisfied by joining a club or playing touch football.

3. The uses-and-gratifications approach assumes that people are aware of their own needs and are able to verbalize them. This approach relies heavily on

surveys based on the actual responses of audience members. Thus the research technique assumes that people's responses are valid indicators of their motives.

A great deal of additional research needs to be done in connection with the uses-and-gratifications approach. In particular, more work is needed in defining and categorizing media-related needs or drives and in relating these needs to media usage. Nonetheless, the current approach provides a valuable way to examine the complex interaction between the various media and their audiences.

SUGGESTIONS FOR FURTHER READING

The sources listed below are good places to go for additional information on this topic.

BLUMLER, JAY, AND ELIHU KATZ. eds., *The Uses of Mass Communication*, Beverly Hills, Calif.: Sage Publications, 1974.

FAUCONNIER, GUIDO, *Mass Media and Society*, Louvain, Belgium: University of Louvain Press, 1975.

KLAPPER, JOSEPH, *The Effects of Mass Communiction*, New York: The Free Press, 1960.

MCQUAIL, DENIS, *Towards a Sociology of Mass Communications,* London: Collier-MacMillan, 1969.

RUBIN, ALAN M., "Uses and Gratifications," in Joseph R. Dominick and James Fletcher, eds., *Broadcasting Research Methods,* Boston: Allyn and Bacon, 1985.

————, "Uses, Gratifications, and Media Effects Research," in Jennings Bryant and Dolf Zillmann, eds., *Perspectives on Media Effects*, Hillsdale, N.J.: Lawrence Elbaum Associates, 1986.

TAN, ALEXIS, *Mass Communication Theories and Research*, Columbus, Ohio: Grid Publishing, 1981.

WRIGHT, CHARLES R., *Mass Communication: A Sociological Perspective*, New York: Random House, 1959.

Chapter 3

International and Comparative Mass Media Systems

It's a cold winter night in Moscow, Idaho, sometime in the late 1980s. Inside a typical house a typical family is spending a leisurely Thursday evening relaxing with the mass media. Our Idaho family subscribes to the local paper, the Moscow *Idahonian,* and a regional weekly paper. In addition, from the thousands of magazines available to them, our family regularly reads six: *TV Guide, Time, Sports Illustrated, People, Seventeen,* and *Reader's Digest.* Three local radio stations are available to them in Moscow plus several that can be received from nearby cities with formats ranging from country to Top 40. If the family chooses to watch television, there are three network affiliates available, four independent stations, and three public TV stations, plus all the premium channels available on the cable. All of these TV channels provide a mix of entertainment and information. For example, on this Thursday night, the family watches "The Cosby Show," "A Different World," and MTV. With the exception of the pay movie channels on cable and the Public Broadcasting Stations, all of the media available to the family carry copious amounts of advertising.

Now let's travel thousands of miles to Moscow, U.S.S.R., and see what is available to a typical Russian family on this same cold Thursday night. The Soviet family buys two national newspapers, *Pravda,* the voice of the Communist party, and *Izvestia,* the government newspaper. The family also reads *Trud,* the organ of the national trade union leadership (in the Soviet Union, all newspapers are published by the party, by the government, or by trade unions). Although there are no news magazines in the style of *Time* and *Newsweek,* several magazines are available. The family reads *Pionerskaya Pravda,* a children's magazine, two women's magazines, and the *Literaturnaya Gazeta* (Literary Gazette) and *Sovietski Sport* (Soviet Sports). The radio is usually tuned to the state-controlled Moscow Radio Network. Four basic radio services are available. The First Program is the main channel broadcasting news, music, and sports. The Second Program is an information and music service. The Third and Fourth Programs are devoted to classical music, literary works, and profiles of Soviet artists. For example, in mid-1988 our Soviet family could hear a theater review, a concert by the State Television and Radio Orchestra, and a discussion about music on the First Program. There are four television channels that serve Moscow; two are national in scope, one is local, and one is educational. On this particular Thursday evening, our Moscow family had a choice of such shows as "Spotlight on Restructuring," "Folk Melodies," a "PM Magazine"-style show called "Good Evening Moscow," exercises, and a soccer game between Hungary and England. One thing is missing, though: Advertising, as our American family thinks of it, is nonexistent.

Our Idaho family would note other differences. Much of the content in newspapers and broadcasting has to do with political news or factory and farm production. A column in *Pravda,* for example, entitled "News from the Fields," talks about what crops farmers are planting in the various regions of the Soviet Union. Personalities are downplayed. Features on movie stars and recording artists are rare.

In years past, our U.S. family would have noted even greater differences. Negative news was downplayed; criticism of the government was hard to find. Information was tightly controlled. In the last few years, however, thanks to a new government policy of openness, called *glasnost,* the picture has changed. News of dissent and dissatisfaction with the government and the party can now be found in newspapers, periodicals, and on TV and radio. Restrictions on the flow of information have been eased. President Reagan, during his 1988 visit to Moscow, addressed the Soviet people on live TV. Moscow residents could watch Dan Rather, Peter Jennings, and Tom Brokaw report live from Red Square. The Soviet Union stopped jamming Voice of America broadcasts. A recent Soviet program on life in the United States actually carried commercials for Pepsi, Visa, and Sony. A Detroit radio station even broadcast its morning show from Moscow during the Reagan visit. An American–Soviet Film Initiative was set up to trade films between the two countries and a recent Moscow Film Festival featured entries from the United States and Britain. In short, although our Idaho family would notice marked differences in the media content of the two countries, the differences are not as pronounced as they were some years earlier.

This chapter has a twofold purpose. First, it will highlight the fact that mass communication doesn't stop at borders. International mass media are growing in

A Soviet family watches President Ronald Reagan addressing the Soviet nation on Soviet television; the address was also broadcast on American television. (Sovoto)

both economic and political influence. In fact, thanks to communication satellites, it is now fairly easy for one country to communicate with another, but this ability creates many new problems. Consequently, the first section of this chapter examines the rapidly changing world of international communication. The second purpose of this chapter is to illustrate that the mass media system in the United States is not the only possible system. There are major differences among countries in the way mass communication operates. In fact, there may be differences in media performance within the borders of a single country. Appreciation of the variation that occurs throughout the world is helpful in understanding the nature and function of our own system. Moreover, knowing about other systems helps us appreciate the difficulties in covering news in other countries (as we shall see, some countries define the news differently than we do, and reporters are expected to act differently). Thus the second part of the chapter examines comparative mass media systems.

INTERNATIONAL MEDIA SYSTEMS

The study of international mass media systems focuses on those media that cross national boundaries. Some media may be deliberately designed for other countries (as is the case with Radio Moscow, the Voice of America, and the international edition of *Newsweek*); other media simply spill over from one country to its neighbors (as happens between the United States and Canada). Let's look first at those media designed for international consumption.

Global Print Media

Many newspapers provide foreign-language or international editions. The popular ones fall into two categories: general newspapers and financial newspapers. As far as U.S.- and British-based publications are concerned, the following were the leaders at the close of 1988:

- The *International Herald Tribune,* published by the *New York Times* and the *Washington Post* and headquartered in France, has a worldwide circulation of about 170,000, most of it in Europe. The paper, which recently celebrated its hundredth anniversary, is printed in ten cities around the world, including Miami, Singapore, and Hong Kong.

- *USA Today International* is a newcomer to the scene with a circulation of about 40,000, again mostly in Europe. The Gannett-owned paper is printed in Switzerland, Singapore, and Hong Kong. Most of its readers are U.S. citizens traveling abroad.

- *WorldPaper,* published by the World Times Company in Boston, is distributed as a newspaper supplement primarily in Latin America, Asia, and the Middle East. It's printed in twenty different countries and boasts a circulation of 650,000.

- *The Financial Times of London,* as its name suggests, specializes in economic news and has a circulation of about 300,000.

- *The Economist,* also based in London, carries financial news and analysis. Easily available in the United States, the paper is printed in Virginia, London, and Singapore. It reaches about 300,000 readers.

- *The Wall Street Journal*'s international editions reach about 75,000 people, mainly in Europe and Asia.

Other papers that enjoy international status are the *New York Times, Le Monde* (France), *El País* (Spain), *The Times* (Great Britain), *The Statesman* (India) and *Al Ahram* (Egypt). *Pravda* is also becoming more prominent on the world scene now that an English-language version is available. In fact, some U.S. papers now offer the English *Pravda* as a supplement to their readers.

As far as magazines are concerned, the *Reader's Digest* publishes 39 international editions in 15 languages that are distributed in nearly 200 countries. The *Digest* has about 10 million readers in foreign countries, making it a formidable vehicle for global advertising. Time Warner Inc., in addition to the international edition of *Time,* which has a circulation of 1.3 million in 190 countries, also publishes *Asiaweek, President* (in Japanese), and *Yazhou Zhoukan,* a newsweekly in Chinese. Many business magazines, including *Business Week, Fortune,* and the *Harvard Business Review,* also have significant foreign readership.

Note that most of the leading newspapers and magazines are published by the industrialized nations. As we shall see, developing nations fear that the mainly Western content in these publications represents a threat to their cultural sovereignty.

Global Broadcasting

About 150 countries engage in some form of international shortwave radio broadcasting. Most of these services are government run or at least government supervised and seem to have a political purpose: A good deal of the content on many services would be labeled propaganda. Over the last few years, however, private international broadcasting has grown in popularity. In the early 1980s, WRNO, New Orleans, became the first licensed commercially supported station to aim at an international audience. Other stations located in the United States and its island possessions followed suit. Nonetheless, the leading major international services continue to be state supported. Listed below are the five leaders based on broadcast hours in 1987:

- The Voice of America (VOA), now in its fifth decade of operation, broadcasts news, editorials, features, and music in more than forty languages. The VOA estimates that about 120 million people, about half of them in the Soviet Union and Eastern Europe, are regular listeners. VOA's propaganda role changes significantly with each new president. Under Jimmy Carter, the VOA's role was educational and informational; under Ronald Reagan, its propaganda role was emphasized. The United States also operates Radio Free Europe and Radio Liberty, both targeted to the people of Eastern Europe, and Radio Martí, a special AM service beamed at Cuba.

- Radio Moscow (RM) is probably the most extensive and the best financed international radio service now in operation. RM's budget is approximately three times that of VOA. Broadcasting more than 2200 hours per week, RM transmits programs in 80 languages to all parts of the globe. Broadcasts to North America, for example, are carried on fifteen different shortwave frequencies. RM's content might best be described as subtle propaganda with news and commentary dominating most of its programming time.

- The World Service of the British Broadcasting Corporation (BBC) has a worldwide reputation for accurate and impartial newscasts because, in theory at least, it is independent of government ownership. Along with its news, the BBC also carries an impressive lineup of music, drama, comedy, sports, and light features. The BBC pioneered the international radio call-in show in which prominent people, such as Prime Minister Margaret Thatcher, answer calls from listeners around the globe. The BBC broadcasts in 37 languages and has about 120 million worldwide listeners.

- Radio Beijing (Peking), which is difficult to pick up in the United States, transmits about 1400 hours of programming weekly in 40 foreign languages. Radio Beijing carried strident anti-American propaganda until the early 1970s when improved relations led to a mellowing of their tone. The Soviet Union, however, still remained a popular target. Most of Radio Beijing's programming consists of news, analysis, commentary, and cultural information about China.

- Deutsche Welle (DW), "German Wave," broadcasts about 800 hours per week in 26 languages. DW's transmitters are located in West Germany and in Africa and Asia. It has a large audience, particularly in Africa.

Probably the biggest change in international broadcasting in the eighties has been the increased use of communication satellites to carry TV signals across borders. Ted Turner's Cable News Network (CNN) has been a pioneer in this area. CNN International now broadcasts to 54 countries, including 25,000 European hotel rooms and 8 British cable TV systems. During the 1988 political conventions CNN was feeding a signal to Telemundo, a Spanish-language network, and to "Vremya," the Soviet Union's nightly newscast. CNN also carries "CNN World Report," a compilation of unedited and uncensored news segments from around the world as originally reported by native journalists. International TV news exchanges, such as VISNEWS and UPITN, send pictures and audio to stations around the globe. The U.S. Information Agency's Worldnet supplies video to about fifty countries. Segments from Russian TV have been carried live by the Discovery Cable Network in the United States, and some special programs, such as ABC's "Capital to Capital,"

Popular TV Shows Around the World

Capsule descriptions of the most popular locally produced TV shows in various countries in the late 1980s follow. In spite of the different languages, most shows will be familiar to U.S. viewers.

- West Germany: "The Legacy of the Guldenburg Family," a prime-time soap opera along the lines of "Dallas" and "Dynasty."

- Brazil: "Roda de Fogo," a nightly series about a corrupt businessman with a fatal disease.

- Australia: "60 Minutes," the Australian version of the U.S. show.

- Sweden: "Varuhuset" (Department Store), a prime-time soap opera about the professional and personal lives of the staff of a Stockholm department store.

- Canada: "Hockey Night in Canada" (self-explanatory).

- France: "Cocoricocoboy," a puppet show aimed at adults, and "Roue de la Fortune"—you guessed it—the French version of "Wheel of Fortune."

Popular Movies Around the World

Note how American movies dominate the following list of top box-office attractions in selected foreign cities in 1988.

- Rome: 1. *Fatal Attraction;* 2. *Wall Street;* 3. *32nd of December* (local production).

- Copenhagen: 1. *Fatal Attraction;* 2. *Pelle the Conqueror* (local production); 3. *The Last Emperor.*

- Sydney: 1. *Three Men and a Baby;* 2. *Fatal Attraction;* 3. *Dirty Dancing.*

- Paris: 1. *Life Is a Long Quiet River* (local production); 2. *Wall Street;* 3. *Three Men and a Baby.*

- Munich: 1. *Fatal Attraction;* 2. *Man spricht Deutsch* (local production); 3. *Dirty Dancing.*

- Stockholm: 1. *Strul* (local production); 2. *Fatal Attraction;* 3. *Empire of the Sun.*

have been transmitted live to both the United States and the Soviet Union. Japanese TV carries "The MacNeil/Lehrer NewsHour," "CNN Headline News," the BBC news, and "ABC World News Tonight," along with several Asian news programs.

In Europe, the Sky Channel, owned by Rupert Murdoch, and the Super Channel beam English-language entertainment programs to cable systems that serve subscribers in several European countries. Plans are in the works to launch programming in German and Dutch as well. Murdoch is also studying a pan-European news channel (to rival CNN) and a sports channel. MTV Europe is available on cable in twelve European countries as well as Japan and Australia.

In sum, as one CNN executive put it, it won't be long before "everyone will be looking inside everyone else's electronic window."

Along with the increasing satellite volume, a good deal of global media traffic consists of videocassettes and films that are shipped from one country to another and broadcast on the native country's TV system or played back on VCRs or shown at local movie theaters. The trade imbalance that exists in many areas of the U.S. economy does not exist in TV and film. The United States imports less than 2 percent of its TV shows. In contrast, European and African nations import an average of 30 and 40 percent, respectively. As more people around the world acquire VCRs, the popularity of American movies on cassette will increase dramatically.

American films dominate the box office of many foreign countries. In the mid-1980s, for example, American-made movies accounted for more than half the film revenues in France and Italy (see boxed material).

Finally, another aspect of international media is the problem of cross-border spillover. TV signals, of course, know no national boundaries and the programs of one nation can be easily received in another country. The problem has caused some friction between the United States and Canada. Shows on ABC, NBC, and CBS are just as popular in Canada as they are in the United States and they take away audiences from the Canadian channels. Fearful of a cultural invasion of U.S. values and aware of the potential loss of advertising revenue to U.S. stations, the Canadian government has instituted content regulations that specify the minimum amount of Canadian content that must be carried by Canadian stations.

This poster advertising the American film The Killing Fields *at a Madrid theater demonstrates the popularity of American films in foreign countries. (Larry Mangino/The Image Works)*

This domination of international mass communication by the United States and other developed countries makes it somewhat easier to understand the fears of many Third World nations (such as those in Africa and Latin America) and some industrialized nations (such as Canada) that they are being victimized by cultural imperialism, a topic explored in more detail later.

COMPARATIVE MEDIA SYSTEMS

Let's now turn our attention to media systems as they exist in individual nations. Before we start, we should note that the media system that exists in a country is directly related to the political system in that country. The political system determines the exact relationship between the media and the government. Over the years, three main theories have developed concerning this relationship. In the sections that follow, there are several examples of these theories in operation.

Theories of the Press

The press in England between the fifteenth and eighteenth centuries operated under strict government control. The theory that characterizes such a relationship is perhaps

"The Repeal, or the Funeral Procession, of Miss Americ-Stamp." Colonial newspapers operated under the authoritarian philosophy as practiced by the British government. This English cartoon, published in 1766, satirized the repeal of the Stamp Act, an attempt to suppress hostile opinion by placing a tax on the pages of colonial newspapers. (The Granger Collection)

the oldest of the theories that deal with the relationship between the government and the press. The **authoritarian theory** arose in sixteenth-century England about the same time as the introduction of the printing press to that country. Under the authoritarian system, the prevailing belief held that a ruling elite should guide the masses, whose intellectual ability was held in low esteem. Public dissent and criticism were considered harmful to both government and the people and were not tolerated. Authoritarians used various devices to enforce cooperation of the press including licensing, censorship of material before publication, the granting of exclusive printing rights to favored units of the press, and the swift, harsh punishment of government critics. In fact, in certain societies, not only is the press prohibited from criticizing the government, but it is also required to perform functions for the good of the state. These might include omitting certain news reports that would be embarrassing or harmful to the government and explaining other events in a light favorable to the ruling powers.

The **libertarian theory** is directly opposed to the authoritarian theory. Libertarians assume that human beings are rational and are capable of making their own decisions and that governments exist to serve the individual. Unlike the authoritarians, libertarians hold that the common citizen has a right to hear all sides of an issue in order to distinguish truth from falsehood. Since any government restriction on the expression of ideas infringes on the rights of the citizen, the government can best serve the people by not interfering with the media. In short, the press must be free of control.

The libertarian theory was compatible with the freewheeling political climate and rugged individualism of early America. By the twentieth century, however, media industries had consolidated and technology had made possible instantaneous broadcasts to millions of people. As a result, the old theories covering the dissemination of information became somewhat outdated. Today, few countries would subscribe to the libertarian viewpoint. In 1947, the Commission on Freedom of the Press, a private organization financed by magazine publisher Henry Luce, constructed the **social responsibility theory,** which was more in tune with the changed marketplace. According to this theory, although the press had a right to criticize government and other institutions, it also had a responsibility to preserve democracy by properly informing the public and by responding to society's interests and needs. Probably the most significant contribution of the social responsibility theorists is their view that it is more important for citizens to have the right of access to information than it is for the press to achieve complete freedom of speech. It is not enough that increasingly large media and economic structures have the freedom to do as they please. They are also obligated to respond to society's needs. Many economically developed countries, including the United States, endorse this social responsibility theory.

Control and Ownership of the Media

One helpful way of distinguishing among the various media systems throughout the world is to classify them along the dimensions of (1) ownership and (2) control. Finnish Professor Osmo Wiio has developed a useful analysis scheme, presented in Fig. 3.1. As can be seen, ownership can range from private to public (public ownership usually means some form of government ownership), while control can range from centralized to decentralized. Note that this typology is an oversimplifi-

FIGURE 3.1 *Typology of media ownership and control. (From Osmo Wiio, "The Mass Media Role in the Western World," in L. Martin and A. Chaudhary (eds.), COMPARATIVE MASS MEDIA SYSTEMS, Copyright © 1983 by Longman Inc. Used with permission.)*

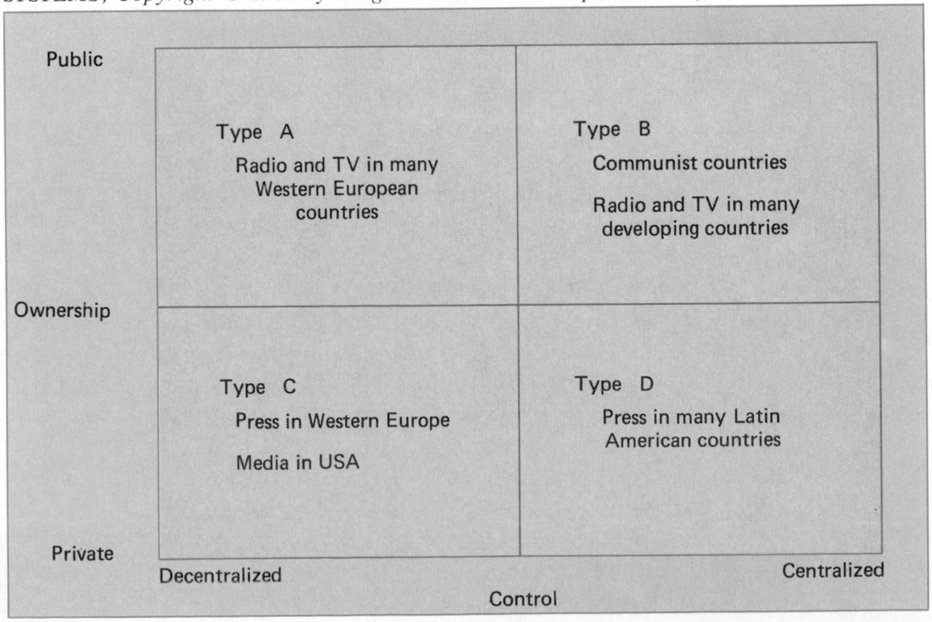

Public

Type A
Radio and TV in many Western European countries

Type B
Communist countries
Radio and TV in many developing countries

Ownership

Type C
Press in Western Europe
Media in USA

Type D
Press in many Latin American countries

Private

Decentralized   Centralized

Control

cation. In many countries, there are mixed media systems in which part of the broadcasting system is owned by the government and part by private interests. In some countries, the print media could be placed in one cell of the matrix and the broadcasting system in another. Nonetheless, this model is helpful in displaying some of the major differences among systems.

In the upper left cell are type A systems. These consist of decentralized control and public ownership, a type best illustrated by the broadcasting systems in European countries such as France, Denmark, and Italy. The broadcasting media are publicly owned, but no single political or special-interest group can control their messages. In Great Britain, for example, the British Broadcasting Corporation is a government-chartered, public owned corporation that is relatively immune to government censorship and interference.

In the upper right cell are Type B systems. This arrangement is typical of communist or socialist countries in which the media are owned publicly and controlled by the dominant political party. Our typical family in Moscow, U.S.S.R., is familiar with such a system.

In the lower left cell is the decentralized control, private ownership model. This is the system that currently operates in the United States and in many European countries. The media are owned by private companies and there is little, if any, centralized control.

The lower right cell contains the centralized control, privately owned system. In many countries, particularly in the developing countries of Africa and Latin America, the media are owned by private organizations but are firmly controlled by the government.

Let's take a more detailed look at ownership and control as they exist around

In mid-1986, the Soviet Union attempted to maintain a news blackout about the explosion and fire at the Chernobyl nuclear power plant, which led to a great deal of misinformation about the accident appearing in the Western media. This Soviet television coverage purports to show the damage to the reactor. When the same photo was shown on CNN in the United States, the right-hand portion was enhanced to clarify the damage. (AP/Wide World Photos)

In contrast to the media coverage of the Chernobyl disaster, information about the devastating earthquake in Armenia was immediately forthcoming and more detailed. Mikhail Gorbachev is shown here visiting a town in the earthquake zone. (AP/Wide World Photos)

the globe. First, we will examine the communist world, the countries that would fall in cell B of the matrix. In communist countries, control of the media is exercised by the Communist party. Freedom of the press belongs not to the media but to the state. Communist countries feel that it is necessary for their media to speak with one voice, and antigovernment or antiparty criticism is forbidden. (Note how the communist system endorses the authoritarian theory of the press mentioned above.) Crime news, family violence, and other sensation-oriented items are not allowed in the communist press unless there is some overriding lesson that might be learned from them. For example, alcohol abuse was a serious problem in the Soviet Union, but the press ignored it until the mid-1980s when a campaign was launched to curtail the problem. Newspaper and TV stories appeared that stressed the harm done by the abuse of alcohol: loss of productivity, traffic deaths, family breakups. The stories were calculated to educate the audience about the dangers of the problem. In mid-1986, during the Chernobyl nuclear accident, this philosophy was once again apparent. The government clamped a blackout on news for the first few days following the disaster. Many Soviet citizens had to rely on Western media to find out what was happening in their own country. Of course, under *glasnost* this control has relaxed somewhat.

Press control in communist countries is exercised in at least four different ways. First, the government controls the source. Printing and broadcasting equipment are given only to approved organizations. Next, journalists are state trained and state approved. Third, news agencies are state owned and news sources are state controlled. Finally, a department of censorship checks all facts before they are broadcast or published.

Next, we'll examine that region known as the Third World. These are the developing nations of Asia, Latin America, and Africa whose media systems would fall in cells B and D of the matrix. In Third World countries, government control can be direct or indirect. Some countries have resorted to police or military takeovers of newspapers and broadcasting facilities. Other, less drastic, forms of control over the print media include requiring an annual permit for publication, licensing journalists, and restricting the supply of newsprint and ink. In most Third World countries, broadcasting is government owned and consequently easy to control. In many Third World countries ownership of the print media is in private hands. For example, six African countries—Gambia, Kenya, Liberia, Morocco, Zimbabwe, and South Africa—have private ownership of newspapers. Nonetheless, their content is carefully monitored.

In most Western countries (those that would fall in cells A and C), ownership of the broadcast media can be either public or private, while print media ownership is usually private. In any case, control is minimal. The United States has the First Amendment, which guarantees a free press. In the United Kingdom, there is a long tradition of acknowledging freedom of expression and of the press. Sweden has a Freedom of the Press Act, and several Scandinavian countries have laws that provide unrestricted access to all public documents (except military secrets). Most of these same countries, along with West Germany, give journalists the legal right to protect their sources. The media in countries such as Japan, New Zealand, Canada, and Australia are also generally free from control.

Role of the Media in Various Countries

The role of a mass media system in a given country will differ according to its place in the above typology. For example, in many developing countries where there is strong centralized control over the media, the principal role of mass communication is to help develop and build the nation. Not surprisingly, many Third World countries are primarily concerned with economic and political development. This concern is translated into a rather focused definition of the role of mass media. In general, the media are expected to help further modernization or other national goals. In fact, a new term, **developmental journalism,** has been coined to describe this philosophy. In short, developmental journalism means that the role of the media is to support national interests for economic and social development and to support objectives such as national unity, stability, and cultural integrity. On the one hand, developmental journalism entails finding ways to make abstract stories about commodity pricing, agriculture, and educational goals understandable to readers and to highlight the developmental goals achieved by the nation. On the other hand, developmental journalism can also mean that the press refrains totally from any criticism of the government and will print only what the government deems helpful to its cause. The philosophy of many Asian, Latin American, and African developing nations falls somewhere between these two conceptions of developmental journalism.

In the communist world, the role of the media is clear cut: They are tools of propaganda, persuasion, and education. They function only secondarily as sources of information. This philosophy dates all the way back to Lenin, who decreed that the communist press was to help further the revolution. The political significance of the media is also clearly seen in the high priority that they occupy in the government bureaucracy. Only the Communist party, the party-controlled government, and party-directed organizations, such as trade unions, are permitted to operate media.

What is the primary function of the media in such a situation? To paraphrase a recent Soviet press guidebook, it is to treat all information as simply material to be used in the service of the Communist party's task of shaping public opinion along desired party lines. This does not mean, however, that the Soviet media function solely as one gigantic public relations agency for the government. They perform other tasks as well. Mark Hopkins, in his seminal *Mass Media in the Soviet Union,* points out that the Soviet media also serve as mobilizers, moral guardians, mass entertainers, and social critics. The mobilization role is easily seen in the way the media promote the various economic plans of the central government. For example, when a new five-year plan for agriculture was announced in the 1970s, it was the job of the media to publicize it in its most favorable light. Soviet media serve as moral guardians by conveying to the audience what is considered correct behavior or desirable values. Characters in Soviet TV dramas, for example, are honest, patriotic, and love their work. The entertainment function of the media is becoming increasingly apparent. Even *Pravda,* the stodgy party newspaper, has a sports section and theater listings. Much TV and film content falls in the entertainment category. Lastly, the Soviet media provide a forum for social criticism. Editorials and letters to the editor provide in a limited way for public debate and discussion. There are, however, unwritten guidelines that indicate what topics are fair game for critics and what topics are immune.

As we saw in Chapter 2, Western media inform and entertain, but their content is somewhat different from communist and Third World media. Most of the information carried by the media in the Western democracies is geared to the specific political and economic needs of the audience. An examination of the press in the United States and Canada, for example, would reveal a large amount of news about the local and national government, some of it unfavorable and critical. The role of government watchdog, based on the ideas presented in the social responsibility theory, is a function that would be unsettling to many of the countries in cells B and D of the matrix in Fig. 3.1. Moreover, a great deal of content in the Western media is consumer oriented, consisting of advertising and news about business. On the entertainment side, the content of Western media generally lacks the cultural heritage dimension found in many Third World countries and does not emphasize the national history aspect as heavily as do the communist media. Further, there is, relatively speaking, little regulation of the content of the entertainment media. Aside from some regulations governing pornography and prohibitions against certain content on the broadcasting media, the government takes little interest in entertainment content.

It's the interpretation or editorial function where the biggest differences are found. The United States and other Western countries have a tradition of press freedom that recognizes the right of the media to present ideas to try to persuade the audience to some point of view. The philosophy of the ''free marketplace of ideas'' is endorsed by most countries in cells A and C of Fig. 3.1. All relevant ideas concerning an issue are examined in the media, and a ''self-righting'' process occurs. Given the autonomous nature of the Western media, it would be difficult for the government to mobilize the media to support some national goal, as is typically done in developing and communist countries. There is a built-in tension and adversary relationship between press and government that makes such efforts rare.

Economic Differences

In the United States, advertising plays a key role in media support (see Chapter 16). Newspapers, magazines, radio, and television all derive a significant amount of their total income from the sale of advertising time or space. Direct government subsidy or support of the media is minimal, limited to the funds given to public broadcasting. (Of course, the government also helps indirectly to support the media by buying a lot of advertising.) In Western Europe, there are several countries that provide indirect subsidies to the media, such as cheaper mailing privileges and tax concessions. Some Scandinavian countries have a system whereby newspapers controlled by various political parties are given direct financial assistance. There are several different systems that are used to support broadcasting. In the United Kingdom, for example, the British Broadcasting Corporation (BBC) is state chartered and gets its operating funds from an annual license fee paid by the owners of TV sets. At the same time, the independent TV networks make their money from the sale of advertising time, in much the same way as do their U.S. counterparts. Many other Western countries follow this same model.

It is difficult to generalize about the means of economic support for media in the Third World. Where the print media are privately owned, money comes from circulation fees and advertising. Publishers are generally free to keep all profits, but in many countries space must be provided free of charge for government announcements. Advertising and license fees are the two major sources of income for broadcasting.

In the communist countries, most economic support for the media comes directly from the government. Since the media are state owned, money for their operation is simply set aside in the government's budget. Newspapers and magazines make a little extra money from circulation, but this is tiny in comparison to their state-derived funds. Because of this subsidy, single-copy costs are quite cheap. A Moscow daily newspaper, for example, costs less than a dime. In all communist countries except the Soviet Union, broadcasting derives additional monies from license fees on receivers. There are annual fees for TV sets, home radios, and an extra fee for a car radio. In the Soviet Union, license fees were done away with in 1962 because,

Beware of the Van

Many countries, including Great Britain, fund their state-run TV systems by an annual tax or license fee imposed on the owners of television sets. This system works fine as long as everybody pays their annual fee. But what about those who decide to ignore the tax (about $110 a year for color TV set owners in 1989) and watch TV anyway, figuring that no one will ever find out they're sneaking a peek?

This is where the van comes in.

To catch people illegally receiving signals, the British Licensing Record Office has a fleet of twenty-two TV-detector vans that cruise up and down the streets of the United Kingdom looking for violators. Each van is equipped with a device that can monitor signals to determine whether a house has its TV set on. If it has, the personnel in the van check their records to see if the residents paid the annual fee. If not, the van stops and the homeowner is confronted with the evidence and given a citation. About a quarter of a million Brits a year are prosecuted for nonpayment.

The employees who drive the vans have heard some wondrous excuses. One couple admitted their TV set had been on but argued that they shouldn't have to pay the fee because only their pet monkey watched TV. One man claimed that there was some mistake because his TV set was broken. When the van driver pointed out the top of the TV was still warm, the man said his cat had been sleeping on it. Neither alibi was accepted.

interestingly enough, people resisted their payment. In their place, the Soviet Union imposes a special tax on the sale of all radio and TV sets. There is also something called "advertising" in all communist media, but it is an insignificant source of revenue and does not resemble Western advertising. Most ads are of a purely informational nature: Such-and-such a product is now available at such-and-such a store. Many newspapers also have small sections devoted to what those in the West would call classified ads, but again, the revenue from these is minimal.

Examples of Other Systems

Let us now take a more detailed look at the mass media in three different countries. One is an industrialized nation, Japan. The second is Brazil, a developing nation, and the third is Poland, which will serve to illustrate the media system in a communist country.

Japan. About 120 million people live on this nation of islands. Japan has the highest living standard of all Asian nations and a literacy rate of about 100 percent. Naturally, its media systems are elaborate and pervasive. There are about 115 papers in Japan with a combined daily circulation of about 65 million, a total that exceeds that of U.S. dailies. Japan has fifteen papers with daily circulations over the million mark, whereas the United States has three. There are five national newspapers, of which the *Yomiuri Shimbun, Asahi Shimbun,* and *Mainichi Shimbun* are the largest. (As you may have deduced by now, *Shimbun* is the Japanese word for newspaper.) The *Yomiuri Shimbun* (literally translated as the Read-Sell Newspaper) has a combined morning and evening circulation of more than 13 million, making it the world's largest daily in terms of circulation. (By comparison, *USA Today* has a circulation of about 1.4 million.) Along with the national papers, Japan supports other regional and local dailies and about a dozen sports papers. Tokyo alone has twelve newspapers, three of them in English. By American standards, Japanese papers have circulations and penetrations that are unheard of. *Kyoto Shimbun,* in a city with a population of 1.5 million, has a circulation of 1.5 million. About 98 percent of the households in Japan subscribe to at least one newspaper.

Japan also has two news magazines, a picture-oriented news weekly called *Focus* and an influential business magazine. New leisure magazines are also making their appearance in Japan. One such publication is called *BOX,* which usually has features on clothing, investments, health care, and housing. The Japanese equivalent to *TV Guide* is also popular. In addition, Asian editions of such familiar publications as *Time, Newsweek,* and the *Reader's Digest* are widely available.

Japan has one of the most technologically advanced broadcasting systems in the world. The state-run noncommercial Japan Broadcasting Corporation (*Nippon Hoso Kyokai,* or NHK) is patterned after the BBC and has an annual budget of more than a billion dollars, all of which comes from a license fee imposed on all TV sets in Japan—$50 a year for a color TV and $30 for a black and white set. Competing with the two NHK channels are five commercial TV networks. TV and radio reach virtually 100 percent of the population as 11,000 transmitters blanket the country. Almost all of the programs on Japanese TV are locally produced. The only popular American show on Japanese TV in the late 1980s was "Airwolf." About 14 percent of all Japanese homes are equipped for cable. At present, however, cable is used to retransmit regular TV into areas that suffer poor TV reception. About 69 percent of all homes have VCRs, and the video software business is booming.

Because of its mountainous terrain, Japan is developing a direct broadcast satellite system (DBS). Plans call for a satellite launch in 1990 that will provide High-Definition TV (HDTV) to NHK viewers.

Japan also has a thriving film industry, with both domestic productions and U.S. imports doing well at the box office. The sound recording industry is well developed. The trade imbalance that the United States generally faces with Japan in other areas does not extend to popular music. Very few Japanese records are hits in the United States, but about one-third of all Japanese record sales come from U.S. or British performers.

Brazil. Brazil is the largest country in South America. Its population is about 145 million, much of it concentrated around urban areas. São Paulo and Rio de Janeiro are its two largest cities. Literacy rates vary, with about 80 percent of those living in metropolitan areas able to read. In the rural sections, literacy is much lower. Annual per capita income averages about $2000, fairly high by Third World standards, but recent inflation has reduced purchasing power. For example, in some cities a copy of the newspaper costs more than a loaf of bread.

Brazil has about 320 daily newspapers with a circulation of about 5 million. *O Globo,* published in Rio, is the leading paper in terms of circulation with almost 300,000 copies sold daily. Every day *O Globo* averages forty-eight pages, emphasizing national and regional news, sports (horse racing in particular), and, to a lesser extent, international news. Its comics page would be familiar to American readers since many U.S. favorites appear in a Brazilian context. "Beetle Bailey" is called "Recruit Zero" and all references are to the Brazilian army. In addition, there are large newspapers in the other Brazilian cities.

The most widely read magazines in Latin America are in Brazil. *Manchete,* the largest, is a weekly news magazine published in Rio with a heavy emphasis on pictures. *Veja,* another large circulation magazine published in São Paulo, resembles *Time* in format. Along with these, the Portuguese-language edition of the *Reader's Digest* is also quite popular, as is *Visions,* a news magazine that is circulated all over Latin America.

Broadcasting in Brazil began in 1922. Currently, there are about 2000 radio stations in the country, about 95 percent of which are privately owned. There are more than 40 million TV sets in operation, many in public settings such as bars, community centers, and schools. TV is the main electronic medium in Brazil, and even the poorest of families has access to the medium. Ads are allowed on virtually all TV and radio stations. In fact, there are four commercial networks, one owned by the magazine *Manchete,* and another owned by the newspaper *O Globo.* Entertainment, features, and sports programming dominate Brazilian TV. In late 1988, two American imports, "Magnum P.I." and "Moonlighting" were both popular. The government operates a TV channel that is primarily educational. Additionally, each commercial station is required to give the government an hour each day for cultural and instructional programs. Cable TV has yet to catch on, but home video is growing among those 4 million Brazilians who can afford the price of a VCR. In fact, in well-to-do neighborhoods, there are videoclubs on almost every block, providing legitimate and pirated videotapes. VCR rentals brought in $60 million in 1987.

In radio, the government operates a national network and the Rural Educational Radio network. The motion picture industry is mainly confined to the urban areas. Brazil has about 1600 theaters, but about 150 sites in Rio and São Paulo account for about 80 percent of the total revenue across the country. Admission is about $1.30 but inflation has recently reduced moviegoing. A company known as Embrafilms, controlled by the government, is the biggest distributor in the country and also finances about two dozen films a year. Because of a massive foreign debt, the government is restricting the importing of U.S. films.

Official state censorship of the media came to an end in 1978. Currently, the Brazilian media are relatively free of government interference. Nonetheless, there are official pressures and guidelines. For example, newspapers are generally free to criticize the government. The government, however, owns the company that distributes newsprint to newspapers. If a paper truly offended the government, it might find its paper supply cut off. The four TV networks are licensed to a progovernment corporation, again providing some indirect leverage. Moreover, television and radio have special obligations placed on them. The Brazilian Telecommunciations Code states that the goals of broadcasting are educational and cultural, even in information and entertainment programming. Thus, commercial stations must provide a minimum of five hours per week of educational programs, and 5 percent of daily programs must be informational. The amount of time given each hour to commercials is also regulated. Radio stations are required to broadcast government-produced programs that teach literacy skills to adults.

Poland. At first glance, Poland may seem an unlikely choice to illustrate the media operations of a communist-controlled country. Upon closer examination, however, it is a good nation to examine since it clearly illustrates that there are wide variations in media systems even within a communist-controlled country. Poland had the freest press in the communist world for a little more than a year in 1980–1981. Then the military took over and in a matter of hours, Poland was at the other extreme: Its media system became the most controlled and most censored in the world. In the late 1980s, under the Soviet philosophy of *glasnost,* things loosened up a bit, but the extent and duration of the new relaxed policy are uncertain.

Poland has about 37 million people. The literacy rate is about 98 percent. There are 44 daily newspapers with a circulation of about 10 million. Another 2500 periodicals are also published. The vast majority of newspapers and magazines are controlled by the Communist party. The party controls the largest publishing group in the country, RSW Prasa. This publishing group also has control over all the distribution channels, making it doubly difficult for nonsanctioned voices to be heard. Before 1982, religious publications and trade union publications were permitted to publish their own newspapers and journals. The crackdown on the Solidarity union organization, however, meant an end to these and other privileges.

Although there are a few exceptions, most Polish newspapers are published in the morning. All papers would seem thin by Western standards, comprising no more than eight to ten pages. Their content could only be described as serious. The largest circulation paper is the *People's Tribune,* required reading for all party members, with about a million copies sold daily. Magazines have a more popular slant, covering sports, women's interests, and youth activities.

Broadcasting in Poland is controlled by the government. There are about forty radio stations and seventy TV stations serving the country. The capital, Warsaw, is the home base for national radio program services. These networks broadcast music, news, educational programs, and a small amount of drama. In addition, the government sponsors an educational channel. There are two national TV channels, and Polish TV is a little more entertainment oriented than Polish radio. Production, distribution, and exhibition of films are all under government control. There are about 2000 film theaters nationwide. Film attendance has been declining over the past two decades, primarily due to economic conditions and competition from TV.

As mentioned above, the relationship between Polish media and the government has varied over the past few years. Most recently, the media have been one of the points of friction between the Solidarity labor movement and the central authorities. In 1980, Polish workers were demanding, among other things, a liberalization of the media. To some extent, this was achieved as a new, more lenient censorship law was enacted, and the Catholic church and trade unions were granted access to the media. As Solidarity consolidated its power, the Polish media underwent a change unique to communist-ruled countries. New magazines and newspapers flourished; radio and television programs were given new freedom. Solidarity itself published a newspaper that instantly became a best-seller. In short, the Polish media had moved away from the communist philosophy of mass communication.

In the midst of these developments, the Polish government declared martial law. Almost immediately, strict rules were placed on the press. Only party-controlled newspapers were allowed to publish. Rigid censorship was imposed, and nothing was to be published without official approval. Only the government-controlled radio network and TV network were allowed to broadcast. TV newscasters were told to put on military uniforms. The government took pains to make ineffective any noncontrolled communication network. Thus the Polish media were brought back into compliance with communist press philosophy.

Then, in the late 1980s, the government loosened its grip. *Res Publica,* an underground magazine, was given legal status in 1987. A Polish rock group called Perfect encouraged its fans to burn Communist party newspapers at one of its rock concerts. Polish TV went so far as to carry a live speech by then-Vice President George Bush in which he was critical of the Polish government. The pope's visit also got extensive TV coverage. Further, almost a million Western-made VCRs have been shipped into Poland since 1981 and the Poles seem to have an insatiable appetite for Western entertainment. A 1987 survey disclosed that the most popular cassettes were Tom Cruise movies and the *Police Academy* series. Although concerned about the cultural and political implications of this influx of Western videocassettes, the government has tolerated their presence. All in all, the Polish media are gradually regaining some of the freedom they had in the early 1980s, but everyone realizes that the political climate could suddenly change.

The "New World Information Order"

As the preceding discussion suggests, there are major differences among countries in the function and role of their mass communication systems. Not surprisingly, these differences often lead to friction. In recent years, the most prominent of these differences had to do with what is generally referred to as the "New World Information Order." In simplified form, here is what this debate is about.

The developing nations feel that the existing system of international communications is controlled by the developed countries of the West. It is further argued that the global coverage of news is dominated by such U.S. organizations as the Associated Press, United Press International, the *New York Times, Newsweek, Time,* CNN, and the three major U.S. TV networks. Under such a system, say the developing countries, news from the Third World is scant, and what news there is reflects unfavorably on the developing nations. Positive news is never carried. Moreover, critics of the existing system argue that Western countries control the available broadcast spectrum and the technology needed to produce and distribute TV and radio programs. These foreign-produced programs tend to dominate the broadcasting systems of the developing countries, who do not have the resources to

Rock and Roll in the U.S.S.R.

The popularity of rock music is worldwide. In the Soviet Union, Western rock made its first appearance with the Beatles, who took the country by storm. Their popularity led the government to approve a tightly controlled rock music industry. Officially approved rock groups with names such as the Songsters, the Optimists, and the Happy Fellows were the hot Soviet rock groups during the 1970s. Their hit songs would probably never make it to the U.S. charts: "How Wonderful the World Is," "It's Not Your Flowers That I love," and the ever-popular "I'll Take You Away to the Tundra." Recently, however, Russian rock has gotten more sophisticated. A 1986 concert for the victims of the Chernobyl nuclear accident featured Soviet rock stars in studded leather surrounded by flashing lights, smoke, lasers, and other special effects.

Glasnost has even found its way into Soviet rock and roll. In 1987, Melodia, the state agency responsible for manufacturing and distributing records, pressed more rock albums than ever before. The Soviet Union still recognizes "official" bands, which belong to a trade union and must submit their music to arts councils for approval, but lately some unoffi-cial groups have been tolerated. Members of official groups get better pay and have readier access to equipment (an important consideration since a Yamaha DX-7 synthesizer costs about 11,000 rubles, twice the price of a new car). Nonetheless, the unofficial groups are surviving and introducing innovations to Soviet rock. Some popular groups are Aquarium (which actually has an album available in the United States), Kino, and Gorky Park, recently signed to a contract by Polygram. Soviet television has recently begun to feature Soviet- and European-produced music videos. In fact, a heavy metal concert featuring Bon Jovi, Motley Crue, and Cinderella took place in Moscow in summer, 1989. The concert is to be shown on pay-per-view TV in the United States.

The biggest problem for the Soviet music industry is outdated production equipment. Russian experts suggest that their country is about twenty to thirty years behind the times. The poor quality of Soviet discs is well known, and most Russians don't buy cassettes, which have a reputation for destroying tape players. Plans for improving Soviet facilities were announced in 1988.

produce their own programs. Thus, the cultural values of the West, particularly those of the United States, are replacing the traditional culture of the developing country. In short, the Western media practice a form of media colonialism over many of the Third World nations.

The forum for much of this debate has been the United Nations, and UNESCO (United Nations Education, Scientific and Cultural Organization) has become deeply involved. In 1980, UNESCO adopted a resolution on the topic that substantially reflected the concerns of many Third World nations (and the Soviet Union). The UNESCO resolution endorsed the philosophy that nations should control the news and entertainment that cross their borders. To be specific, each nation would be entitled to monitor all transborder information, monitor and control foreign media and journalists, and require prior consent for direct broadcasting into the country. It went on to suggest that all journalists should submit to a process that resembled a form of licensing.

The response of Western media professionals to this general argument and the UNESCO resolution was predictable. The Western nations sponsored research to show that Third World nations received their fair share of balanced coverage. Further, the Western tradition of freedom of the press sees any type of control as a threat to journalistic freedom and the free flow of information throughout the world. Journalists should not be licensed and countries should not attempt to draw up official codes of conduct for reporters. There should be no censorship and access to news events should be unrestricted.

Critics of the existing system replied that the research that purported to show balanced coverage was ill planned and shortsighted, and that the free flow of information espoused by those in the West simply meant that the West wanted to keep open profitable Third World markets for its media products.

The participants in this debate were able to agree on at least one thing: Third World nations needed help with their communications development. Accordingly, the International Program for the Development of Communications was created in 1980. Its primary function was to gather and exchange information and arrange consultation in order to help communication systems and services in the developing countries. Western nations have given limited financial support to this program and continue to carefully scrutinize its workings.

The debate between developing and developed countries over information flow is not likely to subside in the future. In fact, this conflict was one of the reasons behind the United States' decision in 1984 to withdraw from UNESCO. (A new secretary general of UNESCO took over in 1987, and his initial statements seemed to indicate that he was willing to take some of the politics out of the organization. Whether the United States uses this opportunity to rejoin UNESCO remains to be seen.) The essence of this disagreement has to do with philosophy. The West, along with some developing countries, believes in a press free from the state and in the right of the press to criticize government and to publicize all points of view. Other developing countries, along with the Soviet bloc, believe that the press has an obligation to support the government, suppress dissent, and help achieve national goals. As is the case with most philosophical disagreements, this one will be hard to settle.

SUGGESTIONS FOR FURTHER READING

The following books contain more information about the concepts and topics discussed in this chapter.

DUNNETT, PETER, *The World Newspaper Industry,* London: Croom Helm, 1988.

GERBNER, GEORGE, AND MARSHA SIEFERT, eds., *World Communications: A Handbook,* New York: Longman, 1984.

HOPKINS, MARK, *Mass Media in the Soviet Union,* New York: Pegasus, 1970.

HOWELL, WILLIAM, *World Broadcasting in the Age of the Satellite,* Norwood, N.J.: Ablex, 1986.

KURIAN, GEORGE, *World Press Encyclopedia,* New York: Facts on File, 1982.

MARTIN, JOHN, AND ANJU CHAUDHARY, eds., *Comparative Mass Media Systems,* New York: Longman, 1983.

MERRILL, JOHN, ed., *Global Journalism,* New York: Longman, 1983.

MICKIEWICZ, ELLEN, *Media and the Russian Public,* New York: Praeger, 1981.

———, *Split Signals: TV and Politics in the Soviet Union,* New York: Oxford University Press, 1988.

Part Two

The Print Media

Chapter 4

History of the Print Media

I t had to be true. There it was, printed in black and white in the August 25, 1835, edition of the *New York Sun*. Sir John Herschel, working with a huge telescope at his new observatory in Cape Town, South Africa, had discovered life on the moon! The August 25 issue quoted Sir John as he described a "moon buffalo":

> Its tail was like that of our *bos gruniens;* but in its semicircular horns, the hump on its shoulders, the depth of its dewlap and the length of its shaggy hair, it closely resembled [the bison]. It had, however, one widely distinctive feature . . . a remarkably fleshy appendage over the eyes.

All of this was pretty hard to believe, but the *Sun* reported that it had taken the story straight from the Edinburgh *Journal of Science*.

Three days later, the *Sun* announced even more fantastic news: Humanlike creatures were flying about the moonscape!

> They averaged four feet in height, were covered, except on the face, with short and glossy copper-colored hair, and had wings composed of a thin membrane, without hair, lying snugly upon their backs, from the top of the shoulders to the calves of the legs. The face, which was a yellowish flesh-color, was a slight improvement upon that of the large orangutan, being more open and intelligent in its expression, and having a much greater expanse of forehead.

The great moon story brought new readers to the *Sun;* its circulation zipped past the 19,000 mark. Suddenly, disaster struck. In an incredible instance of carelessness, Sir John had accidentally left his great telescope facing the sun, and its rays had burned a gaping hole in the lens. No more moon stories.

This last piece of news was too much for some to believe. Scientists demanded to see the original issue of the *Journal of Science* where Herschel's stories had appeared. Letters were on their way to South Africa for confirmation. Finally, a man named Richard Adams Locke had a little too much to drink one night and confessed that he had made up the whole moon story as a gimmick to attract readers to the *Sun*. The *Sun*'s competitors quickly labeled the moon stories as lies, and the *Sun* had to confess to the deception. But it took credit for temporarily diverting the public's attention from the somber cares of the day. The *Sun*'s readers were generally amused and forgiving. The paper never lost its increased circulation.

Newspapers, magazines, and books are in the business of attracting readers. The above example represents an extreme tactic in this process, but it does serve to emphasize a key point. The history of the print media is characterized by political, social, economic, and technological developments that have changed the shape of the newspaper, magazine, and book industries but, in the final analysis, those publications that have succeeded, persisted, and prospered have all been able to attract readers. This short historical sketch will trace the development of newspaper, book, and magazine publishing and briefly illustrate the type of content that managed to get people's attention and interest.

EARLY HISTORY OF PRINTING

The technology necessary to print a newspaper is a simple one—ink is pressed onto paper. The technology necessary to make the newspaper a mass medium is more complicated, and we will begin our brief history with a consideration of the growth of early printing technology. Many historians suggest that the Chinese first invented movable type and also discovered the process for making paper. We do know that Marco Polo described Chinese printing upon his return to Venice in 1295. Nevertheless, prior to the mid-fifteenth century most books and pamphlets available to Europeans were expensive and often inaccurate, handwritten manuscripts. The invention of the printing press and the introduction of movable type to the Western world is usually associated with a German, Johann Gutenberg. Little is known about Gutenberg except that he loved wine, was skilled in metallurgy, had miserable luck as a businessman, and defaulted on several loans (lawsuits filed against Gutenberg provide the only real documentation for naming him father of the printing press). Gutenberg cast his type in soft metal rather than carving it in wood blocks. He borrowed an idea from winemaking and built a crude press that would force the ink onto the paper. Others copied Gutenberg's ideas, and presses spread from Germany throughout Europe during the last half of the fifteenth century. William Caxton, for example, introduced the printing press into Great Britain in 1487 and established a profitable London printing company that published the leading books of the day. Although book publishing was not considered to be a socially important force, Henry

Johann Gutenberg, a German, is usually associated with inventing the printing press and introducing movable type to the Western world. (Culver Pictures)

VIII recognized its potential in 1530 when he required all printers to obtain a royal approval before setting up shop. This notion of publishing "under authority" from the government would figure prominently in the future of the newspaper.

The idea of a mass-circulated newspaper followed the invention of printing. The bulk of early printed matter consisted of books and religious tracts. As more books went into print, more people were encouraged to learn how to read. As literacy grew, more people turned to education, and universities expanded. As education grew, more people became curious about how they lived, how others lived, and how their government was run. Merchants and businesspeople realized that a knowledge of economic conditions and commercial information from other towns and other countries could be beneficial to their own efforts. It wasn't long before publications sprang up across Europe to meet these needs. In Holland, printers began turning out **corantos,** or currents of news, around 1620. Corantos spread to Britain where news about the Thirty Years War was in great demand. These early forerunners of the newspaper carried mainly foreign and commercial news. The corantos were published on and off for the next twenty years, finally expiring because of circulation and license fee problems. They were replaced by the **diurnals,** daily reports of domestic and local events usually concerned with the doings of the king and parliament. This period also saw the rise of the printing of religious books. The Bible and hymnals were widely distributed, as well as a large number of books detailing the controversy surrounding the Reformation and Counter-Reformation. Along with an increase in book publishing came in increase in book suppression. Censorship was common. Even John Milton, the famous English poet who wrote *Areopagetica,* a defense of freedom to publish, was later a government censor.

JOURNALISM IN EARLY AMERICA

In 1686, Benjamin Harris, who had been pilloried in London for printing anticrown pamphlets, arrived in Boston. Four years later, displaying a certain lack of judgment, he published the first American newspaper, *Publick Occurrences Both Foreign and Domestick,* which again contained material offensive to the ruling powers. (One story alleging an affair between the King of France and his son's wife infuriated Boston's Puritan officials. They were aghast that such an account, impugning the integrity of a Christian king, could have reached the residents of their city.) Because of this and other controversial stories, the paper was suppressed after one issue. The idea of a free press had yet to surface in colonial America, and the majority believed that a paper had to have royal consent to be published. Harris' paper had no such consent, and that alone would have been basis enough for the governor of the colony to halt its publication. Fourteen years would pass before another attempt would surface. In 1704, the *Boston News Letter* was published by John Campbell, the local postmaster. Since he owed his position to the local authorities, Campbell tried hard not to offend them, duly licensing his publication with the colony's government and printing the words "Published by Authority" on the front page. His cautious approach resulted in a paper that was safe from suppression, but one that was also lackluster and dull. No stories of philandering kings were found in the *Boston News Letter* pages. Most of Campbell's news consisted of articles clipped from foreign papers, some stories more than five months old. There were notices of ships arriving and departing, summaries of sermons given by local clergy, and death notices. Campbell's paper was a sideline job for him, and it never turned much of a profit. Circulation was probably around 300 subscribers. In 1719, Campbell lost his job as postmaster and his replacement immediately started a rival paper, the *Boston Gazette.*

Campbell did not take kindly to competition. He wrote of the new paper: "I pity [its] readers. Its sheets smell stronger of beer than of midnight oil."

Competition grew as a third newspaper was started in New York and a fourth appeared in Boston. The new arrival in Boston was significant for two reasons. First, it was published by James Franklin (Ben's older brother); and, second, it pioneered a new idea in press philosophy. The elder Franklin correctly noted that other papers carried routine news releases and were careful never to say anything to upset local authorities. Franklin decided that his paper, the *New England Courant,* would be

A front page from The New England Courant, *1722, published first by James Franklin and later by his younger brother Ben. The Franklins resisted the idea of licensing newspapers. (Historical Pictures Service, Chicago).*

THE [N° 58

New-England Courant.

From MONDAY September 3. to MONDAY September 10. 1 7 2 2.

Quod est in corde fobrii, est in ore ebrii.

To the Author of the New-England Courant.

SIR, [No XII.

IT is no unprofitable tho' unpleasant Pursuit, diligently to inspect and consider the Manners & Conversation of Men, who, insensible of the greatest Enjoyments of humane Life, abandon themselves to Vice from a false Notion of *Pleasure* and *good Fellowship.* A true and natural Representation of any Enormity, is often the best Argument against it and Means of removing it, when the most severe Reprehensions alone, are found ineffectual.

I WOULD in this Letter improve the little Observation I have made on the Vice of *Drunkenness,* the better to reclaim the *good Fellows* who usually pay the Devotions of the Evening to *Bacchus.*

I DOUBT not but *moderate Drinking* has been improv'd for the Diffusion of Knowledge among the ingenious Part of Mankind, who want the Talent of a ready Utterance, in order to discover the Conceptions of their Minds in an entertaining and intelligible Manner. 'Tis true, drinking does not *improve* our Faculties, but it enables us to *use* them; and therefore I conclude, that much Study and Experience, and a little Liquor, are of absolute Necessity for some Tempers, in order to make them accomplish'd Orators. *Dic. Ponder* discovers an excellent Judgment when he is inspir'd with a Glass or two of *Claret,* but he passes for a Fool among those of small Observation, who never saw him the better for Drink. And here it will not be improper to observe, That the moderate Use of Liquor, and a well plac'd and well regulated Anger, often produce this same Effect; and some who cannot ordinarily talk but in broken Sentences and false Grammar, do in the Heat of Passion express themselves with as much Eloquence as Warmth. Hence it is that my own Sex are generally the most eloquent, because the most passionate. "It has been said in the Praise of some Men, "(says an ingenious Author,) that they could talk "whole Hours together upon any thing; but it "must be owned to the Honour of the other Sex, "that there are many among them who can talk "whole Hours together upon Nothing. I have "known a Woman branch out into a long extempo- "re Dissertation on the Edging of a Petticoat, and "chide her Servant for breaking a China Cup, in all "the Figures of Rhetorick."

BUT after all it must be consider'd, that no Pleasure can give Satisfaction or prove advantageous to a reasonable Mind, which is not attended with the Restraints of Reason. Enjoyment is not to be found by Excess in any sensual Gratification; but on the contrary, the immoderate Cravings of the Voluptuary, are always succeeded with Loathing and a pal-

led Appetite. What Pleasure can the Drunkard have in the Reflection, that, while in his Cups, he retain'd only the Shape of a Man, and acted the Part of a Beast; or that from reasonable Discourse a few Minutes before, he descended to Impertinence and Nonsense?

I CANNOT pretend to account for the different Effects of Liquor on Persons of different Dispositions, who are guilty of Excess in the Use of it. 'Tis strange to see Men of a regular Conversation become rakish and profane when intoxicated with Drink, and yet more surprizing to observe, that some who appear to be the most profligate Wretches when sober, become mighty religious in their Cups, and will then, and at no other Time address their Maker, but when they are destitute of Reason, and actually affronting him. Some shrink in the Wetting, and others swell to such an unusual Bulk in their Imaginations, that they can in an Instant understand all Arts and Sciences, by the liberal Education of a little vivifying *Punch,* or a sufficient Quantity of other exhilerating Liquor.

AND as the Effects of Liquor are various, so are the Characters given to its Devourers. It argues some Shame in the Drunkards themselves, in that they have invented numberless Words and Phrases to cover their Folly, whose proper Significations are harmless, or have no Signification at all. They are seldom known to be *drunk,* tho they are very often *boozey, cogey, tipsey, fox'd, merry, mellow, fuddl'd, groatable, Confoundedly cut, See two Moons, are Among the Philistines, In a very good Humour, See the Sun,* or, *The Sun has shone upon them;* they *Clip the King's English,* are *Almost froze, Feavourish, In their Altitudes, Pretty well enter'd,* &c. In short, every Day produces some new Word or Phrase which might be added to the Vocabulary of the *Tiplers:* But I have chose to mention these few, because if at any Time a Man of Sobriety and Temperance happens to *cut himself confoundedly,* or is *almost froze,* or *feavourish,* or accidentally *sees the Sun,* &c. he may escape the Imputation of being *drunk,* when his Misfortune comes to be related.

I am SIR,
Your Humble Servant,

SILENCE DOGOOD.

FOREIGN AFFAIRS.

Berlin, May 8. Twelve Prussian Batallions are sent to Mecklenburg, but for what Reason is not known. 'Tis said, the Emperor, suspecting the Designs of the Czar, will secure all the Domains of the Duke of Mecklenburg. His Prussian Majesty, to promote the intended Union of the Reformed and Lutherans in his Dominions, has charged the Ministers of those two Communions, not to make the least mention in the Pulpits of the religious Differences about some abstruser Points, particularly the Doctrine of Predestination, and to forbear all contumelious Expressions against one another.

Hamburg, May 8. The Imperial Court has order'd the Circles of Lower Saxony, to keep in Rea-

Advertising Colonial Style

Early advertising resembled what we today would call classified ads. Ads were set with no display type and were typically found in a column on the last page of the paper. The articles advertised were many and varied. In fact, if you were to read the ads in an early paper, you might not know what was being sold. For example, a 1752 paper advertised the following: durants, duroys, dowlahs, shaloons, camblets, alopeens, and sagathies.

Ben Franklin was one of the first ad copywriters. The following was the text for one of his ads touting a product called "Super Fine Crown Soap":

It cleanses fine Linens, Muslins, Laces, Chinces, Cambricks, with Ease and Expedition, which often suffer more from the long and hard rubbing of the Washer, through the ill qualities of the soap than the wearing.

(Incidentally, the soap Franklin was describing was made by his brothers John and Peter. A shrewd businessman, Franklin endorsed the idea of keeping the money in the family.)

different. He published without the approval of local government. His independence quickly got him into trouble, however, and the colonial magistrates threw him into prison and later forbade him from publishing a newspaper without their prior approval. James neatly got around this latter proscription by naming Ben as the new publisher of the *Courant*. The paper prospered under Ben's tenure as publisher and his writings were highly praised. Sibling rivalry eventually intervened, and Ben moved to Philadelphia where he started the *Pennsylvania Gazette*. Ben Franklin retired from a successful publishing career at the age of forty-two. During this time he started the first newspaper chain, founded the first American foreign-language paper, published one of the first American magazines (see the section on "Magazines of the Colonial Period"), ran the first editorial cartoon, proved that advertising copy could sell merchandise (see boxed material) and, perhaps most important, demonstrated that journalism could be an honorable profession.

The Beginnings of Revolution

Tensions between colonies and crown were rising during Franklin's tenure as publisher, and this controversy sparked the development of the early press. One example of this tension was the trial of John Peter Zenger. In 1733, Zenger was persuaded by his influential backers to publish a newspaper that was openly critical of the British-born Royal Governor of New York. The governor promptly jailed Zenger and charged him with criminal libel. Famous lawyer Andrew Hamilton defended Zenger and capitalized upon the growing colonial resentment of Britain to win his case. Hamilton argued that despite precedents in British law to the contrary, truth could be used as a defense against libel and that a jury of Americans ought not feel bound by laws formed in England and not approved in America. The jury agreed and rendered a not-guilty verdict, thus striking a symbolic blow for press freedom.

Newspapers grew in numbers in the period before the Revolutionary War. Most of them were partisan, siding with the colonies or with the crown; others tried to steer a middle ground. In any case, this period marks the establishment of the **political press,** which openly supported a particular party, faction, or cause. The early newspaper editors, divided though they might be over some issues, were united

A good deal of time and energy was required to publish even a simple newspaper on early colonial printing presses like the one depicted here. (Culver Pictures).

as never before by the passage of the Stamp Act of 1765. The act imposed a penny tax per issue upon each newspaper and was despised by nearly all editors, who saw it as an attempt to put them out of business and as one more example of taxation without representation. The opposition to the act was so vehement that it was repealed the next year.

As the revolution commenced, the colonial papers were thoroughly politicized. In addition to news, the papers reprinted excerpts from the many political pamphlets that were circulating at this time. In fact, the Declaration of Independence was published in the *Pennsylvania Evening Post* on July 6, 1776.

As the war intensified, the press became even more polarized, splitting into propatriot and pro-British factions. Most were prorevolution. About thirty-seven papers were published as the war began, and twenty of these survived. Several new papers sprang up during the war, and enough of these managed to stay in business so that by the end of the conflict approximately thirty-five newspapers were published regularly.

Magazines of the Colonial Period

In colonial times, the word "magazine" meant warehouse or depository, a place where various types of provisions were stored under one roof. The first **magazines** printed in America were patterned after this model; they were to be storehouses of varied literary materials gathered from books, pamphlets, and newspapers and bound together under one cover.

It was Ben Franklin who first announced plans to start a magazine in the colonies. Unfortunately for Ben, a competitor named Andrew Bradford got wind of his idea and beat Franklin to the punch. Bradford's *American Magazine* was published a few days before Franklin's *General Magazine* in 1741. The two publications carried political and economic articles aimed at an intelligent audience. Both were ambitious ventures in that they were designed for readers in all thirteen colonies and deliberately tried to influence public opinion; however, both quickly folded because of financial problems. The next significant attempt at magazine publishing occurred in Philadelphia when another Bradford (this one named William) started the *American Magazine and Monthly Chronicle* in 1757. This publication also contained the usual blend of political and economic articles mixed with a little humor; it was well edited and able to support itself for a year.

As America's political relations with England deteriorated, magazines, like newspapers, assumed a more significant political role. Thomas Paine, who, in his rousing pamphlet *Common Sense,* argued for separation from England, became editor of the *Pennsylvania Magazine*. This publication strongly supported the revolution and was a significant political force during the early days of the war. It became an early casualty of the conflict, however, and closed down in 1776. Other magazines appeared during and after the war, but they were seldom profitable and usually ceased publication within a year or two.

To summarize, it is clear that all these early magazines were aimed at a specialized audience—one that was educated, literate, and primarily urban. They contained a variety of articles dealing with the arts, practical science, and politics, and a list of authors who contributed to them would include most of the major poets, essayists, and statesmen of the period. Their overall impact was to encourage literary and artistic expression and to unify the colonies during America's struggle for independence from England.

Books of the Colonial Period

In 1640, the Puritans in Cambridge, Massachusetts, printed the *Bay Psalm Book*. About 90,000 other titles were to follow it as book publishing took hold in the American colonies. In addition to locally published books, many volumes were imported from England. Among the more popular books printed in the colonies during the second half of the seventeenth century were *The Practice of Piety, a Sure Guide to Heaven,* and *Day of Doom*. Reading was a popular pastime of the early settlers and public libraries sprang up to serve their needs. Benjamin Franklin was instrumental in starting a library in Philadelphia. In a short period, other libraries opened in New York, Rhode Island, and South Carolina. During the Revolutionary War, many book printers turned out political pamphlets. Thomas Paine's *Common Sense* sold 100,000 copies in ten weeks.

Content: Topical Items and Partisan Politics

Newspapers and magazines in the colonial period carried a variety of items dealing with politics, crime, commerce, travel, and happenings in Europe. Benjamin Harris' *Publick Occurrences* contained a wide smattering of news items (in addition to the ones that landed him in trouble). Harris informed his early readers about the Indians selecting a day of formal Thanksgiving, an unnamed man committing suicide, the easing of the small-pox epidemic in Boston, and war news. Although the paper made perfect sense to the inhabitants of late-seventeenth-century Boston, some items would be unintelligible for the reader of the 1990s. For example, one item began with the following: "There lately arrived in Piscataqua, one Papoon from Penobscot in a small Shallop. . . ."

The *Pennsylvania Gazette* was notable for several innovations in content and style. Ben Franklin's paper had a cleaner makeup, with rules dividing the various stories and classified ads. The type was easier to read, and Franklin made an attempt to set off what we might call headlines from the rest of the items. He made use of short paragraphs to compress the news into a limited space. Here, for example, was one such news item that illustrated this trend and revealed a little bit about colonial crime and punishment:

> Last Week William Kerr . . . was indicted and convicted at the Mayor's Court of counterfeiting . . . Pieces of Eight . . . for which he received sentence as follows: To stand in the Pillory one Hour To-Morrow, to have his ear nail'd to same, and the part nail'd cut off and on Saturday next to stand another hour in the Pillory and to be Whipt 39 lashes . . . and then to pay a fine of 50 Pounds.

Perhaps the most interesting of Franklin's achievements was his skillful writing of advertising copy. (See boxed material earlier in chapter.)

During the years of the Revolution, news of war and politics dominated the pages of the young nation's newspapers. The most famous of the revolutionary papers was Isaiah Thomas' *Massachusetts Spy.* Although Thomas tried to maintain neutrality during the early years of his publishing career, the pressures for independence in his city were too great and eventually the *Spy* became a revolutionary paper. Thomas has the distinction of being the first war correspondent, and below is a sample of his reporting of the battle of Lexington:

> The [British] troops in the meantime . . . had crossed the river and landed at Phipp's farm. They immediately . . . proceeded to Lexington . . . with great silence. A company of militia, of about eighty men, mustered near the meeting house; the troops came in sight of them just before sunrise. The militia, upon seeing the troops, began to disperse. The troops then set out upon the run . . . and the commanding officer accosted the militia in words to this effect, "Disperse, you damn'd rebels—Damn you, disperse." Upon which . . . one or two officers discharged their pistols, which were instantaneously followed by the firing of four or five of the soldiers; and then there seemed to be a general discharge from the whole body. Eight of our men were killed and nine wounded.

Magazine content in the colonial period was quite varied. An early issue of Franklin's *General Magazine,* for example, carried ten pages of poems, sermons, book reviews, an article on the currency problem in the colonies, and a news section. Later articles would discuss a religious revival in the colonies, an orphanage recently founded in Georgia, and "A New Method of Making Molasses." Franklin's many interests and pursuits were clearly visible in his magazine.

Of all the magazine writers in the period of the political press, William Cobbett was the best known. A British refugee, Cobbett began editing *Porcupine's Gazette and Daily Advertiser* in 1797. Cobbett made no pretense of being objective; he lashed out at all politicians who displeased him with unrestrained invective. He called Benjamin Franklin's grandson, Ben Franklin Bache, "Lightning Rod Junior." Cobbett didn't stop there; this is what he wrote of Ben Franklin: ". . . a crafty and lecherous old hypocrite . . . whose very statue seems to gloat on the wenches as they walk the State House Yard." It was no wonder that a rival editor called Cobbett "the celebrated manufacturer of lies, and retailer of filth." Cobbett's writings typified some of the more extreme editorial invective of that period.

The content of Joseph Dennie's *Port Folio* magazine was of unusually high quality. Its first issue featured an article by John Adams, "Tour through Silesia."

Political articles became more numerous in succeeding issues, and in 1804 Dennie devoted an entire issue to an examination of the causes of the Alexander Hamilton–Aaron Burr duel. *Port Folio* was a diverse publication, however, and not all of its contents were somber. Here, for example, is a joke from an 1802 issue: "A gentleman, informed by a bill on a window of a house that apartments were to let, knocked at the door and, attended by a pretty female took a survey of the premises. 'Pray my dear,' said he smiling, 'are you to be let with the lodgings?' 'No,' [she] replied . . . 'I am to be let alone.' " Not exactly *Playboy's* Party Jokes, but Hugh Hefner was still more than a century away.

Book content during the colonial period was primarily concerned with religion. There were, however, several publications that were more secular in tone. Benjamin Franklin's *Poor Richard's Almanack* sold about 10,000 copies a year. Sentimental novels, many of them imported from England, were also popular.

The Political Press: 1790–1830

The politicization of newspapers did not end with America's victory in the Revolutionary War. Instead, partisan leanings of the press were transferred into another arena—the debate over the powers of the federal government. The lineup of those who were participants in this controversy included some of the best political thinkers of the time: Alexander Hamilton, James Madison, Thomas Jefferson, John Jay. Newspapers were quick to take sides in this debate, and their pages were filled with Federalist or anti-Federalist propaganda. Hamilton and his Federalists used the *Gazette of the United States* as the "official" outlet for their views. The leader of the anti-Federalists, Thomas Jefferson, sought to counteract the influence of the *Gazette* by starting a rival paper in 1791, the *National Gazette*. Heated political debate gave way to name-calling and quarreling between these two groups, and the content of many newspapers became colored by volatile and inflammatory language. A typical example of the rhetoric in these early papers is found in the anti-Federalist *Aurora*, edited by Benjamin Franklin Bache ("Lightning Rod Junior"). Concerning President Washington, Bache wrote, ". . . if ever a nation was debauched by a man, the American nation has been debauched by Washington." Supporters of Washington and Federalism wrecked Bache's office and beat him up (communication scholars would call this an example of negative feedback).

At the vortex of this debate between Federalists and anti-Federalists was the Constitution of the United States. Although the original document made no mention of the right of a free press, a series of ten amendments, popularly called the Bill of Rights, did contain such a provision. The **first amendment** held that "Congress shall make no law . . . abridging the freedom of speech, or of the press. . . ." Thus the idea of a free press, which had grown during the revolutionary period, became part of the law of the new nation when Congress ratified this amendment in 1791.

Unfortunately, even after the amendment had been passed, the notion of a free press was not completely accepted. Press attacks on political leaders continued unabated. Freed from repressive government regulation, early newspapers found it easy to go to extremes. A controversy regarding U.S. relations with France touched off a journalistic battle filled with invective. Here, for example, is what Federalist editor William Cobbett had to say about our friend Benjamin Franklin Bache: ". . . This atrocious wretch . . . is an ill-looking devil. His eyes never get above your knees. He is of sallow complexion, hollow-cheeked, dead-eyed, and [looks] like a fellow who has been about a week or ten days [hanging on a gallows]." Bache seemed to inspire strong feelings. When another angry rival editor, James Fenno, ran into Bache on the street, Fenno beat him with a cane (another example of negative feedback).

In the late 1790s, with Federalist John Adams as president, the government sought to curb press criticism of its policies and check the volatile writings of other irritating journalists by passing the **Sedition Act.** This act made it a crime to write anything about the U.S. government or Congress that might be ''false, scandalous or malicious.'' Public opinion, however, was not on the side of this repressive law and it was allowed to expire in 1801.

Newspapers grew with the country in the first twenty years of the new century. The daily newspaper began in 1783 and grew slowly. By 1800, most large cities had at least one daily paper. By 1820, there were 24 dailies, 66 semi- or tri-weeklies, and 422 weeklies. Circulations were not large, usually around 1500, except for the big-city papers. The number was small because these newspapers were read primarily by the upper socioeconomic classes; early readers had to be literate and possess money to spend on subscriptions (about $10 per year or 6 cents an issue—a large sum when you consider that during these years 5 cents could buy a pint of whiskey). The content was typified by commercial and business news, political and congressional debates, speeches, acts of state legislatures, and official messages. Still, the audience was growing. As the population moved westward, so did the printing presses. A paper was started in St. Louis in 1808. Frontier Detroit had a newspaper, the *Gazette,* in 1817. By 1833, there were approximately 1200 papers printed in the country.

During this period, several newspapers arose in response to the needs and interests of minority groups. *Freedom Journal,* the first of over forty black newspapers published before 1860, was founded in the late 1820s by the Reverend Samual Cornish and John Russwurm. Written and edited by blacks, the paper championed the cause of black people by dealing with the serious problems arising from slavery and by carrying news of foreign countries such as Haiti and Sierra Leone that appealed to its black audience.

At about the same time, another minority group, the Cherokee Indian nation, was being pressured by the federal government to abandon its tribal lands in Georgia and relocate further west. A Cherokee scholar named Sequoyah became fascinated with the written prose of the whites, for he was convinced that the secret of their superior power lay in their ability to transmit knowledge through a written language. Subsequently, he set out to develop a system of writing for his own people. After experimenting for over a decade, he developed an alphabet, consisting of eighty-six characters, by which the Cherokee language could be set down in written form. His new system enabled his people to learn to read and write. The tribe set up schools where Sequoyah's alphabet was taught and published books in the Cherokee language. Eventually, the first Indian newspaper, the *Cherokee Phoenix,* written in both Cherokee and English, appeared in 1828.

Magazines After the Revolution

Like the prerevolutionary publications that preceded them, magazines popular during the late eighteenth and early nineteenth centuries contained a mix of political and topical articles directed primarily at an educated elite. The birth of the modern news magazine can also be traced back to this period. *Niles Weekly Register,* which reported current events of the time, was read throughout the country. The *North American Review,* started in 1815, was more parochial in its contents, focusing primarily on New England art and politics.

The influence of the political press was also reflected in magazines of the period. One of the most influential was the *Port Folio,* edited by the colorful nonconformist Joseph Dennie. Dennie's intended audience was a select one; he wished to reach "Men of Affluence, Men of Liberality, and Men of Letters." Although the major thrust of the paper was political, Dennie interspersed travelogues, theater reviews, satirical essays, and even jokes, some of them mildly suggestive. It was politics, however, that got Dennie into trouble and got the *Port Folio* tremendous visibility. Dennie was an admirer of all things British and despised the new Republic. He once called the Declaration of Independence a "false, flatulent and foolish paper." He declared democracy a mistake. The government indicted him for seditious libel (another form of negative feedback), but Dennie was finally acquitted. *Port Folio* went on publishing until 1827.

BIRTH OF THE MASS NEWSPAPER

Benjamin Day was only twenty-two years old when he developed the idea of a newspaper for the masses. Day probably had no idea that he was starting a revolution in the communications industry when he launched his *New York Sun* in 1833. Nonetheless, journalism would be profoundly altered by his new approach. Several conditions had to exist before a mass press could come into existence.

1. a printing press had to be invented that would produce copies quickly and cheaply

2. enough people had to know how to read in order to support such a press

3. a "mass audience" had to be present

Day would never have been able to launch his newspaper without significant advances in printing technology. Frederick Koenig had perfected a two-cylinder press in 1814 that printed both sides of the paper at once and could turn out copies at the rate of 1100 per hour. The next step was to harness an outside power source to the press to increase its speed. In 1822, Dan Treadwell took this idea literally and harnessed a real horse to his machine, thus creating a true one-horsepower printing press. The horse's career in journalism didn't last long, as the animal was quickly replaced by steam power. In 1830, the U.S. firm of R. Hoe and Company marketed a press that could produce 4000 double impressions an hour. By 1833, the technology had advanced enough to justify the production of an extremely cheap newspaper that almost everybody could afford.

The second element that led to the growth of the mass newspaper was the increased level of literacy in the population. The first statewide public school system was set up during the 1830s and, in addition to a large number of private elementary schools in the major cities, there were also at least fifty colleges scattered about the various states. The increased emphasis on education led to a concomitant growth of literacy as many people in the middle and lower economic groups acquired reading skills.

The third element was more subtle and harder to explain. The mass press appeared during an era that historians call the age of "Jacksonian democracy." It was an age in which ordinary people were first recognized as a political and economic force. Property requirements for voting had died out. Every state but one in 1832 chose presidential electors by popular vote. In addition, this period was marked by the rise of an urban middle class. The shift from homemade goods to factory-made goods encouraged by the Industrial Revolution was plainly evident in the United States at this time. The trend toward "democratization" of business and politics fostered the creation of a mass audience responsive to a mass press. All of these factors made it possible for Day to attract readers to his paper.

THE PENNY PRESS

Day had seen others fail in their attempts to market a mass-appeal newspaper. Nonetheless, he forged ahead. Day's paper would be a daily and would sell for a penny. This was a significant price reduction when compared to the other New York City, Boston, and Philadelphia dailies, which went for six cents a copy. (The price of six cents was also typical for many weekly papers in other parts of the country. Since they came out less frequently, these papers were cheaper than the *Sun* on an annual basis. Thus although the penny press did not mark a drop in the overall price of American newspapers, it did signal a decrease in the price of urban dailies.) Local happenings, sex, violence, features, and human-interest stories would constitute his content. The first issue contained news of a suicide, police and crime items, shipping information, weddings, obituaries, and feature stories. Conspicuously absent were the stodgy political debates that still characterized many of the six-cent papers. Within six months the *Sun* achieved a circulation of approximately 8000 issues, far ahead of its nearest competitor. Day's gamble had paid off, and the **penny press** was launched.

Others imitated the success of Day's new penny paper. Perhaps the most significant and certainly the most colorful of these individuals was James Gordon Bennett. In 1835, Bennett launched his *New York Herald*. The paper started in humble surroundings—a cellar on Wall Street equipped with two chairs and a desk made by balancing a plank on two flour barrels. Bennett was able to move into more spacious surroundings soon afterward because the *Herald* was even more of a rapid success than the *Sun*. Part of Bennett's success can be attributed to his skillful reporting of crime news, the institution of a financial page, sports reporting, and an aggressive editorial policy. Bennett looked upon himself as a reformer, and in one of his fulsome editorials he wrote: "I go for a general reformation of morals. . . . I mean to begin a new movement in the progress of civilization. . . . Get out of my way ye driveling editors and driveling politicians." This pugnacious attitude was not without risk, and on one occasion one of those rival "driveling editors" cornered Bennett and beat him about the head and shoulders with a cane (more negative feedback).

Another important pioneer of the era was Horace Greeley. His *New York Tribune* appeared in 1841 and would rank third behind the *Sun* and *Herald* in daily circulation, but its weekly edition was circulated nationally and proved to be a great success. Greeley's *Tribune* was not as sensational as its competitors. He used his editorial page for crusades and causes. He opposed capital punishment, alcohol, gambling, and tobacco. He favored a high tariff, trade unions, and westward expansion (the famous quotation usually attributed to Greeley, "Go west, young man," was actually first said by an Indiana newspaperman, but Greeley would have agreed with its sentiment). Greeley also favored women's rights. In 1845, he hired Margaret Fuller as literary critic for the *Tribune*. In addition to her commentary on the fine arts, Fuller published articles dealing with the hard lot of prostitutes, women prisoners, and the insane. Her work attracted strong public interest, and today she is regarded

The New York Times, *first published in 1851, was one of the major newspapers of the penny-press era. This front page from 1862 describes some of the events of the Civil War and includes a map depicting the activity of the Army of the Potomac. (The Bettmann Archive)*

as one of the finest critics of her generation. She also became the first woman foreign correspondent. Greeley's decision to hire Fuller is typical of his publishing philosophy: Like Fuller, he never talked down to the mass audience and attracted his readers by appealing to their intellect more than to their emotions.

The last of the major newspapers of the penny-press era that we shall consider began in 1851 and, at this writing, was still publishing. The *New York Times*, edited by Henry Raymond, promised to be less sensational than the *Sun* or the *Herald* and less impassioned than Greeley. The paper soon established a reputation for objective and reasoned journalism. Raymond stressed the gathering of foreign news and served as foreign correspondent himself in 1859. The *Times* circulation reached more than 40,000 before the Civil War.

Finally, all of these publishers had one thing in common. As soon as their penny papers were successful, they doubled the price.

Significance of the Penny Press

At this point, we should consider the major changes in journalism that were prompted by the success of the mass press during the 1833–1860 period. In short, we can identify four such changes. The penny press changed

1. the basis of economic support for newspapers

2. the pattern of newspaper distribution

3. the definition of what constituted news

4. the techniques of news collection

Before the penny press, most of a newspaper's economic support came from subscription revenue. The large circulation of the penny papers made advertisers realize that they could reach a large segment of potential buyers by purchasing space. Moreover, the readership of the popular papers cut across political party and social class lines, thereby assuring a potential advertiser of a broadly based audience. As a result, advertisers were greatly attracted to this new medium, and the mass newspapers relied significantly more on advertising revenues than did their predecessors.

Older papers were distributed primarily through the mails; the penny press, although relying somewhat on subscriptions, also made use of street sales. Vendors would buy 100 copies for 67 cents and sell them for one cent each. Soon it became common to hear newsboys hawking papers at most corners in the larger cities. Since these papers had to compete with one another in the open marketplace of the street, editors went out of their way to find original and exclusive news that would give their paper an edge. Page makeup and type styles changed in order to attract the attention of the casual passerby.

The penny press also redefined the concept of news. The older papers were passive information collectors; they printed information that others might have sent them or news that might have been published first elsewhere. Thus stories appearing in the foreign press were reprinted, letters from congressmen were reproduced, and official reports from the federal government and presidential speeches were carried verbatim. There was no systematic search for news. The penny press changed that by hiring people to go out and look for news. Reporters were assigned to special "beats": police, financial, sports, and religion, to name a few. Foreign correspondents were popular. Even Karl Marx served as a London correspondent for the *Tribune* (he quit when Greeley forced a salary cut on him). The penny papers created the role of the paid news gatherer. Newspapers changed their emphasis from the affairs of the commercial and political elite to the social life of the rising middle classes.

This shift meant that news became more of a commodity, something that had value. And, like many commodities, fresh news was more valuable than stale news. The increased competition among the papers of the era further emphasized this fact. Any scheme that would get the news into the paper faster was tried. Stories were

News carriers first appeared in the streets of New York to sell Benjamin Day's Sun. *This group of American newsboys poses outside the office of the Greek newspaper* Atlantis. *(Atlantis Photographs, Balch Institute for Ethnic Studies)*

sent by carrier pigeon, pony express, railroads, and steamships as the newspapers kept pace with the advances in transportation. The biggest innovation in news gathering of this time was the invention of the telegraph in 1844. The Mexican War of 1846 made fast news transmission especially desirable, and many newspapers first used the telegraph to carry news about this conflict. All in all, the penny papers increased the importance of speed in news collection.

Magazines in the Penny-Press Era

While the penny press was opening up new markets for newspapers, magazine publishers were also quietly expanding their appeal and coverage. The *Knickerbocker* (as the name suggests, a New York publication), *Graham's Magazine,* and the *Saturday Evening Post* all started between 1820 and 1840 and were written not so much for the intelligentsia as for the generally literate middle classes. By 1842, *Graham's,* under the direction of Edgar Allan Poe, had a circulation of 40,000. The growing social and economic importance of women was illustrated by the birth of *Godey's Lady's Book* in 1830 and *Peterson's* in 1842. These two magazines offered articles on fashion, morals, diets, and health hints and printed elaborate hand-colored engravings in their pages. *Godey's,* under the editorship of Sarah Hale, was a pioneer for women's rights and was the first magazine to campaign for wider recognition of women writers. By 1850, *Godey's* had a circulation of more than 150,000.

Technological improvements in printing and in the reproduction of illustrations also helped to expand the magazine audience. In 1850, *Harper's Monthly* was started as a magazine that would present material that had already appeared in other sources (rather like the *Reader's Digest,* except that the articles were reprinted in full).

During the late 1800s, magazines and newspapers expanded their audiences by the introduction of elaborate woodcut illustrations. Illustrated articles introduced pictures as a significant element of journalism and opened the door for acceptance of photographs. Some of the finest woodcuts of the period ran in Harper's Weekly: *This illustration publicizes the erection of the Statue of Liberty in New York Harbor. (Harper's Weekly).*

Harper's also included elaborate woodcut illustrations along with its articles in double-sized issues. *Harper's Weekly* was instituted seven years later and was to become famous for its illustrations of the Civil War. In 1863, this magazine began publishing reproductions of Mathew Brady's war photographs.

The sensationalist and crusading approach of the penny press also translated itself into at least two magazines. *Frank Leslie's Illustrated Newspaper* was a sixteen-page weekly that sold for a dime and concentrated on lurid illustrations of murders, morgues, and mayhem. The *New York Ledger,* started in 1855 by Robert Bonner,

THE TAMMANY TIGER LOOSE.

The scathing editorial cartoons of Thomas Nast are credited with the downfall of the "Tammany Hall" group of political bosses under the direction of William Tweed. One of Nast's most famous cartoons, "The Tammany Tiger Loose—What Are You Going to Do About It?" incited voters and resulted in Tweed's eventual indictment for grand larceny. (Brown Brothers).

printed the best work of the period's popular writers and ran melodramatic serials in issue after issue. Bonner promoted his magazine heavily and would occasionally print the first few pages of a detective story in a local newspaper and then break off with "continued in the *New York Ledger,*" thus hooking his readers. He would also buy full-page ads in the newspaper that proclaimed "THE NEW YORK LEDGER WILL BE ON SALE TOMORROW MORNING THROUGHOUT THE UNITED STATES AND NEW JERSEY," which probably did little for his popularity in New Jersey.

The crusading spirit was evident in *Leslie's* campaign against contaminated milk in 1858. The magazine took on the power structure of New York City, and the exposé showed that the magazine as well as the newspaper could be used for civic and social reform. The most famous crusade, however, was probably that of *Harper's Weekly* against the corrupt political administration in New York in 1870. Under the control of William "Boss" Tweed, a group of unscrupulous politicians managed to bilk the city out of approximately $200 million. The editorial cartoons of Thomas Nast were credited with helping to bring down this ring.

Books in the Penny-Press Era

The change in printing technology and the growth of literacy also helped the book publishing industry. Many of the publishing companies still active today can trace their roots to this period. Many publishers specialized in professional and educational books, while others addressed their efforts to the general public. Book prices declined and authors such as James Fenimore Cooper and Henry Wadsworth Longfellow were popular, as were the works of English authors. Public education and the penny newspaper created a demand for reading materials. The number of public libraries tripled between 1825 and 1850. Book reading became a symbol of education and knowledge. Paperback books made their debut during the 1830s, but an unfavorable ruling by the postal department ended their popularity by the mid-1840s.

Content: Popular Appeal of the Penny Press

The goal of the print media to reach a mass audience was made possible by advances in printing technology and by a rise in the literacy level of the population. Whereas content of earlier publications had been aimed primarily at an educated elite, news-papers and magazines now hastened to appeal to the interests of new readers in the middle and working classes. The following capsule description of the contents of Ben Day's first issue of the *Sun* on September 3, 1833, will help illustrate the appeal of the penny press. Page size was eight by eleven inches, with three columns to the page, four pages in all. The first column on page one was devoted to news of sailing times for ocean-going vessels. The remainder of page one carried a feature story about "An Irish Captain" who had been in six duels. There was no indication if the story was fact or fiction. On page two was news of a suicide, followed by nine items under the headline "Police Office." Shorter items told of an approaching execution, a murder, a burglary, a fire, an earthquake, a murder trial, cholera in Mexico, and, somewhat out of place, a dinner given for the Postmaster General in Nashville. Page three carried news about another murder, a prison uprising, shipping news, weddings, and death announcements; the rest of the page carried ads. The last page contained a long poem, a table containing the current prices of bank notes (private banks of that period issued their own money), and eight more ads. The political opinion commonly found in the six-cent papers was not present in the *Sun*.

As mentioned earlier, James Gordon Bennett was another prominent figure in the penny-press era. Bennett craved attention and was not averse to using the pages of his *Herald* to brag of his success (he once wrote that his paper would receive $30,000 in revenue for the next two years) and to make plain his lofty goals ("I am determined to make the *Herald* the greatest paper that ever appeared in the world."). Bennett was never one for modesty: "I have infused life, glowing eloquence, philosophy, taste, sentiment, wit and humor into the daily newspaper. . . . Shake-speare is the great genius of the drama . . . and I mean to be the genius of the daily newspaper press." Bennett's desire for self-publicity was perhaps best exemplified by his announcement of his forthcoming marriage, printed in the June 1, 1840, *Herald:*

> I am going to be married in a few days. The weather is so beautiful; times are getting so good . . . that I cannot resist the divine instinct of honest nature any longer; so I am going to be married to one of the most splendid women in intellect, in heart, in soul, in property, in person, in manner, that I have yet seen in the course of my interesting pilgrimage through life. . . . I must give the world a pattern of happy wedded life.

Bennett, of course, was already married in spirit to his newspaper, and he used his upcoming wedding to get in a plug for it: "Association, night and day, in sickness and in health . . . with a woman of the highest order of excellence, must produce some curious results in my heart and feelings, and these results the future will develop in due time in the columns of the *Herald*." Bennett married Henrietta Crean shortly thereafter, took her to Niagara Falls, and continued to send back columns to the *Herald* all during his honeymoon.

The efforts of magazines to appeal to a wider audience are evidenced by a brief examination of the contents of two leaders during this period: *Knickerbocker* and *Graham's*. Washington Irving and James Fenimore Cooper were frequent contributors to *Knickerbocker,* and the work of Nathaniel Hawthorne and Henry Wadsworth Longfellow also appeared in its pages. In 1846, the *Knickerbocker* capitalized on the growing interest in the American West and serialized Francis Parkman's *The Oregon Trail*. *Graham's* content was varied. An 1842 issue contained a love story, a Longfellow poem, and an article by Edgar Allen Poe in which he analyzed the handwriting of some well-known figures of the day. These early magazines succeeded in bringing the work of well-known literary figures to a wider audience.

The novels of Charles Dickens and Walter Scott continued to be best-sellers during this period, as were books by Herman Melville and Henry David Thoreau. Specialized books also appeared. In the late 1840s, textbooks were profitable, as were reference, medical, and engineering books. Noah Webster's *Dictionary of the English Language* appeared in 1828 and the *Encyclopedia Americana* the next year. The first *McGuffey's Reader* was published in 1836. The most significant book of the period, however, was probably Harriet Beecher Stowe's *Uncle Tom's Cabin*, published in 1852. It sold 300,000 copies in its first year and was credited with converting many readers to an antislavery position.

A SURGE IN GROWTH

Newspapers Become Big Business

The Civil War, which altered so many things in the United States, also changed American newspaper journalism. A new reporting technique emerged as telegraphic dispatches from the war zones were transformed into "headlines" to give the reader the main points of longer stories that followed. Because telegraph lines were unreliable and often failed, the opening paragraphs of the news story, the "lead," told the most important facts. The rest of the story contained details. If the telegraph line broke during a story, at least the most important part would probably get through. Thus the "inverted-pyramid" style of reporting was developed.

After the war ended, the country underwent major social changes. From 1870 to 1900 the total population doubled, and the urban population tripled. Mass production techniques changed the economic structure. Immigration brought even more people to the cities, especially in the North and East. Newspaper growth was even greater than that of the population. The number of dailies quadrupled from 1870 to the turn of the century; circulation showed a fivefold increase. One trend was clear: Newspapers were becoming big business. As circulation went up, so did operating costs and initial investments. Bennett was able to start the *Herald* for around $500. Greeley invested $44,000 in the *Tribune* in 1841. Ten years later, the *Times* was started on an investment of $50,000. In 1883, the *New York World* was sold for $346,000. Eleven years later, the *New York Morning Journal* was sold for $1 million. But rewards were also high. It was estimated that the *World* made about $1 million a year in profits by the mid-1890s. A second trend also stood out: The newspaper industry was dominated in this period by several powerful and outspoken individuals. We will consider three who had a significant impact on American newspapers—Pulitzer, Scripps, and Hearst.

Joseph Pulitzer came to the United States from Hungary. He was not a promising candidate for the most-likely-to-succeed award. He first tried a career in the military but was turned down by the British Army, the Austrian Army, and the French Foreign Legion. He was finally accepted into the Union Army during the Civil War but was nearly court-martialed for striking a noncommissioned officer. Unable to find work in New York after the war because he could speak little English, he asked his friends where he should go in order to learn his new language. His friends evidently played a practical joke on him and directed him to St. Louis, a city that then had the largest proportion of non–English-speaking immigrants in the country. After working at a string of unsuccessful jobs in St. Louis, Pulitzer became interested in journalism and realized he had found his calling. In 1878, he bought the *St. Louis Post-Dispatch* and quickly turned it into a success. Just five years later, he was ready to try his hand in the high-stakes world of New York City journalism. The *New York World,* a paper in financial trouble, was for sale. Pulitzer bought it. In a little more than a year, circulation increased from 15,000 to 100,000. Two years later it topped the quarter-million mark.

Pulitzer had obviously found a formula for newspaper success, and his innovations are worth considering. First, Pulitzer introduced new practices that appealed to advertisers: He reserved more space for ads and sold his paper on the basis of circulation. Second, Pulitzer used illustrations, clean page makeup, and simple writing to extend his paper's appeal to immigrants with few skills in English. Third, the *World* never failed to promote itself in its own pages. Circulation figures were printed on the front page. Stunts were used to promote circulation. Pulitzer sent reporter Nelly Bly on a round-the-world trip to break the time mentioned in Jules Verne's *Around the World in 80 Days*. Ms. Bly spent a night in a haunted house, went down in a diving bell, and worked in the Salvation Army. Her stories on these experiences helped Pulitzer build readership. Fourth, Pulitzer attracted a mass readership by reintroducing the sensationalized news of the penny-press era into his paper. In his first issue, Pulitzer led with a report of a storm that devastated New Jersey and included on his front page an interview with a condemned slayer, an item about a hanging, and a tearjerker about a wronged servant girl. Pulitzer loved headlines with alliteration. If alliteration could be mixed with sex, crime, and violence, so much the better, as these examples indicate: ''Little Lotta's Lovers,'' ''Baptized in Blood,'' ''Jim-Jams in the Jury,'' and ''A Preacher's Perfidy.'' Finally, Pulitzer endorsed the notion that a newspaper should promote the general welfare of its readers, especially the underprivileged. Although Pulitzer did not originate the idea, he went to great lengths to put it into practice. The paper crusaded against the abuses of big business and corrupt politicians. In 1883, a heat wave caused many infant deaths in New York's overcrowded slums. The *World* quickly produced headlines: ''How Babies Are Baked,'' ''Little Lines of Hearses.'' (Alliteration was also mixed in with crusades.) Naturally, the *World*'s support of the working class made it a favorite among the many low-income immigrants then living in New York.

Attempts to reach a working-class audience were not confined to the East. In the Midwest, E. W. Scripps started papers in Cleveland and Cincinnati, both growing industrial cities with large populations of factory workers. The Scripps papers featured concisely edited news, human-interest stories, editorial independence, and frequent crusades for the working class. In 1889, Scripps formed an alliance with his business manager, Milton McRae, allowing McRae to head the day-to-day operations of the paper so that Scripps could fade into the background and concentrate on policy matters. Thus in 1890, Scripps, at age thirty-six, went into ''retirement.'' Scripps and McRae pioneered the idea of the newspaper chain and expanded their

William Randolph Hearst, the successful publisher of the San Francisco Examiner *and later the* New York Journal, *employed sensationalism ("yellow journalism") to win the circulation wars of the late 1800s. He created a major publishing empire consisting of a chain of newspapers, a wire service, and four syndicates. (Culver Pictures)*

operations into other cities. By 1911, there were eighteen papers under their control. (Scripps was a colorful character in American journalism. Although he championed the cause of the poor, he lived in regal splendor on a huge ranch near San Diego. He bragged that he consumed a gallon of whiskey a day—probably an exaggeration— and smoked cigars incessantly. When he died at age seventy-one, he was worth about $50 million.)

Perhaps the most well-known of these three newspaper giants, thanks to the film *Citizen Kane,* which was loosely based on his career, was William Randolph Hearst. While Pulitzer was succeeding in New York and Scripps was acquiring papers in the Midwest, twenty-four-year-old Hearst was given control of the *San Francisco Examiner,* thanks to the generosity of his wealthy father. Hearst went after readers by appealing to their emotions. His first issue carried a story of the mismanagement of a local orphanage with headlines such as "Hapless Babes—Tales of Cowardly Cruelty," "Physicians Who Aid in Murder," and "Infants Purposely Mangled at Birth." Fires, murders, and stories about love and hate were given splashy coverage. Hearst banked heavily on sensationalism to raise his readership level. It worked. The *Examiner* shot to the number-one position.

Yellow Journalism

Hearst, like Pulitzer before him, then invaded the big league—New York City. In 1895, he bought the *New York Journal.* Soon, Pulitzer and Hearst were engaged in a fierce circulation battle as each paper attempted to out-sensationalize the other. As one press critic put it, the duel between these two spread "death, dishonor and disaster'' all over page one. Sex, murder, popularized medicine, pseudoscience, self-promotion, and human-interest stories filled the two papers. This type of reporting became known as **yellow journalism** (named after a cartoon character, the Yellow Kid, who wore a bright yellow nightshirt), and whatever its faults, it sold newspapers.

The battle between Pulitzer and Hearst reached its climax with the Spanish-American War in 1898. In fact, many historians have argued that the newspapers were an important factor in shaping public opinion in favor of hostilities. When the

The New York Journal, *one of the leading publications of the yellow journalism era, emphasized crime and violence on its front pages. (Newspaper Collection, The New York Public Library: Astor, Lenox and Tilden Foundations).*

Yellow Journalism and the "Bucket of Blood"

New York was not the only hotbed of the new sensational journalism. A brief look at the *Denver Post* in the rip-roaring era around the turn of the century might convince some that this period represents the bad old days of the American newspaper. The *Post* was taken over in 1895 by Harry Tammen and Fred Bonfils, two gentlemen who had questionable credentials in journalism. Bonfils sold insurance and real estate and later operated lotteries. Tammen started out as a pinboy in a bowling alley and went on to be a bartender. The duo met while Tammen was pouring drinks in a Denver bar and immediately went into the newspaper business.

They started by touting the *Post* as a crusader for the citizens of Denver. Slogans such as "The Paper with a Heart and Soul," "Your Big Brother," and "So the People May Know" graced the paper's pages. In addition, the duo attacked everybody in sight. Led by their sports editor, a man with the rather melodious name of Otto Floto, the *Post* went after politicians, corporations, the governor, quack doctors, and ironically enough, given Bonfils' background, lottery operators. Their enthusiasm occasionally exceeded their facts, and "Who's suing the *Post* for libel now?" was a common question among Colorado reporters as the new century opened. The *Post* was a hit with readers, however, and its increased profitability enabled the publishers to afford good lawyers, and none of the charges ever held up in court.

Encouraged by their success, the two moved into a new building and had their office painted red to match the red ink used in the *Post*'s screaming headlines. Bonfils and Tammen called it the "Red Room," but the residents of Denver nicknamed it the "Bucket of Blood." From their new surroundings, the pair carried on their attacks, sometimes with bizarre results. In one instance, the paper's advice-to-the-lovelorn and gossip columnist, Polly Pry, wrote a story in which a man allegedly murdered and ate his business partner during a search for gold. This man's lawyer, naturally enough, resented the story; he showed up in the Red Room one day and fired a volley of shots at the two publishers. His aim was terrible, and he was finally restrained by Polly Pry herself. In another instance, striking transit workers, infuriated by the *Post*'s support of management, broke into the newspaper building and were systematically wrecking the editorial offices until they were restrained by the authorities.

Not all of the *Post*'s efforts had unsavory results. The paper crusaded for child-labor reform and did much to encourage Colorado as a vacation spot. By 1926, the paper was making a million dollars a year and had a daily circulation of more than 150,000. Under more sedate management, the *Post* today is rated as one of the best papers in the West.

battleship *Maine* was blown up in Havana harbor, the *Journal* offered a $50,000 reward for the arrest of the guilty parties. Circulation jumped over the million mark. War was finally declared in April, and the *World* and the *Journal* pulled out all the stops. Hearst chartered a steamer and equipped it with printing presses. He also brought down his yacht and sailed with the U.S. fleet in the battle of Santiago. The *Journal* put out forty extras in a single day.

Yellow journalism tapered off after this episode, although traces would persist for another decade. Pulitzer, in ill health, finally withdrew from the battle with

Hearst around 1900. Although the period of yellow journalism cannot be said to have been the proudest moment in the history of the American newspaper, some positive features did emerge from it. In the first place, it brought enthusiasm, energy, and verve to the practice of journalism. Aggressive reporting and investigative stories were emphasized by the *World* and the *Journal*. Second, it brought wide exposure to prominent authors and led to some fine examples of contemporary writing. Stephen Crane, Frank Norris, Dorothy Dix, and Mark Twain all wrote for newspapers during this period (1880–1905). Further, yellow journalism helped popularize the use of layout and display devices—banner headlines, pictures, color printing—that would go on to characterize modern journalism.

The Magazine Boom

In 1860, there were approximately 260 magazines published in the United States; by 1900, there were 1800. Why the surge in growth? The primary factors were more available money, better printing techniques that lowered prices, and especially the Postal Act of 1879, which gave magazines special mailing rates. It was possible to aim for a national market on a mass scale, and several magazines set out to do just that.

The most successful of the magazines seeking a mass market was the *Ladies' Home Journal*, founded by Cyrus Curtis in 1881. The first issue, eight pages long, contained an illustrated short story, an article on growing flowers, fashion notes, child-care advice, needlework hints, and recipes. Curtis was the first to realize the potential for national advertising in the magazine industry. He convincingly demonstrated that a magazine could be sold for less than the cost of producing it and still make a profit by using its large audience as a selling point to attract advertisers. Curtis drew well-known authors to his magazine and promoted it heavily. After 1889, the magazine became even more successful under the editorship of Edward Bok (see boxed material, p. 98). By 1893, the *Journal* had a circulation of 700,000.

Inspired by Curtis' success, other magazine publishers hastened to try out the same techniques on a more general audience. *McClure's, Munsey's*, and *Cosmopolitan* were three inexpensive monthlies (*Munsey's* cost only a dime) that started in 1893. They contained articles designed for widespread popular interest, and advertisers looking for ways to reach a national audience flocked to these newcomers.

The general crusading spirit of the press spilled over onto the pages of leading magazines of the late 1890s and early 1900s. Theodore Roosevelt dubbed the magazines that embraced this reform movement **muckrakers.** Corrupt practices in big business was the first topic to activate the muckrakers' zeal. *McClure's* ran an exposé of the Standard Oil Company by Ida M. Tarbell. Although it carried the innocuous title of "History of the Standard Oil Company," the article was filled with dynamite, for it revealed bribery, fraud, unfair business practices, and violence. Shocking stories on political corruption in big cities and another series on crooked practices in the railroad industry followed Tarbell's initial effort. Other magazines joined in. *Cosmopolitan* published "The Treason of the Senate" in 1906. It followed up with attacks on the International Harvester Company. *Collier's* joined in with a report on the fraudulent patent medicine business, and published articles advocating women's suffrage, pure-food laws, direct election of senators, and an income tax. By 1912, the crusading and exposé trend had spent itself. Many of the problems it uncovered had been remedied. The major investigative writers had turned to other pursuits, but most importantly, the public had grown tired of it and magazines had to search for other ways to attract readers.

Edward Bok and the *Ladies' Home Journal*

The most well known and successful of all the editors of the early mass circulation women's magazines was a man—Edward Bok. When Bok was still a boy, he came up with the idea of printing brief 100-word biographies of famous Americans on the back of illustrated cards that were given away with cigarette packs. A tobacco company bought the idea and was soon paying Bok ten dollars for each biography. As the idea became more popular and more biographies were needed, Bok hired others to do the writing at five dollars per biography. This kind of business skill did not go unnoticed for long, and in 1889 Bok, still in his middle twenties, was hired as editor of the *Ladies' Home Journal*. Bok started an advice page in which young women were invited to bring their problems to "Ruth Ashmore" (Bok's pen name). Ruth Ashmore received more than 158,000 letters in the sixteen years that the feature stayed with the magazine. "She" became so popular that Bok had to hire three full-time stenographers to answer "her" correspondence. Eventually, the problems and topics that were raised in these letters became so intimate that Bok felt uncomfortable with them and hired a woman to take over as "Ruth Ashmore."

Bok's advice to young women was traditional and conservative. ". . . Learn to say no. There is in that little word much that will protect you from evil tongues." He did not care for women in business: "The atmosphere of commercial life has never been conducive to the best interests of women engaged in it. . . . To be in an office where there are only men has never yet done a single girl any good; and it has done harm to thousands. . . ."

There were areas, however, in which Bok was sympathetic to expanding women's right. The magazine offered college scholarships to those women who sold a large number of subscriptions. Bok published an editorial about venereal disease in 1906. Shocked advertisers canceled their orders. Such a topic was taboo for women in 1906. Bok argued that 70 percent of special surgical operations on women were caused by venereal disease and that his audience deserved to know the truth.

Bok was a crusader in other ways as well. An environmentalist, he campaigned against killing birds for their feathers to adorn women's hats. He successfully prevented huge billboards from being erected at Niagara Falls and the Grand Canyon. In 1904 and 1905 Bok went after the patent-medicine business and was influential in persuading Congress to pass the Food and Drug Act of 1906. There was one area, however, in which Bok's crusades boomeranged. In 1909 and 1910, he set out to deemphasize the importance of French fashion in America, a situation he thought to be unpatriotic. "American fashions for American women" became his slogan. Bok ran illustrations comparing American and French designs, showing how the American models were as good as or better than their French counterparts. The campaign flopped. Because of the free advertising, more French fashions than ever were sold in the United States, and some unscrupulous operators began manufacturing bogus French labels to be sewn into American products. Bok recognized defeat and abandoned his efforts. He would stay on as editor, however, for thirty years.

The Paperback Boom

During the Civil War, soldiers turned to reading to fill the idle time between campaigns. This created a demand for cheap reading material, and before long a series of paperbacks priced at ten cents apiece flooded the market. These "dime novels'' included the popular Frank Merriwell stories and the Horatio Alger stories. Both series of books stressed a common theme: Virtue, hard work, and pluck were always triumphant. The Alger books were the more commercially successful, selling a total of 250 million copies. The competition between paperback publishers intensified as more companies entered the market. By 1880, about one-third of all the books published in the country were paperbacks, and fifteen different firms were selling the softbound volumes at prices ranging from five to fifteen cents. Many of the best-selling paperbacks were pirated editions of the best-sellers in England and other European countries. By the late 1880s, this problem was so bad that a new copyright law was adopted. The effect of this new law combined with years of cutthroat competition and price cutting spelled the end of this era of paperback popularity.

TRENDS TOWARD CONSOLIDATIONS AND SPECIALIZATION

Newspapers in the Early Twentieth Century

In the first two decades of the new century, the economics of mass production would figure heavily in the evolution of the newspaper. Centralization and consolidation were already noticeable in the railroad, grocery, hotel, and department store industries, and it was only a matter of time before the factors operating in those areas would make themselves felt in the newspaper business. Statistics show that there were 2200 daily newspapers in 1910. By 1930, there were 1942. The number of cities with competing daily papers fell from 689 to 288 in the same period. All of this was happening while population showed a 30 percent increase, daily circulation nearly doubled, and newspaper advertising revenue tripled. Why this decline in competition? There were several reasons.

In the first place, innovations in printing—linotype machines, high-speed presses, engraving plants—meant that purchases of new equipment and operating expenses were making newspaper publishing a costly venture. Many marginal papers

Innovations in the early 1900s such as the high-speed rotary press pictured here made newspaper publishing easier but more costly. (The Bettmann Archive)

could no longer compete. Second, advertisers showed a marked preference for the paper with the largest circulation. Large-circulation papers, in turn, were able to afford the latest equipment and turned out a paper at a more efficient per unit price. In many cities, this spelled the end for smaller papers. Third, in their quest for larger readership figures, newspapers turned increasingly to standardized content. The growth of the wire services and syndication companies meant that much of the same news, cartoons, columnists, and features would appear in different papers. Newspaper personality blurred as one daily looked pretty much like another, and a person saw little need of reading more than one. Lastly, many papers went under because of planned business consolidations. Many people who had seen consolidation successfully used in other fields now tried the same tactic with newspapers. In New York, Frank Munsey (mentioned above), who had made a fortune running hotel chains, folded six of the thirteen papers he acquired in an attempt to start a profitable chain. In Philadelphia, Cyrus Curtis, the magazine publisher, reduced the number of dailies in that city by folding or merging three existing papers. In Chicago, Herman Kohlsaat, a chain bakery owner, reduced the number of dailies from eight to four. Two large newspaper chains, bearing names we have already mentioned, also led the way toward concentration. The Hearst chain folded sixteen papers between 1918 and 1928; the Scripps-Howard group closed down fifteen in about the same period. Chains grew quickly. By 1933, six chains—Hearst, Scripps-Howard, Patterson-McCormack, Block, Ridder, and Gannett—controlled eighty-one dailies with a combined circulation of 9 million, about one-fourth of all daily circulation.

Jazz Journalism

Appearing with the consolidation trend and enjoying a short but lively reign was **jazz journalism.** At the end of World War I, the United States found itself facing a decade of prosperity: the "Roaring Twenties." The radio, Hollywood, the airplane, Prohibition, and Al Capone were all topics that captured national attention. It was perhaps inevitable that newspapers would reflect the times. The papers that best exemplify jazz journalism all sprang up in New York between 1919 and 1924; all were characterized by two features that were common in jazz journalism: (1) they were **tabloids,** printed on a page that was about one-half the size of a normal newspaper page; and (2) they were all richly illustrated with photographs.

The *New York Daily News* debuted first. After a slow start, by 1924 the *News* had caught on. Its tabloid size was easier for people to handle while reading on buses and subways; it abounded with photos and cartoons; writing style was simple and short. The *News* also blended in large portions of entertainment with its news. Comic strips, gossip columns, advice to the lovelorn, horoscopes, and sports were given large chunks of space. And, in a throwback to the 1880s, it emphasized the sensational: crime, sex, gangsters, murder trials, and Hollywood stars. The biggest content innovation of the *News* and the most noticeable was the lavish use of pictures. The entire front page was frequently given over to one or two pictures, and a two-page photo spread was included on the inside. Sports coverage, including detailed racing news, sometimes accounted for 20 percent of the paper's content, but murder trials and love affairs were the areas in which tabloids pulled out all their stops. In 1926, the tabloids discovered the marriage of a wealthy real-estate tycoon to a fifteen-year-old clerk. The tabloids nicknamed them "Daddy" and "Peaches," and news of their torrid romance filled their pages. In the same year, the *Mirror* unearthed a four-year-old murder in New Jersey and through its coverage succeeded in having the victim's widow indicted for the crime. The high point (if it can be called that)

The New York Tabloids in the Roaring Twenties

In 1927, Judd Gray, a corset salesman, teamed up with his girlfriend, Mrs. Ruth Snyder, and murdered poor, unfortunate Mr. Snyder. After a sensational trial, which was played up by the New York tabloid papers, the duo was sentenced to death. The coverage of their execution was to represent the extreme of this era of jazz journalism. As their January death date neared, one of the tabloids published a full-page drawing of an artist's conception of what the pair would look like as they were strapped into the electric chair. The New York *Graphic*, not surprisingly, was anything but restrained in its coverage. The *Graphic* got an exclusive interview with the condemned Ruth Snyder. It promoted the piece with the following blurb:

Don't fail to read tomorrow's *Graphic*. An installment that thrills and stuns. A story that fairly

pierces the heart and reveals Ruth Snyder's last thoughts on earth; that pulses the blood as it discloses her final letters. Think of it! A woman's final thoughts just before she is clutched in the deadly snare that sears and burns and FRIES and KILLS! Her very last words! Exclusively in tomorrow's *Graphic!*

The *Daily News,* however, scored a somewhat questionable scoop on this story when one of its reporters smuggled a small camera into the death chamber by strapping it to his ankle and snapped a picture an instant after the current was turned on. The *News* enlarged the picture, and it filled the entire front page of its January 14, 1928, edition. It was captioned, "When Ruth Paid her Debt to the State!" (Exclamation points were used a lot in jazz journalism.) The picture was such a hit that the *News* had to run off an additional 750,000 copies.

in the battle of the tabloids occurred during the coverage of the Gray–Snyder murder trial (see boxed material above).

Success bred imitation; in 1924 Hearst started the tabloid *Daily Mirror,* and Bernarr MacFadden, publisher of *True Story* magazine, started the *Daily Graphic* (called by many the porno-*Graphic*). Hearst's paper tried to copy the *News,* and there were days when it was hard to tell the two apart. The *Graphic,* which did not even bother to subscribe to a wire service, was easy to spot—it was the most sensationalized of the three. News of murder, rape, divorce, scandal, bootlegging, and sex virtually jumped off the pages of this paper. Rather than running photographs, the *Graphic* ran what it called cosmographs, faked composite photos of events that might have happened. After Rudolph Valentino's funeral, one cosmograph showed the actor, dressed in flowing white robes, entering heaven. Neither the *Mirror* nor the *Graphic,* however, was able to match the success of the *News.* Hearst sold his paper in 1928, and the *Graphic* expired in 1932. The Depression effectively marked the end of the jazz journalism era, but before moving on we should note that not all tabloids were like the *Graphic.* Many conventional-appeal papers appeared in this format. Moreover, sensationalism did not end with the passing of the tabloid era. It would crop up again from time to time in the years to come.

The Impact of the Depression

The Depression had great social and economic impact on newspapers and magazines. During the 1930s, total daily newspaper circulation increased by about 2 million; the total population increased by 9 million. The total income of the newspaper industry, however, dropped about 20 percent in this decade. This shortage of revenue meant that marginally profitable papers were unable to stay in business, and approximately sixty-six dailies went under.

Although worsening economic conditions were one cause of the newspaper's decline, more important was the emergence of radio as a competitor for national advertising dollars. In the period from 1935 to 1940, newspapers' share of national advertising revenues dropped from 45 to 39 percent, while radio's share jumped from 6 percent to more than 10 percent. These cuts hurt the print media and, not surprisingly, newspapers saw radio as the villain. Hostility between the two industries grew, ultimately leading to the short but nasty Press–Radio War (see Chapter 8). By 1940, however, thanks to increased revenue from local advertisers, newspaper revenues were back up and hostilities had lessened. Nevertheless, the economic picture was still not rosy, and the number of daily papers declined to 1744 in 1945, an all-time low.

The other significant media trend during the Depression was the press' negative reaction to the excesses of tabloid journalism, a reaction that was transformed into an attempt to respond to the increasingly complex nature of modern life. The 1930s and 1940s were notable for the growth of interpretive reporting. Reporters took on the task of explaining the complicated economic programs of the New Deal in simple terms that the average reader could understand. Foreign correspondents covering international problems and the tense situation in Europe hastened to include the ''why'' perspective, along with information regarding who, what, and where. Two papers that specialized in interpretive and financial reporting, the *Christian Science Monitor* and the *Wall Street Journal*, gained in popularity during these years, as did magazines such as *Harper's, Atlantic,* and *The New Republic*.

Magazine Development

The most striking characteristic of magazine development during the twentieth century was a trend toward specialization. This movement was given impetus by the increasing importance of national advertising to economic success within the industry (magazines received forty-two cents out of every dollar spent on national advertising in the major media in 1929). A magazine not only had to please its readers, but also had to attract an audience that would be valuable to advertisers. And so magazine publishers had to become experts in marketing procedures. Sometimes their audiences were large; other times the audience might consist of a highly specialized group (see Fig. 4.1).

Shifting economic conditions and changing life-styles in the decades following World War I also influenced magazine development. As some of the prewar circulation leaders went into a decline, new publications—many similar to the shorter format, richly illustrated tabloids of the jazz-journalism era—sprang up to take their place. Three distinct types evolved in the years between World War I and World War II: (1) the digest, (2) the news magazine, and (3) the pictorial magazine.

The pioneer digest was the *Literary Digest,* which, although started in the 1880s, became popular after the war, reaching a circulation of 2 million. Hardly literary and seldom a digest, this magazine was one of the few ever written with scissors. Editors clipped stories from the nation's newspapers on current issues and pasted them up side by side. The finest example of this genre, *The Reader's Digest,* appeared in 1922. Although this magazine also reprinted articles that had appeared elsewhere, it first condensed and edited the material so that it would be read by people in a hurry. The busy and booming twenties were very conducive to the

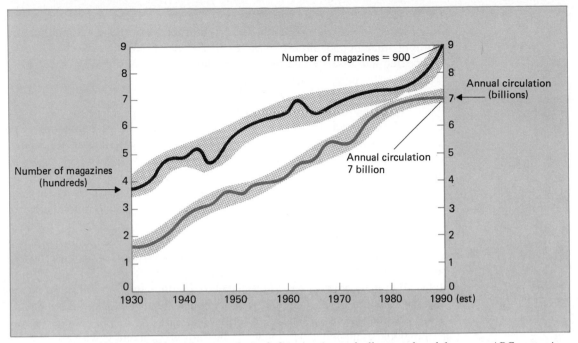

FIGURE 4.1 *Magazine growth, including comics and all general and farm non-ABC magazines listed in Standard Rate and Data Service.*

success of such a venture, and the *Digest* watched its circulation grow, passing the million mark by 1935.

The idea of a news magazine was not new—examples could be found in the nineteenth century. *Time*, however, borrowed little from its predecessors. From its beginning in 1923, *Time* based its format on an original concept: the distillation and compartmentalization of news under various departments. Other innovations included the use of the narrative style to report news stories; group journalism produced by the pooling of the efforts of reporters, writers, and editors into anonymous articles; the institution of a large research department; and a brash, punchy, jargonish writing style. The magazine prospered slowly, but by 1930 it was turning a substantial profit. Two imitators, *Newsweek* and *U.S. News*, appeared in 1933. These magazines served somewhat as national newspapers, providing information and interpretation to the entire country.

In the mid-thirties, two magazines, *Life* and *Look*, revived the tradition of the pictorial weekly originated by *Harper's* and *Leslie's*. Capitalizing on an increased interest in photography, *Life* was launched in 1936 and had almost a quarter of a million subscribers before the magazine even had a name. The tabloids had shown that people liked to look at pictures; the news magazines had shown that people wanted to learn about current events; the movies had made people "picture conscious." *Life* brought all of these elements together. Photojournalism was given wide coverage, and many of *Life*'s photos of World War II were hung in the Museum of Modern Art in New York. Public figures caught in unguarded moments, photo essays, occasional glamour shots, and articles on the arts all went into the early issues. *Life* itself would live for thirty-six years (it would reappear in the late 1970s in a totally different format). *Look* hit the newsstands in 1937, just two months behind *Life*. *Look* lacked the current-affairs emphasis of its forerunner and concentrated more on personalities and features. Over the years, it evolved into a family-oriented magazine. *Look* expired in 1972. The success of these two publications, as you might imagine, inspired copies. *Focus, Peek, Foto, Picture, Click, Pic,* and *See* appeared and disappeared in the years surrounding World War II.

Books in the Early Twentieth Century

The period from 1900 to 1945 saw the commercialization of publishing. Prior to this time, many of the publishing companies were family owned and specialized in publishing one particular kind of book. Publishers were a closely knit group, and their dealings with one another resembled what might take place in a genteel private club. Several events altered this situation. First, a new breed of literary agents, concerned with negotiating the best "bottom line" for their authors, entered the scene. Forced to pay top dollar for their rights to books, the publishing business lost its former "clubby" atmosphere and turned into a business. Second, many publishing houses expanded their publishing efforts into the mass market, publishing popular works of fiction. To compete effectively in the mass marketplace, modern promotion and distribution techniques were introduced to the book industry. Third, a depression in the 1890s and a subsequent sluggish economy meant that the book industry was forced to depend more on banks for finance capital. The banks, of course, insisted that the book companies be run with the utmost efficiency with an eye toward increasing profits. By World War II, all of these factors combined to make the book industry more commercially oriented.

The content of popular books was highly variable during this time period. Outdoor adventures written by such authors as Jack London and Zane Grey were popular at the turn of the century. *Tarzan of the Apes* sold nearly a million copies on the eve of World War I. During the Roaring Twenties, light fiction, such as *The Sheik* and P. G. Wodehouse's *Jeeves* were best-sellers, but serious works sold equally well. H. G. Wells' *Outline of History* and Will Durant's *Story of Philosophy* reached the million mark in sales during this period. Detective fiction by Erle Stanley Gardner (Perry Mason was his hero) and Ellery Queen sold well during the Depression. In 1936, two books broke the two million mark in sales, Dale Carnegie's *How to Win Friends and Influence People* and Margaret Mitchell's *Gone With the Wind*.

ECONOMIC INFLUENCES: 1945–1969

Postwar Newspapers

After World War II, economic forces continued to shape the American newspaper, magazine, and book industries. Some trends of the postwar period were created by advances in print and electronic technology, but others had begun even before the war. For example, the postwar economy forced the newspaper industry to move even further in the direction of contraction and consolidation. Although newspaper circulation rose from approximately 48 million in 1945 to about 62 million in 1970, the number of dailies stayed about the same. There was actually a circulation loss in cities with populations of more than a million, and several big-city papers went out of business. Moreover, the number of cities with competing dailies dropped from 117 to 37 between 1945 and 1970. This meant that about 98 percent of American cities had no competing papers.

In 1945, sixty newspaper group owners ran sixty chains that controlled about 42 percent of the total daily newspaper circulation. By 1970, there were approximately 157 chains that accounted for 60 percent of total circulation. Why had the number of chains continued to grow? One factor was the sharp rise in costs of paper and labor during the postwar years. Newspapers were becoming more expensive to print. The large chains were in a position to share expenses and to use their presses and labor more efficiently. Under a single owner, several papers could "share" the services of feature writers, columnists, photographers, and compositors, thus holding down costs. This movement toward consolidation resulted in a large number of multiple owners controlling the market, with no single chain dominating circulation. The largest group owner in 1970, for example, accounted for only 6 percent of total circulation. The consolidation trend was also present across media, as several media conglomerates controlled newspapers, magazines, radio, and television stations.

Another continuing trend was the competition among media for advertising dollars. Even after inflation had abated, the total amount of advertising revenue spent on all media nearly tripled between 1945 and 1970. Although the total spent on newspapers did not increase at quite this pace, the amount spent on television increased by more than a threefold factor. The rising television industry cut significantly into the print media's national advertising revenue. Although newspapers could take up the slack by increasing local ads, general circulation magazines were not so lucky.

Postwar Magazines

Magazines of the postwar era reflected publishers' firm belief that the one way to become profitable was to specialize. Increased leisure time, made possible by technological advances, created a market for sports magazines such as *Field and Stream, Sports Afield, Golf Digest, Popular Boating,* and *Sports Illustrated.* Scientific advances also generated a resurgence of a popularized version of *Scientific American* and a publication called *Science Illustrated.*

The rapid expansion of urban communities and urban life-styles gave rise to many specialized publications. Liberalized attitudes toward sex prompted such ventures as *Confidential* (1952) and the trend-setting *Playboy* (1953). During the 1960s, the rebirth of an interest in urban culture encouraged the rise of "city" magazines, of which *New York* is probably the best example. The minority community was recognized by the debut of *Ebony* in 1945 and *Jet* in 1951. Magazines of opinion and reflection also sprang up: *The Reporter* (1949), the *National Review* (1955), and *Ramparts* (1962). All in all, magazines reflected the increasing diversity and complexity of twentieth-century life.

Although the total number of magazines published between 1945 and 1970 increased from 5880 to 9573, television cut magazine revenue from 12.5 percent of total mass media ad revenue in 1945 to 7 percent in 1970. Hardest hit were the mass circulation magazines with general appeal. *Collier's* and *Woman's Home Companion* ceased regular publication in 1956; *Coronet* in 1961; *Look* in 1971; and *Life* in 1972. *TV Guide,* on the other hand, turned competition into profit, reaching more than 9 million readers in 1963.

Postwar Books: Paperbacks and Consolidation

Shortly after the end of World War II, new paperbacks published by Bantam, Pocket Books, and New American Library appeared. These books were popular because of their twenty-five–cent price and because new channels of distribution were used to market them. Wire racks filled with paperbacks appeared in train stations, news-stands, drug stores, and tobacco shops. A whole new audience was thus exposed to paperbacks. In 1950, the "quality" paperback appeared. These were serious non-fiction or literary classics that found their prime markets in education.

Speaking of education, the United States received a shock in 1957 when the Soviet Union launched an Earth satellite. In response, the U.S. educational system received a general upgrading and more and more emphasis was placed on schooling. Libraries and classrooms increased their holdings of books. The textbook and educational publishers found themselves in a period of prosperity.

Moreover, expanded leisure time and more disposable income made book reading a popular means of recreation. All in all, the book publishing business looked like a good investment for the future. Consequently, large corporations began acquiring book companies. To name just a few: CBS, Inc., acquired Holt, Rinehart and Winston; Litton Industries acquired Van Nostrand; and ITT purchased Bobbs-Merrill. Between 1958 and 1970, there were 307 mergers or acquisitions of publishing companies. These mergers brought new financial and management resources to the book industry, which helped it stay profitable during the 1970s.

THE PRINT MEDIA IN THE 1970s AND 1980s

The Impact of USA Today

On September 15, 1982, the nation got a look at a colorful new entrant on the newspaper scene. Delivered by satellite to printing plants across the country, *USA Today* was designed to be a national newspaper. Although the paper lost $233 million in its first five years, it emerged into the black in 1987 but lost money again in 1988. The brainchild of Gannett chairman Allen Neuharth, the paper has had significant impact on the newspaper industry. Some of the innovations introduced by *USA Today* include:

- Splashy graphics and liberal use of color.

- Short, easily digested stories—the longest average about 1000 words.

- Extensive use of graphs, charts, and tables. The sports section in particular is crammed with statistics.

- A full page devoted to weather.

- The use of factoids. (A factoid is a list of boiled-down facts with a little dot in front of them—much like this list.)

Several press observers criticized *USA Today* for superficial coverage and for putting a happy gloss on most of its stories. Nonetheless, the paper was quite popular with its readers.

USA Today has a problem attracting advertisers primarily because many of its sales are from vending machines. Purchasers are anonymous, which doesn't make them appealing to advertisers. In addition, *USA Today* is competing with news magazines (it attracts a similar audience), and news magazines get passed from person to person, giving them more readers per copy. *USA Today* tends to be thrown away more quickly and has only about three readers per copy, whereas news magazines have four or five.

Other areas in the print media in which notable developments have taken place in the last decade are (1) ownership, (2) reporting, and (3) marketing.

Changing Patterns of Ownership

During the late 1980s, the declining value of the dollar, the lack of rules concerning foreign ownership of American publishing firms, and the general attractiveness of books, magazines, and newspapers lured foreign investors as never before. Australia-born media baron Rupert Murdoch, now an American citizen, led the charge when he acquired papers in Chicago and New York (he ultimately sold both), a book publishing company, and several magazines. Others quickly followed. The newspaper industry was affected the least, primarily because sale prices of the papers were so high. As of 1988, about 150 U.S. papers, 9 percent, were foreign owned, with two Canadian publishers, Hollinger and Thomson, owning most of these.

In the magazine industry, Hachette, a French company, bought most of the magazines that were formerly published by CBS. A British company, Reed International, controls more than fifty U.S. trade magazines through its American subsidiaries. Other European companies, such as Bertelsmann AG (West Germany), Maxwell Communications (Great Britain), and Elsevier (Netherlands) were on the prowl for other U.S. magazine properties.

In book publishing, Bertelsmann's acquisition of Doubleday, Dell, and Bantam made it the second largest book publisher in the country. Hachette acquired reference book publisher Grolier, and British-based Pearson acquired New American Library and E. P. Dutton. Harcourt Brace Jovanovich restructured itself to avoid being taken over by Maxwell Communications. Maxwell responded by buying Macmillan.

All in all, a significant number of companies that produce American literary and cultural products are now owned by foreign firms. The impact that will have on the content of U.S. publishing is yet to be determined.

Additionally, the ownership pattern of American publishing companies has become more concentrated. In the newspaper area, the independent, family-owned paper is rapidly becoming extinct. More than four out of five Americans read a paper published by a group owner. Magazines are less concentrated than newspapers, but the trend toward centralization is apparent as large companies acquire more publications. The book publishing arena also saw the number of independent companies decline as many were absorbed by large conglomerates. For example, a planned merger of Warner Communications Inc. and Time Inc., announced in 1989, would create an empire with annual revenue from book and magazine publishing topping the $2.5 billion mark.

Reporting

During the mid- to late 1960s, a specialized reporting for a specialized audience developed in the United States—the underground or alternative press. Growing out of the antiestablishment feelings of the time, the **underground press** concentrated on politically liberal news and opinion or on cultural topics such as music, art, and film. Perhaps the most influential papers were the *Village Voice*, the *Los Angeles Free Press,* and *Rolling Stone*. Many alternative papers ran out of steam in the 1970s, and others lost their original flavor. The *Village Voice* and *Rolling Stone,* for example, are now more in line with the mainstream establishment press.

Investigative reporting had roots that could be traced back to the muckrakers, but it enjoyed a rebirth in the 1970s. Best known were the efforts of *Washington Post* reporters Bob Woodward and Carl Bernstein in untangling the Watergate story, which eventually led to the resignation of President Nixon. Their efforts spanned a two-year period from 1972 to 1974 and thoroughly infuriated the White House. At one point, President Nixon, commenting on their coverage of this story, said he had never seen such "outrageous, vicious, distorted . . . frantic, hysterical reporting" (an example from the 1970s of negative feedback).

New attention was focused on investigative reporting in 1981 when a *Washington Post* reporter was forced to return a Pulitzer Prize after it was learned that the award-winning story about an eight-year-old heroin addict was a fabrication. Another reporter was fired after it was revealed that he made up a story about the fighting in Northern Ireland. Moreover, a book had to be recalled by its publisher because of unsubstantiated facts. These episodes brought new emphasis on the importance of accuracy in reporting and writing. Magazine, book, and newspaper editors tightened up their fact-checking procedures.

Marketing

In an era when so many media compete for the attention of the audience, it's only natural that the print media are paying more attention to marketing. The trend in newspapers, magazines, and to a lesser extent book publishing is toward a philosophy that stresses the importance of consumer satisfaction with the product. Audience research is an important component of this marketing-centered approach. Both magazines and newspapers are relying increasingly on readership studies, satisfaction measures, and focus groups that help them fine tune their products. This emphasis on marketing does not sit well with some in the newspaper industry who argue that the tenets of good journalism are being sacrificed for the sake of making a profit. These critics fear that solid news reporting will be replaced by soft or sensational stories that have mass appeal.

Market segmentation is another factor crucial to the success of today's magazine and newspaper. A product that appeals to a homogeneous audience group attractive to advertisers will usually succeed. Magazines, of course, have honed this approach to a fine art. Newspapers are becoming more conscious of this concept and many now include sections that make the content more appealing to upscale, affluent consumers, the kind that advertisers like to reach.

Promotional efforts are also emphasized. Many newspapers now purchase advertising time on local TV and radio stations. Many magazines, such as *TV Guide, Sports Illustrated,* and even *Psychology Today* have run TV ad campaigns designed to increase circulation. Book publishing companies, less dependent on advertising for their revenue, have yet to go quite this far (although TV ads have aired for some romance novels). Nonetheless, publishers are putting more money into point-of-purchase displays and print advertising. Major national newspaper and advertising budgets for new releases now routinely top the $100,000 mark.

RECENT CONTENT TRENDS

Newspapers Standardize; Magazines and Books Diversify: 1940 to the Present

As newspapers moved into the last half of the twentieth century, several trends in their content were apparent. Most obvious was a change in newspaper typography and layout, all with the ultimate goal of making the modern newspaper easier to read. Photography and color were being used more liberally, and many papers showed a willingness to depart from the typical eight-column format that has been traditional. Second, many papers were carrying more of what might be called "feature" stories. Sections entitled "Life," "Lifestyle," "Living," and "Leisure" were becoming more common as papers blended more of this material with their traditional "hard" news. Many big-city papers were attempting to compete with the more localized weeklies by including suburban editions that concentrated on news outside of the core city. The trend toward consolidation also had an impact on newspaper content. The standardization of content and makeup that generally go along with group ownership prompted critics of this trend to charge that newspaper content had become as uniform as a Big Mac. (*USA Today,* from the Gannett organization, was commonly called McPaper by its critics.)

Trying to describe the content of modern magazines would take far more space than we have available since magazine content is as diversified as magazines themselves. On a general level, one content analysis of fourteen national magazines from 1938 to 1976 indicated that fiction has been on a sharp decline and that national-affairs content has increased, as has cultural content and food and nutrition stories. Although these statistics may be helpful, probably the best way to find out about the content of modern magazines would be to scan a local newsstand and note how many different topics are covered by the publications on sale.

Turning to books, the first big paperback best-seller following World War II was Dr. Benjamin Spock's *Baby and Child Care*. Other notable paperbacks followed. Mickey Spillane's Mike Hammer was a hard-boiled private eye who appeared in six novels during the 1950s that sold 17 million copies. *Peyton Place,* a novel famous for its racy parts, sold 10 million in paperback. All in all, from 1940 to 1965, paperback sales were dominated by light fiction and an occasional how-to book.

Hard-cover content during this period was hard to categorize. In nonfiction, cookbooks have enjoyed steady popularity, as have diet books. The late 1960s and early 1970s saw a trend toward self-help and inspirational books such as *I'm OK– You're OK* and *Your Erroneous Zones*. Subsequent years saw physical fitness books become popular, as exemplified by *The Complete Book of Running* and *Jane Fonda's Workout Book*. The early 1980s saw business-oriented books capture surprising sales. *In Search of Excellence* and *The One Minute Manager* both topped best-seller lists. The late 1980s saw a rash of psychological self-help books aimed at women: *Women Who Love Too Much, Men Who Hate Women and the Women Who Love Them, Women Men Love, Women Men Leave,* etc.

In fiction, authors such as Judith Krantz, Robert Ludlum, and Tom Clancy were popular. Some of the best-selling authors in mass-market paperback fiction were John Jakes (*North and South, Love and War*), Danielle Steele (*Fine Things, Changes*), Sidney Sheldon (*Windmills of the Gods*), and Stephen King (a whole slew of horror novels). All in all, the varied content of popular books reflected the eclectic tastes of the modern reading audience.

SUGGESTIONS FOR FURTHER READING

The books listed below are good sources for additional information about the history of newspapers and magazines.

DAVIS, KENNETH, *Two-Bit Culture: The Paperbacking of America,* Boston: Houghton Mifflin, 1984.

EMERY, EDWIN, AND MICHAEL EMERY, *The Press in America,* 6th ed., Englewood Cliffs, N.J.: Prentice-Hall, 1988.

HYNDS, ERNEST C., *American Newspapers in the 1980s,* New York: Hastings House, 1980.

JONES, ROBERT W., *Journalism in the United States,* New York: E. P. Dutton, 1947.

MOTT, FRANK LUTHER, *American Journalism,* New York: Macmillan, 1962.

PETERSON, THEODORE, *Magazines in the Twentieth Century,* Urbana: University of Illinois Press, 1964.

TEBBEL, JOHN, *The Compact History of the American Newspaper,* New York: Hawthorn Books, 1969.

———, *The American Magazine: A Compact History,* New York: Hawthorn Books, 1969.

———, *A History of Book Publishing in the United States* (4 vols.), New York: R. R. Bowker, 1981.

WOOD, JAMES PLAYSTED, *Magazines in the United States,* New York: Ronald Press, 1971.

Also, the scholarly publications *Journalism History* and *Journalism Quarterly* frequently carry articles dealing with newspaper and magazine history.

Chapter 5

Structure of the Newspaper Industry

The modern newspaper industry is in a paradoxical situation. On the one hand, business is good: revenues are healthy, profit margins are high, costs are manageable, and newspapers are being bought for record prices. On the other hand, despite counter-efforts, newspaper readership has been declining for about four decades, with younger people, in particular, more likely to be nonreaders. Newspaper penetration per household has decreased by almost 50 percent since 1946 and competition for readers' time from other media, particularly TV, continues to increase. Literacy skills are down, and a more mobile population is less interested in the local paper. Why is the industry doing so well when all the long-term signs look bleak? Several reasons:

1. Newspapers have been able to carve out an almost exclusive base of economic support. They are still the preeminent vehicle for local advertising. Despite increased competition from radio, TV, cable, and direct mail, the advertising base is strong.

2. Most existing newspapers have a monopoly in their service area. As in nature, only the strong survive and the pressures of the marketplace have forced weak papers out of business.

3. Newspapers, more than other media, tend to share ideas. Hence successful marketing, editorial, and technological concepts are likely to spread to the entire industry.

4. Newspapers have the innate qualities that go with a print medium. They're permanent, browsable, convenient, and relatively inexpensive.

Nonetheless, the ominous signs are not lost on publishers. Consequently, the last few years have seen tremendous changes in newspaper makeup, content, audience research, and marketing as the industry tries to halt the circulation drain and attract loyal readers.

This chapter will examine the changing structure and organization of the newspaper industry and detail how newspapers continue to meet the challenge of delivering what their readers need.

TYPES OF NEWSPAPERS

Ralph Waldo Emerson, who had something to say about virtually everything, once said ''the newspaper . . . does its best to make every square acre of land and sea

111

give an account of itself at your breakfast table.'' If Emerson could see the 1990s version of the newspaper, he might also add that the newspaper does its best to get to your breakfast table before you turn on the ''Today'' show or ''Good Morning America'' or leave to drive to work. The newspaper industry is currently examining how well it fits with modern life-styles and what it must do to keep and attract readers in an age in which competition for their time has become intense.

The newspapers that are published in this country are many and varied. They range from the *Wall Street Journal,* a nationally oriented financial daily, to the *Journal of Commerce,* a small financial paper published in Portland, Oregon; from the *National Enquirer* to the *Daily Lobo,* the college newspaper of the University of New Mexico; from the million-plus-circulation New York *Daily News* to the 7000-circulation Gallipolis *Daily Tribune* in Gallipolis, Ohio. Obviously, there are many ways to categorize an industry as diverse as this one. For our purposes, we will group papers by frequency of publication (dailies and weeklies), by market size (national, large, medium, small), and, finally, by their appeal to specialized interest groups.

Dailies

To be considered a daily, a newspaper has to appear at least five times a week. In 1988, there were about 1643 dailies, down 2 percent from 1985, and about 7600 weeklies. Whether a daily or a weekly, the chief concern of a newspaper is its **circulation,** the number of copies delivered to newsstands or vending machines and the number delivered to subscribers. Daily newspaper circulation has leveled off at approximately 63 million, a figure that has shown little change from 1970 to 1988 (see Fig. 5.1). At the same time, the population of the United States has been growing. Consequently, the ratio of newspapers per household has declined. To illustrate, in 1960, 111 newspapers were sold per 100 households; in 1988, about 72 newspapers were sold per 100 households. This circulation crunch has not hit all papers with equal force, and this becomes evident when we divide daily newspapers into market groups.

National Newspapers. Only a handful of papers fall into this category. These are publications whose content is geared not for one particular city or region but for the entire country. These papers typically use satellites to transmit images and information to regional printing plants where the papers are assembled and distributed. The newest addition to this category is the Gannett publication *USA Today,* started in 1982. With a circulation of about 1.4 million, the paper's use of color and graphics and focus on such topics as sports and weather made a significant impact on other newspapers. The *New York Times* started a national edition in 1980. Also printed via satellite, it had a circulation of about 120,000 in 1987. Two other, more specialized papers are also in this category. The *Wall Street Journal,* concentrating mainly on financial news, was published in seventeen printing plants across the country. By 1988, its circulation had topped the 2 million mark. The *Christian Science Monitor* concentrates on interpretation of news events and features dealing with literature, music, and art. As of 1988, the *Monitor* had a circulation of about 150,000.

Large Metropolitan Dailies. The decline in circulation has hit these papers the hardest. Although the total population of the top fifty metropolitan areas increased more than

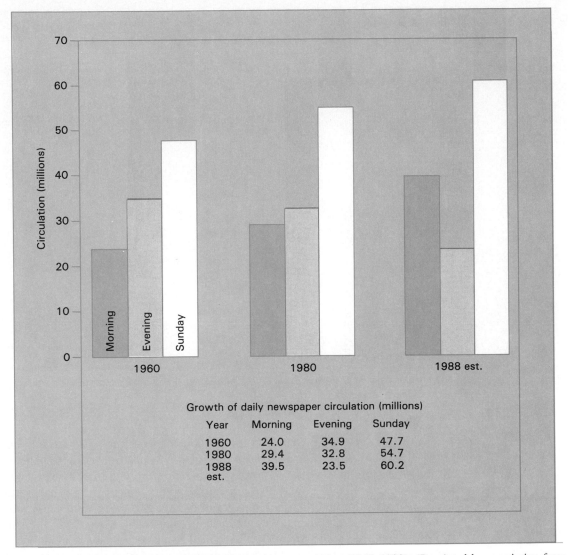

FIGURE 5.1 *Growth of daily newspaper circulation (1946–1988). (Reprinted by permission from the 1988* Editor & Publisher International Yearbook.*)*

30 percent from 1960 to 1988, the circulation of newspapers published in these cities dropped about 40 percent. In addition, the last ten years have seen the demise of several well-known big-city papers: the *Chicago Daily News, Philadelphia Bulletin, Boston Herald-Traveler, Cleveland Press, Washington Star, Baltimore News-American,* and *St. Louis Globe-Democrat.* Why the drop in circulation? Several factors that seem to account for the decline include readers leaving the central city for the suburbs, transient populations, rising costs of newspaper distribution, and increased competition from other media, especially TV.

Suburban Dailies. Although suburban communities of between 100,000 and 500,000 residents are home to only 6 percent of total newspapers, they account for about 31

A newsroom at a small Pennsylvania daily. Small-town newspapers are a valuable source of local news and advertising. (Tom Kelly)

percent of all circulation. Suburban dailies, located in these areas, surrounding the larger cities, are experiencing a period of growth. Circulation of these papers grew by about one-fifth during the 1970s and continued to grow in the 1980s. One reason for this increase is the growth of suburban shopping centers, which have attracted many merchants formerly located in the central cities. To these merchants, suburban papers represent an efficient way of reaching potential customers. In addition, suburban residents are apparently less inclined to go to the city at night for dinner and entertainment, a factor that has cut down newsstand sales of city papers. Perhaps the best known suburban paper is *Newsday,* aimed at the residents of Long Island. In 1988, *Newsday* had a circulation of about 680,000, thereby making it the ninth largest daily paper in the country.

In a quest to regain readers, large metro dailies have taken on the suburban press on the smaller papers' own turf. Big-city newspapers are putting out more **zoned editions,** sections geared to a particular suburban area. The *Philadelphia Inquirer,* for example, has eight "Neighbors" sections designed to compete with the twenty or so suburban papers that surround metro Philadelphia. The *Los Angeles Times* now runs three daily regional editions and six twice-weekly suburban sections. The metro dailies are also building more suburban printing plants to make delivery easier and cheaper.

This competition has become even more intense because about 40 percent of suburban papers are owned by large chains and are able to fight back with the financial resources of the parent company. Some successful suburban papers are taking the offensive. *Newsday,* the successful Long Island paper, started an edition aimed at the New York City market. Even smaller papers are not sitting idle. Doings Newspapers, which operates in the Chicago suburbs, recently started a weekly newsmagazine to go along with its papers. Other suburban papers are forming circulation networks and offering special rates to advertisers.

Small-Town Dailies. This category of newspapers has also made circulation gains. From 1979 to 1988, newspaper circulation in towns with 100,000 or fewer inhabitants grew by 19 percent. Recently, circulation among papers in this category has leveled off, although dailies in towns with populations of between 5,000 and 50,000 have shown modest circulation gains. Surveys have shown that readers of these papers perceive the papers to be sources of local information, for both neighborhood news and advertising.

Weeklies

The number of weekly newspapers in the United States has remained fairly stable at about 7500 over the last 18 years. The circulation of weeklies, however, has increased about 65 percent for this same period, from about 29 million in 1970 to 53 million in 1988. Despite this increase in circulation, the rising expense of printing and distribution has made many weekly publishers more cost conscious. Some have adopted cheaper offset printing, while others have sold their presses altogether and made use of central printing plants. Such plants may handle the needs of several weeklies located in the same general area. Like the daily papers in small towns, weeklies are strong on neighborhood and local news.

The first weekly papers were published in small towns and in rural areas that did not have a large enough population to support a daily. Although many weeklies are still located in these communities, the last few decades have seen the emergence of weekly papers in local suburban neighborhoods. In the late 1980s, it was estimated that about one out of three weekly papers was published in suburbia. Suburban weeklies have one obvious advantage over small-town weeklies. Because suburban papers are located in more populous areas, they have the potential to attract a larger audience and more advertising revenue. On the other hand, suburban weeklies are likely to have more competition from suburban-based dailies and the suburban editions of nearby big-city papers.

Recapturing Readers

No matter what their size or frequency of publication, all newspapers are faced with the task of maintaining their loyal readers while attracting new ones. In this era of increased competition, newspapers are courting readers and potential readers as never before. What are some of the things they are doing?

- They are using more color. Sparked by *USA Today,* a large number of papers have increased the use of colors throughout their pages.

- They are changing their content. Almost 70 percent of U.S. papers have altered the kinds of articles that they run. Some common changes were more business news, more sports news, and more local news.

- They are trying to appeal to young readers. Many papers have increased their use of graphics, modernized their look, introduced more short and snappy stories, and emphasized topics of interest to the eighteen-to-thirty-five age group.

- They are closely monitoring audience reaction to their papers. Specially designed audience research studies and readership surveys are used to gauge consumer reaction to the paper.

Special-Service Newspapers

As the name suggests, special-service newspapers are those aimed at several well-defined audience segments. These papers may be published daily, weekly, bimonthly, or even monthly and include publications designed for minority groups, students, professionals, and shoppers.

There are, for example, many newspapers published specifically for the black community. The black press in this country has a long history, dating back to 1827. Most early papers were started to oppose discrimination and to help gain equal rights and opportunities. The black press reached its circulation peak in the 1960s when approximately 275 papers had a circulation of about 4 million. Since that time, the black press has seen a significant decline in both numbers of papers and circulation.

In 1987, black papers were publishing in thirty-four states and the District of Columbia. Florida, California, Georgia, and New York were the states with the most black papers. Two black papers are dailies: the *Atlanta Daily World* and the *Chicago Daily Defender;* the rest are weeklies. Although some black papers were doing well, others were facing financial problems. In general, the problems faced by the black press stemmed from increasing competition from white-owned papers, decreasing circulation (which made it more difficult to attract advertisers), inflation, and criticism from many in the black community that the papers were too conservative and out of date. In an attempt to recapture readership and advertisers many black papers have changed their format and editorial focus and have begun to concentrate on local news. Additionally, a black press agency, the National Black News Service, was started in order to provide member papers with a steady supply of national and regional news of interest. In the late 1980s it was estimated that the total combined circulation of all black newspapers was about 2 million, down almost 50 percent from the 1960s. In an attempt to gain readers, many black newspapers were trying to appeal to upscale black readers by emphasizing news about education, medicine, and economics. Many papers had added color and updated graphics.

The Spanish-language press dates back to 1835. In the approximately 150 years of its existence, it has grown to include about 100 magazines and periodicals, 8 daily newspapers, and about 45 weeklies. The most prominent daily Spanish-language paper is the New York City tabloid *El Diario-La Prensa,* with a circulation of about 69,000. In Miami, Florida, the *Diario Las Americas* distributes approximately 63,000 copies. The Dallas *El Sol De Texas* has a weekly circulation of 125,000. Several English-language newspapers have recently begun to turn more attention to their Spanish-speaking readers. The *Miami Herald, Chicago Sun-Times,* and *Arizona Republic* introduced Spanish-language sections.

Another special type of newspaper is exemplified by the college press. Although numbers are hard to pin down, as of 1987 there were about 1740 college papers published at four-year institutions with a total circulation of more than 6 million. College newspapers are big business; consequently, more and more papers are hiring nonstudent professionals to manage their operation. Two of the largest college papers in terms of circulation are the University of Minnesota's *Minnesota Daily* and Michigan State University's *State News,* both with circulations around 40,000. College newspapers get high readership scores. One survey noted that about 96 percent of students read at least part of their campus paper.

Another type of special newspaper is the "shopper" or "pennysaver." As the name suggests, shoppers consist primarily of advertisements with some feature material such as astrology columns or helpful hints mixed in. Most shoppers are distributed free and are delivered weekly, usually on Wednesday or Thursday, in anticipation of weekend shopping trips. Shoppers now have their own professional organization, the Association of Free Community Newspapers, which represents about a thousand publications. Shoppers are big business. They have a combined circulation of about 23 million and have been so profitable that big corporations, such as Harte-Hanks, the Tribune Company, and Capital Cities, are currently publishing them.

NEWSPAPER OWNERSHIP

The two most significant facts about newspaper ownership are the following:

1. Concentration of ownership is increasing as large group owners acquire more papers.

2. There has been a decrease in the number of cities with competing papers.

The biggest newspaper group is the Gannett Company with eighty-eight dailies and a combined circulation of about 5.9 million. Knight-Ridder Newspapers Inc. controls twenty-nine dailies with about 4.6 million circulation. Other newspaper chains that own dailies with a combined circulation of more than 2 million are Newhouse Newspapers, the Tribune Company, Dow Jones, and the Times Mirror Company.

The Growth of Newspaper Chains

It was pointed out in Chapter 4 that concentration of ownership is not a recent trend in the newspaper business. In 1900, there were eight major group owners (chains) in operation. The number of chains grew steadily over the years until by the end of 1970 there were 157 chains in operation, which, among them, owned about half of all the country's daily newspapers. By 1987, the number of group owners had decreased by fourteen, but these 143 groups now controlled about three-fourths of all U.S. dailies and more than 80 percent of circulation. The pace of newspaper sales in both 1986 and 1987 was feverish as chains increased their holdings and the amounts paid for newspapers were surprisingly high. Gannett got the *Detroit News* in a package that went for more than $700 million. (Gannett was to spend more than $1 billion in 1986 on new acquisitions.) The Hearst Corporation paid $415 million for the *Houston Chronicle* while the other Houston paper, the *Post,* was sold for about $150 million. The Denver *Post* went for about $95 million, and even the *Morristown* (N.J.) *Daily Record,* with a circulation of 70,000, went for about $125 million. The consequences of this trend may be troubling for American journalism. In many instances, the acquiring company in these deals incurs a huge debt as a result of the deal. There is great pressure from the stockholders and owners of the company to pay attention to the bottom line, squeezing as much profit as possible from the papers, even to the detriment of good journalism, to help pay off some of this debt.

The trend toward chain ownership is apparent in both the major and secondary newspaper markets. While Gannett, Knight-Ridder, and Times Mirror are names familiar to everybody in the industry, companies such as Donrey, Park, and Freedom also have a strong grip on the industry at the mid-market level. These chains and several others control nearly 500 dailies and nondailies with circulations usually less than 100,000. Park, for example, as of 1987 owned fifty-eight papers; the largest was the 18,000 circulation Lockport, New York, *Union-Sun and Journal*.

What are some of the reasons behind the growth of newspaper chains? In the first place, newspapers tend to be a moneymaking investment. With a profit margin of between 15 and 20 percent, buying more newspapers is a profitable way for newspaper chains to increase their earnings. Second, the U.S. tax laws encourage the growth of chains. When a newspaper chain earns a profit and returns this profit to its shareholders in the form of stock dividends, the shareholders must pay taxes on this money. On the other hand, if the chain uses its profits to acquire another newspaper, this money is not taxed and shareholders are happy because their stock increases in value. Additionally, many independent papers are sold to chains after the death of the principal owner to pay the inheritance taxes on the property. In fact, some papers have been sold before the owners' death in an attempt to keep inheritance taxes low. Other newspapers, which are hard pressed to keep up with the rising costs of newspaper production, are persuaded to sell their operation to a chain in return for a substantial sum. In recent years, the Gannett Company paid $165 million for the *Des Moines Register,* and the Times Mirror Company bought the Hartford, Connecticut, Courant company for $106 million. In each of these cases, the purchase price was more than thirty times the company's net income. When offered a chance to make profits like these, many owners are hard pressed to say no.

Newspapers Without a Home

In many parts of the country, newspapers have dropped the name of the local town, city, or region from their titles. Thus many papers wind up being called simply *The Tribune, The Record, The Herald,* or *The Evening News.* For example, Oakland, California, Scranton, Pennsylvania, Warren, Ohio, and Wisconsin Rapids, Wisconsin, all have a paper called simply *The Tribune,* with no place name. Why this trend toward generic newspaper titles? From a marketing standpoint it makes some sense. Many papers try to serve a population in more than just a town or city. Putting a place name in the title might make the paper seem foreign to some subscribers. Moreover, as many readers left the cities for the suburbs,

the city papers dropped their urban designations. In New Jersey, for example, the *Trenton Times* became simply *The Times* and the *Atlantic City Press* was renamed *The Press.*

Some papers, however, have bucked the trend. The *Chicago Sun-Times* became simply the *Sun-Times* in the 1970s but reverted back to its original title in 1985. The Detroit papers kept their city as part of their names despite a tremendous exodus of readers to the suburbs. Even the *Asbury Park Press* resisted temptation to become *The Press.* The paper's executives figured that if Asbury Park was OK for Bruce Springsteen, it was fine with them as well.

In a trend similar to that in other media industries, there is a good deal of cross-media ownership among newspaper companies. For example, Affiliated Publications, which publishes the *Boston Globe,* publishes seven magazines. The Gannett Company owns eight TV and fifteen radio stations. The New York Times Company owns twenty-six daily papers, eleven magazines, and radio and TV stations. Advance Publications controls twenty-six papers and several magazines, radio-TV stations, and cable systems. This trend is likely to continue as more newspapers enter the cable television field.

The Decline of Competition

Coupled with the growth of chains is the decline of newspaper competition within single markets. Back in 1923, more than 500 cities had two or more competing daily papers, including 100 that had 3 or more. By 1988, there were only 43 cities where competition existed, and in 18 of these competition was kept alive only through a **joint-operating agreement (JOA)**. A JOA is formed, under approval by the Justice Department, to maintain two newspapers in a city when otherwise one would go out of business. Functions of the two papers—circulation, advertising, and production—are combined to save money. Only the editorial staffs remain separate and competitive. JOAs exist between papers in Nashville, Cincinnati, El Paso, Tucson, and Birmingham to name just a few. In the past, the Justice Department has almost routinely okayed requests for JOAs, but in 1987 it turned down a request from the two Detroit papers for such an arrangement. The request was granted on appeal, but a group opposed to the merger succeeded in getting an injunction against the JOA. As of this writing, the situation was still unresolved.

The Pros and Cons of Group Ownership

The pros and cons of group ownership and decreasing competition are topics that have been widely debated among newspaper executives and press critics. Critics maintain that fewer competing papers means a loss in the diversity of opinions available to the audience. They also claim that top management in group operations places profits above newspaper quality. A newspaper owned by a chain, say these critics, would likely avoid local controversy in its pages in order to avoid offending advertisers. It has also been charged that chain newspapers are usually under the direction of absentee owners who may have little knowledge of or concern for local community interests.

On the other hand, those who favor newspaper groups argue that group owners can accomplish certain things that smaller owners cannot. For example, a large group owner could afford to improve news coverage by having correspondents and news bureaus in the state capital, Washington, D.C., and foreign cities—an arrangement too expensive for a small owner to maintain. The chains are also better able to afford the latest technical equipment, thereby making newspaper production more efficient. Lastly, chains have the resources to provide for more elaborate training and public-service programs than do individually owned papers. The validity of each of these arguments depends in great measure on the particular group owner involved. As Ernest Hynds concluded in his book *American Newspapers in the 1980s,* "Some group-owned newspapers are among the nation's best; some newspapers belonging to groups are at best mediocre."*

---

* Ernest Hynds, *American Newspapers in the 1980s* (New York: Hastings House, 1980), p. 144.

PRODUCING THE NEWSPAPER

Departments and Staff

The departmental structure and staffing of a newspaper vary with its size. Obviously, a small-town weekly with only a half-dozen employees will not have the same arrangement as the *New York Times*. All papers, however, have certain common aspects. They have a publisher and are generally divided into three main departments. The publisher is in charge of the entire operation of the paper. He or she sets the paper's editorial policy and is responsible for the tone and overall personality of the newspaper. The three main departments at most newspapers are (1) business, (2) production, and (3) news-editorial. Figure 5.2 is a simplified departmental chart for a typical newspaper.

FIGURE 5.2 *Departmental chart for a typical newspaper.*

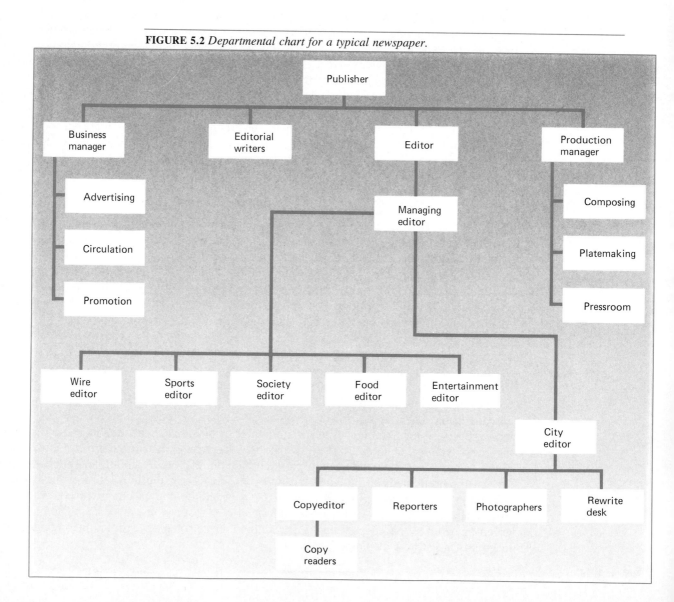

The Business Department. The business department has the primary responsibility of keeping the paper financially solvent. Within the business department, duties are generally subdivided into three major areas: advertising, circulation, and promotion. The advertising division handles local retail advertising, national accounts whose ads are placed by advertising agencies, and classified ads. Since the newspaper will decline or prosper according to its number of readers, the circulation division is an important part of the organization. Typically headed by the circulation manager, this division handles taking orders, delivering the paper to the local community and surrounding areas, handling mail subscriptions, and keeping up-to-date subscription records. The promotion division is responsible for increasing circulation, building advertiser and reader interest in the paper, building goodwill, and demonstrating that the paper is interested in community affairs. Newspaper promotion can involve sales and subscription programs, or it might take the shape of sponsoring concerts, races, athletic leagues, and other special events.

The Production Department. The production department prints the newspaper. Since most dailies are now printed by offset printing and cold-type methods, the arrangement of this department has changed markedly over the last few years. The major subdivisions of the production department are the composing room, where computers and phototypesetters are used to lay out a newspaper page; the platemaking area, where surfaces that will reproduce the printed page are constructed; and the pressroom itself, where ink actually meets paper.

The News-Editorial Department. The department that has the most complicated arrangement in the typical paper is the news-editorial department (see Figure 5.2).

The first thing to note in Fig. 5.2 is the division between the news and editorial sides of the operation, with each side reporting directly to the publisher. This division

The More Things Change . . .

A joke in the modern, high-tech world of newspaper publishing is that the paper is put together on electronic video-display terminals with satellite-fed wire copy, composed on multimillion-dollar computerized typesetting equipment, printed on high-speed presses in an automated plant run by robots, routed to state-of-the-art fuel-efficient delivery trucks, and then given to a twelve-year-old on a bicycle who throws it in the bushes in front of your house.

Well, this may not be entirely true any more: The era of the preteen newspaper carrier—the "little merchant system," typical of Horatio Alger—is drawing to a close. What's causing the demise of the little merchant system? First, most papers are shifting to morning publication. This means that the young carrier would have to get up before dawn to get started. Few youngsters are that committed. Second, the pay isn't very good. In an affluent society, not many kids get excited about making $25 a week. They could easily make that with a lot less effort mowing lawns or baby-sitting. Finally, the suburbanization of society has created housing that is less concentrated and less accessible by bike or foot. Consequently, more and more papers are turning to adult independent contractors or route agents. They pick up the papers at a central distribution point, proceed by truck to subscribers' homes along their appointed routes, and, every once in a while, throw the paper into the bushes in front of your house.

reflects the historical fact that news and opinion are kept separate. The editorial columns contain opinion, while the news columns contain objective reporting.

In the news operation, the central position is that of the managing editor. The managing editor oversees the total day-by-day operation of the news department and coordinates the work of the several departments in the newsroom. The wire editor scans the thousands of words transmitted over the wires of the major news services, Associated Press and United Press International, and selects those stories most relevant to the paper, edits them, and adds headlines. The city editor supervises the newspaper's local coverage. He or she assigns stories to local ''beat'' reporters or general-assignment reporters. Beat reporters have a specified area to cover: city hall, courts, police station. General-assignment reporters handle a variety of stories, ranging all the way from fires and accidents to the local flower show. The city editor also assigns photographers to go along with reporters on selected stories. The copy editor usually works inside a special U-shaped desk (called the slot) in the newsroom and supervises the editing, headline writing, and changes in stories submitted by local reporters.

Finally, there are specialized departments in the paper that generally have their own editor and staff. These may vary from paper to paper, but typically they include the sports, business, family, real estate, and entertainment departments.

Publishing the Newspaper

Getting out a newspaper is a twenty-four-hour-a-day job. News happens at all hours, and many stories happen unexpectedly. Not only that, news is perishable; it becomes less valuable as it ages. Trying to cope with the never-ending flow of news and the constant pressure to keep it fresh requires organization and coordination among the paper's staff. This section will illustrate the coordination by sketching how a newspaper gets published.

A newspaper reporter conducts a telephone interview and types his notes into a computer; later he can compose his story at this VDT. (Alan Carey/The Image Works)

There are two basic sources of news copy: local reporting and the wire services. Early in the day, the wire editor will scan the output from the wire machines and flag possible stories for the day's paper. At the same time, the city editor is checking his or her notes and daily calendar and making story assignments to various reporters. The city editor must also keep track of the location of reporters in case a story breaks unexpectedly during the day and someone has to be pulled off a regular assignment to cover it. While all of this is going on, the managing editor is gauging the available space, called the **newshole,** that can be devoted to news in that day's issue of the paper. This space will change according to the number of ads scheduled to appear on any one day. The more ads, the greater the number of pages that can be printed and the larger the newshole. The editor also checks over available material such as copy that didn't get into the edition of the paper it was meant for or copy that is timeless and can be used to fill space on an inside page.

As the day progresses, reporters return from assignments and write their news stories at the keyboard of a **video-display terminal (VDT).** The finished story is transmitted electronically to a computer, where it is stored. These stories are ''called up'' by copy editors, who trim and make changes in the stories and code them for use in the paper. If, upon further reflection, the managing editor decides that the story is not newsworthy enough for inclusion, the story can be purged from the machine. The managing editor can also instruct the computer to store the copy for future use. The newsworthy stories are then sent back to the computer for processing. Decisions about page makeup and the amount of space to be devoted to a story are made as the deadline for publication appears. Other decisions are made about the ratio of wire copy to local and state news. Photographs and other artwork are selected for inclusion; headlines are written; space is cleared for late-breaking stories; updates are inserted in breaking stories.

In the composing room, high-speed computerized **photocomposition machines** take electronic impulses and translate them into images and words. The stories are printed on strips of photographic paper. These strips then go to the makeup room where, along with ads, photos, artwork, and headlines, they are pasted up into full newspaper pages. (Computers are now being developed to do this layout task. See below.) This pasted-up page looks and reads just like the final printed page. Throughout the day, each page in the paper, including the special sections such as sports, family, classifieds, entertainment, and so on, is pasted up. The paste-ups are taken to the camera room, where a photograph is made of the whole page. This results in a negative, which is sent to the platemaking area. An **offset plate** is made by placing the negative between glass and a sheet of photosensitive metal and exposing the plate to bright light. The finished product is a plate with two areas: those parts that were exposed to light (any place there was a letter or a dot) and the rest of the plate. Some newspapers use plastic instead of metal plates for direct printing.

As the plates are being readied, huge rolls of newsprint are threaded into the presses. The plates are then attached to the press, and the printing process begins. Finished and folded papers emerge from the press and are sent by conveyor belt to the distribution area. The distribution staff counts and bundles the newspapers and then hands them over to the circulation truck drivers, who then deliver them to newsstands and carriers. Figure 5.3 is a simplified illustration of this process.

Technology in the Newsroom

Newspaper technology is now almost all computer-driven, and most publishers continue to automate their operations as new technology becomes available. Pagin-

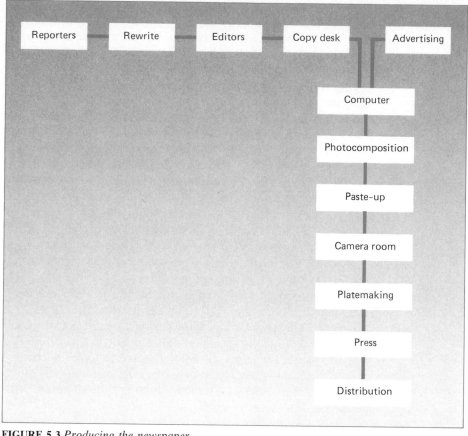

FIGURE 5.3 *Producing the newspaper.*

ation systems, although not quite perfected, made their debut in the late 1980s, and electronic page makeup of display ads with graphics became a reality. Eventually, electronic makeup should eliminate typesetting on photosensitive paper, paste-up of mechanicals, and film used in turning pages into plates. By mid-1988, about 250 papers were using electronic pagination. This new system should make newspaper composition more flexible and ultimately cheaper.

Personal computers are everywhere at today's newspaper. Reporters write stories on them, editors edit on them, advertisers send ads to the papers on them, artists use them for graphics, circulation specialists use them for maintaining subscription lists, and sales departments use them for billing. It's hard to find a department that's not dependent on PCs for one or more major tasks.

Technology has also been at work on another messy problem for newspaper publishers—ink rub-off. The tendency of newspaper ink to come off on hands and clothing is one of the principal reasons subscribers cancel. To attack this problem, many companies are experimenting with treated oil inks that adhere strongly to the paper and are less likely to darken fingers.

On the printing side, **flexographic printing,** a system that uses a plastic plate and has a device that controls excess ink, was adopted by several papers. "Flexo," as it's called, has the advantages of better printing quality, less paper waste, and use of a water-based ink that helps the rub-off problem. About twenty or thirty papers are using flexo in 1989.

Photos as well as words can be transmitted electronically from reporters out in the field. Here, Boston Globe *employees watch a demonstration of the latest electronic phototransmission equipment. (Kenneth Martin/Amstock)*

On another front, experts are predicting that newspaper photography as it now exists will be replaced by filmless electronic photography. The next generation of news photographers will record pictures on videotape or with electronic cameras and transmit them via modem to newspaper computers. An editor will view the picture on a computer monitor, crop it to fit available space, and add a caption. The new system means no more silver-based film, darkroom, and traditional photo morgue. Sony and Canon have already developed the prototype for such a system.

Electronic Publishing

One technology that has not yet caught on is the electronic newspaper. Many newspaper companies had hoped to remake the news and information business by relying on two new electronic services: teletext and videotex. Teletext consists of "pages," or screens of information, that are sent in the unused portion of a regular TV channel. Subscribers purchase a special decoder to receive the system and use a keypad to select and hold the various pages of news as they go by. Videotex is a more ambitious service. It's a two-way system that allows a subscriber with a terminal or personal computer to retrieve information stored in the service provider's main terminal. Most of the services had from three to six newspapers that could be retrieved. Customers could also use the service as an electronic bulletin board, send electronic mail, play games with other subscribers, and shop and bank at home.

Some big companies that tried to develop videotex and teletext services wound up with big losses. Knight-Ridder, for example, spent five years and $50 million before giving up its Viewtron project. The Times Mirror Company lost about $30 million, and Time Inc. dropped about $25 million on their projects. By 1988, most media companies had given up. Why did the electronic newspaper fail? First, it was too expensive. Consumers had to invest in a computer, special terminal, or decoder as well as paying a monthly subscription bill and a hourly use fee. Costs were running $30 to $40 a month, about five times the cost of the daily newspaper. Second, it was hard to use. Videotex users had to wade through pages of menus and submenus to get to where they wanted to be. It was much easier to find a story in the daily paper. Finally, the need just wasn't there. Customers weren't ready to give up the daily paper for the electronic alternative. After a couple of weeks, the novelty effect wore off and customers basically ignored the service.

It's still too early to write the obituary on teletext and videotex. A few companies are still in the videotex business. The biggest, Compuserve, has about 380,000 subscribers, but its main attraction does not seem to be the newspapers it stores in its data banks. Also, specialized business videotex services, such as Dow Jones News/Retrieval service, are doing quite well. Teletext is popular in Europe. Great Britain has about 30 percent of its sets hooked into a teletext service. Other companies are still optimistic about its future. IBM, Sears, and CBS recently announced a joint videotex venture first called Trintex and later renamed Prodigy (CBS ultimately backed away from the deal). Local phone companies are interested in creating an electronic version of the Yellow Pages and other data bases. For the time being, however, the conventional paper will still be around.

ECONOMICS

Newspapers derive their revenue from two sources: advertising, which provides 75-80 percent of the total, and circulation (revenue from subscriptions and single-copy sales), which accounts for about 20-25 percent. Advertising revenue is closely related to circulation since papers with a large circulation are able to charge more for ads that will reach a larger audience.

Despite little change in circulation and rising costs, the financial status of the newspaper industry has improved, and the long-term outlook is positive. Total newspaper advertising volume topped the $31 billion mark in 1988, an increase of about 90 percent since 1980. Newspapers continued to rank number one in the total share of all advertising revenue in 1988, attracting about 26 percent of all advertising dollars. This figure is down a bit from 1980, but total newspaper advertising revenue was just slightly less than the combined total for radio and television. The increased advertising revenues that newspapers have received over the years were the result of rate increases for the ads and of increased sums spent for advertising in all media. Local advertising was still the primary source of income, accounting for about 85 percent of a typical newspaper's revenue in 1988. Overall profit margins in 1986 were about 19 percent. Newspapers had a pretax income in 1986 of about $2.5 billion. Gannett was the revenue leader with 1986 revenues totaling $2.2 billion. The Times Mirror Company placed second with $1.7 billion, and Knight-Ridder placed third with $1.69 billion.

Advertising Revenue

Advertising revenue comes from four separate sources: (1) national advertising; (2) local advertising; (3) classified advertising; and (4) preprints. Local retail advertising is the most important source of newspaper income, accounting for about 40–50 percent of all revenue. Classified ads come next, followed by national ads and preprinted inserts. National advertising originates with manufacturers of products who need to reach a national market on a mass basis. The majority of these include cigarette and tobacco products, automobiles, food, and airline services. Local advertising is purchased by retail stores and service establishments. Department stores, supermarkets, auto dealerships, and discount stores are the businesses that buy large amounts of local advertising space. Some national businesses such as Sears, J. C. Penney, and Montgomery Ward do most of their newspaper advertising through their local outlets. Classified advertising, which is bought by local businesses and individuals, is generally run in a special section at the back of the paper. Buyers as well as sellers purchase classified ads. The ads are grouped by content and contain diverse elements. Local governments publish official legal notices in the classifieds; individuals place personal ads to exchange greetings. Preprints are advertising supplements put together by national, regional, and local businesses that are inserted into the copies of the paper. The paper charges the advertiser for the distribution of the preprints.

The newspaper industry, however, has realized that the market for the advertising dollar is becoming more competitive. Consequently, the industry has taken three major steps to maintain its favored position with advertisers. First, the newspaper industry adopted the Standard Advertising Unit (SAU) in 1984. This marked the first time since 1820 that the industry adopted a standardized measure. Before the SAU, advertisers had to cope with different page sizes and column widths in different papers. The use of the SAU made it easier for advertisers to buy standardized space for their ads. Second, in response to advertisers' complaints that not all homes in a market are exposed to a newspaper, many newspapers sent out free weekly papers, containing articles and ads from the daily, to all nonsubscribers, thus helping advertisers achieve more market coverage. Third, newspapers recognized that direct-mail advertising was becoming a significant competitor. Newspapers started a concerted lobbying effort for higher third-class postal rates. This lobbying campaign paid off in 1988 when the U.S. Postal Service approved higher third-class rates.

The amount of advertising included in a newspaper has a direct bearing on the amount of news the paper can print. The more advertising that is sold, the more pages that can be printed and the more news that can be included. The ratio of advertising to newscopy has stayed about the same since 1970. A typical paper contains about 65 percent ads. The total number of pages in the typical paper has increased from forty-seven in 1970 to about seventy-five in 1986. As a result, the amount of newscopy has also increased, from about nineteen pages in 1970 to twenty-six pages in 1986.

Circulation Revenue

Circulation revenue includes all the receipts from selling the paper to the consumer. The newspaper, however, does not receive the total price paid by a reader for a copy of the paper because of the many distribution systems that are employed to get the newspaper to the consumer. The most common method is for the paper to sell copies to a juvenile carrier or distributor at wholesale prices, usually about 25 percent less than the retail price. Other methods include hiring full-time employees as carriers and billing subscribers in advance (as do magazines). These methods show promise, but they also increase the cost of distribution.

One closely studied factor important in determining circulation revenue is the effect of increased subscription and single-copy prices. In 1970, 89 percent of

Reprinted by permission of Tribune Company Syndicate, Inc.

newspapers were priced at a dime a copy. In 1988, none were priced at a dime; 1 percent sold for 15 cents, and 2 percent for 20 cents. Around 58 percent had raised their price to a quarter and about 40 percent cost more than a quarter. Sunday papers have shown similar increases. In 1970, the typical price was 25 cents. By 1988, it had more than quadrupled. The rising price of newspapers has probably had some negative impact on circulation revenue. Most industry experts agree that increased prices have discouraged families from subscribing to more than one newspaper. Moreover, several papers have noticed that there is a decrease in subscriptions among older, fixed-income residents following a price increase.

General Expenses

The costs of running a newspaper can be viewed in several ways. One common method is to divide the costs by function. This technique shows (1) news and editorial costs; (2) expenses involved in selling local, national, and classified ads; (3) mechanical costs, including typesetting, plate production, camera, and engraving; (4) printing costs such as newsprint (the paper), ink, and the cost of running the press; (5) circulation and distribution costs; and (6) general administrative costs such as secretarial services, clerical services, soliciting for subscriptions.

Some of these costs are variable. For example, the printing costs will increase as the number of printed copies increases. Distribution costs will also increase with circulation size (more trucks will have to make more stops). Other costs are fixed. The expense of sending a reporter to the airport to cover a visiting dignitary will be about the same for a paper with a circulation of 10,000 and for one with a circulation of 100,000. This means that the cost of running a newspaper will depend somewhat on the size of the paper. For a small paper (circulation about 25,000), general administrative costs would rank first, accounting for about one-third of all expenses. The cost of newsprint and ink ranks second, followed by mechanical costs. Total expenses for this size of daily would run about $3 million to $5 million per year. In the case of a big-city daily (circulation 200,000), newsprint and ink costs rank first, followed by administrative expenses and mechanical costs. Newsprint prices were stable from 1984 to 1985 but jumped about 14 percent over the next two years. On the average, newsprint accounts for about 25 cents of every dollar spent by a paper.

In an attempt to cut paper costs, publishers are experimenting with a wood paper substitute called **kenaf.** This soft, fibrous shrub is easier to make into pulp

On the Rack

Few people think about this area of newspaper distribution, but somebody has to keep those coin-operated, self-dispensing newspaper racks in working order. *USA Today,* for example, has on the streets about 120,000 newsracks worth about $30 million. The life span of a typical rack is about four to six years, with most succumbing to terminal rust. Some racks, however, are put out of commission much earlier after suffering a variety of indignities. For example, *USA Today* reports the following:

- When the paper first appeared in Pittsburgh, seventy-eight racks wound up in the Allegheny River.

- In Seattle, after a large number of racks mysteriously disappeared from the streets, police discovered that a local fraternity was requiring pledges to steal the racks as part of their initiation.

- In New York, on the Fourth of July, pranksters threw M-80 firecrackers into the racks to see what would happen. (A firecracker usually blows off the door.)

- In the New England states, pouring molasses into the coin trays is a popular pastime.

- Also in Pittsburgh, several racks had faulty coin mechanisms that would accumulate a large number of coins and then spew them out like a slot machine to lucky purchasers.

- Perhaps most bizarre, on a hot day in Portland, Oregon, after the paper announced a price increase, somebody kneaded ten pounds of leavened bread dough into one of the racks. Needless to say, the dough rose but sales didn't.

than is wood-based paper and is naturally strong. Kenaf mills are already in operation in Texas and the substance has shown itself to work quite well as newsprint. Further refinements should bring the price of kenaf down to where it is competitive with paper.

Another cost-cutting technique involves robots. A Japanese newspaper plant is currently using advanced robotics in its platerooms and pressrooms. Newsprint at the plant is never touched by human hands. Rolls are delivered by automated trucks, spliced and trimmed by robots, and loaded into the press. Although the initial cost of building such a system is expensive, companies are able to save money in the long run because of reduced labor costs.

CAREERS IN THE NEWSPAPER INDUSTRY

The newspaper industry is a big employer. In 1988, newspaper employment exceeded 477,000 people. In fact, newspapers now rank first in the Labor Department's listing of the nation's manufacturing employees. Of these 477,000, about 70,000 are employed in the editorial side of the paper; an additional 50,000 work in promotion and advertising, and another 60,000 in the administrative area. The remainder work in the circulation and production departments. More women are entering careers in journalism. The 1988 workforce was about 42 percent female. Competition for jobs at big-city papers can be stiff, but newspapers located in small and medium-sized

A newsboy throws the paper onto a front porch. The newspaper delivery system begun in the penny-press era is much the same today, even as the techniques of printing and reporting news have changed dramatically. (Dan Chidester/ The Image Works)

communities are having trouble attracting skilled employees. In some regions of the country in the late 1980s there were more jobs available than people to fill them. One of the reasons for this shortage was decreasing enrollment of newspaper majors at colleges. Of the 85,000-90,000 students enrolled in journalism schools in 1988, only about 10-15 percent were actually planning careers in newspapers. A second reason was the low starting salary of entry-level jobs. A 1987 survey revealed that the beginning salary for editorial employees at daily newspapers was about $12,500, somewhat less than starting salaries in other fields. Salaries for other than entry-level jobs at a newspaper tend to be more competitive.

Entry-Level Positions

Students interested in becoming reporters should try to major in journalism. A good course of study includes copyreading, editing, reporting, feature writing, and mass communication law. In addition, a newcomer to the profession should have a well-rounded education in the liberal arts, especially political science, economics, history, literature, and the social sciences. This stress on a well-rounded education is reinforced by the fact that the Accrediting Council on Education in Journalism and Mass Communication, the main organization that accredits journalism schools, recommends that three-fourths of a student's work be taken outside the journalism area.

In fact, some editors prefer to hire reporters who have a liberal-arts degree with a minor in journalism.

A person seeking an entry-level job as a reporter has the best chance of landing a job at a small daily paper or weekly. Starting out at a small paper will give a newcomer experience in several areas of newspaper work since the division of labor at these papers is less clear. A reporter might also function as a photographer, edit wire copy, write headlines, and even assist in paste-up work. One possible way to break into the profession is to secure a summer job or an internship at a daily or a weekly. Most newspapers are always on the lookout for new talent, and a good number sponsor their own summer internship programs. The Newspaper Fund sponsors an internship program, and the Journalism Council has a summer internship program for minority students. Additionally, there are other avenues of entry into the news-editorial side. Although the jobs are not glamorous, some people break into the profession as proofreaders, rewrite persons, or researchers. Once inside the newspaper, these people then hope to move up to more responsible positions.

Other entry-level jobs can be found in the business side of the paper. Students who are interested in this type of work should have a background in business, advertising, and economics, along with a knowledge of mass communication. Since advertising is such an important source of newspaper revenue, most newspapers will gladly accept a newcomer who wishes to work in the sales department. Advertising salespeople might work on selling and planning display advertising for local merchants. Or a person might break in with the classified ad department, where he or she would write ads for people who call the paper with items to sell or positions to fill or would solicit ads for the classified section.

Opportunities also exist in the circulation department for those interested in working with distributors and local carriers. Skills in organization and management are needed for these positions. Since controlling costs has become an important factor in operating a profitable paper, there are also beginning positions for accountants, cost analysts, and market researchers. The production side of the newspaper is staffed by people with technical training and mechanical skills. Most beginners in this department enter it directly from vocational schools or from apprentice programs.

Upward Mobility

In selecting an entry-level position in newspapers and other mass media, it is important to consider where your job might lead and how long it will take you to get there. In short, you should pay attention to the potential for advancement in the particular department you choose. In the case of a reporter, upward mobility can come in one of two ways. A reporter can advance by becoming skilled in editing and move up to the position of copy editor or perhaps state editor, regional editor, or wire editor. The ultimate goal for this person would be the city editor's or managing editor's slot. Other reporters might not wish to take on the additional administrative and desk work that goes with a managerial position. If that is the case, then career advancement for these people consists of moving on to larger circulation papers in big cities or increased specialization in one field of reporting. A beginning reporter, for example, might specialize in covering the business beat. He or she might then advance to become editor of the paper's business section. Eventually, this person might supply a daily business column to the paper. Another reporter might specialize in covering political news. This person might eventually advance to become the paper's Washington correspondent and might even head the paper's Washington bureau.

On the business side the route for advancement in the advertising department usually leads from the classifieds to the national advertising division. This department works with manufacturers of nationally distributed products and services and plans display advertising for these companies. The national ad staff often works hand in hand with the newspaper's national sales representative. The national ''reps'' have offices in major cities where they solicit ads for local papers. Those who begin in the circulation department can eventually rise to the position of circulation manager, while those who start in the advertising side can advance to advertising director. Ultimately, the top job that can be reached, short of publisher, is that of business manager, the person in charge of the entire business side of the paper.

SUGGESTIONS FOR FURTHER READING

The following books contain more information about concepts and topics discussed in this chapter.

BOGART, LEO, *Press and Public,* Hillsdale, N.J.: Lawrence Erlbaum, 1981.

COMPAIGNE, BENJAMIN, *The Newspaper Industry in the 1980s,* White Plains, N.Y.: Knowledge Industry Press, 1980.

FINK, CONRAD, *Strategic Newspaper Management,* New York: Random House, 1988.

HYNDS, ERNEST, *American Newspapers in the 1980s,* New York: Hastings House, 1980.

RANKIN, W. PARKMAN, *The Practice of Newspaper Management,* New York: Praeger, 1986.

SMITH, ANTHONY, *Goodbye Gutenberg,* New York: Oxford University Press, 1980.

Chapter 6

Structure of the Magazine Industry

The key words in the magazine industry are **market segmentation** and **target audience.** Almost every demographic or life-style grouping is served by one or more magazines. Consider: *Seventeen* goes after hip teen females; *Sassy* appeals to the more precocious hip teen females; *Modern Bride* goes after those same females when they are a little older. *Ms., Savvy, Working Woman*, and *Good Housekeeping* are next in line. And for those women and men who no longer find themselves in the *Family Circle*, there's *Divorce* magazine. For those willing to take the plunge again, there's *New Family*. And eventually, everybody is ready for *Modern Maturity*.

Has audience segmentation gone too far? In the list below some authentic magazines are mixed with some fictitious titles that were submitted as comic entries in a contest sponsored by *Advertising Age*. Can you tell the real magazines from the bogus ones?*

King: The magazine for Elvis impersonators

Outlaw Biker: Not for the run-of-the-mill cyclist

Popular Litigant: The magazine for people who sue

Trillion: For people who handle a lot of money

Nip 'n' Tuck: For those who have had cosmetic surgery

Of all the media discussed in this book, magazines are probably the most in tune with social, economic, demographic and sociological trends. As consumer and business needs change, new magazines appear and existing publications fine tune their content to fulfill them. For example, the increased popularity of home computers spawned dozens of magazines: *PC World, Byte, Run, Ahoy, Computer World*, and so on. Television and its related technologies prompted the birth of *TV Guide* and a host of other magazines such as *Orbit, Video Software*, and *Channels*. Popular programming on TV was behind such ventures as *Soap Opera Digest, Music Video Review,* and a host of wrestling magazines. *Runner's World* and *Runner* capitalized on the jogging fad. The "maturing" of the population was reflected in the circulation figures for *Modern Maturity* (published by the American Association for Retired People) and *Lear's* (for the woman over 40).

In an age that seems to be dominated by the electronic media, magazines are still surviving and doing fairly well. Their circulation is up, their revenues are

Outlaw Biker and *Trillion* are real; the others are fictitious.

Consumer magazines fall into major general-interest categories such as sports, news, and women's interests, as these examples illustrate.

holding steady, and they have the confidence of their investors. Magazines serve a narrowly defined audience spread out over a wide area and present information and illustrations in a convenient form: People can read them wherever and whenever they want. All in all, it's a stable industry, well-suited for the future. This chapter will examine the structure and organization of the magazine business and note how it has capitalized on market segmentation.

ORGANIZATION OF THE MAGAZINE INDUSTRY

One of the problems in discussing the magazine industry is deciding what exactly is a magazine. The dictionary defines a magazine as a "periodical publication, usually with a paper cover, containing miscellaneous articles and often with illustrations or photographs." This definition is broad enough to include *TV Guide*, with a circulation of more than 16 million; *Gondolier*, a magazine for boating enthusiasts; *Sky*, given away to airline passengers by Delta Airlines; *Successful Farmer*, the magazine of farm management; *Go,* distributed to Goodyear tire dealers; *The Journal of Social Psychology; Gloria Pitzer's National Homemakers Newsletter;* and the *Swine Flu Claim and Litigation Reporter*. As best as we can tell, there are probably around 12,000–14,000 magazines published in the United States. The number and diversity of these publications are staggering. For example, *Standard Rate and Data Service* lists ninety-one fishing and hunting magazines, forty-eight boating and yachting publications, and four periodicals devoted to snowmobiling. There are more than 2600 magazines sold regularly on newsstands, and the number of new consumer

Specialized Editions

As was mentioned at the beginning of this chapter, specialization and market segmentation are two modern characteristics of newspapers and magazines. In the case of magazines, two examples of these trends are regional and demographic editions. A regional edition of a magazine is one that is distributed in only one region or state and contains certain pages that appear only in that edition. Regional editions are useful for businesses that market their products in a specific area. Advertisements in a regional edition reach only those prospects in the business' immediate market area and avoid the inefficiency of reaching people living in other parts of the country who are not likely customers. About seventy national magazines offer regional editions. *Time*, for example, puts out seven. *U.S. News and World Report* has about twenty; *Playboy* about ten. *Better Homes and Gardens* has nine regions that are divided up into one hundred regional editions.

Another example of regional specialization is found in the growth of city or regional magazines. More than seventy-five of these magazines are now published; most of them started in the 1970s. *New York, Philadelphia, Chicago,* and *Los Angeles* are the best known city magazines, but others exist in smaller cities and regions. Among them are the *Arkansas Times, Alabama Monthly, Shenandoah Valley, The Roanoker, Naples Now, Alaska, Back Home in Kentucky, Dayton, Nutmegger of Connecticut,* and *Sandlapper* (the magazine of South Carolina).

Other magazines offer demographic editions. *Time* has the following:

1. *Time* Major Metros: goes to important U.S. markets for wine sales, foreign cars, and airline travel.

2. *Time* Campus: goes only to students enrolled in colleges and universities and is published from September to May.

3. *Time* Zips: covers subscribers who are prime prospects for luxury products.

4. *Time* Top Management: goes only to top managers in the business community.

Specialized editions are not just the province of general-interest magazines. *Farm Journal* has four specific editions that target dairy, hog, beef, and high-income farmers.

---

titles continues to go up: 171 in 1984, 234 in 1985, 372 in 1986, about 200 in 1988. Total circulation of the 1900 publications audited by the Audit Bureau of Circulations was 350 million. Obviously, classifying the magazine industry into coherent categories is a vexing problem. For our purposes, we will employ two organizational schemes. The first classifies magazines into five main content categories:

1. general consumer magazines

2. business publications

3. literary reviews and academic journals

4. newsletters

5. public relations magazines

The second divides the magazine industry into the three traditional components of manufacturing: production, distribution, and retailing.

Content Categories

General Consumer Magazines. A consumer magazine is one that can be acquired by anyone, through a subscription or a single-copy purchase or by obtaining a free copy. These magazines are generally shelved at the corner newsstand or local book store. (Other types of magazines are usually not available to the general public.) These publications are called consumer magazines because readers can buy the products and services that are advertised in their pages. One noticeable trend in the content of consumer magazines is, as we have mentioned, the movement away from broad, general appeal to the more specialized. *Standard Rate and Data Service (SRDS)*, a monthly directory of advertising rates and other pertinent information about magazines, lists approximately fifty content groupings of consumer magazines, ranging from "Babies," with fourteen publications, to "Women's," with ninety-two titles. Some of the better known consumer magazines are *People, Time, Reader's Digest, Newsweek, Sports Illustrated,* and *Playboy* (see Table 6.1).

Business Publications. Business magazines (also called trade publications) serve a particular business, industry, or profession. They are not sold on newsstands, and their readership is limited to those in the profession or business. The products advertised in these publications are generally those that would be purchased by business organizations or professionals rather than by the general public. *Business Publications Rates and Data,* a companion publication to *SRDS,* lists approximately 4000 different titles of business magazines. Most of these magazines are published by independent publishing companies that are not connected with the fields they

Magazines such as these are targeted to specific audiences; such publications address the specialized interests of the mass audience.

TABLE 6.1 Top Ten Consumer Magazines (December 1988)

TITLE	CIRCULATION (IN MILLIONS)
Modern Maturity	19.3
Reader's Digest	16.5
TV Guide	16.3
National Geographic	10.6
Better Homes and Gardens	8.1
Family Circle	5.9
Woman's Day	5.6
Good Housekeeping	5.2
McCall's	5.1
Ladies' Home Journal	5.1

Source: *Advertising Age*, February 20, 1989, p. 12.

serve. For example, McGraw-Hill and Cahners are two private publishing companies that publish business magazines in a wide variety of areas. Other business publications are put out by professional organizations, which publish the magazine as a service to their members. The degree of specialization of these magazines is seen in the medical field, which has approximately 375 different publications serving all of the various medical specializations. Leading business magazines include *Computerworld, Oil and Gas Journal*, and *Medical Economics*. Business publishers are also active in supplying data bases and computer bulletin board systems to their clients.

Literary Reviews and Academic Journals. Hundreds of literary reviews and academic journals, generally with circulations under 10,000, are published by nonprofit organizations and funded by universities, foundations, or professional organizations. They may publish four or fewer issues per year, and a large number do not accept advertising. These publications cover the entire range of literary and academic interests, including such journals as *The Kenyon Review, Theater Design and Technology, European Urology, Journalism Quarterly, Poultry and Egg Marketing*, and *The Journal of Japanese Botany*.

Newsletters. Newsletters are publications of typically four to eight pages set in typewriter face. They are either distributed free or sold by subscription. In recent years, publishing newsletters has become big business. In fact, there is even a *Newsletter on Newsletters*, published for those who edit newsletters. Newsletters specialize in narrow coverage, whereas magazines strive for broad perspective. Most newsletters try to give their readers inside information; they attempt to achieve a personal tone between writer and reader. In fact, a lot of newsletters begin with ''Dear Client'' or ''Dear Reader.'' Newsletters are extremely specialized with small circulations (typically under 10,000) but high subscription prices ($200 or more for some newsletters).

In addition, many of today's leading magazines are also publishing newsletters. Some are spinoffs from the main publication, such as *Omni*'s *Longevity*, circulation 60,000, and the *Smithsonian*'s *Travel News*. Others are aimed at potential advertisers. The *GQ Newsletter* goes to fashion retailers and contains news about the menswear industry, foreign trends, and a calendar listing upcoming events.

Some well-known newsletters are *The Kiplinger Newsletter*, the *Granville Market Newsletter,* and *Chemical Insight*. In the mass communication area, the *Gallagher Report* and the *Media Monitor* cover events in the print and broadcast industries, and *Communication Booknotes* reviews new books about the mass media.

Public Relations Magazines. Public relations magazines are published by sponsoring companies and are designed to be circulated among the company's employees, dealers, customers, and stockholders. These publications typically carry little advertising, apart from promotional items for the sponsoring organization. There are thousands of public relations publications, and they have developed their own professional organization, the International Association of Business Communicators.

There are several types of public relations magazines. Perhaps the most common are employee magazines, which contain news of interest to all those who work for the company. A new pension plan, possible layoffs, and safety procedures would be common topics for this sort of publication. Other public relations magazines might be sent to customers, stockholders, and dealers.

Function Categories

A second useful way of structuring the magazine industry is to divide it by function into the production, distribution, and retail segments.

The Production Function. The production phase of the industry, which consists of approximately 2000-3000 publishers, encompasses all the elements necessary to put out a magazine—copy, artwork, photos, titles, layout, printing, and binding. A subsequent section will describe in more detail how a magazine is produced.

The Distribution Function. The distribution phase of the industry handles the job of getting the magazine to the reader. It is not a simple job. In fact, the circulation department at a large magazine may be the most complex in the whole company.

If It Works . . .

Sports Illustrated's annual swimsuit issue has become a tradition and almost always draws big circulation numbers. Not to be outdone, one *SI* competitor, *Inside Sports*, put out its own swimsuit spread. If it works for sports magazines, why not for others? Why not for *Pizza Today*, the trade magazine that is sent to pizza parlor managers? In its preconvention issue, *PT* featured a ten-page pictorial of swimsuit-wearing models posing at various spots around Las Vegas, the site of Pizza Expo '87. Reaction was mixed, but everyone agreed the layout helped *Pizza Today* shed its crusty image.

Pizza Today
cover.

As with newspapers, circulation means the total number of copies of the magazine that are delivered through mail subscriptions or bought at the newsstand. There are two main types of circulation. **Paid circulation** means that the readers pay to receive the magazine, either through a subscription or by purchasing it at the newsstand. Paid circulation has two main advantages. First, periodicals that use paid circulation qualify for second-class postal rates, which are lower than other rates. Second, paid circulation provides a revenue source to the publisher in addition to advertising. On the negative side, paid-circulation magazines gain a wide coverage of their area by expensive promotional campaigns designed to increase subscriptions or to sell single copies. Paid-circulation magazines also have the added expense of collecting subscription payments and record keeping. Most consumer magazines use paid circulation.

The alternative to paid circulation is free or **controlled circulation.** Controlled-circulation magazines set specific qualifications for those who are to receive the magazine and send or otherwise distribute the magazine to those who qualify. Magazines that are provided to airline passengers or motel guests are examples of controlled-circulation publications. The advantages of controlled circulation are, first, that publications that use it can reach all of the personnel in a given field and second, that these publications avoid the costs of promoting subscriptions. On the negative side, controlled-circulation magazines gain no revenue from subscriptions and single-copy sales. Further, postage for controlled publication costs more. Controlled circulation has generally been used by business and public relations magazines. No matter what method is chosen, the circulation of a magazine is an important number. Advertising rates are based on circulation figures, and the larger the circulation, the more the magazine can charge for its advertising space.

For a paid-circulation magazine, distributing copies to its subscribers is a relatively simple affair. Address labels are attached to the magazine, and copies are delivered by mail. The complicated (and expensive) part of this process is getting subscribers. There are no fewer than fourteen methods that are used by magazines to build subscription lists. They include employing "cash-field" agencies, which have salespeople make house-to-house calls in order to sell subscriptions directly to consumers; direct-mail agencies such as Publishers Clearing House ("You may have already won $100,000 or other valuable prizes! See inside."), which generates 10 million magazine subscriptions a year; direct-mail campaigns sponsored by the publisher; and, finally, what are called "blow-in" cards, those annoying little cards that fall out of a magazine as soon as you open it.

Single-copy distribution to newsstands and other retailers is a multistep process. The publisher deals with only one party, the national distributor. There are about a dozen national distributors that work with the nation's publishers. The national distributor handles anywhere from a dozen to fifty or more titles. At least once every month, representatives of the magazine sit down with the national distributor and determine the number of magazines to be distributed for an upcoming issue. The national distributor then delivers the magazines to the approximately 500 wholesalers who sell magazines and paperback books within specified areas. In any given month, a wholesaler might receive 1000 or 2000 magazines to distribute to dealers. The actual distribution is done by route people who drive a truck around to their various retailers on a predetermined schedule, deliver new issues of the magazine, and pick up unsold copies.

The Retail Function. The retailer is the last segment of the industry. Best available figures indicate that there are approximately 140,000 different retail outlets in the

Why It Pays to Renew Subscriptions Early (Particularly If You're the Publisher)

Many of you may have had the experience of getting one of those form letters from a magazine publisher informing you that your subscription "expires shortly" and urging you to send a check to renew immediately. Many companies send these notices out some seven months before the expiration date. Why? Simple economics. *People* magazine has about 1.4 million subscribers. Suppose 10 percent of them (140,000) send in their renewals with a check for, say $50 (let's use round numbers for this hypothetical example). *People* would have $7 million on hand about six months before it was due. The magazine could invest this money at, say 6 percent annual interest, and collect more than $200,000. The advantages of early renewal are obvious, at least from where the publisher sits.

United States. Retail outlets may be corner newsstands, drug stores, supermarkets, tobacco shops, convenience stores, and bookshops. Of these, the convenience store is becoming a major force in magazine retailing. In the mid-1980s, the 7-Eleven chain was selling about $60 million annually in magazines and other publications. When a dealer receives a magazine, he or she agrees to keep the magazine on the display racks for a predetermined length of time (usually a week or a month). At the end of this period, unsold copies are returned to the wholesaler for credit.

A big problem is getting the right number of magazines to the newsstands. If too many copies are supplied, the publisher must absorb the cost. On the other hand, too few copies might inhibit the growth of the audience for the magazine.

Magazine Ownership

A major trend of the late 1980s saw the management of the magazine divisions of media conglomerates band together to purchase their departments when their parent organizations were forced to reduce debt or to streamline. For example, Peter Diamandis, the head of CBS Magazines, led a management group which bought the magazine operation from CBS (he later sold it to Hachette Publications; see below). Similarly, management groups at both Harcourt Brace Jovanovich and Lorimar bought their company's magazine operations. A second trend saw more foreign involvement in the U.S. magazine industry as a weak dollar and attractive investment potential lured foreign investors as never before. From 1983 to 1987, foreign buyers accounted for 75 percent of major magazine sales. The biggest deal was the purchase of Diamandis Communications by Hachette, a large French publishing firm. Hachette paid $712 million for Diamandis, a company formed in 1987 when management bought out CBS magazines. Hachette was also a fifty–fifty partner with Rupert Murdoch's company in publishing *Elle* magazine. In addition, Australia's Fairfax Magazines launched *Sassy*, similar to their Australian publication *Dolly*, and Cahners, the U.S. subsidiary of Reed International, a British publishing company, bought *Modern Bride* and *Variety*.

Consolidation has also affected the magazine business as major publishers acquired new titles. *Time* bought *Southern Living*, Gannett bought *Family Weekly*, Condé Nast bought the *New Yorker*, and Hearst acquired *Esquire*. And in late 1988, Rupert Murdoch bought Triangle Publications, owner of *TV Guide* and other magazines, in a $3 billion deal. Although the magazine industry is not yet as concentrated as the newspaper industry, major publishers do account for a great deal of the revenue generated. In 1984, the top five publishers accounted for about one-third of the total revenue generated by consumer magazines. In 1988, the comparable figure was nearly 46 percent. Some companies that publish more than ten consumer magazines are Condé Nast, Hearst, Petersen, and Hachette. The business publication field is dominated by about a dozen publishers, with Edgell Publications (formerly Harcourt Brace Jovanovich) and McGraw-Hill leading the way.

PRODUCING THE MAGAZINE

Departments and Staff

A glance at the masthead (the page that lists the magazine's personnel) of a few magazines will show that although there are many variations, a typical magazine is generally headed by a publisher who oversees four main departments: (1) circulation, (2) advertising, (3) production, and (4) editorial. Figure 6.1, page 142, shows a typical arrangement.

The publisher sets the general policy for the publication. He or she is responsible for budgeting, maintaining a healthy advertising position, keeping circulation high, and making sure the magazine has a consistent editorial direction. Strictly speaking, the publisher directs both the business and the editorial side of the publication, but most publishers tend to pay more attention to the financial operations and generally let the editor-in-chief make decisions concerning the content of the publication.

The Circulation Department. This department, under the supervision of the circulation director, is responsible for getting new readers and keeping current readers satisfied. If the magazine is losing readers, the circulation director must find out why. If the publisher thinks the magazine can attract another 50,000 subscribers, the circulation director has to figure out a way to get them. On most magazines, the pressure-filled job of circulation director is an important cog in the magazine's machinery. Responsible to the circulation director are the heads of three divisions: (1) the subscription manager, who tries to increase the number of people on the magazine's subscription list; (2) the single-copy sales manager, who works with the national distributors, wholesalers, and retailers; and (3) the subscription-fulfillment director, whose division is in charge of making sure that the magazine gets to subscribers by taking care of address changes, renewals, new subscribers, complaints, and so forth.

One circulation problem that plagues the subscription department of all magazines is late delivery. In 1988, surveys disclosed that 73 percent of monthly magazines and 52 percent of weeklies were delivered late by the postal service.

The Advertising and Sales Division. Under the supervision of an advertising director, the advertising and sales division is responsible for selling space in the magazine to potential advertisers. Also working in this department are the sales promotion manager, who is responsible for putting together new programs to enhance sales; the sales staff, which does the actual selling; and the research director, who studies the audience and compiles data of interest to advertisers.

The Production Department. The production department is concerned with actually printing and binding the publication. In charge of this department is the production manager, who buys paper, handles contracts with printers, orders new typesetting

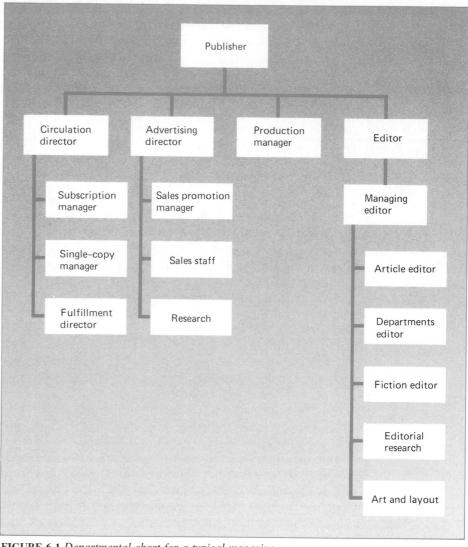

FIGURE 6.1 *Departmental chart for a typical magazine.*

and computer equipment, and makes frequent visits to printing plants to make sure production is going smoothly.

The Editorial Department. The editorial department handles the nonadvertising content of the magazine. The person in charge may be called the executive editor, the editor-in-chief, or simply the editor. On most publications, the job of editor is primarily one of administration, and much of the editor's time is spent in supervising the editorial staff, planning topics that might be used in upcoming issues, informing the advertising department about plans, and taking part in various public relations activities. The day-to-day operation of the magazine falls on the shoulders of the managing editor. Making sure all articles are completed on time, selecting artwork, writing titles, changing layouts, and shortening stories are all functions performed by the managing editor. Helping the managing editor with these tasks are several

---

Building Circulation: Specialized Lists

One of the ways used by circulation managers to build their subscription base is a direct-mail campaign to people likely to subscribe to their magazine. The specialized nature of these lists reflects the specialized nature of the magazine business. Some of the mailing lists currently available:

- people who purchased denim jackets

- buyers of tweezers, nail clippers, and other beauty products

- people who quilt (this list had 345,000 names)

- owners and builders of wooden boats

- buyers of children's books about Judaism

- owners of quality watches—those that cost more than $700

- mechanical engineers (more than 96,000 of them)

- former smokers

- purchasers of personalized golf tees (200,000)

- people who have bought mail order products they saw advertised on cable TV: flea-zappers, ginsu knives, easy-cycle exercisers, and so on (50,000 on this list)

---

editors who handle articles, fiction, or other departments that appear regularly within the magazine. Since the managing editor is usually more skilled in the verbal department than in the visual, an art director designs the magazine, selects typefaces for headlines, and supervises the display of photos and other illustrations.

The computer has had an impact on almost all of the departments at a typical magazine. In circulation, computers are used to maintain subscription lists, generate promotional mailing lists, and do accounting. In the advertising department, computerized data bases are used to generate data that are helpful to potential clients. Special computers have been developed for use in editorial work. Along with word processing, these devices have a split-screen feature that allows editors to make marginal comments or rewrite whole paragraphs without altering the original text. Computerized searches of photo files are also possible. Recent advances in computerized composition made it possible to automate typesetting and integrate art and photos into page makeup, thus eliminating manual paste-ups. In the production department, computers are used to track paper flow, maintain schedules, and monitor quality control. In fact, *Folio* magazine publishes ads for thirty different software/ hardware systems for publishers.

Publishing the Magazine

Everything moves in cycles. When the first American magazines were published by people such as Bradford and Franklin, the editorial and production functions went hand in hand. Early magazine publishers were printers as well as writers; some even ''wrote'' at the type case as they picked up the letters of each separate word and fitted them into their composing stick. During the nineteenth century, however, the production function was divorced from the editorial function. One set of people wrote and edited the copy while another group set it in type. Many magazines have now gone full circle: Computers allow writers and editors to set their words into type and make up pages, reuniting the production and editorial functions.

Nonetheless, even the computer hasn't changed one thing: Except for weekly news magazines, producing a magazine still requires a great deal of lead time. Most issues are planned several months or at least several weeks in advance. It is not uncommon for an editor to be planning a Christmas issue while sweltering through a late-summer heat wave.

The first step in all magazine production is preliminary planning and the generation of ideas for upcoming issues. Once the overall ideas are set, the next step is to convert the ideas into concrete subjects for articles. It is at this point that preliminary decisions concerning article length, photos, and accompanying artwork are made. Once this step is completed, the managing editor starts assigning certain articles to staff writers or freelancers. It is also at this juncture that the magazine's stockpile of completed manuscripts is checked for any material that might be germane to the scheduled issue. It is possible that some of the magazine's staff may have already completed an article on a relevant topic or that a freelance writer may have submitted a piece that would fit in with the planned issue.

The next step involves putting together a miniature **dummy.** A dummy is simply a plan or blueprint of the pages for the upcoming issue that shows the contents in

A TV Guide *magazine editor and art director look over slides and artwork in preparation for a forthcoming issue. Layouts from past issues are displayed on the wall. (AP/Wide World Photos)*

their proper order. At this stage, the dummy is created by folding and trimming regular-size sheets of blank stationery into the total number of pages that will be published. The editor takes the miniature dummy and blocks out those pages that will carry advertising, notes those pages that are normally assigned to regular departments, and labels those pages that will be devoted to assigned articles. The editor can then visualize what the completed magazine will look like.

At about this same time, schedules are drawn up that assure that an article will get to the printer in time to be included in the forthcoming issue. A copy deadline is set—this is the day the writer must hand in the story to the editor. Time is set aside for the editing, checking, and verification of all copy. A timetable is also set up for illustrations and artwork. This production schedule represents the master blueprint that brings together all the elements that will make up the finished copy.

Most articles are now written and edited at the computer. Once they are in acceptable form, a computerized typesetter sets the copy in body and display-size type. Photocopies of the pages can be read to catch errors and changes can be made easily at the keyboard. At the same time, photos and other illustrations are processed by a special camera that fixes them on a special printing plate. After the copy is corrected, the words and illustrations are made up into a mechanical, a page ready to be photographed and transferred to a printing plate. A separate mechanical is required for each color being printed. The mechanicals are photographed and negatives developed. The pages are then positioned in sequence in a special mask, and a press plate is created by shining light through them. The plates then go to the printing press where they are printed.

Many magazines are using satellite transmission to speed up their production process. News weeklies, in particular, are sending copy and illustrations to printing plants located around the country. The new technology allows news magazines to move their deadlines back so that late-breaking news stories can be included. Last-minute insertions and corrections are also much more easily handled.

After the magazine has been printed, it goes to the binding room where it is trimmed and stapled together. Mailing labels containing the names of subscribers are affixed to the magazine and the issues are sorted according to zip codes, bundled, and delivered to the post office. Magazines that will be sold on the newsstand are tied into bundles of fifty to seventy-five each and are shipped to wholesalers.

You Light Up My Ad

Ads in magazines have gotten more ambitious over the years. First it was the pop-up ad, then scratch-and-sniff strips, then microchips that played music. Now a company called Laserlight, Inc., is making magazine ads that actually light up. Here's the secret: A paper-thin battery is connected by printed ink circuit to a tiny LED bulb. When inserted between two pages, the LED bulb (or bulbs) can light up both sides of the ad in one or more colors. Tiny fiber connectors can make a string of bulbs light in sequence, thus giving the illusion of motion. Laserlight is even working on a "commercial on a page" concept that shows the Statue of Liberty, complete with illuminated fireworks, moving ships, and a fifteen-second audio message on a microchip. Some advertisers, including Absolut Vodka, think this is a pretty bright idea and have already shown interest in lighting up their magazine ads.

ECONOMICS

There are three basic sources of magazine revenue: subscriptions, single-copy sales, and advertising. At the beginning of 1989, the magazine industry was collecting more than $18 billion annually from these three sources. Nevertheless, it should be pointed out that this $18 billion figure is not an accurate estimation of the money that is actually received by magazine publishers. For example, a magazine that sells for $2 an issue and sells 500,000 copies generates $1 million in revenue; however, the national distributor, wholesaler, and retailer get a cut of this money. After all these sectors are paid, the publisher receives about half of the total revenue, or in this example, about $500,000. The $18 billion figure also includes gross advertising revenue. Most advertising space is purchased through advertising agencies, which collect a 15 percent commission for their efforts. Thus if an advertiser purchases $100,000 worth of space, the magazine actually receives $85,000 after the agency deducts its fee.

In general, magazines were in good, if not great, economic health at the end of the decade, with pretax profits averaging about 11 percent, a figure virtually unchanged since 1985.

According to the U.S. Department of Commerce, total spending for advertising in U.S. magazines was up less than 5 percent from 1986 to 1987 with a total of about $8.5 billion. Nonetheless, the magazine industry's share of national advertising has been constant for the last five to six years at about 21 percent. Many analysts interpret this as bad news, since magazines were not able to pick up the slack when TV—the magazine industry's biggest rival for national ad dollars—saw its revenues flatten out and even slightly decline over the same period. Others suggest that the industry is doing well just holding its own, given the softness of the advertising market, competition from direct-mail ads, and cutbacks in ad purchases by cigarette and liquor manufacturers in response to public opinion. In any case, if the total amount does not grow, publishers will face a much more competitive market as more magazines battle for a fixed share of the pie.

A major change in magazine economics that has occurred over the last five or ten years is the increasing importance of the consumer in supporting the magazine industry. About three-quarters of the gross revenue of the magazine industry in 1987 came from consumer magazines, with the remainder accounted for by business magazines. A 1986 survey by the Magazine Publishers' Association found that subscriptions accounted for 34 percent of the typical magazine's revenue and single-copy sales for another 18 percent, for a total of 52 percent. Advertising revenue accounts for the other 48 percent. According to the survey, this is the lowest share yet for advertising support. Thus consumer spending for magazines has become more important than advertising revenue for a magazine's support.

Of course, the relative importance of subscriptions, single-copy sales, and advertising revenue varies tremendously from magazine to magazine. *Reader's Digest* gets 60 percent of its revenues from subscriptions, 35 percent from ads, and only 5 percent from single-copy sales. On the other hand, *Penthouse* gets 13 percent of its revenues from advertising, only 5 percent from subscriptions, and a whopping 82 percent from single-copy sales. To give some perspective on advertising fees, as of 1988, a full-page color ad in *Reader's Digest* cost $97,000. The same ad in *Rolling Stone* would cost $29,000 and $5,250 in *Dirt Bike*.

From the point of view of the consumer, one obvious fact of life is that magazines are getting more expensive. In 1987, the average single-copy price of a magazine was about $2.10, an increase of 56 percent since 1980. Subscription costs have increased less, averaging about $23.24, up 40 percent from 1980. Magazines are costing the consumer more because they are more expensive to produce. From 1970 to 1988, the cost of producing the average magazine more than doubled. The typical expense dollar for a magazine breaks down as follows:

Advertising expenses	10¢
Circulation costs	31¢
Editorial costs	10¢
Manufacturing and distribution	39¢
Other operational costs	3¢
Administration	7¢

The two items included under manufacturing and distribution that have increased at the fastest rate are postage and paper. After a few years of stability, the cost of paper and postage both went up in 1988. Second-class postage rates went up 18 percent, and some magazines were examining alternative means of delivery, such as private carrier firms, as an option. *Newsweek*, for example, found that the postal increase will cost $2.4 million in 1988. Most publishers intended to pass this increase along to consumers through higher subscription prices. One survey done in mid-1988 found that nearly one-third of all publishers surveyed were contemplating a subscription rate increase in 1989. If that wasn't enough to deal with, paper costs jumped about 13 percent from 1987 to 1988.

John H. Johnson, founder of Ebony *magazine, the largest black-oriented publication in the world, had to borrow $500 against his mother's furniture to finance* Negro Digest, *an early venture and one of the first black magazines. (AP/Wide World Photos)*

Magazines may also face a new rival for advertising dollars: catalogs. Bloomingdale's, Spiegel, and The Sharper Image have published ad pages in their catalogs. Revenue from catalog advertising was expected to top $25 million in 1987, which hardly compares to the billions spent on ads in consumer magazines but is enough to get the attention of magazine publishers.

Starting a big-circulation magazine is a risky business. Although no hard figures are available, industry experts estimate about twenty to thirty consumer magazines fold every year. In addition, starting a new general-interest publication requires a great deal of cash on hand to carry the magazine through its first years, which are likely to show a loss. Many publications go several years without making a profit. Henry Luce reportedly spent $30 million on *Sports Illustrated* before it showed a profit. It took $13 million to keep *Viva* afloat during its early years. Experts suggest that at least $1 million should be available to support a new general consumer magazine.

On the other hand, a small-circulation narrow-interest magazine can be started on a shoestring. *Computer Language* got under way with $50,000; *Cape Cod Life* was launched with $40,000, and the *Rug Hooker News and Views* was started with about $10,000.

Specialization is a strength of magazines, but it also makes starting a new publication a risky venture. For example, magazines that appeal to the audience that sprouts up around an innovation or fad have their destiny tied to that innovation. Consider the fate of *CB Times*, a publication that did well during the CB craze but faded when the craze subsided, or *PCjr*, which quickly folded after IBM stopped manufacturing this model. In fact, the general slump in home computer sales was accompanied by the demise of many computer magazines, a publishing area that had experienced tremendous growth only a year earlier.

CAREERS IN THE MAGAZINE INDUSTRY

As best anyone can tell, there are only about 113,000 people employed in the magazine industry, thus making it a rather difficult industry to break into. Additionally, the headquarters of large magazine publishing companies tend to be located on the East Coast, especially around New York City. For example, of the top ten magazine group publishers in terms of circulation, eight are located in New York. Additionally, the Los Angeles area is another region that contains a significant number of magazine publishers. This means that someone serious about a career with a major magazine might consider relocating.

Entry-Level Positions

Most jobs in the magazine industry are found at small publications or at business and trade magazines. In the editorial department, the most common entry-level job is that of editorial assistant. This job is really a training position in which a beginner learns about the actual workings and day-to-day chores that go on in the production of a particular magazine. Editorial assistants do a little bit of everything. Some typical duties might include proofreading, research, replying to authors' letters, coordinating production schedules, filing, indexing, cross-referencing, and answering readers' mail. In specialized publications, editorial assistants might be assigned duties somewhat afield of actual editorial work. During her first days on the job, one editorial assistant at a fashion magazine spent her time carrying around clothing for one of the magazine's photographers. A young man who went to work as an editorial assistant for a motorcycle publication spent his first two weeks repairing motorcycle engines.

Another beginning-level position at some magazines is that of researcher. A researcher spends his or her time pulling together assorted facts and data for staff writers or compiling folders and research notes for articles that are in the planning stage. This particular job requires a person who has a general education, is skilled at using the library, and is familiar with reference books. The researcher might be collecting facts on the storm-door industry one week and compiling data on volcanoes the next. The large newsmagazines *Time, Newsweek*, and *U.S. News and World Report* employ large research staffs.

At other publications, many newcomers start out as readers. When articles or stories arrive at the magazine, they are assigned to a reader who studies them, summarizes them for an editor, and may even make recommendations about what to publish. Some beginners become staff writers. The assignment editor gives the staff writers assignments such as preparing a calendar of upcoming events of interest to the readers or editing a section of helpful household hints. In time, staff writers move on to more challenging assignments.

It should be noted that some beginners attempt to break into magazine work by freelance writing. Magazines give some of their assignments to freelance writers who are paid per story. Other freelancers submit articles or stories on speculation, hoping that the magazine will be impressed enough with their work to buy it. The amount a freelancer gets paid for his or her work varies widely with the particular magazine. Some publications may pay $200 for a typical article; others might go as high as $3000–5000.

Some larger magazines also prepare small publications that are distributed to their employees. Jobs on these in-house publications represent important entry-level positions for newcomers since they allow their work to be seen almost immediately by magazine executives. An employee who does an outstanding job on one of these in-house publications usually makes a quick transition to the parent magazine's editorial staff.

Newcomers in the circulation department are usually found in the subscription-fulfillment department where they update subscription lists, send out renewal notices, and handle complaints. Other beginning-level positions in this department are subscription salesperson, assistant to the subscription director, or single-copy sales manager. In the advertising department, entry-level positions are typically "assistants to" a staff member. Assistants to an advertising copywriter help prepare copy for leaflets and display cards, compile various reports, and assist in the preparation of direct-mail letters. Assistants to the sales promotion manager spend their time compiling and verifying statistical tables and charts, checking copies of promotional materials, handling routine correspondence, and suggesting new promotional ideas.

Upward Mobility

Career advancement in the editorial department can follow one of two different routes. Editorial assistants move up the ladder to become assistant editors, usually assigned to a specific department of the magazine. The next step up is that of associate editor, a position that carries increased responsibility. Typically, after spending some time as associate editor, the next position is senior editor. From there, if the person has talent and initiative, he or she may go on to be managing editor or perhaps even editor-in-chief. Another possible upward route finds the editorial assistant moving into the assistant copyeditor's slot. In this capacity, the person will spend most of his or her time working with other people's manuscripts and getting them in shape for publication. The assistant copyeditor then progresses to the rank of copyeditor. From this position it is possible, although not probable, that the person can become the managing editor.

In the circulation department, the next step up after an entry-level position is into the subscription director's or single-copy sales manager's slot. Advancement from this position consists of moving into the top management ranks by becoming circulation director. For many, the circulation director's job has led to a position as associate publisher or even publisher. In the advertising department, upward mobility consists of moving into the position the newcomer was formerly assisting. Assistants to copywriters become full-fledged copywriters. Assistants to the sales promotion manager follow a similar course. Another route upward is to join the magazine's sales staff. Ultimately, the top position to aspire to in the advertising department is that of advertising director, a member of the magazine's top management team. The job of advertising director frequently serves as a springboard to the publisher's position.

SUGGESTIONS FOR FURTHER READING

The following books contain additional information about the magazine industry.

CLICK, J. W., and RUSSELL BAIRD, *Magazine Editing and Production*, Dubuque, Iowa: William C. Brown, 1986.

The Handbook of Magazine Publishing, New Canaan, Conn.: Folio Publishing Corp., 1983.

Magazine Industry Marketplace, New York: R. R. Bowker, 1985.

MOGEL, LEONARD, *The Magazine,* Englewood Cliffs, N.J.: Prentice-Hall, 1979.

RANKIN, W. PARKMAN, *Business Management of General Consumer Magazines*, 2nd ed., New York: Praeger, 1986.

TAFT, WILLIAM, *American Magazines for the 1980s,* New York: Hastings House, 1982.

WOLSELEY, ROLAND, *Understanding Magazines,* Ames: Iowa State University Press, 1972.

————, *The Changing Magazine*, New York: Hastings House, 1973.

Chapter 7

Structure of the Book Industry

When the manuscript first crossed the desk of Robert Asahina, an editor at Simon & Schuster, it didn't cause much excitement. Written by Allan Bloom, a philosopher and a professor of social thought at the University of Chicago, it was a scholarly work developed from an article called "Our Listless Universities" that had been published in *The National Review*. Entitled *The Closing of the American Mind: How Higher Education Has Failed Democracy and Impoverished the Souls of Today's Students*, the book's rather bleak thesis was that American universities no longer acquaint students with the basic core knowledge of Western civilization. Instead, the universities had sold out to trendy, career-oriented studies and were turning out shallow, uninformed, culturally illiterate and misguided graduates. Bloom was highly critical of rock music ("Rock . . . has one appeal only, a barbaric appeal, to sexual desire . . . undeveloped and untutored"), divorce, and the women's movement.

The manuscript was filled with allusions to the classics and classical thinkers. Plato, Homer, Freud, Nietzsche, and a host of other intellectuals were frequently cited. In the era of MTV, *People*, Stephen King novels, and "Wheel of Fortune," this book did not look like a best-seller. Asahina felt the book would receive critical praise but had little hope of a commercial success. Even Bloom conceded that the book would have only about 5000 buyers, "75 percent of whom I know." Simon & Schuster agreed with Bloom and ordered only 10,000 copies printed.

Then something astonishing happened. The *New York Times, Washington Post,* and *Wall Street Journal* gave the book favorable reviews. *The Closing of the American Mind* started appearing on nonfiction best-seller lists. Simon & Schuster rushed more copies into print. The book topped the *Times'* nonfiction best-seller list for fifteen straight weeks. People started talking about it. Education became a hot political issue. Tests of "cultural literacy" appeared in many magazines and newspapers. Bloom's book touched a cultural nerve; it was plugged in to the current social scene. During the summer of 1987, when people generally chose books about sex, glitz, and scandal for their beach reading, *Closing* sold nearly a half-million copies. It promises to sell far more in paperback. In an age when the electronic media have taken center stage, the importance of the book was once again illuminated.

This vignette holds several lessons about the publishing industry. In the first place, there's a lot of uncertainty involved. No one knows for sure why some books are popular and some aren't. Second, there are many publishers who will overlook the profit motive and publish a book purely on its artistic, intellectual, or cultural merit. Consequently, books are an important part of the cultural heritage. Third, books are read by a relatively small audience. A top-rated TV show will have about

The Ayatollah Versus *Verses*

The tremendous cultural and social impact that a book can have was convincingly demonstrated in early 1989 by the furor over British author Salman Rushdie's novel *The Satanic Verses*. The book, at times comical and at times philosophical, takes a long, sardonic look at the clash of cultures between East and West. Praised by critics, the book would probably have been read mainly by Western intellectuals had not Rushdie included a dream sequence in which one of his characters satirically recounts the origins of the Islamic religion. This outrageous passage grievously offended many Muslims, who found the book blasphemous.

A few weeks after publication, there were protests and demonstrations against the book in India, Pakistan, Great Britain, and Saudi Arabia. In one particularly violent protest in Islamabad, the capital of Pakistan, six people were killed and hundreds injured. The furor reached its peak when Iran's Ayatollah Ruhollah Khomeini declared that Rushdie and anyone else involved in publishing the book must be killed for the sin of insulting Islam. Some of Khomeini's followers offered a $5 million reward for carrying out the Ayatollah's sentence. Shaken, Rushdie and his family went into hiding.

The shock waves soon hit the United States. Rushdie's U.S. publisher closed its New York office after receiving several bomb threats. Fearing for the safety of their employees, the three largest bookselling chains in America pulled the novel from their shelves, at least for a while. Rushdie and his wife, a novelist, canceled U.S. book tours. The Authors Guild came to Rushdie's defense and several famous U.S. authors took part in a public reading of the book. Thanks to all the controversy and despite the difficulty in obtaining it, the book became an international best seller.

40 million viewers for each of its episodes. It took about forty years to sell 20 million copies of *Gone With the Wind*, but more than 50 million people watched the movie version in a single evening when it came to television. Even a flop TV show might have 15 million-20 million in its audience. These numbers are beyond the wildest imaginings of most authors. A popular hardcover book might make the year's best-seller list with 125,000 copies sold. Even a mass-market paperback such as *Red Storm Rising* by Tom Clancy might sell only about 3 million copies. Books are the least "mass" of the mass media. Lastly, books can have cultural impact that far outweighs their relatively modest audience size. The *Closing of the American Mind* is simply one of the many books that have influenced their times. *Uncle Tom's Cabin* is credited with helping to change a nation's attitudes toward slavery. Dr. Spock and his *Baby and Child Care* altered the way parents brought up their children and made its author the target of critics who blamed him and his permissive theories for the social unrest of the 1960s.

This chapter examines the book publishing industry. Although we will concentrate primarily on the more practical and concrete aspects of the industry—structure, methods, and economics of publishing—the cultural and social contribution of publishing should not be forgotten.

ORGANIZATION OF THE BOOK INDUSTRY

The book publishing industry can be divided into three segments: publishers, distributors, and retailers.

All Time Best-Sellers

The following are the all-time best-sellers in hardcover and mass market paperbacks. (Dictionaries and the Bible are not included in this list.)

Hardcover		
Title	Copies Sold	Date
1. *Betty Crocker's Cookbook*	22 million	1950
2. *Better Homes and Gardens Cookbook*	21 million	1930
3. *The Joy of Cooking*	10 million	1931
4. *Mr. Boston's Bartender's Guide*	9 million	1935
5. *The Tale of Peter Rabbit*	8 million	1902
Mass Market Paperbacks		
Title	Copies Sold	Date
1. *Baby and Child Care*	32 million	1946
2. *How to Win Friends and Influence People*	15 million	1940
3. *The Hobbit*	13 million	1972
4. *The Exorcist*	12 million	1972
5. *1984*	12 million	1950

Dr. Spock's Baby and Child Care *is the all-time best-selling mass market paperback with sales that top 32 million. The book influenced parents and sparked criticism in the 1960s for the new methods of child-rearing that it promoted. (Alan Carey/The Image Works)*

Publishers

The publishing segment consists of the 2000 or so establishments that transform manuscripts submitted by authors into books that are sought by readers. Every year these companies will publish 45,000–50,000 new titles. Book publishing is a highly segmented industry. Over the past fifteen years, publishers have developed a classification system for the industry based upon the market that is served. The following are the twelve major divisions suggested by the Association of American Publishers.

1. *Trade books* are aimed at the general consumer and sold primarily through bookstores. They can be hardbound or softbound and include works for juveniles and adults. Trade books include hardcover fiction, nonfiction, biography, cookbooks, art books, and several other types.

2. *Religious books* include Bibles, hymnals, prayer books, theology, and other literature of a devotional nature.

3. *Professional books* are aimed at doctors, lawyers, scientists, accountants, business managers, architects, engineers, and all others who need a personal reference library in their work.

4. *Book clubs* at first may sound more like a distribution channel than a division of the publishing segment, but some book clubs publish their own books and almost all prepare special editions for their members. Thus, it makes sense to include them here.

5. *Mail order publications* consist of books created for the general public and marketed by direct mail. These are different from book clubs because the books are marketed by the publisher, and customers do not incur any membership obligations in an organization. The Time-Life Company, among others, has marketed books dealing with cooking, home repair, the Civil War, Western history, aviation, World War II, and other topics.

6. *Mass market paperbacks* are softbound volumes on all subjects that have their major sale in places other than bookstores. Typically, these are the books sold in wire racks in supermarkets, newsstands, drug stores, airports, chain stores, and so on.

7. *University presses* publish mostly scholarly titles or books that have cultural or artistic merit. University presses are typically run on a nonprofit basis and most of their customers are libraries and scholars.

8. *Elementary and secondary textbooks* are hard and softcover books, workbooks, manuals, and other printed materials, all intended for use in the classroom. Logically enough, schools are the primary market for these publishers. (This division is also referred to as "elhi" publishers—from *el*ementary and *hi*gh school.)

9. *College text* publishers produce texts and workbooks for the college market.

10. *Standardized tests* comprise a relatively small segment of the industry. These publishers put together tests of ability, aptitude, interest, personality, and other traits. For example, the Educational Testing Service publishes the Scholastic Aptitude Test and the Graduate Record Exam.

11. *Subscription reference books* consist of encyclopedias, dictionaries, atlases, and the like. They are usually marketed in packages to schools, libraries, and individual consumers.

12. *Audiovisual and other media* supply tapes, films, slides, transparencies, games, and other educational material to schools and training companies.

Table 7.1 shows the relative importance of each of these segments to the industry. As can be seen, trade, professional, and textbook publishing are the major divisions accounting for 74 percent of sales.

Distributors

Only a few kinds of publishers (subscription books, book clubs, mail order) sell their books directly to readers. Most books go to wholesalers and jobbers who, in turn, distribute them to retail and other outlets. There are about fifteen to twenty major wholesalers or jobbers across the country, and these companies usually stock large inventories of trade and/or textbooks. In the mass market paperback field, there are three channels of distribution. National distributors usually distribute both magazines and paperback books. Most national distributors also act as a link between publishers and independent wholesalers (IDs). IDs operate in special geographical areas and are locally owned. There were about 120 independent wholesalers in operation in 1988. The third distribution channel for paperbacks is jobbers. Jobbers service wide geographical areas and differ from independent wholesalers in that jobbers usually do not handle magazines or have their own fleet of delivery trucks. Figure 7.1, page 156, illustrates the distribution process.

Retailers

There are more than 20,000 bookstores in the United States, along with about 200,000 drug stores, supermarkets, airports, and specialty shops where books are also sold. Overall, however, there are five main channels through which books get to the consumer. General retailers include bookstores, book sections in department

TABLE 7.1 Sales by Publishing Industry Division, 1987

DIVISION	PERCENTAGE OF SALES
Trade	27
Religious	5
Professional	21
Book clubs	5
Mail order	4
Mass market paperback	8
University press	1
Elhi text	13
College text	13
Standardized tests	1
Subscription reference	2
AV and other media	1

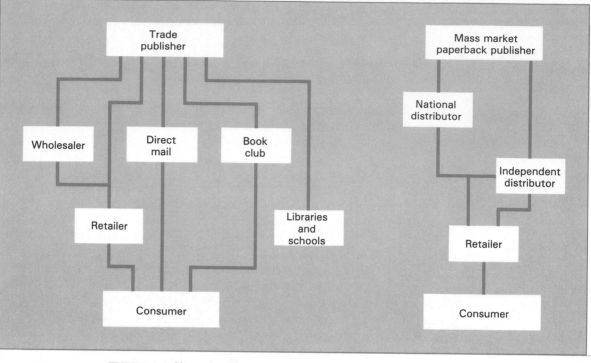

FIGURE 7.1 *Channels of book distribution.*

stores, newsstands, book racks in supermarket and drug stores, specialty stores, and many others. In recent years, large chain bookstores, usually located in shopping malls, have become more prevalent. Waldenbooks has about 1000 stores; B. Dalton, about 780. College bookstores are the principal means of selling books in higher education. Of course, these bookstores also sell many noneducational books as well. The third channel, libraries, includes public, university, and special research libraries.

Many retail booksellers, such as B. Dalton, have stores located in shopping malls. (Courtesy of B. Dalton)

There are approximately 30,000 of these nationwide. Schools and institutions comprise local school systems, book depositories, classrooms, resource centers, and related facilities. The last channel, direct to consumer, includes publishers who directly market to the consumer by mail, telephone, or face to face.

Table 7.2 shows the estimated consumer expenditure in each of these segments in 1987. Not surprisingly, the general retail channel accounts for the largest share of the consumer dollar, followed by college bookstores. These two outlets have also shown the most growth since 1972.

Ownership

The two major trends that have characterized ownership in the book industry in the last five years are (1) acquisitions of American publishing firms by foreign companies and (2) consolidation. Thanks to a weak dollar, foreign investment in the U.S. book business has never been higher. Fifty-five percent of book publishers that changed hands from 1984 to 1988 went to foreign buyers. In one of the biggest deals, the Bertelsmann Publishing Group of West Germany acquired Doubleday, its subsidiary Dell, the Literary Guild, a textbook company, and several printing plants for more than $475 million. In addition, Rupert Murdoch's British-based News Corporation bought Harper & Row for $300 million, Penguin, another British firm, bought New American Library and E. P. Dutton, and yet another British firm, Maxwell Communications, acquired Macmillan, Inc.

Consolidation was evident in several transactions. Time Inc. bought Scott, Foresman, and Harcourt Brace Jovanovich acquired Holt, Rinehart and Winston and W. B. Saunders. Random House bought Crown Books and sold its textbook division to McGraw-Hill. On the retail level, the biggest deal was the merger of B. Dalton with Barnes & Noble. As a result, the book publishing industry is now dominated by conglomerates. To illustrate, here are the five companies that generally dominated the industry in sales during the late 1980s with some of their corporate holdings:

1. *Simon & Schuster*: owned by Paramount Communications, Inc., a large conglomerate itself, the publishing division includes seven companies in the college text area, seven in the elhi market, three trade press publishers, a paperback publishing company, *Webster's New World Dictionary*, computer software, and a mass market distribution service. Revenues in 1987 exceeded $1 billion.

2. *Bertelsmann*: a multinational corporation whose U.S. holdings include Doubleday, Bantam, and Dell book publishers, RCA and Arista Records, several

TABLE 7.2 Percentage of 1987 Consumer Expenditures on Books in Various Outlets

OUTLETS	PERCENTAGE OF SALES
General retailers	45
College stores	18
Libraries	9
Schools	12
Direct to consumer	14
Miscellaneous	2

A college bookstore displaying stacks of textbooks arranged by discipline. Textbooks, used in almost every classroom in America, generate the largest revenues of any segment of the U.S. book publishing industry. (Ellis Herwig/The Picture Cube)

book clubs, three printing plants, and several magazines, including *Young Miss*. Revenues of its American operations for 1988 will exceed $1 billion.

3. *Time Inc.*: this large communications company owns or holds an interest in sixteen magazines, publishes Time-Life Books, owns two additional publishing companies, the Book of the Month Club, HBO pay cable channel, HBO Movies, and 80 percent of ATC, a multisystem cable operator. In 1989, Time Inc. merged with Warner Communications, creating the world's largest media company.

4. *Reader's Digest Association*: this company is best known for magazine publishing, but it is also active in book publishing and mail order book selling (condensed books). It also has holdings in television and computerized data bases, and it even markets insurance to its magazine subscribers.

5. *McGraw-Hill*: the McGraw-Hill Publishing Company makes most of its money from college and elhi textbooks. It also publishes numerous business magazines and newsletters as well as owning several TV stations. The company also specializes in electronic information systems.

PRODUCING THE BOOK

Departments and Staff

Figure 7.2 depicts the organizational arrangement at a typical publishing house. The titles may vary at other companies, but the functions will be basically the same.

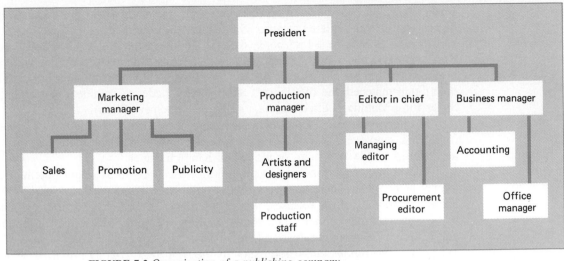

FIGURE 7.2 *Organization of a publishing company.*

There are four major departments in the publishing company: (1) editorial, (2) production, (3) marketing, and, (4) general administration or business.

The editorial department is in charge of dealing with authors. Essentially, it has a twofold task: the selection of manuscripts to be published and their preparation for publication. It is in the performance of the first task that editors and authors initially meet. Some editors specialize in procurement and visit potential authors to solicit their work. Other editors read manuscripts, write reports on them, and recommend acceptance, rejection, or revision. Once an accepted manuscript is completed, copy editors sift through it, checking grammar, punctuation, language, internal consistency, and accuracy.

As the name implies, the production department oversees the planning and design of the physical book. Type style, composition, paper, printing, and binding are the responsibilities of this division. Since many books might be entering production at any given time, the production manager and staff must keep track of many tasks, not the least of which is keeping the book on schedule.

The marketing department supervises several activities, including sales, promotion, and publicity. The actual type of sales activity depends upon the kind of book being marketed. Publishers of elhi textbooks sell mainly to school systems; college text publishers to individuals or committees of professors. Mass market paperbacks must be sold to retailers, who in turn must sell them to the general public. Promoting the book begins long before the book is finished and can take several forms. Advertising in trade magazines, listings in publishing catalogs, and posters are common promotional methods. For trade books, ads in literary magazines and reviews of the book in respected publications can be influential. In the mass market field, some publishers have relied on magazine and television ads. *Gone to Soldiers*, for example, was published with nine different covers and promoted by a quarter-million-dollar radio–TV ad campaign. Some publishers now use holograms (see Chapter 23) on their covers. The title of the book can also be important. *The Squash Book* sold a meager 1500 copies. It was renamed *The Zucchini Cookbook* and sold 300,000.

Joint promotions between publishers and other manufacturers have become an important marketing tool. For example, when Ken Follett's *Lie Down with Lions* was released in paperback, the book was packaged with a Bic pen. The in-store display said ''Ken Follett's favorite Bic pen can now be yours . . . Free.'' All you had to do was buy the $4.95 book. To take another example, Clairol and Bantam Books worked out a deal whereby Clairol's Pazazz Sheer Color Wash would be promoted within the pages of a romance novel trilogy. Each of the heroines had hair colors that matched one of Clairol's Sheer Color shades (Adelaide's hair color was Sheer Fire; Matilda's, Sheer Cinnamon; Sydney's, Sheer Plum).

Promotion is also effective at the retail level. At a Waldenbooks store in California, employees promoted the opening of a new horror book section by dressing up as Dracula, the Wolfman, or a Stephen King character.

The publicity section spreads the news of the book to as many potential customers as possible. There are many tools available to this department: early review copies of the book, press releases, news conferences, publisher's parties, and author appearances on radio and TV talk shows. Getting the book reviewed by a reputable publication is also a tremendous help. This is a challenging task, however. For example, a prestigious publication such as the *New York Times Book Review* might receive anywhere from 12,000 to 15,000 books a year out of which only 10–15 percent might be reviewed.

The business manager at a publishing company is responsible for several functions. One of the most important is accounting. This department oversees processing orders, controls credit, and provides balance sheets on the firm's overall operation. Further, it prepares budgets and makes long-range financial forecasts. The business department's responsibilities include dealing with internal personnel policies and supervising the general day-to-day operational needs of the company.

Publishing the Book

Editors get their books from three main sources: those submitted by agents, unsolicited books sent in by authors, and book ideas generated by the editor. Most trade manuscripts are submitted through literary agents. Editors prefer to receive them this way since agents are known quantities and will not generally submit manuscripts that they know are unacceptable to the editor. Unsolicited manuscripts are given an unflattering name in the business: ''slush.'' As they come in, these manuscripts are put in the slush pile and eventually read, if the author is lucky, by an editorial assistant. Most of the time they are rejected with a form letter, but every once in a while an author gets lucky. *The Office Humor Book*, for example, went from the slush pile into five printings. Editors also generate ideas for books. If an editor has a good idea for a book, he or she will generally talk to one or more agents, who will suggest likely candidates for the assignment. This is another good reason why writers should have agents. In any case, the author typically submits a proposal consisting of a cover letter, a brief description of the planned book, a list of reasons why it should be published, an analysis of the potential market, an outline or a table of contents, and perhaps one or two sample chapters. The proposal usually goes to an acquisitions or procurement editor and is evaluated. If the publishing decision is favorable, then a contract is signed and the author begins work in earnest.

Editorial work starts as soon as the author submits chapters to the publisher. Editors look at the overall thrust of the book to make sure it makes sense and achieves its original intent. Moreover, the mechanics of the book are checked to make sure that the general level of writing is acceptable, that all footnotes are in order, that all necessary permissions to reproduce material from other sources have been obtained, and that all artwork is present. Eventually both author and editors will produce a manuscript that is mutually satisfactory.

Doing It Yourself: The Vanity Press and Self-Publishing

If an author has a manuscript that has been turned down by the traditional publishing companies and if the author still has faith that the manuscript has potential and if the author has some funds to invest, he or she might turn to a vanity press (also called a subsidy publisher) to get the manuscript into print. There are about a dozen firms that actively advertise for and solicit authors. For a fee, they will turn a manuscript into a finished book.

Here's how it usually works. After examining a manuscript, a vanity publisher will notify the author if it's been accepted for publication (almost everything is accepted, unless the manuscript is likely to cause a lawsuit). The publisher agrees to print a certain number of books for the author and send out review copies. Most subsidy publishers also supply distributors with press releases and yearly catalogs of their new books. The publisher also agrees to pay a generous royalty to the would-be author. This sounds good so far, but there are strings attached.

In the first place, in return for these considerations, the author agrees to pay the publisher a certain sum of money (anywhere from $5,000 to $20,000, depending on the length of the manuscript and the number of copies to be printed). This allows the publisher to make a profit even if not a single book is sold. Second, the author is given only the minimum of editorial guidance. Usually just spelling errors and gross grammatical mistakes are corrected. Third, the publisher has no sales staff. If the author wants the new book to sell, he or she must become the salesperson. Last, the vanity press doesn't enjoy a positive reputation among distributors and retailers. Many won't carry subsidy-published books. Nonetheless, some authors do succeed with a vanity press. Statistics suggest that about one in ten authors manage to make back their investment and maybe even turn a small profit.

If the vanity press isn't appealing, an aspiring author might take the plunge and venture into self-publishing. In this arrangement, the author performs all the publishing functions or hires professionals to do them. For example, an author could pay an editorial consultant to edit the manuscript, pay someone to prepare camera-ready copy, and negotiate with a local printer and binder to produce a limited number of copies of the finished book. When all of this is done, the author must also sell the book to the appropriate distributor or retail outlet. It's a long, hard, and expensive path to follow but some authors have succeeded. The paperbacks *Winning Through Intimidation* and *The Great Depression of 1990*, for example, started their lives as self-published books and eventually made the best-seller list.

While all of this editing is going on, other decisions are being made about scheduling, designing the interior "look" of the book, and the cover design. When everything is in order, the production phase—consisting of typesetting, printing, and binding—begins. Most books are typeset using one of three basic methods: hot type, photocomposition, or electronically. Hot type is the traditional **Linotype** method of typesetting. Recently, almost all books are created using other methods. **Photocomposition** involves taking pictures of pages of print. The film is developed and used to make the forms for offset printing (see Chapter 5). The most recent form of typesetting involves computers and is generally known as electronic publishing. In this system, the author uses a computer with a word processing program and writes the book on floppy discs instead of paper. Using a modem, a device which permits computers to exchange information over phone lines, the manuscript is transmitted electronically to the publisher, where it is edited on another computer. When the editorial process is completed, the publisher can then typeset the manuscript and make up the pages using other computerized equipment. For example, one system contains a graphics scanner (a device that converts photos and line art to digital information), a preview screen that displays page layout, and a laser typesetter. If for some reason the author prefers to produce the traditional paper manuscript instead of an electronic one, optical character readers exist that "read" typed pages electronically and input the material into the publisher's computer.

Once the text has been typeset, the printing process begins. Most books are produced using the photo-offset method since it is usually faster and less expensive. The images to be printed are lightly etched in the surface of a metal plate and ink adheres to these areas. These images are then transferred (or offset) onto another drum covered with a rubber blanket. This rubber-covered drum rolls against and prints onto the paper. Photo-offset presses come in two varieties: sheet fed or continuous (called a web press).

After the sheets of the book are printed, they are fed through a series of machines that fold them into the proper order and trim them to the correct size. The actual binding of the book can be done in a number of ways. The traditional method uses a special sewing machine to thread all of the pages together. This method is still used in some large reference or art books that are expected to receive heavy use. A more common process is "perfect" binding. In this technique, the pages are held tightly in place while a special knife shaves away part of their back edges. Next, a special glue is applied and the cover is wrapped around them and everything is joined together. (You can check the book that you're now reading for an example of perfect binding.) The finished books are then sent to the warehouse to await distribution.

ECONOMICS

The overall book industry enjoys economic health. More than $14 billion worth of books were sold in 1988, up 9 percent from 1987, making it the best year in the book business since 1983. Trade books, paperbacks, and college texts all made strong gains over 1986. The U.S. Commerce Department forecast an even better year for books in 1989. Why are books doing so well? First, the population is getting older; the fastest growing age group is thirty-five to forty-nine years old—the age when people buy the most books. Second, the economic climate has been generally good and people have more disposable income to spend on books. Finally, federal and local governments continue to make education a funding priority. Per-pupil expenditures at the elementary and high school levels have increased and are expected to grow in the future, enhancing the market for texts, workbooks, and standardized tests.

At the consumer level, it's obvious that books have gotten more expensive. The average price of a hardcover book in 1988 was $29.99 and the average price of a paperback was up to $4.58. In fact, many paperbacks were selling for $4.95 and some publishers were talking about breaking the $5 mark in the near future.

A publisher has two main sources of income: (1) the money that comes from book sales and (2) money from other sources such as subsidiary rights (money from book clubs, foreign rights, paperback rights, and reprint permissions). Of these two, the income from book sales is the most important. It should be noted, however, that the publisher does not get all the money from the sale of a book. The list price is discounted for wholesalers and booksellers. These discounts might amount to 40 percent for many books.

The costs a publisher incurs are many. First, there is the cost of manufacturing the book itself. This includes the cost of printing, typesetting, and royalties paid to the author. These costs are variable and are tied to the number of books printed. For example, paper costs would be more substantial on a book with a press run of 20,000 than on one with a run of 2,000. There are also operating expenses, including editorial, production, marketing, and general administration expenses. Table 7.3 shows a hypothetical operating statement for an adult trade hardcover book published by a typical publishing company. It is assumed that the book has a list price of $20 (all numbers are rounded off for convenience) and 10,000 copies were printed. After a year, 2000 copies were unsold and were returned to the publisher for a credit. This means that 8000 copies were sold. Allowing a 40 percent discount from the list price leaves the publisher with revenues of about $12 per book. Multiplying 8000 times $12 gives us the gross sales amount: $96,000. From this is subtracted the costs of returns and allowances, leaving a balance of $77,000 in net sales revenue. Manufacturing costs and author royalties amounted to $45,400. This sum is subtracted from the net sales to find the gross margin on sales (the amount that net sales exceeded the cost of sales), in this case, $31,600. Table 7.3 also assumes that the publisher sold some subsidiary rights (to a book club or a paperback publisher) and received $6900 in return. So far, the total income from the book is $38,500. From this, however, we must deduct operating expenses of $34,600, leaving the book with a net profit of $3,900 for the year, about 5 percent of its net sales.

These figures, of course, would vary for other publishers. Profit margins among the various divisions of the publishing industry typically varied from 2 to 15 percent between 1985 and 1988. Advances and acquisition rights are a couple of the big expenses in publishing. For example, romance novelist Barbara Taylor Bradford received $9 million for three planned novels; author Joseph Heller received $4 million

---

TABLE 7.3 Profit/Loss Statement of Trade Hardcover with $20 List Price

Press run	10,000 copies		
Returned	2,000 copies		
Gross sales	8,000 copies @ $12	=	$96,000
Returns and allowances		=	19,000
Net sales		=	77,000
Cost of sales			
Manufacturing		=	27,700
Royalties		=	17,700
Total cost of sales		=	45,400
Margin of net sales over cost of sales		=	31,600
Other income		=	6,900
Operating expense			
Editorial		=	4,500
Production		=	1,600
Marketing and fulfillment		=	18,500
Administration		=	10,000
Total operating expense		=	34,600
Net income		=	3,900

Cliff and His Notes

OK, it's late. There's a big English exam tomorrow and you just haven't had the time to reread and study *Macbeth*. Not to worry. *Cliffs Notes* to the rescue. For a mere three dollars or so, you can buy one of those eye-catching yellow and black student guides that give you a quick plot summary and character analyses that might be enough to get you through the exam. Should you buy one, you won't be the first. *Cliffs Notes* have been around for thirty years and have sold more than 85 million copies.

There really is a Cliff behind *Cliffs Notes*. He's Clifton Hillegass, a septuagenarian who borrowed $4000 in 1958 and started the business in his basement, first summarizing the sixteen major plays of Shakespeare. By 1965, he was selling more than 2 million units a year. Business has been booming since.

Not every educator is pleased with Cliff's success. Many teachers think Cliff's abridgements are a crutch and actually discourage students from reading the original. Cliff disagrees. He thinks his notes keep a lot of students interested in literature by making it understandable.

There's one thing everybody agrees on. *Cliffs Notes* have been a financial success. Cliff was recently offered $50 million for his business. To put it briefly, he turned it down.

for two upcoming books, one a sequel to his best-selling *Catch-22*. The paperback rights to Scott Turow's 1987 hit, *Presumed Innocent*, brought $3 million.

RECENT DEVELOPMENTS

Probably the most notable development in retailing has been the diversification of products available at the bookstore. Most bookstores now stock magazines, calendars, maps, and games alongside their books. But perhaps the most notable additions to the inventories of many book stores is a selection of cassettes and videotapes. One recent survey found that 80 percent of stores were selling videotapes and 90 percent were carrying audiotapes. Publishing houses are also sensing that books on cassette might be a profit center and Warner Audio and Random House, among others, are expanding their efforts in this area. Self-help and self-improvement cassettes are the ones that seem to be selling best, but fiction is quickly gaining, thus creating a new job in publishing houses—the abridger. This is the person who takes a 400- to 500-page novel and condenses it to a 25,000- to 30,000-word script designed to be read aloud in 180 minutes.

In the marketing area, the last few years have seen a boom in the sale of quality paperbacks. Quality paperbacks are different from the regular mass market paperback in several ways. They tend to be slightly larger; their cover designs are flashier, sometimes resembling record album covers; and their prices are higher, $6.95 to $7.95 a copy compared to the typical $4.95 paperback. For the most part, these paperbacks contain high-class fiction. The first book of this type to make it big, for example, was Jay McInerney's *Bright Lights, Big City*, for Vintage Press, which eventually sold more than 300,000 copies. Most publishers of quality paperbacks, however, specialize in books that were critical successes in hardcover but lacked the commercial appeal to do well as mass market paperbacks. Publishing one as a quality

Dr. Seuss signs a book. Personal appearances by authors at bookstores are a popular promotional device. (Vincent Maggiora/San Francisco Chronicle)

paperback might sell an additional 40,000–50,000 copies of a highly regarded book.

Finally, books were always thought of as the permanent medium, a place where an author's words might live forever. Unfortunately, that's not the case. Book deterioration has become a significant problem at libraries across the country. For example, the Library of Congress has more than *twelve acres* of books that have decomposed to the point of being unreadable. Ironically, books printed before 1860 are not a problem. They were printed on rag paper with a low acid content and are holding up well. After 1860, however, books were printed on wood pulp paper which has a high acid content, and these books are falling apart. Putting books on microfilm or microfiche is not the answer. Librarians are now discovering that whole reels of microfilm are decomposing and the film emulsion separating from the base. What can be done? Using low-acid paper is one solution, but at present only 25 percent of all books are printed on this type of paper. Deacidifying existing wood pulp books is possible, but it's expensive and the books must be kept in a climate-

---

Making it Difficult to Tell a Book By Its Cover

If you want privacy while you read, here's a product you should know about: Book Gloves. Manufactured in five different colors, book gloves fit over the cover of your hardback or paperback book so that only you know what you are reading. Now you can take that lurid paperback on the plane or train and not feel self-conscious—you can even read your text-book without fear of ridicule. Book Gloves' slogan: "No more naked books."

---

controlled environment forever. The ultimate solution may be transferring the books to digital form and storing them on optical discs (much like compact discs, or CDs). One disc can hold about 15,000 pages of print. In any event, the book deterioration problem is now recognized as a serious one.

CAREERS IN BOOK PUBLISHING

Book publishing is a small industry; there are only 70,000–75,000 jobs nationwide in the entire business. Consequently, there is a lot of competition for many of the jobs, particularly those on the editorial side. Moreover, since most of the large publishing houses are located on the East Coast, it may be necessary for many hopefuls to relocate.

There are two general areas to pursue in book publishing: editorial and business. For someone interested in editorial work, the best training consists of courses in English and composition with a strong emphasis in writing skills. Entry-level positions are competitive, and most newcomers typically join a publishing company as editorial assistants. There are numerous clerical tasks to be performed in publishing: answering authors' letters, reading manuscripts, writing reports about manuscripts, checking facts, proofreading, writing catalog copy, and so on. Editorial assistants do these and countless other tasks.

The next logical step up the career ladder is to become an assistant or associate editor. These individuals work with senior editors in several different areas: manuscript acquisition, copy editing, design and production, artwork, and so on. Eventually, this path leads to a position as an editor. After getting the necessary experience, editors are promoted to senior editors, managing editors, or executive editors, positions which carry a good deal of administrative responsibility.

On the business side there are several career paths open. Many people start as a sales representative and sell their company's books to the appropriate customers. Sales and marketing experience is so vital to the well-being of the industry that the path to top management usually begins in the sales department. At many companies, presidents and vice presidents are almost always former salespeople with extensive experience in marketing. Sales is a challenging profession and top salespeople are usually well rewarded.

Another potential career route that is generally not crowded with new applications is the subsidiary rights department. This job deals with selling the company's books to foreign publishers, translators, book clubs, and paperback publishers. The subsidiary rights department is an excellent place to learn about finances, contracts, and the commercial side of publishing. It can be a path to top management.

Finally, there are usually opportunities for newcomers in the advertising, promotion, and publicity areas of publishing. Copy for print and broadcast ads must be

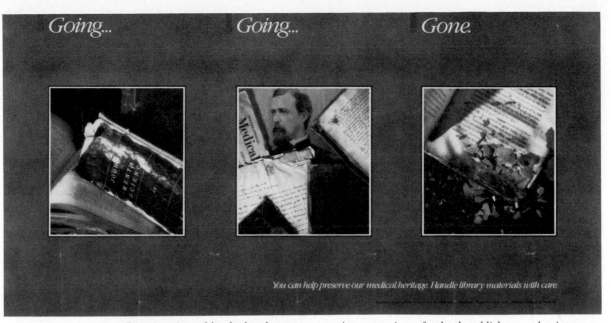

Deterioration of books has become a very important issue for book publishers and printers, as this poster graphically illustrates. (Preservation Section-National Library of Medicine, National Institutes of Health)

written, author tours must be planned, promotional material must be distributed, press releases written, and special events planned. All of these duties would be the responsibility of people working in this area. The usual career path is to find an entry-level position as an ''assistant to'' someone and gradually work your way up to the advertising, promotion, or publicity director for the company.

Before closing, it should be mentioned that it is not always necessary to work for a publishing company to find employment in this area. Many people work as freelance editors, designers, proofreaders, indexers, artists, and photographers. These typically are people who have had some experience and have branched out on their own.

SUGGESTIONS FOR FURTHER READING

The following books contain more information about concepts and topics discussed in this chapter.

BALKING, RICHARD, *A Writer's Guide to Book Publishing*, New York: Hawthorn Books, 1977.

The Book Publishing Annual, 1986, New York: R. R. Bowker, 1985.

The Business of Publishing, New York: R. R. Bowker, 1976.

DAVIS, KENNETH, *Two-Bit Culture*, Boston: Houghton Mifflin, 1985.

DESSAUER, JOHN, *Book Publishing: What It Is, What It Does*, New York: R. R. Bowker, 1981.

————, *Book Industry Trends*, 1987, New York: Book Industry Study Group, 1987.

GEISER, ELIZABETH, ed., *The Business of Book Publishing*, London: Westview Press, 1985.

Also see *Publishers Weekly*, the leading trade magazine of the industry.

Part Three

The Electronic Media

Chapter 8

History of Radio and Recording

How would you like to go home after class one day and listen to the latest album by INXS or U2 on your quadraphonic zonophone? Or maybe you'd rather drop a quarter through the slot in the top of your radio and hear an hour's worth of music brought to you under the watchful eye of the United States Navy? Sound strange? These are just some of the things that might have happened if the recording and radio industries had evolved a bit differently.

A basic knowledge of mass communication is incomplete without examining how media develop and change. Accordingly, this chapter will present a brief history of the sound media industries—recording and radio—and a summary of important content trends. Most discussions of media history generally treat radio and television together and examine sound recording separately (if at all). The current operations of the radio and sound-recording industries are so closely connected, however, that they should be considered together. Further, both media went through similar stages in development: big-business wheelings and dealings, legal fights over patents, technical problems, and formidable competition. Besides, when they started, no one had a clear idea of what good they were.

EARLY YEARS OF THE SOUND-RECORDING AND RADIO INDUSTRIES

In the last half of the nineteenth century, inventors on both sides of the Atlantic were interested in sound; some tried to capture it, while others tried to make it more elusive by sending it across space without wires. In America, Thomas Edison recorded "Mary Had a Little Lamb," using a hand-cranked device with a cylinder wrapped in tinfoil that preserved the sound. This invention perplexed Edison. He wasn't sure what commercial value his 1877 prototype of the **phonograph** possessed. For many years this "talking machine" was exhibited at lecture halls, vaudeville houses, and exhibition tents as a curiosity. Finally, Edison decided his new invention might best be suited to the business world where it would aid dictation. At that time, the idea of the phonograph as home entertainment was too wild to imagine.

Edison's phonograph faced new competition when Chinchester Bell and Charles Tainter patented a device called the **graphophone,** a machine in which Edison's tinfoil was replaced by a wax cylinder. In 1887, more competition emerged when yet another American, Emile Berliner, patented a system that used a disc instead of a cylinder. He called his new invention a **gramophone.**

Meanwhile, across the ocean, others were caught up in more ethereal pursuits. A Scottish mathematician and physicist, James Clerk Maxwell, published a paper in

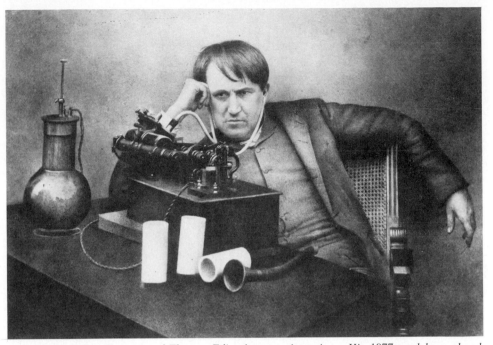

The phonograph is just one of Thomas Edison's many inventions. His 1877 model was hand-cranked, and the sound waves were preserved as scratches in tinfoil. (The Bettmann Archive)

1873 that suggested that an electromagnetic signal could be sent through space without using wires. In 1887, a German physicist, Heinrich Hertz, verified the correctness of Maxwell's theories in a series of experiments in which Hertz actually sent and detected radio waves. Since Hertz was a theoretical physicist, the practical applications of radio held little interest for him. In fact, he would later argue that radio waves could not be used for communication. Nonetheless, as a tribute to his accomplishment, the basic unit of frequency, the **hertz** (abbreviated **Hz**), is named for him. An Italian, Guglielmo Marconi, refined and improved on Hertz's efforts. In 1896, he could send a wireless signal over a two-mile distance (''wireless'' was radio's early name). A businessman as well as inventor, Marconi saw that wireless had promising commercial aspects in maritime communication (ship-to-shore and ship-to-ship messages). At age twenty-three he went to England and established the Marconi Wireless Telegraph and Signal Company, later shortened to British Marconi. By World War I, this company and its U.S. subsidiary, American Marconi, had become a powerful force in maritime and transatlantic communication.

Marconi was sending Morse code—dots and dashes—a system that required special training in order to understand the message. Two Americans, Reginald Fessenden and Lee De Forest, provided the breakthroughs that opened up radio for the general public. Fessenden, building on the work of Nikola Tesla and using a high-speed generator he developed with the help of General Electric, made what might be considered the world's first broadcast in 1906, on Christmas Eve. His audience consisted primarily of ships with wireless receiving sets in New York Harbor. Allegedly, when the shipboard operators heard Fessenden's broadcast of phonograph music, violin solos, and Bible readings, they were so awestruck that many thought they were hearing the voices of angels. Lee De Forest invented the vacuum tube, which made it much easier to receive voice and music transmissions.

A lover of classical music, De Forest broadcast a classical phonograph concert from the Eiffel Tower in 1908. Two years later, he would broadcast the voice of Caruso at the New York Metropolitan Opera.

One reason that radio did not progress faster during the first fifteen years of the new decade had to do with the problem of conflicting patents. These early disputes were long and expensive and contributed to the commercial failures of both De Forest and Fessenden. When World War I broke out, the U.S. Navy saw the military advantages of radio and arranged a moratorium on patent suits. In effect, the Navy was able to pull together all available technical skills and knowledge. This led to significant improvements in radio by the end of the war. It also meant that the Navy would be a powerful force in determining radio's future.

By 1890, three machines that recorded and played back sound were on the market: the phonograph, the graphophone, and the gramophone. At about this time, big business entered the picture as Jesse Lippincott, who had made a fortune in the glass-tumbler business, moved from glass to wax and purchased the business rights to both the phonograph and graphophone, thus ending a bitter patent fight between the respective inventors. Lippincott had dreams of controlling the office-dictating market, but stenographers rebelled against the new device and the talking-machine business fell upon hard times. Strangely enough, relief appeared quickly and financial solvency returned—a nickel at a time.

One of Lippincott's local managers hit upon the idea of putting coin-operated phonographs in the many penny arcades and amusement centers that were springing up all over America. For a nickel you could listen through a pair of stethoscopelike

A "symphony" orchestra makes a recording before the days of electrical recording. Note how the musicians are crowded close to the large horn and the strange-looking horn gadgets that were used to amplify the tones of certain instruments for recording. (Clark Collection of Radioana-Smithsonian Institution Archive Center)

earphones to a cylinder whose two-minute recording had a technical quality that could only be described as awful. Still, these **nickelodeons** were immensely popular, and the demand for "entertainment" cylinders grew. Companies quickly scrambled for a share in the new recording production business.

The two decades spanning the turn of the century were a time of intense business rivalry in the recording industry as competitors tried desperately to drive each other under. While the two major companies, the Columbia Phonograph Company and Edison's North American Phonograph Company, fought one another, Berliner's United States Gramophone Company perfected the process of recording on flat discs. These discs had several advantages over the older cylinder in that they had better sound qualities, could not be illegally copied as easily as the cylinder, and were easier to store. Ultimately, Columbia recognized the superiority of the disc and attempted to break into the market by selling the zonophone, its own version of the disc player. As for Berliner, along with machinist Eldridge Johnson, he formed the Victor Talking Machine Company, which had as its trademark the picture of a dog peering into the bell of a gramophone ("His Master's Voice"). Thanks to aggressive marketing, this new company was highly successful and in 1906 introduced the Victrola, the first disc player designed to look like a piece of furniture. By 1912, the supremacy of the disc over the cylinder was established. Even Edison's company, champion of the cylinder for forty years, joined the trend and began marketing discs.

On the eve of World War I, record players were commonplace throughout America. A dance craze in 1913 sent profits soaring, a trend that was to continue throughout the war. Twenty-seven million records were manufactured in 1914; 107 million were produced in 1919 following the end of the war. The record industry had entered a boom period.

It didn't last.

Recording Pioneer Emile Berliner

The hundredth anniversary of phonograph recording on a flat disc was reached in 1988. This technology was created by Emile Berliner, an immigrant from Germany, who had supported himself working as a stock clerk in a clothing store while investigating on his own the intriguing world of sound amplification and recording. Berliner quickly noted that the cylinders used by Edison had too many disadvantages to be practical. He perfected a way to encode the sound on a flat disc that could be easily duplicated by using a master mold, much like pressing waffles in a waffle iron.

His invention was slow to catch on in the United States, thanks to competition from Edison, but it was a success in Europe. Eventually, Berliner introduced to the American market the phonautograph, which he renamed the gramophone. This eventually replaced the cylinder.

In one area, Berliner clearly saw the future. He predicted that prominent singers and performers would collect royalties from the sale of his discs. He was wrong on another count, however. He thought that musicians and artists who were unable to appear at a concert would simply send a record to be played on-stage instead.

Berliner also developed the prototype of the modern microphone and both his inventions, the disc and the microphone, came together when electronic recording was perfected during the 1920s. Even the modern CD owes him a debt. Like his original invention, the CD stores information in a spiral on a flat rotating surface.

In the beginning, no one in the record industry regarded radio as a serious threat. Record company executives were sure that the static-filled, raucous noise emanating from a radio would never compete with the quality of their recordings. They were wrong.

THE EVOLUTION OF RADIO AS A MASS MEDIUM

It began modestly enough. A quarter-pound of No. 24 double cotton-covered wire wrapped around an empty Quaker Oats carton, a piece of tinfoil, a lump of galena, a thin piece of wire called a cat's whisker, a pair of headphones and you were in business. You had built a radio. In the years following World War I, all across the country, in attics, garages, on front porches, people were hunched over primitive crystal sets, engaged in the new national craze—listening to radio.

For many people radio seemed to be no more than a toy, a passing fad for hobbyists and those who tinkered with electronics. Early radio broadcasting was crude, amateurish, and thoroughly unpredictable. Occasionally, no one would show up at the local station to perform, and the station would not go on the air. Early microphones overheated, so performers had to be careful not to burn their lips. You could hear far better music on the Victrola. The telephone was a far better way of communicating. Many thought that radio would never amount to much. However, several remarkable events were to change their minds.

Big Business Steps In

While radio development before World War I had been characterized by individual inventions, during the postwar years it would be characterized by corporate maneu-

A young boy listens to an early version of the radio. (National Archives)

vers. Shortly after the war, the Marconi Company started negotiations to acquire rights to Fessenden's generator in an attempt to establish a monopoly in U.S.–European radio communication. The United States, with the lessons of the war still fresh, did not want to give a foreign-owned company access to that much power. Moreover, there were many in the United States who did not want the Navy to maintain the amount of control over radio's development that it had amassed during the war. After much negotiation and bargaining, the Marconi Company agreed to sell its American interests to General Electric. In turn, GE set up a new company, the Radio Corporation of America (RCA), to receive the Marconi assets. Stock in RCA would be held by American Telegraph and Telephone (AT&T), Westinghouse, and GE. All of this happened in 1919, before any of these companies had a clear idea as to what radio's future role would be, and none of them seriously considered broadcasting to the general public as a viable moneymaking activity. Nonetheless, by 1920 it was obvious that radio's future lay in the hands of American private enterprise.

Radio Reaches a Mass Audience

The second element necessary for radio's emergence as a mass medium started in Frank Conrad's garage. Up to this point, radio was looked upon as a competitor to the telephone and telegraph industries. The fact that it was public, that everybody could receive it with the proper equipment, was looked upon as a drawback. No one could quite understand why anybody would want to send messages to a large group of anonymous individuals. Enter Frank Conrad, Horne's Department Store in Pittsburgh, and Westinghouse. Conrad was a Westinghouse engineer who tinkered with radio as a hobby. He had built a radio transmitter in his garage and spent his weekends playing records, reporting sports scores, and even showcasing the musical abilities of his sons in front of the microphone. Other amateurs began to send Conrad postcards requesting certain musical selections. In a short time, he had developed a small but dedicated audience. Horne's Department Store saw an opportunity: The store took out a newspaper ad that highlighted Conrad's broadcasting activities and offered their customers a $10 ready-built wireless set that could be used to listen to the Conrad broadcasts. Westinghouse saw an even bigger opportunity. The company proposed to build a station that would broadcast programs on a more or less regular

Broadcasting's Young Pioneers

One of the striking facts about broadcasting is that it was invented and developed by young people. Marconi was only twenty-three when he developed his wireless transmitter. William Paley became president of CBS at the age of twenty-seven. David Sarnoff was twenty-eight when he became chief operating officer of RCA. Heinrich Hertz was thirty when he did his most significant work with radio waves. The alternator was invented by Ernst Alexanderson at age thirty-one. Reginald Fessenden made his first radiophone broadcasts when he was thirty-four. Lee De Forest was the same age when he invented his audion. Frank Conrad was the grand old man of the group; he was forty-two when he started his experimental radio station. Of course, the youngest inventor of them all was Philo Farnsworth, who, at the tender age of sixteen, diagramed an invention called "television."

basis and would, the company hoped, encourage a large audience to listen. Westinghouse would manufacture the radio sets and, in turn, would receive "free" advertising because of its identification with the station. The idea worked. KDKA went on the air November 20, 1920. (It is still on the air as of this day, making it the oldest station.)

After a slow start, sales of radio sets reached the half-million mark in 1924. The next year roughly 2 million were sold. Other companies recognized a good thing when they saw it. RCA started broadcasting in 1921; General Electric in 1922. Westinghouse opened additional stations in Massachusetts, New Jersey, and Illinois. AT&T opened a station in 1922. Radio was on its way. By discovering that an audience existed for broadcast programs *intended* for the general public, radio had found the role it was to play for the foreseeable future.

The Development of Improved Receivers

The third major factor in radio's evolution as a mass medium was due, in part, to Gimbel's Department Store. If you were walking down New York's 33rd Street in May of 1925, you couldn't help but notice. There, in Gimbel's window, was the latest model vacuum tube radio set, which gave far better reception than any of the old crystal sets. For only $15 down, $99 in all (a rather significant amount in 1925), you could buy the new Freed-Eisemann Neutrodyne five-tube receiver with one Prest-O-Lite battery, two 45-volt B batteries, a phone plug, an antenna, and your choice of loudspeakers. Gimbel's entire fifth floor was given over to the sale, and 240 clerks were waiting to serve you. (They sold 5300 receivers the first day.)

Early radio receivers (a) were bulky, cumbersome affairs requiring constant tuning and a knowledge of electronics. However, by the mid-1920s, radios that ran on household current were being sold as popular and fashionable pieces of furniture (b). (Both, Brown Brothers)

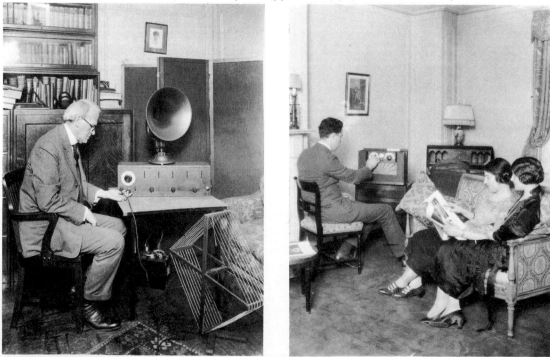

(a)   *(b)*

Before radio could become a true mass medium, an affordable, easy-to-use, relatively efficient receiving set had to be mass marketed. Westinghouse, Atwater Kent, and Crosley led the way in manufacturing, and Gimbel's and other large department stores helped retail the sets. But radio was still not ready for the living room. By and large, 1925 receivers were cumbersome affairs. You needed an assortment of bulky batteries (which had an irritating tendency to leak acid all over the floor), and ugly wires led from the set to the condensers and ground (usually a water pipe). Tuning the early sets required a steady hand, patience, and a knowledge of electronics. You couldn't tune the set and sit back and listen since the two batteries needed constant tuning as they supplied current to the receiver's tubes.

Many of the inconveniences associated with the early receivers had been resolved by 1926. Radios that ran on ordinary house current were being marketed in more and more retail stores. Although the new radios were initially expensive (one set sold for $250), they were quickly bought up. Between 1925 and 1930, 17 million radio sets were sold at an average cost of about $80 per set. Furthermore, this later version was no longer just a curious collection of electronic parts but was designed as a fashionable piece of furniture. Made of mahogany and equipped with built-in speakers, large cathedral-style sets took their place next to the sofa and coffee table. Some of the deluxe models had push-button tuning and a built-in phonograph and even picked up police calls. Families could now gather around the radio set, and listening changed from a solitary to a group activity. The refinement of the radio receiver during the 1920s eased radio's access to the mass audience.

Radio Goes Commercial

One of the curious things about early radio broadcasting was that very little of it was done by broadcasters. The early stations were owned by a polyglot of organizations. WLS in Chicago was owned by Sears, Roebuck (*World's Largest Store*); WGN by the Chicago Tribune (*World's Greatest Newspaper*); WSM in Nashville by the National Life Insurance Company (*We Shelter Millions*); and WHB in Kansas City by the Sweeney Automotive and Electrical School. People went into broadcasting for a variety of reasons. Set manufacturers wanted a service to sell their radios; department stores liked the exposure; universities were convinced that radio would aid education. Some people started radio stations because it was fun. Others started broadcasting for no particular reason at all.

In the beginning money wasn't much of a problem. In 1925, it cost only $3000 to get a station on the air and, once broadcasting, operating expenses weren't high, probably around $2000 per year. It didn't last. Tighter technical standards meant that an engineer was needed; talent started demanding payment; better equipment cost money. The bigger stations felt the squeeze first. In 1927, one large station paid about $350,000 to stay on the air. Even a small station might be faced with annual operating costs of about $25,000. Faced with this inflation, stations looked for a method to collect revenue.

Nobody quite knew how to do it. Some felt that listeners should send in voluntary contributions. One station invented an "Invisible Theater" and asked for contributions according to an imaginary floor plan. Another scheme proposed a coin box on top of the receiver in which listeners would deposit quarters; yet another suggested a tax on tubes in the receiver. These ideas, which might have worked, would have taken years to implement. What was needed was a plan that would bring money flowing in immediately. It was the phone company that hit upon the solution.

In the 1920s, AT&T suffered from tunnel vision. It couldn't convince itself that radio was different from the telephone. Consequently, WEAF (AT&T's showcase station in New York) started to broadcast "toll" programs. To the phone company, the arrangement was obvious. If you made a long-distance call, you paid a special toll. Broadcasting was a special instance of making a long-distance call simultaneously to a large number of people. If you had the money, WEAF had the equipment. The most logical candidates for this new form of conference call were companies that had things to sell. Thus in 1922, the Queensboro Realty Company paid $300 for five radio "talks" that praised the benefits of living in the country. (The company also had country lots they could sell you.) Other companies quickly realized the advertising potential of this system and followed suit. Other stations began to copy WEAF's arrangement, and the problem of financing radio was solved—broadcasting would be supported by advertising.

Radio Commercials: From Queensboro Realty to Things that Glowed, Whistled, Decoded, and Even Looked Around Corners

Early radio commercials were polite and unobtrusive. It was almost as though the companies were embarrassed to invade the privacy of the home with their messages. Commercials were limited to merely mentioning the name of the product or the sponsor. Direct selling or quoting prices over the air was forbidden. Some people argued for a tone to precede the commercial so as to warn listeners of what was to come. There was even a good deal of discussion about the propriety of broadcasting commercials for a product so personal as toothpaste. These attitudes didn't last long.

At first, product names were incorporated into program names as indirect advertising became more accepted. Early listeners were treated to programs such as "The Eveready Battery Hour," "The Gold Dust Twins," and the "Balkite Hour." Other advertisers named performers after their products: the A & P Gypsies, the Clicquot Club Eskimos. From this it was only a short step to direct advertising over radio, and in 1928 Henry Field of KFNF in Shenandoah, Iowa, became one of radio's pioneer salesmen when he invited listeners to buy seeds, bacon, auto tires, fresh hams, prunes, paint, coffee, shoes, and pig meal from his general store. By 1930, the Depression had made most other stations accept direct advertising, and the sixty-second spot announcement became the most widely accepted format. Radio commercials became more ambitious and more elaborate. Dramatic situations were used to sell soap products. Wheaties, Pepsi-Cola, and Barbasol developed the singing commercial. But perhaps the form of advertising that will be best remembered from radio is that of the premium. All it took was a box top and maybe a dime and you could be the proud owner of a Little Orphan Annie Ovaltine Shake-Up Mug, a Tom Mix periscope ring to check around corners, a Captain Midnight Code-o-Graph, a Green Hornet Sign Ring, or a Lone Ranger Special Glow-in-the-Dark Belt. Most premiums were aimed at children, but the adults were not left out. The loyal listeners of "Clara, Lu, 'n' Em" could send in a box top from Super Suds Soap along with a dime and in return they would be sent a package of "Hollywood Flower Garden" seeds. In ten days half a million seed packages were sold. Nonetheless, children were the prime targets for these offers. And no wonder. What kid wouldn't want a Buck Rogers Alien Detector Magic Ring? If you put this ring in the palm of an earthling, it would glow in the dark. If, however, you gave the ring to a Venusian and led him into a darkened room, the ring was guaranteed not to glow. It has not been determined how many Venusians were uncovered by this method.

The Emergence of Networks

The fifth element in radio's evolution also came about because of money. If a station in Philadelphia and a station in New York each had to produce a program to fill one hour's time, each station would wind up paying a bill. It would be cheaper for both to share the costs of a single program and, through a system of interconnection, to broadcast the same show on both stations. This arrangement of interconnecting stations became known as a **network.** Additionally, if enough stations were connected, an advertiser could deal with only one organization and still buy time on the network, thus reaching large audiences by making a single phone call. The economic benefits of a network were apparent to the early broadcasting companies.

The first network was NBC, a wholly owned subsidiary of RCA, set up in 1926. In actuality, NBC instituted two networks. One was formed from the stations that were originally owned by RCA. The second was formed when RCA purchased AT&T's stations and other broadcast assets. (The phone company had decided to end its direct involvement in the broadcasting business. It maintained an indirect involvement by leasing its lines to the networks for station interconnection.) In order to avoid confusion, the two NBC networks were called the Red and the Blue Network.

Shortly after the birth of NBC, a second network, United Independent Broadcasters (UIB), was established. In financial trouble from the start, UIB eventually merged with the Columbia Phonograph Record Company in 1927 to form the Columbia Phonograph Broadcasting System. Eventually, control of this new network, which was subsequently renamed the Columbia Broadcasting System (CBS), was acquired by the Paley family. Among other things, the Paley family owned the Congress Cigar Company, which had been among the first advertisers to sign on with UIB. Sensing the potential of radio, William S. Paley at the age of twenty-seven became the new president of CBS, thus beginning an affiliation that would extend into the 1980s.

In 1927, NBC listed 28 stations as affiliates, while CBS reported 13. Ten years later in 1937, NBC affiliates had grown to 111, while CBS would number 105. National advertising dollars flowed into these young operations. By 1930, advertisers were spending approximately $27 million on network advertising. In this same year, NBC showed a pretax profit of $2.1 million, while CBS reported income of a little less than one million. It was obvious that the network-affiliate arrangement would persist for some time to come.

Government Support and Regulation

The sixth and last element necessary to ensure radio's growth as a mass medium was provided by the federal government. An early attempt at regulation came in 1912 when the Congress passed the Radio Act, which empowered the Secretary of Commerce to issue licenses and to specify frequencies of use. Like everyone else, Congress in 1912 did not conceive of radio as a broadcasting medium, and the Radio Act was written with the idea that radio would prove most useful in maritime communications. During the early 1920s, when more and more stations went on the air, it became obvious that the early legislation would not do the job. Interference became a tremendous problem. Stations switched frequency, changed power, and ignored the operation times specified in their licenses. The situation was aggravated when a 1926 court decision effectively stripped the Secretary of Commerce of the little regulatory power he had. Obviously, a new set of regulations was needed to keep the new medium from drowning in a sea of interference and static.

Congress finally acted to resolve this situation by passing the **Radio Act of 1927.** This act set up the Federal Radio Commission (FRC), a regulatory body that would issue licenses and try to clean up the chaos that existed. Eventually, the FRC made some headway. The commission defined the AM broadcast band, standardized channel designations, abolished portable stations, and moved to minimize interference. By 1929 the situation had improved, and the new radio medium was prevented from suffocating in its own growth.

The Impact of Radio on the Record Industry

As radio's fortunes were on the rise, the recording industry's were waning. By the end of 1924, the combined sales of players and records had dropped 50 percent from those of the previous year. In the midst of this economic trouble, the recording companies quietly introduced electronic recording, using technology borrowed from their bitter rival, radio. The sound quality of records improved tremendously. But despite this improvement, radio continued to be thought of as the medium for "live" music while records were dismissed as the medium of "canned" music.

In 1926, the record industry joined the radio bandwagon and began to market radio–phonograph combinations, an obvious testament to the belief that the two media would coexist. This attitude was also prevalent at the corporate level. In 1927, rumors were flying that the Victor Company would soon merge with RCA. Frightened by this, Columbia, Victor's biggest rival, tried to get a head start by merging with the new (and financially troubled) radio network, United Independent Broadcasters. All too soon, however, the record company became disillusioned and dissolved the deal. The radio network retained Columbia's name and became CBS. Ironically, in 1938, when CBS was in much better financial shape, it would "reacquire" the phonograph company. The much discussed RCA and Victor merger came about in 1929, with the new company dominated by the radio operation.

SHIFTING FORTUNES: 1930–1944

The Great Depression

The Great Depression of the 1930s dealt an economic blow to both radio and sound recording. In the case of radio, the industry was merely stunned; for sound recording, it was nearly a knockout punch.

By most standards, radio was not hit as hard as other industries. For example, the total dollar amount spent on radio advertising grew from 40.5 million in 1930 to 112.6 million in 1935. In fact, the broadcasting economic climate was so favorable that a fourth network (or a third if you count NBC's two nets together) was formed in 1934. The Mutual Broadcasting System (MBS) grew from 4 stations in its initial year to 160 stations in 1940. In addition, the radio audience was expanding. About 12 million homes had radios in 1930, about 46 percent of the U.S. total. By 1940, radio sets were in 81 percent of American homes and had been installed in an additional 7 million cars. New research firms sprang up to tap the needs of radio's growing audience, and broadcasters began to pay attention to the ratings. Although profits were not as high as they might have been in better economic times, the radio industry was able to weather the Depression with relatively little hardship.

The recording industry did not fare nearly as well. Thomas Edison's record manufacturing company went out of business in 1930. Record sales dropped from

$46 million in 1930 to $5.5 million in 1933, and several smaller labels also folded. The entire industry was reeling.

In the midst of all this gloom the recording industry was saved once again by the nickel. Coin-operated record players, called juke boxes (the origin of this term is obscure), began popping up in the thousands of bars and cocktail lounges that mushroomed after the repeal of Prohibition in 1933. These juke boxes were immensely popular and quickly spread to diners, drug stores, and restaurants. Starting in 1934, total record sales began to inch upward; by 1939, sales had increased by more than 500 percent.

While records were enjoying a renaissance, radio was experiencing some growing pains. The first problem had to do with the newspapers. Faced with growing radio competition for advertising dollars, newspaper publishers pressured the wire services to cut off the supply of news to radio networks, thus starting the **Press–Radio War.** Eventually, because of economic reasons, the wire services retreated and the flow of news copy resumed. A second skirmish occurred between stations and the American Society of Composers, Authors, and Publishers (ASCAP). When radio went commercial, ASCAP granted licenses to stations to broadcast music for an annual fee. As radio became more profitable, ASCAP raised its fees. In 1937, faced with another increase, the broadcasters rebelled and started their own licensing organization, Broadcast Music Incorporated (BMI). ASCAP also retreated. Taken together, these two events demonstrated that radio was becoming aware of its economic muscle.

The most significant legal development concerning the sound media during the Depression years was the formation of the **Federal Communications Commission (FCC).** President Roosevelt wanted to create a government agency that would consolidate the regulatory functions of the communications industry in the same way that regulatory powers were consolidated under the Federal Power Commission and the Interstate Commerce Commission. In response to the president's demands, Congress passed the **Communications Act of 1934,** which consolidated responsibilities for broadcast and wire regulation under a new seven-member Federal Communications Commission. Aside from the expanded size of the commission and its increased duties, the fundamental philosophy underlying the original Radio Act of 1927 remained unchanged.

World War II

Radio did well during the war. The amount of dollars spent on radio ads nearly doubled from 1940 to 1945. Helped by a newsprint shortage and an excess-profits tax that encouraged companies to advertise, radio broadcasting outpaced the newspapers as a national advertising vehicle in 1943. By war's end, radio was pulling 18 percent of all ad dollars.

Although the number of new stations that went on the air during the war years was relatively small (only thirty-four new AMs from 1942 to 1945) and major alterations to existing stations were frozen by the FCC, the shape of modern broadcasting would be significantly altered by a court ruling that came in the middle of the war. In 1943, the Supreme Court ruled that NBC must divest itself of one of its two networks. NBC chose to sell the weaker Blue network to Edward Noble, who had made his fortune selling Life Savers candy. Noble renamed his network the American Broadcasting Company (ABC) and by the end of the war, ABC had 195 affiliates and was a full-fledged competitor for the older nets.

The record industry did not do as well, primarily for two reasons. The U.S.

During the 1940s, the local record shop was the place to ''hang out'' with friends and listen to the latest releases. (Nina Leen, Life *Magazine,* © Time Inc.)

government declared shellac, a key ingredient of discs, vital to the national defense and supplies available for records dropped drastically. Second, the American Federation of Musicians, fearful of losing jobs because of ''canned'' music, went on strike. The strike lasted from 1942 to 1944, and, as a result, record sales increased slowly during the war years. It was also during the war that Capitol records embarked on a novel approach to record promotion. The company mailed free records to radio stations, hoping for air play. This marked formal recognition of a new industry attitude: Radio could help sell records.

CONTENT TRENDS IN RADIO AND RECORDS TO 1945

Early Radio: Live Music, Variety, and Drama

Music was the main ingredient of the earliest radio programs, and despite the poor reception on the early 1920s–style receiving set, musical programs were quite popular. As early as 1921, remote broadcasts from hotel dining rooms featuring famous bands were common. All in all, before the networks began to dominate broadcast programs, approximately 70 percent of a local station's programs consisted of musical selections. Almost all of this music was performed live. Records were not thought proper content for radio in the 1920s.

Early radio was curiously formal. Announcers had to dress in tuxedos (even though the audience couldn't see them), and studios were decorated with sofas and potted palms. Odder still, announcers didn't give their own names over the air; they used code names instead. (Evidently, early station managers were afraid that announcers would develop personal followings, ask for more money, and generally become hard to handle.)

By 1929, network broadcasting accounted for about fifty-one hours per week of evening programming. Most of this was music (a good portion classical), but variety and dramatic programs were also making their debut. Foremost among the variety programs was a throwback to the days of vaudeville—the comedy variety programs. Eddie Cantor, George Burns and Gracie Allen, Jack Benny, Ed Wynn, and Fred Allen were all early pioneers of this format. In 1928, two comedians working in blackface, Charles Correll and Freeman Gosden, began broadcasting a program for NBC called "Amos 'n' Andy." By its second season, the show was listened to by half of the people who owned radios. It was a top-rated program for the next five years and literally became a national habit.

The Depression meant that more and more people turned to radio for free entertainment; thus popular radio programs of this period reflected a need for diversion and escape. In 1933, "The Lone Ranger" started the action-adventure format of radio drama and was soon followed by "Gangbusters," "The Shadow," "Dick Tracy," and "Buck Rogers." A Chicago station, WGN, carried a program called "Clara, Lu 'n' Em," which was to become the first of many soap operas. Following in this program's footsteps were "Helen Trent" (about the plight of a woman over thirty-five), "Our Gal Sunday" (a small-town girl marries into English nobility), and "Backstage Wife" (self-explanatory). By 1940, there were forty different soaps on the air.

The Growth of Network News

One other trend was notable during the 1930s: the growth of network radio news. From a somewhat shaky beginning, the networks by 1930 were providing newscasts five days a week. Special-events coverage was also becoming important. CBS

George Burns and Gracie Allen were pioneers of early radio comedy, a format that harkened back to the days of vaudeville. (National Broadcasting Company)

rearranged its entire program schedule to cover the 1932 election. H. V. Kaltenborn reported a battle during the Spanish Civil War while hiding in a haystack. Edward VIII of England abdicated with his famous "The Woman I Love" speech. Coverage of these events drew huge audiences. In September of 1938, with Hitler threatening Europe, CBS and NBC sent more than a thousand foreign broadcasts to the United States from a staff of more than 200 reporters.

Not surprisingly, this trend accelerated during World War II as millions turned to radio for the latest news from the front. Edward R. Murrow gained fame through his reports from London (he once reported during an air raid). George Hicks of CBS recorded the Normandy landings, and in the Pacific, Webley Edwards reported live from a B-29 during an air raid over Japan. The total amount of time spent on news doubled from 1940 to 1944. By 1945, the four radio networks were providing a total of thirty-four hours of scheduled news broadcasts each week. Dramatic programs and music were still popular, however, and some local stations filled about 50 percent of their broadcast day with music, some of it recorded.

Popular Music: Sentiment and Innovation

The nickelodeon established popular records when recording companies discovered that certain artists attracted more nickels than others. Two superstars of this turn-of-the-century era were John Philip Sousa (and the Marine Band) and George H. Diamond (whose big hit was "Have One on the Landlord on Me"). Another popular musical form that developed in the 1890s was ragtime—a musical form characterized by a lively, syncopated rhythm. One of the most distinguished ragtime artists was Scott Joplin, a classically trained black pianist whose "Maple Leaf Rag" (1899) earned him the title of "King of Ragtime."

In general, the songs that were popular during the 1890s were steeped in sentiment. A few representative titles from this period are "Gold Will Buy Most Anything but a True Girl's Heart," "A Bird in a Gilded Cage," "Say *Au Revoir* but not Goodbye," and "The Fatal Wedding." By the turn of the century sentimentality was still present, but many popular songs were in a lighter vein. On the Hit Parade from 1900 to 1915 were "Fido Is a Hot Dog Now," "Meet Me in St. Louis, Louis," and several songs that reflected the continuing popularity of ragtime. A soprano with the interesting name of Alma Gluck became the first recording artist to sell a million records when her old standard "Carry Me Back to Ole Virginny" topped that mark in 1918.

The years after the First World War ushered in the Jazz Age, a period named after the spirited, popular music of the Roaring Twenties. **Jazz,** which emerged from the roots of the black experience in America, was spontaneous, individualistic, and sensual. Because of its disdain for convention, jazz was widely denounced as degenerate during its early years (about thirty years later, another spontaneous and sensual musical innovation, rock and roll, would also be denounced). However, the work of great jazz musicians like Louis Armstrong, "Jelly Roll" Morton, and Bix Beiderbecke eventually was recognized all over the world.

Ironically, another source of content for the recording industry during the 1920s came from a new competitor—sound movies. Movie musicals were proving to be very successful, and recording studios rushed to release versions of songs featured in these films. Jeanette MacDonald, Maurice Chevalier, and Rudy Vallee were all performers who signed contracts with RCA Victor during this time. Hollywood would continue to be a fertile source of popular music throughout the 1930s. By the end of that decade the "Big-Band" era had begun, and the most popular recordings featured selections from Benny Goodman, Glenn Miller, Tommy Dorsey, Duke

Ellington, and Count Basie. The big-band sound would remain popular through the war years of 1941–1945.

INNOVATION AND CHANGE: 1945–1954

The nine-year period following World War II was marked by great changes in both the radio and recording industries, changes that ultimately drove them closer together. The development of television delayed the growth of FM radio, altered the nature of network radio, and forced the radio industry to rely on records as the most important part of a new programming strategy. For its part, the record industry began to use radio as an important promotional device.

FM

The radio industry was in generally good economic shape as the postwar years started. There was one group of broadcasters, however, who might not have shared this assessment: the owners of FM radio stations. Despite the fact that FM sounded better than AM, was static free, and could reproduce a wider range of sound frequencies than AM, AM broadcasting had started first and FM had to struggle to catch up. Following the war, two events occurred that curtailed the development of this new medium. FM had the misfortune of beginning its development at the same time as TV; in addition, because of technical considerations, both FM radio and TV are suited for about the same place in the electromagnetic spectrum. In 1945, the FCC decided to give the rapidly expanding TV service the space formerly occupied by FM. The commission moved FM ''upstairs'' to the 88- to 108-MHz band (where it is today), thus rendering obsolete about half a million FM radios. In addition, many AM operators took out FM licenses as insurance and convinced the FCC that it was in the public interest to ''simulcast,'' that is, to duplicate the content of the AM station over the FM channel. As a result, since little new programming was available, the public had little motivation to purchase FM receivers. It took FM more than thirty years to overcome these (and other) handicaps.

TV

Of course, the biggest change in radio's fortunes came about because of the emergence of television. (We will have more to say about the development of TV in another chapter.) For the time being, it is important to note that by 1948 it was apparent that TV would take over the mass entertainment function currently served by network radio. The emergence of TV meant changes in the content, economics, and functions of radio. Although many individuals believe that television cut into the revenues of the radio industry, no such thing happened. In fact, the revenue of the radio industry rose steadily from 1948 to 1952 and, after a brief drop from 1953 to 1956, continued to rise. The part of the industry upon which TV did have a drastic effect was *network* radio. The percentage of local stations with network affiliations dropped from 97 percent in 1947 to only 50 percent by 1955. Network revenue dropped by 60 percent for approximately the same period. Faced with this loss, stations relied more heavily on revenue from ads for local businesses. In short, they redistributed the makeup of their revenue dollar. As TV became the new mass medium, local stations cut back on their budgets, relied more heavily on music, talk, and news, and began searching for a formula that would allow them to exist with television. The recording industry was to figure heavily in radio's future.

Innovations in Recording

While radio was adjusting to the coming of TV, several important events were permanently altering the shape of the record industry. Using techniques and ideas that were developed in Germany during the war, the 3M Company introduced magnetic recording tape in 1947. The arrival of tape meant improved sound quality, easier editing, reduced cost, and multitrack recording.

The next year Columbia introduced the 33⅓ long-playing record (LP). The new discs could play for twenty-five minutes a side and were virtually unbreakable. Rather than adopt the Columbia system, RCA Victor introduced its own innovation, the 45-rpm extended play record. The next few years were described as the "Battle of the Speeds," as the record-buying public was confronted by a choice among 33⅓, 45, and 78 records. From 1947 to 1949, record sales dropped 25 percent as the audience waited to see which speed would win. In 1950, RCA conceded and began issuing 33⅓ records. Columbia won only a partial victory, however. The 45 would become the preferred disc for single pop recordings while the 33⅓ would dominate album sales. The 78 became obsolete. There were also changes in record players. High-fidelity sets came on the market in 1954, followed four years later by stereophonic record players. Record sales more than doubled during this period.

Two other events were also important: the formation of small, independent recording companies and the emergence of radio as a promotional device. Because the increased importance of tape in record production had cut costs, small companies could now afford to compete with the larger labels. The unbreakable LP could be sent easily through the mail, and profitable mail-order operations were soon thriving. All of these factors favored the formation of new labels. Moreover, the relationship between records and radio became more firmly established. It was recognized that air play was essential to sell a significant amount of records. The emergence of a promotion staff at the record companies signaled this change in marketing technique. In the future, the relationship between the sound recording and the radio industries would be close, sometimes too close, as we shall see.

GROWTH AND STABILIZATION: 1955–1970

Faced with a loss of programs from the networks and increasing rivalry from an ever-growing number of competitors on the radio dial (the number of stations on the air increased from 3343 in 1955 to 5569 in 1965), radio looked for a way to build an image and attract an audience that could be sold to advertisers. The answer was format or formula radio. ("Format" radio attempts to appeal to a particular audience segment.) The first format to develop was middle-of-the-road (MOR), followed in some big cities by a rhythm and blues (R&B) format and by a country/western (CW) format by some stations in rural markets. In the mid-1950s, however, a new format called "Top 40" made its debut. This format demanded strict adherence to a set playlist based on record sales, a distinctive announcing style, rapid pace, and special production gimmicks (like an echo chamber). By 1960, literally hundreds of stations had adopted this format. Very quickly, the Top-40 format became identified with a young audience—a young audience that, as it happened, had a good deal of money to spend on the records they heard played by their favorite disc jockey.

Naturally, the record industry was delighted. Sales skyrocketed from $227 million in 1955 to over $1 billion in 1967. Business had never been better. Radio stations, or at least most of them, were also doing well. Radio industry revenues topped the billion-dollar mark in 1968. Because of this new format, a new figure became important in the marketing of records—the local DJ. Since DJs chose what records were to be played on their programs, they were the focus of attention of dozens of promotional representatives from the record companies. Of course, the record companies were willing to do whatever was necessary to get air play. They began plying the DJs with gifts (followed later by outright bribes) to favor their releases over the competition. It got so bad that it was estimated that some DJs in major markets could supplement their salaries by $50,000 to $100,000 a year by accepting **payola,** as it came to be called. The situation ultimately came to the attention of Congress, and after a series of hearings on the subject the Communications Act was amended in an effort to curtail the practice.

Despite the ''payola'' scandals, both the radio and recording industries continued to grow during this period. By 1970, there were more than 7700 stations on the air, and total revenue exceeded the $1.2 billion mark. The record business also

Payola

In the 1950s the disc jockey (DJ) became an important figure in radio programming. In fact, many promoted themselves to such an extent that they became stars in their own right. DJs sent out glossy pictures of themselves to their fans; they appeared at supermarket openings and record hops; they were the emcees at personal appearances by rock-and-roll groups. As the DJs became more influential, they also began to program their own shows. They picked the records that they would play during their airshift.

Record promoters also realized the tremendous importance of air play in the marketing of a hit. The more a record was played on the radio, the more it sold. Quite naturally, record promoters and DJs began to develop close ties. In the beginning, it was innocent enough. Promoters would make sure that DJs got the latest releases their companies were offering, and they also put in a good word or two about their companies' products. Competition got intense, however, and by 1959 there were about 250 new records released every week. Some unscrupulous promoters resorted to more than words to advance their records. At first, they might send the DJs an elaborate Christmas gift, a case of Scotch, a set of golf clubs, a hi-fi. If that didn't work, some even ''hired'' the DJ as ''creative consultant'' and paid the disc jockey a fee every month. Others would cut the DJ in on the action and offer to pay a penny to the DJ for every record sold in the market. Eventually, most promoters stopped these charades and simply passed the DJ an envelope filled with money in return for air play of their company's songs. In 1958 and 1959, record distributors reportedly spent over a quarter of a million dollars in the larger markets to promote their records artificially.

The news of this illicit business practice did nothing to help the image of rock and roll or of broadcasting. Section 508 was added to the 1934 Communications Act to stop this practice, but it was not altogether successful. New payola scandals broke out in the industry in the early 1970s. At least one record company was accused of offering drugs to station personnel in return for increased air play, and some concert promoters were accused of offering several monetary bribes. Payola resurfaced in 1986 when the U.S. Senate announced plans to investigate illegal practices in record promotion. It's a problem that doesn't seem to disappear.

survived the scandal in good economic shape. In 1970, there were more than 5600 singles released along with about 4000 LPs. Total revenue from record sales had reached $1.1 billion by 1970.

In 1959 another technological development that was to spur sales was introduced by the Ampex Company—the four-track tape. This innovation helped to bring the cost of tape within range of the cost of records. Soon afterward, the development of tape cartridges and tape cassettes that eliminated threading from one reel to another further increased the potential of the tape market. By 1970, tape was accounting for over one-fourth of all recording industry receipts.

The trend toward specialization continued in radio during this period and even reached the network level. In 1968, the ABC radio network splintered into four different services—Contemporary, Informational, Entertainment, and FM—with over 1300 affiliates.

1970 TO THE PRESENT

The ABC network experiment was successful enough to prompt at least two other networks to institute innovative services. The Mutual Network offered a special black network with news and other programs designed to appeal to the black audience. In the mid-1970s, NBC tried to start an all-news radio network (called NIS) but was unable to secure the necessary number of affiliates for a profitable venture. This experiment was abandoned in 1977. Special networks, however, gained popularity in the early to mid-1980s. As of 1988, there were about 25 major radio networks including NBC, ABC, CBS, Mutual, United Radio Networks (United purchased the RKO network in 1985), the Satellite Music Network, CNN Radio network, and National Public Radio. Westwood One purchased Mutual in 1985 and bought NBC network radio three years later. Moreover, network revenues climbed, increasing about 10–15 percent from 1984 to 1985, but they dropped to about 8–9 percent in 1987–1988.

The most significant development in the radio industry during the 1970s was the successful emergence of FM. As noted earlier, FM radio faced several hurdles in its development. By the early 1960s, however, conditions had improved enough for more individuals to consider buying FM stations. Licenses for AM stations were becoming harder to get. People who wished to invest in a broadcast station found it easier to procure an FM license. In 1965, the FCC had passed the **nonduplication rule,** which prevented an AM–FM combination from duplicating its AM content on its FM channel for more than 50 percent of the time. Faced with this ruling and the knowledge that specialized formats were becoming successful in radio, FM stations developed their own kind of sound (many stations adopted a rock format) that capitalized on FM's better technical qualities. Between 1960 and 1970, the number of FM stations tripled. The economic picture also brightened. In 1976, FM broadcasting went into the black as the industry as a whole reported earnings of $21.2 million (see Fig. 8.1).

Profits continued to increase for FM as it captured more and more of the listening audience. In 1988, FM accounted for about 70 percent of all audience listening time, with AM accounting for 30 percent. The only age group where AM garnered more listening time than FM was among people fifty or over. AM station executives began rethinking programming strategy in an attempt to stop the audience erosion. AM stereo was introduced in the early 1980s, but the general lack of radio sets designed to receive it lessened its impact. In general, however, the radio industry continued

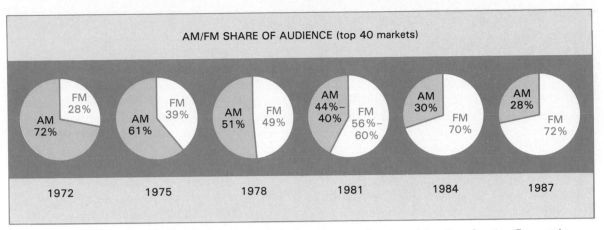

FIGURE 8.1 *Division of AM and FM audiences. Courtesy of Cox Broadcasting Corporation.*

to be profitable. In 1982, the profit margin for the whole industry was about 9 percent on revenues of more than $4 billion. On the regulatory front, the biggest impact on radio came from the 12–12–12 rule, which increased the number of stations one group or company could own from seven to twelve.

More and more radio stations were competing for the same basic advertising, which accelerated the trend toward more refined formats (*Broadcasting Yearbook* for 1988 listed more than sixty). Country music was the most widely programmed format on radio stations in 1987 followed by adult contemporary. Stations were relying heavily on program consultants and audience research to get the exact sound they need to keep their operations profitable. The overall outlook continues to be favorable for radio.

The sound-recording industry went through a boom period from 1974 to 1978 when revenue nearly doubled. The boom was followed by a slump, however, which lasted from 1980 to 1982. In 1983, though, the record industry underwent a revival, thanks in part to Michael Jackson, whose *Thriller* album sold more than 27 million copies, making it the biggest seller in history. Revenues increased about 9 percent over 1982 and increased even more the next year. What factors caused the sudden turnaround?

- The industry cuts costs and watched spending.

- Music videos represented a new and potent source of promotion and exposure.

- Music and film tie-ins were extremely popular. (The sound track of *Flashdance* sold more than 4.5 million albums; *Footloose* did almost as well.)

- Compact discs became popular and attracted new buyers to the stores.

These same factors would help the music industry prosper for the rest of the decade, with revenues topping the $6 billion mark in 1988.

Of all the above, the one factor that probably had the biggest impact on the sound-recording industry was the surprising popularity of music videos and MTV. The videos quickly became an important avenue of exposure for new groups. Radio stations used MTV to pretest additions to the playlists. If a record received heavy play on television, then it was a pretty safe bet that it would be popular on radio as

---

Quest for Ratings

The competition between radio stations for listeners has become intense. One tactic involves paying people to listen. Usually this is done by having something like a Cash Call Jackpot where a station periodically announces that a specific sum of money is in the jackpot. The station then calls someone and if that person knows the correct amount in the jackpot, he or she wins the entire amount. Of course, to know the correct sum, a person has to be listening to the station. A few years ago, in one market, this arrangement got a little out of control. Station A first offered about $500 in their jackpot. Not to be outdone, their competition, Station B, offered $1000. Station A raised their stakes to $2000; Station B countered by going to $5000. Station A then raised the ante to $10,000. By this time Station B could no longer profitably compete. Instead, it resorted to another tactic. Station B began to announce the precise amount that was in Sta-

tion A's jackpot, meaning that a person could listen to Station B and still win Station A's money. Dirty trick, said Station A and began announcing the amount in Station B's jackpot. Eventually both stations dropped the promotion.

More recently, a similar event occurred, but these days the stakes are much higher. In 1985, at least two stations ran a promotion in which a million dollars would be given to a lucky listener whose name was announced over the air. The person had to call the station within twenty minutes to be eligible for the prize. This promotion prompted the formation of a company called GameSitter. For a $6 fee, the company listens twenty-four hours a day to the station and calls you if your name happens to be announced. About 500 people subscribed to the service in its first few weeks of existence. None of them won any money.

---

well. In fact, there were many performers who owed their popularity to MTV: Duran Duran, Eurythmics, Prince, Heart, Madonna, to name a few. Ratings for MTV dropped during 1986 but the channel went back to its roots and played more hard rock and heavy metal and its viewership increased.

The biggest technological advances in the record industry concern **compact discs (CDs)** and **digital audio tape (DAT).** CD sales have grown so much that most experts predict that the traditional LP will be extinct in about ten years. About a million CD players were sold in 1985; in 1988, more than 4 million were sold. Sales of CDs increased more than tenfold over the same period.

DAT uses digital technology but encodes the music on tape instead of disc (see pages 232–233). The big advantage of DAT is that it's cheaper than discs and, like other tapes, can be used for recording. Legal problems have kept DAT players and tapes out of the United States, but most experts agree they will not be long in coming.

Home taping continues to be a big concern. One study found that for every seventeen people who purchased a hit record, fifteen taped it. At mid-decade, the record companies were asking Congress to impose a special royalty tax on blank tape.

CONTENT TRENDS: 1945–PRESENT

Shortly after World War II ended it became apparent that most of radio's biggest stars would soon make the transition to TV. In the beginning, some popular radio programs were simulcast on television, with radio carrying only the audio portion.

Soon the simulcast programs abandoned radio altogether, and the radio networks decided to fill the gap with music and quiz programs. By 1956 it was obvious that the networks would no longer be the potent programming source they had been in the past. In that year, radio networks were carrying only about thirty-five hours of sponsored evening programs each week. Finally, by 1960, all the once popular evening programs and daytime serials had come to an end. Radio network service was limited primarily to news and short features, usually amounting to no more than two or three hours of time a day.

Specialized Formats

Local stations soon adapted to this change. Now that they no longer were tied to the networks for the bulk of their programming, the locals were free to develop their own personalities. Most did it by adopting a specialized format, a sound that had distinctive appeal to a certain segment of the audience. In the beginning, most stations resorted to a "middle-of-the-road" format, a throwback to the networks' influence. Others began to experiment. The most successful experiment occurred in the Midwest where a station began monitoring the sales of records and sheet music and playing those tunes that were selling the most. Hence, the Top-40 format was born. A key element in this format was the **clock hour,** which specified every element of programming. The sound had to be continuous, bright, and exciting. No dead air was permitted. The disc jockey had to complement the format. Since one Top-40 station sounded like any other Top-40 station, it was the DJ who gave each station its particular personality. It was not long before DJs became stars in their own right. One of the first was Alan Freed, who left Cleveland and became one of New York's top DJs. Another was Murray the K, who eventually called himself "the fifth Beatle" during the 1960s. Wolfman Jack is another example. The success of this Top-40 sound encouraged radio stations to experiment with other specialized formats. By 1964, at least a dozen different formats had sprung up.

This trend toward specialization continued through the 1970s and into the 1980s. All-talk and all-news stations have specialized without relying on music. Ethnic

Radio Formats for the 1980s . . . and Beyond

The trend toward specialization in radio may have gone about as far as it can go. From California (where else?) comes a format called "Music From the Hearts of Space," described as "music intended to be a caress, carried on the wind like soft brushstrokes of an autumn sunset . . . a reminder of the dream dance from which we've come." Some listeners described it differently. "New Wave Muzak," said one. "Synthesized slush," said another. Enough people liked it, however, to have an hour-long sample of the format carried on more than 100 noncommercial radio stations.

Back closer to Earth, a Canadian radio station has instituted a format that is really a mosquito repellent. Station CINE in Quebec broadcasts to the Laurentian Mountains outside Montreal, a popular vacation site. During the summer, however, mosquitoes can be a problem. Hence, CINE's innovative programming. Between every song, the station plays the high-pitched sound of male mosquitoes flapping their wings. Female mosquitoes, the ones who are out for blood, can't stand this sound and when they hear it, they buzz off, as it were. The station hopes the sound will not have the same effect on its human listeners.

stations have become popular along with stations that program a religious format. Recycling is also evident as many stations have turned to a "Golden Oldies" format, and the radio networks have begun to supply original variety programs in the evening.

In the mid-1980s at least one station was broadcasting nothing but cuts from popular comedy albums while another presented an "all-kids" format. Many classical and easy-listening stations were carried on local cable TV channels, making their formats more available. Among FM stations in the top 100 radio markets, the most popular format was adult/contemporary (a blend of soft rock and some oldies), but the contemporary hits format (Top 40) was making a comeback. The AM band was showing a tendency to rely more on news, talk, and middle-of-the-road formats. New formats that cropped up were the soft jazz–New Age–"lite" rock fusion called The Wave and a blend of black urban contemporary and Top 40. On the AM band, the late 1980s saw all-sports and all-financial formats emerge. One Cincinnati station even premiered an all-Elvis format.

Sound Recording

After World War II, the most popular recordings were made by the soloists and featured artists who had performed in front of the big bands. Peggy Lee (featured with Benny Goodman), Frank Sinatra (with Tommy Dorsey), Doris Day (with Les Brown), and Dinah Shore (with Xavier Cugat) all had hit records during the postwar years. This music was designed to appeal to all age groups and was, at times, oversentimentalized. Consider these top songs, popular between 1949 and 1954: "Ghost Riders in the Sky" (Vaughn Monroe); "Doggie in the Window" (Patti Page); "Oh My Papa" (Eddie Fisher); and "Three Coins in the Fountain" (The Four Aces). Around 1954, however, music changed. It would never be the same.

The Coming of Rock and Roll

It started with the car. Teenagers had more spending money in these postwar years, and for the first time many of them could afford a car. Pretty soon the car became a symbol of identity; many teenagers customized their cars so that no one would confuse it with the family auto. After the cars came the clothes. By the 1950s, teenage clothes no longer resembled adult clothes. Denim was popular, and leather jackets (à la James Dean and Marlon Brando) were sported by many. Hair styles and makeup became distinctive. After cars and clothes came the movies: *Rebel Without a Cause, The Blackboard Jungle, The Wild One*. Before long sociologists were talking about a "youth culture." One thing this youth culture lacked was a distinctive form of music. Rock and roll would fill that void. The importance of this new form of music to the record industry cannot be minimized. Consequently, our examination of the evolution of popular music content must from this point on focus on the changing trends in rock-and-roll (later shortened to rock) music.

Rock had its roots in black rhythm and blues, commercial white popular music, country and western, and jazz. The first national exposure of rock and roll came in July of 1955 when Bill Haley and the Comets moved into the number-one spot on the charts with "Rock Around the Clock." The song remained there for eight weeks (until replaced by Mitch Miller's version of "The Yellow Rose of Texas"). But Haley was more of a popularizer than a pioneer, for his music sounded a bit like a swing band that had suddenly discovered the big beat. In any event, his popularity quickly faded.

Less than a year later another performer who would enjoy a far more substantial career came on the scene. "Heartbreak Hotel," recorded by a then relatively un-

(a)

(b)   (c)

(a) The one and only Elvis. (b) Chuck Berry introduced the Chicago sound—a mixture of blues, guitar chords, and a heavy beat—to early rock and roll. (c) Lesley Gore was one of the popular female performers of the 1960s. (a, The Bettmann Archive; b, Charles Stewart/Photo Trends; c, Culver Pictures)

known Elvis Presley, would stay at the number-one position for seven straight weeks. A few months later a second Elvis hit, ''Don't Be Cruel,'' would go to the number-one slot, followed by yet another number-one hit in 1956, a change of pace called ''Love Me Tender.'' It was with Elvis that rock and roll first blossomed. Combining a country and western style with the beat and energy of black R&B music, Elvis' records sold millions. He appeared (from the waist up at least) on Ed Sullivan's network TV show. Through Elvis rock and roll gained wide recognition, if not respectabilty.

Presley's success inspired other performers from the country and western tradition. Jerry Lee Lewis combined Mississippi boogie-woogie with country music to produce a unique and driving style. His "Whole Lotta Shakin' Going On" sold 6 million copies in 1957–1958. At about this time, Buddy Holly and the Crickets made the charts with "That'll Be the Day." Holly's music went back to his Texas roots and combined the warm tone of regional country and western music with inventive arrangements and vocal gymnastics to create a novel sound.

Several rock pioneers came from traditional black rhythm and blues music. Perhaps the most exciting (certainly the most energetic) was Richard Penniman, or, as he called himself, "Little Richard." Except for a period of three months, Little Richard had a record in the Top 100 at all times from 1956 to 1957 (best known are "Long Tall Sally" and "Tutti Frutti"). Both his music and his stage performances boiled over with unrestrained energy. About the same time, on the south side of Chicago, Chuck Berry was singing blues in small night clubs. Discovered by the owner of a Chicago-based record company, Berry was the first artist who paid more than passing attention to the lyrics of rock and roll. His style would later influence many musical groups, including the Beatles.

Rock Goes Commercial

By 1959, through a combination of bizarre events, all the pioneers of rock had disappeared. Elvis went into the Army. Buddy Holly was killed in a plane crash. Jerry Lee Lewis married a thirteen-year-old girl said to be his cousin and dropped from sight. Little Richard was in the seminary. And Chuck Berry, arrested for violating the Mann Act, ultimately entered federal prison. Thus the way was open for a whole new crop of stars. Economics dictated what this new crop would look and sound like.

About this time record companies realized that huge amounts of money could be made from the rock-and-roll phenomenon if it was promoted correctly. Unfortunately, rock and roll had an image problem. In 1959, the record industry was shaken by the payola scandals, which, coming on top of years of bad publicity and criticism that blamed rock and roll for most of society's ills, threatened rock's profitability. Since rock and roll had too much moneymaking potential to be abandoned, the record companies decided to clean up rock's image instead.

As the 1960s opened, the "new look" in rock was characterized by middle-class, white, clean-cut, and more or less wholesome performers. Rock stars were young men and women you wouldn't hesitate to bring home and introduce to your parents. On the male side, Ricky Nelson, Bobby Vee, Bobby Vinton, Fabian, Paul Anka, Frankie Avalon, and The Four Seasons were popular. Although there were fewer examples on the female side, those who had hits included Annette, Connie Francis, Brenda Lee, and Lesley Gore. All fit the new image of rock and roll. Consequently, the early 1960s saw few musical innovations. In 1963, however, the music changed again.

The British Invasion

Their name was inspired by Buddy Holly and the Crickets, but instead of the entomologically correct "Beetles," the group chose the spelling "Beatles" (which, it was later explained, incorporated the word "beat"). In early 1964, they took the United States by storm. Musically, the Beatles were everything that American rock and roll was not. They were innovative, especially in vocal harmony, and introduced

Morbidity and Rock and Roll

One of the strangest trends in the evolution of popular rock-and-roll music has been a small but persistent genre of records that can only be classified under the somewhat macabre title of "morbid rock." Although its roots probably go back further, it became especially notable in the 1960s. Among the first songs to become a hit was "Teen Angel," the tale of an unfortunate couple whose car stalled on the railroad tracks. Although the young man of the song is smart enough to run like crazy, the young girl shows a complete lack of judgment and goes back to the car to retrieve her sweetheart's high school ring. The train arrives at the same time. End of romance. Another early example was J. Frank Wilson's "Last Kiss," a tragic tale of a guy and girl out on a date who plow into a disabled car. He survives. She doesn't. End of romance. "Tell Laura I Love Her" told the teary story of a young man who needs money to continue his romance with his lady friend and so resorts to stock car racing to provide extra income. He totals his car and himself. End of romance. "Patches" con-cerned the romance between a girl from the wrong side of the tracks and a middle-class young man. Despondent, the young woman drowns herself in the river. At the end of the song, the young man is contemplating the same thing. Even wholesome Pat Boone got into the act with "Moody River," a song that also told the story of two people who throw themselves into the river and drown. The trend was less noticeable in the early seventies, but a song entitled "Billy Don't Be a Hero" enjoyed wide popularity. This effort was about a young man who goes off to war, against the wishes of his girlfriend, and gets killed. End of romance. (For those who are true fans of this genre, Rhino Records has collected ten teen tragedy songs ranging from "Last Kiss" to the little-known but nonetheless moving "The Homecoming Queen's Got a Gun." Incidentally, the back cover of the LP doubles as a tissue dispenser.)

In any event, this trend has not resurfaced during the 1980s. Perhaps it's . . . dead.

---

the harmonica as a rock instrument. Ultimately, they would change the shape of the music business and American popular culture. The Beatles had seven number-one records in 1964; they held down the top position for twenty of the fifty-two weeks that year. They would have six more chart-toppers over the next two years. When they appeared on the Ed Sullivan show in 1964, it was estimated that 73 million people watched.

Their success paved the way for a veritable British invasion. Most British rock at this time resembled American rock: cheery, happy, commercial, and white. Not surprisingly, some of the first groups that followed the Beatles represented this school (Herman's Hermits, Freddie and the Dreamers, the Dave Clark Five, Peter and Gordon, to name a few). There was another style of British rock, however, far less cheery, as represented by the Rolling Stones and the Animals. This style, which would also enjoy popularity, was blues based, rough hewn, slightly aggressive, and certainly not bouncy and carefree. (One young girl, when asked how she could be a fan of both the Beatles and the Stones, reportedly replied that she liked the Beatles because they were "cute" and sort of liked the Stones because they were "so ugly.")

American artists were not silent during this influx of British talent. Folk music, as performed by Bob Dylan and Joan Baez, was also popular. It was only a matter of time before folk merged with rock to produce "folk rock" ("Mr. Tambourine Man" by the Byrds was one of the first records in this style). Soul music, as recorded on the Motown label, also made its mark during the sixties. The Supremes and the Four Tops had eleven number-one songs between them for this label from 1964 to 1967.

Recent Trends

The late 1960s was a time of cultural transition. Freedom, experimentation, and innovation were encouraged in almost all walks of life, and popular music was no exception. Sparked by the release of the Beatles' *Sgt. Pepper* album, a fractionalization of rock began to take place. Several trends of this period are notable. In 1968, Blood, Sweat and Tears successfully blended jazz, rock, and at times, even classical music. The Band introduced "country rock." The Who recorded a rock opera, *Tommy*. In the midst of all this experimentation, commercial formula music was also healthy. The Monkees, a group put together by ads in the newspaper, sold millions of records. Proponents of "bubble-gum rock," The Archies, kept "Sugar, Sugar" at the top of the charts for a month in 1969 (it replaced, oddly enough, a song by the Rolling Stones, "Honky Tonk Woman").

Still, perhaps the most significant trend in this period was one that changed music again. Toward the end of the sixties and the beginning of the seventies, rock music became part of the counterculture; in many instances, it went out of its way to break with the establishment. Musically, many of the songs of this era were characterized by the **heavy-metal** sound; amplifiers and electronic equipment began to dominate the stage along with the performers. The artists also broke sharply with tradition. The pioneers in this style of rock were all vaguely threatening, a trifle unsavory, and definitely not the type you would bring home and introduce to the family. Consider Janis Joplin, Jimi Hendrix, Sly and the Family Stone, Alice Cooper, Rod Stewart, and David Bowie. They are a far cry from Frankie Avalon and Annette.

Perhaps as a reaction to all this volume, the early 1970s found a softer, more personal style of music gaining popularity. James Taylor, Carole King, Melanie, Carly Simon, and Joni Mitchell were the prime examples of this trend. The most significant development of the early to mid-1970s, however, was the intermingling of rock music with country and western music. During this period and, indeed, even to the present, it is not uncommon to find the top C/W single also high on the pop charts. Many country performers were able to cross over into the pop arena with consistent success. Kris Kristofferson, John Denver, Glen Campbell, Dolly Parton, Anne Murray, Linda Ronstadt, and Olivia Newton-John, among others, have made the distinction between rock and country less clear.

As the 1970s gave way to the 1980s, this trend in crossovers had not diminished; it was not uncommon to find many albums on both the country and the rock best-seller charts. The disco craze faded but gave birth to a new style of heavy-beat dance music. Several other boomlets seemed to have come and gone, among them a phenomenon known as punk rock. The most significant trend in the 1980s was the emergence of "new wave" music, which in a slightly toned-down version became known as simply the "new music" (see Fig. 8.2). This style replaced the guitar as the central rock musical instrument with the synthesizer and keyboard and introduced new and innovative rhythm arrangements.

Metal, Rap, and Retro Rock

In recorded music three big trends characterized the late 1980s: the revival of an established rock style, the mainstreaming of another, and the renaissance of many

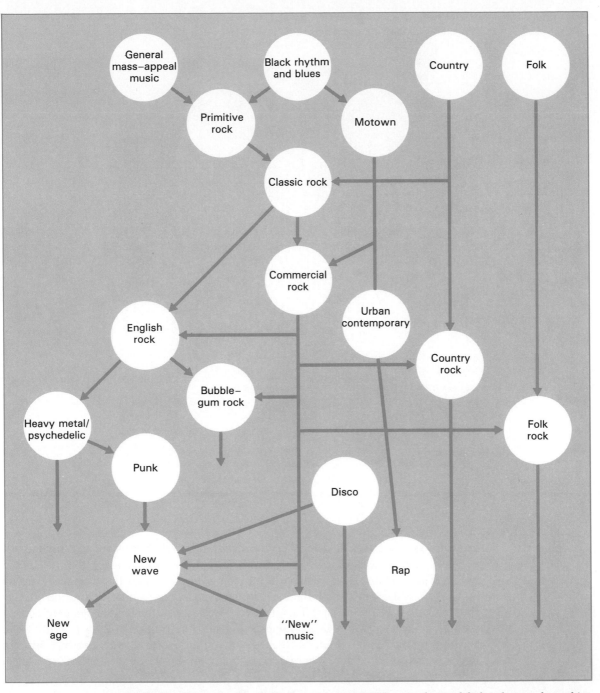

FIGURE 8.2 *The rock-and-roll family tree, circa (1990), greatly simplified and somewhat subjective. If you disagree, draw new arrows and circles.*

of rock's early stars. The music that revived itself in 1987–1988 was heavy metal. Groups such as Bon Jovi, Whitesnake, and Def Leppard enjoyed their highest popularity ever. Black urban contemporary music and rap increased their base of popularity and were frequently heard on mainstream Contemporary Hit Radio stations. Jody Whatley, Club Nouveau, and Run-D.M.C. were groups that got new

Run-D.M.C., a 1980s rap group popular with young listeners. (Gene Bagnato/Retna)

exposure to a mass audience. The biggest trend, however, saw a resurgence in popularity of some rock performers who have been around since the 1960s and 1970s. The Grateful Dead released a hit album and had their first runaway Top-40 hit in 1987. Starship (nee Jefferson Airplane) had several hits, as did the Moody Blues, George Harrison, and Tina Turner. Movie soundtracks that featured oldies, such as *Dirty Dancing* and *La Bamba*, sold into the millions. Classic oldies were showing up on Album-Oriented Rock, Adult Contemporary, and Contemporary Hit Radio stations. Somebody even wrote a book claiming Elvis was still alive. All in all, it was a time of recycling for rock.

SUGGESTIONS FOR FURTHER READING

These books represent a good place to go for further information.

The History of Radio

BARNOUW, ERIK, *A Tower in Babel*, New York: Oxford University Press, 1966.
————, *The Golden Web*, New York: Oxford University Press, 1968.

————, *The Image Empire*, New York: Oxford University Press, 1970.

LICHTY, LAWRENCE, AND MAL TOPPING, eds., *American Broadcasting: A Source Book on the History of Radio and Television,* New York: Hastings House, 1975.

STERLING, CHRISTOPHER, AND JOHN KITTROSS, *Stay Tuned: A Concise History of American Broadcasting,* Belmont, Calif.: Wadsworth, 1978.

The History of Sound Recording and Record Content

CHAPPLE, STEVE, AND REEBEE GAROFOLO, *Rock 'n' Roll Is Here to Pay: The History and Politics of the Music Industry,* Chicago: Nelson-Hall, 1977.

DENISOFF, SERGE, *Tarnished Gold: The Record Industry Revisited,* New Brunswick, N.J.: Transaction Books, 1986.

JAHN, MIKE, *Rock: From Elvis Presley to the Rolling Stones,* New York: Quadrangle, 1973.

ROXON, LILLIAN, *Rock Encyclopedia,* New York: Workman, 1969.

SCHICKE, C.A., *Revolution in Sound,* Boston: Little, Brown, 1974.

SKLAR, RICK, *Rocking America,* New York: St. Martin's Press, 1984.

DISCOGRAPHY

A few albums that help illustrate some of the trends in popular music would be the following:

BEATLES, *Sgt. Pepper's Lonely Hearts Club Band*, Capitol MAS 2653.

BOB DYLAN, *Bob Dylan's Greatest Hits*, Columbia KCS 9463.

DEF LEPPARD, *Hysteria*, Mercury 8306751.

MICHAEL JACKSON, *Thriller*, Epic QE 38112.

ELVIS PRESLEY, *Elvis Presley*, RCA LSP 1254.

LITTLE RICHARD, *Little Richard's Grooviest 17 Original Hits,* Specialty SPS 2113.

THE ROLLING STONES, *Let It Bleed*, London NPS-4.

BRUCE SPRINGSTEEN, *Born in the USA*, Columbia QC 38653.

THE WHO, *Tommy*, Decca DXSW 7205.

Chapter 9
Structure of the Radio Industry

In 1956, listeners in the south-central Virginia town of Gretna could hear seven radio stations. Out-of-town stations were weak and sounded fuzzy, but WMNA-AM and FM were located in Gretna and their signals came in loud and clear. WMNA was a home-town station. It carried the local high school football games, a "Swap Shop" program, a lost and found service, announcements about local church spaghetti suppers, and news about the annual Sorghum Festival in a nearby town.

Now, a little more than thirty years later, thanks to more stations and FCC decisions that allowed existing stations to increase power and redirect their antennas, a Gretna resident can pick up twenty-eight AM and FM stations from larger communities nearby, and five more stations are being built. Almost all of these distant stations are newcomers to the Gretna area and are owned by big companies in other cities. Some stations have already been sold two or more times. But all of these out-of-town signals come in loud and clear thanks to better transmitting equipment and better radio receivers. Gretna listeners can choose from the latest in Top 40, Album rock, easy listening, country, talk, and news—the same things people in Roanoke, Richmond, and even Washington, D.C., are listening to.

But what about WMNA? It's still there, still trying to be a home-town station. The high school games are still carried on Fridays, "Swap Shop" is still going strong, and the station airs a daily reading of obituaries that is sponsored by local funeral homes. Nonetheless, many things have changed. The station now gets part of its news from the Virginia Satellite Network and carries auto races courtesy of the Motor Racing Network of Daytona Beach, Florida. Its playlist features the traditionally popular country and bluegrass, but it recently introduced adult contemporary artists. Most significantly, however, WMNA is barely surviving. National advertising revenue from chain stores and fast-food franchises no longer goes to WMNA; it goes to those stations in the nearby larger communities who have ratings books to show ad agencies. The future does not look rosy, but WMNA plans to stick it out. Unlike many of the newcomers, WMNA has deep roots in its community. People call the station to help find lost pets and the station's staff frequently get gifts of pies and cakes from long-time listeners. Time will tell.

In microcosm, WMNA's story sums up what has been happening in the radio industry lately. The key trends have been increased competition, consolidation, and homogenization. The industry overall is generally prospering but recent changes in regulation, economics, and technology have raised questions about whether community-oriented radio stations with distinct personalities—like WMNA—can survive.

This chapter will examine the fast-changing and highly competitive radio business.

This small-town radio station features turntables, mikes, CD players, and other broadcast equipment all in one room, in contrast to major-market stations where the equipment and functions are located in several areas. (Tom Kelly)

ORGANIZATION OF THE RADIO INDUSTRY

There are more than a half-billion working radio sets in the United States. That works out to about two radios per person or one radio for each car. There are about 10,500 radio stations in operation. Radio is ubiquitous. Think for a moment how many working radios are in your house. The typical household has about a half-dozen. When it comes to individual listening time, the average person listens to radio about twenty-five hours per week, just five hours less than are spent watching TV.

Radio is everywhere. Sets are common in the bedroom (where they put people to sleep and wake them up), in kitchens, in cars, in offices, on city streets, on beaches, at ball games, and in a dozen other places. Additionally, in the past twenty years, there has been a tremendous increase in the number of radio stations serving the United States. Thanks in part to an FCC philosophy that encouraged competition, the number of stations grew from about 6,900 in 1970 to about 10,500 in 1989, an increase of more than 50 percent. To understand how this rapidly growing business is organized, we will examine it from several perspectives: programming, technology, format, and ownership.

Local Stations, Nets, and Syndicators

Local radio stations consist of the 10,500 or so stations that operate in cities, towns, and villages across the country. Big cities have many stations. New York City has forty-five; Los Angeles, forty-six. Smaller towns may have only one or two. White-fish, Montana, for example (population 4000), has two stations. Programming for these stations is provided by networks and by program syndication companies. Technically speaking, the distinction between a net and a syndication service is that all stations on a network carry the net program at the same time while syndicated programming is carried at different times by the stations. In practice, however, much syndicated radio programming is satellite-delivered and carried simultaneously, and many network affiliates tape net programming and broadcast it later. To make it even more complicated, the traditional networks also offer syndicated programs. Consequently, the distinction between the two services may no longer be meaningful.

Historically, networks were important programming sources during the earlier years of radio. After the emergence of TV, the importance of radio networks diminished and they provided only news and public affairs programs to their affiliates. In the mid-1980s, network radio staged a resurgence. By 1989, there were about twenty-five networks, each offering a specialized service. ABC, for example, had seven different networks, ranging from the ABC Information Network (specializing in news and talk) to the ABC-FM network (specializing in features and entertainment). NBC, which sold its networks to Westwood Broadcasting, had three nets: a youth-oriented network called The Source, the more adult-oriented NBC Radio Network, and NBC Talknet. CBS had two networks, as did United Stations. Other networks that were prominent included the AP and UPI news networks, the Satellite Music Network, Mutual Broadcasting, and Transtar. Advertising billings on network radio totaled $425 million in 1988, more than double that of 1980. Although this gain is impressive, radio is still a local medium. The $425 million figure amounts to only about 5 percent of total industry revenues.

Program syndication companies offer stations short- or long-form programming of a highly specialized nature. As of 1989, there were more than fifty companies providing syndicated programs. For example, the Beethoven Satellite Network (it calls itself a network, but most industry sources classify it as a syndicator) provides a classical music service from midnight to 6 A.M. for a $750 a month. Bonneville Broadcasting offers its "Ultra" service to easy listening stations and Churchill has a similar format called "Softsongs," targeted at women aged thirty-five to forty-nine. All Star Radio offers short "drop in" comedy vignettes to subscriber stations, and the Creative Radio Network has a six-hour "Elvis Tenth Anniversary Radio Tribute," a three-hour "Memories of Elvis," and the ever-popular "Elvis Hour."

Thanks to the networks and syndicators, program directors at local stations can now choose from a diverse menu of music, news, features, and specials.

AM and FM Stations

Radio stations speak in two voices. Stations are either AM or FM. **AM** stands for amplitude modulation, one way of transmitting a radio wave, and **FM** stands for frequency modulation, another form of transmission. As we saw in Chapter 8, since about 1975 the fortunes of FM radio have been increasing while those of AM stations were on the decline. In 1988, almost three-quarters of listenership went to the FM stations. Keep in mind, however, that some AM stations, particularly those in large markets, were doing quite well. In 1988, AMs in Chicago (WGN), San Francisco (KGO), Detroit (WJR), and Pittsburgh (KDKA) were the top-rated stations.

All physical factors being equal, radio signals sent by AM travel farther, especially at night, than signals sent by FM. This is because AM radio waves bounce off a layer of the earth's atmosphere called the ionosphere and back to the ground.

The AM dial on a typical radio set illustrates the precise frequencies in the electromagnetic spectrum where the AM station operates. AM stations are further classified by channels. There are three possible channels: clear, regional, and local. A clear channel is one with a single dominant station that is designed to provide service over a wide area. Typically, these dominant stations have a strong signal because they broadcast with 50,000 watts of power. For example, the 720 spot on the AM dial is a clear channel with WGN, Chicago, the dominant station, operating at 50,000 watts. The 770 position is also a clear channel with WABC, New York, dominant. A regional channel is one shared by many stations that serve fairly large areas. A local channel is designed to be shared by a large number of stations that broadcast only to their local communities.

FM signals do not travel as far as AM, but FM has the advantage of being able to produce better sound qualities than AM. FM radio is also less likely to be affected by outside interference such as thunderstorms. Similar to AM, FM stations are organized in classes. Class C FM stations are the most powerful, operating at 100,000 watts. Class B and Class A stations are less powerful. A glance at the FM dial of a radio reveals that FM stations operate in a different part of the electromagnetic spectrum than does AM. Figure 9.1 is a simplified diagram of the spectrum showing where AM, FM, and television signals are located. The number of radio stations sharing this spectrum is about to increase. As of mid-1988, the FCC had issued construction permits to another 761 stations.

Station Formats

Perhaps the most meaningful way we can organize radio stations is according to their **format,** a type of consistent programming designed to appeal to a certain

FIGURE 9.1 *A simplified diagram of the electromagnetic spectrum.*

Cosmic rays	Gamma rays	X–rays	Ultraviolet rays	Visible light	Infrared rays	Radio waves	Electrical energy

UHF TV channels	TV channels 7-13	FM radio	TV channels 5 and 6	TV channels 2, 3, and 4	AM radio	

535
Kilohertz

890
Megahertz

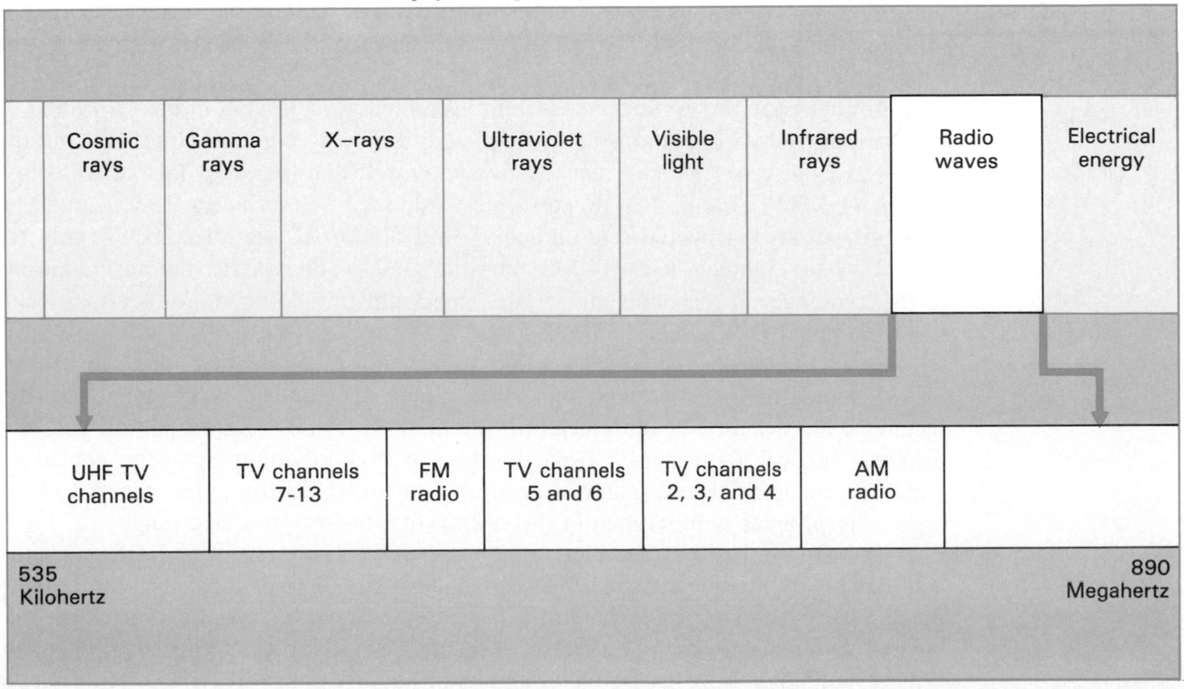

segment of the audience. Formats are important because they give a station a distinctive personality and attract a certain kind of audience that advertisers find desirable. In fact, the development of radio after 1960 is marked by the fine tuning of existing formats and the creation of new ones that appeal to people in distinct demographic and life-style categories. Most modern stations can offer an amazingly precise description of the kind of listener they want their format to attract. An adult contemporary station, for example, might set its sights on men and women, aged twenty-five to forty-five, with college educations, making more than $40,000 a year, who read *Rolling Stone,* drive either a BMW or Volvo, and go to the mall at least twice a week. In our discussion we will cover four basic categories of radio formats: music, talk, news, and ethnic.

The Music Format. This is the largest category and includes many subdivisions and variations. In the late 1980s, the two most listened to music formats were Adult Contemporary (AC) and Contemporary Hit Radio (CHR). AC was a big favorite among FM stations but a few AMs were also carrying it. The general format is a blend of current soft rock hits and suitable oldies, usually about 20 percent current and 80 percent oldies. For example, Fleetwood Mac, the Moody Blues, James Taylor, and Paul Simon were commonly heard on AC stations along with Bruce Hornsby, the Miami Sound Machine, and Whitney Houston. There are three main subdivisions of AC. One specializes in "less talk, more music" and emphasizes a softer rock sound. This format is geared for the target audience aged thirty-five to fifty-four. The second type is the full-service AC station, which puts more emphasis on personalities, news, and weather, especially during "drive time" (6 A.M.–10 A.M. and 4 P.M.–7 P.M.). The third type mixes more Top-40 hits with the oldies and tries for more eighteen- to twenty-four-year-olds.

Contemporary Hit Radio was a derivative of what used to be called Top 40. CHR featured a small playlist of hit records in a fast rotation. There was about a 40–50 percent overlap in the songs played by CHR and AC stations, but CHR stayed with more traditional rock music and featured artists such as Van Halen and INXS, two acts that would rarely be heard on AC stations. CHR tried to appeal to the twelve-to-twenty-five age group.

Another popular format was Album-Oriented Rock (AOR). This format was used primarily by FM stations and specialized in playing popular album cuts put out by a particular type of rock artist. Many people felt that the AOR format was close to that of MTV. Featured AOR performers included Whitesnake, Poison, and Def Leppard, artists that would seldom appear on CHR or AC stations. AOR's primary appeal was to eighteen- to thirty-four-year-old males. Some AOR stations are aiming at the audience on the older end of that spectrum by adding more "classic" cuts from the late 1970s and early 1960s.

Beautiful Music stations play lush instrumental selections that are arrangements of old standards, popular hits, and show tunes. The music is designed to fill a listener's environment without calling attention to itself. (Some people call this format "musical wallpaper.") Typically, long periods of commercial-free music are featured. Beautiful Music stations appeal to an older demographic group and are especially popular with women in the twenty-five-to-forty-five age range.

Country stations, as the name suggests, play hit country and western singles and employ DJs who are down home, friendly, and knowledgeable about country music. In recent years, the dividing line between country and popular music has blurred somewhat as many entertainers (e.g., Olivia Newton-John, Willie Nelson, Waylon Jennings) have crossed over and had hits in both the AC and country charts.

What's in a Name? Choosing the Right Call Letters

Most successfully marketed products promote brand awareness. In radio, brand awareness means that people are aware of the name of their radio station. To make their names easier to remember, many radio stations have distinctive call letters.

Some identify themselves with their cities. A San Francisco station is KABL (cable); Las Vegas has KENO and KLUC (luck); Atlantic City has WIIN: Anchorage, Alaska, has KYAK (kayak); Chicago, the Windy City, has WIND as well as WLUP, the Loop; Waco, Texas, has (what else?) WACO.

Other stations highlight their formats. The "Power" formula has several adherents: WPOW, Miami; WWPR, New York; KPWR, Los Angeles; to name just a few. Rock stations tend to like calls such as WHTZ, Newark; WQHT, New York; KROQ, Los Angeles, and WROQ, Charlotte, North Carolina.

Foxes run about the airwaves: KFQX, Abilene, Texas; WFOX, Atlanta, Georgia; WFQX, Front Royal, Virginia; WFXX, South Williamsport, Pennsylvania; WFXZ, Washington, North Carolina; and WFXA, Augusta, Georgia. Eagles soar all over: WEGL, Auburn, Alabama; WEGX, Philadelphia; KEGL, Fort Worth; KEAG, Anchorage; and WEGA, Puerto Rico.

Lots of stations are magical: KMGC, Dallas; KMGX, Hanford, California; KMGQ, Goleta, California; WMGQ, New Brunswick, New Jersey; WMGX, Portland, Maine; and WMJC, Battle Creek, Michigan.

Talk formats use their calls to tell about themselves: KMNY programs financial news; WFAN carries nothing but sports and sports talk; KFYI is an all-news station; and KMDY runs a comedy format.

We could go on but it probably wouldn't be WISE (Asheville, North Carolina). And by now you're probably thinking WHEW (Fort Myers, Florida).

The biggest appeal of the country format seems to be among twenty-five- to sixty-four-year-old men and women. Country music was the format played by the greatest number of radio stations, but country stations have been facing aging audiences, a general decline in country music popularity, and increasing competition from rock stations. Program directors have been looking for ways to attract a younger audience. Many stations adopted a "lite country" format that is somewhat in the direction of AC programming. Other country stations went in the opposite direction, going back to the basic country sound. In addition, the country format was helped in the late 1980s by the emergence of younger artists such as Randy Travis, Rosanne Cash, and Dwight Yoakam, who appealed to the twenty-five-to-thirty-four age group.

The Middle of the Road (MOR) format, which is widely used among radio stations, is somewhat hard to describe. As the name implies, this format avoids extremes such as hard rock and semiclassical selections. In their place, the MOR station uses contemporary music and an occasional soft-rock AC hit. Recordings by artists such as John Denver, Neil Diamond, and Barry Manilow are common on MOR stations. Further, MOR stations rely on the personality of their DJs to draw an audience. Particularly important are the morning and evening drive time DJs, who are on the air when the station has its biggest audience. The prime appeal of MOR stations is to twenty-five- to forty-five-year-olds.

A couple of new formats have recently emerged. The most popular of these was "The Wave," a format with little talk that fuses light jazz, soft rock, and New

Country music programming is one of the most widely played commercially successful radio formats. RoseAnne Cash is one of the medium's emerging popular performers. (Larry Busacca/ Retna)

Age music. Designed to reach the baby-boomers, The Wave format offers such artists as Earl Klugh, Andreas Vollenweider, and Spyro Gyra along with Dire Straits, Toto, and Peter Gabriel. Although referred to as "audio Valium" by its critics, The Wave had been adopted by many large-market stations and was holding its own against the more established formats.

A second emerging format was Churban–a cross between CHR and black urban music. The format featured such artists as Club Nouveau and Run-D.M.C. and was doing extremely well in large cities with multiethnic populations. In addition to these, other music formats programmed by smaller numbers of stations include jazz, oldies, big band, and classical.

The Talk Format. The talk format attracts listeners in the thirty-five- to sixty-five-year-old age group. Common types of programs that appear on stations using the talk format are interview shows featuring well-known guests who respond to questions from outside callers; advice shows, which also take questions from the audience; and pure call-in shows, in which the audience calls in to discuss a specific topic suggested by the host. News, weather, traffic reports, and feature material are blended in with these programs. Unlike the music formats that do not demand their listeners' close attention, the talk format requires that its audience concentrate on the program in order to follow what is said. More and more AM stations have adopted the talk format.

In an attempt to win back listeners, several large-market AM stations went to a "shock" radio format in the late 1980s. Controversial hosts like Howard Stern presided over programs that touched on previously taboo topics on radio. Some stations featured content that the FCC considered indecent, and it cracked down on this format. The "shock jocks," as they were called, toned it down a bit. At the other end of the spectrum, another popular talk format featured religious programming. Although their TV counterparts ran into some problems in the late 1980s, radio evangelists remained popular, as evidenced by the more than 550 stations that carry this format.

The News Format. The news format emphasizes information. National, regional, and local news reports are broadcast periodically throughout the day. Sports, weather, editorials, public-affairs programs, and an occasional feature round out the programming day. All-news stations appeal primarily to a male audience in the twenty-five- to fifty-four-year-old age category. As with the talk format, all-news stations are primarily on the AM band.

There have been some innovations in the news and talk categories in the last five years. A New York City station went to an all-sports format. KMNY in California adopted twenty-four–hour financial news and talk programs. A Florida station introduced an all-motivation format. Perhaps the most innovative was KPAL-AM in Little Rock, Arkansas, which introduced a full-time format aimed exclusively at children.

Howard Stern, the controversial radio talk show host, is shown here at a rally at the United Nations. His prison garb demonstrates his claim that he is a prisoner of censorship as a result of the FCC's recent move to enforce tighter bans on indecent and offensive material on the air. (UPI/Bettmann Newsphotos)

Consisting of a blend of stories, features, poetry, and music, the station's programming has won numerous awards.

Black and Ethnic Formats. These formats aim for special audiences that are defined primarily by race and nationality. There are about 165 stations that program for the black audience and another 160 Spanish-language stations. About thirty stations are aimed at other ethnic groups. For many years, black and ethnic formats were targeted toward a general audience, offering a mix of music, news, and features. Recently, black and ethnic stations have begun to specialize in their choice of music. Like all radio stations, black and ethnic stations are paying closer attention to their demographics.

Format Homogenization

If you've ever taken a long auto trip and listened to the radio stations in the various communities along your route, one of the things you might have noticed is that radio stations sound pretty much alike no matter where you are. Almost all of the major music formats are represented in the large and medium markets and it seems that every market has its morning "zoo crew," an AC station that specializes in "the classic hits" of the sixties, seventies, and eighties, a CHR station that calls itself "Power" or "Z" or "Q" something-or-other, an easy listening station with a "warm" format that dedicates love songs at night, and maybe even an AM station that specializes in "golden oldies." Even the DJs sound pretty much the same.

There are several reasons behind this trend toward homogenization. First, many large-market stations are owned by groups and what works for a group owner in one market is likely to work in another. Second, satellite-delivered music services (see below) are becoming more common. This means that stations all over the country are playing standardized music. Finally, radio has become so competitive that programming decisions are based on the recommendations of program consultants and audience research firms that compile playlists based on audience surveys and focus groups. There aren't many of these consultants and firms around, and the same records tend to score high from market to market. Consequently, the recommendations tend to be the same from radio station to radio station. Many stations prefer to adopt a "safe" format, one that has worked in similar markets, rather than risking a sizable amount of money on an untested format.

Ownership

Federal Communications Commission regulations state that no one person or organization can own more than twelve AM and twelve FM stations (unless minority-controlled, in which case the number is fourteen each). This puts an upper limit on the amount of station ownership concentration allowed in radio. There are other rules that mitigate against concentration. For example, except in large markets, one organization cannot own two AM or two FM stations that serve the same basic market. Thus in most markets, a single owner can control only one AM and one FM station, a common pattern of ownership, with about 70 percent of FM stations owned by organizations that also operate AM stations in the same area.

The enactment of the 12–12–12 Rule and a change in tax laws prompted a record selling binge in radio in 1986 and 1987 when more than $5 billion worth of radio stations changed hands. When the dust settled, it was obvious that in terms of listenership, the industry had become concentrated with several firms, such as Infinity, Jacor, Emmis, and Malrite, dominating the larger markets.

The trend toward concentration is even more pronounced at the network level. In 1985, Westwood One, a radio network which distributes programming to about 3800 stations, acquired the Mutual Broadcasting System with its 775 basic affiliates. In 1987, Westwood bought the oldest broadcasting network in the country, the NBC Radio Network, from General Electric, for $50 million. This means that the network radio business is dominated by three major players, Westwood, ABC, and, to a lesser extent, CBS.

PRODUCING RADIO PROGRAMS

Departments and Staff

The departmental structure of a radio station varies according to its size. Obviously, a small station with five or six employees has a different departmental setup than a large station with a hundred-person staff. Figure 9.2 illustrates the arrangement at a typical medium-sized station.

FIGURE 9.2 *Departments and staff at a medium-size radio station.*

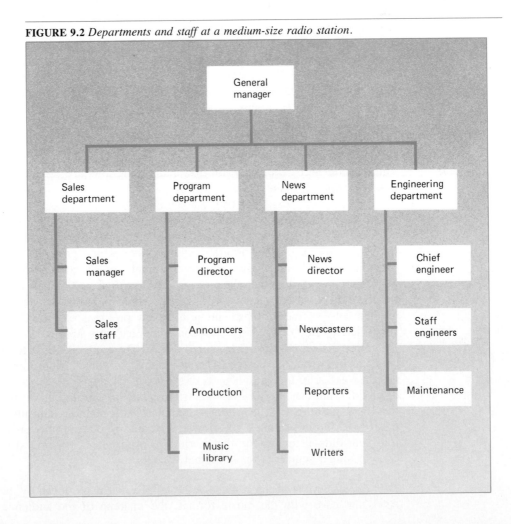

The two top management positions are the general manager and the program director. The manager has the responsibility for planning and carrying out station policy, maintaining contact with the community, and monitoring program content, audience ratings, and sales information. The program director is responsible for the station's sound. He or she supervises the music or other program material that the station broadcasts and is also responsible for the hiring and firing of announcers and DJs.

Most stations are divided into the four departments shown in Fig. 9.2. The sales department consists of the sales manager and the station's sales force. The news department is responsible for compiling the station's local newscasts and rewriting the wire-service reports of national and regional news. The programming department includes DJs, copywriters, and promotion personnel. The engineering department, under the supervision of the chief engineer, is staffed with technicians responsible for keeping the station on the air and maintaining the equipment. Computers have made a big impact on all departments of a radio station in both large and small markets. Special software packages are available for stations to help them bill clients, make budgets, track ratings, list spot availabilities, manage their record inventories of commercial time, plan record playlists, and prepare news copy.

Use of compact discs is now the norm at many stations. Their better quality and ease of storage offer significant advantages over conventional LPs and tapes. Digital audio tape (DAT), a system that converts audio signals to numbers that are read by a computerized sound processor, is on the way (assuming its legal problems are settled) and offers radio stations even more advantages than CDs. DAT has the same sound quality and is easier to handle and maintain than CDs, and, above all, it's cheaper. A 1000-cut record library would cost about $1000 on DAT. A comparable library on CD would run nearly $100,000. The biggest problem with DAT is that cuts are hard to cue up.

Putting Together a Program

This section will concentrate on how radio programs are produced for the music, talk, and news formats.

Music Format. Radio programs are put together either by the station's program director and DJs, who receive records from record companies and local retail record outlets, or by an outside programming service, which provides the station with a package of music and voice. For the moment, let us examine how the staff of a local station puts together their program. The first step is generally to lay out a **format wheel** (also called format clock), which is simply a pie chart of an hour divided into segments representing different program elements. Figure 9.3 is a simplified version of a wheel for a contemporary rock station.

Note that the music is structured to flow from one segment to another. Album cuts and hits from the past are spread around the wheel. Additional wheels would be constructed for the various parts of the broadcast day (i.e., one wheel for morning drive time, another for 10 A.M.–4 P.M., another for evening drive time, and another for 7 P.M.–midnight). The 7 P.M.–midnight wheel might contain more hits from the past if the station's rating book showed a greater proportion of twenty-five- to thirty-four-year-olds listening for that period. Morning and evening drive time might contain longer segments for news and weather.

Talk Format. Most of the content of the talk format is produced by the local station. As is the case with the music format, the makeup of the audience is taken into

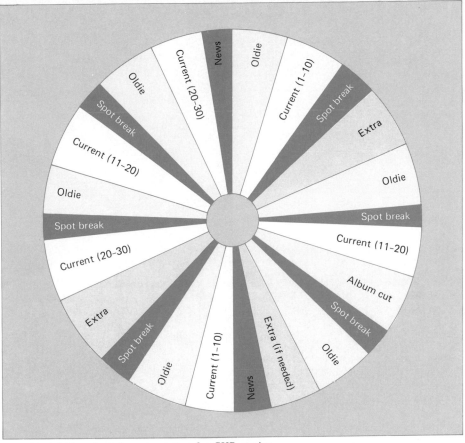

FIGURE 9.3 *Hot clock format rotation for CHR station.*

account in scheduling the type of show to be broadcast during different parts of the day. During drive time, talk segments should be relatively short and liberally interspersed with news, weather, and traffic reports. The audience for the 10 A.M.– 4 P.M. day segment tends to be primarily female and, therefore, topics for discussion should reflect the interests of this group. The early evening audience is generally younger and contains more males. Many talk stations program a sports call-in show during this time period to attract a younger audience.

Producing a talk show requires more equipment than does a simple DJ program. Speaker telephones and extra telephone lines are needed, as well as a delay system. This device gives the talk-show moderator a seven- to thirty-second delay period during which he or she can censor what is said by the caller. Another important part of the talk show is the telephone screener, who intercepts phone calls from the audience before they are taken by the host or hostess. The screener ranks the waiting calls for importance, letting the most interesting callers go first, and filters out crank calls or calls from regulars who contact the station too frequently.

All-News Format. The all-news station also works with a programming wheel, similar to that of the music format. Instead of music, however, the news wheel shows the spacing between headlines, weather, news, sports, business reports, and commercials. It also illustrates the **cycle,** the amount of time that elapses before the program order is repeated. By way of illustration, Fig. 9.4, page 212, shows a simplified news wheel with a thirty-minute cycle.

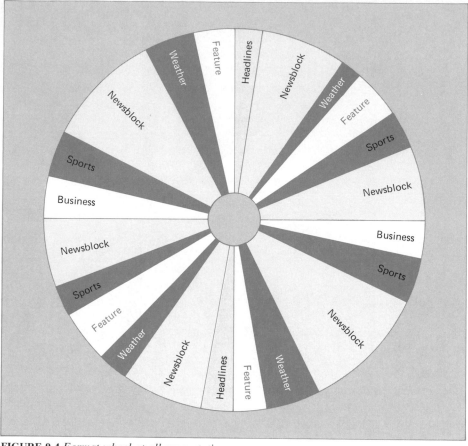

FIGURE 9.4 *Format wheel at all-news station.*

The all-news format is the most difficult to produce. A large staff, consisting of anchor persons, a managing editor, local reporters, editors, rewrite people, a traffic reporter, and stringers (freelance reporters who are paid per story), is needed. The list of necessary facilities is also long: radio wire services, sports wire, weather wire, mobile units, police and fire-frequency scanners, short-wave receiver, and perhaps even a helicopter.

Local Versus Outside Production

Local stations that rely on music for much of their programming get most of their records free or for a nominal cost. Record companies realize that radio play for their releases is necessary to sell their product. Consequently, most record companies employ promoters, who visit the most influential radio stations in a community and deliver their company's latest releases. Other stations subscribe to a service that sends them current material. In some markets, radio stations arrange a deal with retail record outlets whereby the record store sends the station new releases and in return the station plays commercials for the store.

Local production involves patter by the DJs, newscasts, play-by-play reports of sports events, interviews, call-in shows, traffic reports, editorials, and public-affairs programs. Talk and all-news stations fill most of their air time with locally produced material.

As mentioned, a growing number of stations—perhaps 1500 or so—are depending more and more on programming done outside the station, either by a network or by a program syndication service, and delivered by satellite. The switch to network or syndication generally means that the station can cut back drastically on its on-air staff (saving money in the process). Programming fees generally run from $700 to $1500 per month, but most nets and syndicators will waive the fee in large markets in order to be represented. The net retains two minutes per hour to sell on a national basis and the local station can sell all of the other commercial availabilities. Basically, all the station needs to function is a satellite dish and a sales staff.

In addition to saving money, the satellite service offers other advantages. The music programming is put together by experts using audience research that some stations cannot afford. Further, the sound is slick and more professional than many stations could achieve. On the downside, satellite-delivered programming has been criticized for sounding bland and for a general lack of excitement. Additionally, the programming is not geared for a local market. A disc jockey sitting in an LA or New York studio has no idea about what's going on in local markets in Iowa or Alabama or wherever the show is airing. To overcome this disadvantage, many satellite services offer subscriber stations prerecorded promos and announcements personalized to the local market.

ECONOMICS IN THE RADIO INDUSTRY

The profit picture for radio has generally been good in recent years. In 1988, the entire radio industry reported revenues of about $7.7 billion, up slightly from 1987. Profits were up every year from 1974 to 1978 but dropped a bit in 1979–1981. Profits were up the next two years, and in 1988 the average profit margin was about 6 to 8 percent.

Sources of Revenue

Radio stations earn their money by selling advertising time. The amount that a radio station charges for time is included in its rate card. A typical radio commercial costs several hundred dollars in large cities. The same commercial in a small town might cost only a few dollars. WMNA, the station mentioned at the opening of this chapter, charges about $3 for a thirty-second spot.

Like the television industry, the radio industry has three different sources of income from the sale of commercial time. The first comes from the sale of spots on network programs to national advertisers trying to reach a broad market. The second is the sale of time on local stations to advertisers who wish to reach a specific region (e.g., the Northeast) or a specific type of market (e.g., rural areas). This is called national spot advertising. The third source is advertising purchased by local establishments that want their commercials to be heard only in the immediate community. In 1988, each of these sources represented the following amounts of each dollar of radio revenue:

Network	1¢
National spot	21¢
Local	78¢

Although big-city stations employed large numbers of people and were usually owned by big companies, the radio industry was essentially an assortment of small to

Music Licensing: ASCAP and BMI

The Copyright Law of the United States holds that no one may legally perform a musical work for profit without the permission of the copyright holder. The courts have also held that playing a record over a commercial station constitutes such a performance. This law poses a potential problem for radio broadcasters who play dozens of records per day. How do they go about getting permission from the hundreds of copyright owners of the songs they wish to play? How do the copyright holders go about granting permission and collecting payment from the thousands of radio stations that use their material? To solve this dilemma, music licensing organizations were created. They negotiate for permission for the performance of music by stations that wish to use it and secure payment for permission on behalf of the copyright owners. There are two major licensing organizations: the American Society of Composers, Authors and Publishers (ASCAP) and Broadcast Music Incorporated (BMI).

Radio stations enter into contracts or licenses with these organizations. The stations usually arrange for "blanket" licenses, which allow them to use all the compositions that are listed by the organization for an unlimited number of performances. Both ASCAP and BMI charge fees for this license. These fees amount to about 1 to 2 percent of the station's gross receipts. The copyright holders, in turn, are paid by ASCAP and BMI. The amount that is paid is determined in two ways. First, all network radio and television content is monitored by ASCAP and BMI to discover what songs are played and how often they are performed. Second, frequency of use by local radio and TV stations is determined by sampling a small number of stations and projecting these figures to arrive at a total for all stations. The copyright holders are then paid based on the number of calculated performances.

medium-sized stations that derived most of its money from local home-town businesses. As the numbers indicate, the overwhelming amount of revenue in radio came from local commercials.

General Expenses

Expenses in radio are divided into five areas: (1) technical, (2) program, (3) selling, (4) general administration, and advertising. Technical expenses include the payroll for the engineering staff and the cost of maintaining and replacing technical equipment. Program costs cover salaries paid to talent, cost of tape and records, and music fees paid to the music licensing organizations (see boxed material). Sales costs are made up of the salaries of the sales staff and all of the other expenses that go with selling. General administrative expenses include the salaries of all management, secretarial, and clerical personnel, the depreciation of physical facilities, the cost of office supplies, and any interest that is due on loans to the station. As of 1988, the expense dollar was allocated among these five areas as follows:

Technical	4¢
Program	21¢
Sales	24¢
General administration	41¢
Advertising/Promotion	10¢

The low cost of programming reflects the fact that many radio stations pay little or nothing for the records they receive.

Increasing Competition

The proliferation of radio stations has made the industry one of the most competitive in all the media. The overall revenue pie has been sliced into smaller and smaller pieces. In the large markets, which account for the most revenue, the number one station in the market seldom has more than a 10 percent share of the total average listening audience. Further, as Figure 9.5 shows, the gap between the leading station and its competitors has narrowed over the years.

In large markets, listeners generally have several different versions of the same format to choose from. At last count, Los Angeles had nine AC stations; New York had four AOR stations. Increasingly, the same format is competing with itself for listeners. In situations like this, most stations are doing more and more promotions and giveaways to attract listeners (see boxed material).

FIGURE 9.5 *Difference in audience share of number one, number five, and number ten rated stations in Top-Ten markets 1976–1988. Courtesy Katz Radio Group.*

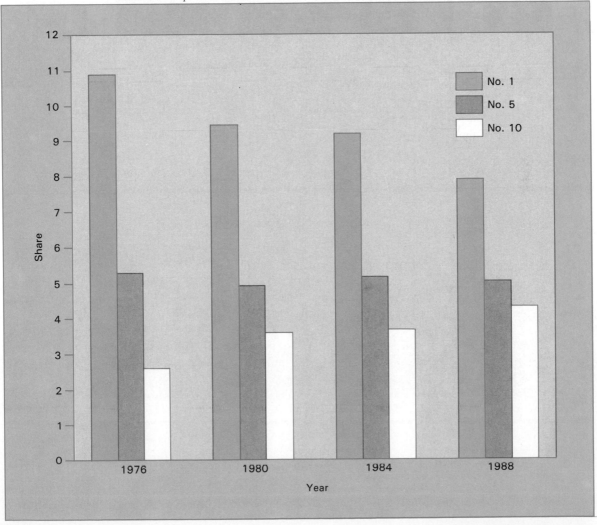

Getting Listeners: Station Promotions

In the highly competitive world of radio, when several stations in a market are programming basically the same format, the difference between a successful station and a failing station may be the amount of money, time, and effort a station devotes to promotion. The traditional station promotion usually involved giving away money to lucky listeners. In some big markets, stations were giving away more than a million dollars in prize money in '988. Other stations were sponsoring more unusual promotions.

- A Washington, D.C., station awarded Super Bowl tickets to a listener who was willing to stomp on 150 pounds of oranges and surf on the resulting orange juice.

- A Dallas station sponsored a "Mr. Puniverse" (as in puny) contest open only to males who weighed less than 145 pounds. Contestants had to appear in swimsuits and answer inane questions. The winner got a vacation to a beach resort and was told to watch out for bullies who might kick sand in this face.

- A Denver station offered $10,000 to anyone who would legally change his or her name to the station's slogan. The winner was Mr. The New Q-103 FM.

- A Nashville station offered a breast enlargement operation as the grand prize in one of its promotions. The same station also ran a contest in which a lucky (?) listener was covered with honey and then permitted to roll around in a swimming pool filled with $100,000. The winner got to keep whatever stuck.

Perhaps the most bizarre promotion, however, was a kind of reverse giveaway. To prove how effective his station's promotions were, a Dallas DJ, asked listeners to send him $20. He promised them nothing in return. No contests. No winners. He just asked each listener for $20. The DJ expected maybe a few dozen responses. Three days later the DJ had received nearly a quarter of a million dollars. At last report, the station was still trying to figure out what to do with the money.

(Scott Baker—Y107)

Noncommercial Radio

Many of the early radio stations that went on the air during the 1920s were founded by educational institutions. As the commercial broadcasting system became firmly established, many educational stations were bought by commercial broadcasters, and the fortunes of noncommercial radio dwindled. In 1945, with the coming of FM broadcasting, the FCC was persuaded to set aside several frequencies for educational broadcasting. This action sparked a rebirth of interest in educational broadcasting so that by 1988 there were about 1300 noncommercial radio stations on the air.

Most noncommercial radio stations are owned by colleges, universities, high schools, or other educational institutions. Others are owned by private foundations. Noncommercial radio gets its support from the institutions that own the stations. Ultimately, much of this support comes from tax revenue since taxes support most public educational institutions. Other sources of support are endowments (gifts), grants from foundations or the federal government, and listener donations.

Noncommercial stations are served by two networks. National Public Radio (NPR) was founded in 1970. NPR provides program service to about 300 affiliates across the country. Member stations pay a fee ranging from $2,000 to $20,000 per year and receive in return about fifty hours of programming a week. Many of these shows are produced at NPR's headquarters; others are produced by member stations and distributed by NPR. Probably the best known NPR program is the award-winning *All Things Considered*. The other noncommercial network is American Public Radio, whose best known show was Garrison Keillor's "Prairie Home Companion." (Keillor left and then returned to radio in 1988 but his future with APR was still unknown.) It's estimated that about 10 million people listen to public radio every week.

CAREERS IN RADIO

There are about 150,000 people employed at radio stations and radio networks. The average station will employ about fourteen full-time people. Competition is tight, but thousands of young people find jobs in radio every year. As in most other industries, radio stations prefer to hire experienced people. How does a newcomer gain experience? One good way is to volunteer to work at your college or university radio station. Try to do as many jobs as possible and learn as much as you can. Another possibility is to arrange for an internship at a local station.

If you intend to look for a job as talent (someone who works in front of the microphone—DJ, announcer, newscaster), you will need to put together an audition tape. This is a five- to fifteen-minute sample of your work. If you're applying for a job at a music format station, the audition tape should include your introduction to appropriate records, some chatter, and a commercial or two. If you're looking for a job as a newscaster, the tape should include your reading of some straight news stories and your integration of some taped interviews into the program. The audition tape allows a potential employer to hear your voice, delivery, style, and general air personality. It constitutes your audition for the job.

Entry-Level Positions

The best place to break into radio is at a small-market station. There are generally more beginning-level jobs in small markets, and the competition is not as fierce as it is in major markets. Another advantage to working at a small-market station is the wide variety of experiences you're likely to have. Small stations hire people who are versatile. A DJ might have to work in sales. A salesperson might have to write commercial copy and produce radio ads. Secretaries and receptionists may cover news stories. It would be virtually impossible to get this sort of experience at a large station.

Most employment counselors recommend that a beginner in radio take any job that is offered to him or her at a station, even if the job is not exactly what the person wants to do. Landing a job is probably more important than starting off in the department that was your first choice. Once inside the organization, it is easier for you to move to your preferred area.

The two areas where most entry-level jobs occur are the programming and sales departments. Of these two, the programming area is the more competitive. Many people who enter the radio field seem to want jobs as announcers or DJs. As a result, there is an oversupply of people in this area. Nonetheless, it is possible to find a job if you are persistent and willing to work unusual hours. Volunteer your services for the midnight to 7 A.M. shift or express a willingness to work weekends or holidays. Tell the program director you're willing to substitute any day any time for a DJ who gets sick. Once you get your own air slot, you can prove yourself as a steady, competent professional and move to better things. Roughly the same sort of advice would apply to those interested in radio news. Make yourself available on the weekends. Offer to work as a stringer. Be persistent.

The best chance of landing a beginning job in radio can be found in the sales department. Radio stations, especially those in smaller markets, are usually in need of competent salespeople with a knowledge of and an interest in radio. If you are able to handle a sales job, it could be the start of a lucrative career in radio.

For comparison purposes, here are some 1987 salary figures. A general manager in a large market (more than 2.5 million) averaged about $107,000 in salary; a general manager in a small market (less than 25,000) made about $29,000. Large-market DJs averaged about $37,000 (some big-market superstars made much more); small market, about $12,500. A sales manager averaged $84,000 in a large market and $24,000 in a small market. Program directors in large markets averaged $53,000; their small-market counterparts, about $14,000.

Upward Mobility

The first job in radio is seldom a lifetime commitment. It usually leads to more challenging positions with more responsibility, more opportunity for creativity, and a larger salary. For talent, there are two distinct avenues of upward mobility. For DJs, it consists of moving up to larger markets and better time slots. The ultimate goal of most DJs is a drive-time air shift in one of the top ten markets. In addition, many DJs progress within a station by moving up to the chief announcer's spot and from there to program director. Radio news reporters also strive to move into the big markets, and those with an interest in administration move into the director's slot. An occasional program director or news director moves up to the general manager's job.

The sales department offers the best route for upward mobility. Competent salespeople are given bigger and more profitable accounts to service. Some will move up to the sales manager position. From sales manager, many will progress to general manager. Salespeople are skilled at making money for the station. They are also used to dealing with people and have many contacts in the community. All of these factors help them move into top management positions. It is an established fact that most radio station managers got their start in the sales department.

Before closing our discussion of radio careers we should point out that radio stations are not the only places of potential employment. Program syndicators such as Drake Chenault hire announcers and those experienced in programming music formats. Companies that produce packaged feature programs need producers, writers, and directors. Radio wire services such as the Associated Press and United Press International need reporters and writers. In short, there are opportunities outside the scope of traditional radio stations.

SUGGESTIONS FOR FURTHER READING

The following books contain more information about the concepts and topics discussed in this chapter.

BITTNER, JOHN, *Professional Broadcasting*, Englewood Cliffs, N.J.: Prentice-Hall, 1981.

BUSBY, LINDA, AND DONALD PARKER, *The Art and Science of Radio*, Boston: Allyn and Bacon, 1984.

FORNATALE, PETER, AND JOSHUA MILLS, *Radio in the Television Age*, Woodstock, N.Y.: Overlook Press, 1980.

HILLIARD, ROBERT, *Radio Broadcasting*, New York: Longman, 1985.

KEITH, MICHAEL, *Radio Programming*, Boston: Focal Press, 1987.

KEITH, MICHAEL, AND JOSEPH KRAUSE, *The Radio Station*, Boston: Focal Press, 1989.

SHERMAN, BARRY, *Telecommunications Management: Radio, TV, Cable*, New York: McGraw-Hill, 1986.

Chapter 10
Structure of the Recording Industry

There's people out there turning music into gold.
John Stewart, Gold, *RSO Records*. Copyright © 1979 by Unichappell Music, Inc. and Bugle Publishing. All rights controlled by Unichappell Music, Inc. International Copyright Secured. All Rights Reserved.

Gold. Platinum. Millions. These are the favorite words of the record industry. After some lean years early in the decade, the industry is now hearing its favorite words much more often. Thanks to MTV, compact discs (CDs), the reemergence of contemporary hit radio, some hot movie soundtracks, and the revival of classic rock,

Bon Jovi, one of the hottest rock-n'-roll bands in America in the late 1980s. (Gary Gershoff/Retna)

the roller coaster record industry was back at the top. In the early part of the decade only a few albums went platinum (sales of more than a million) and hardly any went double platinum (sales of more than 2 million). In contrast, consider these figures from 1987–1988: the rock group Bon Jovi sold 8 million copies of *Slippery When Wet;* the *Dirty Dancing* soundtrack sold 6 million; Michael Jackson's *Bad* and Whitney Houston's *Whitney* each sold 5 million; even mall denizen Tiffany sold 3 million of her debut album. The record industry was doing so well that there was talk it might have to introduce another precious metal to denote huge sales. Maybe plutonium is next. Whether this prosperity will last is anybody's guess, but, for now at least, the record industry is on a growth curve. This chapter will examine the structure of this unpredictable but exciting industry.

ORGANIZATION OF THE RECORD INDUSTRY

The recording industry consists of the various creative talents and business enterprises that originate, produce, and distribute records to consumers. Rock music accounts for about 60 percent of the total sales of the record industry; country and rhythm and blues account for another 10 percent each; gospel, jazz, and classical account for the rest. Although this chapter concentrates on rock music, remember that the other music styles are also part of the industry. For our purposes, we will divide the business into four major segments: (1) talent, (2) production, (3) distribution, and (4) retail.

Talent

The talent segment of the industry consists of all the singers, musicians, song writers, arrangers, and lyricists who hope to make money by recording and selling their songs. The words "hope to make money" are important because far more performers are laboring in virtual obscurity in and around Detroit, Austin, Nashville, New York, and Los Angeles than are cashing royalty checks from their recordings. Exactly how many people are "out there" hoping to make it big is impossible to pinpoint. We do know that almost $3 billion of musical instruments are sold every year and a great deal of this money is spent by the 30,000–50,000 aspiring performers estimated by industry experts to be looking for a big break.

Performers start out as a beginning act. The initial motivation may be simply personal pleasure. Many begin performing during high school. Bob Dylan (then known as Bob Zimmerman) started out with a high school band in Hibbing, Minnesota. These beginning acts rarely last. Most break up with some members dropping out of music and others reforming into new groups. Some group members leave their groups and become single performers; some single performers join groups.

The novice musician or musical group eventually graduates to a "traveling act," which plays anywhere and everywhere to gain experience, a little money, and maybe some recognition. Traveling acts play in bars and clubs where they are little more than human jukeboxes providing accompaniment or background music. REM and REO Speedwagon played college clubs in Athens, Georgia, and Champaign, Illinois, respectively, while getting their acts together. Terence Trent D'Arby first toured Germany with a group called Touch and later played clubs in Britain as a single after the group disintegrated. INXS got together in high school and toured Australia for eleven years before becoming an international success. Cyndi Lauper spent a great deal of time in total obscurity with a group called Blue Angel before she found orange hair and fame. The income for beginning acts is meager, and the work is exhausting. For most performers, this stage is one in which they learn the trade and pay their dues to the profession. In the early years, the main goal of most acts is to survive.

If the act is talented and lucky, it may be noticed by an A&R (artist and repertoire) scout from a record company, an independent producer, agent, or manager. If things work out right, the act is signed to a contract by a recording company.

Production

The entrance of the recording company marks the transition to the production phase of the industry. The company brings the act to a recording studio where a large number of songs are recorded. Audio engineers and elaborate sound-mixing facilities are used to get exactly the right sound. Eventually, a single or an album is put together. The company also supplies publicity, advertising, merchandising, and packaging expertise. Promotion, which in the recording industry consists primarily of getting the record played on influential radio stations and getting the music video on TV, is also the responsibility of the company. There are dozens of record companies, but five dominate the business. They are CBS (Sony), Warner, Polygram, EMI/Capitol, and RCA.

Distribution

There are three main outlets for record distribution: (1) direct retail, (2) rack jobbers, and (3) one-stops. Of these three outlets, the rack jobber is the most important, accounting for approximately 65 percent of all record sales. Retail stores are a distant second, accounting for about 15–20 percent. Direct retail refers to regular record stores that specialize in the sales of records, tapes, and related equipment. Many retail stores are chain operations with several outlets in different parts of the country. Chains having more than 100 retail stores include two that are typically located in shopping malls, Camelot and Record Bar, and several that are "free standing": The Wherehouse, Musicland, and Western Merchandisers.

Rack jobbers service the record racks that are located in variety or large department stores. Such large concerns as Sears, J.C. Penney, and K-mart all have their record departments serviced by rack jobbers. The rack jobber chooses the records that are sold in these locations. The department stores are then relieved of the task of keeping track of what's popular, ordering new releases, reordering, returning unused merchandise, and so on. In some arrangements, the rack jobber makes money by collecting a percentage of the price of each record that is sold. In other cases, the rack jobber simply leases space in the store and owns as well as operates the record department.

One-stops purchase records from record companies and resell them to retail stores and juke box operators who are not in a position to buy directly from the record company. For example, a small, independently owned retail store might not qualify for credit from the record companies and so might purchase its records from a one-stop.

There are two channels of distributing records to these three outlets: independent distributors and branch distributors. Independent distributors (called "indies") are independently owned companies that contract with various labels to physically distribute their records to their accounts. A branch distributor is linked to one of the big five record companies mentioned above, and the local distribution offices are owned by the record company. After some bad years, independent distributors staged a comeback in the late 1980s. In fact, there were more independently distributed singles in the top hundred in 1986 than in the three previous years combined. The independents were helped particularly by the increased popularity of urban contemporary, rap, and rhythm and blues music. Hit groups, such as Run-D.M.C. and the Timex Social Club, also helped the independents get more air play on radio stations, which in turn upped the sales of their products.

During the middle to late 1970s, retail stores were given a 100-percent-return option; that is, they could return to the distributor for credit all of the records that they couldn't sell. When record sales started to decline in 1979 and 1980, this unlimited-return policy was changed and retail outlets were given credit for only 20 percent returns. This prompted retail stores to order smaller quantities of records—a fact that in turn led record companies to produce fewer copies of a single or album for distribution. Even with the turnaround in record sales in the mid-1980s, record companies were still being conservative in the number of records and tapes shipped to retailers. Figure 10.1 summarizes the distribution process.

Retail

The trend in record retailing has been consolidation; as a result, a few large chain stores now dominate the business. The biggest chain, Musicland, which also operates

FIGURE 10.1 *Record distribution channels.*

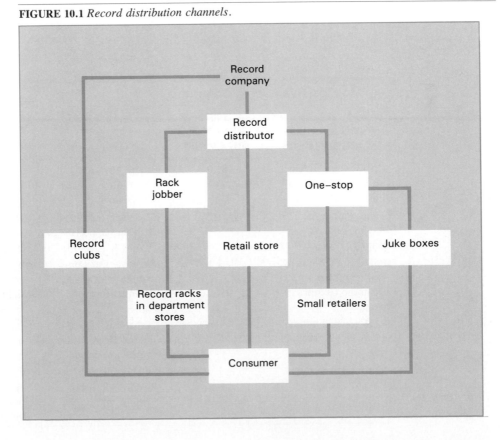

under the names Sam Goody and Discount Records, has 631 locations; Target Stores has 332; Trans World Music, which includes Peaches and Recordland, has 319. In addition, consumers purchase discs and tapes at the record sections of numerous department stores and through the various record clubs that operate through the U.S. Postal Service.

Ownership

One story dominated the U.S. record business in the late 1980s: Almost all of it is now foreign-owned. In 1986, the huge West German conglomerate Bertelsmann AG paid $300 million to General Electric for RCA/Ariola records. The next year CBS sold its record division to the Sony Corporation of Japan for a whopping $2 billion. Two other recording leaders are owned by European companies: EMI/Capitol is owned by Thorn/EMI of Great Britain, and PolyGram is owned by the Phillips Company of the Netherlands. Only one major company, Warner, is U.S. owned. Consequently, the record business is now almost fully under the control of global electronics and communication conglomerates. Table 10.1 summarizes the holdings of the five major companies.

This pattern of ownership highlights the international nature of the recording business. About 80 percent of the music sold in Germany is in English. In Japan, about half is in English. In fact, along with Great Britain, these two countries represent the biggest foreign markets for U.S. records.

TABLE 10.1 Top Five Record Companies

COMPANY AND MAJOR LABELS	1987 REVENUE (BILLIONS)	TOP STARS	OTHER INTERESTS
CBS Records (owned by Sony): Columbia, Epic	$1.7	George Michael, Billy Joel, Barbra Streisand, Neil Diamond	Electronics, CD pressing plants, research, batteries
Time Warner Inc.: Asylum, Electra, Atlantic	1.5	U2, Whitesnake, Anita Baker, Genesis	Home videos, *Mad*, movies, cable TV, book publishing
PolyGram (owned by Phillips): Mercury, Deutsche Grammophon	1.5	Bon Jovi, Def Leppard, Dire Straits, Vladimir Horowitz	Defense weapons, home appliances, lighting fixtures, data systems, toothbrushes
RCA (owned by Bertelsmann): Ariola, Arista	1.3	Aretha Franklin, Grateful Dead, Bruce Hornsby, The Judds	Printing, book clubs, magazines, film, record clubs, banks, TV
Thorn/EMI: Capitol, EMI Manhattan	1.0	Pet Shop Boys, David Bowie, Bob Seger, Natalie Cole	Consumer electronics, appliances, information technology, light bulbs

PRODUCING RECORDS

Departments and Staff

There are seven departments within the typical recording company:

1. artists and repertoire (A&R)
2. sales and distribution
3. advertising and merchandising
4. business
5. promotion
6. publicity
7. artist development

Figure 10.2, page 226, shows a common arrangement.

The A&R department consists of talent scouts for the record industry. The title "artist and repertoire" is a throwback to the 1950s when the A&R department actually matched talent with potential songs. In those days the A&R person even signed talent to contracts and provided creative guidance to the performers by arranging their music and supervising their recording sessions. More recently, performers have become more sophisticated in their approach to music and seldom accept advice from the A&R people. Performers now go to independent producers, who assist them in putting together a demonstration record. In fact, many stars, including Stevie Wonder, Ric Ocasek, and Todd Rundgren, function as both performers and producers. As a result, much of the creative work done by A&R people has been replaced by administrative functions: how much it will cost to sign the act, whether the contract should be for a single or single plus album, what promotional strategies should be used, and so on. Even though the A&R department no longer has the creative clout it once had, it still remains an important part of the industry because the industry depends on new talent and the A&R department is responsible for supplying that talent. A major part of an A&R person's job is to listen to demonstration tapes sent in by hopefuls and to attend auditions. Major companies also send their A&R people out on the road where they move from one club to another, enduring a succession of fourth-rate bands (in the slang of the business, such acts are called "garage bands") in the hope of discovering another Prince or Bon Jovi.

The sales and distribution department, as the name suggests, first sells the company's products and then makes sure that the records get to the record stores where consumers can buy them. As mentioned previously, there are three types of accounts that can be sold: retail stores, rack jobbers, and one-steps. The actual selling of the record occurs about a month prior to the record's release. The distribution of the record is usually done through branch distributors.

The advertising and merchandising department aids record sales by planning media ad campaigns and point-of-purchase displays in record outlets. The advertising campaign goes hand in hand with the efforts of the promotion department (see below) to get air play for the record. It includes television and print ads that remind

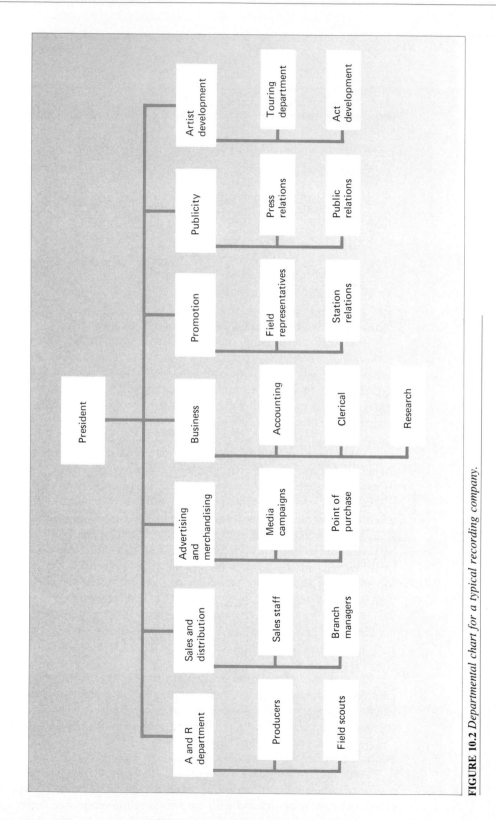

FIGURE 10.2 *Departmental chart for a typical recording company.*

consumers of the record that they have been hearing on the local radio stations. Point-of-purchase displays include posters, mobiles, neon signs, and life-size cutouts that are set up in the record store to help trigger a sale. Market research has indicated that point-of-purchase displays are important in spurring sales, and record companies spend large sums of money for these marketing aids. The advertising and merchandising department also handles other promotional devices such as T-shirts, buttons, and bumper stickers that are used to push the record.

The business department includes lawyers, accountants, market researchers, financial analysts, and secretarial and clerical staffs. It functions in the record business in the same way that such a department would operate in any other business or industry.

In the record business, promotion means getting the record played on radio stations. Since air play is crucial to the success of the record, the promotion department is an important part of all record companies. Since many contemporary stations restrict the records they play to a tightly controlled playlist, the job of the promotion department is a challenging one. Radio stations like to stick with tried and true hits; record company promotion people want to convince the station to play their company's new releases. With about 5000 singles and 2500 albums released in the United States each year and only four or five slots open on a given radio

A sophisticated mixing board such as this one handles as many as forty-eight separate sound tracks that contain recordings of many different instruments and vocals. These boards now contain computer memory devices that retain previously mixed recordings, making the process easier and faster. (Alan Carey/The Image Works)

station each week to devote to new records, the job of the promotion department is made all that much harder. The stakes are high. Unless a record gets air play, it has little chance of becoming a hit.

With the advent of music videos, a whole new avenue of promotion opened up. Now it is almost obligatory for a record company to release a video along with an album or single. The popularity of music videos makes it easier to introduce new acts on a national scale. MTV has more than 20 million subscribers and reaches the whole country. In addition, MTV is willing to experiment with new artists and songs. Songs that would usually not break into the playlist of a contemporary hits station are featured on MTV, thus increasing their popularity and making it possible for them to crack through to radio air play. Surveys have shown that MTV has become an important influence in record and tape buying. About half the people in one national survey reported that they had purchased or intended to purchase a recording by a performer they had seen on MTV. On the other side of the coin, music videos are not cheap to produce. Budgets typically range from about $50,000 for a simple performance video to about $250,000 for a complicated concept video. Many record companies tried to get MTV and other stations using music videos to pay a fee for their use. In sum, music videos significantly changed the nature of record promotion, another example of the media symbiosis mentioned in Chapter 1.

The publicity department attempts to get press coverage for its new performers and new releases. This department also has the responsibility of getting new acts and albums reviewed by critics in such publications as *Rolling Stone* and *Creem*. The publicity department also makes sure that the consumer and trade press is supplied with all the information and photos they need for feature stories and interviews with the label's stars.

The artist development department carries on a wide range of activities. All of this department's efforts are designed to further the career of a group or performer. Some of the duties supervised by this department include coordinating tour dates, making sure that the act has a well-produced concert show, and arranging for television appearances.

Making a Record or Tape

In order for a performer or group to win a recording contract, they need to convince someone in a record company that they have a sound that will sell. The first step in the process is to produce a demonstration tape (called a **demo**) that can be sent to the appropriate persons. A demo is usually done in a studio with four-track mixing facilities and does not have to sound as good as the finished product released by the major studios. All the demo has to do is highlight the strengths of the group or performer and capture the attention of record company executives.

The second step is to sell the demo. Sending an unsolicited tape to a record company is probably the worst way to sell it. Although there are some exceptions (the Doobie Brothers were signed by Warner on the strength of an unsolicited tape), most of these tapes are never listened to. A better way is to hire a manager or agent to sell the demo for the act. If the agent is successful, step three entails going to the recording studio and making a master tape.

Resembling something you might see at NASA's mission control center, with banks of modern equipment, blinking lights, and digital readouts, the modern recording studio does multitrack recording. Professional studios have machines capable of recording up to forty-eight different tracks. This means that different instruments and vocals can be recorded on different sections of the same piece of tape. For

Play It Again, Sam ... Backward

Backmasking is the technical name for hiding in a record or tape a message that can be heard only by playing the record or tape backward. Controversy has surrounded this technique as many religious and social reform groups claim backmasking is being used to present harmful subliminal messages about Satan and other unsavory topics. Some groups have even burned records and tapes that they claim contained these backward messages.

The first well-known case of backmasking occurred in 1968 on the Beatles' *White Album*. At the time, there was a totally unfounded rumor circulating that Paul McCartney was dead. People who believed this rumor claimed that if the song "Revolution Number Nine" was played backward, you could hear something that sounded like "turn me on, deadm'n," a reference, they claimed, to the departed Paul. Other listeners claimed that it took a powerful imagination and repeated close and careful listening to hear anything resembling an intelligible message.

The other well-known example concerns the group Led Zeppelin and "Stairway to Heaven." The song was written by Jimmy Page and sung by Robert Plant, two performers with an interest in the occult. When played backward, one passage of the song sounds like "so here's to my sweet Satan" or something close to that. Other music scholars have suggested that there are at least a half-dozen references to Satan backmasked in other parts of the song. Did Plant and Page deliberately backmask a message? Probably. The hidden message can be heard only in the studio version of the song and doesn't come across in the concert version, suggesting that it was carefully engineered. Were Plant and Page deliberately trying to plant (no pun intended) satanic visions into the minds of their listeners? Maybe, but it seems more likely that they were merely making an obvious point in a clever way. Proceed backward down the stairway to heaven and you'll wind up with the devil.

In any case, "Stairway" must have started a trend. E.L.O.'s album, aptly entitled *Secret Messages,* contains the message "welcome to the show" when played backward. "Snowblind," by Styx, allegedly contains the backmasked message "ooooh, Satan, move in our voices." Others suggest it sounds more like "ooooh, stakem moota roy hoopskirt." In any case, because of all the publicity, Styx actually did place a backmasked message (the Latin phrase on the dollar bill) in their next album.

Do people unconsciously perceive these messages and sell their souls to Satan? Not likely. Studies have shown that people have enough trouble trying to understand the forward versions of rock lyrics—let alone backward messages.

Nonetheless, the controversy will not stop. Only recently another group of music reformers claimed that after listening countless hours to the backward version of the "Mr. Ed" television theme ("A horse is a horse . . ."), they were able to make out the word "Satan." This, of course, immediately brings up the question of why anyone would spend countless hours listening to the "Mr. Ed" theme being played backward . . . or, for that matter, forward.

example, a piano might be recorded on one track, drums on another, bass on another, lead vocal on another, background vocal on yet another, and so on. So that one track docs not leak onto another, the studio is set up with careful placement of microphones and wooden baffles—soundproof barriers that keep the sound of one instrument from spilling over into the mikes recording the other instruments. Before the actual recording begins, audio engineers experiment with different microphones, mike placements, and amplifier settings to achieve the right sound. Once the session starts, the producer makes most of the creative decisions. Some groups do their best on the first "take"; others may need to play the same music a dozen times before it's acceptable. The producer decides when the performers take a break, when the tune has to be played over because of a bad note, when the tape should be played back so that the group can hear itself and perhaps make changes in the arrangement, etc.

The advent of multiple-track recording has revamped the music-making process. Currently, it isn't even necessary for a band to record together. The instrumentalists can come in one at a time and "lay down" their tracks, the lead singer or singers can add the vocals later, and everything can be put together at the mixing console. Further, many new recording studios are equipped with satellite uplinks and downlinks, which make it possible for artists in different states to record an album without ever seeing each other. A singer in New York, for example, sings to background music previously recorded on a digital tape recorder and sent via satellite to New York. The solo is sent back to Hollywood where it is taped on another digital machine. The two tracks are then balanced and mixed together.

Modern studios are also equipped with digital sampling synthesizers that are capable of "memorizing" any sound and playing it back on a keyboard over the full musical spectrum. Musician Jan Hammer used a synthesizer to create the sound of horns, drums, woodwinds, guitars, and vibraphones on the "Miami Vice" theme. None of the instruments heard on that piece of music was played by a live musician.

Of course, the biggest change in recording technology has been the move to digital recording. Conventional sound recording attempts to reproduce on tape or disc a picture of the sound wave it is recording. Music, for example, is represented by a continuous signal. The tiny wiggles and curves in a record groove are "analogous" to the sound we hear; hence, analog recording. The problem with analog recording occurs when the original "picture" of the sound wave is reproduced; the copy is less distinct than the original and a copy of a copy is even less distinct and so on. Eventually the quality becomes so poor that a new original must be made.

This problem can be circumvented by assigning a number, or digit, to each tiny particle of sound and storing this number on magnetic tape, hence, digital recording. Figure 10.3 shows how this works. The first part illustrates a raw sound wave. The second part shows six points at which the sound wave is sampled and a numerical value assigned to the sound at each point (in digital sound, a binary number system, using 0's and 1's, is substituted for the regular numbers). The third part depicts the sound as it would be recovered from the digital code. Note that the recovered wave is similar to but is in no way identical with the original. The reason is that we used an amplitude scale with only six divisions and sampled only six points on the sound wave. Sophisticated digital recording systems sample a far greater number of points on the sound wave and use thousands of distinct amplitude levels. This system is so delicate that two drum beats that sound exactly the same to your ear may have different numerical signatures. To illustrate:

Drum beat 1—1001001111011110
Drum beat 2—1001001111011101

The digital system is a big improvement over the traditional analog system. Any machine that can read the digital tape can duplicate the sound wave. Moreover, since no copy of a copy is made, the ten thousandth record or tape made from a digital master is as good as the first. Digital recording also virtually eliminates "hiss" from a record or tape. Both compact discs and digital audio tape make use of this process.

After the recording session, the next step is called the **mix-down.** This is the

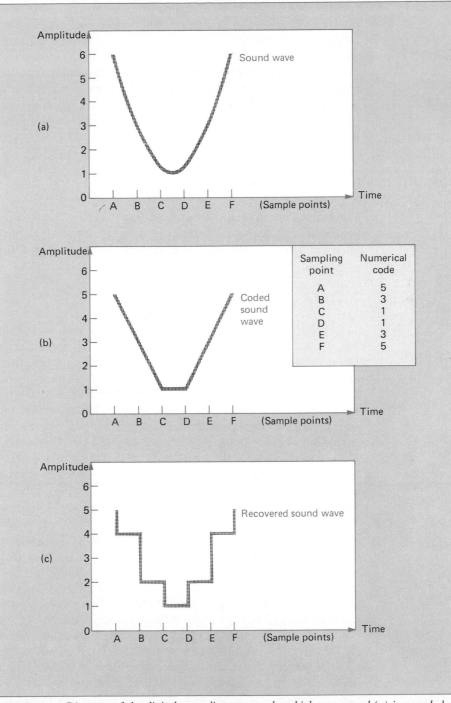

FIGURE 10.3 *Diagram of the digital recording process by which raw sound (a) is sampled and a numerical value assigned at each point (b), so that the sound can be recovered from the digital code (c).*

technically exacting job of mixing down the multiple tracks onto a two-track stereo master. In the mix-down, each track is equalized; echo, overdubbing, or other special effects are added and certain passages are scheduled for rerecording. If an album is being produced, each track has to be precisely placed on the stereo spectrum. A track can be placed in the left or right speaker or in the center, where it is heard as equal in both speakers. Mixing a sixteen- or twenty-four-track tape down to two tracks can take several days. The job has been made somewhat easier in recent years thanks to computerized mixing boards, which quickly recreate a previous mix that can then be modified. After the mix is completed, the master is reproduced on tape and disc for manufacture. At the same time, the promotion department is given a preview of the new release, and the advertising and publicity departments begin their efforts.

ECONOMICS OF THE RECORDING INDUSTRY

We will approach the topic of economics at two levels. First we'll examine the economic structure of the industry as a whole. Next we'll focus on a more personal level and investigate the financial ups and downs of a typical musical group trying to make it in the recording business.

Economic Trends in the Industry

The record business, as mentioned, is a volatile one; in 1988 the industry was on a hot streak, with revenue reaching a record $6.25 billion in the United States and about $17 billion worldwide. The growing popularity of CDs accounts for much of this economic boom. When a person buys a CD player, he or she usually buys about twenty-five to thirty-five CDs in the first year of ownership, about a $300–$400 investment. Let's assume that 2 million new CD players are sold in the United States in a given year (a reasonable assumption) and let's further assume that each new owner buys twenty-five CDs at a retail cost of $10. That alone would generate $500 million in revenue for the industry. Further, the baby-boomers, those in the twenty-five- to forty-year-old category who were raised on the rock music of the 1960s, are continuing to be fans of popular music. This demographic segment is important because it's the group that can afford to spend $200–$300 for a CD player and $10–$12 per disc. Not surprisingly, music from the 1960s is a big seller in this age group. When four of the Beatles' albums were reissued on CD, they quickly sold 2 million copies at retail prices of $12–$16. Consequently, as long as CDs keep gaining in popularity, the revenues of the record industry should be robust.

Not all is rosy, however. On the technological side, the introduction of digital audio tape (DAT) may be troublesome. DAT cassettes are the tape equivalents of compact discs. They are smaller than ordinary cassettes but can hold more music. Since they are processed digitally, there is no background hiss and nothing is lost in the transfer from master tape to cassette. DAT is not compatible with ordinary cassette players; a special machine, which might initially retail for about $1000, is needed. On the one hand, DAT will help the record industry by stimulating sales as cassette fans switch to the new DAT format and buy more tapes. On the other, the problem is that, unlike CDs, you can record on DAT, making it easy to duplicate the crystal-clear sound of a CD. Record manufacturers are worried that bootlegged CDs on DAT would seriously hurt sales. Accordingly, the U.S. record industry has opposed the introduction of DAT players, now manufactured and available in Japan, to this country. Moreover, Congress is considering legislation that would require insertion of a "spoiler" microchip to prevent copying in all DAT players sold in the United States. (To make the DAT story even more interesting, Sony is a leading

Popular, mass-produced music plays an important role in our society, particularly among younger listeners. Here, Michael Jackson's Bad *album is on sale in New York in various forms: LPs, tapes, and CDs. (Ricki Rosen/The Picture Group)*

proponent of DAT technology in Japan. Its entrance into the U.S. record industry through the acquisition of CBS Records might accelerate DAT's introduction to this country.)

Moreover, record counterfeiting and piracy, the illegal copying and selling of ordinary tapes and discs, still hurts the industry to the tune of about $1 billion a year. Despite stricter laws and harsher penalties, this problem shows no signs of abating. The introduction of DAT would make this problem worse.

Revenues from Record Sales

As of 1987, about 55 percent of all recording industry revenue came from the sale of tapes, about 34 percent from CDs, 8 percent from LPs, and 3 percent from singles. Table 10.2, page 234, breaks down the typical costs associated with producing and marketing a CD at a list price of $12.98. Keep in mind that the figures are approximations and subject to change, particularly if the retail prices of CDs continue to decline.

The manufacturer's profit on a typical LP would be about half that of a CD. At the retail level, an LP on sale for $6.99 generates a profit of about $1.75. With their higher profit margins, CDs have obvious appeal for both the record companies and retailers.

TABLE 10.2 Costs and Profits of a Typical CD

Manufacturer's costs	
Recording expense	$ 0.40
Manufacturing cost	0.80
Packaging	1.00
Advertising and promotion	1.00
Artist's royalty	1.10
Freight	0.07
Payment to musicians' trust fund	0.50
Manufacturer's profit	4.00
Distributor's expenses and profit	1.75
Retailer profit	2.36
TOTAL	$12.98

Rock Performers: The Bottom Line

Now let's turn our attention to the finances connected with an individual or group involved in making records. There are many stories about the fantastic sums of money earned by pop music stars. Well, some stars do make a lot of money. Others, however, are not quite as lucky. Let's look at some numbers. A new artist or group will receive a royalty rate of about 7–9 percent of the suggested retail price of an LP or cassette. A more established act might negotiate a rate that's a little higher, maybe 10–12 percent. Really successful performers might get around 15 percent. (Royalty rates on CDs are currently in a state of flux but have historically been calculated on the same price basis as those of LPs.) Royalty rates on singles run about 6–9 percent. For simplicity, let's say a hypothetical group of four performers is getting a 10 percent royalty rate. This works out to about $1 for each LP, tape, or CD sold and about 15 cents per single. It doesn't take a genius to see that the sale of a million albums will generate about $1 million in royalties plus whatever a hit single would sell. Even split among a group of four, it still comes out to a healthy sum for a few months work. Sounds pretty good so far . . . but it's not that simple.

There are two main sources of income for recording artists—record royalties, mentioned above, and personal appearances. If an individual or a group is well known and consistently able to put out hits, then it is true that they will earn large sums of money. Unfortunately, not all groups and performers are able to do this. In fact, only relatively few are able to command huge incomes. The rest do their utmost to survive. The riches are disproportionately divided, with a small number at the top earning most of the money. Moreover, the odds on any newcomer's making it big in the recording industry are slim. Although the figures are rough estimates, about 30,000 young and not-so-young hopefuls try to break into the business in any given year. Perhaps twenty or so will crack the hit lists, putting the odds of success at about 1500 to 1.

Furthermore, the fact that an act is lucky enough to put out one hit album is no immediate guarantee of riches. Getting started in the recording business takes money. Usually, this money is lent to a new group or single by the recording company as an advance against future royalty income. In some cases, a group that brings in a million seller finds itself barely breaking even once all advances and expenses are paid back. To illustrate, let's pretend that you're a member of a four-person rock group that is lucky enough to land a recording contract. The first thing your group will probably need is top-of-the-line instruments and equipment. (Your competition will surely have them.) These do not come cheap. A good guitar goes for about $800. A five-piece set of drums costs about $2000, and amps retail for about the same price. Then, of course, your group will need some money to live on while you're making your records. The record company will also advance you this sum from your future royalties. Then there is the cost of producing the album. This expense is also charged against your royalties. Some record companies might even subtract another 10 percent or so for the packaging of the record. For purposes of illustration, let's say that the record company advances your group about $25,000 for new equipment and living expenses and $200,000 for the cost of recording your album. So far your group is in the hole for $225,000.

Now let's pretend that the group hits it big and sells 400,000 copies of the album and 800,000 copies of a single from the album (a rather optimistic assumption). This nets the group about $400,000 in royalties from the LP and about $120,000 in royalties from the single, for a total of $520,000. Before you can go out and buy a Porsche 944, you learn that the record company will deduct 15 percent for "free goods," records and tapes given away to customers to promote sales. Fifteen percent of $520,000 equals $78,000, so your earnings now total $442,000. Paying back the advance and recording session costs still leaves the group $217,000. (We're assuming the company cheerfully picked up the $50,000 tab for your music video.) Sounds good so far. Unfortunately, we've left out some key expenses. Every group has a manager and the manager's fee is 15 percent (sometimes more) of royalty income, or in our example $78,000. Most groups also hire on a part-time basis a publicity agent, an accountant, and a lawyer. Your group will need a lawyer because most record company contracts are about thirty-five to sixty single-spaced pages long. Legal fees can run from $2000 to $8000 for a recording agreement. Let's say these combined costs total $20,000. Left for the group, $119,000.

The other major revenue source for a group is a tour. Tours are important because they help promote the album. Most record companies insist that a new group go on tour. Let's pretend that your manager has booked the group on a forty-night tour playing various clubs and arenas across the country. Let's also pretend that the group collects $6000 per night as a fee. Working the road is not a pleasant experience for most groups, and many acts split up because of it. But, assuming your group stays together, forty nights at $6,000 per night yields $240,000. Again, things look good. The road, however, has its own special expenses. Airline fees, hotel bills, meals, costumes, transporting equipment, roadies, insurance, and so on, all must be paid for. Touring has become so expensive that many recording artists are linking up with a commercial sponsor who picks up part of the costs. In recent years, Reebok underwrote a Bruce Springsteen tour and Miller, Coca-Cola, and Sun Country Wine Coolers have sponsored tours in return for a little advertising during the concert. Returning to our example, let's say that expenses run $3500 per night. To complete a forty-night engagement tour might require fifty nights on the road (probably more). This amounts to a total tour expense of at least $175,000. Fifteen percent of your gross income goes to the manager ($36,000) and another 20 percent to your road manager and booking agents ($48,000). Then there's the cost of replacing broken gear and equipment and miscellaneous expenses such as extra musicians. As a rough figure, let's say $10,000 goes to miscellaneous expenses. Total tour expenses: $269,000. Total tour income: $240,000. Net loss for the tour: $29,000.

The *Dirty Dancing* Surprise

Dirty Dancing, 1987's biggest musical hit movie, almost never got made. It was rejected by every major studio before a new company in some financial difficulty, Vestron Pictures, agreed to produce it on one condition: It had to be made on a budget of less than $5 million—a drop in the bucket as most movies go. Not surprisingly, RCA records didn't invest much in the movie's soundtrack. It recorded only a couple of new songs and took the rest from the archives of 1960s hits. The soundtrack was put together for less than $200,000.

The rest, as they say, is history. The film became a megahit. The soundtrack went platinum. The videocassette also sold well. A TV series based on the movie appeared on a TV network's 1988–1989 schedule. A stage show featuring some singers from the movie toured the country. Inspired, RCA issued another album of 1960s hits—called, to no one's surprise, *More Dirty Dancing*—which spent about forty weeks on the best-seller charts.

Dirty Dancing enterprises have grossed about $375 million. RCA's share alone amounted to more than $110 million in 1987, about one-fourth of its total domestic revenue. If a corporation could sing, RCA would probably be crooning, "We had . . . the time of our lives . . . ."

So the bottom line is this: royalty income, $119,000; touring losses, $29,000; total income for the group, $90,000. Divided four ways, this yields $22,500 per member (before taxes). Not bad, but a little out of the Porsche range. Maybe a Honda Civic would do instead.

Of course, if you personally write some of the songs on the album, you would receive more royalties as the songwriter. You would also make some money from TV appearances, record sales overseas, and merchandising deals. Most artists, however, don't see much money until they've had a couple of hits back to back. After two years, the Grateful Dead were about $180,000 in debt to their record company. Northeastern rock group Rubber Rodeo wound up owing $500,000 to their company even after four years of recording and touring. The Long Ryders were in debt even after releasing a successful album and appearing in a national ad campaign for Miller Beer. The only group to stay out of this debt situation in recent years was 'til tuesday. This group took only a modest advance and cut recording and touring costs. Also, keep in mind that we optimistically assumed that our hypothetical group's first single and album did well. Most groups usually don't sell that many copies. Remember that all the advances and costs of making a flop album would be recouped against the earnings of future successful records, another reason why most groups start off in debt. Finally, we would also have to take into account the potential earning power of a group over time. There is no guarantee that a group's subsequent albums would do well. You can probably generate a long list of groups that had one hit and then faded into obscurity. All in all, big money can be made in the record industry, but few are lucky enough to cash in.

CAREERS IN THE RECORDING INDUSTRY

Of all the mass media, the recording industry employs the fewest employees. Not counting performers, there are only about 15,000–18,000 people in the entire industry. This section will emphasize careers in the nonperformance side of the business. Those of you interested in pursuing careers as performers, writers, and arrangers obviously should concentrate on developing musical skills.

Entry-Level Positions

Basically, there are at least three distinct career paths within the recording business: (1) engineering, (2) creative, and (3) business. We will examine each of these in turn.

Over the past two decades, the technical aspects of sound recording have become tremendously complex. The control room of a twenty-four-track studio resembles something like the bridge of the starship *Enterprise*. Sometimes it takes two engineers to operate the giant control panel—one to run the tape machines and the other to do the actual recording. If the engineering side of the industry is of interest to you, it would be of some advantage to study at a college that has its own recording studio so that you may become familiar with the equipment. Failing that, the Recording Institute of America (RIA) offers courses in multitrack engineering and sound production. Alternatively, you might volunteer your services as an apprentice at a local recording studio and learn the skills by watching others. There are recording studios all across the United States. Although many of them are located in New York, Nashville, and Los Angeles, there are others in Atlanta, Memphis, Philadelphia, Orlando, Miami, Toronto, Cincinnati, Seattle, Minneapolis, Chicago, Detroit, Ogden (Utah), and Bogalusa (Louisiana).

If your interests lie more in the creative area and you wish to become a record producer, college courses in mass media, business administration, and music are relevant. Some colleges offer courses in the music industry, and a few even offer a bachelor's degree in the music business. You will also need some practical experience in directing a recording session. This can be done by working at a college that has a recording studio or, as suggested above, by volunteering your services at a local commercial studio. Another possible route is to start out at a record company in a low-level position, perhaps in the warehouse or mailroom, and work your way into the A&R department and try to gain experience as a demo producer. From there, you might advance to a regular staff producer. In every case, you should try to learn as much as possible about the record business. Producers also must have some knowledge about sales, accounting, and the legal aspects of production.

If the business side of the profession appeals to you, a college background in business administration and mass media would be most helpful. Those interested in promotion and sales should start out by checking to see if there's a branch office of a major label or independent distributor located nearby. The big-five companies have about twenty branches in various cities across the country. Send a resumé, telephone, appear in person, or do whatever else is necessary to meet the local manager. Your goal should be an entry-level position as a local promotion person or a sales representative in a particular market.

The same advice holds for someone interested in advertising and merchandising. A branch office might be able to start you off at a beginning position from which you can move up to the parent company. An alternative route would be to gain some experience at an advertising agency, preferably one that has a record label as an account, and then move to the record company. Those seeking careers in publicity usually have a college background in journalism or public relations. Many entry-level positions in this area can be found at small record companies. Other publicists work as independents and are hired by an artist's manager or agent.

It is a little more difficult to provide advice on how to get started in the A&R department. Many A&R people come from the promotion department. Others start off at the bottom as secretaries or clerks and work their way up within the division. A good ear and a knowledge of what will sell and how to sell it are essential for a career in this area.

Upward Mobility

There are several paths that lead toward advancement in the recording industry. Again, the precise nature of job advancement will depend upon the particular starting place. Beginning audio engineers progress to staff engineers and ultimately to senior supervising engineer. Some engineers do cross over and become record producers, but this is generally rare. Once you've committed yourself to a technical career in the control room, you'll generally stay there.

People who start out as producers advance by becoming staff producers with major labels. The next step up would be the position of executive producer. At major companies, executive producers are basically administrators. They approve budgets, settle disputes among artists, producers, and studio personnel, and oversee the efforts of the A&R department. The executive producer in the record business is analogous to the executive producer in motion pictures or TV. Another upward path sometimes followed by producers is to start off with an established label and then go into independent production. Independent producers freelance from one label to another, taking on projects that interest them and that promise to make money. Independent producers make money by receiving royalties from the records they produce. Many independent producers go on to form their own labels.

Those who start off in one of the business departments at a record company advance by moving up the corporate ladder. Salespeople move up to regional manager and then to sales director. Promotion people progress from smaller to larger markets. Advertising department employees advance first by taking on more important and lucrative accounts and later by moving up into management and administration. The most common route to top management has been through either the production or sales and distribution department.

In closing, it should be mentioned that we have discussed only the most common types of careers in the recording industry. There are related careers such as agent, or personal manager, or positions in the areas of concert promotion, music publishing, retailing, and marketing. Furthermore, although the record business is hard to break into, the rewards come fast. Since most popular music is performed and purchased by young people, many top managers and producers are also young. Many people become top executives in their late twenties and early thirties. Similarly, many successful producers are in this same age range. Although this can be an advantage, it also means that a person has to make a mark early in his or her career. If a person is not on the way up by his or her middle thirties, the road to advancement becomes harder.

SUGGESTIONS FOR FURTHER READING

The following books contain more information about the concepts and topics discussed in this chapter.

BASKERVILLE, DAVID, *Music Business Handbook,* Los Angeles: Sherman Co., 1985.

SCHEMEL, SIDNEY, AND WILLIAM KRASILOVSKY, *This Business of Music,* New York: Billboard Publications, 1985.

SIEGEL, ALAN, *Breakin' in to the Music Business,* Port Chester, N.Y.: Cherry Lane Books, 1983.

ZALKIND, RONALD, ed., *Contemporary Music Almanac,* New York: Schirmer Books, 1980.

Chapter *11*

History of Film and Television

S tanding in line was nothing new to the crowd of New Yorkers congregated in front of Koster and Bial's Music Hall that mild spring evening. Many of them had stood in line to see a vaudeville show before. But tonight, April 23, 1896, was different. The crowds walking up Broadway and across Herald Square were coming to see the first public exhibition of Thomas Edison's latest invention, the **Vitascope,** a machine that actually projected moving pictures onto a screen large enough for everybody in the theater to view them at once. The first half of the program consisted of skits and songs by the European singer Albert Chevalier. But the real star of the evening was hidden under blue brocade in the second balcony of the theater. Resembling the gun turret on a destroyer, the projection booth housed two Vitascopes (one was a spare), loaded with film and ready to run. When the vaudeville stopped, attention was focused on a twenty- by twelve-foot screen in the middle of the stage. The projectors started whirring, sending forty-six frames of film past the lens every second, and immediately the audience was enthralled. Two young dancers in pink and blue dresses (each frame of film had been tinted by hand) performed an umbrella dance. Next, scenes of surf breaking on the beach amazed the spectators. A comic boxing match, a vaudeville skit, and another dance routine quickly followed. The audience cheered and cheered. A reviewer for the *New York Times* calls the presentation "wonderfully real and singularly exhilarating." The movies had arrived.

Koster and Bial's Music Hall is gone now, replaced by Macy's Department Store. But even today, if you walk the streets of New York or any town across the country on a balmy spring evening, you are likely to see people standing in line, waiting to see moving pictures on a screen.

Motion pictures and television both integrate sight and sound in their presentations. Their histories at first seem to be separate, but on closer examination the two media have much in common. Both depend on the same perceptual mechanism to achieve the illusion of motion; their economics are intertwined; directors and stars from one medium cross over into the other; and, in the future, new technologies will further erase the differences between them. Thus this chapter treats the evolution of motion pictures and television simultaneously. We will, of course, have more to say about film, because it developed earlier than TV.

EARLY HISTORY OF THE MOTION PICTURE

Motion pictures and television are possible because of two quirks of the human perceptual system: the **phi phenomenon** and **persistence of vision.** The phi phenomenon refers to what happens when a person sees one light source go out while another one close to the original is illuminated. To our eyes, it looks like the light is actually moving from one place to another. In persistence of vision, our eyes continue to see an image for a split second after the image has actually disappeared from view. First observed by the ancient Greeks, persistence of vision became more widely known in 1824 when Peter Roget (who also developed the *Thesaurus*) read a paper about it before the British Royal Society of Surgeons. Roget demonstrated that human beings retain an image of an object for about one-tenth of a second after the object is taken from view. Following Roget's pronouncements, a host of toys that depended on this principle sprang up in Europe. Bearing fanciful names (the Thaumatrope, the Zoetrope), these devices made a series of still pictures appear to move. In the Zoetrope, for example, a strip of pictures, each differing slightly from the others, was placed inside a topless revolving drum. As the drum spun around, the viewer looked through vertical slits to see hand-drawn acrobats, clowns, and horses appear to come alive. These primitive playthings, of course, were illustrating the technique we now use to produce cartoons—animation. In fact, if Mickey Mouse were ever to trace his roots, he would find that they led back to a Frenchman, Emile Reynaud, and his magical device, the Praxinoscope. By combining the Zoetrope with a primitive slide projector, Reynaud became the first person to project his drawings onto a large screen. In the late 1880s, Reynaud added a frame and tiny settings and began to charge admission to a small room he dubbed the Théâtre Optique.

Unfortunately, Reynaud and his imitators had to draw each of their pictures by hand—a long, painstaking, and arduous task. The development of the motion picture would have taken far longer if this method had been the only one available. Luckily, at about this same time, tremendous advances were being made in the field of still photography. Louis Daguerre invented a photographic process that used burnished

An early version of Emile Reynaud's Praxinoscope. Later models would be able to project a moving image onto a large screen for many people to view at once. (The Bettmann Archive)

metal as a base and produced splendidly clear and detailed photographs. Never one for modesty, Daguerre called the picture produced by this process the daguerreotype. Nevertheless, despite their fine quality, daguerreotypes sometimes took thirty minutes to expose and the subject had to remain rigid and motionless throughout. (This is the reason many of our ancestors appear to be somewhat stiff.) Moreover, the daguerreotype could not be used to make copies. Eventually, flexible celluloid film replaced the metal, exposure times were shortened, and photography became more practical.

Before long, several people realized that a series of still photographs could be used instead of hand drawings in variations of the Zoetrope and Praxinoscope. In the 1860s, an American, Henry Heyl, mounted a series of still photos on a glass disk and by spinning this disk in front of a bright light that was masked periodically by a shutter device, he projected the images onto a screen. In 1878, a colorful Englishman later turned American, Edward Muybridge, attempted to settle a $25,000 bet over whether the four feet of a galloping horse were ever simultaneously off the ground. He arranged a series of twenty-four cameras alongside a race track in order to photograph a running horse. Rapidly viewing the series of pictures produced an effect much like that of a motion picture. Muybridge's technique not only settled the bet (they were) but also demonstrated, in a backward way, the idea behind motion picture photography. Instead of twenty-four cameras taking one picture each, what was needed was one camera that would take twenty-four pictures in rapid order. It was Thomas Edison and his assistant, William Dickson, who finally developed what might have been the first practical motion picture camera and viewing device. Edison was apparently trying to provide a visual counterpart to his recently invented phonograph (see Chapter 8). When his early efforts did not work out, he turned the project over to this assistant. Using flexible film, Dickson solved the vexing problem of how to move the film rapidly through the camera by perforating its edge with tiny holes and pulling it along by means of sprockets. In 1889, Dickson had perfected a machine called the **Kinetoscope** and even starred in a brief film demonstrating how it worked.

These early efforts in the Edison lab were not directed at projecting movies to large crowds. Still influenced by the success of his phonograph, Edison thought a similar device could make money by showing brief films to one person at a time for a penny a look. The Kinetoscope reflected this idea; it was much like a modern-day peep-show machine. Edison built a special studio to produce films for this new invention, and by 1894 Kinetoscope parlors were springing up in major cities. The long-range commercial potential of this invention was lost on Edison. He was dead set against developing motion picture projection equipment. He reasoned that the real money would be made by selling his peep-show machine. If a large number of people were shown the film at the same time, fewer machines would be needed. Edison once argued that only ten projectors would be needed to show films to everyone in the entire country. His estimate was a little off. Furthermore, when Edison took out patents for his devices, he neglected to pay an addition $150 to secure international patent rights, an oversight that would return to haunt him.

In Europe, other inventors quickly seized upon Edison's ideas. Since they could use his equipment without paying royalties, several Europeans borrowed freely from Edison's ideas and improved upon them. The most noteworthy of these entrepreneurs were the Lumière brothers. In 1894 they had developed a device that not only took motion pictures but projected them as well. By the next year, they were showing films to paying customers in the basement of a Paris café. Other projection devices were developed in both Europe and the United States. In 1895, audiences in several major American cities were able to attend demonstrations of this new equipment. In

Hale's Tours and Scenes of the World

George C. Hale, ex-firechief of Kansas City, Missouri, was one of the first people to make a million dollars in the film industry. Hale mounted a camera on the rear platform of a speeding train and shot film of the landscape as it whizzed by. He then took an old railroad car and converted it into a motion picture theater. When customers paid their money to the ticket collector, dressed as a train conductor, they were ushered in to one of the train's seats. Then, when the ''train'' was full, the conductor would yell ''All Aboard,'' bells would clang, and the whole car would be rocked back and forth, simulating the motion of a moving train. Finally, the lights would darken and the motion pictures that Hale had taken earlier were projected onto a screen, thus recreating the illusion of travel for the delighted ''passengers.''

Hale's Tours were introduced at the 1903 St. Louis Exposition and were an instant hit. During the next two years, Hale's Tours sprang up around the country and became something of a national fad. Hale himself was reported to have made two million dollars from this idea.

the face of all this competition, Edison finally changed his mind. His Vitascope, a projection version of the Kinetoscope, premiered at Koster and Bial's in 1896.

Vaudeville theaters across the country were soon showing films as part of their programs. These early films were simply bits of action—acrobats tumbling, horses running, a man sneezing, prizefighters, jugglers, and so on. The novelty of seeing things in motion was sufficient to impress and even awe early moviegoers. When the film portrayed a locomotive roaring down the track toward the camera, many in the audience actually jumped out of the way. The novelty effect quickly wore off, however, and before long films were used as ''chasers''—appearing at the end of the vaudeville shows to clear the theater for the next performance. Once the newness was gone, the attraction of the motion picture began to wane.

Public interest was soon rekindled when early filmmakers discovered that movies could be used to tell a story. In France, magician Georges Méliès produced a science fiction film that was the great-great-grandfather of *Star Wars* and *Star Trek*. Called *A Trip to the Moon*, it can be appreciated by modern film fans for its technical sophistication. Méliès, however, did not fully explore the freedom in storytelling that film was capable of. His films were basically extravagant stage plays photographed by a stationary camera. It was an American, Edwin S. Porter, who in his *Great Train Robbery* (the ancestor of dozens of John Wayne westerns) first discovered the artistic potential of editing and camera placement. These new narrative films were extraordinarily popular with audiences and proved to be financially successful. Almost overnight, fifty- to ninety-seat theaters, called nickelettes or nickelodeons because of the five-cent admission price, were springing up in converted stores throughout the country. In Pittsburgh, the projectors of the Harris and David Nickelodeon ground away from eight in the morning until midnight. Soon the theater was averaging about 20,000 nickels ($1000) a week in 1905. The growth of these nickelodeons was fantastic; over a hundred more were to open in Pittsburgh within the next year. In New York, licenses were being issues to new establishments at the rate of one a day.

Nickelodeons depended on audience turnover for their profits. To keep the audience returning, films had to be changed often—sometimes daily—to attract repeat customers. This policy created a tremendous demand for motion pictures, and new production companies were quickly formed. (In these early days, films were regarded as just another mass-produced product; hence, early film studios were called ''film factories.'') New York and New Jersey served as the bases for these early film companies.

Birth of the MPPC

Events in moviemaking during the decade 1908–1918 had far-reaching effects on the future shape of the film industry. As the basic economic structure of the film industry developed, the center of filmmaking moved to the West Coast, and independent film producers, having survived attempts by the major studios to stamp them out, became an important force in the industry. The tremendous demand for new pictures brought enormous competition into the field. Small film companies cut corners by using bootlegged equipment (for which they paid no royalty fees) and started making films. Competition quickly reached the cutthroat level; lawsuits were filed with alarming frequency. In an effort to bring order to the business (and to cut down legal expenses), the leading manufacturers of films and film equipment banded together, pooled their patents, and formed the **Motion Picture Patents Company (MPPC).** It was the intent of this organization to restrict moviemaking to the nine companies that made up the MPPC. Film exhibitors were brought into line by a two-dollar-per-week tax, which entitled the theaters to use projection equipment patented by the MPPC. Failure to pay this tax meant that the theater owners would no longer be supplied with MPPC-approved films. Eventually, in order to accommodate the growing industry, a new role, that of film distributor, was created. The film distributor served the function of a wholesaler, acquiring films from the manufacturers and renting them to exhibitors. This three-level structure—production, distribution, and exhibition—is still with us today. The MPPC was quick to take control of film distribution also.

To call the MPPC conservative would be an understatement. The organization refused to identify actors and actresses appearing in their films, for they were afraid that if some of their performers were identified and became popular, they might demand more money. They didn't want to pay some actors more than others because they sold film by the foot, and film was priced the same per foot no matter who was in it. In addition, they were convinced that audiences would not sit through movies that ran longer than one reel in length (about ten minutes). The MPPC also refused to use close-ups in their films, arguing that no one would pay to see half an actor.

Instead of squelching competition, the MPPC actually encouraged it. Annoyed by the repressive regulations, independent producers began offering films to exhibitors at cheaper rates than MPPC members. Full-length feature films, several reels in length, were imported from Europe. The MPPC declared war. ''Outlaw'' studios were raided and equipment smashed. Violence broke out on more than one occasion. In an effort to escape the harassment of the MPPC, independent producers fled New York and New Jersey. They were looking for a location with good weather, interesting geography, low business costs, and proximity to a national border so that the independents could avoid the MPPC's subpoenas. Several areas were tried. Florida proved to be too humid; Cuba was too inconvenient; Texas was too flat. Finally, they found the perfect environment—a rather sleepy suburb of Los Angeles called Hollywood. By 1913, this new home had so encouraged independent filmmaking that the MPPC could no longer contain its growth. By 1917, for all practical purposes, the patents organization had lost its power.

The Star System

The street is a little tawdry now, but the stretch of Hollywood Boulevard between La Brea and Vine is still called the Walk of Fame. Bronze medallions bearing the names of stars dating from the days of the nickelodeon to the present have been inserted in the sidewalk. Moving west along the boulevard toward Beverly Hills, one comes to the Chinese Theater, originally conceived by master Hollywood show-man Sid Grauman. In the forecourt of this ornate movie theater are slabs of concrete bearing the footprints and handprints of the stars.

This aura of glamour surrounding Hollywood and its stars might not have arisen if the MPPC had not been so stubborn. Whereas the patents company refused to publicize its performers, the independents quickly recognized that fan interest in film actors and actresses could be used to draw crowds away from the movies offered by the MPPC. Thus it was that Carl Laemmle, an independent producer, shrewdly publicized one of his actresses who possessed a poetic name—Florence Lawrence—until she became what we might call the first movie star. As Florence's fame grew, her pictures brought in more money, spurring other independents to create their own ''stars'' to maintain pace. Theda Bara (the original vamp), Lillian Gish (who was still appearing in movies over seventy years later), and William S. Hart were among other early performers to gain celebrity status. The two artists who best exemplified the growth of the star system, however, were Mary Pickford and Charlie Chaplin. In 1913, Chaplin was working in movies for $150 a week, a good salary in those days. Just four years later he was paid a million dollars for making eight pictures. Mary Pickford, nicknamed ''America's Sweetheart,'' was paid $1000 per week in

Charlie Chaplin, one of the first movie superstars created by the Hollywood star system, delighted film audiences throughout the world. This scene is from his 1925 comedy The Gold Rush. *(The International Museum of Photography at the George Eastman House, © United Artists)*

1913. By 1918, she was making $15,000–$20,000 per week in addition to a cut of up to 50 percent of her films' profits. In 1919, the star system reached its natural conclusion. Both Chaplin and Pickford joined with other actors, actresses, and filmmakers to start their own production company—United Artists. The employees now owned the shop.

The star system had other more subtle effects. Once stars became popular, their public demanded to see them in longer movies. However, feature-length films that ran one to two hours were more expensive to make. Furthermore, audiences couldn't be expected to sit for two hours on the wooden benches found in many of the nickelodeons. A need had been created for large, comfortable theaters that could accommodate thousands of patrons and, at the same time, justify higher admission costs. These new motion picture palaces were not long in coming. In 1914, the Strand opened in New York. With seats for more than 3000 people, it occupied a whole city block and had space for an entire symphony orchestra. The Rialto, which opened down the block in 1916, featured deep pile carpeting and an interior done in ivory. On the West Coast, Sid Grauman opened his Egyptian Theater (across from the Chinese Theater) in 1922 at a cost of almost a million dollars. His usherettes were dressed in Cleopatra costumes. Clearly, the nickel was no longer the symbol of the movies.

CONSOLIDATION AND GROWTH

The increased cost of filmmaking made it imperative for the producer to make sure that the company's movies were booked into enough of these new theaters to turn a profit. Under this economic pressure, the film industry moved in the direction of consolidation. Adolph Zukor, whose company would ultimately become Paramount Pictures, combined the production and distribution of films into one corporate structure. It was only a matter of time before the big studios had extended their influence into the exhibition end of the business as well. Paramount and its chief rival, Fox, began building their own theaters. The trend toward consolidation was also picked up by theater owners. Marcus Loew, owner of a large chain of theaters, purchased his own studio (later to become MGM). Studio owners could exert control over independent exhibitors by another policy known as **block booking.** In order to receive two or three top-flight films from a studio, the theater owner had to agree to show five or six other films of lower quality. Although this policy was not very advantageous to exhibitors, it assured the production companies of steady revenue for their films. Of course, all of this was taking place while World War I was devastating Europe. When the war ended in 1918, the American film industry was the dominant force in the world, accounting for upwards of 80 percent of the worldwide market. By the beginning of the twenties, the major production companies were comfortable and prosperous and enjoyed as firm a lock on the film business as had the old MPPC, which, ironically, they had replaced only a few years earlier.

The Roaring Twenties

In the early years of the Roaring Twenties, the film industry continued its move toward consolidation and growth. The prosperity boom that followed the war exploded in Hollywood with more force than in other business sectors. Profits were up, and extravagance was the watchword as filmmakers endorsed the principle that the only way to make money was to spend money. Before long, film costs were soaring. Between 1914 and 1924, there was a 1500 percent increase in the cost of a feature film. Salaries, sets, costumes, props, rights to best-sellers all contributed to the mushrooming costs of films. Even the lawyer for United Artists was paid $100,000 a year. By 1927, the average film cost about $200,000, and many films easily topped that. *Ben Hur* (1925) was made for a reported $6 million.

Huge salaries created a boomtown atmosphere in Hollywood, and many people—some still quite young—were unprepared to deal with the temptations that came with sudden wealth. It wasn't long before newspapers were reporting stories about orgiastic parties, prostitution, studio call girls, bootleg whiskey, and drugs. Hollywood was dubbed "Sin City." Scandals were inevitable. In 1922, within a few short months, comedian Fatty Arbuckle was involved in a rape case, two female stars were implicated in the murder of a prominent director, and popular actor Wallace Reid died while trying to kick his drug addiction. Public reaction to these revelations was predictable: indignation and outrage. By the end of 1922, politicians in thirty-six states had introduced bills to set up censorship boards for films. The motion picture companies hired a well-respected former Postmaster General, Will Hays, to head a new self-regulatory body for the industry. Called the Motion Picture Producers and Distributors Association, this organization was successful in heading off government control, and the basic standards it laid down would be in force for almost four decades.

By the mid-1920s theater expansion had peaked, and it was obvious that lavish, expensive films would not always bring in enough profits to cover their costs. Hollywood embraced the techniques of budget control and cost accounting that had helped other industries cut expenses. Consequently, a new title was introduced to filmmaking—the production supervisor. These individuals, typified by MGM's Irving Thalberg, decided how studio money should best be spent. They planned what stories to film, what director to hire, how much should be spent on props, and how to organize filming to minimize costs. Although these people brought financial stability to the business, they sometimes went to excess (one production supervisor decided that his studio could save money by straightening out and reusing bent nails) and many creative people were forced out of the business. The increased power of the production supervisor also meant that studios wanted pictures that would sell. The easiest thing to sell was a picture that imitated a recent success (notice how this philosophy is still with us: *Rambo II, Rocky II, Poltergeist II*, etc.). As a result, the mid-1920s saw the birth of the "formula" picture with proven ingredients for success—big stars, successful and familiar stories, expensive-looking sets. Hollywood films had adopted commercial and industrial practices that would last for the next few decades.

Telling Stories with Film: Content Trends to 1927

Trends and directions in film and television content are best illustrated by examples. Consequently, this and subsequent sections examining content contain the titles of many films or television programs. Of course, if you've never seen the particular film or program that's mentioned, the example may not be entirely effective. Nonetheless, the titles are listed here in the hope that those who have not seen them will make an effort to view these examples, perhaps at film revivals, media history courses, on videocassettes or discs, or on late-night TV. This section will become more meaningful the more you view the films and TV shows that are mentioned.

Horses jumping hurdles, trains rushing by the camera, acrobats tumbling—the earliest films simply recorded motion. As photographic techniques improved, it

Intolerance, *completed in 1916 for the then unbelievable cost of $2 million, included lavish sets such as this one. Despite the large production investment, this early film epic was a box-office flop. (Culver Pictures)*

became possible to take the camera to news events and record them on film. Prizefights, inaugurations, and battle scenes (many of them faked) were popular film subjects at the turn of the century.

After the narrative films of Georges Méliès and Edwin Porter proved that movies could tell a story, film topics became more varied. Still, the majority of these early films ran for only one reel and were aimed at a mass audience composed primarily of working-class immigrants, recently arrived in America. Despite some innovative film techniques such as special effects, sequences of scenes, and crosscutting, the camera remained a stationary spectator to theaterlike productions.

The decade between 1906 and 1916 proved to be an important period for the development of film as a unique means of artistic expression. In 1912, film producer Adolph Zukor decided to copy European filmmakers who were making longer, more expensive films aimed at a middle-class audience. He acquired the four-reel French film *Queen Elizabeth,* starring Sarah Bernhardt, the most famous actress of the period, and distributed it in the United States at the then unbelievable price of a dollar a ticket. His experiment was successful, proving that American audiences would pay more and sit still for longer films. Nevertheless, *Queen Elizabeth* remained essentially the filming of a stage play.

It was an American, D. W. Griffith, who eventually took full advantage of the film medium and established film as its own art form. His brilliant Civil War drama, *Birth of a Nation,* was released in 1915 and became the most expensive American film produced to that date ($110,000). The three-hour movie, which was shot without a script, introduced history as a film topic. It also was a milestone in cinematography. Griffith explored the potential of the camera for visually enhancing story line as well as capturing and communicating the intense emotions of this actors. In addition, through masterful editing, he showed how to control both time and space, to prolong suspense, and to emphasize central themes. He went on to top *Nation*'s figures with an even bigger epic, *Intolerance,* a piece composed of four scenarios dealing with life's injustices. The movies was completed in 1916 at a cost of about $2 million (the same film made in the 1990s would easily cost $40 million to $50 million). Griffith's later productions still demonstrated his skills in set design, editing, and cinematography, but his stories were oversentimentalized, ponderous, and preachy. He was unable to sense the changing tastes of the filmgoers of the 1920s and never mastered the technology of sound as he had the eye of the camera.

While Griffith was producing lavish and highly serious spectacles, other Americans were developing a totally different form of film—the comedy. The pioneer in this area was a former co-worker of Griffith's named Mack Sennett. The slapstick antics of his wondrously incompetent Keystone Cops entertained audiences throughout World War I. It was Sennett's protégé—a former comic in English music halls named Charlie Chaplin—who, dressed in oversized pants and a too-small coat and twirling a cane, created a character known as "The Tramp," probably the most successful comic character in film history. Chaplin's films were popular throughout the entire world. The film that showed him at his best was the 1925 production *The Gold Rush.* Second only to Chaplin in popularity were the films of Buster Keaton, sometimes called the "Great Stone Face" because of the deadpan expression his character maintained even in the most chaotic situations. He is best remembered for his 1926 classic, *The General.*

Two other film forms—the western and the nonfiction film—also gained prominence during the 1920s. After Porter's *The Great Train Robbery,* cowboys, Indians, covered wagons, outlaws, and cattle drives became popular subjects with filmmakers. In fact, the western film (along with radio soap operas) was one of the few uniquely American entertainment forms to be developed in the twentieth century. The foremost director of western thrillers was Thomas Ince, whose films were characterized by strong plots and lots of shoot-'em-up action. Ince also made famous the strong, silent cowboy hero. "Bronco Billy" (G. M. Anderson) was the first cowboy star, but he was soon followed by a whole posse of others: William S. Hart, Tom Mix, Buck Jones, Hoot Gibson, and Ken Maynard, to name a few. The early 1920s also saw the birth of the epic western, in which the sprawling, wild American West itself became a star in the film, a genre that would reappear in the films of the 1960s (*How the West Was Won*), 1970s (*Jeremiah Johnson*), and the 1980s (*Silverado* and *Pale Rider*).

Many films of the postwar decade focused on a topic popular during the Roaring Twenties—sex. Exotic (and erotic) red-hot romances offered an escape to the 1920s moviegoer. This type of film got off to a flying start when a 1921 desert romance, *The Sheik,* starring a smoldering Rudolph Valentino, enjoyed phenomenal box-office success. This led to a whole caravan of sun-scorched romances: *Arabian Love, Tents of Allah, When the Desert Calls, Burning Sands,* and many more. When the desert theme wore out, other action-adventure films starring such leading men as Ramon Navarro and Douglas Fairbanks took its place. The heroes of all these films were

A Cecil B. DeMille Production

As America progressed through the early part of the 1920s, probably the best known Hollywood director was the master showman Cecil B. DeMille. Among the first to realize that the moral climate of the nation following World War I was becoming more permissive, DeMille turned out a string of sophisticated comedies that dealt with mature topics: infidelity, sexual adventures, eroticism, and immorality. "See your favorite stars commit your favorite sins" was a line in one of the ads for a DeMille film.

His films also glorified the bathroom. When one of DeMille's stars took a bath, it was not in your basic tub. Sumptuous and opulent bathrooms, filled with ornate decorations and big as living rooms, were a characteristic of his films. A bath was a ceremony, not some sanitary necessity. (It was also a marvelous excuse to show his leading ladies in various forms of undress.)

When the industry became more strict about depictions of immorality, DeMille found an ingenious way to get around their guidelines. He put his erotic adventures into biblical films such as *The Ten Commandments* (1923) and *The King of Kings* (1927). Showing sin was okay, as long as it was ultimately punished. Furthermore, how could anyone be against a film that featured Moses and God in leading roles?

Of course, DeMille's great contribution to film was his emphasis on production values. His films were visually ornate with meticulous attention paid to details—costumes, sets, props, makeup, scenery. A "Cecil B. DeMille Production" was a film that had a certain style or class all its own. He knew how to please his audiences. None of his films ever lost money.

passionate and aggressive lovers (had the word been popular during the 1920s, they would have been called "macho"), who literally swept a woman off her feet and rode off into the sunset. Speaking of women, several leading ladies of the period portrayed liberated, sexually aware, and sophisticated characters. Greta Garbo, Joan Crawford, Norma Shearer, and Gloria Swanson were among the actresses who specialized in playing these more daring roles. All in all, many movies of this period, especially those of director Cecil B. DeMille (see boxed material), demonstrated a new attitude toward sexual themes.

The Coming of Sound

Silent films, of course, were never silent. Full orchestras, big Wurlitzer organs, sound effects, and narrators had all brought sound to the early screen. As far back as the 1880s, there had been experiments to synchronize a disc recording to the picture. Advances in radio technology, especially those by Lee De Forest, led to a primitive sound system for movies in 1922. Since optical recording of sound on film had been feasible since 1918, why did Hollywood wait until the late 1920s to introduce sound films? Money.

Business was good during the 1920s, and the major studios did not want to get into costly experimentation with new techniques. Warner Brothers, however, was not as financially sound as the other studios. Since Warner did not own theaters in the big cities and could not exhibit all its pictures in the most lucrative markets, the company was willing to try anything to get its films into movie theaters. Primarily as a novelty, in 1926 Warner released *Don Juan,* a silent film starring John Barrymore, which played with synchronized musical accompaniment. The program included music by the New York Philharmonic Orchestra, singers backed by the Metropolitan Opera Chorus, and solo violinists. Neither the industry nor the audience was overly impressed. However, in 1926 Warner followed up *Don Juan* with *The Jazz Singer,* in which Al Jolson not only sang but spoke from the screen. There were only 354 words in the entire film, but the movie was a huge success, and within two years the silent film, for all practical purposes, was dead.

The coming of sound ended many promising film careers. Big, brawny heroes of action-adventure films who had squeaky, high-pitched voices could not make the transition to the new era; neither could beautiful leading ladies with accents too thick for the audience to understand. Directors were suddenly faced with learning how to direct for the microphone as well as for the camera; some didn't learn quickly enough. In addition, mobile camera techniques, so painstakingly developed by directors such as Griffith, suffered a setback, because cameras had to be immobilized in soundproof booths to keep microphones from picking up their whirring sound.

The production of sound films cost Hollywood industries millions of dollars in investments in new equipment, new technicians, and new creative talent. A significant percentage of this cash came from banks, insurance companies, and investment firms, all of which wanted a say on how their funds were to be spent. As a result, production-line filmmaking that encouraged certain conventions of acting, directing, and writing was favored over creative innovations. The early talkies became highly stylized. Nevertheless, in a remarkably short time, the creative side of the industry adjusted to the new demands of sound, and good movies continued to be produced.

By 1930, the industry had improved its technical resources for reproducing sound; the camera and microphone could be moved together, and a more effective

Al Jolson sings into the mike in The Jazz Singer *(1927). This film convinced the public that talkies were possible, thus ushering in a new era in Hollywood. (Culver Pictures)*

balance between picture and sound emerged. The novelty of sound gave a boost to the film industry, despite the economic effects of the Depression. In 1929, average weekly movie attendance was 80 million; by 1930 it had reached 90 million—a fact that led many to regard filmmaking as a Depression-proof industry. They were quickly proven wrong as attendance dropped in 1931 and again in 1932. New innovations were needed to attract audiences. *Becky Sharp* was filmed in the new Technicolor process in 1935. Theaters also began the practice of showing **double features,** two feature films on the same bill. Animated cartoons were also emerging as a force to be reckoned with in the film industry. All this new activity called for Hollywood to produce even more films—almost 400 per year during the 1930s—in order to meet the demands of the market. This high production volume was a boon to major studios since they could churn out large numbers of films more economically. Moreover, the tremendous amount of money needed to convert to sound and the poor financial conditions created by the Depression forced many small companies out of business and left eight major studios with a lock on the film industry.

The Studio Years

The twenty years from 1930 to 1950 were the studio years, with MGM, 20th Century Fox, RKO, Warner Brothers, Paramount, Universal, Columbia, and United Artists dominating the industry. The corporate offices of Hollywood's film moguls controlled the key personnel of the major studios. These studios created hundreds of acres of back-lot movie sets, constructed elaborate sound stages, and built up showy stables of creative talent, carefully groomed for stardom. Audiences adored and emulated their favorite screen idols, who were presented as larger-than-life gods and goddesses inhabiting a glamorous fantasyland.

Different studios left their imprint on the films of the period as certain studio products took on a distinct personality. For example, during this period, Warner Brothers became best known for its gangster films; 20th Century Fox for its historical and adventure films; and MGM for its lavish, star-studded musicals. Let's take a closer look at the content of films in the studio era. The successful premiere of *The Jazz Singer* and the arrival of sound drastically altered the content of films. One new film form—the musical—was created immediately; a well-established film genre—physical and slapstick comedy—virtually ceased to exist; and another established form—the western—suffered a temporary setback.

Since music was easier and cheaper to put on film than dialogue, musical films quickly became popular among Hollywood producers and directors. At first, Broadway shows popular in New York were simply transported to Hollywood and filmed. *Rio Rita* (1929), *Showboat* (1929), and *Gold Diggers of Broadway* (1929) were among the first to appear. Because early sound cameras were awkward and cumbersome, these first efforts were primarily filmed versions of stage plays, photographed by a single, stationary camera. Then in 1930, a New York dance director named Busby Berkeley came to Hollywood and invented the musical extravaganza. Taking advantage of technical advances that made the sound camera more mobile, Berkeley filmed dance numbers that were totally different from stage numbers. Berkeley had his camera shoot straight down on the dance floor where dancers performed kaleidoscope routines; props were animated so that they seemed to glide by themselves across the stage. Although his dance numbers were usually inserted into clichéd backstage musicals, Berkeley's productions (perhaps best exemplified by the film *Gold Diggers of 1933*) still remain among the purest blends of sight and sound ever to show up on film.

The physical and visual comedy practiced by Chaplin and Keaton did not make an entirely successful transition to sound. Only the silent-film comedy team of Laurel and Hardy was able to maintain its popularity in sound films, probably because of a sense of timing that carried over from slapstick comedy into dialogue. The new comedy stars, such as W. C. Fields and the Marx Brothers, relied on snappy one-liners, amusing delivery, wisecracks, and outrageous puns.

The western was also hampered initially by ungainly sound cameras, which were so clumsy that they could not be taken out for location shooting. The visual appeal of wide open spaces and panoramic views of mountains and deserts, however, had been an important factor in the popularity of silent westerns. As a result, not a single western was filmed in the two-year period following the arrival of sound. Eventually, when portable cameras reopened the potential of this genre, moviemakers discovered that sound provided a new, dramatic dimension to traditional cowboy-and-Indian films.

A variety of film genres flourished during the 1930s. Adventure and romance were common themes, popularized by swashbuckling heroes like Errol Flynn and Douglas Fairbanks and tragic beauties like Garbo in *Camille*. There was also a smattering of exotic fantasies, from Johnny Weismuller's jungle series, *Tarzan* and its sequels, to *Frankenstein* (1931) and *King Kong* (1933), a film distinguished by its fine miniature creations and its special effects. After 1935 several literary classics and best-selling novels were adapted to the large screen, among them *Lost Horizon* (1937), *The Good Earth* (1937), *Pygmalion* (1938), and *A Christmas Carol* (1938).

As the 1930s wore on, films blending romance with light banter and comedy arising from the situation became increasingly popular. Director Frank Capra was responsible for several of these, including *It Happened One Night* (1934), *Mr. Deeds*

Clark Gable and Claudette Colbert share a unique sleeping arrangement in Frank Capra's screwball comedy It Happened One Night. *(Culver Pictures)*

Goes to Town (1936), and *Mr. Smith Goes to Washington* (1937). Generally, Capra's films follow the adventures of a naive and sincere ''ordinary guy'' who goes up against rigid convention or corrupt social forces and eventually emerges victorious. Clark Gable, Gary Cooper, and Jimmy Stewart were all leading men who played the honest but shrewd protagonist.

In the field of drama, the 1930s saw a rise in popularity of the gangster film, a genre that introduced the American public to yet another character type: the world-weary tough guy. Jimmy Cagney, Humphrey Bogart, and Edward G. Robinson personified these hard-boiled leading men in films such as *Little Caesar* (1930), *The Public Enemy* (1931), and *The Petrified Forest* (1936).

The potential of suspense and mystery dramas was explored by a notable British director, Alfred Hitchcock. Hitchcock became well known in the United States during the pre-World War II period for films such as *The 39 Steps* (1935), *The Lady Vanishes* (1938), and *Suspicion* (1941). Another foreign-born director, Josef von Sternberg, teamed with the most famous and glamorous female star of this period, Marlene Dietrich, to produce several sophisticated romances. Usually playing a worldly, somewhat cynical seductress, Dietrich was at her sultry best in *The Blue Angel* (1930), *Shanghai Express* (1932), and *Blonde Venus* (1934).

Perhaps the most significant period for motion picture achievement during the early sound era were the years 1939–1941. In 1939, David O. Selznick produced the monumental Civil War epic *Gone With the Wind,* which proved to be an effective showcase for the newly developed Technicolor process (*Gone With the Wind* was rereleased in 1989 with its original color restored). Another film that used color effectively was released that same year, the perennially popular fantasy *The Wizard of Oz.* Yet a third classic was to premiere during 1939, the western epic *Stagecoach,* starring John Wayne in his first major role. Two years later, a young Orson Welles revolutionized filmmaking techniques with his controversial first film, *Citizen Kane.* Loosely based on the life of William Randolph Hearst, Sr., the movie failed at the box office but became a favorite of critics and students of film. Making use of deep focus, innovative camera angles, special lighting techniques, and dissolves from scene to scene, Welles created a work that some critics have hailed as America's single best film.

When World II broke out, it did not take Hollywood long to turn out a number of patriotic films. Although several focused on the fighting overseas (*Wake Island,* 1942; *Bataan,* 1943), the most successful films were those portraying the life-style and cultural values that the United States was trying to preserve. Consider the most popular films during the war years: *Yankee Doodle Dandy* (1942), *Meet Me in St. Louis* (1944), *Bells of St. Mary's* (1945), and *Spellbound* (1945). The first two are escapist musicals, the third is a celebration of old-fashioned values, and the fourth is a mystery thriller. Very few popular movies of the day depicted the actual combat.

To summarize, the financial backing and diverse holdings of the studio system helped the film industry survive the Depression. Attendance and profits began climbing in 1934 and held steady throughout World War II. During the 1940s, going to a movie was just as much a part of American life as looking at television is today. In fact, the all-time peak for filmgoing was 1946, when average weekly attendance reached over 90 million. By 1947, however, all of this was to change.

COMPETITION AND CHANGE: TELEVISION

During the late 1920s, while the film industry was experimenting with the addition of sound to pictures, some enterprising inventors were busy working on ways to add pictures to sound. The product of their endeavors would drastically change the economics and the content of motion pictures. The two people associated with the early development of electrical television, Philo Farnsworth and Vladimir Zworykin, could not have been two more different individuals. Zworykin was the organization man, working first with Westinghouse and later with RCA. He made full use of these companies' large labs and research money and by 1928 had perfected a primitive television camera tube, the iconoscope. At the other end of the spectrum was Farnsworth, the prototype of the individualistic, lone-wolf, and somewhat eccentric inventor. In 1922, at the age of sixteen, when most teenagers were worrying about the prom, Farnsworth diagramed his idea for a television system on the chalkboard before his somewhat stunned high school science teacher. Because he carried out most of his later research in apartment laboratories behind closed blinds, Farnsworth's work aroused curiosity and suspicion. (In fact, his laboratory was once raided by police, who thought that only someone manufacturing illegal drugs and/or alcohol could be using all those glass tubes.) Farnsworth's hard work paid off in 1930 when he got a patent for his TV system. Television might have gotten off to a faster start, but the Depression slowed down its growth as well as that of the film industry.

Picture quality on the early television systems was poor, but technical developments during the 1930s indicated that improvements were possible. With the help of Zworykin and under a patent arrangement worked out with Farnsworth in 1939, RCA set out to develop the commercial potential of the new medium. NBC, owned by RCA, gave a public demonstration of television at the 1939 New York World's Fair with regular two-hour broadcasts. After the fair opened, RCA had TV sets with five-inch picture tubes on display in department stores. Filmmakers did not take the new invention seriously. Like radio in its infancy, early TV was looked upon as a toy, something that would never amount to much. Consider the following: In the early days of TV, performers had to wear thick green makeup to appear "normal" to the TV camera. Lights were incredibly hot and made the green makeup melt and run down the actors' faces. The heat was so intense that performers had to swallow salt tablets. Who could have had the foresight to predict that one day this bizarre, amusing, new toy would challenge and change the film industry?

Government Intervention

Back in 1938, the Justice Department had filed suit against Paramount and the other major film companies, charging that the industry's vertical control of production, distribution, and exhibition constituted restraint of trade and monopolistic practices. The case had been set aside during the war, but by 1948 the courts had ordered the major studios to get rid of at least one of their holdings in these three areas. Most chose to divest themselves of their theater chains. The court also eliminated the block booking system and thus deprived the studios of guaranteed exhibition for all their films. As a result, the studios had to cut back on film production and reduce costs as foreign films and movies made by independent producers cut into the major studios' revenues.

Television itself faced some uncertain times. During World War II, the FCC put a freeze on new TV stations, and most efforts were redirected away from TV to radar. When peace returned in 1945, however, new technology developed during the war was soon applied to the television industry. New picture tubes required drastically less light to perform; microwaves and coaxial cable were used to link stations into networks. Big-screen TV sets were being manufactured in large quantities. All of the signs pointed to big things ahead for TV. There were eight stations on the air in

1945; there were ninety-eight by 1950. Only 8000 homes had TV in 1946. Ten years later, almost 35 million households had TV sets.

TV's rapid success caught the industry and the FCC off guard. Unless technical standards were worked out, the TV spectrum was in danger of becoming overcrowded and riddled with interference. To guard against this possibility, the FCC imposed a freeze on all new applications for TV stations. The freeze, which went into effect in 1948, would last for four years, while the FCC gathered information from engineers and technical experts. When the freeze was lifted in 1952, the FCC had established that twelve VHF and seventy UHF channels (see page 301) were to be devoted to TV. In addition, the commission drew up a list that allocated television channels to the various communities in the United States and specified other rules to minimize interference. Also, thanks largely to the efforts of Frieda Hennock, the first woman to serve on the commission, TV channels were set aside for educational use.

The Structure of Early Television

The structure of early television was modeled after that of radio. Local stations provided a service for their communities and in turn might be affiliated with networks. There were four early TV nets: CBS, NBC, ABC, and DuMont, a smaller network that went out of business in 1956. The Mutual radio network did not make the transition into television.

One of the big problems in early TV was the difficulty in "storing" programs. In the 1950s, most shows were either broadcast live from the networks' New York studios or filmed on the West Coast using conventional Hollywood techniques. Live programs, of course, lacked the potential to be run again, and often they had to be repeated for the West Coast audiences. These programs could not be recorded on film for later showing since film was too expensive to use and took too long to process and edit. Kinescopes (films of the TV screen) were of poor quality but were used because they were the only means available. What was needed was an electronic medium for storing television pictures much in the same way audio tape stores sound. In 1956, the Ampex company solved the storage problem with the invention of videotape. With the new tape, programs could be prerecorded, edited, and polished before broadcast. Tape was much cheaper than film, could be played back at once, and, best of all, could be reused. By the beginning of the 1960s, most of TV's live programming had switched to tape.

UHF, Color, and Network Dominance

After the freeze, both new TV stations and new TV sets rapidly multiplied. Total advertising revenue passed the billion-dollar mark in 1955, and by the close of the 1950s there were 559 stations on the air and almost 90 percent of all American homes had TV. On the negative side, broadcasters and the FCC began to notice that the high hopes expressed in 1952 for the future of UHF television had been too optimistic. Few sets equipped with UHF receivers were made in the 1950s. If you wanted to receive these signals, you spent an additional $25–$50 for a converter. UHF stations also had a smaller coverage area than VHF operations, and most network affiliations and advertising dollars went to the more powerful VHF stations. As a result, UHF TV, much like FM radio, started off at a major disadvantage.

Another technological breakthrough took place in the 1950s with the introduction of color television. Led by NBC (RCA, the parent company, was manufacturing

Live ... From New York

Much of early television was done live. You saw it as it actually happened in a studio in New York or Chicago. There were no opportunities to stop the videotape and do it over. It was an exciting time because you knew that if you watched long enough, if you watched closely enough, and if you watched carefully enough, you would see something go wrong. For example, in one live show actor Lee Marvin had to make a quick move to get out of one scene set in an apartment and into another that took place in a phone booth. The idea was that the camera would tilt down from Marvin to a cigarette smoldering in an ash tray and stay on it until Marvin dashed across the set and into a mock phone booth in the wings. In dress rehearsals, no matter how fast Marvin ran, the camera still spent twenty to thirty seconds on that smoking cigarette, waiting for Marvin to get into the booth. That was too long and everybody looked for a way to shorten Marvin's run. Just before air time, the director had a brainstorm. He put the phone booth on wheels and moved it just off the edge of the apartment set. Marvin should make it easily.

Unfortunately, the director forgot that the studio was built on a slight incline and the phone booth was now at the top of it. He also forgot the rush of adrenalin that actors get when they perform live before the cameras. Anyway, the show went on the air and Marvin must have been running about twenty miles an hour when he jumped in the phone booth. He

hit it so hard that the thing began to roll down the incline and across the studio. Astonished, the studio camera operators had no choice but to follow the booth. Viewers at home were surprised to see a traveling phone booth pass in front of the lighting crew, in front of bare studio walls, and even in front of a half-naked actress changing for the next scene, thinking she was comfortably out of camera range. The phone booth eventually thudded against the wall at the far end of the studio in total darkness. The director finally regained his composure and cut to a commercial while the technical crew ran to guide Marvin back to the set.

On another occasion, a live TV drama had a scene in which one man supposedly shot another. In early TV this had to be handled carefully so as not to injure the sensitive microphones with a loud sound. What was usually done was to have the actor point the gun and pull the trigger, while an offstage technician, far enough from the microphone not to cause harm, would fire a blank. When the show was being telecast live and the time for the shooting scene arrived, the first actor pointed the gun and squeezed the trigger. Nothing happened. The first actor again pointed and pulled the trigger. Again, no sound, nothing. The second actor, the supposed victim of the shooting, quickly grasped his chest and cried out, "My God! Where did you get that silencer?" as he crumpled to the floor.

It was an exciting time to be in the TV audience.

color sets), the networks were broadcasting about two to three hours of color programming per day in 1960.

The 1950s also saw the networks rise to primary importance as programming sources for their local affiliates. NBC and CBS were the two networks that usually dominated television ratings while ABC trailed behind. In the early days of TV, most network prime-time programs were produced by advertising agencies that retained control over their content. After the scandal that followed the discovery that some quiz shows were "fixed" in 1959, the networks began to assert their own control over programming. This trend away from advertiser control of programs has continued. The networks now allow independent producers to supply most of their evening programming (the networks, however, still share in the cost of producing the shows).

CHANGING CONTENT TRENDS IN TV

The changing content of television programs can be accounted for by both economic and social reasons. When TV service first started in the late 1940s, it was in a period of experimentation. Most of the early programs were based on formats developed during radio's era of great popularity. In fact, some of the early TV shows were actually simulcasts of radio programs. Typical low-cost formats included game shows such as "Face the Music" and "Charade Quiz" and interview shows such as "Meet the Press" and "America's Town Meeting of the Air," as well as a variety of westerns, soap operas, and comedies, all directly transposed to television. Another popular feature was the sports program. In a typical week in 1948, fully twenty-five hours in prime time were devoted to sports.

The Golden Age of Television

The 1950s are known as the "golden age" of television. This was a period marked by tremendous growth and innovation. Every program was a pioneer. The show that best typified early TV, however, was the variety show. In a way, this format marked the return of an entertainment style not seen since the motion picture spelled the end of vaudeville. "Ted Mack's Original Amateur Hour" premiered in 1948, as did "Arthur Godfrey's Talent Scouts," Ed Sullivan's "Toast of the Town," and the long-running "Texaco Star Theater," starring ex-vaudevillian Milton Berle. When the definitive history of early TV is written, several pages will have to be devoted to this pioneer comedian, whose incredible popularity soon won him the title of "Mr. Television." Berle probably sold more TV sets than any other human being as people bought the new invention just to see what wacky costume "Uncle Miltie" would show up in next.

A second trend—the first demonstrable trend in television programming was due in large measure to economic factors. Many buyers of early TV sets were people of above-average income and education who tended to live in urban areas, especially the New York City region. This audience had long enjoyed live theater, and it was only natural that popular shows during the late 1940s and early 1950s should feature "live" dramas that would appeal to these sophisticated viewers. "Studio One" (1948–1958) featured plays by Rod Serling, Gore Vidal, and Reginald Rose. "The U.S. Steel Hour" (1953–1963) featured Broadway stars such as Tallulah Bankhead, Rex Harrison, and Gary Merrill. In the mid-fifties, U.S. Steel presented Cliff Robertson in a play called *The Two Worlds of Charley Gordon*. In 1968, Robertson recreated this role in the film *Charly* and won an academy award. Other programs that featured prestige drama were "Robert Montgomery Presents" (1950–1957), "Armstrong Circle Theater" (1950–1963), and "Kraft Television Theater" (1947–1958).

A second trend—the rise of the "adult western"—was also the result of monetary factors. In 1953, ABC merged with Paramount Theaters, which had recently been severed from Paramount Pictures because of the Justice Department's decree. ABC was looking for a program format that was guaranteed to be popular yet relatively inexpensive to produce, and Paramount had experience in producing westerns, a format that had enjoyed steady popularity since 1903. As it happened, ABC

Mr. Television, Milton Berle, dressed in one of the outrageous costumes that became his trademark on the "Texaco Star Theater." (Personality Press)

could not afford the tremendously expensive location shooting associated with the traditional western, so they modified the genre into something more affordable—the "adult western," in which character and motivation took precedence over huge battles between wagon trains and Indians. Two such programs premiered in 1955: "The Life and Legend of Wyatt Earp" (1955–1961) and "Gunsmoke" (1955–1975). These shows started a trend that spawned many imitators: "Cheyenne," "Wagon Train," "Rawhide," "Have Gun Will Travel," and "Maverick." By 1959, the high-water mark for the western, there were twenty-six westerns in prime time. Networks had long since discovered that it paid to copy each other's successful programs.

Economics lay behind a third programming trend of the late fifties. After about 1958, TV became less exclusively an urban medium. As set prices dropped, television set ownership became more widespread. Stations sprang up in small towns, and TV antennas sprouted in rural areas. Soon, television programmers, in their quest for higher ratings, began providing shows that catered to this new audience. One early forerunner was the "Tennessee Ernie Ford Show" (1956–1961), which was followed by "The Andy Griffith Show" (1960–1968) and "The Real McCoys" (1957–1963). The quintessential show of this genre was the highly popular "The Beverly Hillbillies" (1962–1971), which attracted as many as 60 million viewers every week. Other shows, mainly from CBS ("Green Acres," "Petticoat Junction," "Gomer Pyle," "Mayberry RFD"), were quick to imitate this series' success.

The Reaction of the Film Industry

When television began building a sizable audience during the late 1940s, it cut into the motion picture industry's profits. The first reaction of the film industry was to

One of the problems with 3-D movies was the uncomfortable plastic glasses that audience members had to wear in order to appreciate the three-dimensional effects. (J. R. Eyerman, Life *Magazine,* © *Time Inc.)*

fight back. Studios stubbornly refused to advertise their films on TV, and they would not release old films for showing on the newer medium. Many studios wrote clauses into the contracts of their major stars forbidding them to appear on TV. None of their efforts had an appreciable effect on television's growing popularity—more and more Americans bought TV sets, while film attendance slipped even further.

Hollywood looked for ways to recapture some of its audience from TV. By the early 1950s, the film industry thought it had found the answer—technical wizardry. The first technical gimmick was 3-D (three-dimensional film). The audience wore special polarized glasses to perceive the effect and were treated to the illusion of spears, trains, arrows, knives, birds, and Jane Russell jumping out at them from the film screen. Unfortunately, the glasses gave some people headaches, and the equipment was too expensive for most theater owners to install. Audiences quickly became bored with the novelty. It soon became apparent that 3-D was not the answer. The second technical gimmick concerned screen size. Cinerama, which involved the use of three projectors and curved screens, surrounded the audience with film. It was too costly to achieve widespread use. Less expensive techniques that enlarged screen size, such as Cinemascope, Panavision, and Vistavision, were ultimately adopted by the industry but did little to stem Hollywood's loss of money.

The attitude of the movie companies toward TV during these early years was a clear example of shortsightedness. The film studios were still closely allied with their theater outlets. TV was hurting the neighborhood theater; therefore, TV was the enemy. What the film companies failed to see was that they could have played a dominant role in TV's evolution. Because major networks were not eager to supply early television programs, film companies would have been logical sources for television shows. However, the studios held so much animosity toward the new medium that production of early television series went to the advertising agencies, which assumed the role almost by default. Somewhat belatedly, Hollywood recognized that it was in its best interests to cooperate with television. In the late 1950s, the studios began to release their pre-1948 films to TV and also began to supply programs to the networks. In 1960, post-1948 theatrical films were made available to the smaller TV screens.

Recapturing an Audience: Film in the TV Age

During the postwar period, Hollywood produced several films that were more realistic in content and focused on social problems. By the 1950s, however, when it became clear that TV would be a formidable competitor, the film industry hastily cast about for new and unusual gimmicks to draw audiences back to the theaters. First it tried spectacle, complete with big budgets, lavish sets, and a cast of thousands: *Ben Hur*

A salesman taking an order in a 1950s television and radio store. (The Bettmann Archive)

William Castle: Master of the Horror Film

In Hollywood's struggle to recapture the audience from television, no one was more imaginative than low-budget horror film producer William Castle. Early in his movie career Castle realized that if you couldn't attract audiences with a film, you might be able to do it with a gimmick. Without doubt, Castle raised the film gimmick to an art form. Consider these achievements: *Macabre* (1958) was filmed in nine days and cost a paltry $90,000. Castle knew the film was nothing special, but he had the foresight to take out a policy with Lloyd's of London insuring every ticket buyer for $1000 in case they dropped dead of fright during the film. Castle parked hearses in front of the theater and hired fake nurses to stand around in the lobby. Audiences loved it. Most people came not so much for the film but to see if some poor soul would slump over dead in his seat and earn the money. (Nobody ever collected.)

Castle topped himself with *House on Haunted Hill,* starring Vincent Price. The gimmick here was something called Emergo-vision. Each theater was equipped with a black, casket-shaped box installed next to the screen. At a certain point in the film, the box would open and an illuminated twelve-foot plastic skeleton would glide on wires over the audience back to the projection booth. Unfortunately, at the film's sneak preview the equipment failed and the skeleton came crashing down, sending the audience scurrying for the exits. After further refinements, Emergo-vision was installed in theaters all over the country and the audiences went wild. When the skeleton appeared some kids screamed, some ducked under their seats, and others, obviously the more macho ones, threw popcorn boxes and jujubes at the skeleton as it passed overhead.

Castle's greatest artistic triumph, however, was his next film, *The Tingler* (1959). Vincent Price again starred, but he was overshadowed by the The Tingler, an ugly organism that resembled a cross between a lobster and a scorpion. The Tingler supposedly lived in everyone's spinal column and came to life only when a person was frightened (it accounted for that tingling sensation on your backbone when you got really scared). The only way to kill this unpleasant creature was to scream. At one point in the film The Tingler breaks loose in a movie theater and kills the projectionist. In the real theaters, the screen would go blank, a silhouette of The Tingler would crawl past the projector's beam, and a voice would frantically announce, ''Attention. The Tingler is loose in this theater. Please scream for your life.'' The audience, naturally, would start screaming at the top of its lungs. This gimmick would have been enough for most mortals, but Castle didn't stop here. He had small devices, much like the handshake buzzers used in practical jokes, installed under the seats. At the precise moment The Tingler was supposed to be in the audience, presumably looking for its next victim, the projectionist would activate the buzzers, causing audience members to experience a definite tingling sensation in their posterior regions. Pandemonium would generally ensue. (Legend has it that in one city the buzzer devices were installed under the seats the night before *The Tingler* was to open. That night a group of elderly women were invited to the theater to watch a special screening of *The Nun's Story.* During the movie, the projectionist decided to test *The Tingler* buzzers. Many women left the theater convinced that they had had a religious experience.)

(1959), a remake of *The Ten Commandments* (1956), *El Cid* (1960), *Spartacus* (1960), and the highly touted production of *Cleopatra* (1962), starring Elizabeth Taylor and Richard Burton, that failed to recoup its $44 million price tag. Ironically enough, another trend was taking place during this same period at the other end of the financial spectrum—the cheap film. Movies like *I Was a Teenage Werewolf* (1953), *I Was a Teenage Frankenstein* (1954), and *Hercules* (1956) were all made for less than $300,000, a sum the studios could make back after playing for several weeks at local theaters.

With the relaxation of content restrictions, films began addressing subject matter that could not be shown on TV. *Peyton Place* (1957), *From Here to Eternity* (1953), and *Advise and Consent* (1962) dealt respectively with promiscuity, adultery, and homosexuality. In addition to controversial themes, another film genre that came across more effectively on the big screen than on TV was the musical. Subsequently, wholesome and light musicals that made use of vivid color, expensive props, and elaborate costumes and settings (items that could not be matched in a small TV studio) made an appearance. *An American in Paris* (1951), *Singin' in the Rain* (1952), and *The Bandwagon* (1953) were perhaps the best examples.

Although difficult to categorize, the films of the late fifties and early sixties generally continued to rely on subject matter or production techniques that were ill suited for television. For example, big-budget spectaculars were successful: *West Side Story* (1961), *The Sound of Music* (1965), *Doctor Zhivago* (1965). Additional hit films were drawn from popular literature, as action-adventure capers, spiced with sex and featuring indestructible heroes like James Bond (*Thunderball*, 1965; *Goldfinger,* 1964), became audience favorites. In 1967, the release of Arthur Penn's *Bonnie and Clyde* marked a pivotal point in the evolution of film content. Capitalizing on the newly emerged "youth culture," the picture reflected the changing concerns of its audience: dissatisfaction with traditional values, a desire to protest, and a preoccupation with individuality and an unencumbered life-style. Other films ex-

Hollywood vs. TV: Dollars and Scents

As the motion picture industry tried to cope with the rising competition of television, it tried many technical gimmicks to get the audience away from the tube and into the theater. Increased screen size and 3-D were, as has been pointed out, the techniques that got most attention. Lesser known but no less imaginative was another piece of gimmickry that TV could never hope to imitate—Smell-O-Vision.

Smell-O-Vision, also known by the more genteel name of "Aromarama," was first developed in 1959. The following year, producer Mike Todd backed a film called *The Scent of Mystery,* which was accompanied by odors. The smells came from little pipes built into the backs of the theater seats. It worked like this: An early scene in the film showed a rose garden next to a monastery in Spain. While this scene was projected, the faint scent of roses was piped into the theater. Scenes at the seashore were accompanied by the appropriate sea smells. The clue to unraveling the mystery had to do with a certain brand of pipe tobacco that had a distinctive aroma. Unfortunately, it was difficult for the theater's air-conditioning system to eliminate one odor before the next was piped in. As a result, some smells hung in the air and mixed with the next odors that came wafting out from behind the seats. Toward the end of the film, many odors were floating about the theater, and their combination caused an overall disagreeable smell that many audience members complained about. The technique was never tried again, although John Waters tried something similar in his *Polyester.* It wasn't very successful either.

ploring the conflict between nonconformists and the establishment quickly followed: *The Graduate* (1967) and *Cool Hand Luke* (1967). The youth cycle reached its peak during the late sixties with *Easy Rider, Alice's Restaurant,* and *Medium Cool.*

MODERN TRENDS IN FILM AND TV

Waning Power: The 1960s Film Industry

In the film industry, the 1960s were marked by the waning power of the major studios and by a closer affiliation with their old competitor, television. The continued rise of the independent producer led to a concomitant loss of power by the studios. As major production houses cut back, they released many actors, writers, and directors who, naturally enough, formed small, independent production companies. Using the big studios for financing and distribution, these independents and the artists they employed frequently took small salaries in exchange for a percentage of the film's profits. By the mid-1960s, roughly 80 percent of all American films were independent productions.

The poor economic climate brought about other changes. Large studios, faced with ever-worsening financial conditions, were absorbed by larger conglomerates. United Artists became part of the TransAmerica Corporation (it would later be absorbed by MGM, and MGM itself would later be acquired by Turner Broadcasting); Paramount, a division of Gulf + Western; and Warner Brothers, a part of Kinney National. The twilight of the studios extended into the next decade. In the early 1970s, both the MGM and 20th Century Fox studios were sold to make room for real estate developers. Universal, the only studio to remain more or less unchanged, has done so by supporting itself through TV production and by becoming a major tourist attraction for visitors to southern California.

The late 1960s also saw a change in the regulatory climate that surrounded films. The Supreme Court issued several decisions during this time that loosened controls on content, and filmmakers were quick to take advantage of their new freedom. In 1968, the Motion Picture Association of America liberalized its attitudes toward self-regulation. Whereas the old Production Code attempted to regulate content, the new system attempted to regulate audiences by instituting a G-PG-R-X labeling system.

The relationship between film and television became even closer in the 1960s, as movies made expressly for TV appeared in the middle of the decade. By 1974 about 180 of these "TV movies" were shown on network television. In that same year, the major film companies distributed only 109 films to theaters. In addition, many directors like Sidney Lumet and Sam Peckinpah, who started in television, went on to successful careers as film directors.

Coming of Age: Television in the 1960s

By the early 1960s, television's ecstatic trial period had come to an end. TV by then had lost much of its novelty and had become just another part of everyday life. During this decade, the number of TV stations increased by 54 percent, and by 1970, 95 percent of all American households owned at least one working television. Advertisers, lured by the potential profits to be reaped from this vast audience, increased their advertising 120 percent. As the influence of television became more apparent, critics of television programming became more outspoken. Parents were

Live TV coverage of the first moon landing in 1969 reached hundreds of millions of viewers. (Ed Carlin/The Picture Cube)

joined by educators, politicians, psychologists, and minority leaders in expressing their concern over the new medium's social and political impact on its viewers. In response to these economic and social pressures, television development during the 1960s moved in the direction of expansion, diversification, and sensitivity to the growing potential of television journalism.

In 1960, the Kennedy–Nixon debates were telecast to an audience of 65 million. Three years later, NBC and CBS expanded their nightly newscasts to thirty minutes (ABC followed suit shortly thereafter), and the heated competition between Walter Cronkite on CBS and the team of Chet Huntley and David Brinkley on NBC began. In November of 1963, TV journalism demonstrated the highest degree of professionalism during its coverage of the assassination and funeral of President John F. Kennedy. The networks also covered the growing civil rights movement during the sixties as well as the social unrest on campus and in the cities. Perhaps the most exciting moment for television news came in 1969 with its live coverage of Neil Armstrong's historic walk on the moon.

Noncommercial broadcasting was also evolving during the 1960s. Educational stations, as they were called then, got off to a rather shaky start since the choice VHF frequencies in the large markets had been snapped up by commercial stations. Despite this drawback, the number of educational stations grew during the fifties and sixties so that by 1965, ninety-nine were on the air. It was obvious, however, that some stable source of financial support was needed to keep many of them from going dark. A report issued by the Carnegie Commission proposed that Congress establish a Corporation for Public Broadcasting. The commission's recommendations were incorporated into the **Public Broadcasting Act of 1967,** which set up the Public Broadcasting Service. Unfortunately, the act did not provide for secure, long-term financing of the new service, an omission that later led to political problems with the executive branch of the government and prompted yet another study by a new Carnegie Commission in the late 1970s.

Another segment of the broadcasting industry was also experiencing growth in this decade—the cable television (CATV) industry. CATV originated as an attempt to bring TV signals to hard-to-reach mountainous areas, but operators soon began to import signals from distant stations to communities in nonmountainous areas that were without full three-network service. By 1960, CATV systems were capable of providing twelve different channels to their subscribers, including specialized news and information channels, movie channels, and even several audio services. Faced with increased pressures from over-the-air broadcasters, the FCC, which initially did not want to get involved in the regulation of CATV, did an about-face in 1966 and issued a set of regulations for CATV that would slow down its growth for the next half-dozen years. Related to the fortunes of CATV were those of the emerging pay-TV industry. The FCC had okayed an experimental over-the-air pay-TV operation in Hartford, Connecticut, in 1960, and in 1968 the commission issued rules governing the new pay operations. By this time, however, pay-TV companies were turning to CATV systems rather than pursuing over-the-air pay TV. Cable operators were also eager to add one or more pay channels to increase the attractiveness of their service. As the 1970s began, the future of these two industries would become more closely entwined.

Years of Turmoil: TV Content in the 1960s

The 1960s were years marked by growing social turmoil—dissent over the Vietnam War and civil rights and concern over outbursts of violence and the economic recession. These volatile social conditions appear to have been the impetus for two major content trends of this period. Having learned that audiences would tolerate a high level of violence, network programmers produced a steady stream of action-adventure shows. Two of the most successful of these were "The Untouchables," based on the exploits of G-man Eliot Ness, and "Naked City," a cops-and-robbers show set in New York. After the Kennedy assassination in 1963, however, public protest against televised violence resulted in a modification of program content. To satisfy viewers who wished to avoid the harsh realities of life, prime-time television presented shows that can best be categorized as fantasy and escapist situation comedies. In the fall of 1964, for example, the following shows were on the networks' schedules: "My Living Doll" (about a glamorous robot), "My Favorite Martian" (about a Martian), "The Munsters" (a family of monsters making a go of it in suburbia), "Bewitched" (about a friendly witch), "I Dream of Jeannie" (about a friendly genie), and "My Mother the Car" (self-explanatory). Other shows featuring escapist fantasy that appeared during this period were "Batman," "The Wild Wild West," "The Man From U.N.C.L.E.," and "Get Smart."

By the late sixties, however, there was another shift in programming. Growing concern over social conditions was reflected in the watchwords of television content during this period: youth and relevance. In 1969 and 1970, the following shows premiered: "The Young Rebels," "The Young Lawyers," "The Interns" (about young doctors), "Storefront Lawyers" (more young lawyers), "The Headmaster" (about young teachers and young students), and "Matt Lincoln" (about young social workers). None of these shows survived into a second season, thus making this the shortest trend on record.

Portrayals of Blacks and Women

During the early years of television, leading female and black performers were restricted to stereotypical roles. Women were either scatterbrained wives (as in "I Love Lucy") or model housewives and mothers ("Leave It to Beaver"). Blacks were practically nonexistent.

In 1965, however, a young Bill Cosby co-starred with Robert Culp in "I Spy" and created a new role for blacks in TV—the assistant to the hero. By the 1970s, several shows featuring black casts appeared in prime time; most were situation comedies, such as "Good Times" and "The Jeffersons." This trend continued through the 1980s. The 1987–1988 season featured five sitcoms with black casts, but few blacks were on dramatic series.

Women appeared sparingly in lead roles during the 1960s. "Honey West," the first female private eye in a leading role in a TV series, lasted one season (1965). Marlo Thomas starred in "That Girl" for six seasons as a somewhat kooky but modern-thinking woman. Other shows portraying women a little more realistically premiered in the 1970s: "The Mary Tyler Moore Show," "Maude," and "One Day at a Time." In the late 1970s, however, producers seemed to select female leads more for their looks and series such as "Charlie's Angels" and "Three's Company" were on the schedules.

By the 1980s, the portrayal of females was a little more diverse, as evidence by "thirtysomething," "The Golden Girls," "L.A. Law," and "Murphy Brown." Nonetheless, in 1989 NBC premiered "Nightingales," a series about nurses that was a throwback to the familiar female as sex object formula.

Upward Trends: The 1970s Film Industry

Film history since the early seventies has been marked by several apparent trends: Revenue went up, as did the budgets of many feature films, and several motion pictures racked up astonishing gross receipts. Foremost among these trends was a reversal of the slump in box-office receipts that began in 1946 and finally bottomed out in 1971. With the exception of temporary declines in 1973 and 1976, the general trend has been upward. In 1977, total box-office gross was about $2.4 billion; by 1981 it had risen to nearly $3 billion, although some of this increase could be attributed to inflation.

With more cash flowing into the box office, more money became available for the budgets of feature films. In fact, films of the late 1970s and early 1980s were reminiscent of the extravaganzas of the 1920s. For example, *Dune* (1984) and *Cotton Club* (1984) each cost about $40 million to make; *Superman III* (1983) and *Raise the Titanic* (1980) each cost about $36 million. Although the expense of making such films seems astronomical, the final movie product offers a chance at fabulous financial rewards. Perhaps the most interesting film phenomenon of the era has been the rise of the super box-office blockbuster. From 1900 to 1970, only two films (*The Sound of Music* and *Gone With the Wind*) managed to surpass $50 million in film rentals; between 1970 and 1980, seventeen films surpassed this mark (Table 11.1). The science-fiction epic *Star Wars,* which cost approximately $10 million to make, had grossed $400 million worldwide by 1979. Interestingly enough, it was not just the big-budget films that were earning big profits. Several small-budget films also returned revenues far in excess of their costs. For example, *Easy Rider,* released in 1969, cost only $370,000 to make but earned more than $40 million. *Rocky* (1976)

TABLE 11.1 All-Time Top Money-making Films

The figures below are based on film rentals, that is, money received by the film distributor from motion picture theaters. This figure is not the same as total box-office gross receipts. Also, the table includes only rentals from the U.S. and Canadian markets.

FILM	YEAR	RENTALS (MILLIONS)
ET	1982	$229
Star Wars	1977	194
Return of the Jedi	1983	168
The Empire Strikes Back	1980	142
Ghostbusters	1984	130
Jaws	1975	129
Raiders of the Lost Ark	1981	116
Indiana Jones and the Temple of the Doom	1984	109
Beverly Hills Cop	1984	108
Back to the Future	1985	104

Source: Variety, January 11–17, 1989, p. 26.

was made for about $1 million and took in $55 million. Even when the effects of inflation are taken into account, it is apparent that a small group of films has dominated revenues in recent years.

One important factor behind the industry's renewed success at the box office was an increased use of market-research data as part of the filmmaking process. During this time period, motion pictures discovered their own well-defined audience. A survey done in the early 1970s confirmed what most in the industry had suspected: The majority of filmgoers were under thirty, well educated, and primarily urban. Hollywood, with few exceptions, takes great care to satisfy this audience. This trend toward appealing to a specialized audience was manifested in the construction of movie theaters as well. Lavish motion picture palaces were no longer being built. Modern theaters were small and often conveniently set in clusters of three or four within suburban shopping centers.

The trend toward closer cooperation between the TV and film industries was reflected by the production of more movies aimed at a television audience. In 1978, Hollywood produced around 180 films expressly for the small screen; only two dozen more were made for release in motion picture theaters. This move toward cooperation was reflected in another way when, at the end of the 1970s, two television networks, ABC and CBS, reversed tradition and began producing films that were to be released to movie theaters. NBC followed suit in 1986.

On another front, after receiving considerable criticism for giving a PG rating to films such as *Indiana Jones and the Temple of Doom* and *Gremlins,* which contained graphic violence, the Motion Picture Association of America instituted a new category—PG-13. This category was designed for those films where parental guidance for children under 13 was recommended.

Increasing Fortunes: Film in the 1980s

The 1980s were good years for films. Although theater attendance increased only slightly, higher admission costs pushed box-office revenue to new heights. The $4 billion mark was passed in 1984 and again in 1987 and 1988. Pay cable and videocassettes eclipsed the theatrical box office as the most important source of film company revenue.

Production was at an all-time high. Sparked by some independent producers, such as Cannon, Lorimar, and New World, more than 500 films were released in 1987.

There were more theater screens than ever before, nearly 23,000 in 1987 with more on the way. Ticket prices also set records. The average was $4 in 1987 but in some big cities admission prices reached $6 or even $7.

Film budgets also set records with the average film costing about $18.1 million in 1988. Nonetheless, the high price tags did not discourage studios from investing in expensive films. In 1987, about fifty films with budgets in excess of $14 million were released. About 40 percent of these turned a profit. As is obvious, moviemaking is a risky business when it comes to big-budget pictures. It is estimated that a film has to make about two and a half times its production costs to break even. In the case of a $20 million film, this means taking in about $50 million at the box office. Some big-budget films were colossal flops. The $27 million *Leonard Part Six* made only $3 million in 1987. The 1986 film *Howard the Duck* cost about $34 million to produce and brought in only about a third of that. The biggest loser, however, was *Ishtar,* a $50 million film that made about $12.5 million at the box office (see Chapter 12). On the other hand, the reward can be great when a studio is lucky enough to come up with a megahit. *Beverly Hills Cop II* cost about $20 million to make and returned four times that. *Back to the Future* cost about $22 million but returned $104 million. The $14 million *Top Gun* made about $80 million.

Home video helped add to these numbers but it was increasingly difficult to find a picture that vastly outperformed its theatrical box office results on videocassette. In fact, in many instances the home video rights were used to pay for the financing of the film and did not figure in the movie's profit equation.

Vertical Integration II

Hollywood is fond of sequels so it's not surprising that the end of the 1980s saw the major studios get back into the business of owning motion picture theaters. In 1948, the Paramount decision barred motion picture producer-distributors from the exhibition business because the Justice Department thought it was restraint of trade. In the 1980s, with a more deregulation-minded administration in power, movie studios were given the green light to return to the exhibition business provided they didn't discriminate against the films released by other distributors or engage in any other monopolistic practice.

Studios "reverticalized" in a grand way. Cannon, Paramount, Tri-Star, United Artists, and Universal all acquired chains of movie theaters. In addition, theater owner Cineplex Odeon announced a partnership with MCA that would allow Cineplex to produce the films that its theaters would show. By the time the buying spree was over, about one-third of North America's theaters had changed hands. Consequently, the large studios are once again firmly entrenched in the production, distribution, and exhibition of motion pictures.

Film Content: 1970–Present

The 1970s saw the reemergence of the director as a major creative force. Francis Ford Coppola, the first major filmmaker to graduate from a college film program, became the first of several talented film students to burst on the scene during the early 1970s. Coppola made three blockbuster films in that decade: *The Godfather* (1972), *Godfather II* (1974), and *Apocalypse Now* (1979). Another film student, Steven Spielberg, directed the hugely popular *Jaws* (1975), the visually attractive but abstruse *Close Encounters of the Third Kind* (1979), the action-packed *Raiders of the Lost Ark* (1981), and the record-breaking *ET* (1982). Yet another film graduate, George Lucas, directed two of the all-time biggest box-office attractions, *American Graffiti* (1973) and *Star Wars* (1977). This last film marked a noticeable trend in film content of the late 1970s—big-budget science fiction films that relied heavily on special effects. In 1979–1980, for example, these films were all released: *Superman, Alien, Start Trek: The Movie, The Black Hole,* and *The Empire Strikes Back.*

Probably the most notable film trend of recent years has been the steady popularity of the sequel—a movie that continues a story started in an earlier film. *Godfather II,* which began this recent trend, was quickly followed by *Rocky II, III,* and *IV, Star Trek II, III,* and *IV, Superman II, III,* and *IV,* and a host of others. In fact, in 1983 a record sixteen sequels were released. Fourteen more followed in 1984. Some sequels were threatening to go on forever. In 1989, *Star Trek V* was released. The motivating factor behind this large number of sequels is an economic one. As films cost more to produce, Hollywood financiers believe it is less risky to finance a story and a cast of characters that already have proven box-office appeal.

The other type of film that was popular in the first half of the 1980s was the comedy. *Ghostbusters, Mr. Mom, Trading Places,* and *Splash* were all big box-office hits from 1983 to 1985. Another type of comedy was also produced in great quantities by Hollywood studios. This was tabbed the ''teenage exploitation'' film and featured young stars in sexy and/or raunchy situations. Some examples of this genre include *Hot Dog, The Movie, Porky's, Porky's II,* and *Weird Science.* These films were obvious attempts to appeal to the prime moviegoing audience—teenagers.

In contrast, the biggest content trend in the last half of the decade saw the motion picture studios releasing films that appealed to audience segments other than teenagers. Some industry observers labeled this trend the ''graying'' of the motion picture audience. In 1984, teens represented about one-third of the movie audience; in 1988, they represented only one-fourth. Conversely, the percentage of people in the over-forty age group in the movie audience increased from 15 percent in 1984 to more than 20 percent in 1988.

A glance at the popular movies of recent years bears out the film industry's interest in these statistics. *Platoon, Fatal Attraction, The Witches of Eastwick, Moonstruck,* and *Hope and Glory* were aimed at a more mature audience. At the same time, however, Hollywood has not given up on the teenage market. Other box office winners in 1987 included *Dirty Dancing, Beverly Hills Cop II, Nightmare on Elm Street III,* and *Predator,* films made with an eye toward attracting young moviegoers. All in all, it appears that the films of the 1990s will aim for broad appeal.

Growing Public Concern: Television in the 1970s

On the television side, as the 1970s began, public concern over the impact of television programming and over local station practices was steadily growing. A scientific advisory panel composed of mass communication researchers was set up by the Surgeon General's office to investigate the impact of exposure to TV violence (see Chapter 22). The report that was released by this group, although it did contain some controversial elements, indicated that TV violence was related in a modest way to aggressive behavior, especially in young children. Following the publication of this report, the three networks issued statements that said, in effect, that they were reducing the amount of TV violence in their shows. Additionally, the FCC exerted informal pressure on broadcasters to come up with a more formal plan to address this continuing concern. In 1975, the networks agreed to the idea of a "family viewing hour," in which programs suitable for the entire family would be aired. A Los Angeles court ruled late in 1976 that this agreement was unconstitutional and came about as a result of unfair government pressure. This 1976 decision was itself overturned in 1979. In late 1984, the case was settled out of court and the family viewing hour quietly faded into history.

The early 1970s were also characterized by the growth of citizen-group involvement in FCC decisions concerning station licensing and station programming policy. Groups such as Action for Children's Television, the Office of Communication of the United Church of Christ, the Citizens Communications Center, and coalitions of minority groups have become more influential in the regulatory process. One other action by the FCC also had important consequences for the TV industry. In 1970, the **Prime Time Access Rule** was issued. The idea behind this rule was to expand program diversity by requiring stations in the larger cities to schedule programs that were not produced or licensed by the three networks. In effect, this rule took the 7:30–8:00 P.M. (EST) time slot away from the nets and gave it back to the locals. Although many would argue over the efficacy of this rule in producing more diversity, it did have one somewhat unanticipated effect on the economic situation of the networks. ABC, which had been a perennial third-place finisher in the ratings race among the three nets, saved money because of this ruling since it no longer had to program (and lose money on) the 7:30–8:00 P.M. time period. Partly because of this fact, the network was able to stage a resurgence, and in the late 1970s, ABC was usually in the top position among the three nets in their quest for the prime-time audience. ABC's dominance didn't last long, however, as CBS took over the top spot and NBC moved up to second. By 1985–1986, ABC was struggling to escape third place while NBC became number one, a pattern that continued into 1988–1989.

Television in the 1980s: The End of Network Dominance

The biggest trend in the TV industry in the 1980s was the continuing erosion of network audiences. In the early 1970s, the three major networks generally pulled down about 90 percent of the viewing audience in prime time. In 1988, thanks to increased competition from independent stations, cable, and VCRs, their share had slipped to about 70 percent. The decrease in network domination showed up in other areas as well. Independent stations no longer relied as much on networks for their syndicated programming. Many local stations began producing their own syndicated fare. Some production companies guaranteed local stations that they would produce enough episodes for syndication even if a network series was canceled before stockpiling enough programs. At least one company, Paramount, bypassed the network market altogether and took its shows directly into syndication (see boxed material). Finally, if the three major networks didn't have enough problems, a fourth network, the Fox Broadcasting Company, went on the air in 1987, providing its affiliates with two nights of programs. Although the network was awash in red ink after its first season, Fox's offerings further diluted the audiences of NBC, ABC, and CBS.

Some effects of this decline have shown up in the networks' advertising revenue, but they seem to be holding their own. The nets took in about 2 percent more ad

To Boldly Go ... Into Syndication

Paramount's "Star Trek: The Next Generation" pushed the TV syndication market a step closer to the final frontier. Instead of producing the series for one of the three major networks or for Fox, Paramount decided to take the series directly to the syndication market and advertise it as one that would compete successfully with or even preempt traditional network shows. Given a production budget of about a million dollars an episode, a record for programming designed for syndication, the series had the look and the feel of a prime-time show. The program was sold in what is called a "barter" arrangement: Paramount kept seven of the twelve commercial minutes built into

each show and sold them to national advertisers at $70,000 per thirty-second spot. This revenue covered a good portion of the show's production cost. Paramount hoped to make money on the second and subsequent runs of the series.

"Star Trek" was more successful in the ratings than Paramount expected. It beat network competition in some markets and several local affiliates preempted the Saturday night network shows to run "Trek." Paramount was so impressed with the series' performance, it decided to use the same arrangement on yet another program: "Friday the 13th—The Series."

dollars in 1987 than they did in 1986. The networks have been able to accomplish this by raising rates in spite of the decline in audience levels. In 1987 and 1988, for example, network rates rose 7 and 10 percent, respectively. Advertisers are willing to pay these higher prices to achieve the huge reach that only network TV can accomplish. Nonetheless, all of the networks have become much more cost-conscious, have significantly trimmed their budgets, and are looking for ways to cut operating costs. One result of this increased emphasis on economy was a deep cut in the budgets of the three networks' news divisions.

Significant acquisitions also characterized the 1980s. Capital Cities Broadcasting merged with ABC in 1985 and GE bought RCA, the parent company of NBC, in 1986. Although ownership did not officially change hands, Laurence Tisch of the Loews Corporation became head of CBS. The FCC's new rule that allowed a person or organization to own twelve TV stations sparked a major acquisition trend at the local station level. Rupert Murdoch acquired MetroMedia for about $2 billion. Gillett Holdings, Inc., bought controlling interest in six stations formerly owned by Storer Communications for about $1.3 billion. Between 1986 and 1987, 260 TV stations changed hands.

On the production front, motion picture companies dominated the prime-time series arena, accounting for more than half of the series in 1988. Many of these series, however, were no longer produced in Hollywood as high costs drove their production companies to other locations in an attempt to save money. "Spenser" was shot in Boston, "Miami Vice" in Miami, and seven series, including "Wiseguy," "MacGyver," and "21 Jump Street," were shot in Canada.

The Rise of Cable

The cable TV industry was showing signs of maturity as the decade drew to a close. After a period of unbridled optimism and too-high expectations in the early 1980s, cable went through a period of reassessment and retrenchment during the middle of the decade. Expensive and underutilized two-way services were phased out. Promises of enough programming to fill 108 channels were forgotten, and rates were increased to more realistic levels. As a result, the industry regained some economic stability in 1987 and 1988. As cable penetrated into more than half of American homes, it attracted more advertisers. Advertising revenues passed $1 billion in 1987 and almost certainly are headed higher. Some big advertisers have discovered the cable market: Procter & Gamble, Anheuser-Busch, and Philip Morris each spent more than $20 million on cable in 1987. Almost all of the basic cable channels and the pay services were in the black as of 1988.

The business of supplying programs to cable systems has also stabilized. The latter part of the decade saw no major channels go out of business. As of mid-1988, there were 37 basic cable networks, 5 superstations, and 11 pay cable networks supplying programming to about 7500 cable systems nationwide.

Cable's most impressive gains, however, were on the legal front. The first was the passage of the Cable Communications Policy Act of 1984. This act basically freed cable from most regulations that had formerly governed it. Perhaps most important, it allowed cable operators to set their own rates. As a result, basic rates went up an average 20 percent, although many systems lowered pay cable prices to compensate. The second major victory was the overturning of the "must-carry" rules by the federal court system. In the past, cable systems had to carry any and all stations that were significantly received in their local markets. The courts ruled this to be unconstitutional, freeing operators to add and drop stations as they pleased. As a result, many in the motion picture and traditional broadcasting business feared that cable was becoming too powerful and asked for reregulation of the industry.

On the business front, the planned merger of Warner Communications and Time Inc. will create a company whose operations will reach more than five million basic cable subscribers. The combining of Warner's motion picture studios with Time's Home Box Office means that the new company can both produce and distribute material for pay TV. Time Warner Inc. would become the nation's number one producer of entertainment.

Zipping, Zapping, and Grazing

A development that had significant impact on both traditional TV and the cable industry was the spectacular growth of VCRs. Fewer than 5 percent of households had VCRs in 1982. By 1989, that figure was expected to reach 60 percent. In fact, the VCR has been adopted faster than any other appliance except television. The effects of the VCR are many. First, the renting of movies on cassettes has become a multi–billion-dollar business, with motion picture studios depending on cassettes for a large part of their revenue. VCRs sparked the growth of the prerecorded videocassette industry. As of 1988, there were about 26,000–28,000 home video rental shops in the United States.

Second, the VCR encourages **timeshifting,** playing back programs at times other than when they were aired. Although this has helped traditional television since it increased the total audience by allowing people who might not otherwise view a program to do so, it has caused some new problems for advertisers. Some viewers have special machines that "zap" commercials: The VCR pauses while the commercial is aired and then starts up again when the program is on. Also, when viewers play back these programs, many will fast forward, or "zip," their way through the ads, diluting their effectiveness.

Finally, the proliferation of the hand-held remote-control device has also caused problems for advertisers and programmers. Remote units are in almost two-thirds of all households and have encouraged the tendency toward ''grazing,'' rapidly scanning all the channels during a commercial or dull spot in a program in search of greener pastures. Advertisers and producers both tried to make their messages so interesting that grazing was discouraged. Nonetheless, it was still a widespread practice.

In other developments, many of the highly touted new technologies failed to catch on. Videotex and teletext (see Chapter 5) cost many media companies a lot of money and most were out of the business by 1988. Some still thought the technique had promise, however, and Sears and IBM announced plans for a system called Prodigy to begin before 1990. **Low-power television (LPTV)**, which would allow a new class of TV stations with a small service area, grew slowly, hampered in part by an unexpected avalanche of applications for stations reaching the FCC. As of 1989, most LPTV stations were marginal operations at best. **Direct broadcasting by satellite (DBS)** also fell by the wayside as many of its biggest backers pulled out of the business. Technological advances, however, will make this service less expensive and might change its outlook.

On the legal side, the key word was ''deregulation.'' The FCC did away with literally dozens of rules. Among those falling by the wayside were the Fairness Doctrine (see Chapter 17), a rule that made buyers of stations hold on to the stations for three years before selling, and various program logging requirements.

In sum, the traditional television industry had been significantly altered by developments in the 1980s. Audiences were able to choose among several alternatives to network television. New and expanded uses of the medium were possible and viewers were quick to take advantage of most of them. This trend toward expanded choices will likely continue as the decade progresses.

TV Content: 1970s to the Present

The early 1970s were the law-and-order years. In 1971, seventeen and a half hours of prime time were devoted to cops-and-robbers programs as the networks introduced viewers to a country cop (''Cade's County''), young cops (''Mod Squad''), Hawaiian cops (''Hawaii 5-0''), crippled cops (''Ironside''), uniformed cops (''Adam 12''), and federal cops (''The FBI''), not to mention a fat private eye (''Cannon''), a blind private eye (''Longstreet''), and a tough private eye (''Mannix''). This trend remained popular until the mid-seventies when it was replaced by one of television's most significant programming developments—the more sophisticated, ''adult'' version of the old situation comedy. The trend began in 1970 with the controversial sitcom ''All in the Family.'' The adult comedies that followed, including ''M*A*S*H,'' ''Soap,'' ''Sanford and Son,'' and ''Barney Miller,'' all dealt with previously taboo topics (for television) such as premarital sex, racial prejudice, and abortion. True to the belief that imitation of success breeds more success, networks did not hesitate to ''spin off'' characters from well-established shows. Leaders in this movement were the highly popular ''Mary Tyler Moore Show,'' which spawned ''Rhoda,'' ''Phyllis,'' and ''Lou Grant,'' and ''All in the Family,'' which led to ''Maude'' and ''The Jeffersons.''

During the late seventies and early eighties, prime-time series began to imitate daytime soap operas as programs that continued a story line from week to week went to the top of the ratings. These shows were typically about a rich and powerful family and featured at least one nasty villain or villainess that the audience evidently enjoyed hating. First show of this genre was the extremely popular ''Dallas,'' which

Home Shopping

One of the biggest programming trends in TV in the mid- to late 1980s was the growth of home shopping networks. The company that started the boom, Home Shopping Network (HSN), started as a local Florida shop-by-TV channel and then went national. Flushed with its early success, HSN bought eleven TV stations and its stock climbed from $18 to $282 a share. Then HSN ran into trouble. Plagued by alleged irregularities in their stock offerings, competition from other shopping channels, and decreasing sales, HSN's stock dropped down to $16 a share.

HSN's problems helped cool off an industry. Revenue projections were scaled down and a few companies went under. Nonetheless, it remained a profitable business. There were eleven national home shopping networks in 1988 with the large ones reaching about 20 million homes. The outlook, however, is still uncertain. Cable operators are concerned about cluttering up their systems with a lot of home shopping services. Also, sales potentials might be drying up. After all, as one critic put it, how many gold chains, cubic zirconium baubles, Capodimonte figurines, and electronic flea collars can a person want to buy?

(Home Shopping Network)

was followed by "Dynasty," "Flamingo Road," and "Falcon Crest." The prime-time soaps maintained their popularity into the 1985–1986 season as both "Dallas" and "Dynasty" were consistently among the top-rated shows. A "Dynasty" spinoff, "The Colbys" premiered in 1985. These shows seemed to demonstrate the fact that audiences love to see that money and power to not necessarily guarantee happiness. This trend had declined by decade's end.

The cast of "21 Jump Street," the Fox Network's highest rated series. The show, about tough young cops who promote good values, has a strong following among teens. (Courtesy of Fox Television)

The mid-1980s marked the comeback of comedies, particularly warm, family-oriented comedies. These shows, dubbed "warmedies" by the trade press, included "Family Ties," "The Cosby Show," "Growing Pains," "Our House," and "Who's the Boss?" One big reason for the popularity of this genre was economic. Family-oriented sitcoms did well in the syndication aftermarket. The warmedies were replaced by "dramadies," shows that were still warm but more reality-oriented and shot without the traditional laugh track. Shows falling in this category were "Slap Maxwell," "Frank's Place," and "The Days and Nights of Molly Dodd." Although these shows were generally praised by critics, audience reaction was lukewarm at best, and these shows generally were not around very long. The last, and perhaps most significant programming trend was the introduction of series with "targeted" demographics. These were shows carefully constructed to appeal to a narrow but desirable segment of the mass audience. The most obvious example is "thirtysomething," a program about and designed to appeal to the upwardly mobile thirty-to-forty crowd, the "yuppies." "Beauty and the Beast" also fits in this category with its female-oriented stories.

SUGGESTIONS FOR FURTHER READING

The books listed below represent some of those available that cover the history of television and film.

BARNOUW, ERIK, *A Tower in Babel*, New York: Oxford University Press, 1966.

————, *The Golden Web*, New York: Oxford University Press, 1968.

————, *The Image Empire*, New York: Oxford University Press, 1970.

————, *Tube of Plenty*, New York: Oxford University Press, 1975.

BOHN, THOMAS, AND RICHARD STROMGEN, *Light and Shadows*, Sherman Oaks, Calif.: Alfred Publishing Company, 1978.

BROOKS, TIM, AND EARLE MARSH, *The Complete Directory of Prime Time Network TV Shows, 1946–Present*, New York: Ballantine Books, 1984.

BROWNLOW, KEVIN, *The Parade's Gone By*, New York: Alfred Knopf, 1968.

ELLIS, JACK, *A History of Film*, Englewood Cliffs, N.J.: Prentice-Hall, 1979.

JACOBS, LEWIS, *The Rise of the American Film*, New York: Teachers College Press, 1939.

KNIGHT, ARTHUR, *The Liveliest Art*, New York: Macmillan, 1957.

LICHTY, LAWRENCE, AND MALACHI TOPPING, *American Broadcasting: A Source Book on the History of Radio and Television*, New York: Hastings House, 1975.

MAST, GERALD, *A Short History of the Movies*, Indianapolis, Ind.: Bobbs-Merrill, 1976.

MONACO, JAMES, *American Film Now*, New York: New American Library, 1984.

SKLAR, ROBERT, *Movie-Made America*, New York: Random House, 1975.

STERLING, CHRISTOPHER, AND JOHN KITTROSS, *Stay Tuned: A Concise History of American Broadcasting*, Belmont, Calif.: Wadsworth, 1978.

UDELSON, JOSEPH, *The Great Television Race*, University: University of Alabama Press, 1982.

WILK, MAX, *The Golden Age of Television*, New York: Dell Publishing Company, 1976.

Chapter 12

Structure of the Motion Picture Industry

Remember the old Hollywood slogan "Movies are better than ever"? Well, that's a matter of opinion, but it's a fact that the movie *industry* was doing better than ever. The late 1980s have seen record box-office figures, increasing videocassette sales and rentals, and more films being made than ever before. As *Variety,* the trade paper that is the industry Bible, puts it, business has been "boffo."

Ironically, the videocassette, once thought to be the enemy of the theater business, is greatly responsible for this boom. Videocassettes have

- created an "aftermarket" for theatrically released movies that is now a primary source of revenue for film companies

- spurred the production of new films, especially by independent producers

- encouraged the growth of medium-budget "quality" films that are attracting a new demographic segment back to theaters

The movie industry, however, is a business that runs in cycles. Bad times inevitably follow good times. In 1989, many observers were predicting that clouds were already forming on the horizon. The cassette business was softening, there were too many movies being produced, and budgets were getting out of control. Or, to quote *Variety* again, the feature film business in years to come will be filled with "zoom and gloom."

This chapter will examine the structure of the unpredictable movie business as it moves through an era of transition.

ORGANIZATION OF THE FILM INDUSTRY

The film industry is a business whose ultimate goal is to make money. This statement may seem crass to many people who believe that film is an art form produced by creative and imaginative people whose primary goal is to achieve aesthetic excellence. Although it may be true that film is an art form, the film industry is in business to make a profit. If an occasional moneymaking film also turns out to have artistic merit, so much the better, but the artistic merit is usually a by-product rather than the main focus. In our analysis of the film industry, we will divide its structure into three levels: (1) production, (2) distribution, and (3) exhibition.

Production

The production side of the industry will be discussed at some length later in this chapter. For now, we will mention only some of the basics.

Films are produced by a variety of organizations and individuals. For many years, the major studios controlled virtually all production, but independent producers have recently become prevalent. In 1987, independents produced almost two-thirds of all feature films. The major studios now finance and distribute many films made by independent companies.

Probably the biggest change in production in the late eighties has been the increased number of films that are released each year. Prompted in part by the additional revenues from home video and the theatrical box office, a total of 513 films were released in 1988, an increase of 55 percent since 1982. The major film production companies (Columbia, Paramount, 20th Century Fox, MGM/United Artists, Disney, Orion, Warner Brothers, Universal) will each produce twelve to eighteen films a year. Table 12.1 shows the share of the domestic box office for each major studio in 1988.

TABLE 12.1 Domestic Box Office Market Shares—1988

Company	Share (%)
Paramount	16
Disney	20
Warners	11
Orion	7
20th Century Fox	11
Universal	10
Columbia	3
MGM/UA	10
Others	12

Distribution

The distribution arm of the industry is responsible for supplying prints of films to the thousands of theaters and drive-ins located across the United States and to cinemas across the entire globe. In recent years, distribution companies have also supplied films to TV networks and to makers of videocassettes and videodiscs. Distribution companies maintain close contact with theater owners all over the world and also provide a transportation and delivery system that ensures that a film will arrive at a theater before its scheduled play date. In addition to booking the film at local movie houses, the distribution company is responsible for making the multiple prints of a film that are necessary when the film goes into general release. They also take care of advertising and promotion for the film. Most of the distribution of motion pictures is handled by the large studios listed above. These companies are firmly entrenched in both the production and distribution aspects of the business.

The distribution picture is changing. The increase in the number of motion picture screens (see page 279) has created a demand for films that the major distributors cannot fill. As a result, more independently distributed films with a specialized appeal are being screened. *A Room with a View,* for example, which would have had a hard time getting into theaters a few years ago, grossed $23 million at the box office. Additionally, box office surveys note that a large number of film fans are renting cassettes of quality films. These fans apparently are encouraged to seek out more current films of the same type at local theaters.

The nature of film distribution, however, assures that the large companies will always control a large portion of the business. First, it's too expensive for an independent producer or a small distribution company to contact theaters and theater chains spread out all over the globe. The big studios already have this communication network set up and can afford to maintain it. Second, the large studios can offer theater owners a steady stream of films that consistently feature big-name stars. A small company could not withstand that competition for long.

Distribution companies also serve as a source of financing for independent producers. These companies lend money to the film's producer to cover all or most of the estimated cost of the film. In this way, the major studios acquire an interest in films that they did not directly produce. This arrangement will be discussed further in the section of this chapter that deals with film economics.

Exhibition

Perhaps the biggest surprise of recent years has been the tremendous expansion of the exhibition side of the industry. In an era when experts believed that movie channels on cable, VCRs, and movies on cassette would keep people away from the theater, the number of theatrical motion picture screens in this country hit an all-time high, about 22,800 in 1988, an increase of almost 15 percent since 1985.

Many new movie theaters have several screens and show a wide range of current films. (Dion Ogust/The Image Works)

Why the increase in screens? First, motion picture distributors realize that it's the theatrical run of a movie that will set the tone for cable and cassette sales. A hit at the box office usually means more money for the studio in cable fees and in cassette sales. The theater is still crucial to the industry. Second, theater owners are banking on the VCR to bring more people back to theaters. They expect that once people get into the movie-watching habit at home, they will go back to theaters to see the most recent releases.

Multiplex theaters, featuring four, six, or eight screens clustered around a central concession stand, are still the rule. Most new theaters seat about 200–400 patrons. The massive movie palaces of the 1920s and 1930s have not reemerged, but there are noticeable changes inside the motion picture theater as exhibitors go after a slightly older market. Soundproofing to prevent spill from adjoining theaters is now common, and concession stands are putting real butter on popcorn, with a few even offering mineral water and cappucino to their customers.

One other trend: Drive-in movies are rapidly becoming extinct. There were only about 1800 left in 1988 as most operators found that they could make far more money by selling the real estate on which the drive-in was located than by keeping it in operation.

The exhibition segment is controlled by large chain owners. Very few independent operators are left in the large markets. Screens owned by the top seven chains account for about 80 percent of all box-office revenue. In addition, motion picture distributors are back into the exhibition segment as several studios have acquired theater chains (see Chapter 11). Consequently, as of 1988, the biggest theater chain was United Artists Theater Circuit, with about 2000 screens, followed by the Canadian-based Cineplex Odeon.

Ownership

Like television, the motion picture industry has given way to conglomerates. In a business as risky as motion pictures, it makes a certain amount of economic sense to join forces with a large and diversified organization. The parent conglomerate provides a reservoir of money, and if the film company has a bad year, the losses can be covered by another division in the conglomerate that had a good year. To illustrate, these are the major motion picture production/distribution companies:

1. Paramount: owned by Paramount Communications (formerly Gulf + Western), a large, international conglomerate with interests in hundreds of industries including publishing, banking, financial services, real estate, home video, and film and TV production.

2. Universal: owned by MCA, Inc., which also controls record companies, book publishers, music publishers, restaurant chains, recreational facilities, home video, and a toy company.

3. 20th Century Fox: part of the 20th Century Fox Film Corporation, owned in part by Rupert Murdoch, this company runs film processing plants, a ski resort, TV production facilities, a home video company, and TV network.

4. Warner Brothers: part of Warner Communications, which owns a cable TV company, a music publishing company, several record labels in the United States and Europe, a comic book company, *Mad* magazine, a book publishing company, and motion picture theaters. Warner Communications recently merged with Time Inc.

Ishtar, The Movie That Didn't Go Better With Coke

The original idea behind *Ishtar* was to do a modern version of one of those Bob Hope–Bing Crosby "road" movies of the 1930s and 1940s. Columbia, Coke's movie company, opened the vault for the film. The studio hired Warren Beatty and Dustin Hoffman for the lead roles at $6 million apiece. Elaine May was called in to direct at a fee of $1 million. She promptly decided that filming a couple of scenes on location in a real nightclub wouldn't work as well as building a fake nightclub on a studio soundstage for $5 million. She also wound up paying construction crews to move sand dunes around so that her shots would be composed better. Not surprisingly, *Ishtar* was quickly behind schedule and over budget.

When filming finally wrapped in March of 1986, the total tab for the film had risen to more than $50 million. Sensing disaster, several of Columbia's top executives took other jobs.

The movie opened in May 1987 to mostly bad reviews. Filmgoers stayed away in droves and the film was able to gross only $12.7 million at the box office and a bit more from overseas markets, cable, and cassette sales. Columbia was saddled with one of the biggest single-picture losses in motion picture history, more than $25 million. Embarrassed, Coca-Cola decided the motion picture business was just too risky and announced plans to spin off Columbia Pictures and eventually withdraw from Hollywood filmmaking. Coke will still be represented at the concession stands but it wants little part of the doings behind the camera.

5. Columbia: part of Columbia Pictures Entertainment, which was formed when Columbia merged with an independent production company, Tri-Star Pictures. In addition to film and video production companies, Columbia also owns motion picture theaters. Columbia had been wholly owned by the Coca-Cola Company, but after its experiences with the film *Ishtar* (see boxed material), Coke apparently decided the movie business was a little too risky. It now owns only 49 percent of Columbia.

6. Disney: The Walt Disney Company has two production companies, Touchstone, for "mature" movies, and Buena Vista, for general films. It also owns amusement parks, hotels, golf courses, and real estate and makes a tremendous amount of money licensing the Disney characters for use by other companies.

7. MGM/UA: the least diversified of these companies, it has the most complicated history. In 1986, the company was bought by Turner Broadcasting, which later sold back most of the company (keeping MGM's film library) to new management. MGM/UA Communications, as it's now called, relies on feature film distribution for most of its money but also has interests in home video and theaters. In 1989, MGM/UA was acquired by Qintex, an Australian firm.

What are some of the implications of large corporate ownership in the motion picture industry? One consequence seems to be that these large companies are less willing to take risks in experimenting with new movie content. A recent study noted that the 1980s were typified by extreme conservatism in corporate moviemaking.

Sequels to successful films and reissues of popular movies were never higher than during this period. In addition, the amount of diversity in movie themes was at an all-time low.

PRODUCING MOTION PICTURES

Departments

Film studios differ greatly in the way they are structured. Figure 12.1 is a common departmental chart. There are three main departments illustrated. The distribution department handles sales and contracts for domestic and worldwide distribution. The production division is in charge of all those elements that actually go into the making of a film. Also illustrated is the TV production division, which would handle all the studio's work in the development and production of series and made-for-TV motion pictures.

FIGURE 12.1 *Departmental chart for a typical motion picture company.*

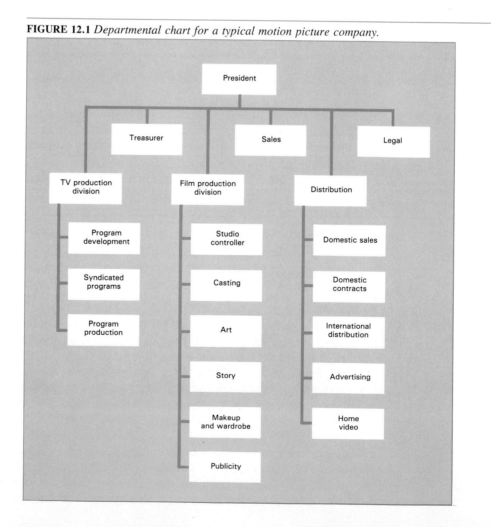

Behind the Scenes

How does a film get to be a film? There are three distinct phases in moviemaking: (1) preproduction, (2) production, and (3) postproduction. Similar to television, all films begin with an idea. The idea can be sketchy, such as a two-paragraph outline of the plot, or detailed, such as a novel or a Broadway play. When an idea is submitted to a producer, it is referred to as a **property.** If the producer is interested in the property, the producer may draw up an **option contract.** As the name suggests, an option contract is an exclusive right to put into effect for a fixed period of time an agreement for rights or services. For example, the producer might want an option on the property for six months. During these months, the producer will try to interest talent and financial backers in the project. If no one is interested, at the end of six months the option is dropped and full ownership of the property reverts to the original author. On the other hand, if there is potential, the producer will exercise his or her option and purchase the rights to the property.

Many of the today's motion picture deals are put together by agents. In fact, many industry experts suggest that big agencies such as William Morris and International Creative Management are the most powerful forces in the motion picture business. Agents put together packages—a star or stars, a director, a producer, and other creative talent—that are sold to studios. In return for their services, agents collect hefty packaging fees.

Once the rights have been secured, the preproduction process continues to the next step—writing the screenplay. In general, the route to a finished motion picture script consists of several steps:

1. Step one is called a treatment. This is a narrative statement of the plot and descriptions of the main characters and locations; it might even contain sample dialogue.

2. Step two is a first-draft script. This version contains all the dialogue and camera setups and a description of action sequences.

3. The third step is a revised script incorporating changes suggested by the producer, director, stars, and others.

4. Finally, step four is a script polish. This includes adding or subtracting scenes, revising dialogue, and other minor changes.

While all this is going on, the producer tries to find actors and actresses (talent) who will appear in the film. The contracts and deals that are worked out with the talent vary from the astronomical to the modest. One common arrangement is for the star to receive a flat fee or salary for his or her services. Sometimes this can be a substantial amount. Sylvester Stallone got about $16 million for *Rambo III*. Robert Redford and Dustin Hoffman routinely get about $6 million per picture. Bruce Willis got $5 million for *Die Hard*. Other actors might get a flat fee and a percentage of the film's revenue after the film shows a profit. At the other end of the scale, the Screen Actors Guild has a contract that spells out the minimum salary that must be paid to actors in minor roles and walk-on parts.

Meanwhile, the producer is also trying to secure financial backing for the picture. We will have much more to say about the monetary arrangements in film in the section on economics. For now, it is important to remember that the financial arrangements have to be worked out early in the preproduction process.

At the same time, the producer is also busy lining up skilled personnel to work behind the camera. Of these people, the film's director is most central. When all the elements have been put together, it will be the director's job to actually make the movie. He or she will determine what scenes get photographed from what angle and how they will be assembled in the final product. Working closely with the director is the cinematographer (the person responsible for the actual lighting and filming of the scenes) and the film editor (the person who will actually cut the film and assemble the scenes in the proper order). In addition to these individuals, a movie crew also contains dozens of other skilled people: set designers, makeup specialists, electricians, audio engineers, crane operators, painters, plumbers, carpenters, property masters, set dressers, caterers, first-aid people, and many others.

Shortly after the director has been signed for the project, he or she and the producer scout possible locations for shooting the film. Some sequences may be shot in the sound studio, while others may need the authenticity that only location shooting can provide. As soon as the locations have been chosen, the producer makes the necessary arrangements to secure these sites for filming. Sometimes this entails renting the studios of a major motion picture production company or obtaining permits to shoot in city streets or other places. The producer must also draw up plans to make sure that the filming equipment, talent, and technical crew are all at the same place at the same time.

Once all these items have been attended to, the film moves into the actual production phase. Cast and crew assemble on the chosen location, and each scene is shot and reshot until the director is satisfied with what has been filmed. The actors and crew then move to another location, and the process starts all over again. Overriding the entire production is the knowledge that all of this is costing a great

Filming of a scene from The Adventures of Baron Munchausen, *using hand-held cameras. The filming of the table, with its fantastical creations, was quite an adventure in itself. (Elliott Erwitt/ Magnum)*

During postproduction, the motion picture film editor selects the most appropriate camera shots and synchronizes sound to the pictures. (David S. Bolton)

deal of money. Shooting even a moderate-budget film can cost $200,000 to $250,000 *per day.* Therefore, the director tries to plan everything so that each dollar is used efficiently.

Most films make use of a production schedule that lists the order in which the scenes are shot, the location, the needed crew, the talent involved, special equipment, props, and transportation. This schedule sets up the most efficient sequence of filming. The first step is to group all scenes according to location. Next, all scenes at one location are divided into interior or exterior shots. To illustrate, suppose the script calls for scenes one and three to be shot inside a bank and scenes two and four to be shot outside in the bank's parking lot. It is more efficient to film scenes one and three first so that the same lighting setup can be used before moving outside. Because of this scheduling, film scenes are generally shot in a sequence different from the order in which they appear in the story. For example, let's suppose a film script calls for a helicopter shot of Yankee Stadium to open the film and a similar shot at the close. Rather than filming those scenes on the first and last day of shooting, it makes more sense to film them on the same day. Thus the helicopter would be rented for only one day, permission to use the stadium would be needed only once, and so on. After the scenes are shot, they can be spliced into their proper place.

The average shooting schedule for the typical film is about fifty days. Each day's shooting (and some days can be twelve to sixteen hours long) results in an average of two minutes of usable film. Exhibitors prefer feature films that are about 100 minutes in length. This means the movie can be shown every two hours with a 20-minute break in between for people to visit the concession stand.

At the end of each day's shooting, the film is sent to the laboratory where it is developed overnight. Also, the film of the previous day's shooting is projected for the director and cast. This is called viewing the "dailies" and lets the director see how the film is coming along. Recently, many directors have been using TV cameras to videotape the scenes as they are being filmed. Since tape can be played back immediately, there is no delay in seeing the dailies.

The postproduction phase begins after the filming has been completed. A film editor arranges the various scenes into a coherent and aesthetically pleasing order. Working with the director, the editor decides where close-ups should be placed, the angle from which the scene is shown, and how long each scene should last. The elaborate optical special effects that some films require are also added during post-production. Once the scenes have been edited into an acceptable form, postproduction sound can be added. This might include narration, music, sound effects, and original dialogue that, for one reason or another, has to be redone. (About 10 to 15 percent of outside dialogue has to be rerecorded because of interfering noises.) Finally, the edited film, complete with final sound track and special effects, is sent to the laboratory where a release print of the film is made. In the case of some films, the final version is shown to special preview audiences. These audiences fill out special preview cards that indicate their reactions to the film. If the reaction is overwhelmingly negative, the film may be returned to the editing room for more work. If the reaction is favorable, the film is made ready for distribution.

ECONOMICS

Since 1970, the box-office receipts of the movie industry have shown more or less steady growth. In 1988, the movie industry posted a record $4.46 billion in revenue (to keep this figure in perspective, the total revenue from the sale and rental of videocassettes during this same period was $7.46 billion). Movies are an expensive medium. The average movie cost about $18 million to produce in 1988, up 20 percent since 1985, and another $7 million to $9 million to advertise and market. Costs have risen so high that few movies—maybe one in twenty—are now profitable from box-office receipts alone. Financial success for most films comes from foreign revenue, cassette sales, and cable fees. Studios hope for a megahit, a blockbuster, to make up for their frequent losers.

Financing Films

Where do producers get the enormous sums of money necessary to make a film? Let's take a look at some common financing methods. If a producer has a good track record and the film looks promising, the distributor might loan the producer the entire amount needed to make the film. In return, the distributor gains distribution rights to the film. Moreover, if the distributor also has studio facilities, the producer might agree to rent those facilities from the distributor.

A second method is to arrange for a **pickup.** Under this arrangement, a distributor guarantees a producer that the distributor will pick up a finished picture at a later date for an agreed-upon price. For example, a distributor might agree to pay a producer $10 million eighteen months in the future provided that the producer delivers a finished picture by that date. Although this money helps, it does not do the producer any immediate good since the money won't appear for a year and a half. Armed with this agreement, however, the producer can arrange for a bank loan to secure the money needed immediately. If the bank is satisfied with the financial status of the distributor and feels that the producer can bring in the picture for $10 million or less, the bank grants the loan. But what happens if the bank feels that the

Credit Where Credit is Due

You can learn a lot if you pay attention to the opening and closing credits of a movie. First of all, keep an eye out for a director named Allen Smithee. What's so special about him? Well, for one thing, he doesn't exist. Allen Smithee is the name chosen by the Directors' Guild to be used on films when the real director doesn't want to be identified. Usually this means the film turned out so bad, for whatever reason, the real director doesn't want to be associated with it.

Also check out the writing credits. An ampersand (&) between two names means that the writers are a team; they worked together on the script. The word *and* between two names usually means that one reworked the other's script. Thus a screenplay credit "Written by Smith and Jones & Green" means that Smith did the original draft and the team of Jones & Green redid it.

You may see some titles you don't understand. Some are easy to explain. A "gaffer" is an electrician and a "grip" is a studio stagehand. Some take a little more effort. In *Made in Heaven,* a James Gierman is listed in the credits as a "Cheese Host." What's a cheese host? The person who serves snacks to the actors during their breaks.

producer won't be able to finish the film in eighteen months or that the movie will go over budget? In this case, a third party, called a completion guarantor, is brought in to make sure that the loan will be repaid.

A third method is to finance the picture through outside investors, most frequently through a **limited partnership.** Under this arrangement, a number of investors put up a specific amount to pay for the film. Their personal liability is limited to the amount they invest; that is, they can't lose any more than what they put up, even if the picture goes over budget. The limited partners have no artistic control over the picture. They simply invest their money and hope to make a profit.

A fourth method is a **joint venture.** Under this arrangement, several companies involved in film production and distribution pool their resources and agree to finance one or more films. The most recent example is Tri-Star Pictures, a joint venture involving Columbia Pictures, CBS, and HBO. (CBS withdrew in 1985.) Tri-Star began business with $200 million in cash and a $200 million line of credit at local banks. Columbia released the films to theaters and then to home video, followed by an HBO exclusive, and finally a CBS airing. Tri-Star had early success with *The Natural* and *The Muppets Take Manhattan* before being acquired by Coca-Cola. (There are also some uncommon methods of financing. Robert Townsend, producer of *The Hollywood Shuffle,* charged the $40,000 he needed to finish the film on his personal credit cards.)

No matter how films are financed, movie studios are becoming more cost conscious. Many are distributing more movies made by independents, who can make films at lower cost; others are moving their productions to Canada or to states other than California to cut labor costs. Disney, for example, built an elaborate studio in Florida.

The producer and distributor also agree on how to divide the distributor's gross receipts from the film (the money the distributor gets from the theater owners, TV networks, pay-TV operations, and videocassette and videodisc operations that show the film). Since the distributor takes the greatest risk in the venture, the distributor is the first to be paid from the receipts of the film. Distribution companies charge a

The Ten Most Expensive Films

Although an average movie cost about $18 million to produce in the late 1980s, many films cost more. In fact, some cost much, much more. The table below lists the ten most expensive films of all time. Please note that the table does not account for the effects of inflation. (Also note that this table contains only films from Western nations.) The most expensive film of all time is probably *War and Peace*, produced by the government of the Soviet Union. The Soviets evidently failed to keep a budget for the film, but some industry experts report it must have cost at least $100 million.

Film	Year	Cost (millions)
Rambo III	1988	$57.0
Superman II	1980	54.0
Who Framed Roger Rabbit	1988	52.0
Annie	1982	51.5
Cotton Club	1984	51.1
Ishtar	1987	51.0
Santa Claus: The Movie	1986	50.0
Inchon	1982	46.0
Dune	1984	42.2
Cleopatra	1962	42.1

distribution fee for their efforts. In addition, there are distribution expenses (cost of making multiple prints of the film, advertising, necessary taxes, insurance), which must also be paid. Lastly, the actual production cost of the film must be repaid. If the distributor or a bank loaned the producer $10 million to make the film, that loan has to be paid off (plus interest). Because of all these expenses, it is estimated that a film must earn two and a half to three times its production cost before it starts to show a profit for the producers.

Independent filmmaker Robert Town-send, who produced and starred in Hollywood Shuffle, *financed the film with his savings account and credit cards until he was able to sign a distribution deal. (Scott Weiner/Retna)*

Merchandising is a large part of motion picture promotion, as evidenced by these items which tie in with Batman. (Gregg Matthews/Black Star)

Dealings with the Exhibitor

The distributor is also involved in other financial dealings—this time with the exhibitors. An exhibition license sets the terms under which the showing of the film will occur. The license specifies the run of the film (the number of weeks the theater must agree to play the picture), holdover rights, the date the picture will be available for showing, and the clearance (the amount of time that must elapse before the film can be shown at a competing theater).

The license also contains the financial terms for the film's showing. There are several common arrangements. The simplest involves a specified percentage split of the money that is taken in at the box office. The exhibitor agrees to split the money with the distributor according to an agreed-upon formula, perhaps fifty–fifty the first week, sixty–forty the second, seventy–thirty the third, and so on, with the exhibitor keeping more money the longer the run of the film. Another alternative is the **sliding scale.** Under this setup, as the box-office revenue increases, so does the amount of money that the exhibitor must pay the distributor. For example, if a week's revenue was more than $30,000, the exhibitor would pay the distributor 60 percent; if the revenue was $25,000–$29,999, the distributor would receive 50 percent, and so on. Another common approach is the ninety–ten deal. Under this method, the movie theater owner first deducts the house allowance (called the "nut") from the box-office take. The house allowance includes all the operating expenses of the theater (heating, cooling, water, lights, salaries, maintenance, etc.), plus a sum that is pure profit for the theater (this sum is called "air"). From the revenues (if any) that remain, the distributor gets 90 percent and the house 10 percent.

A less commonly used practice is called **four-walling.** In this system, the distributor actually rents the theater for a specified fee for a predetermined length of

Promoting and Advertising the Film

About $7 million is spent promoting and advertising the average film. Where does this money go? Obviously, a good deal goes to purchase ads in newspapers and to buy radio and TV spots. In filmmaking, the primary marketing goal is to get a picture to open strongly—if the numbers on the first weekend of release are low, it's hard to get them curving upward. Most of the advertising budget, about 80 percent, is spent to open the film. Another portion goes to producing the "trailer," that brief piece of film that is shown in movie theaters as a preview of coming attractions. The trailer is important because it is shown to film patrons, the precise targets of all film advertising. Newspaper and TV ads are seen by many nonmoviegoers, but there is no wasted effort with a trailer. A poorly constructed trailer can seriously hamper a film's earning power.

Another promotional device is called a merchandise tie-in. Tie-ins consists of T-shirts, posters, record albums, clothing, toys, electronic calculators, pinball machines, and any other product that can be tied in with the film. *Star Wars,* for example, spawned a line of miniature models, toys, clothes, and even bedspreads. It made twice as much in merchandising deals as it made at the box office. *Saturday Night Fever* spun off a successful soundtrack album and items ranging from John Travolta white suits to John Travolta beach towels. The leader in merchandise tie-ins for the late 1980s was *Rambo III*. The film's producers signed fifty licensing contracts that covered approximately seventy-five Rambo-related products, including jungle pants, hunting knives, athletic wear, posters, dolls, T-shirts, a videogame, trading cards, and a Rambo doll, complete with rocket launcher, tanks, and other macho accessories. The revenue from these licensing agreements went to pay off some of the film's $57 million price tag.

The last promotional area concerns using the film industry's achievement awards to promote the film. The Oscars, of course, are the most important awards. Movie studios invest large sums of money in advertising and promoting their nominees among the membership of the Academy of Motion Picture Arts and Sciences. Universal spent $2 million to promote seven films for Oscars in 1986. Ads are taken out in trade papers, special screening parties are held, and special showings of the films are arranged with the Los Angeles CATV systems. Winning one or more Oscars generally increases a film's success at the box office. Some experts estimate that being named best picture is worth at least an additional $10 million in box-office receipts. *Platoon,* the best picture of 1986, saw its box-office revenue increase 43 percent the week after it won.

time and keeps all of the box-office receipts. Four-walling has been used most often by small distribution companies that handle low-budget films such as *The Wilderness Family.* Four-walling has some appeal for exhibitors since they are guaranteed a profit no matter how poorly the picture draws. If the picture draws well, the exhibitor will make money from the sale of popcorn, candy, and soft drinks at the concession stand. Speaking of concession sales, it should not be overlooked that this can be a source of significant income to motion picture exhibitors since the profit margin on items sold is about 80 percent.

All of this means a trip to the movies can be an expensive proposition. For example, consider the costs for two at a theater in New York City in 1989: admission for two, $14; two small boxes of popcorn, $3.50; one package of Twizzlers and one box of Milk Duds, total for both, $3.50; two large Cokes, $4.50. Total tab: $25.50.

CABLE AND HOME VIDEO

Hollywood has seen a drastic shift in the revenue mix for motion pictures in the last few years. Theatrical revenue now takes a back seat to cable and home video. In 1987, an estimated 39 percent of film revenue came from cassettes, 8 percent from pay cable services, and 7 percent from network and syndicated TV, making a total of 54 percent from video. Theater box office and other nonvideo sources now account for only 46 percent of revenue.

The cassette rental business boomed from 1985 to 1987 but has recently showed signs of leveling off. Cassette rentals and sales brought in about $7.5 billion in 1987. About 65 million cassettes were sold in 1987 and a record 3.3 billion were rented. Initial reports for 1988, however, indicate that the rental and sales figures flattened out. Industry analysts suggest that consumer demand is down since many people have rented all of the past hits that they wanted to see, and new releases will be the driving force behind the industry. Moreover, a growing number of consumers are expressing dissatisfaction with local video stores because they seldom have enough copies of hit movies to satisfy demand. Many consumers are unwilling to go back to a store three and four times to find what they want. In addition, VCRs are now in about 60 percent of homes, but sales have leveled off. All of this suggests that the prerecorded cassette market will not grow as fast as previously.

Hollywood's share of the home video pie comes from the sale of cassettes to consumers and to video stores which subsequently rent them to consumers. The **first sale** provision of current copyright law, however, prohibits the studios from making money on cassette rentals. Consequently, studios are encouraging video stores to stress cassette sales and are marketing many top hits at prices from $20 to $30, far below the usual $70–$90 selling price. Tapes that sell for $20–$30 make up the "sell-through" market; the higher priced tapes are designed mainly to be sold to rental stores. Classifying tapes as sell-through or rental is a tough marketing decision for most companies. Further, to capitalize on the home video market, some companies are putting commercials on their cassettes. *Top Gun* was preceded by a Pepsi commercial and a Nestle's ad preceded *Dirty Dancing*.

The home video market is driven by big hits, just like the theatrical box office. Movies that were popular on the big screen are almost always popular on the smaller screen. Table 12.2, page 292, lists the top cassette sellers as of 1988. Note that with the exception of the Disney Classics, all were box-office winners. Some movies that were box-office duds do quite well on videocassette. For example, the $51 million *Cotton Club* made only $15 million in theatrical film rentals (the amount the distributor gets after the exhibitors take their cuts) but 150,000 cassettes have been sold at about $70 each. *Dune,* another box-office bomb ($42 million production cost; $20 million in rentals) earned about $8 million in cassette sales. Home video has been a plus to films with smaller budgets as well. First, home video has opened up a whole new market for small-budget (about $3 million–$4 million) films. Some of these films cover their production costs with up-front money from cable and videocassette rights even before release to local theaters. This technique, however, will not work all the time, particularly with the increased number of films now in distribution. Cassette renters are becoming more choosey. Both Cannon Films and the DeLaurentis Entertainment Group, hoping to make money from cassette rentals, produced too many films in 1986 and 1987. Consumers ignored their product and both companies wound up on the verge of financial collapse. Small-budget movies that got good critical reviews but little box-office success have found new life on

TABLE 12.2 Top Selling Videocassettes

FILM	STUDIO	UNIT SALES (MILLIONS)
ET	Universal	10.0
Cinderella	Disney	4.0
Top Gun	Paramount	2.8
Crocodile Dundee	Paramount	2.1
Lady and the Tramp	Disney	2.0
Sleeping Beauty	Disney	1.8
Beverly Hills Cop	Paramount	1.6
Star Trek IV	Paramount	1.6
Indiana Jones and the Temple of Doom	Paramount	1.4
Raiders of the Lost Ark	Paramount	1.3

cassette. *The Adventures of Buckaroo Banzai* got few theater customers but has sold 100,000 cassettes. *Cross Creek* and *Birdy* made more in home video than they did at the box office. It appears that many people are unwilling to spend $20 to take a family of four to a marginal movie but are willing to spend $2 to rent a cassette. As one video rental customer put it, "If it's lousy, I just do a fast forward and say goodbye."

In the long run, movie studios are betting on **pay-per-view (PPV)**. In this system, the studio feeds movies to cable systems at certain hours when subscribers can view them for a fee, usually $5.00, sort of like an electronic rental system. Nearly 8 million homes are equipped for PPV. The revenue produced by PPV systems is still relatively small, about $200 million in 1989, but experts are predicting that 20 million homes will be on PPV systems by the mid-1990s with revenues topping the billion-dollar mark. PPV has been helped recently by the invention of low-cost devices that allow cable systems to have "addressability"; that is, they must know which homes want the movie and send it only to those homes that want it. On the downside, consumer interest in PPV is still lukewarm. Surveys have shown that given a choice between renting a movie at the local video store and receiving it for the same cost over PPV, only a third of the respondents opted for PPV. Nonetheless, the studios are seriously studying the PPV market.

CAREERS IN FILM

Finding a job in the film industry is difficult but not impossible. Film is a young person's medium; many of Hollywood's top directors are not too many years removed from their college-student days. As a result, motion picture companies are always looking for bright, young talent. Unfortunately, the industry is not large enough to accommodate all of the newcomers who are seeking jobs, and competition is formidable.

A young person who had actual experience in films and filmmaking will probably enjoy more success in finding a job. How do you get this experience? In general, there are two ways: (1) taking college courses that deal with film and (2) making your own films. About 750 colleges and universities now offer courses in film, 227 offer bachelors' degrees, and many offer graduate degrees. The advantages of a university major in film are substantial. In the first place, the university or college provides the student with an opportunity to practice with technical equipment: lights, meters, editing machines, cameras, and so forth. Most students cannot afford to buy this equipment or rent it for long periods of time, and film production companies usually cannot afford to set aside equipment for on-the-job training. Second, students can take courses in film aesthetics and film history and learn by observing how others have made films. Third, students can take courses in other areas that relate to film, such as art, literature, history, music, and photography. Knowledge of these areas can be valuable for filmmakers. Finally, during the course of his or her studies, the student may have the opportunity to make a film as a final classroom project. This finished film can be shown to potential employers as a sample of the student's capability.

The other approach to gaining experience is to become an independent film-maker. This method is valuable because it allows a person to gain knowledge of every aspect of filmmaking. By necessity, the independent filmmaker must learn about financing, writing, producing, editing, directing, accounting, and marketing. A potential employer knows that a person who successfully produces an independent film is dedicated to the film profession and is competent in the mechanics of filmmaking. Of course, this approach requires that the individual have some money to invest in basic film equipment and the time necessary to devote to the film. A person looking to go this route should be prepared for some financial hardships while the film is being made.

Entry-Level Positions

Once a person has some experience, the next step is to find an entry-level job. This requires securing a job interview—not an easy task. The common technique of mailing a résumé to a potential employer seldom works in the film industry. Because of the competition, most unsolicited résumés rarely generate a positive response, and no small number are immediately discarded.

There are three ways to overcome this hurdle. The first is to know somebody. As is the case in most industries, if you have a friend or a friend of a friend in the industry, getting a job interview is less difficult. Unfortunately, most people don't fall into this category.

The second way is to get yourself noticed. A newcomer accomplishes this by seeking out internships or training programs with production companies. The 1987 American Film Institute's *Guide to College Courses in Film and Television* lists such opportunities. Many times help in finding out about and applying for internships can be secured from teachers or placement offices. Once you've gotten yourself into an organization, you will have better success in arranging an interview. Another way to get yourself noticed is to enter the many student film festivals. These events are excellent ways for students to gain public exposure and professional recognition for their work. At last count there were twenty-six different festivals and awards competitions held across the United States. A newcomer who wins one or more awards at these festivals may find getting through the door into the film industry a little easier.

The third way is to be persistent. This is also the hardest way. Make a list of those companies where you wish to work and call on them personally. Since most film production companies are located in southern California and New York, this means that the job seeker might have to relocate. (Most experts agree that you would probably have to make this move eventually if you are serious about a career with the major feature film companies. Hiring takes place in these two areas, and it is necessary to be there to be hired.) Once you've got your list together, start calling on the companies. Bring along a one-page summary of your education and special skills. If you have a completed film that is available for viewing, indicate it in your summary. Don't be discouraged if your first visit is fruitless. Keep checking back. Even companies with immediate openings may suggest others that are hiring. As is the case with television, a newcomer should be prepared to take practically any job as a starter. Once inside the company, the path to more creative and challenging positions is easier to follow.

Upward Mobility

A new employee should try to select his or her first job with an eye toward future advancement. Some routes are better chosen if the person's ultimate goal is producing and directing. Other avenues suggest themselves if top management is the ultimate goal. One early choice an aspiring filmmaker must deal with is the choice between editing and directing. Although there are some exceptions, most people who start in the editing room tend to stay there, advancing ultimately to the post of supervising film editor. Those interested in producing and directing are better advised to begin as production assistants and progress to assistant directors, director, and perhaps producer. To reach high-level management, a person might consider breaking in with the distribution or sales division.

Two last points should be considered. First, what most students think of when they say they are interested in the film industry is a career in Hollywood feature films. This is understandable because this is the most visible part of the industry. It should be kept in mind, however, that there are opportunities in the educational and industrial film areas as well. Many organizations produce their own training or promotional films. There are also several companies that specialize in producing educational films for high schools and colleges. These organizations are potential places of employment. Second, when many students consider film careers, they tend to think only about careers as producers, writers, or directors. Although these jobs are perhaps the most glamorous, it should be remembered that the film industry also needs publicists, advertising experts, promotion directors, business managers, accountants, salespeople, and market researchers. In short, there are opportunities for more than production people.

SUGGESTIONS FOR FURTHER READING

The following books contain additional information about film.

AMERICAN FILM INSTITUTE, *Guide to College Courses in Film and Television,* Princeton, N.J.: Peterson's Guides, 1987.

BLUEM, A. WILLIAM, AND JASON SQUIRE, eds., *The Movie Business: American Film Industry Practice,* New York: Hastings House, 1972.

BOBKER, LEE, *Making Movies: From Script to Screen,* New York: Harcourt Brace Jovanovich, 1973.

FINLER, JOEL, *The Hollywood Story,* New York: Crown, 1988.

GOODELL, GREGORY, *Independent Feature Film Production,* New York: St. Martin's Press, 1982.

JOWETT, GARTH, AND JAMES LINTON, *Movies as Mass Communication,* Beverly Hills, Calif.: Sage Publications, 1980.

KERR, PAUL, *The Hollywood Film Industry,* London: Routledge and Kegan, 1987.

LITWAK, MARK, *Reel Power,* New York: Morrow, 1986.

MAYER, MICHAEL, *The Film Industries,* New York: Hastings House, 1978.

MONACO, JAMES, *American Film Now,* New York: Oxford University Press, 1985.

STEINBERG, COBBETT, *Film Facts,* New York: Facts on File, 1980.

Chapter 13

Structure of the Television Industry

For about thirty years, the structure of the television industry was basically unchanged. The three major networks distributed their programs by microwaves or land lines to the local affiliates who, in turn, broadcast them into people's houses. The network share of the viewing audience was more than 90 percent, the remainder divided between independent stations and public television.

All of that has changed now. Viewers have more choices: basic cable, pay cable, superstations, more independent stations, videocassette recorders (VCRs), and backyard satellite dishes. All of this change, however, has not altered one basic fact of television viewing. People still watch *programs*. If the programs are interesting, it doesn't matter how they are delivered to the home. This chapter will first examine the structure of the conventional TV industry and then discuss some of the newer TV services: cable, home video, and satellite receiving dishes.

ORGANIZATION OF THE TRADITIONAL TELEVISION INDUSTRY

Before we begin, it is necessary to define some of the key concepts and discuss the arrangements between major elements of the industry. The **commercial television system** consists of all those local stations whose income is derived from selling time on their facilities to advertisers. The **noncommercial system** consists of those stations whose income is derived from sources other than the sale of advertising time.

A local TV station is licensed by the Federal Communications Commission to provide TV service to a particular community. In the industry, these communities are customarily referred to as markets. There are 211 markets in the United States, ranging from the number-one market, New York City, with about 6.6 million homes, to number 211, Miles City, Montana, with about 6000 homes. Some of these local TV stations enter into contractual agreements with TV networks. As in the radio industry, a television network is a group of local stations linked electronically so that programs supplied by a single source can be broadcast simultaneously. Three commercial networks in the United States supply programs to local stations: the American Broadcasting Company (ABC), the Columbia Broadcasting System (CBS), and the National Broadcasting Company (NBC). A fourth commercial network, the Fox Broadcasting Company, went on the air in 1987, providing affiliates with limited programming. By 1988, Fox was more than $50 million in the red; although the network announced plans to tough it out, its future was still uncertain. The Public Broadcasting Service (PBS) serves as a network for noncommercial stations. The electronic part of the program distribution is done through microwave and satellite facilities. A local station that signs a contract with one of the networks is an affiliate. Each of the three major commercial networks has about 200 affiliates scattered across the country; Fox has slightly fewer. Local stations that do not have network affiliation are independents. With this background in contractual arrangements, let us now turn to an examination of how the industry is organized.

Much like the film industry, the TV industry is divided into three segments: (1) production, (2) distribution, and (3) exhibition. The production element is responsible for providing the programming that is ultimately viewed by the TV audience. The distribution function is handled by the TV networks and syndication companies. The exhibition of television programs—the element in the system that most people are most familiar with—is the responsibility of local TV stations. It should be kept in mind that there is some overlap in the performance of these various functions. Networks produce and distribute programs; local stations also produce programs as well as exhibit them. Let's take a more detailed look at each of these three divisions.

Production

Pretend for a moment that you are the manager of a local TV station in your hometown. Your station signs on at 6 A.M. and signs off at 2 A.M. That means your station must provide twenty hours of programming every day, or approximately 7000 hours of programming each year. Where do you get all this programming? There are basically three sources:

1. local production

2. syndicated programming

3. for some stations, network programs

Local production consists of those programs that are produced in the local station's own studio or on location with the use of the station's equipment. The most common local productions are the station's daily newscasts, typically broadcast at noon, in the early evening, and late in the evening. Stations have found that these newscasts attract large audiences, which in turn attract advertisers. As a result, the local news accounts for a major proportion of the ad revenue that is generated by a local station. Not surprisingly, local stations devote a major share of their production budgets to their news shows. Many stations are equipped with portable TV cameras, mobile units, satellite news-gathering vans, and even helicopters. Other locally produced programming might consist of local sports events, early morning interview programs, and public affairs discussion shows. It would be difficult, however, for a local station to fill its entire schedule with locally produced programming. As a result, most stations turn to programming produced by other sources.

If the station is affiliated with a network, much of its programming problem is solved. Networks typically supply about 65–70 percent of the programming carried by their affiliates. Not all of this programming is actually produced by the networks. In fact, only network news, documentaries, sports events, talk shows (such as "Today" and "Good Morning America"), some soap operas, and an occasional prime-time series are network productions. The other programs carried by the networks are actually produced by independent production companies or the television divisions of film production companies. Even though the network does not produce the program, it still has as a stake in its performance since the network and the

Anchors Liz Walker and Jack Williams broadcasting the news at Channel 4, Boston. Local newscasts are the most common form of production at local television stations, with as many as five hours of news programming broadcast in some big-city markets. (Bob Kramer/Amstock)

production company combine to finance it. If the program is a hit, both the network and the production company will make a profit. In the case of a motion picture, the network buys the rights to show the film one or more times on TV. Table 13.1 lists some programs produced by independent production companies and TV divisions of major film studios.

If the station is independent, it has to look elsewhere for programming. Most often the source of this programming is a syndication company. (A syndication company is part of both the production and distribution segment in TV broadcasting. We will have more to say about it below.) Many independent production companies sell their shows to syndication films. Multimedia produces ''Donahue'' and Lorimar produces ''She's the Sheriff'' for the syndication market. Tribune Entertainment puts together ''Geraldo'' and King World Productions syndicates ''Wheel of Fortune,'' ''Jeopardy,'' and ''The Oprah Winfrey Show.'' Programs that have already played on the networks' schedules (''M*A*S*H,'' ''Family Ties,'' ''Barney Miller'') can also be bought from syndication companies. In addition, packages of movies, made up of some of the 22,000 films that have been released for television, can be rented or leased from syndication companies. Obviously, an independent station would rely more heavily on syndicated material than a network affiliate.

Distribution

As we have mentioned, the two main elements in the distribution segment of television are the networks and the syndication companies. The network distributes

TABLE 13.1 Examples of Production Companies and Their Programs for the 1988–1989 TV Season

PRODUCTION COMPANY	PROGRAMS
Independents	
The Cannell Studios	"Wiseguy", "21 Jump Street"
MTM	"Newhart", "Annie MacGuire"
New World TV	"Wonder Years", "Tour of Duty"
Lorimar	"ALF", "Midnight Caller"
TV Divisions of Film Companies	
MGM/UA	"In the Heat of the Night", "thirtysomething"
Paramount	"Dear John," "Cheers"
Columbia	"Who's the Boss?", "Married . . . with Children"
Universal	"The Equalizer", "Murder, She Wrote"

programs to its affiliates by transmitting them by satellite. The station then transmits them to its viewers as they are received, or it videotapes them and presents them at a later time period or different day. The affiliation contract between a local station and the network is a complicated document. In simplified terms, the station agrees to carry the network's programs, and in return the network agrees to pay the station a certain amount of money for clearing its time so that the network programs can be seen. (Although it may seem contradictory that the network actually pays the station to carry the network's programming, remember that the network is using the local station's facilities to show the network's commercials.) The amount of money paid by the network varies by market size. For example, in the late 1980s, in

Behind the scenes of "The Oprah Winfrey Show," showing the control panels and video monitors. (Kevin Horan/Picture Group)

Danger Mouse vs. The Mayor

Syndicated programs—particular syndicated cartoons—can attract a remarkably loyal audience. In New York City, station WNYW-TV began a Sunday morning phone-in program in March of 1987 called ''Koch on Call,'' during which viewers could call the mayor and discuss matters of public interest. To accommodate the mayor, the station preempted the popular syndicated cartoon ''Danger Mouse.'' WNYW was besieged by letters asking it to dump the mayor and return the rodent. The New York *Daily News* did the democratic thing to settle the issue. It sponsored a phone-in poll. The results: 660 votes for the mayor; 6540 for ''Danger Mouse.''

Anchorage, Alaska, the local NBC affiliate received about $300 per hour. NBC compensated its local station in Dallas about $2,500 per hour, while it paid its New York affiliate $10,000 an hour. The network then sells time in its programs to advertisers seeking a national audience.

Syndication companies provide another kind of program distribution. These organizations lease taped or filmed programs to local television stations. Sometimes, as mentioned above, the syndication company also produces the program, but more often it distributes programs produced by other firms. Local stations that purchase a syndicated program receive exclusive rights to show that program in their market (a situation complicated by cable TV systems that bring in distant stations; see below). Usually a station buys a package of programs—perhaps as many as 120 episodes or more—and the contract specifies how many times each program can be repeated.

Contractual arrangements take different forms. In a **straight cash** deal, the stations pay a fee for the right to show the program a specified number of times and retains the rights to sell all of the commercial spots available in the program. In a **cash plus barter** deal, the station pays a reduced fee for the program but gives up some commercial spots to the syndication company, which, in turn, sells the spots to national advertisers. In a straight **barter arrangement,** no money changes hands but the syndicator keeps more commercial minutes to sell nationally, leaving fewer spots for the local station to sell. For example, in 1988, ''Webster'' was sold on a straight cash deal while ''Bustin' Loose'' split seven minutes of commercial time, giving three minutes to the distribution company (MCA TV) and four minutes to the stations.

Syndication companies try to sell their shows in as many TV markets as possible. The greater the coverage of the show, the more appealing it is to national advertisers. Shows that have less than 50 percent market coverage usually have a tough time being successful. Top-rated syndicated shows, like ''Wheel of Fortune'' and ''Jeopardy,'' are seen in nearly all TV markets.

Traditionally, tapes of syndicated programs were placed in containers and sent to stations by air or rail express. Recently, however, many syndication companies have distributed their shows electronically by satellite, allowing some programs to treat current topics. ''Entertainment Tonight,'' for example, is distributed the same day it's produced.

Syndication functions as an important ''aftermarket'' for prime-time TV shows. In fact, most prime-time series are produced at a deficit, sometimes $200,000 or

One of the longest running and most successful comedy series, "I Love Lucy," is still being profitably syndicated to hundreds of TV markets. (Howard Frank)

more for each one-hour episode. Production companies gamble that they can make back this money in the syndication market. It's a risk, but if an off-net show hits it big in syndication, it might earn half a billion dollars or more. To be attractive in the syndication market, however, a prime-time show must have enough back episodes stockpiled so that stations can run episodes for a long time without repeats becoming a problem. One hundred seems to be the magic number, and most series usually have a big party to commemorate the production of their hundredth episode. Since only twenty-two or twenty-four new shows are produced each season, it's obvious that those series that last four or five years are the best bets for syndication success.

Exhibition

At the start of 1989, there were approximately 1,100 commercial TV stations and 340 noncommercial stations in the United States. One important difference between TV stations is a technical one. Some TV stations are licensed to broadcast in the very high frequency (**VHF**) band of the electromagnetic spectrum; these stations occupy channels 2–13 on the TV set. Other stations broadcast in the ultra-high frequency (**UHF**) part of the spectrum; these stations are found on channels 14–69. VHF stations have a signal that covers greater distances than UHF stations. Consequently, VHF stations tend to be more desirable to own and operate.

As we suggested earlier, another important difference between stations concerns their affiliation with national networks. As of 1989, more than 80 percent of all commercial stations were affiliated with CBS, NBC, ABC, or Fox. Each of the networks owns and operates stations (called **O and Os**) in the largest markets in the United States. These stations tend to be very profitable and contribute a great deal to the overall revenues of their parent network.

Those stations not affiliated with networks are called **independents.** For many years, independents were hampered because most were UHF stations and had less coverage area than VHFs. The emergence of cable, however, gave UHF independents more of a competitive advantage, since both UHF and VHF stations have the same audience reach on the cable. In fact, one of the major trends of the 1980s has been the growing importance of independent stations in the TV industry. Independent stations' share of the viewing audience increased about 60 percent from 1972 to 1987, with a good deal of this gain coming at the expense of network viewing. The number of independent stations nearly tripled from 1980 to 1988 and annual revenue more than doubled. The boom came to an end, however, in 1987–1988, as increased competition and skyrocketing programming costs caused twenty independent stations to go bankrupt with more probably on the way.

Ownership

American broadcasting saw an unprecedented restructuring in the late eighties. Due in part to their economic situation and the increased competition facing the networks, the following changes occurred. Capital Cities Broadcasting assumed control of ABC. Long known for its emphasis on the bottom line, Capcities immediately instituted drastic cost-cutting measures to stem the company's flow of red ink. In an example of history repeating itself, NBC was taken over by General Electric, one of its original owners back in 1927. Although NBC's ratings were best of all the networks, its new owners also cut back on the budget. Technically, CBS did not change hands, but it came under the control of Laurence Tisch, head of the Loews Corporation. Tisch assumed control of the network with the backing of its founder, William Paley, who came out of retirement to ease the transition (another example of history come full circle). The cost-cutting at CBS received the most publicity as numerous news personnel were laid off. Tisch also sold several CBS properties in order to improve the company's solvency.

As of 1989, then, one network was under the control of a large conglomerate, another was controlled by a parent company with interests in publishing and cable, and a third had become almost completely broadcasting oriented. To be specific:

- NBC is under the control of RCA, which is in turn owned by General Electric. In addition to its holdings in nonmedia areas such as aerospace, aircraft engines, consumer products, and financial services, GE/RCA has interests in home video, owns and operates seven TV stations, has a production company and a corporate video production firm. RCA/NBC recently sold off its record company, the NBC Radio Network, and some of its radio stations.

- Capcities/ABC has interests in magazine publishing and owns seven daily newspapers, Chilton Books, part interest in three cable channels, a video production company, eight TV stations, and twenty-one radio stations.

- CBS Inc. has a video production company, a home video distribution firm, a radio network, and five TV and eighteen radio stations. In its move toward streamlining, CBS sold off its book publishing, magazine publishing, and recording divisions.

At the station level, a 1984 FCC ruling that raised the number of TV stations a person or organization could own from seven to twelve (provided that the twelve stations reached no more than 25 percent of the country's TV households after allowing for a 50 percent UHF "discount") sparked a massive trend toward consolidation in the industry. A change in tax law also accelerated the process, so that in 1985 and 1986 a record 227 TV stations changed hands. When all the dealing was done, it was evident that group ownership was the major defining characteristic of TV broadcasting. As of 1988, 191 groups owned about 77 percent of all the stations in the top 100 markets. Table 13.2 lists the top five group owners.

PRODUCING TELEVISION PROGRAMS

Departments and Staff

There are many different staffing arrangements in television stations. Some big-city stations employ 300–400 people and may be divided into a dozen different departments. Small-town stations may have twenty to thirty employees and only a few departments. Staffing arrangements are diverse. However, Fig. 13.1, page 304, represents one possible staffing structure.

At the top of the chart is the general manager, the person ultimately responsible for all station activities. The rest of the staff is divided into five different departments. The sales department is responsible for selling time to local and national advertisers, scheduling ads, and sending bills to customers. Maintaining all the technical equipment is the responsibility of the engineering department. The production department puts together locally produced programming. Producers, directors, camerapersons, artists, and announcers are part of this department. At many stations the programming function is also handled by this department. Those involved in programming decide what programs should be broadcast and at what times they should be presented. The function of the news department is self-evident. It includes the news director, anchorpeople, reporters, and writers responsible for the station's newscasts. The administrative department aids the station manager in running the station. Under this umbrella are included legal counsel, secretarial help, and the personnel, accounting, and bookkeeping departments.

Television stations have warmly embraced technology. Virtually all large-market stations now use personal computers for programming, administration, and sales.

TABLE 13.2 Top Five Owners of TV Stations

COMPANY	NUMBER OF STATIONS	PERCENTAGE OF COVERAGE
Capcities/ABC	8	24.4
NBC	7	22.3
CBS	5	20.8
Fox Television	7	19.4
Tribune Broadcasting	6	18.7

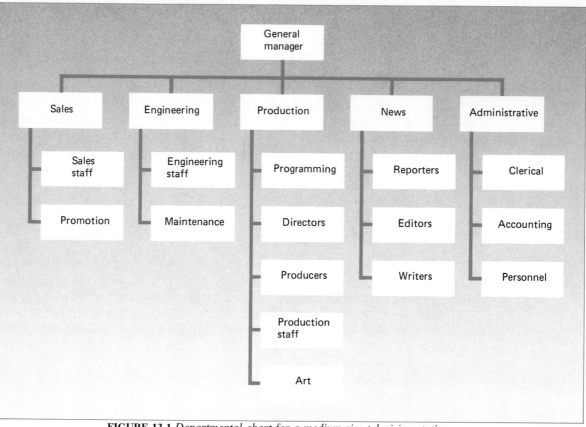

FIGURE 13.1 *Departmental chart for a medium-size television station.*

Almost all have access to a satellite dish and about 40 percent of all stations broadcast in stereo sound.

At the network level, the divisions are somewhat more complicated. Although the three major networks differ in their setups, all seem to have departments that perform the following functions:

1. Sales: handles sale of network commercials and works with advertising agencies.

2. Entertainment: works with producers to develop new programs for the network.

3. Owned and operated stations: administers those stations owned by the networks.

4. Affiliate relations: supervises all contacts with stations affiliated with the network (and generally tries to keep the affiliates happy).

5. News: responsible for all network news and public affairs programs.

6. Sports: responsible for all sports programming.

7. Standards: checks all network programs to make sure they don't violate the law or the network's own internal standards. All nets have recently cut back on this department.

8. Operations: handles the technical aspects of actually sending programs to affiliates.

Getting TV Programs on the Air

Producing television programs ranges from the incredibly simple—two chairs and a potted palm placed in front of a camera for an interview show—to the incredibly complex—the millions of dollars and hundreds of people who produced the miniseries "War and Remembrance." At the local level the biggest effort at a TV station goes into the newscast. Every station has a studio that contains a set for one or two anchorpeople, a weather forecaster, and a sportscaster. The station's news director assigns stories to reporters and camera crews, who travel to the scene of a story and videotape a report. Back at the station, the newscast producer and news director are planning what stories to air and allotting time to each. In the meantime, the camera crews and reporters return; the reporters write copy and editors prepare videotape segments. When the final script is finished (this may be only a few minutes before airtime), it is given to a director, who is responsible for pulling everything together and putting it on the air. In some markets, the production of the local news also includes live reports by correspondents at the scenes of news events. These reports are sent back to the station by microwaves.

In addition to the news, the local station might also produce one or two interview programs. These are usually done in the studio and taped for later broadcasting. Some stations are involved in producing a "magazine" program consisting of segments videotaped on location by portable equipment and later edited into final form. Aside from these kinds of shows, most local stations do little other production.

The networks are the organizations that are heavily involved in program development and production. Because they are responsible for filling the hours when the biggest audience is watching (called prime time, 8–11 P.M., Eastern Standard Time), the three networks must pay special attention to cultivating new shows. For the moment, let's concentrate on how a prime-time series is produced.

Everything starts with an idea. Network executives receive hundreds of ideas every year; some come from independent producers, some from TV departments of motion picture companies, some from network employees, and a good many from amateurs hoping for a break. From this mass of ideas, the networks select perhaps fifty to seventy-five, usually submitted by established producers or companies, for further attention. After examining plot outlines and background sketches of the leading characters for these fifty to seventy-five potential series, the networks trim the list once again. For those ideas that survive, the networks request a sample script and a list of possible stories that could be turned into scripts. If the idea still looks promising, the network and producer enter into a contract for a **pilot,** the first episode of a series. In a typical year, perhaps twenty-five pilots are ordered by each net. Pilots are expensive. The networks spent more than $100 million on seventy-five pilots for the 1988–1989 season; few of them made it into sustained production. If the pilot show gains a respectable audience, the network may order five or six episodes to be produced and may place the program on its fall schedule. From the hundreds of ideas that are sent to the network, only a few ever make it to prime time.

The process does not stop with the fall season. If a program does well in the ratings (see Chapter 20), the network will order enough episodes for the rest of the season. If the show does not do well, it will be canceled and another show will replace it. Meanwhile, network executives are sifting through the hundreds of program ideas for the next season, and the cycle begins once again.

The actual production of these series is done by independent or movie-affiliated production companies. Many of these companies own their own studios and production facilities; others rent or lease the space and equipment they need. There are two basic types of production: film and tape. Film programs are produced through the traditional techniques of motion pictures. There is typically one film camera, and each scene is shot several times from different angles until the director is satisfied. The scenes are shot out of sequence and later spliced into their proper order.

Other programs are shot on videotape with three or more TV cameras. The director selects the best shot from the three cameras to be recorded. In some cases, each episode is taped twice (typically, the dress rehearsal and final performance are recorded), and the director and tape editor select the best scenes from each and assemble them into the final version.

Of course, not all network programs are put together in this manner. Newscasts are usually done live with film and tape segments inserted in them. Shows such as "Good Morning, America" and "Today" are done live. Soap operas and game shows are typically done with multiple cameras and recorded on tape and, after minor editing, saved for future broadcast.

Once the shows have been produced, where and when to place them in the schedule must be decided. This task, known as **programming,** is a crucial one. A bad programming decision might mean failure for a good show while a shrewd decision might make a mediocre show a hit. Programmers at both the network and local level use certain principles to help them in their decisions. For example, one important consideration is **audience flow.** Ideally, the audience from one program should flow to the program that follows it. Mindful of this, programmers tend to schedule similar programs back to back so as to not interrupt the flow. For example, on Thursday nights during the 1987–1988 season, NBC scheduled four situation comedies in a row: "The Cosby Show," "A Different World," "Cheers," and "Night Court." CBS tried to encourage audience flow in the same season on Tuesday nights by scheduling three action-adventure series back to back: "Houston Knights," "Jake and the Fat Man," and "The Law and Harry McGraw." CBS was not successful with its strategy and cancellation notices went up for these shows.

Another principle is **counterprogramming,** airing a program designed to appeal to a different segment of the audience than those on competing stations. To illustrate, during the 1988–1989 season, CBS scheduled "Murphy Brown" and "Designing Women," shows with a lot of appeal to women, against ABC's "Monday Night Football," which drew a large number of male viewers.

Of course, the increasing use of VCRs to timeshift programs further complicates programming decisions.

ECONOMICS

Television has been a profitable industry since 1950, and its total income has increased every year since 1971. In 1988, television advertising revenue amounted to $26 billion, more than double the 1980 figure. The three networks shared $9 billion of this total. The pretax profit margin hovered around a healthy 15 percent. Although the gap was narrowing, VHF stations continued to be more profitable than UHFs, and network affiliates showed more profit than independent stations.

Commercial Time

Where did the $26 billion in revenue come from? It came from the sale of commercial time by networks and local stations to advertisers. A station or a network makes available a specified number of minutes per hour that will be offered for sale to advertisers. There are three different types of advertisers who buy time on TV stations:

1. national advertisers

2. national spot advertisers

3. local advertisers

National advertisers are those who sell general-consumption items: soda pop, automobiles, deodorant, hair spray, and so on. These advertisers try to reach the biggest possible audience for their messages and usually purchase commercial time on network programs.

In contrast, other advertisers have products that are mainly used in one region or locale. For these advertisers, buying time on a network show would not be the most efficient way to spend their money since many people who are not potential customers would be exposed to their messages. For example, a manufacturer of snowmobiles would gain little by having his or her ad seen in Miami or New Orleans. Likewise, a manufacturer of farm equipment would probably not find many customers in New York City. These companies turn to national spot buying. This method affords the advertiser flexibility since ads can be placed in precisely those markets that have the most sales potential. The snowmobile manufacturer would buy spots in several northern markets such as Minneapolis, Minnesota; Fargo, North Dakota; and Butte, Montana. The farm equipment company would place ads in primarily rural markets.

Finally, there are many local businesses that buy advertising time from TV stations. They need to reach only the area from which they get most of their customers. Consequently, they purchase time on one or more TV stations located in a single market. The industrywide figures for 1988 showed the relative importance of these three types of advertising. Network spots accounted for 38 percent of the total amount of advertising dollars, while the remainder was divided about equally between national spot and local advertising.

At the local station level, revenues depend upon the amount of money a station charges for its commercial time. The larger the audience, the more money a station can charge. The prices for thirty- and sixty-second commercials are listed on the station's rate card. The cost of an ad will vary tremendously from station to station. A thirty-second ad might cost only $100–$200 in a small market, while the same time would cost thousands in a major market. The same general pricing principles apply at the network level. Shows with high ratings have higher advertising charges than shows with low ratings. For example, in 1987, the average thirty-second commercial in prime time cost $122,000. Spots on a top-rated show cost twice as much; on a lower-rated show, about $85,000. To give some perspective on how expensive it can get, on the 1988 Superbowl a thirty-second spot was going for $620,000.

Where Did the Money Go?

Network programs are costing more and more to produce. For example, in 1988, one week of prime-time programs cost the three networks about $60 million. A show such as "thirtysomething" cost about $800,000 per episode to produce; "L.A. Law" cost about a million per episode. Some shows cost even more. "Dallas" and "Dynasty" checked in with about $1.2 million per episode and "Moonlighting," which typically ran over budget, wound up costing about $1.5 million per episode.

Twenty-two episodes (about the usual number produced in a season) of the average hour show cost almost $20 million. This heavy production cost is evident in the budgets of local stations. Broadcast expenses come from four areas: technical, program (which includes production costs), selling, and administration. The television expense dollar for 1988 was divided as follows:

Advertising/promotion	6 ¢
Technical	7 ¢
Program	34 ¢
Selling	9 ¢
Administration	31 ¢
News	14 ¢

It is obvious that the pattern of costs in television is quite different from that of radio (see Chapter 9).

In sum, traditional broadcast television has been an industry in transition. The networks were experiencing hard times, some independents were failing, but most stations in large and medium markets were doing well. Traditional broadcasting retained one big advantage over cable television and VCRs: It can be received by nearly 100 percent of American households, whereas cable is in about half and VCRs in just under 60 percent. Consequently, traditional over-the-air TV possesses unique advantages for national advertisers. Even though the network share of the prime-time viewing audience dropped to around 70 percent, the nets still dominate national advertising. This situation may change in the future, but it's still too early to write obituaries for traditional TV.

PUBLIC BROADCASTING

A Short History

In 1987, the act that established the Public Broadcasting Service reached its twentieth anniversary. During those two decades, public broadcasting's achievements were considerable but its evolution was hampered by political infighting, a lack of a clear purpose, and most of all, an insufficient amount of money. Let's quickly review some of the history of noncommercial television in the United States.

Until 1967, noncommercial TV was known as educational television. Most of the programs were instructional and were criticized for being dull. In 1967, following the recommendations of the Carnegie Commission, Congress passed the Public Broadcasting Act, which authorized money for the construction of new facilities and established the Corporation for Public Broadcasting (CPB), an organization that was to oversee noncommercial TV and distribute funds for programs. The government also created the Public Broadcasting Service (PBS), an organization whose duties resemble those performed by commercial networks, that is, promotion and distribution of programming among member stations. Although this arrangement seemed to work well at first, internal disputes soon surfaced concerning which of these two organizations had final control over programming. Another squabble developed in 1974 between public television and the Nixon administration when the White House felt that PBS programs were antiadministration. President Nixon eventually vetoed a CPB funding bill. Organizational problems continued to plague public broadcasting into the 1980s.

In addition, several cable channels began to offer programs that competed for public TV's audience. CBS Cable, with all the formidable resources of its parent company at its disposal, led the way in this area of cultural programming, with a schedule that included drama, ballet, opera, and concerts. Many experts felt that much of the traditional programming on public TV would eventually move to cable or to videocassette. On top of this came further reductions in federal funds for public broadcasting. In fact, the National Telecommunications and Information Administration, which recommends broadcasting policy to the White House, announced in 1983 that it was considering a suggestion that would end *all* federal funding of public TV. The future did not look promising.

Then things started to change. CBS Cable went out of business after losing $30 million. Other "arts" cable networks were struggling along in the red. There was little competition from videocassettes. Somewhat surprisingly, cable turned out to be more of a friend than foe to public TV. Those same must-carry rules that aided independent TV stations also helped public stations. Since two-thirds of all public stations are in the UHF band, carriage by local cable systems increased their coverage area and helped public TV double its audience from 1980 to 1984. The end result was that public TV wound up as the primary cultural channel in the nation with 90 million viewers every week.

The outlook was not all sunny, however. Since the White House appoints the members of the CPB board, political squabbles are constant. Some of the loudest occurred during the mid- to late 1980s, when conservative and liberal board members clashed over the "mission" of public broadcasting.

Also troubling was the overturning of the FCC's must-carry rules governing cable systems. These rules had guaranteed that public stations would be carried by local cable operators. The repeal of these rules made the future of cable-carried public stations uncertain.

Things were not bright on the monetary front either. The Reagan administration cut funds for public broadcasting and proposed to freeze future funding at current levels. Congress restored some of the cuts, but in 1987 the system was struggling to get along on about the same amount of money it had in 1982. Faced with this uncertainty, public TV looked to other sources for funding: corporate underwriting, auctions, viewer donations, and sales of program guides. Some noncommercial stations even briefly experimented with commercials. More than forty stations dropped their on-air pitches for money and many others cut back drastically on televised pledge drives when they finally realized that their televised pleas for viewer donations were counterproductive. The viewing public appreciated it; pledges at stations that cut back on the begging went up 5 percent.

Moreover, the goal of public broadcasting was becoming less clear. Cable channels, such as the Arts & Entertainment Network and the Discovery Channel, carry programs once identified with public broadcasting. Public TV stations themselves further blurred their identity by rerunning shows that were once popular on the commercial networks, such as ''The Avengers,'' ''Leave It to Beaver,'' and ''The Lawrence Welk Show.'' In sum, the twentieth anniversary of public broadcasting was marked by a great deal of analysis of how the next twenty years might be different.

Programming and Financing

Production methods for public television are similar to those of commercial TV. Decisions concerning what programs will be produced, however, are reached in a totally different manner. PBS uses the Station Program Co-operative (SPC) to select many of the programs that will be carried by its member stations. The SPC system is unique to PBS, and its workings are complicated. In short, member stations are given a ballot that includes descriptions of possible programs. Stations vote for those programs that they wish to carry. After several preliminary rounds, the ballot is pared down to the shows receiving the most votes, and an actual purchase round is then conducted. At this point, if a station wishes to carry a program, it must agree to pay part of its production costs. About 30 to 40 percent of the total programming on PBS comes from the SPC. Other programs are underwritten by foundations or by large companies. The large oil corporations are frequent sponsors of PBS programs. (Noting this fact, one critic suggested that PBS actually stands for the Petroleum Broadcasting Service.) Another frequent source is Great Britain; many series aired on PBS appeared first on the British Broadcasting Corporation (a fact that led another critic to suggest that PBS actually stands for Primarily British Shows). In actuality, according to PBS, only 11 percent of its first-run schedule consists of British programs. In fact, in the last few years, PBS programming has taken on much more of an American look with programs such as ''American Playhouse,'' ''Frontline,'' and ''Eyes on the Prize.''

PBS programs have earned numerous awards and substantial praise from critics. ''Sesame Street'' revolutionized children's TV by presenting educational content in an entertaining format. Millions of avid fans gave up other activities to watch the latest episode of ''Jewel in the Crown.'' ''Nova'' and ''Cosmos'' introduced millions to the wonders of science.

Like commercial stations, public TV stations receive licenses from the FCC. As of 1989, there were about 340 public stations operated by about 175 different license holders. Of these 340 stations, about 35 percent are licensed to states or municipalities and many of these are organized into state-operated networks. About 30 percent of public stations are licensed to colleges and universities; another 27 percent are owned by community organization and the remainder by public school systems.

Unlike commercial TV, public TV gets most of its support from the government. About 40 percent of public TV's revenue comes from the federal, state, or local government. Local residents who subscribe to public TV stations by paying a yearly fee to the local station account for about 20 percent. Support of programs by business accounts for another 15 percent. The remaining support comes from foundations, private colleges, and auctions held by some stations. To provide some comparison between the economics of commercial and noncommercial TV, recall that *one week* of commercial TV cost about $60 million. For 1987, the *entire budget* of the Corporation for Public Broadcasting was about $210 million, less than the cost of a month of network programs.

Religious Broadcasting

The proliferation of cable TV channels, independent TV stations, and satellite transmission of TV programs has caused a surge in religious broadcasting that promises to lure millions of viewers into the electronic church. In 1988, there were seven satellite-fed national cable services providing religious programming to their subscribers. The leader, the Christian Broadcasting Network, was available in about 40 million homes, just 6 million behind the leading cable network, ESPN (the entertainment and sports network). Additionally, about eighty-five to ninety independent TV stations also offer religious content.

The size of this audience is difficult to pinpoint, but a recent survey by the A. C. Nielsen Company suggests that about 40 percent of the nation's homes watched at least one of the top ten religious broadcasts during February of 1985. The top-rated religious show was "The 700 Club," which had a projected monthly audience of nearly 29 million. The audience for religious programming tends to be older than that for conventional TV programs (about half of the religious viewers are over 50) and is primarily female (63 percent). Most of the audience use TV as a supplement rather than a substitute for going to church.

The religious programming now being broadcast is a far cry from the traditional preaching and sermons that used to dominate Sunday morning TV. Many of the new channels blend religion with reruns of family-oriented entertainment series that were once broadcast on the three major networks. CBN, for example, cablecasts "Lassie" and "The Flying Nun" as a regular part of its schedule. Even the overtly religious programs have the "look" of network shows. "The 700 Club," for example, uses a talk show format and famous guest stars frequently come on the show to talk about their religious experiences. "The PTL Club" uses a format that is often compared with Johnny Carson's "Tonight" show.

Religious broadcasters do not confine themselves to a discussion of religion. One survey discovered that political issues are discussed in half the programs, while complex theological issues are seldom debated.

Religious broadcasting fell on some hard times in recent years. Oral Roberts was criticized when he asked viewers to send him $8 million to prevent God from "calling him home." Pat Robertson's presidential campaign fizzled and Jim Bakker and Jimmy Swaggart were both involved in sex scandals. Religious broadcasters quickly announced a tougher code of ethics, but many stations and cable systems canceled contracts with "televangelists."

CABLE TELEVISION

Cable television reached a milestone in 1987: It had penetrated into more than half of the homes in America. With its increasing presence came more advertising dollars, more prestige programming, and more political clout. After some rough early going, cable was an industry that was approaching maturity.

History: From Puny Weakling to Bully?

Cable TV (**CATV**) began modestly in the 1950s as a device used to bring conventional television signals to areas that could not otherwise receive them. Communities in mountainous areas or communities too small to support their own stations were

Televangelist Jimmy Swaggart looks to heaven during his ''I have sinned'' sermon, asking for God's forgiveness for his alleged sexual misconduct. His tearful resignation from his ministry was broadcast live and aired on national and local news programs. (UPI/Bettmann Newsphotos)

the first to be wired for CATV. As cable grew, some systems imported signals from distant stations into markets that were already served by one or two local stations. The local stations, as you might imagine, were not pleased since their audiences were being siphoned off by the imported signals. This situation caused some political maneuverings as stations affected by CATV appealed to the FCC and to Congress for help. The FCC vacillated over the question of cable regulation before issuing in 1965 a set of rules that had the effect of retarding the growth of CATV in large markets. In 1972 the FCC enacted a new set of less restrictive rules for cable. These new rules helped spur the growth of CATV systems during the 1970s. By 1980, in a move toward deregulation, the FCC dropped virtually all rules governing CATV.

This deregulation move helped systems grow as various cable companies scrambled to acquire exclusive cable franchises in communities across the nation (see Fig. 13.2). Some companies made extravagant promises to win these contracts: 100 plus channels, local-access channels, community channels, shopping and banking at home, two-way services—and all at bargain prices. After the smoke cleared, the industry quickly realized that economic reality dictated that its performance would fall short of promises:

- There was not enough quality programming available to fill 100-plus channel systems.

- Exotic cable services such as shopping and banking at home and videotex failed to support themselves as viable businesses.

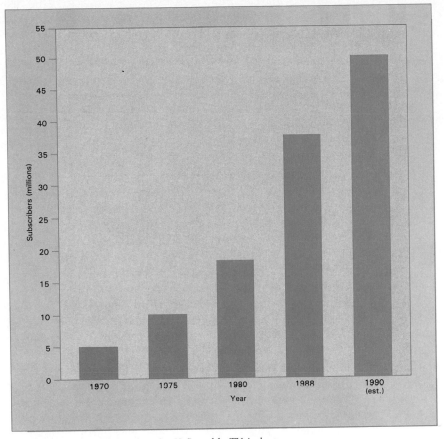

FIGURE 13.2 *Growth within the U.S. cable TV industry.*

- Two-way TV was too expensive for most viewers. Once the novelty effect wore off, it was a little-used feature.

- Advertiser-supported channels such as CBS Cable, TeleFrance USA, Ted Turner's Cable Music Channel, the Arts channel, and the Satellite News Network either folded or were discontinued when bought by other companies.

Cable quickly recovered from these setbacks and continued to grow. As of 1988, there were 7500 cable systems serving about 50 million households. Cable was a fixture in nearly 55 percent of American homes. Keep in mind that this growth occurred despite the fact that cable companies generally avoided expensive urban installations. In 1988, New York City and Los Angeles had 40 percent cable penetration; Chicago had only 35 percent. Once these cities are wired, cable's reach will be greatly increased.

By 1989, cable had begun to flex its newfound muscles. On the political front, the industry was able to steer the 1984 Cable Communications Policy Act through the Congress. This legislation took the lid off cable rates, allowing many systems to increase profits. On the legal front, the court system struck down the must-carry rules, which had required cable systems to carry all local broadcast stations. Now, pending congressional action, cable systems can carry whatever services they want to. Many broadcasters feared that it was only a matter of time before cable systems charged some stations a fee to carry them on the cable. Others voiced concern that cable systems were moving some independent stations from the lower numbered cable channels (2–16) into cable "Siberia" (channels 16 and up), where there are fewer viewers and where independents are less competitive with other cable channels in which the local station has an ownership interest.

On the economic side, cable advertising revenues exceeded $1 billion in 1988. Although still small in comparison to the ad revenues generated by traditional television, this figure would represent an increase of more than 100 percent over 1984, enough to get the attention of traditional broadcasting.

Cable scored several recent programming coups that made traditional broadcasting take notice. ESPN signed a three-year deal with the National Football League to carry prime-time pro football games, breaking the network monopoly on that sport. As more sports programming traditionally carried by over-the-air broadcasters, such as New York Yankees baseball, went to cable, many feared it was only a matter of time before the Superbowl and the World Series moved to the wire. "It's Garry Shandling's Show" gave Showtime a popular and critical hit and greatly increased its visibility. (Ironically, Showtime promptly sold the show to the Fox Network.) Other big-ticket network series were bypassing the traditional syndication route and premiering first on cable. "Miami Vice," "Murder, She Wrote," and "Remington Steele" were the first to make the leap to cable. These shows will offer increased competition to traditional broadcast stations.

Perhaps the one thing that worried traditional broadcasters and programming suppliers most was the increasing vertical integration of the cable industry. Lack of regulation allowed cable operators to become more and more involved with programming, thus controlling both the hardware and the software side of the business. TCI, the biggest cable system operator, owns part of Turner Broadcasting System, which includes superstation WTBS, CNN, and the TNT cable network. TCI also owns half of the American Movie Classics Channel and parts of the Discovery Channel, Black Entertainment Television, and The Fashion Channel. ATC, another large operator, is owned by Time Inc. (soon to be Time Warner Inc.), which also owns HBO and Cinemax. Viacom, which operates systems in seven states, owns Showtime, The Movie Channel, and MTV.

All of these developments have cable's chief rivals, the motion picture and broadcasting industries, charging that cable systems are unregulated monopolies and asking for some kind of reregulation. One network executive likened cable to a "toll bridge into the home," controlling to a large extent what programs Americans got to see on their TV sets. Critics charge that cable is cornering the market on information and entertainment and is putting itself into such a strong position that it can bully its rivals into submission. The cable industry, of course, denied this charge. Nonetheless, some regulators and lawmakers are concerned about the growing power of cable. In 1988, the FCC reenacted the syndication exclusivity rules that protect the programming of local stations against duplication from distant stations brought in by cable. Moreover, the must-carry rules might be resurrected in a different form, and Congress convened hearings examining cable's anticompetitive behavior. The next few years could be highly influential in cable's subsequent evolution.

Ownership

The trend in the cable industry, like that in other media, is toward consolidation. The top ten cable multiple system operators (MSOs) now reach more than 54 percent

TABLE 13.3 Five Largest Cable System Operators

SYSTEM	NUMBER OF SUBSCRIBERS (MILLIONS)
TCI, Inc.	9.5
ATC	3.7
Continental Cable	2.2
Comcast	2.1
Cox Cable	1.4

of the nation's subscribers. The five largest cable systems and the number of their subscribers are listed in Table 13.3.

Structure of CATV Systems

CATV systems are structured differently from those of conventional TV. There are three main components in a CATV system (see Fig. 13.3, p. 316):

1. the head end
2. the distribution system
3. the house drop

The **head end** consists of the antenna and related equipment that receives signals from distant TV stations or other programming services and processes these signals so that they may be sent to subscribers' homes. Some CATV systems also originate their own programming, ranging from local newscasts to weather dials, and their studios may also be located at the head end.

The **distribution system** consists of the actual cables that deliver the signals to subscribers. The cables can be buried or hung on telephone poles. In most systems, the main cable (called the trunk) has several feeder cables, which travel down side

SMATV and MDS

Two services that are connected to the cable industry are MDS (Multipoint Distribution Service) and SMATV (Satellite Master Antenna Television).

An MDS transmitter sends microwaves to special antennas and receivers. MDS is an ideal means to transmit pay programming (such as movies) to apartments and hotels. Sometimes called ''wireless cable,'' MDS has also been sold to homes where cable was not available.

SMATV offers a small-scale version of cable. It is particularly attractive to urban areas where cable is not yet available. Most big apartment buildings have a rooftop master antenna that picks up traditional TV signals. Tenants can plug into this system for better reception. In the SMATV system, a satellite receiving dish is installed that picks up the signals from the national cable networks. Tenants pay a subscription fee and in effect belong to a miniature cable system. Of course, the fortunes of SMATV may change radically when the big cities are wired for cable.

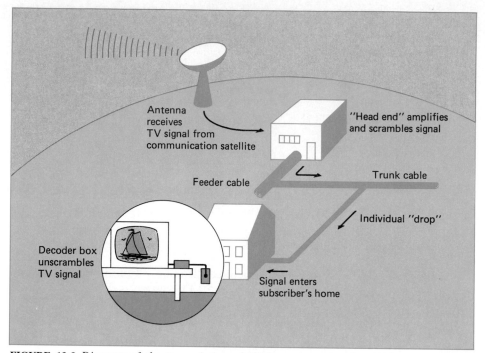

FIGURE 13.3 *Diagram of the transmission of HBO programming from videotape studios, via satellite, to the pay subscriber's television set. At the head end, the signal is assigned to a cable TV channel before being sent on its way to the subscriber's home.*

streets or to other outlying areas. Finally, there are special amplifiers installed along the distribution system, which boost the strength of the signal as it comes from the head end.

The **house drop** is that section of the cable that connects the feeder cable to the subscriber's TV set. Drops can be one way (the signal travels in only one direction—from the head end to the house) or two way (the signal can also be sent back to the head end by the subscriber). Most cable systems built before 1972 provided twelve channels for their subscribers; those built afterward have at least twenty. In some communities, there are fifty-four channels. Advanced two-way systems offer shopping-at-home and banking-at-home services.

Programming and Financing

We will examine these topics from two perspectives: (1) from that of a local cable system operator and (2) from that of a national cable network.

The sources of programming for a local system consist of:

1. Local origination—This might range from a fixed camera scanning temperature dials to local news, high school football, and discussions. Other local origination programs include a government channel, which carries city council meetings or zoning board hearings. Some systems have set aside public-access channels available for anyone to use for a modest fee.

2. Local broadcast television stations—Until recently, cable systems were required by law to carry the signals of all local TV stations. As we have already

seen, this law has been overturned, but most systems continue to carry the local channels. In addition to local channels, some cable systems carry signals from nearby cities.

3. Superstations—These are independent stations whose signals are carried by many systems nationwide. There are five main superstations: WTBS, Atlanta; WGN, Chicago; WWOR and WPIX, New York, and KTVT, Dallas. Superstations primarily broadcast sports, movies, and syndicated shows.

4. Special cable networks—These are services distributed by satellite to cable systems. Most of these networks are advertiser supported. Examples include MTV, The Weather Channel, the USA Network, Black Entertainment Television, and the noncommercial C-SPAN (which covers Congress).

5. Pay services—These are commercial-free channels that typically provide theatrical movies and original programming: HBO, Showtime, The Movie Channel, Cinemax, The Disney Channel.

A local cable system has two basic sources of income, subscription fees from consumers and local advertising. Most systems charge a basic fee for local stations, superstations, and special cable networks. In addition, consumers might pay an additional fee to receive one or more pay channels. Looking at expenses, cable is a capital-intensive industry (this means it takes a lot of money to start a system). The cost of stringing the cable, hardware, maintenance, installations, disconnects, and franchise fees makes it expensive. Once in place, the operating costs of a typical system become more reasonable. A good part of the basic cable monthly subscription fee goes to cover construction and maintenance costs. Cable systems must also pay for their programming. Some national cable channels supplement their advertising revenue by charging cable systems a small fee per subscriber (called a **carriage fee**), which is often passed on to the consumer. In the case of pay services, the consumer fee is split between the cable system and the cable network. For example, if a pay channel costs the consumer $8 a month, $5 might go to the cable network while $3 is retained by the cable operator. Local advertising on cable represents the other source of income for operators. This sum is growing, but it still represents only 5 percent of total income for local systems.

Turning to the national level, cable networks draw upon three major sources for their programming: (1) original production, (2) movies, and (3) syndicated programs. The all-news channel, CNN, relies upon original production for virtually all of its content. Most of ESPN's programming is original as is C-SPAN's. Movies make up most of the content on HBO and Showtime, although both channels have recently relied more on original productions. Superstations program a mix of all three sources, while channels such as the USA Network and the CBN Cable Network depend heavily upon syndicated programs. Many of the programs on cable are reruns of network series from the 1950s and 1960s and recent shows from the networks, giving these shows a second life.

There are three main revenue sources for national cable services: advertising, carriage fees, and subscription fees. Pay-TV channels such as Showtime and HBO make their money from subscription fees paid by the consumer. Some cable networks, such as MTV and ESPN, will charge local operators a carriage fee (also called an affiliation fee) that ranges from about 5 to 30 cents per subscriber. MTV charges 27 cents; CNN, 23 cents. Some channels, such as C-SPAN, support themselves entirely from this money. Other networks will sell advertising in addition to the carriage fee while still others, such as The Nashville Network, support themselves entirely through ads. As mentioned earlier, advertising revenues for cable are growing, but cable still accounts for only a small percentage of the total TV ad dollars. As of 1988, basic cable networks were the fastest growing in the industry, with audience ratings increasing 20 percent in 1987. Most basic cable channels were turning a profit, with only VH-1, Nick at Nite, and the Discovery Channel still hoping to improve their financial situation.

Pay cable channels, Showtime, HBO, Disney, and others, went through a period of growth stagnation in 1984–1986 but, thanks to a multimillion-dollar promotion campaign, showed significant growth in 1987. The Disney Channel increased its number of subscribers about 20 percent, Cinemax jumped 9 percent, and Showtime and HBO about 3 percent. Only The Movie Channel and The Playboy Channel were losing viewers. Pay cable is now in about 28 percent of all TV homes. Table 13.4 lists the top five pay channels services.

HOME VIDEO

The home video industry came into existence because of the tremendous growth of VCR sales. In 1982, only 2 million VCRs were sold. The number doubled in 1983 and doubled again in 1984. Obviously, such a swift pace could not sustain itself forever, and VCR sales plateaued from 1985 to 1987. Nonetheless, 60 percent of U.S. homes were equipped with the device by 1989 and experts predicted that figure would ultimately rise to about 85 percent.

VCR owners use their machines to timeshift, that is, to record TV shows for playback at a more convenient time. As of 1988, the shows that were timeshifted the most were soap operas, movies, and "Late Night with David Letterman." VCRs are also used for playing back prerecorded tapes bought or rented at video counters and video stores. There are more than 24,000 prerecorded cassette titles on the market and an estimated 400 new titles are introduced every month. This pace will probably slacken in the future as all of the most desirable tapes of years past are transferred to cassette, leaving only current releases.

Like most other businesses, home video can be divided into three segments: production, distribution, and retail. The production side of the industry consists of those companies that produce prerecorded cassettes. Since much of the home video market consists of movies, many of the large motion picture studios also dominate the cassette business. In 1986, for example, about two-thirds of videocassette sales went to the ten largest motion picture studios, with 20th Century Fox and Columbia

TABLE 13.4 Top Five Pay Cable Channels

CHANNEL	SUBSCRIBERS (MILLIONS)
HBO	15.0
American Movie Classics	7.0
Showtime	5.7
Cinemax	4.1
Disney Channel	3.2

leading the pack. In fact, as we discussed in Chapter 12, the home video market has become the most important source of revenue for the motion picture industry.

Few of these companies sell directly to dealers. Instead, they sell to distributors, who form the bridge between production and retail. Currently some ninety distributors in the United States handle videocassettes. Major companies include HBO Video, CBS/Fox Video, RCA/Columbia Home Pictures, Vestron, Tri-Star, and Orion. Moreover, the cassette distribution business now resembles record distribution as a new breed of rack jobber is making it easy for many retail and department stores to get into the video renting business. Companies such as Stars-To-Go and CEVAXS install and operate video rental counters in convenience stores and grocery stores, usually paying rent to the store and collecting a percentage of the video rental business in return. Most of the 60,000 or so convenience stores in the United States have or plan to install a video rental area.

Tapes are priced for either the rental or the **"sell-through" market.** Sell-throughs generally are priced lower. For example, exercise or self-improvement tapes generally are priced for sell-through, since it is assumed that customers will want to keep them for their personal video library. Some movies also are priced for sell-through. *Top Gun* and *ET* each had a pricetag under $30 when first released. Other movies carry a $70 or $80 price and are designed to be sold primarily to rental stores. A distributor will sell a $70 tape to a retailer for about $45. The distributor's profit on this transaction will be 12–15 percent. Distributors must pay large sums of money to win the rights to movies. Fees around $10 million are not unheard of.

Father and son at a video rental store where the array of tapes is often enormous, ranging from all categories of motion pictures to instructional and "how-to" videos; some new "supermarket video stores" now carry as many as 12,000 rental options. (Emilio A. Mercado/The Picture Cube)

Video Dogs and Video Babies

You probably know you can buy videotapes that help you exercise, improve your golf game, or teach you how to fix your car. But did you know there are a number of vicarious videos that help you enjoy the benefit of certain things without having to put up with the reality? For example, does your apartment or house lack a fireplace? No problem. Just pop in a cassette of "Video Fireplace" and enjoy forty-five minutes of taped wood burning. No messy ashes to clean. No dangerous sparks burning the rug. You like tropical fish but can't afford a tank? No problem. Just buy "Video Aquarium" and spend forty-five minutes in front of your TV watching fish swim around. No need to buy fish food. No messy cleanups. Want to have a pet but don't have the time to care for one? No problem. Take home

"Video Dog." According to the owner's manual, video dogs are friendly, good natured, never need to go outside, and won't track mud over the floor. Want to experience parenthood without the inconvenience and mess of the real thing? Just cue up "Video Baby." The tape comes with a birth certificate, medical record sheet, and script to help you enjoy video parenting to the fullest. For example, wave when the script tells you to wave and Video Baby waves back. Tell Video Baby to splash in the tub and Video Baby splashes on cue. How do you clean up Video Baby after a messy feeding session? Easy . . . just fast forward to the next segment. (The company that manufactures these vicarious videos has a new one on the drawing board: Video Cat. When you call it, it just looks at you.)

The retail side of the industry is the most volatile. Precise figures are hard to come by because of rapid change, but it was estimated that in 1988 there were about 26,000–27,000 video rental/sales stores in the United States in addition to the thousands of tape counters at grocery and convenience stores. The typical large retail store carries a library of about 3000–5000 different titles, representing a balance of current hits with other titles that have a longer shelf life. In contrast, convenience stores and other outlets stock only 200–500 titles, most of them current hits. Competition has grown so much that video stores now resemble fast-foot franchises since most of them serve customers in about a three-mile radius.

The video rental business is dominated by large chains. Companies such as Erol's, Tower Video, and National Video accounted for more than one-third of all video stores in 1987 and were still growing. Independently owned stores find it tough to compete with the big chains, and hundreds went under from 1985 to 1988. Those that did survive became more specialized, building up an inventory of foreign films, 1940s movies, art films, or films in some other area. Small video stores frequently have a cash flow problem. Suppose a store bought five copies of twenty-five new cassettes a month at an average cost of $50. This amounts to $6250 a month spent for new product. At an average cost of $2.25 a rental, almost 2800 rental transactions would be required just to pay the bill for new releases. Most small stores can't generate that amount of volume.

On the other hand, videocassette sales and rentals constitute big business. In 1987, consumers spent about $7.5 billion on cassettes, with about 80 percent of that sum going to tape rentals and the remainder to tape sales. The industry has shown recent signs of leveling off and revenues are expected to grow more slowly in the future. Competition brought down rental fees. The overall industry average mentioned above was $2.25 per tape, but lower fees—sometimes below $1—are common. A tape has to be rented about thirty times before a retailer can show a profit.

Traditional broadcasters reacted to the increased competition from home video. The networks began offering more shows that attract an older audience (such as "The Golden Girls"), since older viewers were less likely to own VCRs. Further, the networks were scheduling some of their strongest shows on the weekends, when VCR usage is highest, to counterprogram the machine. Some local stations are running promotions that urge viewers to watch their channel while taping the competition's. And if all of this fails, the three major networks have released some of their programs to the home video market.

SATELLITE DISHES

The satellite dish collects faint microwave signals from an orbiting satellite and amplifies them about a million times. A cable carries these signals to a converter where they are changed so that they can be received over a normal TV set. Most satellite dishes (Also called TVROs—for TV Receive Only) also have a remote-control device that permits the viewer to aim the dish at the appropriate orbiting satellite. A TVRO can receive not only all the regular TV channels but also "raw feeds," signals sent by networks and cable channels to local stations and cable systems and not intended for public viewing. A good backyard dish can pick up 75 to 100 channels.

In the early 1980s, owners of TVROs were able to pick up free programming off the satellites and the TVRO business was booming. Then the pay movie services and other cable channels scrambled their signals and the bottom dropped out of the TVRO business. To illustrate, in 1985, before widespread scrambling, about 90,000 dishes a month were being sold. After scrambling, the average dropped to about 14,000.

Currently, most dish owners and potential buyers have accepted scrambling as a given. Consumers are now required to buy a descrambling device, which costs several hundred dollars, and pay a monthly fee to receive the now-scrambled channels. Despite the increased costs, sales have been picking up lately, particularly among people living in rural areas unlikely to receive cable.

A whole new program distribution industry has been springing up to serve TVRO owners. Companies such as the Satellite Broadcast Networks (SBN) uplink stations' signals and sell subscriptions to the service to dish owners. The pay-TV channels (Showtime, HBO, etc.) also offer dish owners subscriptions to their programming for a monthly fee. As of mid-1988, Congress was considering legislation that would regulate this new business.

No matter what the legal outcome, future developments in technology will drastically change this industry. High-power satellites can be received on smaller and cheaper dishes. In fact, one new type of antenna developed by the Japanese is not even a dish. The Matsushita Corporation recently unveiled a flat-plate antenna that is only 15 inches square and can be installed on an outside wall instead of on an ugly concrete slab in the backyard. In the future, these new dishes might be receiving signals from direct broadcast satellites (see Chapter 23 for a description of DBS) providing original programming . . . but that's a story for a future edition.

CAREERS IN THE TELEVISION INDUSTRY

How does a young person get started in a career in television? Where should you look for that first job? Someone hunting for a job in TV quickly discovers that it's a relatively small industry. According to recent figures provided by the FCC, about 78,000 people are employed in commercial TV; 50,000 in CATV; 10,000 in non-commercial television; and about 16,000 at TV networks. This means that there are about 144,000 employees in the entire industry. (To give you some perspective on this figure, General Motors employs 578,000 and IBM, 340,000.)

In any given year, probably 5,000 to 10,000 people are hired by the TV industry. Many of these people are replacing employees who have retired or gone on to other careers, while others are filling newly created positions. Also, in any given year, about 15,000 to 20,000 people are looking for TV jobs. Speaking conservatively, we can say that there are at least two people looking for each available position. In some areas of television, especially for the so-called glamour jobs (TV reporter, network page, on-camera host for an interview show, series writer), the competition will be much more intense.

Entry-Level Positions

Despite this competition, individuals who are skilled, intelligent, and persistent are likely to be successful in finding jobs. Here are some general hints on job hunting in TV.

1. Think small. As in radio, small-market TV stations offer more employment potential than larger-market stations. True, the big markets pay more and have more employees than small markets, but the competition and the number of people looking for jobs will also be greater. Moreover, at a small station, you have a chance to do more and learn more than you might at a larger station.

2. Don't be afraid to start at the bottom. Most industry professionals and employment counselors advise job-seekers to take any type of job that will get them into a TV organization. Once you get in, it is easier to move upward into a position that might be more to your liking. Many successful people in TV started in the mailroom, secretarial pool, or shipping department.

3. Be prepared to move. Your first job will probably not be a lifetime commitment. Most people in TV change jobs several times in their careers. Frequently, the road to advancement in TV consists of moving about and up—from a small station to a large station, from an independent station to a network affiliate, from the station to the network. Most newcomers to TV spend about twelve to eighteen months at their first job.

Upward Mobility

Those interested in producing TV shows might consider looking for jobs as a camera operator, floor manager (the person who gives cues to the talent and makes sure everything in the studio goes smoothly during the telecast), or production assistant (a person who handles all the odd jobs that need to be done during a show). From there you might progress upward to become an assistant director or assistant producer or perhaps a writer. Eventually, you would hope to become a full-fledged director or producer.

Those thinking about a career in TV journalism have to make an early decision. If you are interested in being an on-camera news reporter, your best bet might be to find a general reporting job at a smaller station. If your interests lie behind the camera, your possibilities are varied. You can start out as a news writer or news researcher or even a cameraperson or tape editor. Most people interested in performing before the camera generally stay in that capacity. Upward mobility for general-assignment reporters consists of moving into the anchor position. For anchors, it consists of moving to bigger and more lucrative markets. For those behind the scenes, the first move up will probably be to the assistant news director slot and then on to the news director position.

Sales is the one division that offers the most upward mobility. Unlike radio sales, TV sales usually is harder to break into. Most stations prefer people who have had some experience in selling (many move from radio sales to TV sales). Once a salesperson is established, however, the monetary rewards can be substantial. Salespeople advance their careers by moving to larger markets or by moving up to the sales manager position.

The highest level a person can reach at the local level is the general manager's position. In the past, most general managers have come from the sales department. This trend is likely to continue, but it is also probable that more people who started off in the news departments move into management, since news is becoming more of a moneymaker. Historically, only a few people from the programming side enter top management.

Other Opportunities

A television station is not the only place to look for employment. The cable TV industry is expanding and needs people skilled in every facet of TV—production, sales, programming, and management. As cable provides more local programming and adds more channels, the industry will need more people in promotion, publicity, performance, marketing, and community relations. Allied with cable are the pay-TV services (HBO, Showtime, etc.). These organizations will also need skilled personnel. CATV and pay TV should not be overlooked as potential job sources.

Another emerging employment source is the home video area. The production of prerecorded cassettes and videodiscs represents another area where there are expanding opportunities for those interested in the creative and business side of TV. Finally, many large companies, such as IBM and Xerox, have in-house production facilities. In fact, some companies have studios that are on a par with many large TV stations. These companies use TV to produce employee training programs and to fill other internal communication needs. Although not as visible as some other parts of the industry, this is an important source of employment for a large number of people.

SUGGESTIONS FOR FURTHER READING

The following books contain more information about the concepts and topics discussed in this chapter.

ARMER, ALAN, *Directing Television and Film*, Belmont, Calif.: Wadsworth, 1986.

BALDWIN, THOMAS, AND D. S. MCVOY, *Cable Communication*, Englewood Cliffs, N.J.: Prentice-Hall, 1983.

DOMINICK, JOSEPH, BARRY SHERMAN, AND GARY COPELAND, *Broadcasting/Cable and Beyond*, New York: McGraw-Hill, 1990.

HEAD, SYDNEY, AND CHRISTOPHER STERLING, *Broadcasting in America*, 5th ed., Boston: Houghton Mifflin, 1987.

SMITH, LESLIE, *Perspectives on Radio and Television*, New York: Harper & Row, 1985.

STEINBERG, COBBETT, *TV Facts*, New York: Facts on File, 1980.

Part Four

Special Mass Media Professions

Chapter 14

News Gathering
and Reporting

About 63 million newspapers are sold every day. Nine million people read a weekly news magazine. About 23 million households watch the daily network newscasts. The all-news cable channel, CNN, has about 300,000 homes tuned to it on a given evening. Local TV newscasts are among the top-rated shows in many markets. Obviously, news is important to Americans.

Before anything becomes news, however, it must be reported. A professional reporter must be aware of the qualities that characterize a news story, the types of news that exist, and the differences in the way the various media cover news. This chapter examines these topics and looks at the career possibilities of news gathering and reporting.

DECIDING WHAT IS NEWS

Out of the millions of things that happen every day, print and electronic journalists decide what few things are worth reporting. Deciding what is newsworthy is not an exact science. News values are formed by tradition, technology, organizational policy, and increasingly by economics. Nonetheless, most journalists agree that there are common elements that characterize newsworthy events. Below are listed the five qualities of news about which there is the most agreement.

1. Timeliness. To put it glibly, news is new. Yesterday's news is old news. A consumer who picks up the evening paper or turns on the afternoon news expects to be told what happened earlier that same day. News is perishable and stale news is not interesting.

2. Proximity. News happens close by. Readers and viewers want to learn about their neighborhood, town, or country. All other things being equal, news from close to home is more newsworthy than news from a foreign country. A train derailment in France, for example, is less likely to be reported than a similar derailment in the local trainyard. Proximity, however, means more than a simple measure of distance. Psychological proximity is also important. Subway riders in San Francisco might show interest in a story about rising vigilantism on the New York subways, even though the story is happening 3000 miles away.

3. Prominence. The more important a person, the more valuable he or she is as a news source. Thus, activities of the president and other heads of state

A news reporter in action. Lightweight cameras and videotape recorders as well as electronic news-gathering (ENG) technology now make it possible to broadcast live from the scenes of important stories. (Tom Kelly)

attract tremendous media attention. In addition to political leaders, the activities of sports and entertainment figures are also deemed newsworthy. Even the prominence of the infamous has news value. The past lives and recent exploits of many criminals are frequently given media coverage.

4. Consequence. Events that have an impact on a great many people have built-in news value. A tax increase, the decision to lay off thousands of workers, a drought, inflation, an economic downturn—all of these events have consequence. Note that the audience for a particular news item is a big factor in determining its consequence. The closing of a large factory in Kankakee, Illinois, might be page one news there, but it probably wouldn't be mentioned in Keokuk, Iowa.

5. Human Interest. These are stories that arouse some emotion in the audience; stories that are ironic, bizarre, uplifting, or dramatic. Typically, these items concern ordinary people who find themselves in circumstances with which the audience can identify. Thus, when the winner of the state lottery gives half of his winnings to the elderly man who sold him the ticket, it becomes newsworthy. When a ninety-year-old brickmaker from North Carolina volunteers to go to Guyana to help the local construction industry, it becomes news.

In addition to these five traditional elements of news value, there are other things that influence what information gets published or broadcast. Most journalists agree that economics plays a large role. First, some stories cost more to cover than others. It is cheaper to send a reporter or a camera crew to the city council meeting than to assign a team of reporters to investigate city council corruption. The latter would require a long time, extra resources, extra personnel, and patience. All of which cost money. Some news operations might not be willing to pay the price for such a story. Or, conversely, after spending a large sum of money pursuing a story, the news organization might run it, even if it had little traditional news value, simply to justify its cost to management. By the same token, the cost of new technology is reflected in the types of stories that are covered. When TV stations went to electronic news gathering (ENG), stories that could be covered live became more important. In fact, many organizations, conscious of the scheduling of TV news programs, planned their meetings and/or demonstrations during the newscast to enhance their chances for TV coverage. Further, after helicopters became an expensive investment at many large TV stations, traffic jams, fires, beautiful sunsets, and other stories that lent themselves to airborne journalism suddenly became newsworthy.

The relationship between economics and network TV news was vividly demonstrated in 1987 when CBS and ABC, reacting to declining profits, sharply reduced the budgets of their news departments. CBS cut the deepest: more than 300 people laid off, $30 million slashed from the news budget, and three bureaus shut down. ABC also cut its staff but its reductions were not as drastic. (Even NBC, which had a financial situation more favorable than the other two networks, ultimately reduced its news budget.) These cuts triggered a round of controversy between news staffs and management. Reporters argued that less money and less people would have a negative impact on news coverage. In a personal column appearing on the op-ed page of the *New York Times,* CBS anchor Dan Rather criticized his employer and charged tht CBS news would now cover less news. In response, network executives argued that the cutbacks simply represented good cost management and that the networks had been spending excessive amounts of money on their news divisions for years. The cutbacks, they argued, would not hurt the quality of news reporting. Instead, they would make it more efficient.

This controversy ultimately triggered an unprecedented hearing called by the House Telecommunication Subcommittee to examine how corporate economics have affected news coverage. For three days the committee collected nearly twenty hours of testimony from network executives. When the hearing was over, the committee at least had a better understanding of the business that drives network news. By mid-1988, however, the networks had accepted reduced budgets and smaller staffs as a fact of life. One study of the content of network news noted little difference between precut and postcut newscasts, indicating that the nets were able to cope with their new circumstances.

Newspapers are not immune from the pervasive influence of the bottom line. As more corporations and large newspaper chains dominate the business, more MBAs than journalists are becoming newspaper executives. The topics of greatest interest to this new breed of manager are marketing surveys, budget plans, organizational goals, and strategic planning—not the news-gathering process. This new orientation usually shows up in the newspaper's pages. The paper's "look" improves: more color, better graphics, an appealing design; there are more features: food sections, personal finance columns, entertainment guides, and reviews. In all, the paper becomes a slickly packaged product. At the same time, however, the amount of space devoted to local news decreases, reporters are discouraged from going after expensive investigative stories, and aggressive pieces about the local business community tend to disappear. Many experienced editors fear that the new corporate breed of managers will change the traditional news values of American journalism.

Economics alters news values in other, more subtle, ways. Ben Bagdikian, in *The Media Monopoly,* noted that the rise of media conglomerates (big companies that own newspapers, broadcasting stations, and other properties) poses a problem for journalism. Can a newspaper or TV station adequately cover the actions of its parent company? For example, could NBC news objectively report the activities if GE was involved in some alleged wrongdoing? Or could a Gannett-owned paper adequately cover events at *USA Today,* another Gannett property? Economics plays a part in local markets as well. Newspapers make their money from circulation figures, and it has been charged that some publishers pander to public taste to inflate circulation figures. Media baron Rupert Murdoch was criticized for this when he took over the *New York Post.* He was chastised for placing great emphasis on sensationalism in an attempt to attract new readers. (He eventually sold the *Post* and its new owner has toned it down.) A similar situation exists in local TV news. The local newscast is an extremely profitable item for most TV stations, and competition is fierce. During special ratings weeks—called "sweeps" (see Chapter 20)—when viewing in every local market is measured, a whole new set of news values comes into play at many TV stations. All of a sudden, special programs on teenage prostitution, UFOs, pornography, the singles scene, and similar reports appear on the news. The quest for higher ratings (and revenues) at the expense of traditional news values is evident.

Another influence on news reporting is organizational policy. Sometimes this influence is easy to see. For example, most news organizations have a policy that covers reporting of a civil disorder or a hostage crisis. Further, during an election campaign, news executives often set some time/space allocations for minor candidates. Other times, this influence is more subtle. For example, on the network news level, pressure from local stations requires that the network news be national in scope, so as not to duplicate local efforts. Further, many executives in the print and broadcast media subscribe to the notion that the audience prefers news events that can be told as "stories"; that is, they have drama, action, and a clear story line. Accordingly, news events that emphasize confrontation, controversy, and even violence tend to be given additional news prominence. Other organizations may have policies that require controversial stories to be screened by legal experts and modified before going on the air. And some broadcast news operations prohibit the airing of otherwise newsworthy stories if a hidden camera was used to collect information. The influence of organizational policy, while sometimes subtle, touches a great deal of news.

CATEGORIES OF NEWS AND REPORTING

Generally, news can be broken down into three broad categories: (1) hard news, (2) features or soft news, and (3) investigative reports.

Hard News

Hard news stories make up the bulk of news reporting. They typically embody the first four of the five traditional news values discussed above. Hard news consists of basic facts: who, what, when, where, how. It is news of important public events, such as government actions, international happenings, social conditions, the economy, crime, environment, and science. Hard news has significance for large numbers of people. The front sections of a newspaper or magazine and the lead stories of a radio or TV newscast are usually filled with hard news.

There is a standard technique used to report hard news. In the print media, it is the traditional inverted pyramid form. The main facts of the story are delivered in the first sentence (called the lead) in an unvarnished, no-nonsense style. Less important facts come next, with the least important and most expendable facts at the end. This structure aids the reporter (who uses it to compose facts quickly), the editor (who can lop off the last few paragraphs of a story to make it fit the page without doing wholesale damage to the sense of the story), and the reader (who can tell at a glance if he or she is interested in all, some, or none of the story). This format has been criticized for being predictable and old-fashioned. More literary writing styles have been suggested as alternatives, but the inverted pyramid has survived and will probably be around far into the future.

In the broadcast media, with the added considerations of limited time, sound, and video, the inverted pyramid format is not used. Instead, broadcast reporting follows a square format. The information level stays about the same throughout the story. There's usually no time for the less important facts that would come in the last paragraphs of a newspaper story. TV and radio news stories use either a "hard" or a "soft" lead. A hard lead contains the most important information, the basic facts of the story. For example, "The city council has rejected a plan to build the Fifth Street overpass." A soft lead is used to get the viewers' attention; it may not convey much information. For example, "That proposed Fifth Street overpass is in the news again." The lead is then supported by the body of the story, which introduces new information and amplifies what was mentioned in the lead. The summation, the final few sentences in the report, can be used to personalize the main point ("This means that the price you pay for gasoline is likely to go up"), introduce another fact, or discuss future developments.

Of course, the writing style of broadcast news is completely different. The writing is more informal, conversational, and simple. In addition, it's designed to complement sound bites (the sound of the newsmaker) or videotape segments.

Soft News

Soft, or **feature, news** covers a wide territory. Features may not be very timely or have much importance to the lives of the audience. The one thing that all soft news has in common is that it interests the audience. Features typically rely on human interest for their news value. They appeal to people's curiosity, sympathy, skepticism, or amazement. They can be about places, people, animals, topics, events, or products. Some stories that would be classified as soft or feature news might include the birth of a kangaroo at the local zoo, a personality sketch of a local resident who has a small part in an upcoming movie, a cook who moonlights as a stand-up comedian, a teenager who mistakenly gets a tax refund check for $400,000 instead of $40, and so forth.

Features are entertaining and the audience likes them. Indeed, one of the trends of the mid-1980s was the growing popularity of television and print vehicles based primarily on soft content, for example, "Entertainment Tonight," "USA Today: The TV Show," "Showbiz Tonight," *People,* "Life Styles of the Rich and Famous," *Us* magazine, the *Life* section of *USA Today.* Even the prime-time news magazines "60 Minutes" and "20/20" have substantial amounts of soft news. Likewise, the fiercely competitive early morning network TV shows are turning more to soft news.

The techniques for reporting features are as varied as the features themselves. In the print media, features seldom follow the inverted pyramid pattern. The main point of the feature is often withheld to the end, much like the punch line to a joke.

Other features might be written in chronological order; others might start with a shocking statement such as ''Your secrets just might kill you'' and then go on with an explanation, ''If you have a medical problem, you should wear a Medic-Alert bracelet.'' Still other features can be structured in the question-and-answer format. In short, reporters are free to adopt whatever structure they think is suitable.

TV features are more common than radio features. In some large TV markets, one or more reporters may be assigned to cover nothing but features. Almost all stations have a feature file where story ideas are catalogued. If a local station does not have the resources to produce local features, there are syndication companies that will provide general-interest features for a fee. Broadcast features also use a variety of formats. Humorous leads and delaying the main point until the end sometimes work well, a technique often used by Andy Rooney in his features for ''60 Minutes.'' Other times a simple narrative structure, used in everyday storytelling, will be quite effective, as evidenced by the award winning ''On the Road with Charles Kuralt.'' The interview format is also popular, particularly when the feature is about a well-known personality.

Investigative Reports

As the name implies, **investigative reports** are those that unearth significant information about matters of public importance through the use of nonroutine information-gathering methods. Most day-to-day reporting involves investigation, but the true investigative piece requires an extraordinary expenditure of time and energy. Since the Watergate affair was uncovered by a pair of Washington newspaper reporters, investigative reporting has also been looked upon as primarily concerned with exposing corruption in high places. This connotation is somewhat unfortunate for at least two reasons. In the first place, it encouraged a few short-sighted reporters to look upon themselves as self-appointed guardians of the public good and to indiscriminately pursue all public officials, sometimes using questionable techniques in the hope of uncovering some indiscretion. Much of this investigative journalism turned out to be insignificant. In the second place, this emphasis on exposing political corruption distracted attention from the fact that investigative reporting can concentrate on other topics and perform a valuable public service.

Investigative reports require a good deal of time and money. Because of this heavy investment, they are generally longer than the typical print or broadcast news item. Broadcast investigative reports are usually packaged in thirty- or sixty-minute documentaries, in a series of short reports spread through the week on the nightly newscast (called ''minidocs''), or in a ten- to fifteen-minute segment of a news magazine program (such as ''60 Minutes'' or ''20/20''). Print investigative pieces are usually run as a series of articles. Sometimes newspapers will print a special section devoted to a single report, as did the *Philadelphia Inquirer* in 1983 when it published a sixty-eight–page analysis on the questionable conduct of the Pennsylvania Supreme Court.

Interestingly, the mechanics of investigative reporting are similar in the print and broadcasting media. First, a reporter gets a tip or a lead on a story from one of his or her sources. The next phase consists of fact gathering and cultivating news sources. Eventually, a thick file of information on the topic is developed. These facts are then organized into a coherent piece that is easily digestible by the audience. Here the differences between print and broadcast reporting techniques become apparent. The print journalist can spend a good deal of time providing background and relating past events to the topic. Additionally, the print investigative reporter can draw heavily upon published documents and public records. (The Pentagon Papers story, for example, depended primarily on official government documents.) In television and radio, the investigative report usually has less time to explore background issues. Documents and records are hard to portray on TV, and less emphasis is placed on them. In their place, the TV reporter must come up with interviews and other visual aspects that will illustrate the story. Moreover, the format of the TV report will sometimes dictate its form. As noted above, one of the most popular formats on TV is the minidoc. Minidocs run for a brief period each day for several days. At the beginning of each, the story has to be summarized or updated. Toward the end of the week, the summary might take up the first half of the report.

Some noteworthy examples of recent investigative efforts include these from 1987–1988: WMAQ-TV in Chicago ran a story on lead contamination in the city's parks. Six months later, the station examined the problem again and found that little had been done to correct it. The reports eventually prompted the city to form a task force to address the situation. KYTV-TV in Springfield, Missouri, spent several months investigating drug trafficking in the nearby Ozark Mountains. The station ran the story as a series of minidocs and followed up with a half-hour documentary. The *Charlotte Observer* won a Pulitzer Prize for its coverage of the scandal-ridden PTL club. The *Chicago Tribune* published a lengthy exposé of conflicts of interest among Chicago's city council members, and the *Atlanta Journal and Constitution* printed a multipart series on how area banks were discriminating against black homebuyers who were seeking mortgage loans.

THE NEWS FLOW

As mentioned in Chapter 1, one of the characteristics of mass communication is the presence of a large number of gatekeepers. This fact is easily seen in the gathering and reporting of news. Reporting is a team effort, and quite a few members of the team serve as gatekeepers.

Print Media

Figure 14.1 illustrates the typical organization in a newspaper newsroom. Looking first at the newspaper, there are two main sources of news: staff reports and the wire

FIGURE 14.1 *Organization of a newspaper newsroom.*

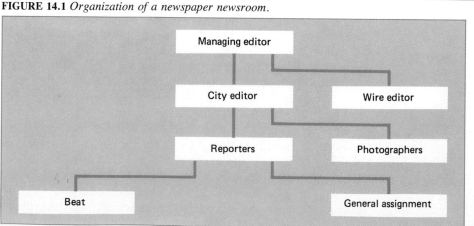

services. Other, less important sources include feature syndicates and handouts and releases from various sources. Let's first examine how news is gathered by newspaper personnel. The city editor is the captain of the news-reporting team. He or she assigns stories to reporters and supervises their work. There are two types of reporters: general assignment and beat. A beat reporter covers some topics on a regular basis such as the police beat or the city hall beat. A general-assignment reporter covers whatever assignments come up. A typical day for the general-assignment reporter might consist of covering an auto accident, a speech by a visiting politician, and a rock concert. Stories from the reporters are passed along to the city editor, where they are okayed and sent to the copy desk for further editing. The managing editor and assistant managing editor are also part of the news team. They are responsible for the overall daily preparation of the paper. Let's review the news flow and the various gatekeepers in the process. The city editor can decide not to cover a story in the first place or not to run a story if the event is covered. The reporter has a wide latitude of judgment over what he or she chooses to include in the story. The copy editor can change the story as needed, and the managing editor has the power to emphasize or deemphasize the story to fit the day's needs.

Broadcast Media

The sources of news for the broadcast media are similar to those for the newspaper. Special wire services cater to television and radio stations, and local reporters are assigned to cover nearby events. In addition, many broadcast newsrooms subscribe to syndicated news services or, if affiliated with a network, have access to the net's news feeds.

The broadcast newsroom, as seen in Fig. 14.2, is organized along different lines from its print counterpart. At the local station, the news director is in charge of the overall news operation. In large stations, most news directors spend their time on administrative work—personnel, budgets, equipment, and so on. In smaller stations, most news directors might perform other functions (such as being the anchorperson) as well. Next in command is the executive producer. This person supervises the work of all the producers in the newsroom. Typically, there are producers assigned to the early morning, noon, evening, and late night newscasts. In addition to looking after the other producers, the executive producer might also produce the evening news, typically the station's most important. As is probably

FIGURE 14.2 *Organization of a TV newsroom.*

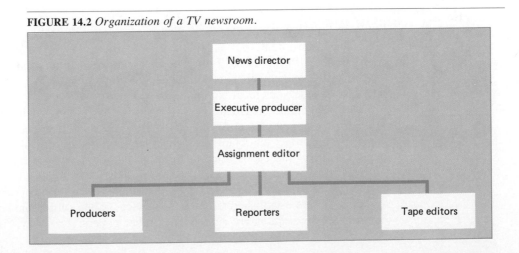

clear by now, producers are important people in TV news. Their actual duties, however, are not well known. In capsule form, here are some of the things that a news producer does:

1. decides what stories are covered, who covers them, and how they are covered

2. decides the order in which stories appear in the newscast

3. determines the amount of time each story is given

4. writes copy for some stories

5. integrates live reports into the newscasts

The assignment editor works closely with the news producer. The assignment editor is in charge of coverage planning and execution. He or she assigns and monitors the activities of reporters, camera crews, and other people in the field. Since speed is important in most broadcast news operations, there is great pressure on the assignment editor to get the crews to the story in the shortest amount of time.

Then, of course, there are the ''glamour'' jobs—on-air reporters and anchors. Most reporters in broadcast news function as general-assignment reporters, although the large-market stations might have one or two regularly assigned to a beat, such as the entertainment scene. In many stations, anchors will occasionally do field reports, but most of the time they perform their work in the studio, preparing for the upcoming newscast. In addition to the people seen on camera, there are quite a few workers that no one ever sees or hears. Photographers usually accompany reporters to shoot the video. Tape editors trim the footage into segments that fit with the time alloted to the story. Big stations also have news writers and production assistants who pull slides and arrange other visuals needed during the newscast.

Obviously, the chain of gatekeepers in broadcast news is a long and complicated one. Starting with the assignment editor and ending with the anchor, usually more than a half-dozen people have some say-so over the final shape of the newscast. Sometimes, the way a story ends up might be drastically different from the way it started at the beginning of the gatekeeper chain. It is not unusual for a reporter to work all day on a story and then be told by a producer that the story will get only forty seconds of air time.

THE WIRE SERVICES

The next time you read your local newspaper, you will probably notice that many stories have the initials AP or UPI in the datelines. The AP stands for Associated Press and the UPI for United Press International. These two organizations are called wire services, and together they provide you with most of the news about what's going on outside your local community.

The Associated Press can trace its roots back to 1848 when several New York newspapers chipped in to cover the cost of sending small boats out to meet incoming ships from Europe to obtain the latest news. This news-gathering service was expanded during the 1850s when it started providing news to member papers via the telegraph (hence the name ''wire'' service). This new organization was called the New York Associated Press. In 1892, a regional press service called the Western Associated Press established a rival wire service, called simply the Associated Press, and began to provide news service to member papers. The New York organization

Local papers and broadcast stations rely on the wire services for national and international stories to which they would not otherwise have access. Here, editors at a worldwide news agency, Agence France Presse, read news tapes arriving on telex transcriptors. (Guy Le Querrec/Magnum)

folded soon after the debut of this new service. Eventually, the Associated Press moved its headquarters to New York, where it is currently located.

United Press was formed in 1907 by newspaper-chain owner E. W. Scripps. Scripps was dissatisfied with the service his papers had been receiving from the AP and started his own news-gathering organization. In 1958, the United Press absorbed the International News Service, a competitor that was founded in 1909 by William Randolph Hearst, and changed its name to United Press International.

In simplified form, here's how the wire services work. A correspondent covers a local news event; for the sake of illustration, let's say it's a fire. He or she reports the event to the bureau chief of the local wire service. If the bureau chief thinks the story is newsworthy enough, the chief will send it on to the state bureau to go out on the state or regional wire. The state bureau chief then decides whether to send it on for inclusion on the national wire. All in all, the wire services are the eyes and ears for local papers and broadcasting stations that can't afford to have people stationed all over the country.

The AP has about a hundred regional bureaus in the United States and about sixty foreign bureaus. Members of the association pay for this service according to their size and circulation. A large paper, such as the *New York Times*, will pay more than a small-town paper. Approximately 1200 papers use AP's service. United Press International also has about a hundred domestic bureaus and a large number of foreign offices. As with the AP, member payment is based on the subscriber's size and audience.

Wire services have facilities to transmit news photos electronically. (Tom Kelly)

Together, the two wire services churn out about 8 million words every day. The news is transmitted in about a dozen different languages. AP and UPI also have facilities to transmit news photos electronically. In addition, both agencies offer a wide range of services to their clients. AP, for example, has a weather wire, a sports wire, and a financial wire. Both agencies also provide a broadcast wire that is used by radio and TV stations in preparing their newscasts. An audio service is also available to radio stations as well as a video service that displays written news summaries electronically on the TV screen and is used by cable TV systems. In the late 1980s, AP had 10,000 customers worldwide, including about 1,300 daily papers. It also served about 4000 domestic radio and TV stations plus another 400 or so cable systems. UPI had about 7000 customers, including approximately 900 newspapers and 3500 radio and TV stations and 500 cable systems. As of this writing, however, UPI had been in financial trouble for several years and had gone through several ownership changes. Its long-term future is uncertain.

AP and UPI are not without competition. The New York Times News Service and the Los Angeles Times–Washington Post News Service are rivals that also offer supplemental news stories, not generally covered by the major wire services, to their subscribers. Some newspaper groups also have their own special news services. For example, the Gannett News Service sends material to all the Gannett-owned local papers and to *USA Today*. There's competition overseas as well. The British-based Reuters agency now has about half a dozen bureaus in the United States. Agence France-Presse is also a formidable worldwide competitor.

The wire services are putting new technology to work. Virtually all of their material is now delivered by satellite. Noisy typewriters and clattering teletypes have been replaced by computer-based equipment. AP is also supplying information for home computer data bases and is linked to several systems that provide teletext services.

MEDIA DIFFERENCES IN NEWS COVERAGE

It doesn't take a genius to see that broadcast journalism is different from print journalism. Over the years these differences have led many to argue which is "better": print or broadcast journalism. Proponents of print journalism correctly point out that the script of a typical network evening newscast would fill up less than one page of a typical newspaper. They argue that the print media have the potential for depth reporting and lengthy analysis, elements that are usually missing from broadcast news because of time pressure. Moreover, some critics have taken to looking down on broadcast journalism, labeling it "show biz" and commenting on its shallowness. The supporters of broadcast news answer that measuring a network newscast by comparing its word count to that of a newspaper is using the wrong yardstick. They suggest it is more appropriate to ask how many pages of a newspaper it would take to print the thousands of different visuals that regularly accompany a TV newscast. The emergence of twenty-four–hour news channels and late night newscasts, say these proponents, now make it possible to cover news in depth. Print journalism is critized for being slow, old fashioned, and dull.

And so the debate goes. Unfortunately, the argument covers up the essential fact: Both print and broadcast news have their own unique strengths and weaknesses. One should not be considered better than the other. Both play important roles in informing the public.

Words and Pictures

Having said that, however, it is also important to add that the inherent characteristics of both media have an impact on what news gets covered and how it gets covered. In the first place, the physical structure of each medium means that there will be some obvious differences. Print journalism is organized in space; TV journalism in time. Hence, the newspaper can contain far more stories than the typical TV newscast. Moreover, there can be more details provided about any one story. Within the limited time constraints of broadcasting (even including the all-news stations), it is hard for radio and television to provide much more than a headline service and in-brief look at a few stories. If a topic is treated in depth, the amount of information and detail included is typically far less than what is contained in its newspaper counterpart. Some observers have said that TV is better at transmitting experience or impressions, while the newspaper is better at facts and information. In any case, stories dealing with lengthy analysis and complicated interpretation tend to be better suited to the print medium.

Second, print news has permanence. A reader can go back and reread difficult and complicated parts as many times as necessary for understanding. An idea missed the first time can be reexamined. Broadcast news does not have this luxury. Radio and TV newscasts are written for a single exposure. This means that complicated and complex stories are sometimes difficult to cover in the electronic media. Newspapers and magazines have a built-in advantage when it comes to reporting these

TV News Coverage of Famine: Brazil and Ethiopia

In 1984, British charitable organizations were trying to publicize the story of famine in two drought-plagued countries—Ethiopia and Brazil. In Brazil, it was estimated that about 20 million people were suffering from the worst drought in modern memory. About 6 million people in Ethiopia faced imminent starvation. Admittedly, it's hard to measure human suffering, but many experts saw the Ethiopian and the Brazilian famines as roughly equal in their seriousness. Nonetheless, the Ethiopian famine became one of the big news stories of 1985 while Brazil's problems went largely unreported. Why? Part of the answer is the visual nature of TV news.

In short, Ethiopia had good pictures, Brazil didn't. The Ethiopian government instituted feeding centers that immediately attracted thousands of starving people. The scenes at these stations furnished the agonizing and haunting TV pictures that were carried on the network news. The impact of seeing thousands of emaciated children and adults all congregated in one place was instrumental in prompting the massive charity drives that were aimed at feeding Ethiopia's hungry. In Brazil, the government also sent aid to the hungry, but there were no large-scale feeding centers to attract crowds. As a result, the famine victims were spread out over 1.4 million square kilometers, and their suffering was much harder to film. There were no dramatic shots of huge crowds of starving people. Second, it rained in Brazil. The rain had no immediate impact on the drought and related famine, but it did turn the earth green—and green was not the best color to dramatize a drought. In Ethiopia, the ground remained parched and brown, providing more striking pictures. These two factors helped get Ethiopia wide TV coverage.

The drought and related famine returned to Ethiopia and neighboring Sudan all through 1987 and 1988. In fact, the more recent famine was much more severe than the one in 1984–1985. Coverage of this new development, however, was not extensive. Finally, the news media broke the story that the Ethiopian government was using the famine to starve out antigovernment rebels living in the drought areas. The government apparently halted food shipments going to the famine areas on more than one occasion. The print media covered this aspect of the story more extensively than did TV. Part of TV's problem was the difficulty in getting pictures from the area primarily because the Ethiopian government was less than cooperative.

The visual dimension of a news story is an important ingredient that often determines the impact the story will have. Pictures of the starving children in Ethiopia, carried in the print media and on television, are ingrained in the national memory. (Sarah Putnam/The Picture Cube)

types of stories. Of course, television news has the advantage of the visual dimension. TV news directors ask if a story has action, visual appeal, something that can be seen. Faced with a choice between two events that are of equal importance, the television news organization will most likely choose the one that has better pictures

Technojournalism

The TV reporter of the future may be a blend of a producer, camera operator, lighting technician, audio expert, and satellite communication engineer. Within the next few years, TV news-gathering operations will switch to lightweight automatic cameras about the same size as and as easy to use as current still cameras. Compact and easy-to-operate editing equipment will let reporters screen material anywhere, even while riding on an airplane. Flyaway uplinks—portable satellite transmitters with a foldable dish that can fit into an oversized suitcase—will enable reporters to file stories from wherever they are standing. Instead of sending a correspondent, producer, camera operator, and audio engineer into the field to tape a report, TV journalism of tomorrow may be a one-person show. It's clear that aspiring TV reporters will need to be a lot more versatile than today's variety.

available. Sometimes the visual dimension of a story may be further enhanced by studio graphics, as happens when a smoking gun or the word "murder" is inserted over the anchorperson's shoulder. Obviously, the visual dimension is important and represents a powerful weapon in the arsenal of TV reporting. Some of the visuals carried by TV news are deeply ingrained in the national memory: the attempted assassination of Ronald Reagan, the starving children in Ethiopia, the hostages in the Middle East, the Chinese students in Beijing. Nonetheless, it is easy for television news to needlessly cater to the visual and run items that have little news value other than their potential for dramatic pictures. There have been many instances of a small, relatively insignificant fire leading a local newscast simply because good pictures were available. Murders and violent events that have occurred half a world away show up on American TV not because of their intrinsic news value but because the pictures were dramatic.

This is not to say that print reporters don't like a visual story. Quite the opposite. The advent of good color reproduction in newspapers and magazines means that a good photo to accompany a story is a real plus. Recall that *Life* magazine brought the news in pictures to eager readers for decades. It is fair to say, however, that the print media are less likely to be influenced by only the visual impact of a story.

Print and Broadcast Journalists

A second key difference has to do with the fact that in TV news, the reporter is an important part of the process. This situation is in direct contrast with print journalism, where the reporter stays relatively anonymous with perhaps only a byline for identification. Very few newspaper reporters become nationally known figures (Bob Woodward and Carl Bernstein, the Watergate reporters, are an obvious exception). In TV, the person reading or reporting the news is part of the story. TV news is not anonymous; each story has a face to go with it. Repeated exposure of newscasters on the local and the network level has turned many of them into celebrities or "stars" in their own right. One of the explanations for this is that some viewers evidently develop what amounts to a personal relationship or a sense of empathy with reporters and anchors. There are many stories that illustrate this peculiar audience–reporter relationship. When Dan Rather replaced Walter Cronkite at CBS, news executives tried all sorts of things to make him look appealing to the audience.

Finally, one winter night in 1982, Rather wore a sweater under his jacket. Few people remember anything about what stories Rather reported that night, but almost everyone remembered his sweater. During her first years on the "Today" show, correspondent Jane Pauley received more comments about the way she wore her hair than about any of the stories she covered. Examples abound at the local level as well. The late Fahey Flynn, longtime anchor at WLS-TV in Chicago, wore a bow tie as his trademark. One year a new management team came to the station and in an attempt to make him look younger replaced his bow tie with the traditional long necktie. The extremely negative response of the audience caught the station's management by surprise, and Flynn quickly reverted to his familiar bow tie. Apparently, audience involvement with reporters is much more prevalent in TV than in print.

As personalities in TV news became more popular with the audience, they were able to command higher salaries. Annual salaries for the three network anchors range from about $1.8 million (Peter Jennings) to $2.5 million (Dan Rather). Even at the local level, salaries between $250,000 and $750,000 are common in large markets. Not surprisingly, with all this money at stake, many well-known broadcast journalists are being represented by agents. The entrance of the agent into the news arena has given TV journalism some problems all its own. Some journalists have negotiated contracts that safeguard them from general-assignment reporting and other less glamorous tasks; others have a contractual clause that guarantees them so much air time per week; still others have been granted total editorial control over their reports. The situation has become so widespread that a session at a recent convention of radio–TV news directors was entitled "The Most Important People in TV News Are Not in TV and Not in News." The session had to do with how to deal with agents representing TV newscasters.

News Consultants

Yet another difference between print and broadcast journalists is the amount of control that outside news consultants have on the news itself. Market research consultants are employed by both newspaper and broadcasting organizations, but their activities are most noticeable at local TV stations. Consultants introduced the audience survey to local stations; they made recommendations to management based on what the public said they wanted to see in local news, not on what journalists thought should be in the newscast—a fundamental shift in the traditional definition of news. The heyday for the consultants was the 1970s, exactly the same time that local TV newscasts were becoming extremely profitable. Station management soon realized that increased news ratings meant increased revenues, and increased ratings were what the consultants promised to deliver. Some of the things the consultants introduced to local TV news made some journalists concerned. "Happy Talk" news, where the anchors bantered back and forth during the newscast, was encouraged. "Top-40" news, where the station tried to cram as many short items as possible into a newscast that moved along at breakneck speed, was another popular recommendation. "Tabloid News," a format stressing crimes, sex, accidents, and other action-filled stories, spread to many stations. ("If it bleeds, it leads," was the motto in these newsrooms.) And, more recently, "Life-style News," a format that emphasizes soft news, has been springing up at local stations. This approach stresses health items, consumer topics, entertainment, food, and careers. The traditional hard news from city hall and the state capital now had more competition from sources that weren't usually defined as news. This phenomenon has not spread to the network evening newscasts, where the influence of consultants has been much less pronounced.

Recently, local TV newscasts have returned to a more traditional approach to covering the news. Of course, there are still many stations that pander to audiences by overdoing crime or entertainment stories, but quite a few others have moved away from the excesses of the past. This doesn't mean that consultants have disappeared; they are still a strong force in local TV news. (It's easy to see their influence, particularly if you travel across the country. The local TV news in Anchorage looks very much like the local TV news in Atlanta. Newscast formats, styles, and even the anchorpeople all seem quite familiar—a direct result of stations all over the country using the same consultants.)

Technology and TV News

The last difference we shall discuss concerns two sets of initials that have had tremendous impact on TV news—**electronic news gathering (ENG)** and **satellite news gathering (SNG)**. We'll look at ENG first.

Back in the 1950s and 1960s, television cameras were clumsy, heavy, and needed a lot of light. Consequently, they were studio-bound equipment. If news was to be covered in the field, it had to be done on film. Film cameras were portable but had one major disadvantage: The film had to be developed before it could be shown on the news. Getting pictures of an event that happened thousands of miles away might take hours since the film had to be shot, sent back by airplane, developed, edited, and broadcast. The ENG revolution in the mid-1970s changed all of that. At the heart of the revolution was technology. Small, lightweight cameras and videotape recorders meant that pictures of news events could get on the air much quicker. Videotape is ready to edit immediately after it is shot. Second, with advances in helicopter, microwave, and satellite technology, ENG made it possible to broadcast live from the scenes of major stories. News could be shown as it was happening. With ENG, TV can cover a war, an attempted assassination, or a disaster in real time, or very close to it. The story may not be as complete as it might be in the next issue of *Time* or *Newsweek,* but it is much more immediate.

This benefit, however, was not without its risks. When ENG first came on the scene, there was a tendency for news directors to use it simply because it was there, without regard for the newsworthiness of the event itself. There were times when reporters did live reports from places where news had happened hours earlier or was about to happen or did live interviews with people where a taped interview might have sufficed. Things that could be covered live suddenly possessed elevated news value. It took a while to learn that immediacy was not an automatic virtue in news reporting.

By the same token, a live interview is an unedited interview. Vulgarity, obscenity, and demagoguery have all been included in many live ENG interviews. The reporter in the live situation has special responsibilities and problems to face (see boxed material). A live broadcast attracts a crowd. Sometimes the crowd is friendly; other times it is nasty or tries to make the reporter's life miserable. More than a few correspondents have been showered with water, beer, or worse while doing a live report.

Live reports also run the additional risk of violating standards of good taste or ethics. There is no eraser in live TV news; the reporter can't go back and do it over. Going live to the scene of an accident carries with it the chance of televising scenes

The Dangers of Live ENG

News reporters are well aware of the many things that can go wrong during a live report from the field. It takes an agile mind to cope with all the complications. For example, a reporter in a northeastern city was assigned to do a story on an increase in bus fares. A perfect spot, thought her news director, for a live interview with some disgruntled bus riders.

The reporter was sent to a metropolitan bus stop where she found three typical bus riders waiting for the 6:10 bus that would take them to their homes far away in the suburbs. This seemed to work out fine because the reporter was scheduled to go on the air live at 6:02 and do a three-minute interview segment. She lined up her three interviewees and waited for her cue. By this time, she only had about five minutes to wait before the news show went on the air.

Then things started to go wrong. A gang of teens rode by on their bicycles and started shouting obscenities at the reporter. Luckily, she and her camera operator managed to chase them away before six o'clock. At one minute after six, the reporter heard through her earpiece that her report was going to be delayed a bit. She and her three bus-riding interviewees waited patiently. At exactly ten minutes after six, the reporter heard the director say that they would be coming to her for her three-minute report in a matter of seconds. She breathed a sigh of relief. Suddenly, the 6:10 bus pulled up and the three riders, not willing to wait another hour for the next bus, got on. The bus doors closed and the bus drove off, leaving the reporter completely alone with not another person in sight. At that very moment, the ENG camera went live and the reporter faced the longest three minutes of her career.

of extreme gore or gruesomeness. ENG offers new opportunities for a reporter to invade someone's privacy. A hostage or terrorist situation presents special problems. In these instances the news value of a live report must be closely examined.

SNG is a relatively recent trend but its effects on the traditional affiliate–network news relationship could be far-reaching. About 150 to 175 TV stations, most of them in the large markets, have specially equipped vans or trucks that enable them to cover and transmit live stories from any location. The SNG vehicle uplinks the story to a communication satellite, which in turn sends it to the local station. SNG allows local stations to be on the scene of national and international news stories, a service that only the networks previously provided. For example, the local station's anchors could travel to Atlanta in 1988 and report live on the impact that the Democratic National Convention has on Portland, Austin, Jacksonville, or wherever they came from. Most local station news directors prefer their correspondents over network reporters when it comes to covering some big stories. The directors like the local angle and the additional prestige that go along with the coverage.

Moreover, the networks and independent companies, such as Conus Communications, provide satellite feeds (pictures and words) of breaking spot news. CBS News, for example, sends out about 150 stories every weekday to its stations. Affiliates put their own local audio over the pictures and use them in their newscasts. Viewers are increasingly seeing the same video coverage on their local and network newscasts. Further, both independent and affiliate stations belong to regional and national satellite services. At Conus, for example, if there's a plane crash in Milwaukee or an earthquake in Palo Alto, a local Conus member covers it and sends

More Dangers of ENG

ENG photographers are typically called on to cover drug busts, hostage takings, barricaded snipers, terrorists, and other dangerous situations and people. Ironically, TV stations spend a lot of money to protect their ENG gear but few have paid attention to protecting the camera operator. Now, thanks to the Video Protection Company, ENG operators can order a specially made lightweight piece of body armor called the Media Tactical Jacket, the same kind of bulletproof vest that law enforcement officers have been wearing for years. The company's motto: ''InVEST in safety.''

the report to Conus, which, in turn, puts it on the satellite for all of its other member stations to use. CNN has a similar service called Newsource, which has seven scheduled feeds a day.

Given these advances, local stations are asking if they still need the network newscast. Many local stations think they can do the job of covering local and

The media cover a Democratic presidential debate in Des Moines, Iowa. (Jim Heemstra/Picture Group)

international news for their market better than the nets. Even the networks themselves are seriously examining the future of their newscasts. As mentioned earlier, the net newscast is expensive and networks are looking for ways to cut back. Network news ratings are down about 15–20 percent from 1981. Most large market stations now run sixty or ninety minutes (or more) of local news before going to the network and many people are ''newsed out'' by then. The nets have already cut back on coverage of live events. Only CNN was on the air when the space shuttle exploded, and CNN provided the only extended live coverage of the confirmation hearings of Supreme Court nominee Robert Bork. Some network executives envision the day when the networks provide merely a video feed and a ''correspondents service'' for their stations. In any case, the shape of network news may have already been changed unalterably by the new technologies.

Similarities in the News Media

Before closing, it should be mentioned that although there are significant differences between print and electronic journalism, there are actually many similarities as well. To keep the topic in perspective, these should also be mentioned. To begin, both print and electronic journalists share the same basic values and journalistic principles. Honesty in news reporting is crucial for both television and newspaper reporters. Stories must be as truthful as humanly possible. The print journalist should not invent fictional characters or make up quotations and attribute them to newsmakers. Electronic journalists should not stage news events or rearrange the questions and answers in a taped interview. High standards of honesty are important no matter what the medium. Another shared value is accuracy. Checking facts takes time, but it's something that a professional reporter must do with every story. Misspelling a name in a newspaper is analogous to mispronouncing it during a news broadcast. Details, big and small, should be checked. A third common value is balance. Every story has two or more sides. The print or broadcast journalist must make sure that he or she does not publicize or promote just one of them. Information should be offered on all sides of a story. Finally, both print and broadcast reporters share the value of objectivity. Objectivity is a difficult concept to define; in fact, the concept includes many of the shared values that we have already discussed. Briefly summarized, objectivity means that the reporter tries to transmit the news untainted by conscious bias and without personal comment or coloration. Of course, complete and total objectivity is not possible because the process of reporting itself requires countless judgments, each influenced in some way by the reporter's value system. Nonetheless, journalists have traditionally respected the truth, refused to distort facts deliberately, and consciously detached themselves as much as possible from what they were reporting.

Second, both print and broadcast reporters must maintain credibility with their audiences. The news media periodically undergo crises of confidence when many people begin to doubt that their newspapers and broadcast stations are telling them the complete and honest truth. Sometimes these crises appear when some journalistically unacceptable reporting is disclosed, as in the 1980s when the *Washington Post* had to give back a Pulitzer Prize because one of its reporters had fictionalized a story and passed it off as fact. Sometimes they occur when the news media seem to be exploited by some self-serving group, as occurred in 1985 during the coverage of an airplane hijacking and subsequent hostage taking by Middle Eastern terrorists. Other times credibility is called into question by legal events, such as libel suits brought by Ariel Sharon and William Westmoreland in the mid-1980s that revealed some questionable reporting practices. Whenever public opinion polls reveal that the news media have slipped another notch or two in credibility, both print and electronic journalists try to regain the lost confidence. After much soul searching, the crisis usually passes. Credibility, however, is not something that should be examined only during journalistic crises. It is important no matter what the medium. If a reader or a viewer loses trust or stops believing what is being reported, the fundamental contract between audience and reporter is undermined and the news organization cannot survive. It matters little if the news organization is a newspaper, magazine, radio, or TV station; credibility is paramount.

CAREERS IN NEWS GATHERING AND REPORTING

The career prospects for a young person interested in the news profession vary with the type of job desired. The job market for newspaper reporters and editors in the late 1980s was quite good. In some parts of the country, there were more jobs at newspapers, particularly weeklies, than there were people to fill them. Copy editors were in more demand than general-assignment reporters, and persons skilled in specialized reporting areas, such as business and financial news, were also in demand. On the other hand, jobs for sports writers were scarce. As a general rule, a person with good writing and reporting skills will have a good chance at landing an entry-level job at a newspaper. In fact, some better journalism students are hired right off the campus by big-city newspapers.

Jobs in magazine journalism are harder to come by, primarily because there are so few of them. Most news magazines look for experienced people. Some even recommend that a prospective employee have a specialty in some area, such as law, finance, or science, along with journalism training. The videotex-teletext area is not a major source of employment for young journalists. As of this writing, there were only about 300 newswriting-reporting jobs across the country in this area.

Things are a bit tighter in broadcast journalism. Deregulation has meant that many radio stations have decided not to increase their news-reporting efforts. Consequently, the job market in radio journalism is sluggish. In television news, the glamour jobs of anchor and on-camera reporter continue to have far more applicants than there are available positions. There is some good news, however. The emergence of two-hour newscasts at large-market stations, the growth of the Cable News Network, and the increased prominence given to news at local stations has meant that there has been some expansion of the job market in news. Getting that first job, however, is still difficult and the market is highly competitive. Most newcomers are content to start in a small market and work their way up.

The outlook is a little brighter in the other positions. ENG camerapersons are in some demand as are tape editors. The news producer position is another one where prospects for employment are favorable. The Cable News Network offers entry-level positions called "video journalists" for people interested in the writing and producing end of TV news. Again, most experts in this area suggest that a newcomer start in smaller markets, gain valuable experience, and then progress to larger cities.

To give you some perspective on TV news salaries, in 1987–1988 the anchors of the local evening newscast in the Chicago market, the third largest in the United States, earned anywhere from $50,000 to $1.5 million a year. Anchors in Charlotte, North Carolina, the thirty-second largest market, had salaries that ranged from $50,000 to $100,000. In Tucson, Arizona, the eighty-first largest market, anchor salaries ranged from $53,000 to $78,000. A general-assignment reporter, who reports from the scene of a news event, averaged about $65,000 in Chicago, $35,000 in Charlotte, and $22,000 in Tucson. A news producer averaged about $100,000 in Chicago, $35,000 in Charlotte, and $23,000 in Tucson.

SUGGESTIONS FOR FURTHER READING

The following books contain more information about the concepts and topics discussed in this chapter.

BAGDIKIAN, BEN, *The Media Monopoly,* Boston: Beacon Press, 1983.

BLAIR, GWENDA, *Almost Golden,* New York: Simon & Schuster, 1988.

CHARNLEY, MITCHELL, *Reporting,* New York: Holt, Rinehart and Winston, 1975.

GOEDKOOP, RICHARD, *Inside Local Television News,* Salem, Wisc.: Sheffield Publishing, 1989.

LEWIS, CAROLYN, *Reporting for Television,* New York: Columbia University Press, 1984.

NEWSOM, DOUG, AND JAMES WOLLERT, *Media Writing: News for the Mass Media,* Belmont, Calif.: Wadsworth, 1985.

STOVALL, JAMES, *Writing for the Mass Media,* Englewood Cliffs, N.J.: Prentice-Hall, 1985.

TEAGUE, BOB, *Live and Off-Color: News Biz,* New York: A&W Publishers, 1982.

WESTIN, AV, *Newswatch,* New York: Simon & Schuster, 1982.

YOAKAM, RICHARD, AND CHARLES CREMER, *ENG: Television News and the New Technology,* New York, Random House, 1985.

Chapter 15

The Structure of the Public Relations Industry

Y ou get in the car, start the motor, put the car in gear, and then, without warning, the car surges forward on its own. Stepping on the brake pedal doesn't help; the car simply goes faster. Ultimately it hits something solid enough to stop it. . . . You've just experienced the sudden acceleration problem.

Quite a few cars, including Cadillac, Volvo, Toyota, and Mercedes-Benz, have had problems with sudden acceleration but none as serious as that of the Audi 5000. Audi's problems and how they responded to them are a classic example of bad public relations.

Problems of unintended acceleration with Audi were first noted in 1978. In 1982, Audi recalled its cars to correct a problem with the floormats—they had a tendency to get tangled up with the accelerator pedal. As problems continued, Audi maintained an official silence but recalled more cars in 1983 and raised the brake pedal a bit so that motorists wouldn't mistake it for the accelerator. Nonetheless, the incidents still occurred and Audi continued to take a no-comment stance. Then, in 1986, the *New York Times* ran an article on unintended acceleration that caught the eye of a Long Island woman who had experienced two sudden acceleration accidents with her Audi. She brought the problem to the attention of the Center for Auto Safety, which had been collecting complaints about the Audi. Eventually the attorney general of the State of New York called the car unsafe and demanded that it be recalled. Bad publicity was mounting. An Audi Victims Network with forty members was established. The company finally responded with another recall, this time to increase the distance between the brake and accelerator pedals. It was apparent that the company was treating this as an engineering rather than a public relations problem. Audi also previewed the crisis-management strategy that it would follow for about the next two years. The unintended acceleration was not the fault of the car. Instead, it was the drivers who caused the problem by mistaking the gas pedal for the brake pedal. In effect, Audi was blaming the victims, a bad public relations strategy that won it no friends.

Then the real firestorm broke. In November 1986, "60 Minutes" presented a devastating report on Audi's problems. Viewers saw smashed-up Audis resting against trees, buildings, and parked cars. One Audi wound up face-down in a swimming pool. In a tearful interview, a woman recounted how her son was killed when her Audi surged out of control. Another owner explained that when his Audi lurched forward he had applied the brakes so hard he developed shin splints, but the car still didn't stop. Audi did not know how to react to the piece. The company blamed ''60 Minutes'' for sensationalizing its report. Audi executives wrote to CBS about the program's inaccuracies. A videocassette was produced showing experts rebutting the ''60 Minutes'' charges. Throughout all of this, the company still maintained that the drivers were to blame for the sudden acceleration. Audi was convinced that there was no problem. The company didn't realize what every good PR practitioner recognized: If consumers perceived a problem, that problem was as real as any mechanical malfunction. Consequently, the company came across as cold and arrogant. Its official explanation said that the problem was caused by ''misapplication of the brake pedal due to a combination of factors that could include . . . driver distraction or driver unfamiliarity with the car.''

Audi sales figures showed how consumers reacted to the company's explanation. Showroom traffic dropped 58 percent. Sales dropped 60 percent. Parking garages banned Audi 5000's. Audis that were bought for $20,000 only a year earlier sold for $6,000.

The company's problem was made even worse because independent tests of the Audi could not locate a mechanical problem. For the executives at Audi, the most plausible explanation still seemed to be driver error. The tests showed that the brake and accelerator pedals in the car were located closer to the middle than in other cars. In a Buick, for example, the distance between right edge of the brake pedal and the center of the front seat was 6.2 inches; in the Audi 5000, it was 1.1 inches. Further, the distance between the pedals was 2.6 inches in a Buick, 2.4 inches in an Audi. Research also turned up the fact that most accidents occurred before the car had been driven 4000 miles, or before the driver had a lot of time to become familiar with the pedal arrangement. Finally, many Audis had a problem with high idle speed, particularly when the car was first started. Consequently, the most logical explanation was that some drivers started the car, shifted into gear, felt a slight but sudden movement caused by high idling, and stepped on what they thought was the brake to stop the car. Unfortunately, the placement of the pedals and the unfamiliarity with the car caused them to mistakenly press the accelerator pedal instead, sending the car careening forward or backward.

From a public relations standpoint, even though this account might be true, stressing it would not be the best tactic, since it tends to vilify the drivers. Audi was stuck with an explanation it couldn't really use. Desperate, the company offered $5000 rebates on a new, different model Audi. A $30 million ad campaign was launched to regain credibility for the company. The commercials showed famous people who drove Audis. The company still declined to mention the sudden acceleration problem in its ads. Sales jumped a little, but by March of 1987 they were still averaging more than 60 percent below normal.

Finally, the company admitted that its stonewall strategy was wrong. A recall was ordered to install a shift lock designed to prevent unwanted acceleration. Audi's publicity stopped emphasizing driver error and stressed the efforts of the company to solve the problem. The Audi 5000 model was phased out and replaced by a new design. Audi was starting to make a comeback, but everyone agreed the company still faced a monumental public relations problem and the process of regaining consumer confidence would be a long and painful one.

Audi's problems are not typical of those faced by PR agencies and corporate PR departments, but they do indicate the tremendous importance that favorable PR plays in the corporate and consumer setting. The rest of this chapter examines the role of public relations in contemporary society.

DEFINING PUBLIC RELATIONS

Before trying to explain what public relations is, it may first be helpful to differentiate it from other concepts. There are, for example, several similarities between advertising and public relations. Both are attempts at persuasion and both involve using the mass media. Public relations, however, is a management function; advertising is a marketing function. Second, advertising uses the mass media and machine-assisted communication settings; it does not involve interpersonal communications. PR utilizes all the various communication settings, including interpersonal communication. A third difference is seen in the fact that advertising is normally sponsored. Public relations messages appear as features, news stories, or editorials, and the space or time involved is not paid for. In many instances, advertising, particularly corporate advertising, is used to help further the public relations program.

Another concept that is sometimes confused with public relations is **publicity**, the placing of stories in the mass media. Publicity is a tool in the public relations process but it is not equivalent to PR. For example, it is perfectly possible for a firm to have extensive publicity and bad public relations. Further, publicity is primarily one-way communication; public relations is two way.

Having examined what public relations is not, we now turn to look at what it is. The term "public relations" has many interpretations and meanings. In fact most of the leading textbooks in the PR field typically lead off with a chapter that attempts to define exactly what public relations is or isn't. Rather than catalogue the many definitions that have been offered, it seems more useful to define PR by examining what PR people do.

First, almost everyone in the PR industry would agree that public relations involves working with public opinion. On the one hand, PR professionals attempt to influence public opinion in a way that is positive to the organization. For example, in the Audi episode, the company wanted to persuade consumers that it was doing everything it could to protect their safety. In short, the belated public relations effort was designed to maintain a favorable public opinion. On the other hand, it is also the function of the PR department to gather information from the public and interpret that information for top management as it relates to management decisions. Again, referring back to the Audi case, the company commissioned several surveys during the crisis to find out how the public viewed the auto in the wake of the problems. Strategic management decisions were made with the results of these surveys in mind.

Second, public relations is concerned with communication. Most people are interested in what an organization is doing to meet their concerns and interests. It is the function of the public relations professional to explain the organization's actions to various publics involved with the organization. Public relations communications is two-way communication. The PR professional also pays close attention to the thoughts and feelings of the organization's publics. Some experts refer to public relations as a two-way conduit between an organization and its publics.

Note that the word "publics" in the preceding section is plural. This is because the organization typically deals with many different publics in its day-to-day operations. Several PR scholars divide these groups into internal and external publics. Internal publics include employees, managers, labor unions, and stockholders. External publics consist of consumers, government, dealers, suppliers, members of the community, and the mass media. Public relations serves as the link for all these various publics.

The PR Campaign to Save Big Boy

Getting the public to notice the client's products is a big part of the job for many PR professionals. Take the case of Big Boy, the chubby, smiling, wavy-haired cherub in the checkered pants who for many years was the mascot of Big Boy Restaurants of America. The company, however, thought Big Boy was "outdated" and "silly." It wanted to send him into retirement. The PR firm representing the company saw it differently. This was a chance to get Big Boy back into the media spotlight. The PR firm started a TV campaign in which viewers were asked whether the company should keep the fifty-year-old mascot. Customers cast ballots at the 835 Big Boy restaurants. A rally was held at a local school and coverage was sent to 700 TV stations across the nation. The story of the campaign to save Big Boy made all the wire services; Johnny Carson mentioned it several times in his monologue.

Protests to keep Big Boy were held in front of several restaurants. Big Boy statues became collector's items. When it was all over, more than 4 million ballots were cast and 90 percent of them wanted to keep Big Boy. The company was pleasantly surprised by the success of the PR effort and hired the PR company on a continuing basis.

In 1988, Big Boy got a new owner, Elias Brothers, but the company agreed that the character was going to stay around for a while. In fact, plans were drawn to make him even more prominent. Regional franchisee names were dropped so that Bob's Big Boy and Abdow's Big Boy became simply Big Boy restaurants. Another $30 million or so was to be spent on an advertising campaign centered around the theme "America Loves Its Big Boy."

Third, public relations is a management function. It is designed to help a company set its goals and adapt to a changing environment. Public relations practitioners regularly counsel top management. Inherent in the specification of public relations is a planned activity. It is organized and directed toward specific goals and objectives.

Of course, public relations involves much more than just the three functions mentioned above. Perhaps it would be easier, for our purposes, to summarize them in the following working definition:

> Public relations is a management function that helps to define organizational objectives and facilitate organizational change. Public relations practitioners communicate with all relevant internal and external publics in the effort to create consistency between organizational goals and societal expectations. Public relations practitioners develop, execute and evaluate organizational programs that promote the exchange of influence and understanding among organizations' constituent parts and publics.*

The above definition may not be graceful, but it does highlight the varied nature of the field.

* Craig Aronoff and Otis Baskin, *Public Relations: The Profession and the Practice* (St. Paul, Minnesota: West Publishing, 1983), p.9.

SHORT HISTORY OF PUBLIC REALTIONS

If the term is interpreted broadly enough, the practice of public relations can be traced back to ancient times. The military reports and commentaries prepared by Julius Caesar can be viewed as triumph in personal and political public relations. During medieval times, both the Church and the guilds practiced rudimentary forms of public relations.

It was not until the American Revolution that more recognizable public relations activities became evident. The early patriots were aware that public opinion would play an important role in the war with England and planned their activities accordingly. For example, they staged events, such as the Boston Tea Party, to gain public attention. They also used symbols, such as the Liberty Tree and the Minute Men, that were easily recognized and helped portray their cause in a positive light. Skillful writers such as Samuel Adams, Thomas Paine, Abigail Adams, and Benjamin Franklin used political propaganda to swing public opinion to their side. As a case in point, note that the altercation between an angry mob and British soldiers became known as ''The Boston Massacre,'' an interpretation well suited to the rebel cause.

Later, the presidency of Andrew Jackson marked the beginning of political public relations. Jackson, born on the frontier, was not a skilled communicator and needed help to get his ideas across to the people. Jackson relied on Amos Kendall, a former newspaperman, to handle his public relations. Kendall wrote speeches, served as press secretary, and arranged public events to help Jackson's cause.

Public relations pioneer Ivy Lee. (The Bettmann Archive)

The Industrial Revolution and the resulting growth of mass production and mass consumption led to the growth of big business. Giant monopolies were formed in the railroad, steel, and oil businesses. Many big corporations tended to disregard the interests of the consumer in their quest for more profits. In fact, many executives felt that the less the public knew about their practices and operations, the better. Around the turn of the century, however, public hostility was aroused against unscrupulous business practices. Led by the muckrakers (see Chapter 4), exposés of industrial corruption and ruthless business tactics filled the nation's magazines. Faced with these attacks, many corporations hired communications experts, many of them former newspaper writers, to counteract the effect of these stories. These specialists tried to combat this negative publicity by making sure that the industry's side of the issue was also presented. These practitioners were the prototypes of what we might call press agents or publicists.

The debut of modern public relations techniques dates back to the first decade of the 1900s. Most historians agree that the first real public relations pioneer was a man named Ivy Lee. In 1903, Lee and George Parker opened a publicity office. A few years later, Lee became the press representative for the anthracite coal operators and the Pennsylvania Railroad. When confronted with a strike in the coal industry, Lee issued a "Declaration of Principles." This statement endorsed the concepts of openness and honesty in dealing with the public; it also marked the shift from nineteenth-century press agentry to twentieth-century public relations. Lee went on to have a successful career counseling people such as John D. Rockefeller, Jr. Among other achievements, Lee is credited with humanizing business and demonstrating that public relations is most effective when it affects employees, customers, and members of the community. Moreover, Lee would not carry out a public relations program unless it was endorsed and supported by top management.

Following World War I, two more public relations pioneers, Carl Byoir and Edward L. Bernays, appeared on the scene. Bernays is credited with writing the first book on public realtions, *Crystallizing Public Opinion*, published in 1923. In 1930, Byoir organized a public relations firm that is still one of the world's largest.

The Depression caused many Americans to look toward business with suspicion and distrust. In an attempt to regain public favor, many large corporations established their own public relations departments. The federal government, in its attempt to cope with the bad economic climate, also used good public relations practices to its advantage. Franklin Roosevelt introduced his New Deal reform program complete with promotional campaigns to win public acceptance. Roosevelt also recognized the tremendous potential of radio in shaping public opinion, and his fireside chats were memorable examples of personal public relations. The government intensified its public relations efforts during World War II with the creation of the Office of War Information.

Since the end of the war, changes in American society have created an atmosphere in which public relations has shown tremendous growth. What are some of the reasons behind the recent surge in this area?

1. Many corporations have recognized that they have a social responsibility to serve the public. Finding the means of fulfilling this responsibility is the task of the public relations department.

2. A growing tide of consumerism has caused many corporations and government agencies to be more responsive and communicative to their customers or clients, a function served by the public relations department.

This idyllic view of an Iowa family in 1942 is an example of the positive image of wartime America created by the Office of War Information. (Jack Delano-OWI/FSA/Library of Congress)

3. The growing complexity of modern corporations and government agencies has made it difficult for them to get their messages to the public without a department that is specifically assigned to that task.

4. Increasing population growth along with more specialization and job mobility have made it necessary for companies to have communication specialists whose task it is to interpret the needs of the audience for the organization.

All of the above have combined to make the last thirty years or so the "era of public relations." The profession has grown from about 19,000 members in 1950 to more than 170,000 people in 1988. More than 80 percent of the top 300 companies in the United States have some kind of public relations department. Along with this growth has come increased professionalization among public relations practitioners. A professional organization, the Public Relations Society of America, was founded in 1947 and adopted a code of standards in 1954. Public relations education has also made great strides. Recent estimates suggest that about 350 colleges across the country offer courses in public relations. In 1967, the Public Relations Student Society of America was founded. It now has 150 chapters and 5000 members.

The last few years have seen public relations assume even greater importance. Mergers, acquisitions, and a 1987 collapse of the stock market meant that corporations had additional responsibilities in communicating with their publics. Moreover, the increasing cost of advertising put more of an emphasis on promotions and other public relations campaigns as alternatives. It seems likely that public relations will remain a growth area for the foreseeable future.

ORGANIZATION OF THE PUBLIC RELATIONS INDUSTRY

Public relations activities are generally handled in two ways. Many organizations have their own public relations departments that work with the managers of all other departments. These departments are part of top management, and the PR director is responsible to the president of the company. For example, General Motors and AT & T both have about 200 people in their PR departments. Other organizations hire an external public relations counsel to give advice on press, government, and consumer relations. In business and industry, about one-third of the PR activity is handled by outside counseling firms. Many major corporations retain an outside agency in addition to their own internal public relations department.

Each of these arrangements has its particular advantages and disadvantages. An in-house department can be at work on short notice; an internal department has more in-depth knowledge about the company, and its operations tend to be less costly. On the other hand, it's hard for a corporate PR team to take an objective view of the company. Further, internal PR departments tend to ''go stale'' and have trouble coming up with fresh ideas unless new personnel are frequently added. An outside agency offers more services to its clients than does an internal department. Additionally, external counselors have the advantage of being objective observers, and many firms like the prestige associated with being a client of a respected PR firm. On the other side of the coin, outside agencies are expensive, and it takes time for them to learn the inner working of their clients' operations.

(Left) The oil spill from the Exxon Valdez *in Prince William Sound, Alaska, has been a public relations struggle for Exxon, as it attempts to explain not only the alleged drunken conduct of the* Valdez *captain but also the critical delays in launching clean-up efforts. At night, sea lions rest on a rock in the oily waters of the Sound. (Right) Exxon chairman L. G. Rawl testifies before the Senate Commerce Science and Transportation Committee. (left: Reuters/Bettmann Newsphotos; right: UPI/Bettmann Newsphotos)*

International Clients

Many PR firms handle international clients and must be familiar with business practices of varying cultures. PR professionals have to be aware of many differences. For example:

- In Bulgaria, shaking your head from side-to-side means "yes"; shaking it up-and-down means "no."

- Pointing at someone or beckoning someone with a finger in a Middle Eastern country is considered an insult, since that is the way dogs are summoned in these countries.

- In the People's Republic of China, never give a client a clock as a gift. Clocks are symbols of bad luck.

- In some Arab countries, it is an insult to bring food and drinks as gifts, since this implies the host cannot afford them.

- In Italy, if you don't use your hands a lot in a conversation, people will think you are bored.

- Many Latin Americans think it is impolite to give a negative answer to a business associate. Instead, they will agree and then explain later that they couldn't do something.

Internal or external, public relations professionals perform a wide range of services. These include counseling management, preparing annual reports, handling news releases and other forms of media coverage, supervising employee and other internal communications, managing promotions and special events, fund-raising, lobbying, community relations, and speech writing, to name just a few.

There have been two major trends in the ownership of PR agencies in the last five years. First, several of the top PR agencies have merged with large advertising agencies. To illustrate, of the top ten PR firms that have major operations in the United States, seven were affiliated with ad agencies. Second, there is now a decidedly British flavor to U.S. PR firms (as there is in advertising; see Chapter 16). Three of the top five firms are British-owned. Hill and Knowlton is part of the British-based WPP Group. Rowland Company Worldwide is part of the giant British ad agency Saatchi & Saatchi. Shandwick, a new arrival on the scene, is based in London.

Public relations is practiced in a variety of settings. Although the general principles are the same, the actual duties of the PR practitioner will vary according to the setting. Below is a brief description of the major areas where public relations is practiced.

1. Business. Public relations helps the marketing process by instilling in the consumer a positive attitude toward the company. Public relations also helps promote healthy employee management relations and serves as a major liaison between the firm and government regulators. Lastly, all businesses have to be located somewhere, and the PR department markets sure the company is a good citizen in its community.

2. Government and politics. Many government agencies hire public relations specialists to help them explain their activities to citizens and to assist the

news media in their coverage of the different agencies. These same specialists also communicate the opinions of the public back to the agency. Government PR is big business; its total expenditures on public information rivals the budgets of the three TV networks. The Department of Defense, for instance, produces thousands of films and TV programs every year. The Department of Agriculture sends out thousands of news releases annually. Political public relations is another growing field. A growing number of candidates for public office hire a PR expert to help them get their message across to voters.

3. Education. PR personnel work in both elementary and higher education. The most visible area of practice in elementary and high school concerns facilitating communication between educators and parents. Other tasks, however, are no less important. In many school systems, the PR person also handles relations with the school board, local and state legislative bodies, and the news media. Public relations at the college and university level, although less concerned with parental relations, has its own agenda of problems. For example, fund-raising, legislative relations, community relations, and internal relations with faculty and students would be concerns of most college PR departments.

4. Hospitals. The rising cost of health care and greater public expectations from the medical profession have given increased visibility to the public relations departments in our nation's hospitals. Some of the publics that hospital PR staffs have to deal with are patients, patients' families, consumers, state insurance commissions, physicians, nurses, and other staff members. Despite the increasing importance of hospital public relations, many hospitals do not have a full-time PR staff. Consequently, this is one area that will see significant growth in the future.

5. Nonprofit organizations. The United Way, Girl Scouts, the Red Cross, and the Salvation Army are just a few of the organizations that need PR professionals. Probably the biggest PR goal in organizations such as these is fundraising. Other objectives would include encouraging volunteer participation, informing contributors how their money is spent, and working with the individuals served by the organization.

6. Professional associations. Organizations such as the American Medical Association, the American Dairy Association, and the American Bar Association employ PR practitioners. In addition to providing news and information to the association's members, other duties of the PR staff would include recruiting new members, planning national conferences, influencing government decisions, and working with the news media.

7. Entertainment and sports. A significant number of PR experts work for established and would-be celebrities in the entertainment and sports worlds. A practitioner handling this type of client has two major responsibilities: get the client favorable media coverage and protect the client from bad publicity. Additionally, many sports and entertainment events (e.g., the Superbowl, a motion picture premiere) have PR campaigns associated with them.

From the above, it appears that the profession requires PR specialists as well as generalists.

DEPARTMENTS AND STAFF

This section discusses the structure of both internal public relations departments and external public relations agencies. The internal department setup will be discussed first. At the outset, it should be remembered that no two company departmental charts are alike, so the precise makeup of the PR department will vary. In any case, Fig. 15.1 displays a common organizational arrangement. Note that the PR director is directly responsible to the president (or the chief executive officer). Since PR affects every department, it makes sense for it to be supervised by the person who runs the entire organization. The figure also illustrates that the department is designed to handle communication with both internal and external publics.

The organization of a public relations agency is more complex. Figure 15.2 shows one possible departmental arrangement. As is apparent, the structure is somewhat similar to that of an advertising agency. Also, note that the range of services provided by the agency is more extensive than that of the internal corporate PR department.

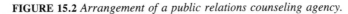

FIGURE 15.1 *Arrangement of a corporate public relations office.*

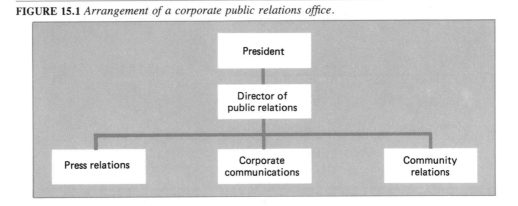

FIGURE 15.2 *Arrangement of a public relations counseling agency.*

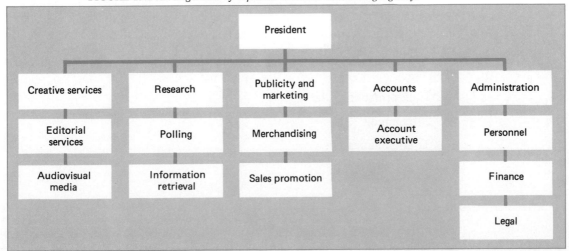

PR for Dolls

People spend $5 billion a year on dolls; they consistently outsell every other toy and are among the top ten most popular items to collect. Nonetheless, the industry still likes to promote itself. A PR firm offered one suggestion: Hold an international awards program. The doll industry liked the idea and instituted the "Doll of the Year" awards (the DOTYs). Plans call for more than 300 manufacturers to submit photos of their entries in twelve categories including fashion doll, baby doll, action doll, and limited edition doll. The preliminary judging will be done by the International Doll Academy, which will narrow the lists to five dolls in each category. The general public will then vote on the twelve dolls of the year. Ballots will be available at toy and department stores and in magazines.

One contender in this competition will surely be the Barbie doll. Barbie is pushing thirty and after countless parties, costume changes, and dates with Ken, Barbie's PR firm has come up with a fresh, new look for her. Barbie is going to be an executive. Her career apparel includes a pink business suit, matching hat, pumps, and an attaché case containing a calculator, credit cards, and her business cards. Her office play set contains fold-out desk, personal computer, phone, and file folder. At last report, Ken was still unemployed.

THE PUBLIC RELATIONS PROGRAM

Pretend you're the public relations director for a leading auto company. The company is entering into an agreement with a foreign car manufacturer to produce the foreign model in the United States. Unfortunately, in order to increase efficiency and centralize its operations, the company will have to close one of its plants located in a Midwestern city. About a thousand employees will have to be transferred or find new jobs, and the community will face a significant economic blow. It will be the job of the public relations department to determine how best to communicate this decision to the community.

The thorny problem outlined above is not an atypical one of the public relations professional. To handle it adequately, however, requires a planned, organized, and efficient public relations program. This section will trace the main steps involved in developing a typical PR campaign.

An effective public relations effort is the result of a four-step process:

1. information gathering

2. planning

3. communication

4. evaluation

Information Gathering

The information-gathering stage is an important one because what is learned from it will influence the remaining stages. Information gathering can be achieved through several means. Organizational records, trade journals, public records, and reference

Getting The Bugs Out
(Warning: Do Not Read This If You Are Squeamish)

You never can tell what you'll be doing when you work in PR. Take the case of the Boasberg Company, the PR firm for American Cyanamid, maker of the Combat Roach Control System. The task: make America aware of Combat. The PR answer: "The Great American Roach Off."

Research showed that most Americans respond to roaches in one of two ways —either sheer horror or gallows humor. The PR program was designed to capitalize on the gallows approach. The idea was simple: Give a prize to the individual who comes up with the largest roach in America. There were only a few rules. Roaches had to be of the *Periplaneta americana* species and they had to be dead but they couldn't be . . . squashed (yuck!).

The campaign started with a "Bug Bazaar" press conference in New York City with a scientist who was an expert in roach behavior. Next came a series of local contests, all less than serious. Florida contestants were reminded that no steroids were allowed. Judges wore headbands topped with roachlike antennas and eyes the size of golf balls. Network TV, *USA Today*, and many magazines covered the contest. As for Combat, sales were projected to increase about $13 million.

The winner? A twelve-year-old Florida girl who submitted a 2.07-inch-long roach that she found on a beach (ick!). The roach wound up as part of a permanent display in the Smithsonian Institution.

books serve as valuable sources for existing data. Personal contacts, mail to the company, advisory committees, and personnel reports represent other sources of information. If more formal research methods are required, they might be carried out by the PR department or by an outside agency that specializes in public opinion polling or survey research. To return to our example, the PR director at the auto company will need to gather a great deal of information. How much will the company save by its reorganization? Exactly how many workers will be transferred? Will the company help to find new jobs for the workers who will be unemployed? What will be the precise economic impact on the community? What will become of the empty buildings that will be left behind? Will the employees believe what the company tells them? What do people expect from the company? Will the company's image be hurt in other areas of the United States?

Planning

Phase two is the planning stage. There are two general types of planning: **strategic** and **tactical**. Strategic plans involve long-range general goals that the organization wishes to achieve. Top management usually formulates an organization's strategic plans. Tactical plans are more specific. They detail the tasks that must be accomplished by every department in the organization to achieve the strategic goals. Plans might be drawn up that can be used only once or they might be standing plans that set general organizational policy.

Planning is a vital part of the PR program. Some of the items involved in a PR campaign involve framing the objectives, considering the alternatives, assessing the risks and benefits involved in each, deciding on a course of action, figuring up the budget, and securing the necessary approvals from within the organization. In recent years, many PR practitioners have endorsed a technique known as **management by objectives (MBO)**. Simply put, MBO means that the organization sets observable and measurable goals for itself and allocates its resources to meet those objectives. For example, a corporation might set as a goal increasing sales by 25 percent over the next two years. When the time elapsed, it would be easy to see if the goal had been achieved. This approach is becoming more popular in PR because top management typically thinks in these terms, and it allows PR practitioners to speak the same language as chief executives. Second, it keeps the department on target in solving PR problems; and, finally, it provides concrete feedback about the efficiency of the PR process. In our hypothetical example, some possible objectives might be informing more than 50 percent of the community about the reasons to move or to make sure that community and national attitudes about the company are not adversely affected.

Communication

Phase three is the communication phase. After gathering facts and making plans, the organization assumes the role of the source of communication. Several key decisions are made at this stage concerning the nature of the messages and the types of media to be used. Because mass communication media are usually important channels in a PR program, it is necessary for public relations practitioners to have a thorough knowledge of the various media and their strengths and weaknesses. Moreover, PR professionals should know the various production techniques for the print and broadcast media. Some common ways of publicizing a message through the mass media include press releases, press kits, photographs, paid advertising, films, videotapes, press conferences, and interviews.

Public relations also makes use of other channels to get messages to its publics. These might include both the interpersonal and the machine-assisted settings. House publications, brochures, letters, bulletins, posters, billboards, and bulletin boards are possible communication channels used by a company to reach its own employees. On a more personal level, public meetings, speeches, demonstrations, staged events, open houses, and tours are other possibilities.

In the hypothetical example, our PR director would probably use a variety of messages and media. News conferences, ads, news releases, and public meetings would seem appropriate vehicles for explaining the company's position to its external public. Meanwhile, house publications, bulletin boards, speeches, and letters could be used to reach its internal public.

Evaluation

The last phase concerns evaluation of the PR program. How well did it work? The importance of evaluation in public relations is becoming greater because of the development of the MBO techniques discussed above. If a measurable goal was proposed for the PR program, then an evaluation technique should be able to measure the success in reaching that goal. There are several different things that might be measured. One easy method is simply to gauge the volume of coverage that the campaign generated. The number of press releases sent out, the number of letters mailed, speeches made, and so on, is simple to compute. In like manner, press clippings and mentions in TV and radio news can also be tabulated. It's important to remember, however, that volume does not equal results. A million press clippings mean nothing if they are not read by the audience. To measure the impact of a campaign on the audience requires more sophisticated techniques of analysis. Some common techniques would include questionnaires distributed to random samples of the audience, telephone surveys, panels, reader-interest studies, and the use of experimental campaigns. It is likely that many of the above techniques would be used by our hypothetical PR director.

Before closing, it should be pointed out that the above discussion talks about these four steps as though they are distinct stages. In actuality, the PR program is a continuous process, and one phase blends into the next. The results learned in the evaluation stage, for example, are also part of the information-gathering phase of the next cycle of the PR program.

ECONOMICS

Large sums of money are spent on public relations. The total amount spent on corporate PR activities is extremely hard to measure, but there is some information about the revenues of PR agencies. In 1987, the top fifty firms with major PR operations in the United States earned about $650 million in fee income. The two giants of the industry, Hill and Knowlton and Burson-Marsteller, between them earned about $225 million of this total. The third-ranking firm, Shandwick, earned $65 million. The PR business can also be volatile, especially among smaller agencies. Fee income might vary anywhere from 40 to 80 percent in a year.

PR agencies earn their money by charging their clients a basic fee for the time spent on their accounts plus charges for any extra costs incurred by the agency. Small public relations firms charge a few hundred dollars a month for their services. The big firms charge much more. Hill and Knowlton, for example, has a monthly minimum fee of $5000, and other expenses are billed to the client at cost. In addition, many firms charge a 17.65 percent markup for handling collateral materials such as photos, printing, research, and related activities. For example, if a particular photo cost $100 to make, the agency would bill the client $117.65.

CAREERS IN PUBLIC RELATIONS

Newcomers to the public relations field typically begin their work in the corporate area, with most people starting off in the public relations department of a medium to large organization. A smaller number go directly into PR counseling firms. Others follow a different career path into the profession by first working at a newspaper or broadcasting station and then moving into public relations. In any case, those in the PR industry recommend that prospective job seekers have excellent communications skills, particularly in writing, since many entry-level jobs entail writing and editing news releases, reports, employee publications, and speeches. Other qualifications that are desirable are a knowledge of public opinion research techniques, business practices, law, and the social sciences. Because of the importance of writing skills, many professionals recommend that young people major in journalism—many journalism schools now offer emphasis in PR. In other colleges, public relations courses might be found in the business school or in the department of speech.

New employees in the PR department are expected to perform a wide range of duties. A recent survey of the field found that media relations, advising top management, publicity, and community relations were the activities carried out most often by PR practitioners. More specifically, a newcomer would be expected to write news releases, update mailing lists, research materials for speeches, edit company publications, arrange special events, produce special reports, films, and tapes, and give public speeches.

The job market in public relations is expanding, but competition for entry-level positions will remain keen. One way that is helpful in gaining initial entry into the profession is to secure an internship with a public relations firm while still in college. A survey of recent graduates now working in public relations revealed that under-graduate internships turned into full-time jobs for about one-fifth of all those surveyed. These internships might carry a modest salary or they may involve no pay at all; some internships carry college credit, others do not. In any event, all internships can be valuable training experience.

Salary data are hard to summarize because of the varied nature of the field, but here are some 1988 figures. Note that the jobs for which information is available are those that require some experience. Entry-level positions would be somewhat less. Account executives at PR counseling firms averaged about $25,000 annually while vice presidents averaged about $51,000. For PR specialists in organizations other than counseling firms, the median salary for assistants was about $23,000 and for manager/supervisors, about $41,000.

As with the advertising area, those considering a career in public relations should develop a portfolio to show prospective employers. This portfolio should consist of news stories, brochures, magazine articles, photos, and scripts that exemplify your work. Applicants having a strong portfolio enjoy a definite advantage in the job hunt. In addition, membership in the Public Relations Student Society of America is also a good way to make valuable contacts.

A note of caution is also appropriate here. Many advertised jobs that are labeled ''public relations'' sometimes turn out to be something else. It's not unusual for sales jobs, receptionist positions, and even bartending slots to be called ''PR positions.'' The newcomer should check each position carefully before applying.

In closing, as in other media-related work, the job applicant should not be too choosy about his or her first job. Most counselors recommend taking any job that is available, even if it lacks the glamour and the salary that the applicant was hoping for. Once inside the firm, it is much easier to move to those positions that are more attractive.

SUGGESTIONS FOR FURTHER READING

The following books contain more information about concepts and topics discussed in this chapter.

ARONOFF, CRAIG, AND OTIS BASKIN, *Public Relations: The Profession and the Practice,* St. Paul, Minn.: West Publishing, 1983.

CUTLIP, SCOTT, AND ALLEN CENTER, *Effective Public Relations*, Englewood Cliffs, N.J.: Prentice-Hall, 1985.

HABERMAN, DAVID, AND HARRY DOLPHIN, *Public Relations: The Necessary Art,* Ames, IA: Iowa State University Press, 1988.

REILLY, ROBERT, *Public Relations in Action,* Englewood Cliffs, N.J.: Prentice-Hall, 1988.

SIMON, RAYMOND, *Public Relations: Concepts and Practices*, Columbus, Ohio: Grid Publishing, 1980.

WILCOX, DENNIS, PHILLIP AULT, AND WARREN AGEE, *Public Relations: Strategies and Tactics*, New York: Harper & Row, 1989.

Chapter 16

The Structure of the Advertising Industry

F ill in the blanks:

Have you driven a _____ lately?
Built for the human race. _____.
_____. The choice of a new generation.
The _____ card. Don't leave home without it.
Please don't squeeze the _____.

The fact that most of us could readily supply the missing words (Ford, Nissan, Pepsi, American Express, Charmin) is a testament to the advertising industry. This chapter will examine its history, structure, and career opportunities.

DEFINING ADVERTISING

Simply defined, advertising is any form of nonpersonal presentation and promotion of ideas, goods, and services usually paid for by an identified sponsor. Note three key words in the above definition. Advertising is nonpersonal; it is directed toward a large group of anonymous people. Even direct-mail advertising, which may be addressed to a specific person, is prepared by a computer and is signed by a machine. Second, advertising typically is paid for. This fact differentiates advertising from publicity, which is not usually purchased. Sponsors such as Coke and Delta pay for the time and the space they use to get their message across. (Some organizations such as the Red Cross or the United Way advertise but do not pay for time or space. Broadcast stations, newspapers, and magazines run these ads free as a public service.) Third, for obvious reasons, the sponsor of the ad is identified. In fact, in most instances identifying the sponsor is the prime purpose behind the ad—otherwise, why advertise? Perhaps the only situation in which the identity of the advertiser may not be self-evident is political advertising. Because of this, broadcasters and publishers will not accept a political ad unless there is a statement identifying those responsible for it.

Advertising fulfills four basic functions in society. First, it serves a marketing function by helping companies that provide products or services sell their products. Personal selling, sales promotions, and advertising blend together to help market the product. Second, advertising is educational. People learn about new products and services or improvements in existing ones through advertising. Third, advertising plays an economic role. The ability to advertise allows new competitors to enter the business arena. Competition, in turn, encourages product improvements and can lead to lower prices. Moreover, advertising reaches a mass audience, thus greatly reducing the cost of personal selling and distribution. Finally, advertising performs a definite social function. By vividly displaying the material and cultural opportunities available in a free-enterprise society, advertising helps increase productivity and raises the standard of living.

Keep in mind that advertising is directed at a **target audience**, a specific segment of the population for whom the product or service has a definite appeal. There are many target audiences that could be defined. The most general are consumers and business. Consequently, **consumer advertising**, as the name suggests, is targeted at the people who buy goods and services for personal use. Most of the advertising that most people are exposed to falls into this category. **Business-to-business advertising** is aimed at people who buy products for business use. Industrial, professional, trade, and agricultural advertising are all part of this category. Consumer advertising is the focus of most of this chapter but we will also take a brief look at business-to-business advertising.

CAPSULE HISTORY OF ADVERTISING

Advertising has been around ever since people have been around. Its earliest beginnings, of course, are impossible to pinpoint, but there are several examples dating back thousands of years. Clay tablets traced to ancient Babylon have been found with messages that touted an ointment dealer and a shoemaker. Ancestors of modern-day billboards were found in the ruins of Pompeii. Later, the town crier was an important advertising medium throughout Europe and England during the medieval period. In short, advertising was a well-established part of the social environment of early civilization.

In more recent times, the history of advertising is inextricably entwined with changing social conditions and advances in media technology. To illustrate, Gutenberg's invention of printing using movable type made possible several new advertising media: posters, handbills, and newspaper ads. In fact, the first printed advertisement in English was produced in about 1480 and was a handbill that announced a prayerbook for sale. Its author, evidently wise in the ways of outdoor advertising, tacked his ad to church doors all over England. By the late 1600s, ads were common sights in London newspapers.

Advertising made its way to the colonies along with the early settlers from England. The *Boston Newsletter* (see Chapter 4) became the first American newspaper to publish advertising. Ben Franklin, a pioneer of early advertising, made his ads more attractive by using large headlines and considerable white space. From Franklin's time up to the early nineteenth century, newspaper ads greatly resembled what today are called classified ads.

The Industrial Revolution caused major changes in American society and in American advertising. Manufacturers, with the aid of newly invented machines, were able to mass produce their products. Mass production, however, also required mass consumption and a mass market. Advertising was a tremendous aid in reaching this new mass audience.

The impact of increasing industrialization was most apparent in the period following the end of the Civil War (1865) to the beginning of the twentieth century. In little more than three decades, the following occurred:

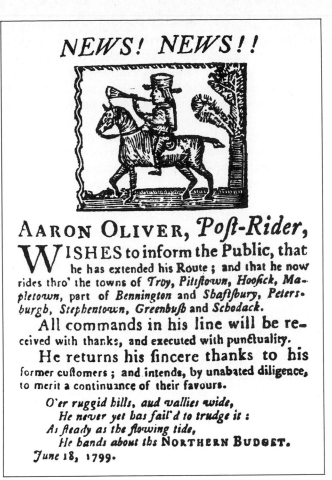

Colonial advertisement (1799) announcing the Post Rider's new mail route. (The Bettmann Archive)

1. The railroad linked all parts of the country, making it possible for Eastern manufacturers to distribute their goods to the growing Western markets.

2. Thanks in large measure to an influx of immigrants, the population of the United States grew quickly, doubling between 1870 and 1900. More people meant larger markets for manufacturers.

3. The invention of new communication media—the telephone, typewriter, high-speed printing press, phonograph, motion pictures, photography, rural mail delivery—made it easier for people to communicate with one another.

4. Economic production increased dramatically, and people had more disposable income to spend on new products.

This improved economic and communication climate helped advertising thrive. Magazines were distributed from coast to coast and made possible truly national advertising. The development of the halftone method for reproducing photographs meant that magazine advertisers could portray their products more vividly. By 1900, it was not unusual for the leading magazines of the period (*Harper's, Cosmopolitan, McClure's*) to run 75–100 pages of ads in typical issue.

Not surprisingly, the increased importance of advertising in the marketing process led to the birth of the **advertising agency**, an organization that specializes in providing advertising services to its clients. The roots of the modern-day agency can be traced to Volney B. Palmer of Philadelphia. In 1842, Palmer bought large amounts of space in various newspapers at a discount and then resold the space at higher rates to advertisers. The actual ad—the copy, layout, and artwork—was still prepared by the company wishing to advertise; in effect, Palmer was a space broker. That situation changed in the late nineteenth century when the advertising agency of N.W. Ayer & Son was founded. Ayer & Son offered to plan, create, and execute a complete advertising campaign for their customers. By 1900, the advertising agency became the focal point of creative planning, and advertising was firmly established as a profession.

This new profession, however, was not without its problems. Around the turn of the century, patent medicine ads that made extravagant claims of curing every known disease were found in many publications. The wild and unsubstantiated claims for these products sparked a consumer revolt, and in 1906 Congress passed the Pure Food and Drug Act, the first federal law to control advertising. Several years later, Congress also created the Federal Trade Commission (FTC), an agency designed to protect businesses from unfair competitive practices. At about this same time, efforts aimed at wiping out fraudulent advertising also began within the advertising profession (Chapters 17 and 18).

The 1920s saw the beginning of radio as an advertising medium (see Chapter 8). The rise of network broadcasting made radio an attractive vehicle for national advertisers. By 1930 about $27 million was spent on network advertising, and many of the most popular shows of the day were produced by advertising agencies. The stock market crash of 1929 had a disastrous effect on the U.S. economy. Total dollars spent on advertising dropped from $2.8 billion in 1929 to $1.7 billion in 1935. It would take a decade for the industry to recover. World War II meant that many civilian firms cut back on their advertising budgets. Others simply changed the content of their ads and instead of selling their products instructed consumers on how to make their products last until after the war.

The growth of advertising from the end of the war in 1945 to the late 1980s can only be described as spectacular. The changeover from a war economy to a consumer economy prompted a spurt in advertising as manufacturers hurried to meet the demand for all the goods and services that people had put off buying because of the war. From 1950 to 1975, the amount of money spent on advertising increased an incredible 490 percent. Also during this period several significant developments took place. The most important was probably television's rise as a national advertising medium. TV's growth had an impact on both radio and magazines. Radio became a medium used primarily by local advertisers. Magazines that aimed at specialized audiences attracted more advertisers, but general-interest publications (such as *Colliers* and *Look*) could not compete with TV and eventually went under. Second, the consumer became a more powerful force in the marketplace. Responding to increased consumer pressure, the FTC introduced corrective advertising during the 1970s (see Chapter 17). Third, direct advertising (much of it done through the mail) increased by more than 800 percent from 1950 to 1980. This increase was due to the growth of computerized mailing lists, the emergence of the telephone as a marketing tool, and the expanded use of credit card shopping. Finally, the advertisers have become more sophisticated in their methods thanks to the emergence of computers and other electronic data processing devices.

ORGANIZATION OF THE CONSUMER ADVERTISING INDUSTRY

There are three main components of the advertising industry:

1. the advertisers

2. advertising agencies

3. the media

Each of these will be discussed in turn.

Advertisers

Advertising is an important part of the overall marketing plan of almost every organization that provides a product or a service to the public. Advertisers can range from the small bicycle shop on the corner that spends $4 on an ad in the local weekly paper to huge international corporations such as Procter & Gamble, which spends more than $1.4 billion annually for ads.

At a basic level, we can distinguish two different types of advertisers: national and retail. **National advertisers** sell their product or service to customers all across the country. The emphasis in national advertising is on the product or service and not so much on the place where the product or service is sold. For example, the Coca-Cola Company is interested in selling soft drinks. It doesn't matter to the company if you buy their product at the local supermarket, a small convenience store, or from a vending machine; as long as you buy their products, the company will be happy. **Retail advertisers** (also called local advertisers) are companies such as local restaurants, car dealerships, TV repair shops, and other merchants and service organizations that have customers in only one city or trading area. The retail advertiser wants to attract customers to a specific store or place of business. Some companies are both national and local advertisers. Sears and K mart, for example, advertise all over the country, but their individual stores use local advertising to highlight their specific sales and promotions. Franchises, such as McDonald's and Burger King, keep up their national image by advertising on network TV, while their local outlets put ads in the paper to attract customers from the local community.

Naturally, the way organizations handle their advertising depends on their size. Some companies have their own advertising departments; a small retail store might have one person who is responsible for advertising and marketing and who may also have other job functions. Large or small, there are several basic functions that must be attended to by all advertisers. These include planning the ads and deciding where they will appear, setting aside a certain amount of money for the advertising budget, coordinating the advertising with other departments in the organization, and, if necessary, supervising the work of an outside agency or company that produces the ad. In addition, some large advertisers have departments that can create and prepare all the advertising materials, purchase the space and airtime for the ads, and check to see if the ads were effective in achieving their goals.

No matter how the advertising is handled, it is likely that quite a few people in the organization are really part of the advertising business. In some companies, the president or chief executive becomes actively involved (for example, Lee Iacocca of Chrysler, Victor Kiam of Remington—he liked the razor so much he bought the company—Frank Perdue of Perdue Chickens). Moreover, sales and marketing personnel keep a close watch on the type of advertising that is planned and where the advertising is to appear. Even the people in the design and production departments are often asked to contribute ideas to the company's ads. In short, it could be said that almost everyone in the company feels that he or she is involved with the company's ads because the advertising represents them in some way.

Agencies

According to the American Association of Advertising Agencies, an agency is an independent business organization composed of creative and business people who develop, prepare, and place advertising in advertising media for sellers seeking to find customers for their goods and services. The big advertising agencies tend to be located in the big cities, particularly New York, Los Angeles, and Chicago. Smaller agencies, however, are located all across the country. In fact, most cities with more than 100,000 people usually have at least one advertising agency. When it comes to income, however, the bigger agencies dominate.

The last few years in the agency business have seen the the spawning of superagencies, or ''mega-agencies,'' resulting from the merger and consolidation of several large ad agencies. In addition, the business has been ''globalized,'' since these new mega-agencies have branches all over the world. The half-dozen mega-agencies listed in Table 16.1 dominated the industry at the close of 1988.

The impact of foreign ownership is apparent in the agency business as in many other media. Three of the megagroups in Table 16.1 are British-owned. The trend began in 1986 when a British agency, Saatchi & Saatchi, acquired DFS Dorland and Compton to form a company that billed more than $11 billion worldwide in 1987. WPP Group is another British-based company that acquired the J. Walter Thompson agency in 1987. A third British company on the list is the WCRS/Belier Company, whose American properties include Della Femina, Travisano and Partners. The other mega-agenices are American-owned. The Omnicom Group was formed in 1986 by the merger of BBDO, Doyle Dane Bernbach, and Needham Harper. Omnicom billed more than $6 billion in 1987. The Interpublic Group included the McCann-Erickson, Lintas, and Dailey agencies and employed about 14,000 people. The Ogilvy Group included Ogilvy & Mather; Sali, McCabe, Solves; and SAGE Worldwide. Eurocom is based in Paris and has agencies throughout Europe and Asia.

TABLE 16.1 Mega-Agencies Ranked by Worldwide Income, 1988

AGENCY	GROSS INCOME (MILLIONS)
Saatchi & Saatchi	$1990
Interpublic Group	1260
WPP Group*	1173
Omnicom Group	986
Ogilvy Group	865
Eurocom	500
WCRS/Belier	335

* In mid-1989, the WPP Group acquired the Ogilvy Group, making the new company number one on the income list.

Agencies can be classified by the range of services that they offer. In general terms, there are three main types: (1) full-service agencies, (2) media buying services, and (3) creative boutiques.

As the name implies, a **full-service agency** is one that handles all phases of the advertising process for its clients; it plans, creates, produces, and places ads for its clients. In addition, it might also provide other marketing services such as sales promotions, trade show exhibits, newsletters, and annual reports. In theory, at least, there is no need for the client to deal with any other company for help on promoting their product.

A **media buying service** is an organization that specializes in buying radio and television time and reselling it to advertisers and advertising agencies. The service sells the time to the advertiser, orders the spots on the various stations involved, and monitors the stations to see if the ads actually run.

A **creative boutique** (the name was coined during the 1960s and has hung on to the present) is an organization that specializes in the actual creation of ads. In general, boutiques create imaginative and distinctive advertising themes and produce innovative and original ads. A company that uses a creative boutique would have to employ another agency to perform the planning, buying, and administrative functions connected with advertising.

Not surprisingly, full-service agencies saw media buying services and boutiques as competitors. Consequently, the full-service agencies improved their own creative and media buying departments. It wasn't long before the services and boutiques began to feel the effects of the agencies' efforts. As it stands now, only a few services and a few boutiques still handle large national advertisers.

What does a full-service ad agency do for a client? To begin with, the agency studies the product or service and determines its marketable characteristics and how it relates to the competition. At the same time the agency studies the potential market, possible distribution plans, and likely advertising media. Following this the agency makes a formal presentation to the client detailing its findings about the product and its recommendations for an advertising strategy. If the client agrees, the agency then launches the execution phase. This phase entails writing and producing the ads, buying space and time in various media, delivering the ads to the appropriate media, and verifying that all ads actually appeared. Finally, the agency will work closely with the client's salespeople to make sure that they get the greatest possible benefit from the ads.

Media

The last part of the advertising industry consists of the mass media. The media serve as the connection between the company that has a service or product to sell and the customers who wish to buy it. The media that are available for advertising include the obvious ones—radio, television, newspapers, magazines—and others that are not so obvious, such as direct mail, billboards, transit cards (bus and car cards), stadium scoreboard ads, and point-of-purchase displays. Chapters 5, 6, 8, 9, and 13 presented a general overview of newspapers, magazines, radio, and television and also discussed their dependence on various kinds of advertising. This section examines them from the perspective of an advertiser and also discusses direct-mail and other out-of-home advertising media.

Even the slickest and most imaginative advertising message will fail if it is delivered to the wrong people. To make sure that this catastrophe doesn't happen, advertisers employ highly skilled media planners to help them place and schedule their ads. With the numerous mass media that are available to deliver the message and the hundreds (even thousands) of individual media outlets to choose from, it is necessary to study closely what each of the various media can offer.

When advertising specialists look at the various media, they tend to evaluate them along four dimensions:

1. Reach—how many people can get the message?

2. Frequency—how often will the message be received?

3. Selectivity—does the medium actually reach potential customers?

4. Efficiency—how much does it cost to reach a certain number of people? (this is usually expressed as cost per thousand people)

Newspapers have good reach; they can go to every geographic location in the country and are read by millions of people. Many newspapers are published daily, which means that advertisers can present their messages to the audience with a high degree of frequency. The newspaper, unless it is a specialized publication aimed at a certain ethnic group, does not score high on the selectivity dimension. Although it gives an advertiser geographic selectivity by being distributed in a certain area of the market, within that area its readership is not specific. It would be inefficient, for example, to use the newspaper alone to reach eighteen- to twenty-five-year old females since the paper is not specifically targeted to that group. In terms of cost, it is hard to generalize because there are so many newspapers to consider. In general terms, the absolute cost of advertising in many papers is inexpensive, but the standardized cost of reaching a thousand people tends to be relatively high.

Magazines tend to have a more limited reach than newspapers. Further, most magazines come out once per month, which means that the potential for frequent presentations of an ad is not high. On the other hand, magazines offer a tremendous degree of selectivity for advertisers. If an advertiser wanted to reach teenage girls, he or she could choose among several publications designed for that audience segment. The cost of magazine advertising tends to be relatively high, but this cost must be evaluated against its efficiency in reaching a target group.

Radio has excellent reach and allows advertisers to present their messages with great frequency. In addition, radio stations aim for specialized audience groups, allowing advertisers to pinpoint a specific group with their messages. The cost of radio advertising is low and represents a good value to advertisers. The problem with radio advertising is that there are so many stations competing for basically the same audience—a situation that makes it difficult for an advertiser to select the most efficient mix of stations.

Television has almost universal reach and allows for frequent repetition of messages. Television is not very selective in the audience it reaches, but the advertiser does have some flexibility. For example, certain programs tend to draw a certain kind of audience. The network news, for example, draws an older audience; soap operas still tend to attract primarily a female following. The potential of selectivity for TV will increase with the widespread growth of cable TV channels. MTV, for example, attracts an audience composed mainly of fifteen- to twenty-five-year-olds. On the cost dimension, television's situation is almost the opposite of newspapers. In absolute terms, the cost of advertising on TV, especially network TV, is high because it reaches so many people. It's so expensive that many smaller companies simply cannot afford it. If the cost for reaching a thousand viewers is calculated, however, it is relatively low.

Billboards and other outdoor advertising media score high in terms of reach and frequency dimensions. With proper positioning and lighting, outdoor advertising can be seen twenty-four hours a day all year long. Its selectivity is limited, however, since its audience will be composed of all people who happen to pass a certain point. Outdoor advertising also tends to be a relatively expensive way to advertise.

Direct advertising, especially direct mail, has the potential for widespread reach. Virtually everybody has a mailbox. It also has the potential for frequent delivery of the message. Direct advertising is probably the most selective of all advertising media. Special mailing lists allow the advertiser to focus on his or her particular target audience. One disadvantage of direct advertising is its high cost. Direct mail in particular has become rather expensive with the recent increases in postal rates.

Finally, of course, in addition to the above considerations, advertisers have to take into account many other factors before deciding on what medium to use. An important part of any decision involves considering the creative limitations imposed by the physical properties of each medium. Television, for example, allows the advertiser to show the product in action. On the other hand, TV ads are short and cannot be used to present a great deal of technical information. A magazine ad can be in full color and can present a large amount of data, but it might not have the same impact as a TV ad. All in all, choosing what media to use in the final advertising mix is a difficult decision.

PRODUCING ADVERTISING

Departments and Staff

Figure 16.1, page 372, shows the departmental chart for a typical advertising agency. Remember also that many large companies have their own advertising departments in the overall corporate organization, and their arrangement would be similar to the one presented here. As can be seen, there are four major departments:

1. creative

2. account services

3. marketing

4. administration

The creative department, as the name implies, actually produces the ad. The people in this department write the advertising **copy** (the headline and message of the ad), choose the illustrations, prepare artwork, and/or supervise the scripting and production of radio and TV commercials.

The account services department is responsible for the relationship between the agency and the client. Because the advertising agency is an organization outside the firm doing the advertising, it is necessary to appoint someone, usually called an account executive (AE), to promote communication and understanding between client and agency. The AE must represent the viewpoint of the agency to the client but at the same time must keep abreast of the needs of the advertiser. Needless to say, since the AE tends to be the person in the middle, his or her job is an important one of the agency.

The marketing services department is responsible for advising the client as to what media to use for his or her messages. Typically this department makes extensive

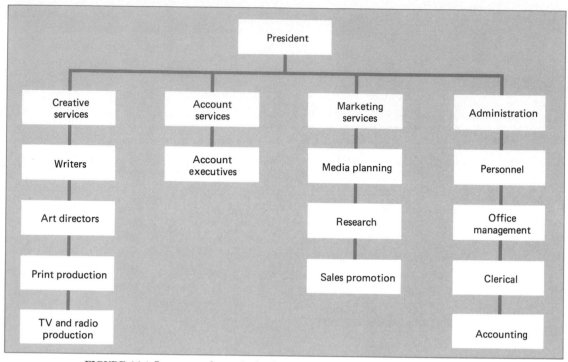

FIGURE 16.1 *Structure of a typical advertising agency.*

use of the data collected by the Audit Bureau of Circulations, Arbitron, Nielsen, and the other audience research services mentioned in Chapter 20. This department is also in charge of any sales promotions that are done in connection with the advertising. These may include such things as coupons, premiums, and other aids to dealers.

Finally, like any other business, the advertising agency needs a department to take care of the day-to-day administration of the agency. This department is in charge of office management, clerical functions, accounting, personnel, and training of new employees.

The Advertising Campaign

Advertising appears in a variety of media, and the production techniques vary with each. In addition, much of the actual creative work involved in putting together the ads takes place before the production process and reflects strategic decisions made during the initial planning process. Consequently, perhaps the best way to illustrate how ads get produced is to present a general discussion of an advertising campaign for a national product. A **campaign** consists of a large number of advertisements all stressing the same major theme or appeal that appear in a number of media over a specified time. Greatly simplified, there are at least six different phases of a typical campaign:

1. choosing the marketing strategy

2. selecting the main appeal or theme

3. translating the theme into the various media

Great Ideas That Failed (Part I)

By now everybody is familiar with the New Coke/Old Coke marketing problem encountered by the Coca-Cola Company. Apparently, somebody misinterpreted the market research results and failed to anticipate the backlash that occurred when the Old Coke (or Classic Coke if you prefer) was taken off the market. Much embarrassed, the company had to backtrack and reintroduce the old product.

Coca-Cola is not alone in having been embarrassed. There have been other notable failures: A product called Clean and Kill was supposed to disinfect as well as clean. The choice of a name, however, left something to be desired. Consumers thought the product was some kind of rat poison and avoided it entirely.

Speaking of bad product names, a few years ago a lot of money was spent advertising Yucca Dew shampoo. Unfortunately, the target audience, teenage girls, did not want to put anything on their hair that sounded like yuk. The product did not stay around long.

Open Air Spinfresh was a product introduced in Australia. An interesting concept, the product consisted of a plastic toilet paper holder with "fragrance-impregnated" beads that gave off a burst of air freshener whenever the paper roll was turned. A half-million dollars was spent on advertising but to no avail. The product failed because someone in the marketing department failed to notice that Australia does not have a standard-size fixture for toilet roll holders. In most Australian homes, Open Air Spinfresh kept falling on the floor, a feature that did not endear it to consumers. (A new, improved version of this product recently appeared in the United States.)

Lastly, even the cleverest advertising ideas can't save a product if the original concept is in bad taste. The case in point: Hippy Sippys. These were hollow plastic hypodermic needles filled with brightly colored candy designed for toddlers. Retailers were so horrified that they refused to carry them.

4. producing the ads

5. buying space and time

6. executing and evaluating the campaign

In the first phase, a great deal of research is done to determine the target audience, the marketing objective, the appropriate price for the product or service, and the advertising budget. It is during this phase that the word **positioning** is often heard. Positioning has many interpretations, but in general it means fitting a product or service to one or more segments of the broad market in such a way as to set it apart from the competition without making any change in the product. For example, Seven Up successfully competed in a soft drink market dominated by colas by positioning itself as the "uncola." Hyundai successfully positioned itself as the car for the cost-conscious consumer. In the $6.3 billion pet food industry, Science Diet positioned itself as a superpremium pet food in an attempt to appeal to the affluent pet owner. Other brands, such as Carnation's Grand Gourmet, Kal Kan's Pedigree, and Quaker's King Kuts also went after this segment. Kellogg positioned its Mueslix cereal as an upscale product, trying to attract the same adult consumer who would buy yogurt and croissants. Bain de Soleil noticed that its consumer research found sunbathers highly conscious of the risk of skin cancer due to overexposure. It repositioned its product to stress the protection angle. The product even changed the

Throwing a Tantrum

Almost everybody has gotten so fed up with some irritating TV ad that they would like to throw a brick at the TV screen whenever the ad comes on. Well, now you can. A British inventor has come up with a product called Tantrum. Tantrum is a rubber brick that contains a switch that will turn off the TV set.

Throw the brick against the screen and, voilá, no more commercial.

A new improved version of the Tantrum will turn the set back on again after a time lapse long enough to make sure the irritating commercial has passed. The cost: about $20. The big question: Will it be advertised on TV?

degree of tanning shown on the model in its print ads. For years the model had been a deep, dark tan, but in 1988 she was several shades lighter.

Sometimes repositioning doesn't work, as was the case with Minute Maid orange juice's attempt to reposition its product from simply a breakfast drink to an all-purpose beverage. Despite an $18 million campaign featuring the message "Not just for breakfast any more," sales of orange juice were sluggish as consumers apparently failed to respond to the theme.

After the product or service has been positioned, an overall idea or theme for the campaign is developed. Once again, considerble research is done to find the proper theme. In the early 1980s, for example, Delta Airlines had positioned itself as an airline catering to the needs of the business traveler. But what specific item should be stressed in Delta's campaign: food, courteous service, extensive routes? Research revealed to Delta that the most important factor to the business flyer was convenience. The business traveler was concerned with when planes left and when they arrived. Hence, Delta's agency came up with the "Delta is ready when you are" theme. The Canon Corporation, maker of single-lens reflex cameras, introduced its new automatic camera in the late 1970s by positioning itself to appeal to college-educated men, eighteen to forty-five, who happened to be the prime buying audience for single-lens cameras. How should Canon appeal to this group? The company's advertising agency decided to emphasize the camera's ease of operation and hit upon the theme: "The Canon AE-1 is so advanced it's simple." The campaign turned out to be a big success. TCBY yogurt, noting that many yogurt buyers were diet and health conscious introduced its ad campaign based on the theme: "Say goodbye to high calories. Say goodbye to ice cream." Heineken beer, seeing a lot of its sales going to other imported beers, launched a campaign whose theme made fun of the "trendy" aspect of its competition: "When you're through kidding around, come back to Heineken."

The next phase consists of translating this theme into print and broadcast ads. Advertisers try to achieve variety in their various ads but with a consistency of approach that will help consumers remember and recognize their product. The recent "It's a good time for the good taste of McDonald's" campaign is a case in point. All McDonald's advertising, both print and broadcast, carried that theme whether for cheeseburgers, McNuggets, or price promotions. McDonald's advertising agency created 1000 variations of that theme in single year. Or take the case of Bartles and Jaymes wine coolers. The product is actually made by the Ernest & Julio Gallo Winery, but the company thought its reputation as a maker of jug wines would not

Innovative pop-up ad for TransAmerica appearing in Time *magazine. The ad startles readers with a three-dimensional view of a manufacturing complex, a city skyline, and a pickup truck. (AP/ Wide World Photos)*

go over well with the wine cooler's target audience, young, upscale consumers. Consequently, the Gallo name is never mentioned in the series of ads that portray two down-home, folksy types lounging on a porch. The spots are all consistent. They have a dry, understated humor, and the Frank Bartles character does all the talking while the Ed Jaymes character remains the silent partner. Variety is achieved in the different ways humor is used to sell the product. One spot touts the wine cooler as a perfect gift to put under the tree on Labor Day. Another shows a chart of all the foods that the wine cooler complements. The only foods it doesn't go with are kohlrabi (a little-known variety of cabbage) and candy corn. The spots were so well received that many people thought that Frank and Ed were the actual founders of the company. The Army used its "Be all that you can be" theme for seven years in its print and broadcast ads and only recently introduced variations.

The actual production of the ad is done much in the same way as other media content is produced. In the print media, the copy, the headline, subheads, any accompanying illustrations, and the layout is first prepared in rough form. The initial step is usually just a thumbnail sketch that can be used to experiment with different arrangements within the ad. The headline might be moved down, the copy moved from right to left, and so on. Next a **rough layout**, a drawing that is the actual size of the ad, is constructed. There are usually several of these rough layouts prepared, and the best of these are used to produce the **comprehensive layout**, the one that will actually be used to produce the ad. Many agencies use outside art studios and printers to help them put together print ads and billboards.

Subliminal Advertising

Subliminal persuasion consists of sending persuasive messages just below the threshold of perception. (In psychology, the perceptual threshold is called a "limen," hence the term "subliminal.") Whether or not subliminal persuasion really works in ads has been an advertising controversy for about thirty years. It all started back in the 1950s with an experiment in a movie theater. While the movie was playing, messages were flashed on the screen for about 1/3000 of a second, too fast for the conscious mind to perceive them. The messages said "Drink Coca-Cola" and "Eat Popcorn." The experimenters claimed that sales figures jumped 57 percent for popcorn and 18 percent for Coke in the six weeks of the study. Was subliminal persuasion at work? Probably not. All subsequent attempts to replicate this finding failed. Quite probably the increased sales were the result of the particular film that was shown—*Picnic*. This movie had plenty of scenes of people eating and drinking in hot summer weather, which probably inspired the audience to imitate the actors. Other experiments have indicated that subliminal persuasion is unlikely. Perceptual thresholds vary tremendously among people. Even if the message was perceived, it would probably be distorted. "Eat Popcorn" might come out "Cheat Your Horn."

The subliminal controversy erupted again in 1972 with the publication of *Subliminal Seduction* by Wilson Bryan Key. The author claimed that advertisers manipulated consumers by deliberately embedding sexual symbols and words within the artwork of their ads. Key's book contained illustrations of this alleged subliminal persuasion. These examples ranged from supposed phallic symbols hidden in the ice cubes in the illustration used for a liquor ad to a four-letter word allegedly hidden in an ad for dolls. Most people who saw Key's examples were hard pressed to find the images he described without a huge dose of imagination and poetic license. It turned out, however, there was at least a tiny particle of truth to Key's charges. Several photographers and photo touch-up artists confessed that they had indeed introduced carefully disguised sexual references to ads as a private practical joke. These instances were few in number, and it hardly constituted a conscious manipulation by the advertising industry.

In any case, there is no proof that ads with camouflaged sexual content sell better than the tamer versions. Subliminal persuasion is fun to talk about but there is little evidence that it exists.

Radio commercials are written and created much in the same way that early radio drama shows were produced. A script is prepared in which dialogue, sound effects, and music are combined to produce whatever effect is desired. The commerical is then either produced in the sound studio or recorded live on location. In either case, postproduction editing adds any desired special effects, and eventually a master tape is prepared for duplication and distribution.

The beginning step in the preparation of a television commercial is the preparation of a **storyboard**, a series of drawings depicting the key scenes of the planned ad. Storyboards are usually shown to the client before production begins. If the client has any objections or suggestions, they can be incorporated into the script before the expensive production begins. Once the storyboards are approved, the commercial is ready to go into production. Most TV commercials are shot on film (although some are now switching to videotape) and the production process is similar to that described in Chapter 12. Television commercials are the most expensive ads

(Open on series of quick cuts of man on a motorcycle, a woman and an outdoor cafe. Shots cut between color and black and white, with pans and hand-held shots)
Music: Over throughout.
Singer (VO): Lord I hear that lonesome train. Sounds like a five oh one. All my life it seems, me and my Levi's jeans we been on the run.
(Super fades in)

Leslie Caldwell, art director
Mike Koelker, writer/creative director
Steve Neely, producer
Leslie Dektor, director
Petermann Dektor Productions, production
  company
Foote, Cone & Belding (San Francisco), agency
Levi Strauss & Company, client

3
(Open on Joe Isuzu on Bonneville Salt Flats)
SFX: Wind.
Joe: How fast is the new Isuzu Impulse Turbo? How does 950 miles per hour sound?
(Super fades in as Joe draws a .357 magnum, aims across flats and fires)
Super: Sounds like a lie.
SFX: Gunshot.
Music: Begins and continues throughout.
(Joe places gun down, runs to car and gets in)
SFX: Car door slam.
(Cut to close-up of bullet flying through air)
SFX: Air rushing.

(Cut to close-up of Joe primping in car's rearview mirror then winking at himself. Cut to car tire as car races off)
SFX: Screeching tires.
(Camera intercuts between close-ups of bullet flying through air and Joe in car. Cut to car approaching slalom course. Cut to bullet. Cut to close-up of Joe in his car. Cut to his car driving over each marker on slalom course. Cut to bullet and Joe taking the lead in background. Cut to close-up of Joe smiling in car. Cut to car speeding past bullet. Then several shots of car screeching to a stop. Cut to bullet. Cut to Joe walking around car, then running to hold target in front of his face)

Joe: The Impulse Turbo. Faster than a speeding...
SFX: Bullet humming, crunch.
(Bullet passes through target. Joe pulls target away from face and is holding bullet in his teeth)
Joe: ...well, you know.
(Fade to tag)

Rick Carpenter, art director
Dick Sittig, writer
Richard Russo, creative director
Sandra Tuttle/Alan Pierce, producers
Ron Travisano, director
Travisano DiGiacomo Films, production company
Della Femina, McNamee WCRS, Inc. (Los Angeles)
  agency
American Isuzu Motors, client

Preparing the ad. A printed storyboard for a TV commercial featuring Joe Isuzu. (Della Femina, McNamee WCRS, Inc., American Isuzu Motors)

Great Advertising Ideas That Worked—Sort of

The California Raisin Advisory Board knew a good thing when they saw it. Foote, Cone & Belding, the Board's ad agency, had just previewed a commercial for California raisins that featured a group of "Claymation" raisins strutting their stuff to the tune of "I Heard It Through the Grapevine." The board okayed the ad immediately and it soon premiered on TV stations across the country. Viewers loved it and remembered it. The ad industry gave the spot a Clio award.

But did it sell raisins? Yes, but not a whole lot. Sales went up about 8 percent after the campaign broke in 1986–1987. Sales the next year, when the Claymation figures were big stars, were up even less and initial figures for the first half of 1988 showed almost no gain.

The public apparently liked the raisin figures much better than the edible kind. Retail sales of merchandise bearing the raisins' likeness exploded. Consumers could buy models of the raisins, raisin pencils, raisin watches, and raisin sheets and blankets. More than sixty companies were granted licenses to use the cute little fruits in their marketing. In 1988, here was the projected box score:

- Sales of raisins: $200 million
- Sales of raisin merchandise: $250 million

---

to produce. A thirty-second commercial can easily cost $150,000. Special effects, particularly animation, can drive the costs even higher. In order to keep costs down, much of the time spent producing TV commercials consists of planning and rehearsal. As with the print media, many agencies hire outside production specialists to produce their commericals.

While the creative department is putting together the print and broadcast ads, the marketing department is busy buying time in those media judged to be appropriate for the campaign. If the product is seasonal (e.g., sun tan lotion, snowmobiles), the ads are scheduled to reflect the calendar, appearing slightly before and during the time people begin buying such items. Other products and services might call for a program of steady advertising throughout the year.

The last phase of the campaign consists of the ads actually appearing. Testing is done during and after this phase to see if consumers actually saw and remembered the ads. In addition, sales data are carefully monitored to determine if the campaign had the desired effect on sales.

ECONOMICS

This section will examine the economics of advertising on two levels. First, we will look at the total industry and trace expenditures in the various mass media. Second, we will narrow our focus and examine how an ad agency makes money.

Advertising Volume in Various Media

About $118 billion was spent on advertising in the United States in 1988. Newspapers accounted for the biggest share of advertising volume—about 26 percent. TV ranked second, accounting for 22 percent, followed by direct mail, radio, magazines, and

The medium of outdoor advertising has grown rapidly over the past decade. Here, a giant lifelike hand reaches for a Pepsi on Robert Keith & Co.'s Third-Dimension billboard. (Markham/Novell Communications)

outdoor advertising. To give some idea of the dollar amounts involved, in 1988 approximately $31 billion was spent on newspaper ads compared to $26 billion spent on TV. About $21 billion was spent on direct mail. Since 1960, newspapers have shown a slight decrease in their relative share of advertising volume, as have direct mail and magazines. Television has shown a significant increase while radio and outdoor advertising have shown modest growth from 1960 to 1988.

Agency Compensation

How an advertising agency makes money is not well known outside the agency and media community. This section will discuss two common methods: (1) media commissions and (2) retainers.

Historically, the major mass media have allowed advertising agencies a 15 percent commision on the time and space that they purchase. This practice came about because the media recognized that agencies saved them a great deal of expense in making sales and collecting fees. In simplified form, here's how the commission system works. Let's assume you have a new product and have enlisted the services of an agency to help you market it. You wish to run an ad in a particular magazine that will cost $1000. Your agency places the order, prepares the ad, and sends it to the magazine. After the ad appears, the magazine sends the agency a bill for $1000. The agency passes this bill on to you. You send $1000 to the agency, which then deducts its 15 percent commission ($150 in this case) and sends the remainder ($850) to the magazine. If the total ad charges were $10,000, the agency would retain $1500 in commission. Recently, however, the traditional 15 percent commission fee has come under fire. Some advertisers feel the figure is too high and negotiate for a lower percentage. The big three automakers, for example, pay about a 12 percent commission. Other advertisers are putting agencies on a sliding scale that's tied to

---

Great Ideas That Failed, Part II

Coca-Cola planned to make headlines in 1988 by broadcasting the world's first 3-D commerical. Coke had heard that ABC's ''Moonlighting'' was planning the first network series episode in 3-D as its 1988 season finale. Coke thought that a 3-D ad during the program would recapture some of the publicity that was going to the new Michael Jackson commercials for Pepsi. Coke agreed to promote the ''Moonlighting'' episode with expensive displays at grocery and convenience stores and to hold a big promotional sweepstakes before the episode aired. Coke also planned to distribute special 3-D viewing glasses developed by the company to more than a quarter-million outlets where Coke was sold, including McDonald's restaurants.

As Coke was gearing up for the event, the Writers Guild of America went on strike, the last episode of ''Moonlighting'' was canceled, and Coke was stuck with an awful lot of 3-D glasses. Undaunted, the company ran the promotion during the 1989 Superbowl. Not to be outdone, Pepsi quickly ran an ad that suggested Coke had a strange view of reality—the ad depicted a group of Coke executives sitting at a conference table wearing those cellophane 3-D glasses.

---

the performance of the advertised product. If sales go up, the agency gets more money. If they go down, the compensation is reduced. Other companies are opting for a fixed fee plus reduced commission arrangement. In fact, by the late-1980s, only about half of all advertisers were using the straight commission arrangement.

The retainer system is somewhat similar to the retainers paid to lawyers or accountants. The agency and the advertiser agree on a minimum monthly or annual fee that the agency is to receive for its services. Sometimes any commissions earned by the agency during this period are charged against this fee. In other instances, the services performed by the agency for the client may not produce commission income (e.g., research, annual report preparation), in which case the flat fee is charged.

BUSINESS-TO-BUSINESS ADVERTISING

As its name suggests, business-to-business advertising is designed to sell products and services not to general consumers but to other businesses. This type of advertising is not as visible as consumer advertising since business advertising is typically confined to specialized trade publications, direct mail, professional journals, and special display advertising planned for trade shows. Recently, however, some business-to-business ads have turned up in the mass media.

Although its visibility might not be high, business-to-business advertising is big business, ringing up about $100 billion in revenue in 1987. Some students ignore a career in business-to-business advertising because they feel it's not as glamorous as consumer advertising. There may be some truth to this: Selling a chemical solvent, bench-top fermenter, or blast furnace is not as flashy as designing a campaign for a sleek new sports car. In its own way, though, business advertising poses greater creative challenges. Coming up with a theme to sell the sports car is probably a lot easier than coming up with a winning idea for the chemical solvent.

An example of a business-to-business print ad in a specialized business publication: CompuServe promotes its information services. (Billy Barnes)

Consumer vs. Business-to-Business Advertising

There are some obvious differences between advertising directed at consumers and business advertising. This section will list four.

First, the target audience in business advertising is much smaller. In some industries, the audience may number in the hundreds. Companies that manufacture storage tanks for petroleum products have determined that there are only 400 people in the United States authorized to purchase their product. In other areas, it may be in the thousands. This means, of course, that the media used to reach the target market must be selected carefully. In the nuclear reactor business, perhaps one or two publications are read by everyone in the market.

Second, most of the products that are advertised tend to be technical, complicated, and high priced. For the advertiser, this means that the ads will probably contain a great deal of technical information and will stress accuracy.

Third, the buyers will be professionals. Unlike the consumer market where anybody can buy the product, the targets in business-to-business advertising are usually purchasing agents whose only job is to acquire products and services for their company. Generally speaking, the decisions of the purchasing agent are based on reason and research. An error of a penny or two on a large purchase might cost the company thousands of dollars. Consequently, business advertising typically uses the rational approach. Additionally, it's important for the advertisers to know exactly who makes the buying decision, since most purchases in large businesses are generally made in consultation with others in the company.

Fourth, personal selling plays a greater role in the business arena and advertising is frequently seen as supporting the sales staff in the field. As a result, ad budgets in the business sector may not be as high as their consumer counterparts.

Media

The media mix for business advertising is also different from consumer advertising. Since the target audience tends to be small, personalized media are best. Business publications tend to be the mainstay of a lot of campaigns. One study suggested that about 60 percent of industrial advertising dollars went to business and trade publications. Trade publications can be horizontal, dealing with a job function without regard to industry (such as *Purchasing Agent*), or vertical, covering all job types in an entire industry, such as *LP/Gas*.

Direct mail is also a valuable business advertising tool. Highly differentiated mailing lists can be prepared and ads sent to the most likely prospects. Research has shown that direct mail is perhaps better accepted among business people than among consumers. Whereas a large percentage of direct mail material is thrown out unopened by the general public, about three-quarters of all business people, according to a survey done in the early 1980s, read or at least scan their direct mail ads.

Advertising in trade catalogs is particularly important to those companies that sell through distributors rather than their own sales staff. Since a catalog is a direct reflection of the company, extra care is taken to make sure it is up-to-date, accurate, and visually appealing.

A business-to-business television ad that appeared during many sports and news programs: Wang promotes its computer networking capabilities to businesses that want to improve their internal communication. (Wang Laboratories, Inc.)

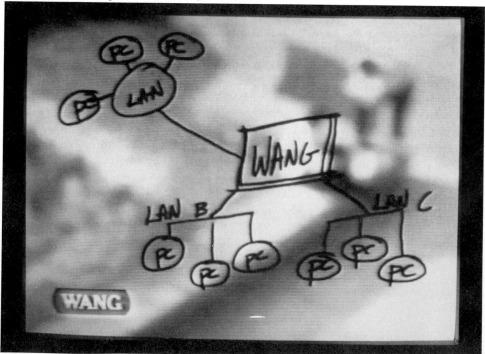

Business-to-business advertising in the mass media used to be rare, but some large companies, such as Federal Express, IBM, and Xerox, have used it to great effect. Federal Express, for example, found that its business increased more than 40 percent after it started to advertise in consumer media. Purchasing time and space in the mass media must be done skillfully because of the expense and the chance of wasted coverage if the right decision makers are not in the audience. Consequently, those firms that do use the mass media buy time on TV shows that draw an older demographic mix, such as "60 Minutes," or buy space in business magazines or general news magazines. *Business Week*, *Fortune*, and *Forbes* are obvious choices. Some publications, such as *Time* and *Newsweek*, have special editions that go to the business community.

Appeals

Close attention is paid to the copy in business-to-business advertising. A lot of consumer ads depend on impression and style to carry their message. The copy tends to be brief and can cater to the emotions. Business copy tends to be longer, more detailed, and more factual. A premium is placed on accuracy and completeness. If the ad contains technical inaccuracy or unsubstantiated exaggeration, the credibility of the product is compromised. Some of the most used formats in business advertising are testimonials, case histories, new product news, and demonstrations.

This is not to say, however, that all industrial ads should be stodgy and dull. In recent years, several ad agencies specializing in business ads have introduced warmth, humor, and creativity into their messages. The philosophy behind this movement is that business people are also consumers and that they respond as consumers to business and trade ads. For example, the headline in an ad for New Zealand Kiwifruit promised to tell grocers "how to rid your store of these ugly little brown things." The body copy stressed the importance of displaying the kiwis next to traditional fruit such as strawberries and peaches, which would encourage shoppers to snap them up. Federal Express ran a print ad that featured a Federal Express Overnight Letter Package next to a plain brown envelope that might be sent though the postal system. Under the Federal Express envelope was "V.I.P."; under the brown envelope, "R.I.P." It's likely that this trend will continue.

CAREERS IN ADVERTISING

Although exact figures are hard to determine, there are more than 200,000 people working in the advertising business, with approximately 85,000 of those employed at advertising agencies. Job prospects appear bright for the future. The increasing amount of consumer goods being produced along with more intense competition among existing companies will create a sustained need for advertising specialists in the years ahead. Many experts think that opportunities will be the greatest in the advertising departments of large to medium size companies. No matter where a person intends to work, there are certain guidelines that are helpful in providing an overall view of the field.

Entry-Level Positions

Most advertising departments or advertising agencies rarely hire generalists; they prefer people with some degree of specialization. Consequently, a job applicant must make some basic decisions early in his or her professional training. Probably the first decision is whether to concentrate on the creative or the business side of the industry.

The creative side, as mentioned earlier, consists of the copywriters, art directors, graphic artists, photographers, and broadcast production specialists that put the ads together. Entry-level jobs would include junior copywriter, creative trainee, junior art director, and production assistants. In most of these positions, a college degree in advertising or the visual arts is helpful, with a secondary concentration in marketing, English, sociology, or psychology also a benefit. For those preferring to work in the creative area, you need to develop a **portfolio**, a collection of the best examples of your professional work. This work might have been done while you were still in school or on the job. Most employees expect to see such a sampling of your work during the job interview.

Working on the business side of the industry refers to choosing a career as an account executive, a media planner, market researcher, traffic manager, or business manager. Proper preparation for this career includes extensive course work in both advertising and business with particular emphasis on marketing. Common entry-level positions in these fields are assistant media buyer, research assistant, junior account executive, account service trainee, or a position in the traffic department. One of the most common entry-level jobs is that of traffic coordinator, the person who makes sure that all production work gets to the proper place at the proper time. Since this job provides a good experience with all of the various departments in the firm, it is a good place for a newcomer to gain valuable experience. Some advertising agencies have training programs (although these are becoming harder to find), and others sponsor internships that make the initial jump into the business a little easier for the newcomer to master. The American Association of Advertising Agencies also has a free pamphlet, *A Guide to Careers in Advertising*, which can be requested from its New York office.

Finally, agency and advertising departments in private companies are not the only places to look for potential employment. There are a significant number of opportunities available in companies that supply their goods and services to advertisers. For example, freelance artists, photographers, jingle writers, film and video tape producers, sound recording specialists, and casting specialists are just some of the people needed by media suppliers. And, as has been pointed out in previous chapters, many people work for the various media in their advertising departments. These include copywriters at radio stations, people who sell newspaper and magazine space or radio and TV time; market researchers, sales promotion experts, and many others.

Upward Mobility

Opportunities for advancement in advertising are excellent. Outstanding performance is rewarded quickly, and many young people progress swiftly through the ranks. Beginning creative people typically become senior copywriters or senior art directors. Eventually, some may progress to become creative director, the person in charge of all creative services. On the business side, research assistants and assistant buyers can hope to become research directors and media directors. Account trainees, if they perform according to expectations, move up to account executives and later may become management supervisors. The climb to success can occur rapidly; many agencies are run by people who achieved top status before they reached forty.

SUGGESTIONS FOR FURTHER READING

The following books contain more information about the concepts and topics discussed in this chapter.

ARLEN, MICHAEL, *Thirty Seconds,* New York: Penguin Books, 1979.

BOVEE, COURTLAND, AND WILLIAM ARENS, *Contemporary Advertising*, Homewood, Ill.: Richard D. Irwin, 1982.

DUNN, S. WATSON, ARNOLD BARBAN, DEAN KRUGMAN, AND LEONARD REID, *Advertising: Its Role in Modern Marketing*, Hinsdale, Ill.: Dryden, 1990.

ENGEL, JACK, *Advertising*: The Process and the Practice, New York: McGraw-Hill, 1980.

RUSSELL, THOMAS, AND RON LANE, *Kleppner's Advertising Procedures*, 11th ed., Englewood Cliffs, N.J.: Prentice-Hall, 1990.

Part Five

Regulation of the Mass Media

Chapter 17

Formal Controls: Laws, Rules, Regulations

Formal controls over the mass media include laws, court decisions that refine those laws, and rules and regulations administered by government agencies. In this chapter we will discuss five different areas where these formal controls are important: (1) the controversy over a free system of mass communication, (2) copyright, (3) restrictions on obscenity and pornography, (4) the regulation of radio and television, and (5) the regulation of advertising. Unfortunately, many students have the idea that the field of mass communication law and regulations is dull and boring. Nothing could be further from the truth. In what other textbook could you read about raunchy magazines, the CIA, soldiers of fortune, mass murderers, women in men's locker rooms, juicy divorces, and a man who owned a submarine?

THE PRESS, THE LAW, AND THE COURTS

A Free Press

As noted in Chapter 4, the idea of a free press did not catch on at first in America. The early colonial papers had problems if they were not "published by authority," that is, open to censorship by the Crown. Through the Stamp Act, the British government attempted to suppress hostile opinion by taxation. Recognizing these dangers to a free press, the framers of the Constitution added an amendment to that document. This amendment (the **First Amendment**) stated in part that "Congress shall make no law . . . abridging the freedom of speech, or of the press." The precise meaning and interpretation of these words, however, have been open to some debate. Let's examine some key instances in which press and government have come into conflict.

Prior Restraint

When the government attempts to censor the press by restraining it from publishing or broadcasting material, it is called **prior restraint.** Such attempts have been relatively rare. Nonetheless, this area does serve to illustrate that the provisions in the First Amendment are not absolute. The Supreme Court has ruled that under certain circumstances, prior restraint or censorship of the press is permitted, but the government faces a difficult task in proving that the restraint is justified. There are some obvious examples of legal censorship. During wartime a newspaper could be prevented from publishing the sailing schedules of troop transports; a radio station could be prohibited from broadcasting the location and numbers of soldiers on the front lines. Other attempts at prior restraint have not been particularly successful; the Supreme Court has generally upheld the right of the press. There are two specific cases in this area that are beneficial for us to examine. One is not widely known; the other made the front pages.

Near Case. During the 1920s, the Minnesota legislature passed a law under which newspapers that were considered public nuisances could be curtailed by means of an **injunction** (an order from a court that requires somebody to do something or refrain from doing something). The motives behind this law may have been praiseworthy because it appears to have been designed to prevent abusive attacks on minority groups. Using this law, a county attorney sought an injuction against the *Saturday Press* and the paper's manager, J. M. Near, on the grounds that the paper had printed malicious statements about city officials. In 1931, the Supreme Court ruled that the Minnesota law was unconstitutional. Said the Court:

> The fact that for approximately 150 years there has been almost an entire absence of attempts to impose previous restraints upon publications relating to the malfeasance of public officers is significant of the deep-seated conviction that such restraints would violate constitutional rights.

It would be forty years before this issue was raised again.

The Pentagon Papers. U.S. Attorney General John Mitchell was anxious to see the Sunday, June 13, 1971, edition of the *New York Times*. Mitchell had attended the wedding of President Richard Nixon's daughter Tricia the day before, and he wanted to see how the *Times* had covered it. On the left side of page one, Mitchell saw a flattering picture of the president with his daughter on his arm. Next to the wedding picture, another story caught Mitchell's eyes: "Vietnam Archive: Pentagon Study Traces 3 Decades of Growing U.S. Involvement." As Mitchell read further he realized that the *Times* article was sure to cause problems.

The basis for the story in the *Times* began three years earlier when then Secretary of Defense Robert McNamara became disillusioned with the Vietnam War and ordered a massive study of its origins. This study, known eventually as the Pentagon Papers, was put together by thirty-six different people and ran for more than 7000 pages. The final report was classified "Top Secret—Sensitive." During April of 1971 one of those Pentagon staff members who compiled the report leaked a copy to a reporter for the *New York Times*. After much study and secrecy (the *Times* rented a suite at a New York hotel for staff members working on the story, furnished it with a safe, and put guards outside), the paper was ready to publish the story in nine different installments. The U.S. Justice Department, under John Mitchell's direction, asked a U.S. District Court judge to halt publication of the stories on the grounds that they would "cause irreparable injury to the defense interests of the United States." The order was granted, and for the first time in history a U.S. paper was ordered by the courts to suppress a specific story. By then, however, other newspapers had obtained copies of some or all of the Pentagon documents and started publishing them. The Justice Department sought more restraining orders, but as soon

The first installment of the Pentagon Papers appeared in the New York Times. *Attempts by the government to halt further publication ended when the Supreme Court ruled in favor of the* Times. *(© 1971 by the New York Times Company.)*

as one paper was ordered to stop publishing another newspaper in another part of the country would pick up the series. It was obvious that the Supreme Court would eventually have to intervene.

The Court did intervene and with uncharacteristic haste. On June 30, 1971, only seventeen days after the papers first appeared and only four days after hearing oral arguments on the case, the Court decided in favor of the newspaper's right to publish the information. Naturally, the staff at the *New York Times* was delighted. The paper called the decision a ''ringing victory for freedom under law.'' Upon closer examination, however, the victory was not quite as ringing as it was made out to be. The Court did not state that prior restraint could never be invoked against the press. Instead, it pointed out that the government ''carries a heavy burden of showing justification'' for imposing restraint. The government, in the opinion of the Court, had not shown sufficient grounds for doing this. The government was free, if it wished, to bring other prior-restraint cases to the courts to establish exactly how much justification it needed to stifle publication. In addition, each of the nine judges wrote a separate opinion that highlighted the ambiguities and complexities surrounding this topic. Perhaps the best summary of the case was put forward by the Twentieth Century Fund's Task Force on Government and the Press: ''While basic issues were

Prior Restraint and the High School Press

A 1988 Supreme Court decision left little doubt that there was one area where authorities could exercise prior restraint—the high school newsroom. The case began in 1983 when a principal in Hazelwood, Missouri, deleted from the high school paper two articles, one on teenage pregnancy and one about divorce, on the grounds that they were inappropriate.

Three students, with the help of the American Civil Liberties Union, filed suit in district court, arguing that their First Amendment rights were being violated. The district court found in favor of the school system. The students appealed this decision and were de-

lighted when the appeals court reversed the district court. Ultimately, however, the case wound up at the Supreme Court, which sided with the district court's decision in favor of the school system.

In its decision, the Court ruled that the paper was an integral part of the school's educational function. The paper was part of the regular journalism curriculum and produced using school supplies and personnel. The staff was restricted to journalism students. As such, it was not a "public forum" and not entitled to First Amendment protection.

posed, basic issues were not resolved." The Task Force went on to say: "The fact remains that there is as yet no authoritative concept of whether publication boundaries exist."

The prior-restraint problem cropped up again three years after the release of the Pentagon Papers when a book, *The CIA and the Cult of Intelligence*, was published with several blank spaces filled only with the word "Deleted." The Central Intelligence Agency had successfully persuaded the courts that parts of the book should be censored because some information had been classified by the agency and the book's author had made an agreement with the CIA nineteen years earlier not to divulge classified information.

In a related case, a former CIA agent published a book called *Decent Interval* without submitting it for prepublication review as expressly required by his employment agreement with the intelligence agency. The government successfully sued the author and won the right to all his royalties stemming from the book. In 1982, Congress passed the Intelligence Identities Protection Act, which made it a federal crime for people to publish anything that they have reason to know will disclose the identity of U.S. intelligence agents. In addition, the Reagan administration, much to the chagrin of the press, managed to keep all civilian reporters and photographers from early coverage of the invasion of Grenada. Some journalists trying to get there were turned back under threat of harm. No reporters were allowed on the island until the third day of the fighting.

The situation for journalists improved somewhat in 1988 when the U.S. Navy started escorting reflagged Kuwaiti tankers through the Persian Gulf. The Department of Defense established a National Media Pool, which granted a limited number of reporters access to the scene. The news media gave mixed reviews to the arrangement, praising the Pentagon for allowing news personnel aboard ships but criticizing the slowness with which stories were transmitted back to the United States.

To sum up, there is a strong constitutional case against prior restraint of the press but, nonetheless, gray areas still exist where censorship might be legal. These areas will probably remain ambiguous until further court cases help define the limits of government authority in this area. It is likely, however, that the barriers against prior restraint will remain formidable.

For its part, the government is free to employ other measures, such as the Grenada ban or controlled media pools, to discourage disclosure of sensitive diplomatic and military information.

PROTECTING NEWS SOURCES

Before we begin an examination of this topic, we should point out that the issues are fairly complicated. Conflicting interests are involved. Reporters argue that if they are forced to disclose confidential sources, those sources will dry up and the public's right to know will be adversely affected. The government arguments cite the need for the administration of justice and the rights of an individual to a fair trial.

Perhaps a hypothetical example will help bring these issues into focus. Suppose you are a reporter for a campus newspaper. One of your sources calls you late one night and informs you that several students have started a drug ring that has monopolized the sale of illegal drugs on campus. To check the accuracy of this report, you call another one of your sources, one who in the past has given you reliable information on campus drug dealing. This second source confirms what your caller told you and adds more details. For obvious reason, both of your sources ask not to be identified and you agree. Based on these reports and some additional research on your part, you publish a lengthy article in the campus newspaper about the drug ring. A few days later you are summoned before a grand jury that is investigating criminal drug dealings. You are asked to reveal your sources. If you refuse, you will be charged with contempt and possibly fined or sent to jail. What do you do?

The Reporter's Privilege

Other reporters have found themselves in the same fix. One was Paul Branzburg. In 1969, Branzburg wrote a story for the *Louisville Courier-Journal* in which he described how two local residents were synthesizing hashish from marijuana. His article stated that he had promised not to reveal their identities. Shortly thereafter, Branzburg was subpoenaed (ordered to appear) by the county grand jury. He refused to answer questions about his sources, claiming, in part, that to do so would violate the First Amendment provision for freedom of the press. The case ultimately reached the Supreme Court, which ruled that the First Amendment did not protect reporters from the obligation of testifying before grand juries to answer questions concerning a criminal investigation. Initially, this ruling was viewed as a setback for reporters' rights. Upon closer examination, however, the Court did suggest some situations in which the reporter's claim to privilege would be valid. These included harassment of news reporters, instances in which grand juries do not operate in good faith, and situations in which there is only a remote connection between the investigation and the information sought. Additionally, the Court suggested that Congress and the states could further define the rights of a reporter to protect sources by enacting legislation (called **shield laws**) to that effect. Approximately half of the states had shield laws on the books or passed them shortly after the Branzburg decision.

After the Branzburg decision, state courts were somewhat inconsistent in their rulings. On the one hand, several cases have ended with the courts upholding the reporter's right to keep his or her sources secret. In Florida, Lucy Ware Morgan, a reporter for the *St. Petersburg Times*, refused to disclose her source for a story about a grand jury report that discussed corruption in city government. She was promptly convicted of contempt of court and received a ninety-day jail sentence. In 1976, however, the Florida Supreme Court overturned the conviction and ruled in Ms. Morgan's favor. Using the Branzburg decision as a guideline, the court concluded that the name of her source was not relevant to the investigation of a crime and that the contempt charge was designed to harass her. Other decisions have narrowly defined the test of relevancy between the case at hand and the reporter's sources. In Virginia, a newspaper reporter refused to identify a source during testimony at a murder trial. The lawyer for the accused argued that the source's name was needed to question the credibility of a prosecution witness. The Virginia Supreme Court ruled in favor of the reporter and stated that a reporter's privilege must yield only when the defendant's need for the information is essential. To be essential, said the court, the information had to (1) relate directly to the defendant's guilt or innocence, (2) bear on the reduction of an offense, or (3) concern the mitigation of a sentence.

Nevertheless, there are other decisions that, from the point of view of working journalists, appear less reassuring. For example, consider the somewhat complicated case of William Farr. In 1971, Farr was a reporter for the *Los Angeles Herald-Examiner*, covering the Charles Manson murder trial. Farr discovered that a potential witness was going to reveal a bizarre plot in which the Manson "family" was going to slay several movie stars. Farr's story made page one and angered the trial judge. (The judge had ordered all participants in the trial not to talk to the press. Someone evidently had violated that order.) The judge subsequently ordered the reporter to reveal his sources. Farr cited California's shield law and refused to divulge his sources, and the judge did not press the issue at the time. After the trial ended, however, Farr left journalism and took a different job. The Manson trial judge once again ordered Farr to reveal his sources, now claiming that Farr was no longer covered by California's shield law. Farr again refused and was given an open-ended jail sentence for contempt. After serving forty-six days, Farr was released pending the outcome of an appeal. In a related action, he was ordered to serve another five days and pay a $500 fine. In 1974, Farr was almost forced to go through the whole ordeal again when he was called before a grand jury investigating perjury charges; once again, he refused to reveal his sources. Farr was initially found in contempt of court, but this action was reversed within a week. To make matters even more complicated, Farr became involved in a libel suit connected with this case and once again refused to answer questions about his sources. Farr's ordeal finally came to an end when the statute of limitations ran out before those bringing the libel suit were ready for trial.

As the 1980s drew to a close, journalists regarded shield laws as helpful, but most realized they were not the powerful protectors of the press that many had hoped for. As of 1988, twenty-six states had passed shield laws, but this number hasn't changed since 1974. In addition, the laws themselves represent a bewildering collection of provisions, qualifications, and exceptions. Some state laws protect only confidential material; some protect the reporter from revealing the name of a source but do not protect the information obtained from sources. Other state laws confer less protection if the reporter is involved in a libel case. In some states, shield laws don't apply to reporters subpoenaed by a grand jury.

Further, many state courts are interpreting the shield laws on a case-by-case basis and ignoring or limiting the interpretation of some of the broad protections contained in the law. For example, in New York, which has a strong shield law, the court ruled that its protection did not extend to TV station outtakes (tape or film segments not shown on the air). A Pennsylvania court recently ruled that its state shield law doesn't apply to some libel cases.

Overall, about a third of the shield law rulings by state courts since the mid-1970s have been against the press. On the positive side, however, is the fact that even in those states that have no shield laws, many have recognized a reporter's privilege to resist a subpoena. On the other hand, to make matters even more complicated, in 1988 a jury granted a sizable monetary award in a breach of contract suit in which a man sued a journalist who had promised him confidentiality and then revealed his name. It's obvious that this is an area where reporters should tread carefully.

Search and Seizure

Finally, there is the troublesome question of protecting notes and other records that might disclose sources. In this regard, the courts have offered little protection. Three particular cases have disturbed the news media. In 1971, four police officers entered the offices of the *Stanford Daily*, the campus newspaper of Stanford University, and produced a search warrant authorizing them to search for photographs of a clash between demonstrators and police that the *Daily* had covered the day before. The newspaper brought suit against the authorities, charging that its First Amendment rights had been violated. In 1978, the Supreme Court ruled that the search was legal. (In 1980, however, Congress extended some protection to newsrooms by passing a bill that would require the government to secure a subpoena in order to obtain records held by reporters. The scope of a subpoena is somewhat more limited than that of a search warrant.)

In the second case, the U.S. Court of Appeals in the District of Columbia decided another case that further eroded reporters' rights to protect sources. In 1974, the Reporters Committee for Freedom of the Press filed suit against the American Telephone and Telegraph Company (AT&T) because the company would not pledge to keep records of reporters' toll calls safe from government scrutiny. (An analysis of these calls might help to locate a reporter's source of information.) The Court of Appeals ruled that it was legal for the government to examine such records without the reporter's knowledge or consent.

The last case involved *New York Times* reporter Myron Farber. During 1976, Farber had been reporting the investigation into mysterious deaths at a New Jersey hospital. The stories led to the indictment of a prominent physician on charges of poisoning five patients. Defense lawyers ultimately subpoenaed notes and documents pertaining to the case that were held by Farber and the *Times*. Both Farber and the paper refused, and both were convicted of contempt of court. Farber was sentenced to six months in jail and a $1000 fine; the *Times* was slapped with a $100,000 fine and was ordered to pay $5000 every day until it complied with the court's order. The *Times* ultimately turned over its files, but a judge ruled that the paper had "sanitized" them by removing some relevant material and reinstated the fine. Farber, meanwhile, had spent twenty-seven days in jail. (The case was complicated somewhat when it was disclosed that Farber had agreed to write a book on the case for a major publishing company. Some felt that Farber was holding out in order to make revelations in his book and thus increase its sales.) Eventually, Farber wound up spending forty days in jail, and the *Times* paid $285,000 in fines. All penalties finally ended with the jury's verdict that the physician was innocent.

New York Times *reporter Myron Farber talks with newsmen after spending forty days in jail for refusing to turn over to the court notes and documents pertaining to the investigation of a murder case. (UPI/Bettmann Newsphotos)*

Judging from the above, perhaps the safest conclusion that we can draw is that a reporter's privilege in protecting sources and notes is unlikely to be absolute. Even those decisions that have favored journalists have been qualified. It also appears that further developments in this area will be put together on a piece-by-piece basis by lower courts unless the Supreme Court generates a precise decision or the legislature passes a comprehensive law. As for reporters, they must carefully consider these issues when they promise confidentiality to a news source.

COVERING THE COURTS

The conflict of competing interests has repeatedly cropped up when news media attempt to cover the courts. On the one hand, the Sixth Amendment guarantees a trial before an impartial jury; on the other, the First Amendment guarantees the freedom of the press. Trial judges are responsible for the administration of justice; reporters are responsible for informing the public about the legal system. Sometimes the responsibilities clash.

Publicity Before and During a Trial

If a potential jury member has read, seen, or heard stories in the news media about a defendant that appear to indicate that person's guilt, it is possible that the defendant will not receive a fair trial. Although research has not produced definitive evidence linking pretrial publicity to prejudice, this concern has been at the heart of several court decisions that have castigated the news media for trying cases in the newspaper or on television instead of in the courtroom.

The 1960s saw a flurry of cases that suggested that the Supreme Court was taking a close look at pretrial publicity. In 1961, the Court for the first time reversed a state's criminal conviction entirely because pretrial publicity had made it impossible to select an impartial jury. The case concerned Leslie Irvin, a rather unsavory character who was arrested and charged with six murders. Newspapers carried police-issued press releases that said ''Mad Dog'' Irvin had confessed to all six killings. The local media seized upon this story with a vengeance, and many stories referred to Irvin as the ''confessed slayer of six.'' Of the 430 potential jurors examined by attorneys, 90 percent had formed opinions about Irvin's guilt—opinions that ranged from suspicion to absolute certainty that he was guilty. Irvin was convicted—hardly a surprise—and sentenced to death. After six years of complicated legal maneuvers, made even more complicated because Irvin managed to escape from prison, the case went before the Supreme Court. The Court ruled that the pretrial publicity had ruined the defendant's chances for a fair trial and sent the case back to be retried. (Irvin, who had been recaptured, was again found guilty but this time was sentenced to life imprisonment.)

Perhaps the most famous case of pretrial publicity concerned an Ohio physician. On July 4, 1954, the wife of Cleveland-area osteopath Dr. Sam Sheppard was found slain in the couple's home. Sheppard became a prime suspect, and the news media, especially the Cleveland newspapers, were impatient for his arrest. ''Why Isn't Sam Sheppard in Jail?'' and ''Why Don't Police Quiz Top Suspect?'' were headlines that appeared over page-one editorials. News reports carried the results of alleged sci-entific tests that cast doubt on Sheppard's version of the crime (these tests were never brought up at the trial). Articles stressed Sheppard's extramarital affairs as a

The murder conviction of Dr. Sam Sheppard (shown here at his first trail) was overturned by the Supreme Court because of the extremely prejudicial publicity surrounding his arrest and trial. In a second trial, Sheppard was found not guilty. (UPI/Bettmann Newsphotos)

possible motive for the crime. After his arrest, the news stories and editorials continued. There were enough of them with headlines such as "Dr. Sam Faces Quiz at Jail on Marilyn's Fear of Him" and "Blood is Found in Garage" to fill five scrapbooks. Every juror but one admitted reading about the story in the newspapers. The sensationalized coverage continued during the trial itself, which produced a guilty verdict. Twelve years later the Supreme Court reversed Sheppard's conviction because of the extremely prejudiced publicity. This case assumed added importance because the Court listed six safeguards that judges might invoke to prevent undue influence from publicity. These safeguards included sequestering the jury (i.e., moving them into seclusion), moving the case to another county, and placing restrictions on statements made by lawyers, witnesses, or others who might divulge damaging information.

The dilemma surfaced again in 1983 when a federal judge prohibited CBS from showing videotapes of former automaker John DeLorean talking to undercover agents during a drug "sting" operation. DeLorean was about to stand trial for conspiracy to import cocaine and the judge felt that the tapes would harm DeLorean's chance for a fair trial. An appeals court overturned the judge's ruling, pointing out that the tapes were not necessarily prejudicial and the trial court judge had not adequately considered other measures to assure DeLorean a fair trial.

These cases and others like them have prompted efforts to develop guidelines to prevent this problem from recurring. The U.S. Justice Department issued a set of rules that would restrict what information could be released to the press when a person was arrested for a federal crime. The American Bar Association adopted a similar but more stringent set of guidelines covering information release. In many states, voluntary agreements between the press and the legal profession have been drawn up.

Gag Rules

Despite these efforts, however, the controversy has persisted. Some judges have announced restrictive orders, or **gag rules,** that restrain the participants in a trial (attorneys, witnesses, defendants) from giving information to the media or that actually restrain media coverage of events that occur in court. For example, a Superior Court judge in a Washington murder trial ordered reporters to report only on events that occurred in front of a jury. Two reporters violated this rule by writing about events that took place in the courtroom while the jury was not present; they were subsequently charged with contempt. The Washington Supreme Court refused to review this ruling. In other cases, the news media have won what might be called hollow victories. To illustrate, in New York in 1971 a judge closed a trial to both public and press. News organizations appealed, and the judge's ruling was ultimately declared incorrect. Although the press may have won a victory in principle, it lost one in fact—by the time the closure rule had been judged invalid, the trial had already been conducted behind closed doors. Two Louisiana reporters also won but lost when they violated a gag order and reported testimony given in open court. They were found guilty of contempt and fined $300. A higher court ruled that the gag order was unconstitutional, but the contempt fine was nonetheless upheld. The gag order, said the court, could not be ignored even though it might be invalid. Reporters must obey judicial orders until they are reversed, or reporters will suffer the consequences.

The whole question of gag orders reached the Supreme Court in 1976. A Nebraska judge had prohibited reporters from revealing certain information about a mass murder case. The Nebraska Press Association appealed the order to the Supreme Court. The Court ruled on the side of the press association and held that reporting of judicial proceedings in open court cannot be prohibited. Once again, upon first examination, this rule appeared to be a significant victory for the press. As time passed, however, it became apparent that the Nebraska decision had left the way open for court-ordered restrictions on what the trial participants could say to the press. The decision also seemed to indicate that some legal proceedings, primarily those that take place before the actual trial begins, might be legitimately closed to the public. By the early 1980s, this was exactly what was happening. Although the press was left free to report what it chose, its news sources were muzzled by judicial order. During the late 1970s, judges began holding pretrial hearings in private in order to limit pretrial publicity. A 1979 Supreme Court decision held this practice to be constitutional. In 1980, the Court did go on record as stating that the press did, in fact, have a constitutional right to attend criminal trials. *Pretrial* events, however, such as those stated above, might still be closed. Because many criminal cases are settled out of court, these pretrial hearings are often the only public hearings held.

In the years 1980–1988, the press has gained wider access to court proceedings. In 1984, the Supreme Court ruled that the jury selection process should be open to the press except in extreme circumstances. In a second case that same year, the Court established standards that judges must meet before they can close a pretrial hearing. A 1986 Supreme Court decision, however, gave the press a major victory in its efforts to secure access to pretrial proceedings. The Court held that preliminary trial proceedings must be open to the press unless the judge could demonstrate a "substantial probability that the defendant's right to a fair trial would be violated." Additionally, lower courts have held that the First Amendment right of access to trials also extends to documents used as evidence. Also in 1986, the Supreme Court ruled that the jury selection process, as well as the trial itself, must ordinarily be open to the public. The Court also provided a set of strict guidelines that would justify a private selection of a jury.

These decisions, however, do not give the press an absolute right of access to all court proceedings. Some parts of trials and pretrial hearings may still be closed if the judge can fulfill the court's guidelines regarding closure. Further, the recent court decisions have not changed the legal status surrounding the privacy of grand jury hearings—they continue to have the right to secrecy. All in all, it might be safe to conclude that the press has been given a green light to report matters that occur in open court with little fear of reprisal. But gag orders on news sources and the closing of various legal proceedings threaten to be an area of tension between the press and the judiciary for some time to come.

Cameras and Microphones in the Courtroom

Photojournalists and reporters for radio and television stations have been at somewhat of a disadvantage when it comes to covering a trial. For many years the legal profession has looked with disfavor on the idea of cameras and microphones in the courtroom. There was a time when this attitude may have been entirely justified. The whole problem seems to have begun in 1935 when Bruno Hauptmann was put on trial for the kidnaping and murder of the son of national hero Charles Lindbergh. Remember that news photography and radio journalism were still young in 1935, and this fact may have contributed to some of the abuses that occurred during this trial (see boxed material). After the trial, the American Bar Association adopted

Canon 35 and the Hauptmann Trial

In 1935, nearly three years after the crime, Bruno Hauptmann was tried for the kidnaping and murder of the nineteen-month-old son of national hero Charles Lindbergh. The trial was held in the small, rural town of Flemington, New Jersey. When it opened, more than 150 reporters were packed into a small area reserved for the press. During the trial, this number swelled to about 700 as members of the press corps prowled the corridors and surrounding rooms of the courthouse in an attempt to cover every aspect of the trial. The wire services transmitted more than 11 million words of trial coverage—a million on the first day. About one hundred telegraph technicians had to be on the premises to operate this system, further adding to the crowd. Photography during the trial was forbidden, but photographers were allowed in the courthouse and some were even allowed in the courtroom itself to take pictures when the trial was not in session.

As the trial progressed, the overcrowding got worse and it became obvious that the trial had turned into a media event. The ban against photography during court sessions was broken, but nothing was done about it. A newsreel motion picture camera was placed in the balcony of the courtroom and, despite a promise from the newsreel people that they would not take films during the trial, footage was taken of the testimony of Lindbergh, Hauptmann,

and others. The film was shown in movie theaters throughout the country. Photographers, many of them freelancers, became more aggressive as the trial progressed and contributed to a general lack of courtroom decorum. The crush of reporters also aggravated the already severe overcrowding in the courtroom. The crowds got so bad that the attorneys for both sides actually subpoenaed their friends in order to make sure that they got into the courtroom. One radio reporter, Gabriel Heatter, had no problem getting a seat. The judge's wife enjoyed his broadcasts so much that she prevailed on the judge to give Heatter a place in the front row. In an attempt to scoop the opposition, an Associated Press employee rigged a secret radio transmitter inside the courtroom. On February 13, 1935, the jury brought in a guilty verdict. (Unfortunately, the Associated Press employee got confused and incorrectly sent out the word that Hauptmann was innocent. Embarrassed, the Associated Press had to send out a correction ten minutes later; the employee was subsequently fired.) Out of all this confusion and carnival like atmosphere came Canon 35, a rule adopted by the American Bar Association that would limit courtroom reporting by photographers and radio and television reporters. Controversies that started in that overcrowded courtroom in Flemington are still debated today.

Canon 35 of its Canons of Professional Ethics. This provision stated that the taking of photographs in the courtroom and the broadcasting (later amended to include telecasting) of court proceedings ". . . detract from the essential dignity of the proceedings, distract the participants and witnesses in giving testimony" and should not be permitted. Although Canon 35 is not law, its language or some variation of it was adopted as law by every state except Colorado and Texas.

In 1965 the Supreme Court entered the picture when it ruled on the Billie Sol Estes case. Estes was on trial in Texas for allegedly swindling several farmers. The trial judge, over Estes' objections, had allowed the televising of the trial. Estes was found guilty, but he soon appealed that decision to the Supreme Court on the grounds that the presence of television had deprived him of a fair trial. The high court agreed with Estes and argued for the prohibition of television cameras from the courtroom. The decision said that broadcasting a trial would have a prejudicial impact on jurors, would distract witnesses, and would burden the trial judge with new responsibilities. But, the Court went on, there might come a day when broadcast technology would become portable and unobtrusive and television coverage so commonplace that trials might be broadcast. Thus the decision in the Estes case was not a blanket provision against the televising of trials.

Since 1965, the trend has been toward a general relaxation of the tension between the legal profession and the electronic press. In 1972, the American Bar Association adopted a new code of professional responsibility. Canon 3A(7) of this document superseded the old Canon 35. Canon 3A(7) still maintained the ban against taking photographs and broadcasting in the courtroom, but it did allow the judge the discretion to permit televising a trial to a press room or to another courtroom to accommodate an overflow crowd. In 1981, the Supreme Court ruled that broadcast coverage of a criminal trial is not inherently prejudicial, thereby clearing the way for the presence of radio and TV in the courtroom. At the same time, however, the Court left it up to the states to devise their own system for implementing such coverage.

As of 1988, several different systems had evolved in various states. For example, three states require the consent of all parties concerned before electronic coverage of a criminal case is allowed; other states simply require the consent of the prosecution and defense; still other states permit no coverage at all. As of this writing, thirty-three states had established some permanent system for electronic coverage. TV and radio, however, are still barred from federal courtrooms, including the Supreme Court.

REPORTERS' ACCESS TO INFORMATION

Government Information

Reporting the doings of the government can be a frustrating task if the government insists that information about its activities be kept secret. After World War II, many members of the press complained that government secrecy was becoming a major problem. Reporters were being restricted from meetings, and access to many government documents was difficult to obtain. In the midst of continuing pressure from journalists and consumer groups, Congress passed the **Freedom of Information Act (FOIA)** in 1966. This law gave the public the right to discover what the federal government was up to—with certain exceptions. The law states that every federal executive-branch agency must publish instructions on what methods a member of the public should follow to get information. If information is improperly withheld, a court can force the agency to disclose what is sought. There are nine areas of "exemption" that do not have to be made public. Some of these exemptions are trade secrets, files of law-enforcement investigations, and oil-well maps.

Journalists, however, have not made extensive use of this law. The primary reason seems to be the length of time necessary to secure the actual information. Reporters usually need information in a hurry, and the long time lag associated with the proceedings under the Freedom of Information Act generally makes it less attractive in the eyes of a reporter. Nonetheless, the act has helped in the development of several major stories. In 1987, the *Seattle Times* used Department of Energy reports obtained under the FOIA to put together an award-winning story on safety problems at a nuclear weapons plant. KRON-TV in San Francisco used the FOIA to get Federal Aviation Administration records for a story on air safety.

A "Sunshine Act" also ensures that regular meetings of approximately fifty federal government agencies will be open to the public. There are, however, ten different situations that might permit the agency to meet behind closed doors, so the right of access to these meetings is far from absolute. In addition, many states have similar laws to ensure open records and open meetings.

Access to News Scenes

We have already mentioned this issue in our discussion of the right of the press to attend certain judicial proceedings. But what about the reporters' right of access to news settings outside the courtroom? The law here appears to be in the developmental stage. In the few decisions that have been handed down, the courts have given little support to the notion that the First Amendment guarantees a right of access. In separate rulings, the courts declared that journalists could be sued for invasion of privacy, for trespassing on private property, and for disobeying a police officer's legitimate command to clear the way at the scene of a serious automobile accident. Three of the most relevant Supreme Court opinions have focused on the question of access to prisons and prisoners. In these cases, the courts have ruled that reporters do not have the right to visit specific parts of a prison, to speak to specific prisoners, or to bring cameras inside. In general, the Court seems to be saying that the access rights of the press are not different from the access rights of the general public. When the public is not admitted, neither is the press.

There have been some rulings, however, that have recognized a limited right of access. A Florida decision found that journalists who are customarily invited by police onto private property to view a news scene cannot be prosecuted for trespassing.

On the other hand, another decision in Florida held that local police could not invite the press along on a raid conducted on private property. In another case, a Wisconsin court found that a TV photojournalist who had entered private property with permission from a police officer responding to a call was guilty of trespass. Other recent cases have also questioned the legality of government officials inviting journalists onto private property. In another case, reporters who followed antinuclear demonstrators through a fence onto the property of a utility company were found guilty of trespass. It is becoming difficult for journalists to rely on the argument that common custom and practice serve as a defense against trespass. Probably the safest thing for a journalist to do is to obtain the consent from the owner before entering private property. This is often difficult, of course, since the owner may not be available during a breaking news event.

The courts have allowed access to news settings in order to halt discrimination among journalists. For example, in one case it was ruled that a female journalist could not be barred from entering a baseball team's locker room if male reporters had been admitted. And it was also ruled that the Tennessee State Senate could not bar the reporters of a particular Nashville newspaper from the Senate floor if it allowed reporters from other organizations to be admitted. In sum, the final words on this topic have yet to be written by the courts. A case as influential as the Branzburg or Estes decision has yet to be adjudicated in the area of press access. It is a good bet, however, that such a test will not be long in surfacing.

DEFAMATION

From the above, it is clear that in its news-gathering activities, the press often collides with the government. In addition, the right of free speech and the rights of a free press sometimes come into conflict with the right of an individual to protect his or her reputation. Protection for a person's reputation is found under the laws that deal with defamation.

In order to understand this somewhat complicated area, let's start with some general definitions:

Libel: written defamation that tends to injure a person's reputation or good name or that diminishes the esteem, respect, or good will due a person.

Slander: spoken defamation. (In many states, if a defamatory statement is broadcast, it is considered to be libel even though technically the words are not written. Libel is considered more harmful and usually carries more serious penalties.)

Libel per se: Some words are always libelous. Falsely written accusations, such as labeling a person a ''thief'' or a ''swindler,'' automatically constitute libel.

Libel per quod: Words that seem perfectly innocent in themselves can become libelous under certain circumstances. Erroneously reporting that Mr. Smith was seen eating a steak dinner last night may seem harmless unless Mr. Smith happens to be the president of the Worldwide Vegetarian Society.

In order for someone to win a libel suit brought against the media, that person must prove five things: (1) that he or she has actually been defamed and harmed by the statements; (2) that he or she has been identified (although not necessarily by name); (3) that the defamatory statements have been published; (4) that the media were at fault; and (5) in most instances, that what was published or broadcast was false.

Not every mistake that finds its way into publication is libelous. To report that James Arthur will lead the Fourth of July Parade when in fact Arthur James will lead it is probably not libelous because it is improbable that leading a parade will cause harm to a person's reputation. (Courts have even ruled that it is not necessarily libelous to report incorrectly that a person died. Death, said the courts, is no disgrace.) Actual harm might be substantiated by showing the defamatory remarks led to physical discomfort (such as sleepless nights) or loss of income, or increased difficulty in performing a job.

Identification need not be by name. If a paper erroneously reports that the professor who teaches Psych 101 at 10 A.M. in Quadrangle Hall is taking bribes from his students, that would be sufficient.

Publication, for our purposes, pertains to a statement's appearance in a mass medium and is self-explanatory.

Fault is a little more complicated. To win a libel suit, some degree of fault or carelessness on the part of the media organization must be shown. As we shall see, the degree of fault that must be established depends on several things: (1) who's suing; (2) what the suit is about; and (3) the particular state's laws that are being applied.

A 1986 Supreme Court decision held that private persons (as opposed to public figures) suing for libel must prove that the statements at issue are false, at least when

Handle With Care

Below are listed some red-flag words and expressions that are typical of those that may be libelous *per se*. Extreme care should be exercised in using these words in news reports:

bankrupt	corrupt	blockhead
intemperate	dishonest	rascal
unprofessional	amoral	scoundrel
communistic	disreputable	sneak
incompetent	illegitimate	deadhead
morally delinquent	hypocritical	fool
smooth and tricky	dishonorable	slacker
profiteering	cheating	skunk
sharp-dealing	unprincipled	poltroon
	sneaky	ignoramus

(This list is also a handy reference guide for insults. Simply choose one word from the left list, one from the center, and one from the right, e.g., "You profiteering, amoral poltroon," or "You incompetent, corrupt deadhead." Just make sure that you don't put it in writing and that no third party is listening. Otherwise, you may get hit with a defamation suit.)

the statements involve matters of public concern. For all practical purposes, however, proving that the media were at fault also involves proving the falsity of what was broadcast or published, so that virtually everyone who brings a libel suit must show the wrongness of what was published.

It should be emphasized that a mass medium is responsible for what it carries. It usually cannot hide behind the fact that it only repeated what someone else said. In most situations, a magazine could not defend itself against a libel suit by claiming that it simply quoted a hospital worker who said a colleague was stealing drugs. If, in fact, the hospital worker's colleague was not stealing drugs, the magazine would have to look to some other defense against libel.

What are some of the defenses that can be used? There are three. The first is truth. If what was reported is proven to be true, there is no libel. This defense, however, is rarely used since it is extremely difficult to prove the truth of a statement. In addition, since the Supreme Court's decision placed the burden of proving the falsity of a statement on the person bringing the libel suit, the defense of truth has become even less attractive. A second defense is privilege. There are certain situations in which the courts have held that the public's right to know comes before a person's right to preserve a reputation. Judicial proceedings, arrest warrants, grand-jury indictments, legislative proceedings, and public city-council sessions are examples of situations that are generally acknowledged to be privileged. If a reporter gives a fair and accurate report of these events, no lawsuits can result, even if what is reported contains a libelous statement. The third defense is fair comment and criticism. Any person who thrusts himself or herself into the public eye or is at the center of public attention is open to fair criticism. This means that public officials, professional sports figures, cartoonists, artists, columnists, playwrights, and all those who invite public attention are fair game for comment. This defense applies only to opinion and criticism, not to misrepresentations of fact. You can report that a certain director's new movie stank to high heaven without fear of a lawsuit, but you could not report falsely that the director embezzled funds from the company and expect protection under fair criticism. However, criticism can be quite severe and caustic and still be protected from lawsuit.

In 1964, the Supreme Court significantly expanded the opportunity for comment on the actions of public officials. In a case involving the *New York Times* and an official of the Montgomery, Alabama, police department, the Court ruled that a public official must prove that false and defamatory statements were made with actual malice before a libel suit can be won. The Court also clarified what is meant by actual malice—publishing a statement with the knowledge that it was false or publishing a statement in "reckless disregard" of whether it was false or not. A few years later, the Court expanded this protection to include statements made about public figures as well as public officials. In 1971, it appeared that the Supreme Court would even require private individuals who become involved in events of public concern to prove actual malice before collecting for a libel suit. Three years later, the Court seemed to retreat a little from this position when it held that a lawyer involved in a civil lawsuit was not a public figure, that he was not involved in an event of public interest, and that he did not have to prove actual malice. Even more protection was extended to the private citizen in 1976 in a case concerning the divorce of Mary Alice Firestone from her husband, tire heir Russell Firestone, Jr. The trial lasted seventeen months and received large amounts of media coverage. Ms. Firestone even called several press conferences while the trial was taking place. When *Time* magazine erroneously reported that the divorce had been granted on the grounds of extreme cruelty and adultery, Ms. Firestone sued for libel. (Her husband had charged her with adultery, but adultery was not cited as grounds for the divorce.) *Time* argued that she was a public figure and contended that Ms. Firestone had to show not only that the magazine was inaccurate but also that it acted with malice. The Supreme Court ruled that she was not a public figure, despite all the attendant press coverage, and drew a distinction between legitimate public controversies and those controversies that merely interest the public. The latter, said the Court, are not protected, and actual malice need not be proved.

The Court affirmed this distinction in 1979 by noting that the fact that someone is involved in a "newsworthy" event doesn't make the person a public figure. When a U.S. senator presented a scientist with a satirical award used to denote wasteful spending of government funds, the scientist sued for defamation. The Court ruled that even though the scientist became the subject of media attention, his public prominence before receiving the satirical award did not merit labeling him a public figure. Therefore, he did not have to meet the actual malice standard. Private citizens, however, do have to show some degree of fault or negligence by the media. In many states, this means showing that the media did not exercise ordinary care in publishing a story. Establishing this will allow a private citizen to collect compensation for any actual damages that stemmed from the libel. The big bucks, however, come from punitive damages assessed against the media. These awards are designed to punish the media for their past transgressions and serve as a reminder not to misbehave again. To collect punitive damages, even private citizens must show actual malice.

The mid- to late 1980s were characterized by a large increase in the size of the dollar awards made by jurors to the winners of libel cases. To illustrate, from 1980 to 1982, only 17 percent of the awards were over $1 million. In 1983–1984, some 75 percent exceeded that figure. By 1986, more than 40 percent of the awards were half a million or more. For example, the *Philadelphia Inquirer* lost a libel suit and was ordered to pay $4.5 million. A man who successfully sued *Philadelphia* magazine was awarded $7 million. A jury awarded singer Wayne Newton about $20

What is "Actual Malice"?

Many people are confused by the meaning of the phrase "actual malice" as it applies to defamation. Some individuals mistakenly think that a person who is defamed has to prove evil motives, spite, or ill will on the part of the person or medium that allegedly committed the defamation. Not so. In the famous *New York Times* v. *Sullivan* case, the Supreme Court defined actual malice as (1) publishing something that is known to be false ("I know what I'm publishing is not true but I'm still going to publish it anyway."); or (2) publishing something with reckless disregard for whether it's true or not ("I have good reason to doubt that what I'm publishing is true, but I'm still going to publish it anyway.").

A recent libel case involving CBS, Inc., and Walter Jacobson, a news anchor and commentator at WBBM-TV (the CBS affiliate) in Chicago, illustrates this definition. The Brown & Williamson Tobacco Corporation (maker of Viceroy cigarettes) claimed that Jacobson libeled their company when he charged during a TV commentary that Viceroy was using an ad campaign to persuade children to smoke. Viceroy, said Jacobson, was equating cigarette smoking with "wine, beer, shaving or wearing a bra . . . a declaration of independence and striving for self identity . . . a basic symbol of the growing up process." The commentary cited as evidence a Federal Trade Commission report that claimed the company had been advised by its advertising agency to launch such a campaign. Brown & Williamson, forced to prove actual malice on the part of Jacobson because of the company's position as a public figure, denied ever having launched such a campaign. In fact, company lawyers argued that Brown & Williamson was so outraged by its ad agency's advice that it fired the advertising firm. Further, Brown & Williamson argued that Jacobson knew this fact before he broadcast his commentary. In court, one of the officials for the tobacco company testified that a researcher for Jacobson had been told that the ad agency had been fired and that the campaign was not used. During the trial, Jacobson said that he had rejected a suggestion from this researcher that a disclaimer should be included in the commentary stating that Brown & Williamson had not used the campaign. Evidently, this fact was enough to convince the jury that Jacobson knew that what he was saying was false—thus establishing actual malice. The jury found in favor of the tobacco company and awarded Brown & Williamson more than $5 million in damages.

For their part, Jacobson and CBS still maintain that the commentary was an accurate summary of the Federal Trade Commission report and that Brown & Williamson had a strategy directed toward children, even if the company didn't fully implement it. In late 1985, CBS announced plans to appeal the decision. The appeal was decided in 1988 in favor of the tobacco company. CBS was ordered to pay $3.05 million in damages.

million after finding that he was defamed by an NBC news report. Obviously, these huge awards greatly troubled the press.

On the other side, 70–75 percent of these awards are reduced on appeal and huge awards, such as those just mentioned, are usually drastically cut. In fact, until 1988, every award over $1 million had been overturned on appeal and reduced. In 1988, however, an appeals court ordered a CBS station to pay more than $3 million to a tobacco company libeled in a news report by one of their owned and operated stations (see boxed material).

Additionally, juries do not always return with verdicts against the media, particularly when public figures are involved. Former Israeli Defense Minister Ariel

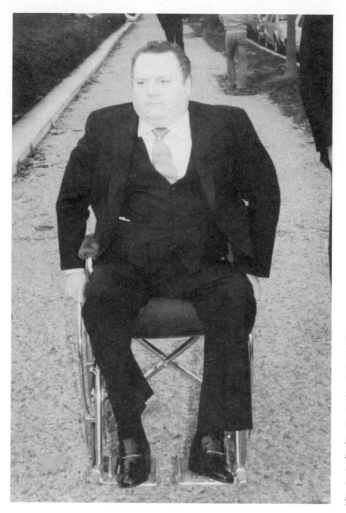

Larry Flynt, publisher of Hustler *magazine, arriving at the Supreme Court, which was reviewing evangelist Jerry Falwell's libel suit against* Hustler *for "emotional distress" caused by a parody of Falwell that appeared in the magazine. The suit was ultimately thrown out of court. (UPI/Bettmann Newsphotos)*

Sharon sued *Time* magazine for $50 million over a paragraph in a 1983 cover story that linked him to a massacre of Palestinian civilians. The jury found that the paragraph in question was indeed false and defamatory and that certain *Time* employees had acted negligently and carelessly. But the jury also found that *Time* had not published the material with actual malice (*Time* did not know the material was false when it was published), something that Sharon had to prove since he was a public figure. Consequently, no cash award was made.

As of the late 1980s, the libel scene had quieted down a bit. The number of newly filed lawsuits against the press was down dramatically. Part of this was due to several court rulings that favored the press. After nearly ten years of litigation, a libel suit brought by a former Mobil Oil president was dismissed by an appeals court and was refused hearing by the Supreme Court. The Supreme Court also threw out a libel suit brought by the Liberty Lobby against columnist Jack Anderson and upheld a lower court's decision that a particularly offensive ad parody in *Hustler* magazine involving TV evangelist Jerry Falwell was not libelous. Moreover, the court went on to rule that Falwell could not recover any damages from *Hustler* for "emotional distress" caused by the ad. In short, for a while at least, the libel crunch had let up.

To summarize, although the laws vary from state to state, it appears that to win a defamation suit a private citizen must show that published material identifying the citizen was false and harmful and that the media bear some degree of fault. Public officials, public figures, and private citizens seeking awards for punitive damages have a harder task. They must also show that the media acted with actual malice—something that is usually difficult to prove.

COPYRIGHT

Copyright provides the author with protection against unfair appropriation of his or her work. Although its roots go back to English common law, the basic copyright law of the United States was first enacted in 1909. In 1976, faced with copyright problems raised by the new communications technologies, Congress passed new legislation. The current copyright statute is found in Title 17 of the United States Code. The new law covers literary, dramatic, and musical works, as well as motion pictures, television programs, and sound recordings. The law also states what is not covered. For example, an idea cannot be copyrighted, nor can a news event or a discovery or a procedure.

Copyright protection lasts for the life of the author plus fifty years. In order to obtain full copyright protection, it is necessary to send a special form, copies of the work, and a small fee to the Register of Copyrights. The owner of a copyrighted work can then reproduce, sell, display, or perform the property.

It is important to note that copyright protection extends only to copying the work in question. If a person independently creates a similar work, there is no copyright violation. As a result, one of the things that a person who brings a copyright suit must prove is that the other person had access to the work under consideration. Thus, if you contend that a hit Hollywood movie was actually based on a pirated script that you submitted to the company, you must show that the people responsible for the movie had access to your work. (To guard against copyright suits, most production companies won't open the envelopes of what look like unsolicited scripts.) Note, however, that you don't have to prove that someone intentionally or even consciously copied your work.

In addition, the law provides that people can make "fair use" of copyrighted materials without violating the provisions of the Copyright Act. Fair use means that copies of the protected work can be made for such legitimate activities as teaching, research, news reporting, and criticism, without penalty. In determining fair use, these factors are taken into consideration:

1. the purpose of the use (whether for profit or for nonprofit education)

2. the nature of the copyrighted work

3. the amount reproduced in proportion to the copyrighted work as a whole

4. the effect of the use on the potential market value of the copyrighted work

Thus, a teacher who reproduces a passage from a long novel to illustrate writing style to an English class will probably not have to worry about copyright. On the other hand, if a commercial magazine reproduces verbatim a series of articles published in a not-for-profit magazine, it is likely that the copyright statute has been violated.

The most recent cases involving copyright law have dealt with the new communication media. In what was popularly known as the "Betamax" case, the Supreme Court ruled in 1984 that viewers who own videocassette recorders could copy programs off the air for later personal viewing without violating the copyright act. Such taping, said that Court, represented fair use of the material. A second area that has copyright implications has to do with the rebroadcasting of the signals of local and distant stations by cable systems without permission or payment of fee. Under the new copyright law, cable systems are free to retransmit distant signals containing copyrighted materials without obtaining permission of the copyright holder, but the system must pay a compulsory license fee, determined by the size of the cable system and whether the distant signal is commercial or educational. The money goes to a Copyright Royalty Tribunal, which distributes the money to program producers, syndicators, and TV broadcasters. As of 1989, this system of payment was being closely studied, and it is likely that some modifications may be forthcoming.

OBSCENITY AND PORNOGRAPHY

Our previous discussion has generally referred to the problems of the working press in their efforts to gather and publish timely and important news and information. The complicated and confusing area of law that surrounds obscenity seldom touches the press; instead, it concerns films, magazines, and books, which function more as entertainment media. Nonetheless, the rights of free speech under the First Amendment can come into conflict with the right of society to protect itself from what it considers harmful messages.

Obscenity is not protected by the First Amendment; that much is clear. Unfortunately, nobody has yet come up with a definition of obscenity that seems to satisfy everybody. Let's take a brief look at how the definition of this term has changed over the years. (If, when we are done, you are a little confused about this whole issue, don't feel bad. You are not alone.)

For many years, the test of whether something was obscene was the **Hicklin rule**, a standard that judged a book (or any other item) by whether isolated passages had a tendency to deprave or corrupt the mind of the most susceptible person. If one paragraph of a 500-page book tended to deprave or corrupt the mind of the most susceptible person (a twelve-year-old child, the village idiot, a dirty old man, etc.), then the entire book was obscene. The standard was written in the 1860s and would be widely used for the next eighty years.

In a 1957 case, *Roth* v. *United States*, the Supreme Court tried its hand at writing a new definition. The new test for detecting obscenity would be the following: whether to the average person, applying contemporary standards, the dominant theme of the material taken as a whole appeals to prurient interests. ("Prurient" means "lewd" or "tending to incite lust.") The Roth test differed from the earlier rule in two significant ways. Not only did the entire work, rather than a single passage, have to be taken into consideration, but the material had to offend the average person, not anyone who saw it. Obviously, this standard was less restrictive than the Hicklin rule, but fuzzy spots remained. Should the community standards be local or national? How exactly would prurient interest be measured?

To give you some idea as to the difficulties in this area, here is one example of how someone tried to use the strict language of this test to beat an obscenity charge. In 1966, the case of Edward Mishkin came before the Supreme Court.

Mishkin, who was appealing his sentence, operated a bookstore near New York's Times Square. The books he sold emphasized sadism and masochism. In his defense, Mishkin argued that his books were not obscene since under the literal interpretation of the Roth test the books he sold would have to incite prurient interests in the average person. Since Mishkin's books appealed to a somewhat deviant crowd, the average person, he argued, would not find them lewd. In fact, the average person would be disgusted and sickened by them. Therefore, they were not obscene. Wrong, said the Court, and let his sentence stand.

The next few years produced more obscenity cases to plague the high court. Other decisions added that the material had to be ''patently offensive'' and ''utterly without redeeming social value'' to be obscene. During the 1960s, the Supreme Court began considering the conduct of the seller or distributor in addition to the character of the material in question. For example, even if material were not considered hard-core pornography, it could be banned if sold to minors, thrust upon an unwilling audience, or advertised as erotic in order to titillate customers. A 1969 ruling introduced the concept of ''variable obscenity'' when it stated that certain magazines were obscene when sold to minors but not obscene when sold to adults.

By 1973, so many legal problems were cropping up under the *Roth* guidelines that something had to be done. Consequently, the Supreme Court attempted to close up loopholes in the case of *Miller* v. *California*. This decision did away with the ''utterly without redeeming social value'' test and stated that the ''community standards'' used in defining obscenity could be local standards, which, presumably, would be determined by local juries. The new test of obscenity would include these principles:

1. whether the average person, applying contemporary community standards, would find that the work as a whole appeals to prurient interest

2. whether the work depicts or describes in a patently offensive way certain sexual conduct that is specifically spelled out by a state law

3. whether the whole work lacks serious literary, artistic, political, or scientific value.

Despite this new attempt, problems weren't long in coming. The language of the decision appeared to permit a certain amount of local discretion in determining what was obscene. The question of how far a local community can go in setting standards continues to be troublesome. The Supreme Court has since ruled that the motion picture *Carnal Knowledge* was not obscene, even though a state court said that it was. The Court has also said that *Screw* magazine and the *Illustrated Presidential Report of the Commission on Obscenity and Pornography* were obscene no matter what community's standards were invoked. The Court further clarified the third of the Miller guidelines in a 1987 case when it ruled that judges and juries must assess the literary, artistic, political, or scientific value of allegedly obscene material from the viewpoint of a ''reasonable person'' rather than applying community standards. The first two guidelines, however, will still be decided with reference to contemporary community standards.

In 1982, the Court ruled that laws banning the distribution of pornographic materials involving children were not violations of the First Amendment. The Court ruled that a state's interest in safeguarding the physical and psychological well-being of children took precedence over any right of free expression. If it strikes you as somewhat bizarre that the members of the highest court of the United States have spent considerable time plowing through publications like *Screw* magazine and looking at such movies as *Deep Throat*, you are not alone. Obscenity is one problem that the Court would probably like to disappear, but it seems that this is highly unlikely to happen.

Over the years it has become apparent that the Court has taken a somewhat more lenient view as to what constitutes obscenity. The Miller case suggests that the Court is encouraging the states to enact laws to deal with the problem at the local level. Given the long history of controversy that surrounds this topic, however, it is unlikely that this predicament will end soon. In fact, the whole issue surfaced again in 1986 when the Justice Department released a report on pornography. The report, which had strong political overtones, called for more stringent laws concerning pornography. One such law, the Child Protection and Obscenity Enforcement Act, took effect in 1988.

REGULATING BROADCASTING

The formal controls surrounding broadcasting represent a special case. Not only are broadcasters affected by the laws and rulings discussed above but they are also subject to additional controls because of broadcasting's unique position and character. When broadcasting was first developed in the early twentieth century, it became clear that more people wanted to operate a broadcasting station than there were suitable frequencies available. An overcrowded spectrum led to problems of interference that threatened the future of the entire industry. As a result, the early broadcasters asked the U.S. Congress to step into the picture. Congress did exactly that when it passed the Radio Act of 1927. This law held that the airwaves belonged to the public and that broadcasters who wished to use this resource had to be licensed to serve in the public interest. A regulatory body, called the Federal Radio Commission (later known as the Federal Communications Commission), was set up to determine who should get a license and whether or not those who had a license should keep it. Because of this licensing provision, radio and television are subject to more regulations than are newspapers, magazines, films, and sound recording.

The Federal Communications Commission (FCC) uses the 1934 Federal Communications Act (an update of the 1927 Radio Act) as the basis for its regulatory power. The FCC does not make law; it interprets the law. One of its big jobs is to interpret the meaning of the phrase "public interest." For example, the FCC may write rules and regulations to implement the Communications Act if these rules serve the public interest. Moreover, the FCC awards and renews licenses if the award or renewal is in the public interest. Over the years, several significant FCC rulings have shed some light on this rather ambiguous concept. One of the first things the commission established was that it would examine programming and determine if the public interest was being served. It was not enough for a station to adhere to the technical operating requirements of its license. It would also have to provide a "well-rounded" program structure. In its 1929 Great Lakes decision, the commission also put broadcasters on notice that the broadcasting of programs that tended to injure the public—fraudulent advertising, attacks on ethnic groups, attacks on religions—would not be in the public interest.

Another facet of the public interest as interpreted by the FCC appears to be diversity. The underlying philosophy of the commission seems to be that the public is better served if it has a large number of competing stations from which to choose.

Consequently, during the 1940s, the commission adopted the **duopoly rule,** which prohibits the ownership of more than one AM, one FM, or one TV station in a single community. The duopoly rule was relaxed in 1989 to permit radio–TV joint ownership in some large markets. In addition, the FCC has ruled that no more than twelve AM, twelve FM, and twelve TV stations can be controlled by a single owner. The commission has also moved to limit the cross-ownership of newspapers and broadcasting stations. The Prime Time Access Rules during the 1970s (see Chapter 11) were another reaffirmation of this emphasis on diversity.

Localism is another important component of the public interest as it has been defined by the FCC. In a 1960 policy statement, the commission stated that programs featuring local talent and aimed at local self-expression were necessary elements in serving the public interest.

What can the FCC do to stations that do not operate in the public interest? It can take several official actions. At the mildest level, it can fine a station up to $20,000 (a large amount for small stations but a relatively small sum for profitable stations in big cities). The next level of severity is to renew a station's license only for a probationary period (usually a year). This action typically puts the station on notice that it has to improve its performance or face even more serious consequences. The most severe form of official action is the revoking or nonrenewal of a license. This is tantamount to the death sentence for a station. Revocation/nonrenewal is more of a threat, however, than a reality. From 1934 to 1978 the FCC took away the licenses of 142 stations. This figure should be weighed against the thousands of renewals that the commission granted each of these years. In fact, it has been calculated that 99.8 percent of all licenses are renewed. Nonetheless, the threat of revocation is a potent one that is universally feared among broadcasters. Despite the fact that it is prohibited from censoring programs, the FCC is able to regulate broadcasters by what is called the "raised-eyebrow technique." This means that the commission will make known its attitude and opinion on a certain questionable practice outside of formal rulemaking; stations generally take the hint and respond accordingly. For example, during the 1970s the FCC issued a notice that radio stations might not be serving the public interest by playing what the commission considered drug-oriented music. Stations that did play such songs would be subject to extra scrutiny at license-renewal time. Radio stations all over the country took the hint.

In the 1980s, as was the case in many industries, the prevailing regulatory philosophy that governed broadcasting was one of deregulation. The FCC had eliminated literally hundreds of rules and regulations, including the controversial Fairness Doctrine (see below). Nonetheless, the basic regulatory structure, as specified by the 1934 Communications Act, is still intact and if the regulatory climate should change, it would be a fairly simple matter to reinstate much of what has been repealed. In fact, at the beginning of 1989, many repealed rules and regulations were being reconsidered by the FCC.

The Equal Opportunities Rule

The **Equal Opportunities rule** is contained in Section 315 of the Communications Act and is thus federal law. Section 315 deals with the ability of bona fide candidates for public office to gain access to a broadcast medium during political campaigns. Stated in simple terms, this section says that if a station permits one candidate for a specific office to appear on the air, it must offer the same opportunity to all other candidates for that office. If a station gives a free minute to one candidate, all other legally qualified candidates for that office are also entitled to a free minute. If a station sells a candidate a minute for a hundred dollars, it must make the same offer to all candidates. Congress has made some exceptions to this law, the most notable of which are legitimate newscasts and on-the-scene coverage of authentic news events. This last exception provided the loophole by which the networks were able to broadcast the recent presidential debates. They were simply covering a news event that was under the sponsorship of another organization.

The Fairness Doctrine

As of 1989, the **Fairness Doctrine** no longer existed. The FCC repealed it in 1987. This doesn't mean, however, that it's dead and buried. There were several proposals in Congress to revive it. In fact, by the time you read this it might be back on the books or it might still be dormant.

When it was still in force, the Fairness Doctrine provided that broadcasters had to seek out and present contrasting viewpoints on controversial matters of public importance. On any issue, broadcasters had to make a good-faith effort to cover all the opposing viewpoints. This didn't have to take place in one program, but the broadcaster was expected to achieve balance over time. Note that the Fairness Doctrine never said that opposing views were entitled to equal time. It simply mandated that some reasonable amount of time be granted.

REGULATING CABLE TV

The regulatory philosophy of the FCC toward cable TV has shown wide variation over the years. In the 1950s, the FCC ruled that it had no jurisdiction over cable. This notion changed in the 1960s when the commission exerted control over the new medium and wrote a series of regulations governing its growth. By 1972, a comprehensive set of rules governing cable was on the FCC's books. The growth of cable during the 1970s led to successful lobbying efforts by the industry to ease many of these restrictions. In the 1980s, in line with the general deregulation philosophy, almost all of the FCC's rules over cable have been dropped. That the FCC has gotten out of the picture does not mean, however, that there are no regulations governing cable. Other organizations have gotten into the act. On the federal level, Congress passed the Cable Communications Policy Act in 1984. Among other things, the new law sets out specific guidelines for the renewal of a cable system's franchise (a **franchise** is an exclusive right to operate in a given territory), gives state and local governments the right to grant franchises, allows cable operators greater freedom in setting rates, provides criminal penalties for the theft of cable services, frees cable systems from most programming regulations, and legalizes backyard satellite dishes but also requires owners to pay to receive programming that has been descrambled. At the state level, cable franchising is regulated by five states, and others have enacted laws governing ownership and public access channels. At the local level, in most states franchising is the province of the local government, and all cable companies must comply with local regulations concerning taxation, employment practices, and general business methods.

REGULATING ADVERTISING

Deceptive Advertising

"Rapid Shave outshaves them all!" At least that's what a 1959 commercial for that shaving cream claimed. In order to drive that point home, a demonstration was included in the ad. As an announcer extolled the benefits of the product, Rapid Shave was applied to a substance that looked like sandpaper. A razor then shaved the paper clean, whisking away every grain of sand. Unfortunately, the substance wasn't sandpaper. It was really sand applied to a sheet of plexiglass. The Federal Trade Commission (FTC) claimed that the commercial was deceptive. The FTC's investigations discovered that Rapid Shave could not shave actual sandpaper unless the sandpaper was first soaked with the stuff for about eighty minutes. The advertising agency that put together the commercial appealed the commission's ruling all the way to the Supreme Court. The Court sided with the FTC.

The problem of deceptive and potentially harmful advertising has been around a long time. The philosophy of *caveat emptor* (let the buyer beware) was dominant until the early 1900s. Exaggerated claims and outright deception characterized many of the early advertisements, especially those for patent medicines. Spurred on by the muckrakers (see Chapter 4), the government took steps to deal with the problem when it created the Federal Trade Commission in 1914. In the early years of its existence, the commission was concerned with encouraging competition through the regulation of questionable business practices such as bribery, false advertising, and mislabeling of products; protecting the consumer was not the main focus. Thus an ad that identified underwear as "wool" when it actually contained only 10 percent wool was deemed unlawful because it hurt the business of those manufacturers who actually produced 100 percent wool underwear and truthfully labeled their product. The consumer started to receive some protection in 1938 with the Wheeler–Lea Act, which gave the FTC the power to prevent deceptive advertising that harmed the public, whether or not the advertising had any bad effects on the competition.

Like the Federal Communications Commission, the Federal Trade Commission has several enforcement techniques available to it. First of all, it can issue trade regulations that suggest guidelines for the industry to follow. In 1975, for example, it ruled that auto ads must contain both the city and highway estimate of gas mileage. The FTC also uses **consent orders.** In a consent order, the advertiser agrees to halt a certain advertising practice but, at the same time, the advertiser does not admit any violation of the law; there is only an agreement not to continue. Somewhat stronger is a **cease-and-desist order.** This order follows a hearing by the commission that determines that a certain advertising practice does indeed violate the law. Violation of a consent order and failure to comply with a cease-and-desist order can result in fines being levied against the advertiser.

In the late 1960s and the 1970s, the FTC took a more active role in the regulation of advertising. The rising tide of interest in the rights of the consumer and the presence of consumer activist groups (such as Ralph Nader's Raiders) were probably behind this new direction. A flurry of activity took place. First, the FTC wanted documentation for claims. If Excedrin claimed to be more effective in relieving pain than Brand X, the advertiser was now required to have proof for that statement. The FTC also ordered "corrective advertising" in which some advertisers were required to clarify some of their past claims. Profile Bread, for example, had been advertised as a weight-reducing aid, with fewer calories per slice than normal bread. (This was literally true. Profile Bread had seven fewer calories per slice, but only because it was sliced thinner.) The company agreed to run corrective ads with copy that included the following:

> I'd like to clear up any misunderstanding you may have about Profile Bread. Does Profile have fewer calories than other bread? No, Profile has about the same per ounce as other breads. To be exact, Profile has seven fewer calories per slice. That's because it is sliced thinner. But eating Profile will not cause you to lose weight. . . .

(Interestingly enough, the corrective ads were so well received by the audience that the company wanted to present them more often than the ruling required.) Ocean Spray Cranberry Drink and Listerine were other products that were subjected to corrective advertising. At about the same time, the FTC also came out for the notion of counteradvertising. This idea would have required TV stations to provide free time to consumer groups in order to reply to TV commercials. If a station ran an auto company's ads for a compact car, it would also have to run ads from a public-interest group that pointed out possible safety problems with that car. This proposal was not greeted with widespread support and eventually was abandoned.

The other area of FTC concern during the 1970s was advertising directed toward children. A 1978 study by the FTC recommended that *all* TV advertising directed at young children be prohibited. In 1980, a new administration took office and the FTC quietly dropped its inquiry into this area. The new chairman of the FTC endorsed less federal control over advertising and was in favor of deregulating much of the industry. This philosophy persisted throughout the decade.

Commercial Speech Under the First Amendment

The 1970s also marked a change in judicial thinking toward the amount of protection that advertising, or commercial speech, as it is called, receives under the First Amendment. Before the 1970s, advertising had little claim to free-speech protection. In the 1940s, F. J. Chrestensen found this out the hard way. Chrestensen owned a former U.S. submarine. There is not much that a private individual can do with a submarine, aside from making a few dollars by charging admission to view it. This was Chrestensen's idea, and he wanted to distribute handbills advertising the sub. No way, said the New York City police commissioner. The city's sanitation code did not allow the distribution of advertising matter in the streets. Chrestensen did discover that handbills of information or of public protest were allowed. Inspired, Chrestensen put his submarine advertising message on one side of the handbill, while the other side was printed with a protest against the City Dock Department. Sorry, said the city, the protest message could be handed out, but the advertising on the other side would have to go. Chrestensen, still stuck with his submarine, appealed and two years later the Supreme Court ruled against him and agreed with the City of New York that advertising merited no First Amendment protection.

Since that time, however, the Supreme Court has retreated from this view. In 1964, it extended First Amendment protection to ads that dealt with important social matters. Seven years later, the Court further extended this protection when a Virginia newspaper editor ran an ad for an abortion clinic located in New York and thus violated a Virginia law against such advertising. The Supreme Court ruled in favor of the editor and stated that the ad contained material in the public interest and merited constitutional protection. Virginia was also involved in the next significant

In the 1940s and 1950s, much cigarette advertising promoted the health benefits of smoking. This ad for Camels suggests that doctors endorse not only this brand of cigarette but also smoking in general. (PAR Archive)

court ruling. A state law made it illegal to advertise the price of a prescription drug. Because of the importance of this information to the public, the Court ruled that the Virginia law was invalid. More recent cases suggest that in many instances commercial speech will fall under the protection of the First Amendment.

In a 1980 ruling concerning advertising by an electric utility company, the Supreme Court enunciated a four-part test for determining the constitutional protection for commercial speech. First, commercial speech that involves an unlawful activity or advertising that is false or misleading is not protected. Second, the government must have a substantial interest in regulating the commercial speech. Part three asks if the state's regulation actually advances the government interest involved. Finally, the state's regulations may be only broad as necessary to promote the state's interest. A 1984 ruling illustrated the use of these principles when the Court upheld a prohibition against posting signs on city property. The Court first noted that although the advertising was for a lawful activity and not misleading, the government has a substantial interest in reducing "visual blight" and that the ordinance directly advanced that interest and was not overly broad. Further, the Court affirmed that corporations also have the right of free speech and granted lawyers, doctors, and other professionals the right to advertise their prices. Although

The *Soldier of Fortune* Case

A simple ad started it all:

> Ex-Marine—67–69 'Nam vet—Ex-DI, weapons specialist—jungle warfare, pilot. M.E., high risk assignments, U.S. or overseas.

This ad was placed in *Soldier of Fortune* magazine by John Hearn. Robert Black saw the ad and contacted Hearn. Four months later, Black arranged to have Hearn murder Black's wife. The wife's parents sued the magazine, claiming that the publication should have foreseen that running the ad would result in a crime, perhaps murder.

At the trial, evidence introduced by the murdered woman's parents established that the magazine had previously run ''hired-gun ads'' that strongly implied that some illegal conduct was contemplated. The editor of the magazine was also aware that at least one such ad, seeking an expert in poisons, had resulted in a solicitation to a murder. These and other facts apparently convinced the jury that *Soldier of Fortune* should have known that the ad might lead to foul play and was negligent in running it.

This verdict raises some knotty problems. What about ads for radar detectors, illegal in many states? Suppose a car equipped with such a device gets into an accident because of excessive speed. Should the publication that advertised the detector be held liable? What about a woman who answers an ad in the personals column of a newspaper and is raped on the first date? Is the newspaper at fault? Must a publisher investigate any and all ads for hidden meanings? This verdict, if affirmed on appeal, has serious implications.

not all of the questions surrounding this issue have been answered, it seems safe to conclude that at least some commercial speech is entitled to First Amendment protection. Its status, however, is less than that given to political and other forms of noncommercial expression. In the future, it's likely that more and more advertising will fall into the category of protected speech.

In another case with repercussions for advertisers, a tobacco company was found partially liable for the death of a smoker from lung cancer, in part because early ads for cigarettes stressed their health benefits for smokers. Although it seems hard to believe, during the 1940s and 1950s many cigarettes were advertised as ''just what the doctor ordered,'' even after information linking smoking to lung cancer and other diseases came to light. This case may have limited impact since it dealt primarily with pre-1966 claims, before health warnings appeared on packs. On the other hand, it raises the broader question of whether advertising contains an implied warranty for the product.

Finally, a federal jury in Texas returned a $9.4 million verdict against *Soldier of Fortune* magazine for running a classified ad that helped one of its readers to murder his wife (see boxed material). This decision, currently under appeal, raised disturbing questions about the extent of liability a publication has for the ads it runs.

CONCLUDING STATEMENT

The term ''half-life'' is a useful concept in physics. It refers to the length of time in which one-half of the radioactive atoms present in a substance will decay. We might borrow this term and reshape its meaning so that it is relevant to this book. The half-life of a chapter in this text is the time it takes for half of the information contained in the chapter to become obsolete. With that in mind, it is likely that the half-life of this chapter may be among the shortest of any in this book. Laws are constantly changing; new court decisions are frequently handed down and new rules and regulations are written all the time. All of this activity means that what is written in this chapter will need frequent updating. In addition, it means that mass media professionals must continually refresh their understanding of the law. Of course, this also means that there will be a continuing stream of colorful characters, intriguing stories, and high drama as the courts and regulatory agencies further wrestle with the issues and problems involved in mass communication regulation.

SUGGESTIONS FOR FURTHER READING

The following books contain more information about the concepts and topics discussed in this chapter.

CARTER, BARTON, MARC FRANKLIN, AND JAY WRIGHT, *The First Amendment and the Fourth Estate,* Mineola, N.Y.: Foundation Press, 1988.

GILLMOR, DONALD, AND JEROME BARRON, *Mass Communication Law*, St. Paul, Minn.: West Publishing Company, 1984.

HOLSINGER, RALPH, *Media Law*, New York: Random House, 1987.

MIDDLETON, KENT, AND BILL CHAMBERLIN, *The Law of Public Communication*, New York: Longman, 1988.

NELSON, HAROLD, AND DWIGHT TEETER, *Law of Mass Communications*, Mineola, N.Y.: The Foundation Press, 1989.

Chapter 18

Informal Controls:
Ethics, Codes,
Self-Regulations, and
External Pressures

L aws and regulations are not the only controls on the mass media. Informal controls, stemming from within the media themselves or shaped by the workings of external forces such as pressure groups, consumers, and advertisers, are also important. The following hypothetical examples illustrate some situations in which these controls might spring up.

1. You're the program director for the campus radio station. You get a call one morning from the promotion department of a major record company offering you a free trip to California, a tour of the record company's studios, a ticket to a concert featuring all the company's biggest stars, and an invitation to an exclusive party where you'll get to meet all the performers. The company representative explains that this is simply a courtesy to you so that you'll better appreciate the quality of his company's products. Do you accept?

2. You're reporter for the local campus newspaper. The star of the football team, who also happens to be the president of the Campus Crusade for Morality, has been involved in a minor traffic accident, and you have been assigned to cover the story. When you get to the accident scene, you examine the football player's car and find a half-dozen pornographic magazines strewn across the back seat. You have a deadline in thirty minutes; what details do you include?

3. You're the editor of the campus newspaper. One of your reporters has just written a series of articles describing apparent health-code violations in a popular off-campus restaurant. This particular restaurant regularly buys full-page ads in your paper. After you run the first story in the series, the restaurant owner calls and threatens to cancel all of his ads unless you stop printing the series. What do you do?

4. You're doing your first story for the campus paper. A local businessman has promised to donate $5 million to your university so that it can buy new

equipment for its mass communication and journalism programs. While putting together a background story on this benefactor, you discover that he was convicted of armed robbery at age eighteen and avoided prison only by volunteering for military duty during the closing months of World War II. Since then, his record has been spotless. He refuses to talk about the incident, claims his wife and his closest friends do not know about it, and threatens to withdraw his donation if you print the story. Naturally, university officials are concerned and urge you not to mention this fact. Do you go ahead and write the story as one element in your overall profile? Do you take the position that the arrest information is not pertinent and not use it? Do you wait until the university has the money and then print the story?

We could go on listing examples, but by now the point is probably clear. There are many situations in the everyday operation of the mass media where thorny questions about what to do or not to do have to be faced. Most of these situations do not involve laws, regulations, legalities, or illegalities but instead deal with the tougher questions of what's right or what's proper. Informal controls over the media usually assert themselves in these circumstances. This chapter will discuss the following examples of informal controls: personal ethics, performance codes, internal controls such as organizational policies, self-criticism, and professional self-regulation and outside pressures.

PERSONAL ETHICS

Ethics are rules of conduct or principles of morality that point us toward the right or best way to act in a situation. Over the years, philosophers have developed a number of general ethical principles that serve as guidelines for evaluating our behavior. We will briefly summarize five principles that have particular relevance to those working in the mass media professions. Before we begin, however, we should emphasize that these principles do not contain magic answers to every ethical dilemma. In fact, different ethical principles often suggest different and conflicting courses of action. There is no "perfect" answer to every problem. Also, these ethical principles are based on Western thought. Other cultures may have developed totally different systems. Nonetheless, these principles can provide a framework for analyzing what is proper for examining choices and for justifying our actions.

Ethical Principles

The Principle of the Golden Mean. Moral virtue lies between two extremes. This philosophical position is typically associated with Aristotle, who, as a biologist, noted that too much food as well as too little food spoils health. Moderation was the key. Likewise, in ethical dilemmas, the proper way of behaving lies between doing too much and doing too little. For instance, in the restaurant example mentioned above, one extreme would be to cancel the story as requested by the restaurant owner. The other extreme would be to run the series as is. Perhaps a compromise between the two would be to run the series but also give the restaurant owner a chance to reply. Or perhaps the story might contain information about how the restaurant has improved conditions or other tempering remarks.

Examples of the Golden Mean are often found in media practices. For example, when news organizations cover civil disorders, they try to exercise moderation. They balance the necessity of informing the public with the need to preserve public safety by not inflaming the audience.

The Categorical Imperative. What is right for one is right for all. German philosopher Immanuel Kant is identified with this ethical guideline. To measure the correctness of our behavior, Kant suggests that we act according to rules that we would want to see universally applied. In Kant's formulation, categorical means unconditional—no extenuating circumstances, no exceptions. Right is right and should be done, no matter what the consequences. The individual's conscience plays a large part in Kant's thinking. The categorical imperatives are discovered by an examination of conscience; the conscience informs us what is right. If, after performing an act, we feel uneasy or guilty, we have probably violated our conscience. Applied to mass communication, a categorical imperative might be that all forms of deception in news gathering are wrong and must be avoided. No one wants deception to become a universal practice. Therefore, a reporter should not represent himself or herself as anything other than a reporter when gathering information for a story.

The Principle of Utility. The greatest benefit for the greatest number. Modern utilitarian thinking originated with the nineteenth-century philosophers Jeremy Bentham and John Stuart Mill. The basic tenet in their formulations holds that we are to determine what is right or wrong by considering what will yield the best ratio of good to bad for the general society. Utilitarians ask how much good is promoted and how much evil is restrained by different courses of behavior. Utilitarianism provides a clear method for evaluating ethical choices: (1) calculate all the consequences, both good and bad, that would result from each of our options; then (2) choose the alternative that maximizes value or minimizes loss. Looking at the mass communication area, we can easily see several examples of utilitarian philosophy. In 1971, the *New York Times* and other papers printed stolen government documents, the Pentagon Papers. Obviously, the newspapers involved thought that the good that would be achieved by printing these papers far outweighed the harm that would be done. (Note that the Kantian perspective would suggest a different course of action. Theft is bad. Newspapers do not want the government stealing their property so they should not condone or promote the theft of government property.) Or take the case of a small Midwestern paper that chose to report the death of a local teenager who had gone East, turned to prostitution and drugs, and was murdered while plying her trade. The paper decided that the potential benefits of this story as a warning to other parents outweighed the grief it would cause the murder victim's family.

The Veil of Ignorance. Justice is blind. Philosopher John Rawls argued that justice emerges when everyone is treated without social differentiations. In one sense, the veil of ignorance is related to fairness. Everybody doing the same job equally well should receive equal pay. Everybody who got an eighty on the test should get the same grade. Rawls advocated that all parties concerned in a problem situation should be placed behind a barrier where roles and social differentiations are gone and each participant is treated as an equal member of society as a whole. Often Rawls' veil of ignorance suggests that we should structure our actions to protect the most vulnerable members of society. It is easy to see the relevance of this principle to the workings of the mass media. If we applied the veil of ignorance to the problem of hammering out the proper relationship between politicians and journalists, Rawls would argue that the blatant adversarial relationship so often found between the groups should disappear. Behind the veil, all newsmakers would be the same.

Inherent cynicism and abrasiveness on the part of the press should disappear as well as mistrust and suspicion on the part of the politicians. On a more specific level, consider the case of someone working in the financial department of a major newspaper who frequently gets tips and inside information on deals and mergers that affect the price of stock and passes these tips on to personal friends who use this information for their own profit. The veil of ignorance suggests that the reporter must treat all audience members the same. Personal friends should not benefit from inside information.

Principle of Self-Determination. Do not treat people as means to an end. This principle, closely associated with the Judeo-Christian ethic and also discussed by Kant, might be summarized as "Love your neighbor as yourself." Human beings have unconditional value apart from any and all circumstances. Their basic right to self-determination should not be violated by using them as simply a means to accomplish a goal. A corollary to this is that no one should allow himself or herself to be treated as a means to someone else's ends. For example, sources inside a government investigation on political corruption leak the names of some people suspected of taking bribes to the press, which, in turn, publishes the allegations and the names of the suspects. The principle of self-determination suggests that the press is being used by those who leaked the story as a means to accomplish their goal. Perhaps those involved in the investigation wanted to turn public opinion against those named or simply to earn some favorable publicity for their efforts. In any case, the press should resist being used in these circumstances. The rights, values, and decisions of others must always be respected.

A Model for Individual Ethical Decisions

There are numerous instances where personal ethical decisions have to be made about what is or is not included in media content or what should or should not be done. These decisions have to be made every day by reporters, editors, station managers, and other media professionals. Too often, however, these decisions are made haphazardly and without proper analysis of the ethical dimensions involved. This section presents a model that media professionals can use to evaluate and examine their decisions. This model is adapted from the work of Ralph Potter.*

DEFINITIONS → VALUES → PRINCIPLES →
LOYALTIES → ACTION

In short, the model asks the individual to consider four aspects of the situation before taking action. First define the situation. What are the pertinent facts involved? What are the possible actions? Second, what values are involved? Which values are more relevant to deciding a course of action? Third, what ethical principles apply? We have discussed five that might be involved. There may be others. Lastly, where do our loyalties lie? To whom do we owe a moral duty? It is possible that we might owe a duty to ourselves, clients, business organizations, the profession, or to society in general. To whom is our obligation most important?

Let's examine how this model would apply to a real situation. In 1987, the State Treasurer of Pennsylvania held a press conference just hours before he was to

---

* Ralph Potter, "The Logic of Moral Argument," in *Toward a Discipline of Social Ethics*, P. Deats, (ed.), Boston: Boston University Press, 1972.

422   PART FIVE   REGULATION OF THE MASS MEDIA

be sentenced for his conviction in a kickback scandal. After 30 minutes of proclaiming his innocence, he pulled a .357 Magnum from a brown envelope, displayed it to the crowd, placed the gun barrel in his mouth, and, in full view of news photographers and TV cameras, pulled the trigger. Available news photos and tapes showed the entire event, and several angles showed the particularly grim aftermath of the gunshot wound. How should a situation like this be handled?

First, we need to specify the key facts. A public figure has committed suicide. Some photos and tapes are available that show blood and gore. We could opt to show all the graphic details, show only a part of them, or not show them at all. What values are involved? Obviously, as journalists we value freedom of expression and the right of society to be informed of all events, no matter how unpleasant. At the same time, we value the right to privacy and the right of people to be spared unnecessary grief. We also value our own sensibilities and those of our readers. Do they need to be shocked by seeing graphic portrayals of the effects of violence?

What principles are involved? Obviously, Aristotle's principle of moderation is relevant. At one extreme, we could publish the goriest of the pictures. At the other, we could publish no pictures at all. The principle of the mean suggests that we look for a middle ground between these two poles. Further, the principle of self-determination applies. If we show these pictures merely to use sensationalism to spur our newspaper's circulation or TV rating, then we are treating the victim and his family as a means toward fulfilling our end goal of selling papers or getting ratings. Further thought indicates that the principle of utility is also germane. The potential harm caused to readers' sensibilities and the victim's family must be weighed against the good that might result from society seeing how abhorrent violence really is. A graphic photo might deter some readers from resorting to violence in the future. As for the loyalty dimension, there are conflicting obligations. As an employee of the media, we have an obligation to the business to make a profit. Sensational photographs will probably sell more papers and get higher ratings. We also have a duty to the profession to report the news as it happens and a duty to society to keep it informed. We also have a duty to ourselves not to exploit sensational events and to maintain standards of our personal conscience. Which takes precedence? Will the journalism profession and society in general suffer from not seeing the violent photos? Must the media depend on violence to keep them solvent?

In this particular instance, different editors at TV stations and newspapers made different decisions. An ABC station in Harrisburg, Pennsylvania, interrupted a rerun of the sitcom "Webster" and ran the entire tape. A station in Pittsburgh did the same. A suburban Philadelphia newspaper ran a series of photos of the suicide, including one snapped an instant after the trigger was pulled, clearly showing blood and gore. These stations and this newspaper justified their decision based on their duty to inform the public about news, no matter how unpleasant. Other stations and papers apparently endorsed the principle of moderation and declined to show the violence. Many stations cut the tape at the point when the man raised the gun to his mouth. Two of the three networks did not show the tape and one cut it just after the gun was revealed. Most newspapers used a photo of the victim with the gun placed in his mouth, a picture that was disturbing enough but did not show the actual suicide.

Consider another example. During the primary campaign for the 1988 Democratic presidential nomination, reporters for a Miami newspaper received a tip about Gary Hart, then the front-running candidate for the nomination: The married Hart would be spending the weekend at his Washington, D.C., townhouse with a young Miami woman who was not his wife. Two reporters staked out Hart's townhouse and finally confronted him and the young lady on a darkened street after the couple emerged from the townhouse. The paper published a story that the two spent the weekend together. The publicity ultimately led to Hart's withdrawal from the race.

Several ethical questions are raised by this story. Should the private sex lives of candidates become a matter of public concern? Should candidates be stalked and staked out by reporters? A follower of Kant's Categorical Imperative would probably argue that secret surveillance is not something that should become a universal law. We don't want other people spying on us; therefore, we should not spy on other people. The Veil of Ignorance would suggest that Hart not be treated differently from other citizens just because he was a politician. The newspaper, however, justified its coverage both on the principle of utilitarianism and on Aristotle's Golden Mean. In the first place, the paper pointed out that Hart was a candidate for the most powerful office in the world and that the value of any information about his character qualifications for that office outweighed any harm that might have come from an invasion of privacy. Additionally, the paper noted that it tried to balance the story by allowing Hart to give his side. Hart at first denied any involvement with the young woman.

Not all journalists agreed with the Miami paper's tactics. Some faulted the paper for sloppy surveillance; others criticized the rush to get the story into print without obtaining more facts and reactions. The newspaper still maintained that its actions were ethically correct. In any event, the private lives of other presidential candidates and their families subsequently underwent intense press scrutiny, opening up a host of other ethical concerns.

Let's look at one further example of applying ethical analysis to a real-life situation. In this case, a Pennsylvania newspaper chose to run a dramatic photo of a paramedic giving mouth-to-mouth resuscitation to an infant victim of a car wreck. (The baby later died.) In his analysis of the situation, the paper's editor clearly relied on the utilitarian principle. He decided that the social good that might result from running this photo outweighed any offense to readers' sensibilities or additional suffering to the victim's family. He wrote:

> In running the photograph we hope it caused everyone to take another look at auto safety and how their family is protected. Are little children sufficiently buckled up? . . . We hope (the photo) gave everyone a new appreciation for the volunteer rescue teams in the region. Perhaps now we won't be so quick to refuse a contribution next time they seek funds for better life-saving equipment.

In addition to matters of taste and exploitation, reporters and editors frequently face instances where they must weigh the public's right or need to know against possible repercussions on individual lives. To illustrate, a man suspected of a robbery has a perfect alibi because several witnesses testify that at the time of the crime he was sharing a motel room with a woman who was not his wife. How much of this story needs to be reported? Is the apparent infidelity a necessary element? Or what of the reporter who gets crucial information "off the record"? Are there circumstances in which this confidence can be violated?

Individual ethical judgments are made in the entertainment area as well. The principle of moderation is often apparent as filmmakers have been known to delete certain scenes in their movies or soften dialogue in order to receive a PG rating instead of an X or an R. Television station managers frequently decide if a network program is suitable for their market. For example, when the network broadcast the Charles Bronson film *Death Wish*, many local stations were faced with a problem.

Situational Ethics

A more recent ethical philosophy was articulated by American theologian Joseph Fletcher. In 1966, Fletcher published *Situation Ethics: The New Morality* in which he argued that the most important aspect of morally correct behavior was not blind adherence to prefabricated rules or ethical principles but an appreciation that the moral quality of an action varies from one situation to another. Traditional ethical guidelines may be compromised or even set aside if a particular situation calls for it. Fletcher suggested that individuals trust their own intuitive sense of justice and their instinctive love of their neighbor to show them the right thing to do. Thus, there may be situations where a reporter might be justified in lying to a source if his or her motives were perceived as morally right and if the lie resulted in the maximization of beneficial consequences to all concerned. (Note how Fletcher's viewpoint shares some of the philosophy of utilitarianism.)

Many critics of situational ethics argue that Fletcher's conceptions depend too much on a person's prior moral training and ethical experience. If a person lacks the insight to recognize that his or her behavior is unjust or morally wrong, situational ethics might be used to justify any kind of behavior, no matter how reprehensible. Nonetheless, situational ethics help us to appreciate that ethical behavior is not static or mechanical but is influenced by the changing and dynamic context of modern life.

The film, even in its edited-for-TV version, was extraordinarily violent and advocated violence as a means to solve personal problems. The value underlying the situation appeared to be a belief that freedom of expression should be preserved even in the case of violent content. Not showing the movie would be a blow against artistic expression. On the other hand, many station executives valued the right of the audience to be free from undue risk. The possibility certainly existed that some people who saw the film might go out and commit copycat violence. There were several ethical principles involved in this situation. The veil of ignorance suggests that the most vulnerable of the audience should be protected against copycat violence. Many managers might have endorsed the categorical imperative that violence is wrong and should not be condoned or encouraged under any circumstances. Other managers felt that there was some balancing point between the extremes of showing the film as planned or not showing it. Still others felt that the harm to freedom of expression caused by not carrying the film was far worse than what might happen if it were broadcast. The loyalties in this situation are not complicated. Station managers have a duty to preserve the safety of their community. They also have a duty to their employees and shareholders to make a profit and keep their station in business (*Death Wish* promised to get good ratings, which would translate into increased profits). Finally, the managers had a duty to other professionals to preserve freedom of expression.

The decisions made by station managers in this case were varied. Some showed the film as scheduled. Others placed warning announcements at the beginning and in the body of the program to alert viewers to the violent content. Other managers taped the program and showed it late in the evening when fewer impressionable children were in the audience. Still others declined to show it at all.

Most of the time, ethical decisions are made in good faith with a sincere desire to serve the public and reflect positively on the profession. Sometimes, however, ethical judgments may be adversely affected by other influences.

One of the factors that influences the judgment of some reporters is a phenomenon known as **acculturation.** Simply defined, acculturation in a media context means the tendency of reporters or other media professionals to accept the ideas, attitudes, and opinions of the group that they cover or with whom they have a great deal of contact. Many political reporters, for instance, come to share the views of the politicians they cover. So do many police-beat reporters. Publishers and station managers who spend a great deal of time with business leaders might come to adopt the point of view of industry. A 1977 study of reporters and legislators in Colorado revealed that political reporters and politicians held quite similar views. The investigation also revealed that many reporters actually identified with capitol legislators, felt a sense of kinship with them, and actually considered that they, the reporters, were part of the legislative process. In the Potter model, these individuals have confused their loyalties. They see their duty to the group they are covering as more important than their duty to the profession of journalism.

Acculturation is not necessarily bad; it can cause concern, however, when it begins to affect judgment. Recently, a California newspaper learned that several off-duty police officers had terrorized a bar and had gotten into fistfights with some of its patrons. The disturbance was so serious that the chief of police recommended that three of the officers be dismissed. The paper, however, sat on the story for almost six weeks. It turned out that in the past the police and the paper had developed an easy sense of cooperation. Police officers had been given the OK to look at the paper's files; in turn, the officers would give the paper "mug shots" if the paper needed a picture of a suspect. It is possible that this close and cooperative atmosphere led some journalists to identify with the police officers and affected their news judgment in handling this story.

PERFORMANCE CODES

Many ethical decisions have to be made within minutes or hours, without the luxury of lengthy philosophical reflection. In this regard, the media professional is not very different from other professionals such as doctors and lawyers, who also face complicated decisions. In these professions, codes of conduct or of ethics have been standardized in order to help individuals in their decisions. If a doctor or a lawyer violates one of the tenets of these codes, it is possible that he or she might be barred from practice by a decision of a panel of colleagues who "police" the profession. Here the similarity with the mass media ends. Media professionals, thoroughly committed to the notion of free speech, have no professional review boards that grant and revoke licenses. Media codes of performance and methods of self-regulation are less precise and less stringent than those of other organizations. But many of the ethical principles discussed above are incorporated into these codes.

The Print Media

During the colorful and turbulent age of jazz journalism (see Chapter 4), several journalists, apparently reacting against the excesses of some tabloids, founded the American Society of Newspaper Editors. This group voluntarily adopted the Canons of Journalism in 1923 without any public or governmental pressure. There were seven canons: responsibility, freedom of the press, independence, accuracy, impartiality, fair play, and decency. By and large, the canons are prescriptive (telling what

Early Codes of Performance and Ethics in the Newspaper Business

One of the first books to consider ethics and performance codes in journalism was *The Ethics of Journalism,* published by Nelson Crawford in 1924. Below are excerpts of performance codes written by press associations and newspapers that Crawford catalogued.

From the Kansas Code of Ethics, adopted by the Kansas Editorial Association:

Reporters should not enter the domain of law in the apprehension of criminals. They should not become a detective or sweating agency for the purpose of furnishing excitement to the readers.

However prominent the principles, offenses against private morality should never receive first-page position. . . .

From the Brooklyn *Eagle:*

Beware of seekers of free publicity. Remember that space in *The Eagle* sells for 25¢ a line. . . . Don't help press agents cheat the advertising department.

Don't emphasize locality in fire or burglary stories or in news reports which give a special section an unsavory reputation.

From the Springfield *Union:*

The Union does not publish the names of persons arrested for drunkenness, nor of "drunks" who are fined nominal amounts by the court. . . . Give them a chance to reform.

In automobile accidents do not give the name of the car, nor in shooting accidents the make of the weapon used.

Don't help publicity agents to cheat the advertising department.

From the Seattle *Times:*

Remember that young girls read *The Times*.

When it is necessary to refer to improper relations between the sexes, the limit permitted in *The Times* is some such statement as "The couple were divorced," or "The couple separated," or "Various charges were made not considered fit for publication in the columns of *The Times*."

From the *Christian Science Monitor:*

Verify all quotations, especially from the Bible, whenever time will permit.

Use words of one syllable rather than those of many—the latter may serve to show off your learning, but the average reader hasn't a dictionary at his elbow. . . .

Never use expressions that suggest nauseating ideas.

The last sentence contains a thought we could all take to heart.

ought to be done) rather than proscriptive (telling what should be avoided). Some of the canons tend to be general and vague, with a great deal of room for individual interpretation. Under responsibility, for example, it is stated that "the use a newspaper makes of the share of public attention it gains serves to determine its sense of responsibility, which it shares with every member of its staff." This is a noble thought, but it is of little guidance when it comes to deciding if a newspaper should include the detail about the pornographic magazines in the football player's car. Other statements seem simplistic. Under accuracy, for example, one learns that "headlines should be fully warranted by the contents of the article they surmount." Before you get the wrong idea, it should be pointed out that these canons should not be dismissed as mere platitudes and empty rhetoric. They do represent the first concrete attempt by journalists to strive for professionalism in their field.

When the canons were first released, *Time* magazine held out grandiose hopes for the future of the profession: "The American Society of Newspaper Editors (ASNE) aims to be to journalism what the American Bar Association is to the legal fraternity." *Time* was overly optimistic. The legal fraternity, through its powerful bar associations, has the power to revoke a member's license to practice. Journalists have fiercely resisted any idea that resembles licensing as a restriction on their First Amendment rights. The ASNE has never proposed licensing or certifying journalists for this reason. In fact, the ASNE has never expelled a member in its seventy-year history, even though it has had ample reason to do so. To illustrate, just one year after the canons were adopted, our old friend Fred Bonfils (see Chapter 4) of the *Denver Post* testified that he had accepted $250,000 to suppress stories about the Teapot Dome oil-lease scandal that was then plaguing the administration of President Warren G. Harding. (Ironically, Harding himself was a former newspaper editor.) Rather than expelling Bonfils, the ASNE decided to stress voluntary compliance with its canons.

Fifty years later, Sigma Delta Chi, the Society of Professional Journalists, adopted a Code of Ethics for those working in the news media. Intended for journalists in all media, the code was modeled after the ASNE canons. The Sigma Delta Chi Code has five main sections: responsibility, freedom of the press, ethics, accuracy, and fair play. Some of the guidelines are fairly specific. Under fair play, for example, one notes that "the media should not pander to morbid curiosity about the details of vice and crime." And under ethics is to be found the following guideline: "Gifts, favors, free travel, special treatment or privileges can compromise the integrity of journalists and their employers. Nothing of value can be accepted." In 1975, the Associated Press Managing Editors Association (APME) adopted a code that also discussed responsibility, accuracy, integrity, and conflicts of interest. As with the ASNE's canons, adherence to these codes is voluntary and neither Sigma Delta Chi or APME has developed any procedures to enforce the codes.

Broadcasting and Film

For many years, radio and television broadcasters followed the National Association of Broadcasters (NAB) Code of Good Practice. This code first appeared in 1929 and was revised periodically over the years. It was divided into two parts, one covering advertising and the other general program practices. In 1982, however, a court ruled that the code placed undue limitations on advertising and the NAB suspended the advertising part of its code. The next year, in order to forestall more legal pressure, the NAB officially dissolved the code in its entirety. Although the code is gone, its impact still lingers on, as many broadcasters have incorporated parts of the code's provisions into their personal operating philosophies.

Codes of conduct in the motion picture industry emerged during the 1920s. Scandals were racking Hollywood at that time (see Chapter 11), and many states had passed or were considering censorship laws that would control the content of movies. In an attempt to save itself from being tarred and feathered, the industry invited Will Hays, a former postmaster general and elder of the Presbyterian church, to head a new organization that would clean up films. Hays became the president, chairman of the board of directors, and chairman of the executive committee of a new organization, the Motion Picture Producers and Distributors of America (MPPDA). In 1930, the Motion Picture Production Code was adopted by the new group. The code was mainly proscriptive; it described what should be avoided in order for filmmakers to get their movies past existing censorship boards and listed

The Legion of Decency

After World War I, during the roaringest part of the Roaring Twenties, the films that grossed the most money had titles like *Red Hot Romance, She Could Not Help It, Her Purchase Price,* and *Plaything of Broadway.* One movie ad of the period stated breathlessly: ". . . brilliant men, beautiful jazz babies, champagne baths, midnight revels, petting parties in the purple dawn. . . ." It wasn't long before public opposition to such sensational movies began to form. The appointment of Will Hays, the creation of the Motion Picture Producers and Distributors of America, and the adoption of the Motion Picture Production Code were designed, in part, to forestall this public criticism. Much of the code was suggested by a Roman Catholic layman, Martin Quigley, and a Roman Catholic priest, Father Daniel Lord. Despite the existence of the code, however, sensational films still appeared in significant numbers. This trend was most disturbing to many segments in society, particularly the Catholic church. Keep in mind that at this time the United States was in the midst of a severe economic depression. Many individuals, including prominent Catholics, connected the country's economic poverty with the nation's moral bankruptcy as evidenced by the films of the period. Additionally, an Apostolic Delegate from Rome took the film industry to task in a blistering speech before the Catholic Charities Convention in New York. In April of 1934, a committee composed of American bishops responded to the speech and to the general tenor of the period by announcing the organization of a nationwide Legion of Decency, whose members were to fight for better films. The Legion threatened to boycott those theaters that exhibited objectionable films and sometimes made good on their threats. The Chicago chapter of the Legion enrolled half a million members in a matter of days and was matched by equal enrollment in Brooklyn. Detroit Catholics affixed "We Demand Clean Movies" bumper stickers to their cars. Other religious groups joined the Legion—Jewish clergy in New York, Lutherans in Missouri. Pope Pius XI praised the Legion as an "excellent experiment" and called upon bishops all over the world to imitate it.

There were 20 million Catholics in the United States in 1934, and naturally the film industry took this group seriously. The Production Code Administration was set up with the power to slap a $25,000 fine on films released without the administration's seal of approval. The Legion's boycotts hurt enough at the box office to force many theaters to book only films that the Legion approved. In Albuquerque, New Mexico, seventeen out of twenty-one theaters agreed not to book a film condemned by the Legion. In Albany, New York, Catholics pledged to avoid for six months each theater that had screened the condemned film *Baby Doll.* Producers, frightened by this display of economic power, began meeting with Legion members to make sure there were no lascivious elements in their films.

By the 1960s, however, the Legion was losing most of its clout. The restructuring of the film industry allowed independent producers to market their films without code approval. Many producers did just that and demonstrated that some films could make money even without the Legion and Production Code approval. The increasingly permissive mood of the country encouraged an avalanche of more mature and controversial films. Moreover, the Legion, renamed the National Catholic Office for Motion Pictures, painted itself into a corner when it condemned artistically worthwhile films like Bergman's *The Silence* and Antonioni's *Blow Up* and endorsed films like *Godzilla vs. the Thing* and *Goliath and the Sins of Babylon.* By the 1970s, this group had effectively lost all its power; it was essentially disbanded in 1980. Nonetheless, during its prime, the Legion of Decency was the single most effective private influence on the film industry.

what topics should be handled carefully so as not to rile existing pressure groups. The 1930 code is remarkable for its specificity; it rambles on for nearly twenty printed pages. The following are some excerpts:

> The presentation of scenes, episodes, plots, etc. which are deliberately meant to excite [sex and passion] on the part of the audience is always wrong, is subversive to the interest of society, and is a peril to the human race.

> The more intimate parts of the human body are the male and female organs and the breasts of a woman.

> a. They should never be uncovered.
> b. They should not be covered with transparent or translucent material.
> c. They should not be clearly and unmistakably outlined by garments. . . .

> There must be no display at any time of machine guns, sub-machine guns or other weapons generally classified as illegal weapons. . . .

> Obscene dances are those: which represent sexual actions, whether performed solo or with two or more; which are designed to excite an audience, arouse passion, or to cause physical excitement.

A few years after the Production Code was drafted, a Roman Catholic organization, the Legion of Decency (see boxed material), pressured the industry to put teeth into its code enforcement. The MPPDA ruled that no company belonging to its organization would distribute or release any film unless it bore the Production Code Administration's seal of approval. In addition, a $25,000 fine could be levied against a firm that violated this rule. Because of the hammerlock that the major studios had over the movie industry at this time, it was virtually impossible for an independent producer to make or exhibit a film without the aid of a member company. As a result, the Production Code turned out to be more restrictive than many of the local censorship laws it was designed to avoid.

The Production Code was a meaningful force in the film industry for about twenty years. During the late 1940s, however, changes that would ultimately alter the basic structure of the motion picture industry also scuttled the code. In 1948, the Paramount case ended producer-distributor control of theaters, thus allowing independent producers to market a film without the Production Code seal. In addition, economic competition from television prompted films to treat more mature subjects. The industry responded during the 1950s by liberalizing the code; however, despite this easing of restrictions, more and more producers began to ignore them. Nonetheless, the code, outdated and unenforceable, persisted into the 1960s. A 1966 revision that tried to keep pace with the changing social attitudes of the 1960s proved to be too little too late. In 1968, the motion picture industry entered into a new phase of self-regulation when the Production Code seal of approval was dropped and a new motion picture rating system was established. Operated under the auspices of the Motion Picture Association of America (successor to the MPPDA), the National Association of Theater Owners, and the Independent Film Importers and Distributors of America, this new system, commonly referred to as the **MPAA system,** places films into one of five categories:

G: suitable for general audiences
PG: parental guidance suggested
PG-13:   some content may be objectionable for children under 13 (a new category added in 1984)

R: restricted to persons over seventeen unless accompanied by parent or adult guardian

X: no one under seventeen admitted

Unlike the old Production Code, which regulated film content, the new system leaves producers pretty much free to include whatever scenes they like as long as they realize that by so doing, they may restrict the size of their potential audience. One possible repercussion of this system may be the steady decline in the number of G-rated films released each year. Producers evidently feel that movies in this category will be perceived as children's films and will not be attractive to a more mature audience. During the first eleven years of the rating system's existence, the percentage of films in the G category dropped, while the percentage of films in the R category increased. X-rated films have never accounted for more than 10 percent of the total number of films submitted for review (of course, many low-budget, hard-core pornographic films are never submitted for classification). In 1987, about 83 percent of all movies released by the well-known studios and independent producers fell into the PG and R categories; only 1 percent was G rated.

In order for the MPAA rating system to work, producers, distributors, theater owners, and parents must all cooperate. There is no governmental involvement in the classification system; there are no fines involved. Moviemakers are not required to submit a film for rating. People evidently think that the system is a good idea. An industry survey done in 1988 disclosed that 67 percent of the adults surveyed considered the ratings to be ''very useful'' guides for children's attendance. How often parents actually pay attention to these classifications is still a bit unclear. One survey done in the 1970s found that only 35 percent of a sample of parents could name a movie that their teenage sons and daughters had recently seen and only 17 percent knew the film's rating.

Other Media Codes of Performance and Ethics

There are several other codes of ethics that are involved in regulating the media. The comic book industry, for example, through the Comics Magazine Association, has developed a forty-one–point code. This code, developed in order to forestall governmental regulation of the industry, tries to discourage excessive violence, nudity, and horror in comic book content. Like the codes in the other media, this one is also voluntary. Publishers whose material is approved display the code seal on their comics.

In the advertising industry, several professional organizations have drafted codes of performance. The American Association of Advertising Agencies first adopted its Standards of Practice in 1924. This code, which covers contracts, credit extension, unfair tactics, and the creative side of advertising, contains provisions prohibiting misleading price claims, offensive statements, and the circulation of harmful rumors about a competitor. The Advertising Code of American Business, developed and distributed by the American Advertising Federation and the Association of Better Business Bureaus International, covers much the same ground. Memberships in these organizations and adherence to the codes are voluntary. In public relations, the Public Relations Society of America adopted its first code in 1954 and revised it during the 1970s. As with the other codes enforcement is essentially voluntary, and the society has no control over a practitioner who is not a member.

INTERNAL CONTROLS

Codes establishd by professional organizations and individual ethics are not the only informal controls on media behavior. Most media organizations have other internal controls that frequently come into play. Written statements of policy can be found in most newspapers, television, radio, and motion picture organizations. In advertising, a professional organization for self-regulation has existed since 1971.

Organizational Policy: Television Networks' Standards and Practices

The three major TV networks have departments whose job it is to make sure that all of the programs they broadcast meet the networks' own standards of performance. Usually labeled "Standards and Practices," these departments have a common goal: providing programs that are acceptable to the majority of the viewing audience. At NBC, the Broadcast Standards Department collaborated with the network's program development section. In a typical season, the Standards Department made about 2000 judgments on entertainment programs and scripts. All of the network standards-and-practices departments made suggestions at all stages of production: proposals, outlines, scripts, shooting scripts, and final program. Feature films made originally for theatrical release were also reviewed by these departments, and many films had sequences edited out or dialogue changed before being presented on TV. Because of the tremendous variety of content, the networks' standards-and-practices organizations generally did not have a comprehensive written policy that covered every situation. Instead, these departments relied mainly on the judgments of their staff members. There were, however, certain general policy statements that were followed. The following are two excerpts from the NBC Statement of Program Standards:

> Language: Unless there is an overriding dramatic justification, NBC avoids the use of profanity, words of obvious disrespect, and obscene or vulgar language.

> Minorities: NBC standards are sensitive to the problems of racial and ethnic minorities and of all disadvantaged individuals. NBC is careful to exclude comic material that could be considered offensive or demeaning while allowing good natured joking that can be socially stabilizing.

In addition to these network policy statements, most local stations also have what is known as a **policy book.** This book typically spells out philosophy and standards of operation and identifies what practices are encouraged or discouraged. For example, most television and radio stations have a policy against newsroom personnel functioning as commercial spokespersons. Radio stations typically have a policy against airing "homemade" tapes and records. Other stations may have rules against playing songs that are drug oriented or too suggestive. Commercials that make extravagant claims or ads for questionable products and services might also be prohibited under local station policy.

Limits of acceptability, of course, are always changing. Back in the 1960s, the network's Standards and Practices Department decreed that Barbara Eden of "I Dream of Jeannie" couldn't show her navel on network TV. By the late 1980s, however, a decreasing network audience share and competition from cable channels pushed back the limits. In the 1988–1989 season, the miniseries "Favorite Son" and a Geraldo Rivera special on satanism contained the most explicit scenes of sex and violence yet seen on network TV.

The networks also prescreen commercials and reject the ads they find too suggestive or in bad taste. Standards in commercials, too, are becoming more liberal. For many years, the nets had a policy proscribing ads that showed live women modeling lingerie. An ad for a bra, for example, showed the product suspended in space or on the torso of a mannequin. In 1987, the nets loosened their policy a bit and allowed an ad that showed a real woman actually wearing a Playtex bra.

Finally, the networks' budget cutbacks have hit the standards-and-practices departments. All the nets have slashed the number of employees in this area and have allowed series producers authority in determining program content. Some series producers, however, went too far and offended both viewers and potential advertisers. As a result, the networks are reexamining their cutbacks. NBC, for one, announced in 1989 a new director for its Standards Department and promised to take a closer look at its shows.

Organizational Policy: Newspapers and Magazines

Newspapers and magazines have policy statements that take two distinct forms. On the one hand, there are **operating policies** that cover the everyday problems and situations that crop up during the normal functioning of the paper. On the other, there are **editorial policies** that the newspaper follows in order to persuade the public on certain issues or to achieve specific goals. Both policies can exert some control over what a particular newspaper or magazine publishes.

Operating policies will vary from paper to paper. In general, however, these policies might cover such matters as accepting ''freebies,'' using deception to gather information, paying newsmakers for a story or exclusive interview (checkbook journalism), junkets, electronic surveillance, use of stolen documents, outside employment of reporters and editors, conflicts of interest, accepting advertising for X-rated films, and deciding whether or not to publish the names of rape victims. Here, for example, are excerpts from the *Rules and Guidelines* used by the *Milwaukee Journal:*

> Free tickets or passes to sports events, movies, theatrical productions, circuses, ice shows, or other entertainment may not be accepted or solicited by staff members.
>
> A gift that exceeds token value should be returned promptly with an explanation that it is against our policy. If it is impractical to return it, the company will donate it to a charity.
>
> Participating in politics at any level is not allowed, either for pay or as a volunteer.
> Public relations and publicity work in fields outside the *Journal* should be avoided.

Some indication of the degree to which journalists have adopted these and similar policies comes from surveys done by Sigma Delta Chi, the Society for Professional Journalists. A 1983 survey found that 88 percent of all journalists ruled out all gift taking (except for inexpensive token gifts). Thirty-five percent said they never accept free trips, and 47 percent reported that their company allowed them to moonlight (hold down another job that did not conflict with their position as a journalist).

Some newspapers and magazines are liberal; some are conservative. Some support Democratic candidates; others support Republicans. Some are in favor of nuclear energy; others against. These and other attitudes are generally expressed in e editorial pages of the newspaper. Editorial policy is generally clear at most ublications. The *Chicago Tribune* has traditionally expressed a conservative point f view. The *New York Times* has a more liberal policy. The editorial policy of a aper will exert a certain amount of control over the material that is printed on its ditorial pages. This, of course, the paper has a perfect right to do. There may be mes, however, when the editorial policy of the paper spills over onto its news ages, and this might cause a problem with the paper's reputation for objectivity, esponsibility, and integrity.

A 1984 article in the *Columbia Journalism Review* illustrates several examples f editorial policy permeating and perhaps injuring news coverage. According to the rticle, the new publisher of a Jacksonville, Florida, newspaper during the late 1970s vas a local real estate and banking mogul with close ties to the business community. When one of the paper's reporters was investigating the business practices of one of he publisher's associates, the reporter was summoned into the publisher's office. There, in the presence of the person she was investigating, she was ordered to reveal er sources and her information. In 1979, when the people of Jacksonville were onsidering whether to build a controversial bridge opposed by environmentalists ut favored by local business interests, the reporter who had provided detailed overage of the problems associated with the bridge was suddenly reassigned to nother beat: covering the local beaches. This probusiness philosophy evidently arried over when yet another new publisher took over the paper in 1983. The ewspaper staff was told to prepare a forty-two–part series of promotional articles outing the city. For forty-two consecutive days, a different aspect of the city was o be featured on a full page with artwork and a news story written in a "positive" style.

This procommunity philosophy, called "boosterism," is not limited to Jacksonville. In Flint, Michigan, the publisher and the editor of the local paper belong to the Chamber of Commerce and sixteen other community organizations. This in itself is not a problem if it does not interfere with news reporting. Unfortunately, there is evidence that it has. In April of 1985, a reporter wrote an investigative story on the possibly improper use of tax and grant money to finance trips by members of the local school board. After a visit to the paper by a school official (and fellow Chamber of Commerce member) the publisher ordered the story killed. Likewise, when the local Fisher Body plant closed, TV networks and newspaper headlines across the state announced the bad news that Flint was about to lose 3600 jobs. When it covered the story, the local Flint paper didn't mention the job loss until the eleventh paragraph on an inside page. "Good news," however, got prominent play. A story about new shrubs being planted at the local Buick facility got front-page coverage while a story about the Civil Rights Department charging the Flint Chamber of Commerce with sex discrimination got covered on page fourteen of the paper's third section.

In 1988, a Pasadena, California, paper carried a column that criticized the city's extravagant and expensive preparations for the Tournament of Roses Parade. A few days later, under pressure from civic leaders, the paper's executive editor apologized in print for the remarks. Two days later the column was permanently dropped.

Owners and publishers can exert editorial control over news policy in several ways. They can hire only those people who agree with their editorial views. (For example, the *New Orleans Times-Picayune* ran an ad in a trade magazine for a business reporter. One of the qualifications was a "probusiness philosophy.") They can also fire those people who produce stories that the owner doesn't like, or they can issue orders to downplay some topics while paying large amounts of attention to others. Walter Annenberg, when he owned the *Philadelphia Inquirer* and the

Editorial Policy and What's "Said": *Time* Magazine and the Presidents

The problem of editorial policy affecting straight news coverage was never a dilemma for *Time* magazine under the direction of Henry Luce. When it was founded in 1923, *Time*'s editors argued that objectivity in presenting the news isn't possible and that *Time* reporters shouldn't hesitate in making a judgment in their articles. More often than not, these judgments were in line with *Time*'s editorial policy. One subtle way of injecting editorial judgment into ostensibly factual news stories is to choose carefully the synonyms used for the word "said" when reporting someone's conversations and speeches. An article by John C. Merrill in a 1965 issue of *Journalism Quarterly* documents that *Time* employed this technique in its reporting about Presidents Truman and Eisenhower.

President Harry S Truman was no favorite of the magazine. When Truman spoke he seldom "said" anything; instead, he "sputtered," "barked," "droned," "preached," or "popped a gasket." When he finally "said" something, he said it "curtly" or "coldly" or said it "flushed with anger" or "grinning slyly." President Dwight D. Eisenhower, however, was liked by the magazine. When he spoke, he "chatted amiably," "pointed out cautiously," "talked with a happy grin," or "spoke warmly." Or, when he preferred not to say anything, he "skillfully refused to commit himself."

News, reportedly became so upset with the management of the Philadelphia 76ers pro basketball team that he limited coverage of them to two paragraphs after a win and one paragraph after a loss.

What is the significance of these examples for the news-consuming public? For one thing, we should point out that the above cases are probably exceptions to the norm rather than the norm itself. Nonetheless, they do illustrate the potential hazards of relying on only one source for news. The intelligent consumer of news and information should rely on several different media to get a more complete picture.

Self-Criticism

Some informal control over media content and practices comes from within—but not much. Compared to the amount of investigative reporting and critical analyses that newspapers, magazines, television, and radio conduct about other facets of society, the amount of internal criticism that they do seems insignificant. True, there are some exceptions. Newspapers and magazines employ critics who comment on films and TV programs, but it is debatable if this criticism has any influence. In the news area, there are several journalism reviews that regularly criticize media performance. The *Columbia Journalism Review* is the best known, but its circulation is only 35,000. The *Chicago Journalism Review* and the *Washington Journalism Review* are the two other well-written publications of this type. There were more journalism reviews at the beginning of the 1970s, but their number has steadily diminished. Television and radio news operations seldom do a serious job of criticizing themselves. Newspapers do a bit more in this area, and the *Wall Street Journal* has occasionally run an in-depth study of the problems facing the newspaper industry. Further, a questionable media tactic, such as the Gary Hart surveillance, will usually prompt a flurry of self-examination. In film, the industry newspaper *Variety* has sometimes published an article critical of the film industry. *Billboard,* the trade publication of the sound recording industry, has run analytical, if not critical, pieces on the recording industry.

Some newspapers have tried to incorporate an idea from Scandinavia into their operations in order to provide some internal criticism. An individual employed by the paper (called an **ombudsperson**) is assigned to handle complaints from readers who feel that they have gotten a raw deal and to criticize in general the performance of the paper's staff. The ombudsperson with the Louisville, Kentucky, newspapers handled between 500 and 1000 complaints during the first three years the paper had this system. The idea, however, has not made a big splash nationwide, and only a few papers maintain such a person. (One of the problems might be the difficult-to-pronounce title, "ombudsperson." The Louisville papers reportedly get letters addressed to the "Omnibus person" or to "Dear Omnipotent.")

Professional Self-Regulation in Advertising

In 1971, the leading advertising professional organizations—the Council of Better Business Bureaus, the American Advertising Federation, the American Association of Advertising Industries, and the Association of National Advertisers—formed the National Advertising Review Council. Its objective is to sustain high standards of truth and accuracy in advertising. The Council itself is composed of two divisions: the National Advertising Division (NAD) and the National Advertising Review Board (NARB). When a complaint about an ad is made by a consumer or competitor, the complaint goes first to the NAD, where it is evaluated. The NAD can dismiss the complaint as unfounded or trivial or it can contact the advertiser for an explanation or further substantiation. If the NAD is satisfied that the ad in question is accurate, it will dismiss the complaint. If the NAD is not satisfied with the explanation, it can ask the advertiser to change the ad or discontinue the message. If the advertiser disagrees, the case goes to the NARB, which functions as a court of appeals. Ultimately, if the case has not reached an acceptable solution, the NARB could call it to the attention of the Federal Trade Commission or other appropriate agencies. Most advertisers, however, are willing to comply with NARB's wishes. Note, however, that the National Advertising Review Council depends totally on moral forces to accomplish its goals. It cannot order an advertiser to stop running an ad, impose a fine, or kick anybody out of the profession.

To give you some idea of the kinds of complaints handled by the NAD, here is a sampling taken from the late 1980s.

Case One—A consumer questioned the accuracy of a TV commercial for macadamia nuts, noting that in the ad the jar contained all whole nuts while in reality the product sold at retail stores was a mixture of whole nuts, half nuts and pieces. When contacted by NAD, the advertiser noted that the product contained about 50 percent whole nuts and only about 2 percent nut fragments. The advertiser also pointed out that the consumer is able to inspect the jar's contents before purchase. The NAD agreed with the consumer that it was misleading to show a close-up of a jar in which no broken nuts were visible. The company agreed to modify the ad.

Case Two—A college student complained that the compact discs he bought after seeing a TV ad for something called "The 50 Best of the British Invasion," marketed by Silver Eagle Records, contained only forty songs. The company responded that the ad carried a message saying "edited for compact disc." The NAD said that wasn't enough and the company agreed to follow NAD's recommendations in future advertising.

Public Relations Society of America Code of Professional Standards for the Practice of Public Relations

Declaration of Principles

Members of the Public Relations Society of America base their professional principles on the fundamental value and dignity of the individual, holding that the free exercise of human rights, especially freedom of speech, freedom of assembly, and freedom of the press, is essential to the practice of public relations.

In serving the interests of clients and employers, we dedicate ourselves to the goals of better communication, understanding, and cooperation among the diverse individuals, groups, and institutions of society, and of equal opportunity of employment in the public relations profession.

We pledge:

To conduct ourselves professionally, with truth, accuracy, fairness, and responsibility to the public;

To improve our individual competence and advance the knowledge and proficiency of the profession through continuing research and education;

And to adhere to the articles of the Code of Professional Standards for the Practice of Public Relations as adopted by the governing Assembly of the Society.

Articles of the Code

These articles have been adopted by the Public Relations Society of America to promote and maintain high standards of public service and ethical conduct among its members.

1. A member shall deal fairly with clients or employers, past and present, or potential, with fellow practitioners, and the general public.

2. A member shall conduct his or her professional life in accord with the public interest.

3. A member shall adhere to truth and accuracy and to generally accepted standards of good taste.

4. A member shall not represent conflicting or competing interests without the express consent of those involved, given after a full disclosure of the facts; nor place himself or herself in a position where the member's interest is or may be in conflict with a duty to a client, or others, without a full disclosure of such interests to all involved.

5. A member shall safeguard the confidences of present and former clients, as well as of those persons or entities who have disclosed confidences to a member in the context of communications relating to an anticipated professional relationship with such member, and shall not accept retainers or employment that may involve disclosing, using or offering to use such confidences to the disadvantage or prejudice of such present, former or potential clients or employers.

6. A member shall not engage in any practice which tends to corrupt the integrity of channels of communication or the processes of government.

7. A member shall not intentionally communicate false or misleading information and is obliged to use care to avoid communication of false or misleading information.

8. A member shall be prepared to identify publicly the name of the client or employer on whose behalf any public communication is made.

9. A member shall not make use of any individual or organization purporting to serve or represent an announced cause, or purporting to be independent or unbiased, but actually serving an undisclosed special or private interest of a member, client, or employer.

10. A member shall not intentionally injure the professional reputation or practice of another practitioner. However, if a member has evidence that another member has been guilty of unethical, illegal, or unfair practices, including those in violation of this code, the member shall present the information promptly to the proper authorities of the society for action in accordance with the procedure set forth in Article XII of the bylaws.

11. A member called as a witness in a proceeding for the enforcement of this code shall be bound to appear, unless excused for sufficient reason by the judicial panel.

12. A member, in performing services for a client or employer, shall not accept fees, commissions, or any other valuable consideration from anyone other than the client or employer in connection with those services without the express consent of the client or employer, given after a full disclosure of the facts.

13. A member shall not guarantee the achievement of specified results beyond the member's direct control.

14. A member shall, as soon as possible, sever relations with any organization or individual if such relationship requires conduct contrary to the articles of this code.

Public Relations Society of America. Used by permission.

Case Three—A rental car firm published newspaper coupons advertising a $39 per week rental price. Several consumers claimed that when they tried to rent a car at the advertised rate, they were told that the cars were unavailable and customers had to rent more expensive models. The company responded by saying that inexperienced counter personnel failed to tell people that the advertised models would be available in a short time. It also agreed to consider refunds to disappointed customers and to change its future ads to stress the limited availability of the models.

OUTSIDE INFLUENCES

The larger context that surrounds a media organization often contains factors that have an influence on media performance. This section discusses four: economics, pressure groups, press councils, and education.

Economic Pressures

Another factor that has influence over media gatekeepers is a potent one—money. In commercial media, the loss of revenue can be an important consideration in controlling what gets filmed, published, or broadcast. Economic controls come in many shapes and forms. Pressure can be brought to bear by advertisers, by the medium's own business policy, by the general economic structure of the industry, and by consumer groups.

Pressure From Advertisers. Films and sound recording are financed by the purchase of individual tickets, albums, and tapes. They earn virtually no money from advertisers and consequently are immune from their pressure. On the other hand, in the print media, newspapers depend on advertising for about 75 percent of their income, while magazines derive 50 percent of their revenues from ads. Radio and television, of course, depend upon ads for all their income. The actual amount of control that an advertiser has over media content and behavior is difficult to determine. To keep the issue in perspective, it is probably fair to say that most news stories and most television and radio programs are put together without much thought as to what advertisers will say about them. Occasionally, however, you will find examples of attempts at control. We will list a few as illustrations.

A 1985 issue of the *Chicago Sun-Times* contained a legitimate cartoon satirizing the owner of a local Cadillac dealership. The owner was involved in the corruption trial of a traffic court judge. The owner testified that he had regularly given the judge and his wife free Cadillacs to drive in return for favorable disposal of traffic tickets accumulated by his car-leasing customers. It turned out that the auto dealership was one of the paper's leading advertisers. The *Sun-Times* later published a front-page apology to the owner of the dealership.

In 1988, a Wisconsin weekly, under pressure from a large pesticide company that bought a lot of ads in the paper, fired an editor who had written an article on the dangers of pesticide poisoning.

In another example in the same area, the May 1985 edition of the newsletter of the Michigan Press Association contained helpful hints on how to design ads that resembled legitimate news stories. Using the same typeface and format as the surrounding story and burying the advertiser logo in the headline or text rather than at the bottom were two of the recommendations.

Advertiser pressure appears to be on the decline. One reason is the drop in the number of markets with competing newspapers. In cities with a single paper, the advertiser has no other place to go to get his or her print message before the public. In fact, many advertisers who have withdrawn advertising from a newspaper have quickly reinstated it. In radio and television, sponsors rarely produce their own programs as they did back in the 1950s. Instead, they buy commercials scattered throughout daytime and evening programming. This means that they can no longer dictate the content. In network television, prime-time commercial minutes are so much in demand that advertisers who pull out are quickly replaced by others, with the result that there is no economic hardship for the network. Additionally, the nets are supported by about 500 advertisers whose median billing accounted for only approximately 0.04 percent of network sales. As you can see, the threatened loss of one advertising account will not cause much concern. Small-market radio stations, especially those losing money or making only a marginal profit, are the most likely to succumb to advertiser pressure.

Business Policies. Economic pressure on media content is sometimes encouraged by the business practices of the media themselves. Some newspapers and broadcasting stations might not report all the details of a news story or might delete certain items in an attempt to give a break to their advertisers. When the Supreme Court of Massachusetts ruled that a creditor could be sued for harassing those who owed money, the Boston newspapers declined to identify the retail store involved in the suit. The store had allegedly made late-night calls to those behind in their payments and threatened them with credit revocation. Why was the name of the store not mentioned? Perhaps because the store in question spent a lot of money on advertising space in the papers. In another example, a TV station taped out the brand names of toys that were being used to demonstrate potentially hazardous playthings. (Toy advertisers spend a lot of money on TV ads.) In San Francisco, two daily papers deleted the names of local companies named in a study of air pollution in the area.

Then there is the problem of what a prominent editor called "revenue-related reading matter." This crops up when a new shopping center or movie theater or department store opens in town and receives heavy news coverage, perhaps more than is justified by the considerations of ordinary journalism, in return for advertising revenue. Formal arrangements of this sort are difficult to document, but the *Wall Street Journal* in a 1966 article turned up a couple. A Texas newspaper ran a Monday business section that apparently covered commerce and industry news in the local area. In fact, the news space was calculated to reflect the amount of advertising each firm had purchased in the paper. In Colorado, a memo from the business news director of a newspaper to its managing editor stated that an agreement was made between the paper and the owners of a new shopping center in which one page of news coverage would be provided for every four pages of ads purchased by shopping center stores. At WLUP in Chicago, talk-show hosts ad-libbed mentions of items they saw in the *Chicago Tribune* but neglected to tell their listeners that the paper paid for each plug. In St. Paul, Minnesota, during the 1987 Christmas season, a local paper treated its readers to dozens of articles about Santabear, a promotional toy sponsored by the Dayton Hudson Company, a department store chain. The paper even published a sixteen-page educational supplement about the toy. Dayton Hudson was the paper's largest advertiser.

It is also difficult to tell how much advertiser influence is exerted on gardening sections, restaurant listings, travel pages, and "special sections." A Florida paper, for example, sent a letter to registrars of southeastern colleges and universities, inviting them to advertise in a special section on education. Each school that chose to advertise would receive "at no additional cost" editorial space equal to the size of the paid ad. The schools themselves were asked to provide content for the "news" story. At least one Philadelphia paper was up-front about it. In its Restaurant Index it printed the following: "Because of space limitations only those restaurants that advertise in our paper are listed in this guide." Another paper ran a column introducing its new food critic and even included a picture for restaurant owners to clip and save.

If some organizations go out of their way to keep potential and actual advertisers happy, other newspapers and TV stations have actually allowed economic considerations to keep some people and places out of news pages and newscasts. A Lansing, Michigan, television station evidently used news blackouts to prod some organizations into paying past-due bills. A memo from the station owner to the sports director, reproduced in the *Columbia Journalism Review*, states in part:

> I heard your story . . . on the Tennis Tournament . . . at the Lansing Tennis Club. These people owe us $1500 . . . and are making no effort to pay us. Considering these circumstances, I do not want to give them any publicity on the Club or any of their activities.

Others have used blackout techniques to exert economic pressure in other ways. In Florida, a newspaper was sued for libel by the management of a local stadium. When the stadium owners refused to settle out of court, the paper instituted a policy of blacking out news about events going on at the stadium. In 1978, the Kansas Press Association supported a newspaper publisher in his news blackout of a political candidate who had bought advertising on radio and television but had bought no space in newspapers.

These activities are not illegal (although the TV station might have a hard time explaining to the FCC at license-renewal time why a news blackout is in the public interest). They do, however, raise questions about the credibility and integrity of any media outlet that would mislead its readers and viewers into thinking that such commercial undertakings are newsworthy or that such actions demonstrate responsible behavior. Lastly, the above illustrations are not meant to criticize or impugn the reputation of any medium or profession. There are probably countless, less publicized examples of situations where newspapers, magazines, television, and radio stations resisted advertising and economic pressure and printed or broadcast what they thought should be publicized. What you should learn from this section is the close relationship that can sometimes exist between advertiser and media and the pressures that can result. Most of the time, this will cause few problems. When professional judgment is compromised by the dollar sign, however, then perhaps the economic pressures are performing a dysfunction for the media.

Economic Structure of the Industry. In the newspaper industry, economic survival depends upon circulation. The higher the circulation, the more advertisers will pay for ads and the more money comes in from subscriptions and single-copy purchases. The newspaper business, as we have mentioned, is highly competitive. Although there are few cities where daily papers compete directly with one another, daily newspapers compete fiercely with weeklies, television, radio, and other leisure-time activities for the attention of the audience. In many urban markets during the 1970s, some newspapers seemed to be losing the battle. The number of people reading a daily newspaper and the number of papers sold in the United States dropped during that decade. Since 1960, New York, Boston, Chicago, Los Angeles, Detroit, Houston, Baltimore, Cleveland, and Philadelphia have seen the death of at least one daily newspaper. Although advertising revenue has remained healthy, newspaper executives still see declining readership as their number-one problem. In order to cope with the decline, newspapers have begun to rely on market research to discover what types of things readers want in a paper. This may not sound like a bad idea, but there is the danger that the traditional obligation of the journalist—to give a truthful, comprehensive, and intelligent account of the day's events—may be short-circuited by marketing experts. Will economic considerations rather than journalistic judgment increasingly dictate the content of newspapers? Or, as the *Columbia Journalism Review* succinctly put it:

> Some [editors] are coming to think of their offering in terms that may sound alien to journalists: news as what sells, or what the marketing experts say will sell; news as . . . a palatable product whipped up by specialists in circulation, advertising and graphics; news as a servant to comfort, flatter or tempt the reader; news as a soothing environment for the advertiser.

The danger in catering too faithfully to readers' preferences is the possibility of distorting the actual news content of the paper. A newspaper-sponsored survey disclosed that stories about accidents, disasters, and crime were what readers read most. In Detroit, an editor, who evidently took the results of this survey to heart, distributed a memo to the newspaper's staff praising an article on rape, robbery, and an auto accident as a "fine example" of the sort of story the paper wanted on page one: "I want at least one [story on page one] that will jolt, shock, or at least wake up our readers." Other examples of what the editor wanted were stories headlined "Nun Charged with Killing Her Baby" and "Prison Horrors Revealed." Even the staid *New York Times* spent $20,000 promoting a search for the Loch Ness monster. Note that in the above cases, economic pressure encouraged papers to develop mass appeal by emphasizing content that was popular, breezy, or sensational. Most newspapers did not try to attract more readers with increased news coverage of economic, educational, scientific, or foreign-affairs news. Instead, they responded with more least-common-denominator news, designed to attract the largest crowd.

The pressure toward least-common-denominator content is even more apparent in broadcast journalism. During the early 1970s, the trend in TV journalism moved toward "eyewitness" or "happy-talk" news, a format stressing a "show-business" approach to TV news. Youthful, attractive, well-dressed anchorpersons and news "personalities" traded quips and witty one-liners while delivering the stories. The "eyewitness" format also stressed the news value of the tried-and-true audience-grabbing topics of humor, violence, human interest, and soft-feature stories.

Similarly, television and radio entertainment programming is designed to please advertisers by attracting the largest possible audience. Given a choice between a program about ballet and another about a tough private eye, the programmers will probably choose the one about the detective because it will likely attract more people. In the early days of network prime-time television, classical music programs appeared in prime time; they were quickly replaced, however, by quiz and game shows with more mass appeal. Furthermore, the 1950s were typified by the airing of prestige drama programs during prime time ("Studio One," "Goodyear TV Playhouse," "Actor's Studio," etc.). As more people bought sets and TV became a mass medium, the prestige drama was replaced by westerns—a program form that appealed to larger numbers and was therefore more attractive to advertisers.

The economic situation of the three networks is interesting because together they create what economists call an **oligopoly,** a situation in which a few firms dominate the market. (The auto industry, the steel industry, and the fast-food industry are other examples of oligopolies.) Oligopolies are marked by several distinct characteristics. First, the firms are mutually interdependent. A successful innovation by one member is usually imitated by the others. If Burger King succeeds in marketing a chicken sandwich or any other new product, McDonald's and Wendy's will probably add that item to their menu as well. In network television, if ABC succeeds with detective shows, expect to see detective shows on CBS and NBC as well. If CBS scores a hit with "60 Minutes," then ABC will counter with "20/20" and NBC with its "NBC Magazine." Second, the product of an oligopoly is essentially interchangeable. It would be quite difficult to tell the difference between steel made by Bethlehem Steel or the U.S. Steel Company. Similarly, over the years, the schedules of the three networks have increasingly begun to resemble one another. Situation comedies on NBC are virtually the same as situation comedies on CBS and ABC. The three schedules are almost interchangeable. In sum, the three major networks involved with prime-time TV behave in line with the classical theory of response to economic pressures. This situation, of course, will change due to the increased competition from cable and VCRs.

Pressure Groups

Various segments of the audience can band together and try to exert control over the operation of mass media organizations. These groups sometimes use the threat of economic pressure (boycotts) or sometimes simply rely on the negative effects of bad publicity to achieve their goal. In radio and television, pressure groups (or citizens' groups, as they are often called) can resort to applying legal pressure during the license-renewal process. Because of broadcasting's unique legal position, it has been the focus of a great deal of pressure-group attention. In 1964, for example, a group of black citizens, working with the Office of Communication of the United

Just Say No, Mighty Mouse

Sometimes pressure groups might go a little too far. In mid-1988, a conservative media watchdog group claimed that a recent episode of CBS's Saturday-morning animated series "Mighty Mouse" showed the cartoon hero sniffing cocaine. A spokesperson for the citizens' group said that close inspection of the program showed that Mighty Mouse, spurned by a female character, reaches under his cloak, removes what appears to be a white powder, and inhales it through his nose.

Not true, responded Ralph Bakshi, pro-

ducer of the series. (Bakshi is best known for his *Fritz the Cat* adult cartoon film.) Mighty Mouse was innocently smelling the crushed petals of flowers that had been given to him earlier by the female character, a flower seller. CBS, however, ordered the three-and-a-half–second segment edited from the cartoon.

The same conservative pressure group had earlier condemned "The Dukes of Hazzard," *A Passage to India,* and *Back to the Future.*

Church of Christ, formed a pressure group and attempted to deny the license renewal of a TV station in Jackson, Mississippi, because of alleged discrimination on the part of station management. After a long and complicated legal battle, the citizens' group was successful in its efforts. This success probably encouraged the formation of other groups. John Banzhaf III headed an organization called ASH (Action for Smoking and Health), which was instrumental in convincing Congress to ban cigarette advertising from radio and television. A local group in Texarkana, Arkansas, negotiated an agreement with a local television station whereby the station would alter some of its programming and employment practices in return for the group's dropping of its legal action. Several Mexican-American groups were successful in persuading the Frito-Lay Company to remove its cartoon character, the "Frito Bandito," from its ads. At about the same time, perhaps the most influential of all the pressure groups interested in broadcasting was formed: Action for Children's Television (ACT). From a modest start, this group was successful in achieving the following:

1. persuading the networks to appoint a supervisor for children's programming
2. eliminating drug and vitamin ads from kids' shows
3. instituting a ban on the host's selling in children's programs (Captain Kangaroo cannot sell bicycles, e.g.)
4. reducing the amount of advertising during Saturday morning programs

In the mid-1970s, other special-interest groups whose primary interest was not broadcasting began to get involved with television programming. The American Medical Association stated that televised violence was harmful to a person's mental health and sponsored research to measure the amount of violence in network shows. The national Parent Teachers Association (PTA) also criticized TV violence and working with another citizens' group—the National Citizens Committee for Broadcasting—identified the most violent TV shows and publicized the companies that advertised during those programs. Implicit in the PTA's listings was the threat of a boycott against companies that sponsor violence. In fact, several companies changed their ads when confronted with the PTA's results.

The National Organization for Women (NOW) has also been active in campaigning against discrimination in hiring practices and for a more representative portrayal of women in the mass media. NOW has not limited its attention to the broadcast media. It has also been concerned with the elimination of sexist language in all media, the image of women in advertising, and the lack of significant women's roles in popular films. In 1985, Mothers Against Drunk Driving (MADD) was instrumental in getting the TV networks to modify their policies toward portraying alcohol use in their programs.

Perhaps the most successful of all pressure groups was the National Legion of Decency, discussed earlier in this chapter, which exerted a surprising amount of control over the motion picture industry during the 1930s and 1940s, primarily by

Members of the National Writers Union march along Fifth Avenue to protest against booksellers that had removed copies of The Satanic Verses *from their shelves. (Clarence Davis N.Y. Daily News Photo)*

using the threat of a boycott. Individual films have upset other groups. *The Godfather* was deemed offensive by some Italian-American groups. The 1988 film *The Last Temptation of Christ* inspired threats of picketing and demonstrations even before it opened. The film eventually took in about $9 million, a little better than it would have done without all the controversy.

Pressure groups organized along political lines have also exerted control over media content and practices. One particularly vicious example occurred in the 1950s during the "Cold War" period when a massive "communist scare" ran throughout the country. A self-appointed group called Aware, Inc., tried to point out what it thought were communist influences in the broadcasting industry. Performers whose background was thought to be even the least bit questionable were "blacklisted" by the organization and were unable to find employment in the industry until they "rehabilitated" themselves by going through a rigid twelve-step process. The blacklist went to the heart of the commercial broadcasting system. Its founders threatened to boycott the products of advertisers who sponsored shows with suspected communists. The investigation techniques of Aware, Inc., were slipshod and deficient. Many innocent persons were put on the blacklist and had their careers permanently damaged. Finally, one performer, John Henry Faulk, sued Aware for libel. After hearing the evidence at the trial, the jury was so aghast at the techniques and tactics used by Aware that they awarded Faulk a record $3.5 million in damages. (Faulk, however, was able to collect only a small part of this sum since the chief defendant died shortly after the trial.)

Disregarding extremist groups like Aware, Inc., we might sum up by saying that there are both positive and negative aspects in the activities of these citizens' groups. On the one hand, they probably have made some media organizations more responsive to community needs and more sensitive to the problems of minorities and other disadvantaged groups. Citizen-group involvement with media organizations has also probably increased the feedback between audience and the media industry. On the other hand, these groups are self-appointed guardians of some special interest. They are not elected by anyone and may not be at all representative of the larger population. In addition, many of these groups have exerted unreasonable power and some, like Aware, may actually abuse their influence and do more harm than good.

Press Councils

The idea of **press councils** was imported from Europe. A press council is an independent agency whose job it is to monitor the performance of the media on a day-do-day basis. The American press councils generally follow the model used in Great Britain, where a council has been operating since 1963. The British council consists of people with media experience and some lay members. It examines complaints from the public about erroneous or deficient press coverage. The council has no enforcement powers; if it finds an example of poor performance, the council issues a report to that effect. Unfavorable publicity is the only sanction the council can bring to bear.

In the United States the National News Council was in existence from 1973 to 1984. In its approximately ten-year existence, the council considered 242 complaints against the news media and found that about half of them were unwarranted. During its tenure, however, the National News Council never won the support of the press. Its proceedings received little publicity and many influential news-gathering organizations refused to cooperate with it. With the National News Council gone, there are only a few local news councils across the country that evaluate press performance.

Education

Education also exerts informal control over the media. Ethics and professionalism are topics that are gaining more and more attention at colleges and universities.

In fact, there has been a recent upsurge in the interest of teaching ethics at many schools of journalism and mass communication. About 40 percent of the schools in the United States (about 117 of 279) offer a special ethics course to their students. Of these 117, about 20 were taught for the first time in either 1983 or 1984. More than half of the approximately forty books specifically devoted to mass media ethics have been published since 1980. Numerous workshops and conferences in how to teach ethics were held during the mid-1980s. Most of the experts in this area agreed that instead of teaching specific codes of ethics to students, a systematic way of thinking about ethics should be stressed, so that individuals can consider things and arrive at decisions rationally.

Even this book can be thought of as a means of informal control. After reading it, it is hoped, you will bring a more advanced level of critical thinking and a more sensitive and informed outlook to your media profession or to your role as media consumer.

SUGGESTIONS FOR FURTHER READING

The books listed below represent a good starting point if you want to find out more about informal controls on the media.

CHRISTIANS, CLIFFORD, KIM ROTZOLL, AND MARK FACKLER, *Media Ethics*, New York: Longman, 1987.

FARBER, STEPHEN, *The Movie Rating Game*, Washington, D.C.: Public Affairs Press, 1972.

FINK, CONRAD, *Media Ethics*, New York: McGraw-Hill, 1987.

GERALD, EDWARD, *The Social Responsibility of the Press*, Minneapolis: University of Minnesota Press, 1963.

HOHENBERG, JOHN, *The News Media: A Journalist Looks at His Profession*, New York: Holt, Rinehart and Winston, 1968.

HULTENG, JOHN, *The Messenger's Motives*, Englewood Cliffs, N.J.: Prentice-Hall, 1976.

KRIEGHBAUM, HILLIER, *Pressures on the Press*, New York: Thomas Crowell, 1972.

LINTON, BRUCE, *Self-Regulation in Broadcasting*, Washington, D.C.: National Association of Broadcasters, 1967.

MEYER, PHILLIP, *Ethical Journalism*, New York: Longman, 1987.

RIVERS, WILLIAM, AND WILBUR SCHRAMM, *Responsibility in Mass Communication*, New York: Harper & Row, 1969.

RUBIN, BERNARD, *Questioning Media Ethics*, New York: Praeger, 1978.

Part Six

Mass Media Audiences

Chapter 19
Audience Characteristics and Patterns of Use

I t's 11:30 P.M. on Friday, and outside the movie theater the line for the midnight show is already forming. One glance, however, tells the casual passerby that this is no ordinary movie line. Several people, dressed in hooded black robes, resemble executioners. Others are wearing skullcap wigs; still others are decked out in eyeshadow and motorcycle grease. The most popular costume, however, worn by both males and females, is high heels, black stockings, a short black slip, whiteface, and lipstick.

Once this crowd is inside the movie theater, it is quickly apparent that this is not the typical movie audience. The film seems secondary, and the audience is intent on entertaining itself. As a wedding scene unfolds on screen, showers of rice cascade from the audience. When one of the film's characters proposes a toast, a dozen slices of cold toast come frisbeeing from the audience toward the screen. On screen the cast of the film engages in a dance called "The Time Warp." At least two dozen audience members dance along in the aisles, their movements choreographed to those on screen. At one point, the "hero" of the movie exclaims, "Great Scott!" A half-dozen rolls of toilet tissue streamers (Scott's, one would presume) unravel toward the screen. And so it goes . . . another routine screening of *The Rocky Horror Picture Show*.

(In 1985, the *Rocky Horror Picture Show* celebrated its tenth anniversary. So far, it's grossed more than $60 million in ticket sales. About 200 theaters have regular midnight showings of the film and there's even a book, *The Rocky Horror Rules of Etiquette*, that instructs new audience members on how to behave properly during the screening. It may be in its second decade, but *Rocky Horror* is still very much alive.)

It's 5:30 P.M. on New York City's Long Island Expressway (sometimes called the World's Longest Parking Lot); traffic is at a standstill. One frustrated commuter snaps on the car radio just in time to hear a local radio station's traffic copter report. "Avoid the Long Island Expressway if humanly possible," says the voice on the radio. The commuter, along with about a half-dozen others in the immediate vicinity, opens the car window and shakes his fist at the heavens.

It's midnight in the college dorm. One roommate is on the phone talking to a prospective date. The other roommate is trying to read a Faulkner short story for tomorrow's English Lit class. After ten minutes, the second roommate, having heard enough of the phone conversation, turns on the stereo, plugs in a set of earphones and reads Faulkner while listening to Bruce Springsteen.

The above examples, diverse as they are, all illustrate people in the mass

Sometimes just being a part of the audience at The Rocky Horror Picture Show *is more important than watching the film. (Boston Globe Photo)*

communication audience. To say that the audience is the most important part of the mass communication process is an understatement. Without the audience, there would be no mass communication. In addition, as has been pointed out in Chapter 1, the audience is the ultimate source of mass media revenue. If the audience was not there to purchase movie tickets and recordings, subscribe to newspapers and magazines, and attend to radio and TV programs, no mass medium could stay in business.

The nature and content of the mass medium also determines the precise composition of the audience. As mentioned in Chapter 6, controlled circulation magazines will be read by a highly specific audience segment. Radio formats, as mentioned in Chapter 9, are designed to appeal to tightly defined demographic groups. Finally, as we will see in the next chapter, audience characteristics shape the feedback from receiver to source.

TYPES OF MEDIA AUDIENCES

As communication media develop and evolve, audiences evolve with them. The notion of media and audience evolution has been suggested by several mass communication scholars. The discussion below incorporates and expands upon ideas put forth by John Merrill and Ralph Lowenstein in their book *Media, Messages and Men* and by Richard Maisel in his article "The Decline of the Mass Media," in a 1973 edition of *Public Opinion Quarterly.*

In general terms, we can identify at least four stages in audience evolution:

1. the elite stage

2. the mass stage

3. the specialized stage

4. the interactive stage

In the **elite audience stage,** the audience for the medium is relatively small and represents the more educated and refined segments of society. In this stage, the audience does not represent the "average man" or "average woman." Media content is geared to elite tastes. In the **mass audience stage,** the potential audience consists of the entire population, with all segments of society likely to be represented. Media content is designed to appeal to what has been called the "least common denominator" in the audience. The **specialized audience stage** is typified by fragmented, special-interest audience groups. Media content is carefully designed to appeal to distinct and particular audience segments. In the **interactive audience stage,** the individual audience member has some selective control over what he or she chooses to see or hear. In effect, the audience member joins in the process as an editor or, in some cases, even as a transmitter of information.

Transitions from one stage to the next are subtle and usually occur over long periods of time. Factors that influence the evolution from stage to stage are social (more education, more leisure time), technological (availability of electricity, printing presses, etc.), and economic (more affluence, presence of commercially based media system). In addition, certain media audiences within a single country may be at different levels of evolution, and audiences within different countries may be at different stages. Lastly, as is the case with most generalizations, these evolutionary stages are better exemplified by some media than others, especially when only a single country (the United States) is examined. Nonetheless, this framework is helpful in analyzing mass media audiences and allows us to gain some indication as to the future trends in audience evolution.

The Print Media Audience

The print media seem to exemplify best the stages in audience evolution. Early books, which were lettered by hand, were usually kept chained to a table in a monastery, and only those privileged people who could read could make use of them. We have already seen how the content of early newspapers and magazines was selected to appeal to elite socioeconomic groups: the policymakers, the educated upper class, and the political leaders who had money to spend and who were interested in business news, sermons, speeches, political events, and book reviews. Newspapers began moving into the mass stage when Benjamin Day realized that technological, economic, and social conditions were right for the penny press in general and his *New York Sun* in particular. Magazines entered the mass stage more gradually. During the late nineteenth century, *McClure's* and *Ladies Home Journal* took the first steps in this direction, and the success of *Reader's Digest, Life,* and *Look* signaled that the mass stage was firmly established by 1930. Of course, not all magazines and newspapers were aimed at a mass audience; some continued to cater to the elite, while others went after more specialized audiences. The point is that we can generally identify consistent patterns in the way audiences change over the years.

Both newspapers and magazines now appear to be in the specialized stage. Magazines in particular illustrate this trend. Almost every occupational and special-interest group has a publication directed at it. In fact, there are only two general-interest magazines left: *TV Guide* and *Reader's Digest*. Although newspapers are

Interactive Fiction and Grues

One of the more popular computer programs that puts the reader in the starring role is "Zork III." As the story starts, the adventurer (the reader) is at the bottom of an endless stairway in a huge underground cavern. It's now up to the reader to solve the riddle of the dungeon and escape with his or her life. The reader moves the story along by telling the computer in what direction he or she wishes to move. For example, at the bottom of the endless stairs, there is a dark winding trail leading to the south.

The reader types, "Walk south."

The computer replies. "It is pitch black. You are likely to be eaten by a grue."

The reader types, "What is a grue?" (a logical question given the circumstances).

Computer: "The grue is a sinister, lurking presence in the dark places of the earth. Its favorite diet is adventurers . . ."

The reader, throwing caution to the winds, types "Walk south."

Computer: "Oh no! A lurking grue slithered into the room and devoured you! You have died."

End of story. Such are the perils of interactive fiction.

---

not yet as specialized as magazines, the trend toward special supplements and inserts indicates movement in that direction. Although neither medium has entered the interactive stage, signs on the horizon suggest that such a transition is already underway. Some newspapers have begun experimenting with systems that "deliver" the news via the television set, with the reader/viewer selecting from a large menu those stories and other items that he or she wishes to read. For all practical purposes, in this setup the audience member takes an active role in editing the news.

As for books, they have moved into the mass audience and specialized stage while still maintaining some of their elite stage characteristics. To elaborate, paperbacks, such as Jackie Collins' *Rock Star* or James Michener's *Alaska*, appeal to a mass audience. A walk through a typical bookstore will also demonstrate the dozens of topics aimed at special audience segments: business, computers, reference, self-help, history, and so on. Finally, the book industry also publishes collections of poetry, art, and drama tailored for the elite audience. Books are also moving into the interactive stage. Many children's and teenage novels are written so that the reader actually selects various plot options and actually constructs the story. Moreover, some computer programs offer interactive fiction. In this arrangement, text appears on the screen and at appropriate times the reader enters a response. The program incorporates this response into the subsequent story. In effect, the reader becomes the main character of the story.

The Radio and Sound-Recording Audiences

Because of its early adoption of the commercial system of support, radio passed briefly through the elite stage. During this period, a large proportion of early broadcast music consisted of classical selections, and educational programs were numerous. The birth of the networks in 1927 and the decline in the number of educational stations signaled radio's passage into the mass appeal stage. By the 1930s, with the tremendous popularity of programs such as "Amos 'n' Andy" and

When radio entered the mass-audience stage during the 1930s and 1940s, young crooner Frank Sinatra developed a national following.
(*Brown Brothers*)

"The Lone Ranger," radio was truly attracting a mass audience. The coming of television pushed radio rather forcefully into the specialized stage. Radio programming turned to distinctive formats, and its audience fragmented into many smaller groups.

The sound-recording medium's transition from elite to specialized stage is less easy to trace. When the recording industry was in its infancy, record players for home use were fairly expensive, and only the more affluent could afford them. Hence a significant proportion of early recordings featured opera stars or selections of classical music, two content forms that appealed to this elite audience. It is difficult to pinpoint the passage of sound recording into the mass-audience stage; however, the tremendous popularity of juke boxes and the surge of record sales during the 1930s made this decade the most likely transitional period. From the late 1930s until the middle of the 1950s, many mass-appeal artists (Doris Day, Frank Sinatra, Bing Crosby) were popular. Then, with the emergence of a youth culture and the birth of rock and roll, the young audience quickly became a distinct consumer segment. More and more records were designed to appeal to this new market. Today, the many variations of rock music currently available on record stands—in addition to the heightened popularity of soul, country, jazz, and folk music—indicate the establishment of various specialized consumer groups. Although the passage of radio and recording into the interactive stage appears to be in the somewhat distant future, the growth of call-in radio programs seems to indicate a step in that direction.

The Film and Television Audiences

It is equally difficult to pinpoint the movement of the motion picture medium from the elite to the mass stage. In the United States, the very roots of the industry were embedded in film's mass-audience appeal. *The Great Train Robbery*, for example, was certainly not designed to be played to an elite crowd. If one were to look overseas, however, one might find evidence of an elite stage in the history of films from other countries. Some scholars have suggested that during the period between 1920 and 1933, German and Russian films went through what might be termed an elite stage. Perhaps the lack of a comparable elite period in American film development is a quirk stemming from the unique economic and social conditions that prevailed during the motion picture industry's development in this country. In any event, by 1920 motion pictures were firmly entrenched in the mass-audience stage. As with radio, it was the arrival of television that brought about change and forced films to specialize.

A glance at the movie section of any big-city newspaper will show that many films still try to appeal to special audience segments. There are films geared to teens (*Dirty Dancing, License to Drive*); "quality" films (*The Moderns, Babette's Feast*); horror films (*Sorority Massacre, Nightmare on Elm Street, Part IV, Friday the 13th, Part* whatever), black films (*The Hollywood Shuffle, School Daze*); and pornographic films. Most films are geared for the eighteen-to-thirty crowd; *Crocodile Dundee I* and *II, Rambo I, II,* and *III, Coming to America*. Recently, however, Hollywood has noted that films with a more general appeal such as *Moonstruck, Roxanne,* and *Who Framed Roger Rabbit?* also do well at the box office. The interactive stage has yet to arrive.

Television passed through the elite stage during the early 1950s when TV sets were so expensive that only the affluent could easily afford them. Consequently, programs such as prestige drama ("Studio One" and "The U.S. Steel Hour") enjoyed popularity during these years. As sets became less expensive and permeated the country, mass-appeal programs such as adult westerns and situation comedies predominated. Of all the media we have considered, television is one still most firmly established in the mass-appeal stage. Nevertheless, there are unmistakable signs that it is moving toward specialization. Pay television and cable systems now provide special public-access channels, movies, sports, news, and special information services such as the Home Shopping Network. Low-power UHF TV stations would enable new stations to provide more local services.

TV is also moving to the interactive stage thanks to some pioneering by toy companies. Mattel recently introduced the Captain Power superjet, which lets kids exchange laserfire with the on-screen characters in the syndicated series of the same name. Another set of toys, MotoMonsters, were set into motion by inaudible electronic signals received by the home TV. Hasbro announced plans for NEMO, a device that allows viewers to control events and outcomes of prerecorded dramatic programs. Plans for an interactive "Wheel of Fortune" and other games were also on the drawing board (see boxed material).

It Can Pay to Watch TV

The Game Channel plans to syndicate an interactive TV game show called "Tele-Quest" in which viewers and on-air contestants can win money.

Viewers over eighteen must pay a one-time $3 fee to The Game Channel. Then, during the live broadcast of the show, registered players can call an 800 number and play as many as four games per show at the cost of $3.50 per game. An MC asks multiple-choice trivia questions with six possible answers and viewers punch in their answers on the phone. A computer tallies up the number of right answers and the winning viewer gets about 20 percent of the game-entry fees. Thus if 3 percent of an average audience of 50,000 play the game, the winner would pocket $1,000. (Of course, if only 1000 watched the program with 3 percent playing the game, the winner would make about $21.) The viewing contestants with the highest scores are invited to come to the show to be an on-air player.

Only three TV stations initially agreed to carry the show, but the Game Channel has high hopes for its future.

PRECONDITIONS FOR MEDIA EXPOSURE

Not every individual is a member of a media audience. In order for a person to be included, certain economic and personal preconditions must be fulfilled. These preconditions vary from medium to medium. For example, to be part of the reading audience, an individual must be literate. (No such precondition exists for those who simply look at the pictures in magazines and newspapers.) Although this might seem a minor precondition for most people, many newspaper publishers feel that the decline in newspaper circulation may be due in part to a decreased level of literacy in the population. Many educators have pointed out that reading achievement scores among the school-age population dropped during the 1970s. As a result, many papers lowered the level of reading difficulty in their pages and instituted the use of numerous pictures and other graphics in order to minimize the literacy precondition. This trend continued during the 1980s.

Time

One major personal precondition is, of course, time. If a person has little free time, it is unlikely that he or she will be a heavy consumer of media offerings. Certain media, however, are less affected by the time precondition than others. To illustrate, an audience member can listen to radio or recordings while doing something else: eating, working, driving, even studying, as noted in one of the opening examples of this chapter. Newspapers, magazines, and books, on the other hand, provide a written record that audience members can put aside or pick up at their convenience. Videocassettes can also be viewed when convenient.

Mobility of a media channel is an important factor in establishing the time precondition. Because radio and, to a lesser extent, record players and tape players are portable, they can accompany an audience member to the beach or to a sporting event. Printed publications are also portable and can be read while traveling on the subway or on a long plane trip. It is difficult to read, however, while performing more demanding activities since reading requires a higher level of concentration. Television is basically stationary. Usually, the audience watches TV in the home, although some viewing is possible while participating in other activities. The medium most affected by the time precondition is that of motion pictures. To see a film, an audience member must leave his or her house, travel to a theater, and have available at least two hours of free time. Films also demand a high level of attention; it is difficult to do anything else (except munch popcorn) while watching a movie.

Economics

Furthermore, in order to become an audience member, an individual must have access to media content. Accessibility may, in turn, have a significant impact on economic preconditions. For instance, if a person is unwilling to make the extra effort needed to travel to a library or to borrow reading material from a friend, then an economic precondition exists. The person must be able to afford the purchase price of a single copy of a newspaper or magazine or the price of a subscription. Publishers are acutely aware of this economic factor and attempt to price their products so that their potential audience is not unduly limited by economic barriers. Note that in the print media, audience members pay only for content; no special receiving equipment must be purchased. Since, apart from adequate hearing ability, the sound-recording audience needs no special skills, the main precondition is also an economic one. Ruling out borrowing, an audience member must be able to afford the cost of reproduction equipment (which can run into a substantial sum for a sophisticated system) in addition to the cost of the content itself (a record or tape). Many people thought that one possible cause of the slump in record sales during the late 1970s was the spiraling prices of records and tapes. Radio may be the medium most accessible to audiences because its preconditions are minimal. No special skills are needed and the cost of the receiving equipment is not great, especially in the case of inexpensive transistor radios. Once the audience member has purchased the receiving set, there is no further direct outlay of money for the programming. From the point of view of the radio audience, sports, music, talk, and news content are all free. (Of course, in radio and television the audience supports the programming indirectly. See Chapters 9 and 13.)

The broadcast television audience finds itself in an analogous situation. Once the initial cost of the TV set has been met (with the advent of inexpensive black-and-white sets, this is not as much of a hurdle as it once was), there is no additional direct charge for TV programs. (This fact has prompted some cynics to state that TV programs are worth exactly what we pay for them.) It should be pointed out that the above statements apply to conventional, over-the-air broadcasting. The audience for cable TV (CATV) is limited because of technological barriers (it's impossible to subscribe to CATV if the cable doesn't pass your house) and economic preconditions (a person must be able to afford the installation fee and a monthly fee). There is also an economic precondition, a monthly or per-program charge, for the pay-TV audience. The audience for videocassettes is limited because of the substantial sum necessary to purchase playback equipment. The drop in price of VCRs and the inexpensive rental fee for cassettes have made this less of a problem.

The motion picture audience must meet the economic precondition of the purchase price of a ticket ($6 in many cities, as of this writing) but does not have to invest in special receiving equipment. Moreover, there are certain informal barriers that will restrict the size of the audience for individual films. An X-rated movie, for example, is restricted to those eighteen years of age or older. Lastly, since the movie audience has to travel to the movie theater, audience members must possess physical mobility.

DIMENSIONS OF THE AUDIENCE

This section presents a capsule sketch of the characteristics that describe the audiences for the various media, including a great many facts and figures. Most of these will be expressed in some numerical form. The use of numbers is virtually unavoidable since a great deal of information about media audiences is expressed in quantitative terms (see the next chapter). Additionally, when media professionals talk about the audience, they tend to speak in numerical terms, for example, circulation, rating, box-office gross, number of records sold, cost of reaching a thousand people, and so on. Students who plan a career in the media might as well start now to become familiar with this perspective.

Many of the generalizations made in this chapter are expressed in terms of averages or other descriptive statistics. It should be kept in mind that this is simply a convenient way to summarize a large amount of information. Convenience, however, does not come without a price. Discussing the average time a person spends with television or any other medium can camouflage the large degree of variability present in audience behavior. There may be no such creature as the ''average TV viewer'' or the ''average newspaper reader.'' These summary statistics allow us to make only general statements; they do not tell the whole story.

A final note on tables, charts, and graphs. It is not necessary that a student memorize all the information contained in the tabular material that goes along with this chapter. Tables and graphs are like paragraphs; each contains a main point. It is generally sufficient to come away with the main idea(s) or trend(s) illustrated by the table or chart. Remembering that the total circulation of all daily newspapers in 1970 was 62,108,000 seems less important than knowing that total circulation has leveled off and that circulation per 1,000 people has actually declined in recent years.

Newspaper Audiences

As of 1988, approximately 63 million copies of morning and evening papers, either purchased at the newsstand or delivered to the doorstep, found their way into American homes every weekday. Daily newspaper circulation, in absolute terms, has been practically steady since 1970, as a glance at Table 19.1 will show. The population, however, has been increasing. To reflect this fact and to provide additional perspective, columns four and five of Table 19.1 present the ratio of circulation to the total adult population of the United States (expressed in thousands). As can be seen, newspaper circulation is not keeping pace with the overall growth of the population. Weekly papers enjoyed a period of growth from 1960 to 1988.

The percentage of adults reading one or more papers every day has declined from about 80 percent in the early 1960s to about 67 percent in 1988. Although this decline in daily newspaper readership encompasses every age group, the most pronounced decline has occurred in the eighteen-to-twenty-nine and thirty-to-fifty-four age groups. Readership also has dropped in all education categories, but the drop is sharpest among those who have not attended college. The overall drop in daily circulation has been most noticeable in urban areas. As Fig. 19.1 shows,

TABLE 19.1 Daily and Weekly Newspaper Circulation

YEAR	ALL DAILY PAPERS	ALL WEEKLY PAPERS	DAILY CIRCULATION PER 1000 ADULTS	WEEKLY CIRCULATION PER 1000 ADULTS
1930	39,589,000	—	455	—
1940	41,132,000	—	415	—
1950	53,829,000	—	487	—
1960	58,882,000	21,328,000	475	172
1965	60,358,000	26,088,000	451	195
1970	62,108,000	29,423,000	428	203
1975	60,655,000	35,176,000	380	221
1980	62,201,840	40,970,000	360	245
1984	63,100,000	43,100,000	341	235
1988	62,955,502	52,919,846	330	272

Reprinted by permission from ANPA, "Facts about Newspapers, 1989."

newspaper circulation in cities with more than a half-million residents has dropped about 9 percent from 1958 to 1986. Conversely, circulation in medium-sized towns with populations from 100,000 to 500,000 has increased 11 percent. Circulation in smaller communities has increased the most, up nearly a third in the same period.

Why the decline? Some have attributed it to the increased mobility of Americans, the increase in single-person households, more expensive subscription and per-copy prices, a general decline in the level of reading ability among young people,

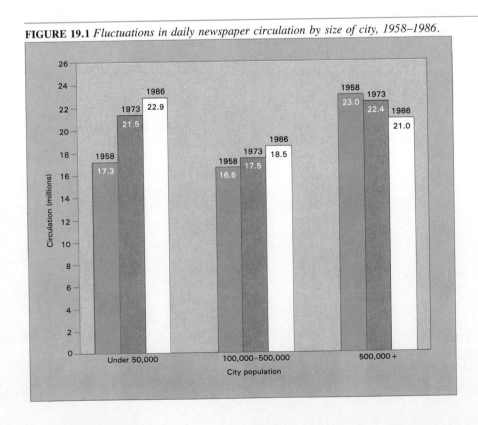

FIGURE 19.1 *Fluctuations in daily newspaper circulation by size of city, 1958–1986.*

The Daily Newspaper Nonreader

Not everybody reads the daily newspaper. In general, research has shown that the nonreader tends to be low in education, low in income, and either young (under twenty) or old (over seventy). In addition, nonreaders are more likely to live in rural areas and tend to have infrequent contact with neighbors and friends. Other studies note that the nonreader has little identification with the community, is less likely to own a home, and seldom belongs to local voluntary organizations.

Why don't these people read a daily paper? The main reasons they give are lack of time, preference for another medium for news (usually radio or TV), a general lack of interest in reading a paper, and the fact that newspapers cost too much.

More recent surveys have indicated that the portrait of the nonreader is more complicated than first thought. There appears to be a group of nonreaders that does not fit the typical demographic profile mentioned above. These people tend to be high in income and fall into the twenty-six- to sixty-five-year-old group. These atypical nonreaders are far more likely to report that lack of time and lack of interest in content are the main reasons why they don't read the paper. Editors and publishers are attempting to bring this atypical group back into the fold of newspaper readers by adding news briefs and comprehensive indexes to help overcome the time crunch and by diversifying newspaper content to help build interest.

and inroads made upon leisure time by television viewing. All these factors probably have had some impact, but as we shall see, magazine readership has not dropped off as sharply as newspaper reading, even though magazines should be affected by the same forces (higher prices, competition from TV, decline in reading skills, etc.). Magazines have avoided a drop in audience levels primarily by specialization. Similarly, weekly newspapers may be attracting readers because of their local appeal.

Newspaper vending machines on a Washington, D.C. street illustrate the variety of papers available; the newspapers here include those targeted for a specialized audience such as Jewish Week *and* Investor's Daily *as well as regional and national papers. (John Schultz-PAR/NYC)*

Perhaps part of the readership decline of daily newspapers can be attributed to the absence of specialized information that appeals to distinct audience groups, especially younger readers.

Of those who do read the newspaper, three-quarters have the paper delivered to their homes and, not surprisingly, the home is the place where most newspapers are read. Once the newspaper is in the household, it is read by approximately two people who spend an average of about twenty-five minutes per day reading the newspaper. In 1965, the comparable figure was about thirty minutes per day, indicating that not only are fewer people reading the newspaper, but on the average, those who are reading it are spending less time at it. The most popular time of day for newspaper reading is after the evening meal.

Figure 19.2 contains information on the demographic characteristics of the newspaper audience. (**Demography** is the statistical study of large groups of people; it focuses on such characteristics as age, race, sex, income, education, etc.) As Fig. 19.2 suggests, those people most likely to read a newspaper are those who are older, more educated, and married.

FIGURE 19.2 *Newspaper readership by demographic characteristics.*

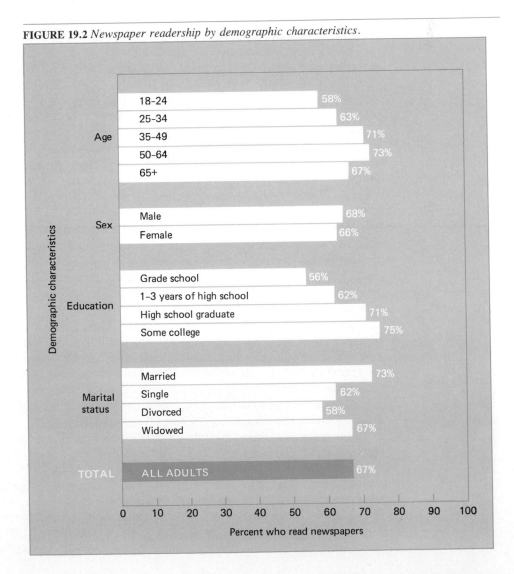

What sections of the paper are read by the audience? A 1980 study sponsored by the Newspaper Advertising Bureau found that general news sections attracted the most readers (94 percent), while four other sections—editorial, entertainment, sports, and radio and TV listings—tied for second place, with 81 percent reporting readership. Comic sections were read by 79 percent, classified ads by 78 percent, food and cooking by 77 percent, and the business section by 55 percent.

Magazine Audiences

Although data on the audience for an individual magazine are readily available, information about the total audience for magazines is hard to come by, primarily because of the difficulty in defining what qualifies as a magazine. Nonetheless, some figures are available. In 1988, as reported to the Audit Bureau of Circulations (see next chapter), total magazine circulation exceeded 324 million copies. Of these, about 27 percent were bought at the newsstand while the remaining 73 percent were delivered as part of a subscription. The 1988 figure represented a 22 percent increase over 1979. If we examine circulation figures per 1000 people, as we did with newspapers, we find that magazine circulation has nearly kept pace with the growth in the adult population during the 1970s and 1980s.

It was mentioned earlier that the audiences for magazines have become more and more specialized. Approximately 40 percent of all magazines have circulations under 150,000. Only four (*Reader's Digest, TV Guide, Modern Maturity,* and *National Geographic*) have what might be called mass circulations of more than 10 million copies. In fact, even specialized magazines are becoming specialized. There is now a magazine for *new* lawyers and another for *young* doctors. This specialization is further reflected in the growing numbers of magazines that are available to the audience. From 1970 to 1984, as reported by the Audit Bureau of Circulations, the number of general consumer magazines increased from 300 to 556, a jump of 75 percent. (These figures do not include thousands of professional and scholarly publications sponsored by nonprofit organizations.)

Mentioning specific examples of this increasing specialization might be the most effective way of documenting this trend. *Casket and Sunnyside* is a magazine that is widely read among funeral home directors. *Poultry Times* is a big seller among chicken farmers. Other magazines with a tightly focused audience appeal, such as those aimed at hunters, audio buffs, or wrestling fans, have also been successful in attracting an audience.

Specialization is apparent in another area as well. Many magazines have become *regionalized*—that is, they appeal to an audience living in a well-defined geographic area. "City" magazines, such as *Los Angeles, Philadelphia,* and *The Washingtonian,* are geared toward specific urban dwellers. *Yankee* directs its appeal to New Englanders, while *Southern Living* is aimed at a regional audience in the South. Even magazines with a national circulation such as *Outdoor Life, McCall's,* and *Nation's Business* create special content for several regional editions.

It appears that almost everybody does some type of magazine reading. In an average month, 94 percent of U.S. adults read at least one copy of a magazine. Most read more. One study reported that adults read or look through an average of ten magazines a month. About 28 percent read a magazine on an average day, and the typical adult spends about twenty-five minutes daily reading magazines. About three-quarters of the audience keep magazines on hand for future reference, and about the same proportion reported that they reread something or referred back to an article or ad. As far as demographics are concerned, the typical magazine reader is more educated and usually more affluent than the nonreader. Magazine readers also tend to be joiners. One survey found them far more likely to belong to religious, science, and professional organizations than nonreaders.

Of course, certain magazines seek out a particular demographic group. For example, some magazines have traditionally appealed to either a male or female audience. Automotive, motorcycle, and golf magazines usually have about an 80 percent male readership. At the other end of the scale, *Family Circle, Harper's Bazaar, Vogue,* and *Glamour* have readerships that are more than 80 percent female. Literary magazines and general-interest publications such as *Reader's Digest* and *TV Guide* have a readership split about evenly between men and women. Within male–female groupings, certain magazines appeal to discrete age groups. Among men, almost half of the readers of motorcycle and automotive magazines are between the ages of eighteen and twenty-four, with a median age of twenty-five. By comparison the median age of men who read business magazines is forty. Among women, approximately half of the readership of *Seventeen* and *Glamour* is under twenty-five.

Book Audiences

Despite competiton from television, the book-reading audience has actually increased from 1955 to 1986. In the mid-1950s, about 14 percent of a national sample of adults reported reading a book on the day prior to the survey. Twenty-one years later, the comparable figure was 22 percent. The person most likely to be a book reader was a college-educated female thirty-five to forty nine years old.

Radio Audiences

There are more radio sets in this country than there are people. In fact, there are about twice as many. As of January 1989, there were more than 530 million radio receivers scattered around the United States, with car radios accounting for about one-third of this number. Virtually every household in the country is equipped with at least one working radio set. On a typical day at least three-fourths of all adults will listen to radio, and the average person will listen, or at least have the radio on, for about three hours. Most people listen to radio in the early morning when they are getting ready for and driving to work and in the late afternoon when they are driving home. These two "day parts," as they are called by those in the industry, consisting roughly from 6 A.M. to 10 A.M. and 4 P.M. to 7 P.M., are called "drive time."

Perhaps the biggest change in the audience for radio over the past fifteen years has been the steady increase in listeners for FM stations. In 1973, only 28 percent of the listening audience was tuned to FM stations. Fifteen years later the figure was 72 percent, as FM listenership surpassed that of AM. The largest increase in FM audiences has occurred among teenagers. Probably because of the trend toward Top 40, album rock, and progressive rock apparent among FM stations, the percentage of teens who reported listening to FM stations from 1977 to 1984 mentioned above more than tripled, increasing from 24 to 90 percent. As far as demographics are concerned, the average listener, regardless of age, sex, or educational background, listens to radio about three hours a day. Of this group, females and young listeners are slightly more represented.

Perhaps the best way to talk about the radio audience is to examine radio station formats and describe the type of audience each attracts. Contemporary Hit stations draw an audience composed primarily of twelve- to twenty-four-year-olds, with females outnumbering males by about a three-to-two margin. Album and progressive rock attract eighteen- to thirty-four-year-olds, with about equal proportions of men and women represented in their audience. Middle of the road, beautiful music, classical, and all-news formats generally attract an older crowd, with most of their audience coming from the forty-five-and-over age groups. Country music stations seem to have a general across-the-board appeal to those over twenty-five.

As a person gets older, he or she tends to evolve out of the audience for one format and move on to another. For example, as a young person leaves the teenage years, he or she will probably listen less to Contemporary Hit stations and more to stations that play progressive, album rock. As that same person continues to get older, he or she will probably tune more to Adult Contemporary stations or even to progressive country formats. A little later, this person might tune to ''good music'' or talk stations. (Of course, it is also true that music styles are changing along with the individual. What is considered progressive rock today might fall into the good music category twenty years from now.) Table 19.2 attempts to summarize some areas of peak listener appeal for selected station formats.

Sound-Recording Audiences

Information regarding the audience for sound recording (records, tapes, and CDs) is somewhat difficult to uncover, partially because the recording industry is supported by audience purchases and not by advertising. This means that recording companies concentrate on compiling statistics relating to overall sales figures and that detailed demographic information about the audience is typically not sought after. True, some record companies have sponsored market research to find out more about their audiences, but the results of these studies are usually not made available to the general public. We do know that by the late 1980s there were approximately 80 million stereos, with perhaps an equal number of tape playback units and 11 million CD players in use. It has been estimated that more than 90 percent of all the households in the country have some means of playing a record, tape, or CD. In the late 1980s, this audience was buying more than 600 million tapes and records every year.

In general, those people who have a sound system have paid about $500–$800 for their equipment and have a typical collection of about seventy albums and approximately thirty singles. They listen to discs and tapes about an hour a day.

TABLE 19.2 Appeals of Selected Radio Station Formats

FORMAT	AGE	SEX	REGION
Adult Contemporary	24–54	Female	All
Album-Oriented Rock	18–24	Male	Urban
Beautiful Music	35+	Both	All
Contemporary Hits	12–34	Both	All
Country	18–49	Both	Rural
Middle of the Road	35+	Both	All
News/Talk	25–54	Both	Urban
Religious	55+	Female	Rural
Urban Contemporary	12–34	Both	Urban

Rock music is responsible for most of the industry's growth. Nearly 70 percent of the money spent on records and tapes is for rock or similar forms of music. In fact, rock is so successful that it now comes in as many brands and packages as breakfast cereal. There is new wave, punk rock, hard rock, and, at the quieter end of the spectrum, soft rock, pop rock, mellow rock, folk rock, and country rock. This audience growth surprised many in the industry who believed that as the children of the post-World War II "baby boom" grew out of their teenage years, record buying would drop off sharply. This has not happened, and the record audience has maintained its buying habits into the twenties and thirties.

Record buying is related to age and sex. About a fifth of all records and tapes in the United States are bought by females between nine and fourteen (this audience segment is called "bubble gummers" by some in the trade). More than half of all records and tapes are bought by sixteen- to twenty-four-year-olds. About a third of record buyers are in the twenty-five to fifty bracket.

Motion Picture Audiences

Much like the data on the sound-recording audience, information on the motion picture audience is sketchy. Hollywood seems to put little faith in detailed audience study, preferring instead to concentrate on the "bottom line," the amount of money a film brings in. Thus although there is considerable financial information, precise audience data are hard to come by. In general terms, we know that after a slump during the early 1970s, movie attendance picked up. Average weekly attendance has been steady for about the last twenty years (see Fig. 19.3). Attendance, however, is nowhere near the levels of the 1930s and 1940s, when film was in its heyday.

The movie audience is a young audience. As Fig. 19.4, on page 464, indicates, three out of every four moviegoers are under thirty. Teenagers are a significant part of the movie audience. Although teens make up only 20 percent of the population, they make up nearly 40 percent of the film audience.

FIGURE 19.3 *Average weekly film attendance in the United States. (Motion Picture Association of America. Used by permission.)*

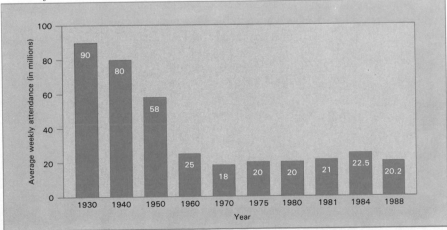

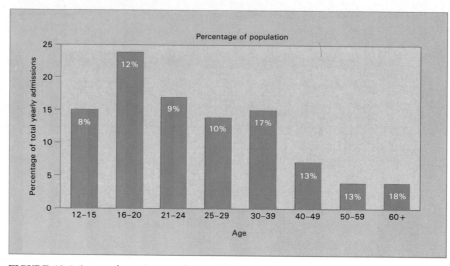

FIGURE 19.4 *Age and movie attendance. (Motion Picture Association of America. Used by permission.)*

The movie audience has changed in recent years. Older fans are now more likely to go out to a theater than they were five years ago. For example, the proportion of forty- to forty-nine-year-olds in the audience has increased 18 percent; fifty- to fifty-nine-year-olds, 26 percent; and those over sixty, 50 percent. Attendance by those under thirty, meanwhile, dropped by about 2 percent. Despite these changes, as Fig. 19.4 indicates, nearly seven out of ten moviegoers are still under thirty and teens still account for a significant part of the audience.

Frequent moviegoers (those who see at least one film a month) account for 87 percent of all film admissions. These frequent fans are generally single, within the sixteen-to-twenty age group (going to the movies continues to be a popular dating activity; only 6 percent of the audience goes to a movie alone), more educated, from middle-class families, and from urban areas.

The audience for movies is largest in July and August and smallest in May. The worst two weeks of the year for moviegoing are the first two weeks in December, when attendance drops 30–50 percent.

What films have attracted the largest audiences? Some indirect information is available if we examine what the industry calls "film rental fees." This is the money that the theater pays to the distribution company to show the film. If we assume that films that earn large rental fees are attracting large audiences (a seemingly reasonable assumption), a list of the most popular films can be compiled. Table 11.1, page 268, contains such a list as of 1988. Probably the main reason for the large number of recent releases on such a list is the fact that Hollywood now aims for the "super grosser," the film that will draw huge audiences and earn for the company what the industry calls "megabucks."

Television Audiences

The TV set has become firmly entrenched in the life of Americans. As of 1988, some 98 percent of all homes in the country had at least one working television set. About 60 percent had more than one. Nine out of ten households had color sets. Cable television (CATV) had more than 49 million subscribers in 1989, roughly 55 percent of all TV households.

Television rating services report that the set in the average household is on for about seven hours a day, with each individual watching an average of more than three hours daily. The TV audience changes throughout the day, steadily growing from 7 A.M. until it reaches a peak from 8 to 11 P.M., Eastern Standard Time. These hours are typically labeled ''prime time.'' After 11 P.M., the audience drops off dramatically. Figure 19.5 details this pattern of audience viewing.

Not surprisingly, the television audience is largest during the winter months, December through March, and smallest during July and August, when people spend more time out of doors. The composition of the television audience changes during the day. Preschoolers and females tend to predominate during the daytime hours from Monday to Friday. On Saturday mornings, most of the audience is under thirteen. Prime time is dominated by those in the eighteen- to forty-nine-year-old age group.

Not everybody is alike in their TV viewing habits. Various demographic factors such as age, sex, social class, and education affect viewership. For example, teen-agers watch the least. People in low-income homes generally watch more television than their middle-income counterparts. People with more education tend to watch less, and women watch more often than men. Cable subscribers are younger, have more children, and are more affluent than the average viewer. They also are dissatisfied with traditional television and want more program variety. Subscribers to the pay-cable channels had younger heads of households, were more affluent, and watched more TV than families in noncable homes.

Those individuals who own a VCR constitute a district audience group. By the end of 1988, VCRs were in more than 55 percent of all TV households. VCRs were more likely to be found in homes of college-educated consumers between the ages of thirty-five and forty-nine with incomes of more than $25,000 per year living in primarily urban areas. A higher percentage of cable homes than noncable homes had VCRs. VCRs are used 4.7 hours per week for playing prerecorded tapes and 2.4 hours for recording TV programs. Three-quarters of the playback time is used for

FIGURE 19.5 *Household viewing of television at various times of day.*

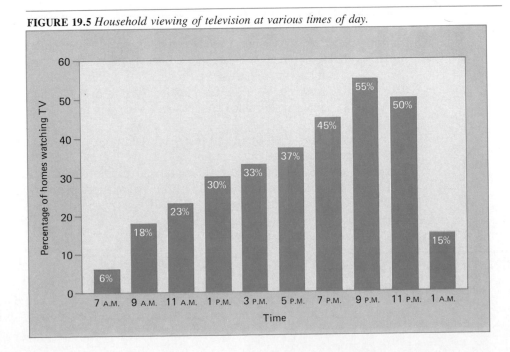

The Television Nonviewers

In the typical household the TV set is on for more than seven hours every day. The average individual watches about three hours a day. TV sets are found in about 98 percent of all households. Given this massive penetration of television into the fabric of the daily lives of Americans, it seems hard to believe that there are people who don't watch it. But there are at least a few who could be called nonviewers. What are these unusual people like?

The best answer to that question is that they are hard to characterize. It is known that nonviewers differ from viewers on specific demographic characteristics. For example, research has shown that nonviewers are more likely to be women, childless, and apparently less religious than viewers. There are no differences between viewers and nonviewers in terms of age and race. Nonviewers also tend to be more educated than viewers. Additional research has discovered that nonviewers are less satisfied with family life, belong to more groups and organizations, and socialize more frequently with friends outside their neighborhoods. All of these facts are difficult to fit together. Nonviewers do not seem to be affected by economic deprivation since they are more likely to be employed and to be more educated than viewers. They do not appear to be socially isolated since they belong to organizations and visit frequently with friends. Perhaps the most intelligent conclusion we can draw is that not watching TV is a complicated behavior (or nonbehavior). People evidently avoid television for a variety of reasons and, as a result, are exceedingly difficult to pigeonhole.

rented or purchased tapes, the remainder for playback of home-recorded tapes. Most videotaped playbacks occur during the weekend. Prime-time programs, movies, and soap operas are recorded the most. Of interest to advertisers is the fact that about one-third of VCR owners delete the commercials while recording off the air and of those that don't delete, about half say they fast forward to skip the commercials during playback. The rental of prerecorded cassettes is becoming increasingly popular, with movies rented most often. Executives at the pay cable channels were closely monitoring the impact of VCR ownership on the viewing of HBO, Showtime, and similar services. At least one service, The Movie Channel, looked upon the VCR as a friend and scheduled feature movies early in the morning hours to facilitate home taping.

One striking fact about the television audience is its great size. Ninety-nine million people saw the final episode of "Roots" in 1977, and 125 million saw the farewell episode of "M*A*S*H." A typical prime-time program might reach as many as 20 million households. What shows are most popular with the audience? Table 19.3 shows the prime-time series that have appeared most often in the top twenty programs of any given year.

INTERMEDIA COMPARISONS

In this section we present responses from people who were asked during the course of several surveys to rate the various mass media on a variety of dimensions. The first of these is a series of polls dealing with news.

TABLE 19.3 Most Popular Prime-Time Series, 1950–1989

RANK	PROGRAM TITLE	YEARS IN TOP 20
1	"I Love Lucy"/"Lucy"/"Here's Lucy"/"The Lucy Show"	17
2	"Red Skelton"	16
	"Gunsmoke"	16
3	"The Ed Sullivan Show"	13
4	"Bonanza"	12
	"Disneyland"/"Wonderful World of Disney"	12
5	"Andy Griffith"/"Mayberry RFD"	11
	"60 Minutes"[a]	11
6	"All in the Family"/"Archie Bunker's Place"	10
7	"Beverly Hillbillies"	8

[a] Still on the air as of 1989.

Since 1959, the Roper Organization, Inc., has conducted periodic surveys asking people to (1) choose their main source of news and (2) name the one medium that they perceive as most credible as a news source. Tables 19.4 and 19.5 summarize the results of these surveys.

Since 1963, television has been named most often as the source of most news. Its lead over the second-place medium, newspapers, has been growing more or less steadily. The percentage naming radio has declined sharply since 1959, while the percentage naming magazines, never high to begin with, has also slightly decreased. In terms of trends in credibility, TV became the most believable medium in 1961 and now has a two-to-one advantage over the newspaper in that department. Radio and magazines, chosen by a small proportion of the survey, have shown a slight decline.

Before leaving this topic we should point out that some individuals have suggested that the actual wording of the Roper question on the source of most news

TABLE 19.4 Source of Most News (Answers in Percentage)[a]

"I'd like to ask you where you usually get most of your news about what's going on in the world today—from the newspapers or radio or television or magazines or talking to people or where?"

SOURCE OF MOST NEWS	1959	1961	1963	1964	1967	1968	1971	1972	1974	1976	1978	1980	1982	1984	1987	1988
TV	51	52	55	58	64	59	60	64	65	64	67	64	65	64	66	65
Newspaper	57	57	53	56	55	49	48	50	47	49	49	44	44	40	36	42
Radio	34	34	29	26	28	25	23	21	21	19	20	18	18	14	14	14
Magazines	8	9	6	8	7	7	5	6	4	7	5	5	6	4	4	4
Other people	4	5	4	5	4	5	4	4	4	5	5	4	4	4	4	4

[a] Note: Columns do not add up to 100 because multiple responses were allowed.

Source: The Roper Organization, Inc., America's Watching, Television Information Office, 1989. Used with permission of the Television Information Office.

TABLE 19.5 Relative Credibility of Media (Answers in Percentage)

"If you got conflicting or different reports of the same news story from radio, television, the magazines and the newspapers, which of the four versions would you be most inclined to believe—the one on radio or television or magazines or newspapers?"

MOST BELIEVABLE	1959	1961	1963	1964	1967	1968	1971	1972	1974	1976	1978	1980	1982	1984	1987	1988
Television	29	39	36	41	41	44	49	48	51	51	47	51	53	53	55	49
Newspapers	32	24	24	23	24	21	20	21	20	22	23	22	22	24	21	26
Radio	12	12	12	8	7	8	10	8	8	7	9	8	6	8	6	7
Magazines	10	10	10	10	8	11	9	10	8	9	9	9	8	7	7	5
Don't know	17	17	18	18	20	16	12	13	13	11	12	10	11	9	11	13

Source: The Roper Organization, Inc., *America's Watching,* Television Information Office, 1989. Used with permission of the Television Information Office.

might give a distorted picture of the results. The phrase "what's going on in the world today" might prompt people to think about international and national events, an area in which TV network news seems dominant, and as a result, people tend not to mention the newspaper, whose focus is usually more local.

This fact is apparent in the second survey we will examine. The American Society of Newspaper Editors (ASNE) sponsored a 1985 survey that focused on media credibility. The results indicated that newspapers were considered more reliable than TV, 72 to 66 percent, in the coverage of local news. The ASNE respondents were also asked a question similar to that used in the Roper surveys. If given conflicting reports of events, about half said that they would believe TV and about 25 percent said the newspapers. Another question asked respondents to rank the honesty and ethical standards of people in twelve different occupations. Members of the clergy, doctors, and police were ranked as having the highest standards. TV news anchors and TV reporters ranked fourth and sixth, while newspaper editors and newspaper reporters were seventh and eighth, with advertising executives and used-car salespersons finishing at the bottom. These results prompted newspaper and TV executives to examine new ways to improve their credibility.

THE SOCIAL CONTEXT

In Chapter 1, we saw that the mass communication audience was large, heterogeneous, spread out over a wide geographic area, self-defined, and anonymous to one another. During the early part of the twentieth century, these characteristics prompted sociologists and mass communication researchers to regard this audience as a collection of isolated individuals who responded in essentially the same way to a message presented via the media. The viewpoint, called the **hypodermic needle approach**, persisted for many years. It was subsequently discovered that audience members do not exist in a social vacuum. They can be placed in definable social categories based on such common characteristics as age, sex, political affiliation, occupation, and education, which will also have an impact on their media behavior. In addition, an audience member's social relationships will have an impact on media use and effect. For example, even though political candidates might spend millions

Age and Media Usage

One of the most important determinants of media usage is a person's age. Exposure to the various mass media changes as each of us gets older. The chart below attempts to profile how our media behavior fluctuates with age. Note that the sound media (radio, records, and tapes) tend to be most used during preteen and teenage years; movies tend to peak around the early twenties. As time devoted to sound recording, radio, and moviegoing begins to decrease during the thirties, forties, and fifties, newspaper and magazine usage begins to pick up. After the teenage years, TV viewing tends to increase.

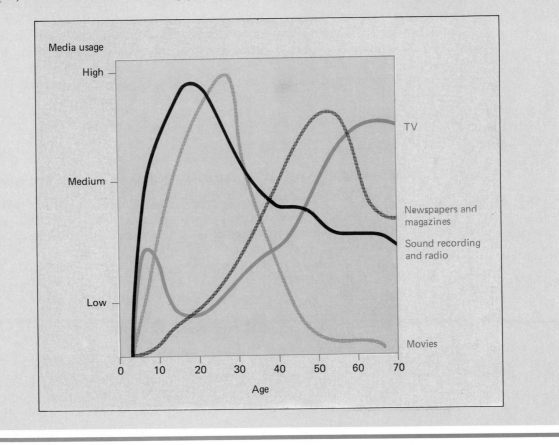

of dollars on commercials, an individual's personal voting choice might be influenced more by the opinions of people in his or her interpersonal communication network—family members, co-workers, boss, or peers.

The relationship of the audience and its social context has great relevance for determining the effects of mass communication, as we shall see in Chapters 21 and 22. In fact, one of the classic theories of the persuasive effects of mass communication, the **multistep flow model** of influence, suggests that mass media alone will be unlikely to change audience opinions on important issues precisely because the media's influence is filtered through a social network of opinion leaders. For our immediate purpose, it is important to note that, in addition to its persuasive aspect, social context also plays a significant role in other areas of media behavior. For example, one study of radio listening among grade-schoolers showed that youngsters with few friends tended to listen more than did their more popular classmates. Other studies suggest that popular teenagers are apt to see more movies than their less popular peers (perhaps because they date more often and attend films as a dating activity). Social characteristics such as occupation and socioeconomic status also affect newspaper and magazine reading. College students frequently develop new musical or film tastes because they are encouraged to sample different offerings by their roommates and friends. Some media activity—attending *The Rocky Horror Picture Show*, for example—has become a social rather than a solitary event. Even such seemingly isolated audience members as those who listen to car radios or recorded music over headphones may have been influenced somewhat by their own social context. ("I have to listen to all-news radio because my boss expects me to know about current events," or "I never liked Bruce Springsteen until my friend explained his music to me.") In any case, even though mass media audiences may be scattered about and isolated from one another, the impact of the individual's social context on his or her media behavior should not be minimized.

SUGGESTIONS FOR FURTHER READING

These sources can be consulted for more information on mass communication audiences.

AMERICAN NEWSPAPER PUBLISHERS ASSOCIATION, *Facts about Newspapers,* 1989.

DEFLEUR, MELVIN, AND SANDRA BALL-ROKEACH, *Theories of Mass Communication,* 5th ed., New York: Longman, 1988.

DOMINICK, JOSEPH, AND JAMES FLETCHER, *Broadcasting Research Methods,* Boston: Allyn and Bacon, 1985.

JEFFRES, LEO, *Mass Media: Processes and Effects,* Prospect Heights, Ill.: Waveland Press, 1986.

MERRILL, JOHN C., AND RALPH L. LOWENSTEIN, *Media, Messages and Men,* New York: David McKay, 1971.

STERLING, CHRISTOPHER H., *Electronic Media,* New York: Praeger, 1984.

STEINBERG, COBBETT, *TV Facts,* New York: Facts on File, 1985.

———, *Film Facts,* New York: Facts on File, 1980.

STONE, GERALD, *Examining Newspapers,* Newbury Park, Calif.: Sage Publications, 1987.

Chapter 20

Mass Media Feedback Systems

Many people who follow the fortunes of the television industry are aware of the Nielsens, the ratings that help measure a show's popularity, but very few people are aware of the unique TV ratings called the Van Dorps. It's about time this unsung hero of audience measurement received due recognition. George J. Van Dorp, a water commissioner for the city of Toledo, Ohio, during the early 1950s, happened to develop his own original system for rating TV shows. Van Dorp noticed that during the course of an evening, Toledo's water pressure would suddenly plummet and then, after a few minutes, would zoom upward again. This curious activity baffled Van Dorp until he noticed that the dips in the water pressure were correlated with the commercials and station breaks in evening television programs. Evidently, people were waiting for these opportunities to take care of natural habits that involved the use of Toledo's water supply. When such an opportunity occurred, Toledo's water pressure dropped dramatically. Van Dorp began charting the peaks and valleys in the water pressure and was able to rank in order Toledo's favorite TV shows. After he announced his findings, other major cities also noted this same link between TV shows and water pressure. Unfortunately for Van Dorp, this novel way of obtaining audience feedback was not greeted with enthusiasm by the TV industry, and the Van Dorps never sent the Nielsens down the drain. Nonetheless, this pioneer ratings expert deserves a place in the audience-measurement hall of fame; his feedback technique was certainly among the most inexpensive ever developed.

It's probably obvious by now that this chapter will deal with mass media feedback systems. As noted in Chapter 1, feedback refers to those responses of the receiver that attempt to affect subsequent messages of the source. It was stressed that feedback in the mass communication setting was more limited than in the interpersonal situation and was usually delayed.

As mentioned in Chapter 19, audience characteristics and feedback are closely related. Feedback helps a mass medium know who is in the audience and aids the source in structuring messages designed to interest that audience. Audience characteristics also determine the exact form of the feedback. For example, audiences for mass media are large, too large to be surveyed in their entirety; therefore, some representative samples must be examined. The audience is scattered geographically; therefore, it takes time to gather feedback. The audience is anonymous; therefore, demographic data are collected to give the audience some identity. Let us now take a more detailed look at feedback mechanisms as they relate to mass media.

FORMS OF FEEDBACK

We will begin by distinguishing between two different forms of feedback. The first, **audience-generated feedback,** occurs when one or more audience members attempt to communicate their opinion or point of view to a mass medium. In this form of feedback, the media are receivers of messages initiated by audience members. This type of feedback is set in motion by the receivers of the message; it requires extra effort on the part of the audience to send but little effort on the part of the media to receive. Some typical examples of audience-generated feedback are letters to the editor of a newspaper or magazine (or to the managers of radio and television stations), petitions delivered to media organizations, phone calls to radio talk shows, cancellations of a newspaper or magazine subscription, and reviews of films and TV shows by critics.

The second form, **media-originated feedback,** consists of information about the audience that media industries must go out of their way to gather. The original impetus for this form of feedback comes from the media organization itself. Reactions from the audience are solicited by the media or related organizations acting on their behalf. Examples of media-generated feedback are ratings in television and radio, circulation figures as charted by the Audit Bureau of Circulations, record popularity as compiled by industry publications such as *Billboard* and *Cashbox*, film box-office revenue as reported in *Variety*, surveys done by broadcasting systems, readership surveys sponsored by newspapers, and lists of best-selling books.

Feedback Characteristics

Table 20.1 lists the general characteristics of audience-generated and media-originated feedback. It is important to separate these two forms (1) because their characteristics are different and (2) because usually, but not always, media-originated feedback is more effective in altering subsequent messages.

First, audience-generated feedback is generally not sent by people who are typical of the entire audience. For instance, the person who writes a letter to the editor of a newspaper or magazine is usually older (over thirty), likely to be a professional, better educated, and earning more money than those in the general population. Individuals who write letters to radio and television stations also tend to be older, better educated, more interested in public affairs, and more likely to live alone than others in the community. A survey of people who phone radio call-in programs found that the callers were older, less mobile, lived alone more often, and

TABLE 20.1 Characteristics of Feedback in Mass Communication

AUDIENCE-GENERATED	MEDIA-ORIGINATED
1. Generally not typical of entire audience.	1. Tries to examine a representative cross section of audience.
2. Travels directly to a media organization.	2. Gathered by a third party.
3. Expressed qualitatively.	3. Expressed quantitatively.
4. Audience determines form and channel.	4. Media organizations determine form and channel.
5. Delayed.	5. Delayed.

had lower socioeconomic status than the general population. Petitions to broadcasting stations are typically presented by special-interest groups. Published reviews of media content represent the view of only one person (the critic), and in many cases a film or a TV series that receives a bad review will be immensely popular. A media organization that relied only on audience-generated feedback would not get a clear picture of its entire audience.

In contrast, media-originated feedback strives to examine a representative cross section of the audience. Television and radio rating firms sample randomly from across the country or from within a specified market. Readership surveys sponsored by newspapers and magazines also are based on random selection. (A large sample, perhaps around 1000 people, chosen at random will usually mirror the characteristics of the larger community fairly accurately.) Surveys of movie attendance and record popularity attempt to examine markets that are reflective of the entire moviegoing and record-buying public.

Collecting and Expressing Data

Second, audience-generated feedback is collected directly by the media organization. Letters to the editor are read by newspaper or magazine employees, and a few are selected for publication. The rest may or may not be kept on file. Phone calls to a radio or TV station are usually logged, and perhaps a rough record is made of their content (e.g., nine people objected to the program; three praised it). On the other hand, a third party, usually a large organization, gathers and records media-originated feedback. In television and radio, stations and networks do not collect their own

Audience-generated feedback during Elizabethan times. The crowd lets the actors know exactly how the play is doing. (Historical Pictures Service)

ratings data. Instead, they rely on firms such as the A.C. Nielsen Company and Arbitron. Newspaper and magazine circulation figures are compiled by the Audit Bureau of Circulations. Information about movie box-office revenue is collected by the trade paper *Variety*, in association with the Standard Data Corporation; record popularity is tabulated by the trade publication *Billboard;* book sales by *Publishers Weekly*.

Next, audience-generated feedback is usually expressed in qualitative rather than quantitative terms. The TV or film critic reports his or her personal reactions to a movie or TV show. The critic does not take a sample of viewers and report what the majority liked or disliked about what they saw. A letter from a reader or viewer generally reports only the qualitative opinion of one person—the writer. In addition, media organizations generally evaluate audience-generated feedback in qualitative terms. An organized letter-writing campaign that produces a thousand identical letters to a TV network is apt to be less influential than a hundred literate and evidently spontaneous letters. True, there are instances when the quantity of audience responses is noted (as in the case when the number of pro and con calls are tabulated), but the qualitative aspects of the responses will also be considered. To illustrate, the TV series "Designing Women" was saved from cancellation one season because the network received letters from fans of the show. It was not so much the number of letters that impressed CBS executives as the fact that they were from intelligent, well-educated, and apparently affluent viewers. By contrast, in media-originated feedback the emphasis is on quantitative information. Every medium relies upon a numerical form of feedback. Newspapers and magazines rely on circulation data, a compilation of how many people buy a newspaper or magazine at a newsstand or have a regular subscription. Book publishers rely on sales figures. In radio and television, program viewing is expressed as the percentage of people viewing or listening. The film and sound-recording industries rely on box-office figures and sales data as the two main forms of feedback, and both are expressed in numerical terms.

Messages and Channels

Each feedback system offers a different choice between feedback forms and channels to the media audience. In the audience-generated situation, the audience determines what form and channel their message will take. If an audience member is upset about a particular TV program, for example, he or she can choose to (1) write a nasty letter to the station, (2) phone the station, or (3) start a petition among other viewers to present to the station manager.

In media-originated feedback, the precise form that information about the audience takes is determined by media organizations. Newspapers and magazines rely on detailed circulation and readership data. Magazines collect elaborate information that identifies the demographic makeup of their audience and even classifies them by the products that they use. Television and radio usage is expressed in the percentages of total people or total households that are viewing or listening. The audience is further subdivided into various demographic groups whose behavior is of interest to advertisers and other media planners. In sound recording and film, the industries choose to collect sales information rather than actual headcounts of their audience. Thus box-office revenue data are gathered about the motion picture audience, and the industry looks at the bottom-line dollar figures and not at individual behavior. In the eyes of the motion picture media, it matters little if twenty different people paid $5 each to see a film or if ten people paid $5 on two different occasions to see the same film twice—the amount of revenue collected in each situation is the same. Similarly, the recording industry collects sales data on records and tapes and also monitors their play on radio stations as a gauge of popularity. In all cases, the media have adopted the precise form of feedback that is most valuable to them and to their advertisers.

Lastly, audience-generated and media-originated feedback have one characteristic in common: In both systems, feedback is typically delayed. As pointed out in Chapter 1, it takes time for a letter, phone call, petition, or canceled subscription to reach the appropriate office or individual in the media organization. Likewise, media-originated feedback takes time to collect. Circulation figures supplied to the Audit Bureau of Circulations are revised only once or twice a year. Box-office and record-popularity information is generally two weeks old by the time it is published. Ratings information is generally from two weeks to several months old by the time it is disseminated (however, many of the larger markets are measured with computer-assisted devices so that overnight ratings are possible).

In the rest of this chapter, we will examine the most common forms of feedback in each of the various media.

FEEDBACK: THE PRINT MEDIA

Letters to the Editor

The most prevalent form of audience-generated feedback in the newspaper and magazine industries is the letter to the editor. This is probably the oldest of all the feedback mechanisms that we shall talk about; letters to newspaper and magazine editors were common during Ben Franklin's time. The *New York Times* started publishing letters in 1851, only a few days after it was founded. Evidently, letters are popular feedback mechanisms with readers since newspapers receive a large number of them. The *Seattle Times*, for example, gets about 7,000 a year, while the *New York Times* receives more than 40,000. One survey reported that about 45 percent of those questioned read the letters section often or almost always. Another survey noted that this section was more popular with older newspaper readers. The main reason people give for writing letters is that it lets them ''blow off steam'' or ''get something off their chests.''

Written feedback from readers does not provide an accurate picture of the print media's audience, however. We have already noted that the people who write these letters tend to be atypical of general newspaper readers. Furthermore, although space is set aside for letters, most magazines and newspapers receive far more than they can print. The *New York Times*, for instance, prints about one out of every twenty letters it receives. Nor is it clear whether the letters that finally do get into print are representative of all mail received.

The ABC

The best known media-originated feedback system in newspapers and magazines is that connected with the **Audit Bureau of Circulations (ABC)**. During the early 1900s, with the growth of mass advertising, some newspapers and magazine publishers began inflating the number of readers for their publications in order to attract more revenue from advertisers. In an effort to check this deceptive practice, advertisers and publishers joined together to form the ABC in 1914. The organization's

Measuring Ad Readership in the Print Media: The Starch Reports

One of the things that an advertiser needs to know is how many people are exposed to his or her ad in a newspaper or magazine. Since the early 1920s, the Starch organization (formal name: Starch INRA Hooper, Inc.) has been providing this form of feedback to the advertising industry. Every year Starch measures approximately 100,000 ads in more than 100 publications, including consumer magazines; business, trade, and industrial publications; and newspapers. Each Starch readership study is based on interviews done with a representative sample of 100–150 readers of the publication under study. Once it has been determined that a respondent actually has read a publication, a Starch interviewer then goes through a copy of the magazine or newspaper ad by ad and asks whether the person can recall seeing the ad and its various components (headline, illustration, copy, etc.).

After all questions are asked, each respondent is classified into one of four categories:

1. Nonreader: a person who didn't remember having seen the ad.

2. "Noted" reader: a person who remembered having previously seen the ad.

3. "Associated" reader: a person who not only "noted" the ad but also saw or read some part of it that clearly indicated the brand or advertiser.

4. "Read-most" reader: a person who read more than half of the written material in the ad.

A Starch Readership Report includes a copy of the publication in which labels have been attached to all of the ads under study. These labels report the readership score of the entire ad as well as reading scores for each of the ad's component parts. For example, for one particular ad, 19 percent of the sample might be classified as "noted" readers, 16 percent as "associated" readers, and 6 percent as "read-most" readers. In addition, the Starch data would also tell the advertiser that 20 percent saw the illustration that went with the ad, 13 percent read the headline, and 11 percent read some of the ad copy, and so on.

By using the feedback provided by the Starch organization, advertisers can compare one ad campaign against another to see which was more effective, compare the scores of their ads with the scores of competitors' ads, and isolate what layout and copywriting factors are related to high readership.

purpose was to establish ground rules for counting circulation, to make sure that the rules were enforced, and to provide verified reports of circulation data. The ABC audits about three-fourths of all print media in the United States and Canada, about 2600 magazine, farm, and business publications and daily and weekly newspapers.

The ABC functions in the following manner. Publishers keep detailed records of circulation data. In the case of a newspaper, these records would include such information as the number of copies delivered by carriers, the number of papers sold over the counter, and the number delivered by mail. Twice a year, publishers file a circulation statement with the ABC, which the ABC in turn disseminates to its clients. Once every year, the ABC audits publications to verify that the figures that have been reported are accurate. An ABC representative visits the publication and is free to examine records and files that contain data on press runs, invoices for newsprint, and transcripts of circulation records. In an average year, the ABC's field staff of ninety travels approximately 300,000 miles and spends about 135,000 audit hours in verifying the facts on member publications' circulation. The cost of the ABC's services, about $5 million per year, is financed through member dues and service fees. As far as fees go, an individual newspaper or magazine audited by the ABC pays an hourly rate of about $50 for the amount of time it takes to do the audit. Most audits take fewer than forty working hours to complete, which means the total tab would be less than $2000. Figure 20.1 is a sample newspaper audit.

FIGURE 20.1 *Sample of the ABC audit report. (Reprinted with permission of the Audit Bureau of Circulations.)*

ABC Audit Report-Newspaper

THE MORNING PROTOTYPE (Morning and Sunday)

THE EVENING PROTOTYPE (Evening)

City (County), State/Province

TOTAL AVERAGE PAID CIRCULATION FOR 12 MONTHS ENDING MARCH 31, (Year):

	AVERAGE PAID CIRCULATION			
	Combined Daily	Morning	Evening	Sunday
1. TOTAL AVERAGE PAID CIRCULATION	116,548	80,600	35,948	102,982

1A. TOTAL AVERAGE PAID CIRCULATION BY ZONES:

CITY ZONE

	Population	Hslds*
(Year) Census:	177,358	53,688
(Year) ABC Estimate:	182,531	55,252

	Combined Daily	Morning	Evening	Sunday
Dealers and Carriers not filing lists with publisher (a)	63,260	32,126	31,134	42,927
Street Vendors	2,430	1,014	1,416	1,453
Publisher's Counter Sales				
Mail Subscriptions	117	94	23	60
School-Single Copy/Subs. See Par. 12(b)	32	32		
Total City Zone	65,839	33,266	32,573	44,440

RETAIL TRADING ZONE

	Population	Hslds*
(Year) Census:	688,042	210,422
(Year) ABC Estimate:	707,479	216,354

	Combined Daily	Morning	Evening	Sunday
Dealers and Carriers not filing lists with publisher	41,346	38,160	3,186	54,607
Mail Subscriptions (See Pars. 12-c and 12-d)	6,129	6,104	25	285
School-Single Copy/Subs. See Par. 12(b)	17	17		
Total Retail Trading Zone	47,492	44,281	3,211	54,892
Total City & Retail Trading Zones	113,331	77,547	35,784	99,332

	Population	Hslds*
(Year) Census:	865,400	264,110
(Year) ABC Estimate:	890,010	271,606

ALL OTHER

	Combined Daily	Morning	Evening	Sunday
Dealers and Carriers	1,672	1,670	2	2,633
Mail Subscriptions (See Pars. 12-c and 12-d)	1,545	1,383	162	1,017
Total All Other	3,217	3,053	164	3,650
TOTAL PAID excluding Bulk (For Bulk Sales, See Par. 5)	116,548	80,600	35,948	102,982

*Hslds—Households

(a) See Paragraph 12-a.

Business magazines and trade publications are audited by the Business Publication Audit (BPA), which uses methods similar to the ABC.

Total Audience Data

In addition to circulation figures, organizations that provide audience feedback in the magazine industry report total audience figures. The total audience is composed of the **primary audience,** those people who subscribe to the magazine or buy it at the newsstand, and the **pass-along audience,** those people who pick up a copy at the doctor's office, while traveling, at work, and so on. The two major companies that measure magazine readership are the **Simmons Market Research Bureau (SMRB)** and **Mediamark (MRI).** Because the magazine-reading audience is highly segmented, both companies must select a large random sample of households so that the audience for each magazine will be statistically meaningful. Personal interviews are then conducted with the residents to get an "exposure score" for a large number of magazines. The interviewer shows the respondent a deck of cards bearing the logos of anywhere from 100 to 200 different magazines. The respondent is then asked to sort the cards into three piles according to whether he or she read, may have read, or didn't read the publication. (Since a respondent is sorting a large number of magazines, it's inevitable that some error creeps into the system. Readers frequently forget or confuse the names of magazines they have read. One study of the sorting technique found that a large number of respondents reported reading a publication called *Popular Sports*. Unfortunately, this magazine never existed.)

At this point, the measurement techniques of the two companies diverge. SMRB shows respondents a stripped-down version of the magazine and readership is again verified by asking if the respondent has read or looked through that particular issue. The interviewer also asks about the place where each magazine was read. Additional data are gathered about ownership, purchase, and use of a wide variety of products. MRI measures recent reading by requesting respondents to go through each card in their "read" or "may have read" piles and asking if the respondent has read the magazine within the last week or month, depending on the publication schedule of the magazine. Since they use different techniques, the results of the two companies are frequently at odds; resolving the differences in their estimates for various magazines has become a vexing problem for the industry.

The reports issued by SMRB and MRI are extremely detailed and encompass many volumes. They contain such specific information as what percentage of a particular magazine's readers earn more than $25,000 per year and detailed product-use data such as how many readers used an upset-stomach remedy in the last month. A small portion from an MRI report is reproduced in Fig. 20.2.

Best-selling book lists are based on several sources of information. The list compiled by *Publishers Weekly* is based on publishers' reports of books shipped and billed to bookstores, libraries, and wholesalers. The *New York Times* best-seller list is compiled from figures taken from a sample of 1600 bookstores, including all the chain outlets.

FEEDBACK: RADIO AND SOUND RECORDING

Radio is supported by the sale of advertising time; the sound-recording industry depends upon the sale of tapes and discs for support. Radio stations are licensed by the Federal Communications Commission and as such are subject to a number of

	ADULTS		MEN		WOMEN		XV FEMALE HOMEMAKERS	
	UNWGT	PROJ ('000)	UNWGT	PROJ ('000)	UNWGT	PROJ ('000)	UNWGT	PROJ ('000)
ALL ADULTS	20330	170599	10059	81025	10271	89573	9708	79371
METROPOLITAN HOME	262	1957	86	670	176	1287	171	1204
MODERN BRIDE	241	2761	31	*292	210	2470	178	1755
MODERN MATURITY	2899	20846	1215	8064	1684	12782	1626	12104
MODERN PHOTOGRAPHY	378	3135	264	2205	114	931	106	759
MONEY	1079	8147	685	4884	394	3263	381	3039
MOTHER EARTH NEWS	364	3200	194	1567	170	1633	164	1553
MOTOR TREND	500	4602	455	4192	45	*410	41	*378
MS.	290	2664	38	*255	252	2408	229	1869
NATIONAL ENQUIRER	1883	19463	698	7309	1185	12154	1113	10446
NATIONAL GEOGRAPHIC	3942	30961	2145	16082	1797	14878	1705	13460
NATIONAL GEOGRAPHIC TRAVELER	396	3294	221	1805	175	1490	167	1390
NATIONAL LAMPOON	277	2863	198	1950	79	913	74	788
NATURAL HISTORY	192	1408	101	707	91	701	86	670
NEWSWEEK	2573	20338	1527	11579	1046	8759	992	7907
NEW SHELTER	220	1746	136	1027	84	719	83	715
NEW WOMAN	459	4007	44	*322	415	3685	389	3187
NEW YORK MAGAZINE	207	1374	110	742	97	632	94	603
NEW YORK TIMES (DAILY)	514	2793	306	1561	208	1232	200	1149
NEW YORK TIMES MAGAZINE	777	4821	436	2633	341	2188	318	1955

FIGURE 20.2 *Excerpt from an MRI report. (Copyright © 1986 by Mediamark Research Inc.)*

rules and regulations. The sound-recording industry is not subject to these restrictions. Because of these differences, the feedback systems that exist in these two media are somewhat dissimilar.

Radio Audience Responses

In the radio industry, there are several sources of audience-generated feedback. First of all, listeners write letters to the station concerning the station's programming practices. Some stations have installed telephone recording devices attached to a special phone number. Listeners are encouraged to dial that number and present their opinions and points of view. These comments may then be spliced together and aired as a public-affairs program. Other stations have call-in shows in which people are asked to present their views on the air (usually with a seven-second tape delay for insurance).

Another form of audience-generated feedback usually comes into play around license-renewal time. The 1934 Communications Act states that an audience member may file a petition to deny the renewal or transfer (sale) of the license of a radio or television station. The person or group filing such a petition must cite factual evidence proving that granting the renewal or transfer would not be in the public interest. In recent years, most petitions to deny license renewals have been filed by groups representing women and minorities. These petitions typically allege that the station has not lived up to its obligations under the Equal Opportunity Employment guidelines or that the station has failed to provide programming that adequately serves the minority community. One recent result of contact between petitioners and stations is the negotiated agreement. In this arrangement, the group agrees to drop its petition to deny in return for assurances from the station that the practices that prompted the original petition will be changed. These agreements continue to be an effective (if somewhat drastic) method of settling specific disputes. Much to the relief of broadcasters, a general trend toward deregulation has meant that petitions to deny have lost some of their former power.

Arbitron and the Diary Method

In the radio industry, media-originated feedback is provided by ratings conducted by professional research organizations. The major company that measures the radio audience is **Arbitron,** a subsidiary of Control Data Corporation, manufacturers of computer hardware and software. Arbitron surveys radio listening in approximately 240 markets across the United States and reports its results to broadcasters and advertisers. Large markets (New York, Los Angeles, Boston, Chicago, Detroit, Philadelphia, San Francisco) are measured at least four times a year, while smaller markets may be examined only once in the same period. All markets are measured during April and May.

Within a given market, Arbitron chooses people at random from a listing of all telephone numbers in the market. Individuals who agree to participate in Arbitron's survey are sent a pocket-sized diary. This diary is designed to travel with a person in order to measure both in-home and out-of-home listening. Participants are instructed to fill in the diary on a day-to-day basis, noting the time spent listening to radio and identifying the stations. The back of the diary asks respondents to provide basic demographic data. Approximately 3000–4000 of these diaries are mailed in a given market, and Arbitron follows up with several reminder calls to persons in the sample. Nevertheless, only 50–55 percent of the diaries are returned in usable form. Figure 20.3 is an example of an Arbitron radio diary. Once all the diaries have been returned, Arbitron begins an analysis that typically takes three to four weeks. The end product of this process is a ratings book, which is sent to participating stations. A sample page of such a book is reproduced in Fig. 20.4, on page 482.

Measurements of radio and television audiences gathered by the diary method are usually expressed in terms of two related concepts: (1) ratings and (2) share of the audience. A **rating** is simply the ratio of listeners to a particular station to all people in the market. To illustrate, suppose that in a market with 100,000 people, 20,000 listen to radio station KYYY from 9:00 A.M. to 9:15 A.M. The rating of KYYY would be 20,000/100,000, or 20 percent. A **share of the audience** is the ratio of listeners to a particular station to the total number of radio listeners in the market. For example, again suppose that 20,000 people are listening to KYYY from 9:00 A.M. to 9:15 A.M. and that in the total market 80,000 people are listening to the radio during the same period. KYYY's share of the audience would be 20,000/80,000, or 25 percent. Shares of the audience divide the listening audience among all stations in the market. When they are summed, shares should total 100 percent. Table 20.2 contains another illustration of the technique of computing shares and ratings.

The cost of these ratings books is shared by all the stations in a market that subscribe to Arbitron. The ratings are extremely important to stations because they are used to establish what rates stations will charge their advertisers. Birch Radio recently began competing with Arbitron in providing radio ratings. Birch uses a telephone recall method in which listeners are asked to report on the previous day's listening activity.

Sound-Recording Audience Responses

Few people write letters to record companies, although some fan mail directed to recording artists provides a rather crude gauge of popularity. Another indirect form of audience-generated feedback is attendance at personal appearances and concerts. In general, feedback is concerned with the bottom line—sales figures.

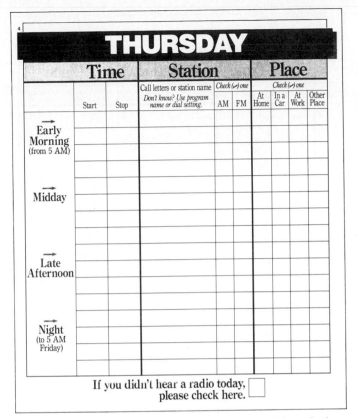

FIGURE 20.3 *Sample of an Arbitron radio diary.* (Arbitron Ratings: Your Radio Ratings Diary. *Copyright © 1988 Arbitron Ratings Company. Reprinted by permission.*)

TABLE 20.2 Calculating Ratings and Share of Audience

Market size:	500,000 people
Stations:	WALL, WISK, WONT, WENT

	Listening at 9 A.M.:
WALL:	15,000
WISK:	20,000
WONT:	50,000
WENT:	30,000
Total listening:	115,000

RATING	SHARE
$\text{WALL} = \dfrac{15,000}{500,000} = 0.03 \text{ or } 3\%$	$\text{WALL} = \dfrac{15,000}{115,000} = 0.13 \text{ or } 13\%$
$\text{WISK} = \dfrac{20,000}{500,000} = 0.04 \text{ or } 4\%$	$\text{WISK} = \dfrac{20,000}{115,000} = 0.17 \text{ or } 17\%$
$\text{WONT} = \dfrac{50,000}{500,000} = 0.10 \text{ or } 10\%$	$\text{WONT} = \dfrac{50,000}{115,000} = 0.44 \text{ or } 44\%$
$\text{WENT} = \dfrac{30,000}{500,000} = 0.06 \text{ or } 6\%$	$\text{WENT} = \dfrac{30,000}{115,000} = 0.26 \text{ or } 26\%$
	$\text{TOTAL} \quad = 1.00 \text{ or } 100\%$

Target Audience
PERSONS 18-49

	MONDAY-FRIDAY 6AM-10AM				MONDAY-FRIDAY 10AM-3PM				MONDAY-FRIDAY 3PM-7PM				MONDAY-FRIDAY 7PM-MID				WEEKEND 10AM-7PM			
	AQH (00)	CUME (00)	AQH RTG	AQH SHR	AQH (00)	CUME (00)	AQH RTG	AQH SHR	AQH (00)	CUME (00)	AQH RTG	AQH SHR	AQH (00)	CUME (00)	AQH RTG	AQH SHR	AQH (00)	CUME (00)	AQH RTG	AQH SHR
WANS-FM																				
METRO	93	561	3.0	10.6	77	391	2.4	9.6	91	549	2.9	12.5	52	396	1.7	16.5	85	505	2.7	13.7
TSA	180	1004			201	675			212	1033			77	718			173	952		
WASC																				
METRO	2	29	.1	.2	4	26	.1	.5	7	40	.2	1.0					14	54	.4	2.3
TSA	2	29			4	26			7	40							14	54		
WBBO																				
METRO	*												*							
TSA																				
WBBO-FM																				
METRO	10	50	.3	1.1	15	74	.5	1.9	12	69	.4	1.7	4	56	.1	1.3	14	71	.4	2.3
TSA	10	60			17	84			15	91			6	75			20	97		
A/F TOT																				
METRO	10	50	.3	1.1	15	74	.5	1.9	12	69	.4	1.7	4	56	.1	1.3				
TSA	10	60			17	84			15	91			6	75						
WCKI																				
METRO		6								6			*							
TSA		6								6										
WCKN																				
METRO	49	269	1.6	5.6	66	254	2.1	8.2	58	318	1.8	8.0	28	212	.9	8.9	46	229	1.5	7.4
TSA	84	513			112	451			114	604			59	460			85	473		
WELP																				
METRO	3	6	.1	.3	2	5	.1	.2	3	28	.1	.4	*9	18	.3	2.8	*5	28	.2	.8
TSA	3	6			2	5			3	28			9	18			5	28		
WESC																				
METRO	7	53	.2	.8	7	40	.2	.9	5	26	.2	.7	*1	10		.3	6	41	.2	1.0
TSA	9	81			7	42			8	39			2	21			6	41		
WESC-FM																				
METRO	129	461	4.1	14.7	83	338	2.6	10.3	64	349	2.0	8.8	34	256	1.1	10.8	64	281	2.0	10.3
TSA	286	1220			193	832			156	899			73	532			138	633		
A/F TOT																				
METRO	136	490	4.3	15.5	90	351	2.9	11.2	69	356	2.2	9.5	35	256	1.1	11.1				
TSA	295	1260			200	846			164	921			75	543						
WFBC																				
METRO	6	43	.2	.7	8	20	.3	1.0	2	40	.1	.3	1	14		.3	1	27		.2
TSA	6	43			8	20			2	40			1	14			1	27		
WFBC-FM																				
METRO	163	669	5.2	18.5	109	374	3.5	13.6	84	444	2.7	11.6	14	204	.4	4.4	29	293	.9	4.7
TSA	279	1148			194	711			150	853			39	420			68	560		
WHYZ																				
METRO	24	80	.8	2.7	33	85	1.0	4.1	18	62	.6	2.5					33	131	1.0	5.3
TSA	24	80			33	101			18	62							38	147		
WLWZ																				
METRO	59	252	1.9	6.7	61	224	1.9	7.6	72	314	2.3	9.9	35	222	1.1	11.1	75	281	2.4	12.1
TSA	63	284			66	256			74	343			35	225			80	328		
WMUU-FM																				
METRO	10	65	.3	1.1	6	60	.2	.7	6	35	.2	.8	1	47		.3	7	55	.2	1.1
TSA	11	78			6	73			6	35			1	61			7	55		
WMYI																				
METRO	39	302	1.2	4.4	43	294	1.4	5.4	43	326	1.4	5.9	10	148	.3	3.2	30	233	1.0	4.8
TSA	139	858			152	761			135	949			35	511			92	669		
WORD																				
METRO	22	85	.7	2.5	7	62	.2	.9	7	45	.2	1.0	1	19		.3	8	46	.3	1.3
TSA	22	85			8	73			7	45			1	19			8	46		
WSPA																				
METRO	22	103	.7	2.5	13	45	.4	1.6	9	64	.3	1.2	2	23	.1	.6	1	28		.2
TSA	22	103			13	45			9	64			2	23			1	28		
WSPA-FM																				
METRO	36	148	1.1	4.1	46	154	1.5	5.7	36	160	1.1	5.0	6	65	.2	1.9	11	79	.3	1.8
TSA	60	306			85	319			77	343			13	167			27	215		
WSSL																				
METRO	3	28	.1	.3	4	20	.1	.5	3	8	.1	.4		4			4	19	.1	.6
TSA	3	28			4	20			3	8				4			4	19		
WSSL-FM																				
METRO	91	438	2.9	10.3	123	378	3.9	15.3	102	461	3.2	14.0	31	225	1.0	9.8	78	338	2.5	12.5
TSA	201	962			213	776			182	911			49	445			165	725		
A/F TOT																				
METRO	94	452	3.0	10.7	127	393	4.0	15.8	105	464	3.3	14.4	31	229	1.0	9.8	82	357	2.6	13.2
TSA	204	975			217	792			185	914			49	449			169	743		
WKSF																				
METRO	11	85	.3	1.3	3	41	.1	.4	5	84	.2	.7	9	99	.3	2.8	9	105	.3	1.4
TSA	87	527			83	470			80	564			52	471			75	546		
WBCY																				
METRO	8	100	.3	.9	6	63	.2	.7	7	105	.2	1.0	1	10		.3	2	23	.1	.3
TSA	61	283			33	169			17	269			6	122			14	96		
WCKZ-FM																				
METRO	17	110	.5	1.9	25	113	.8	3.1	37	164	1.2	5.1	33	97	1.0	10.4	33	158	1.0	5.3
TSA	48	303			40	239			67	426			48	261			67	366		
WROQ																				
METRO	4	25	.1	.5	7	41	.2	.9	3	18	.1	.4	3	28	.1	.9	7	31	.2	1.1
TSA	5	38			9	65			11	145			5	58			13	86		

Footnote Symbols: * Audience estimates adjusted for actual broadcast schedule.   + Station(s) changed call letters since the prior survey - see Page 5B.

ARBITRON RATINGS

GREENVILLE-SPARTANBURG

42

SPRING 1988

FIGURE 20.4 *Excerpt from an Arbitron radio ratings book. (Arbitron Ratings—Radio. Copyright © 1988 Arbitron Ratings Company. Reprinted by permission.)*

Media-originated feedback in the sound-recording industry is characterized by stars, triangles, and bullets. These are the common symbols used in ***Billboard*** magazine's charts of popular records. Stars stand for recordings that are "movers"; they are on their way up in the charts. Bullets go to singles that are one-million sellers; triangles go to two-million sellers. Every week disc jockeys, program directors, and record company executives scan the *Billboard* charts, the most important channel of feedback in the sound-recording industry.

What determines the award of stars, triangles, and bullets? How is the *Billboard* chart put together? In general, the *Billboard* charts are based on two components: (1) exposure and (2) sales. Sales information is gathered in the following manner. *Billboard* selects the top fifty markets in terms of total record sales in the United States (these markets are among the most populous), and within these markets the magazine subjectively chooses the most influential recording outlets. These can be retail record shops, record departments in department stores, and suppliers to jukebox operators. *Billboard* then hands out reporting forms on which sales data for the hottest-selling discs and tapes are recorded. About 185 outlets are surveyed weekly.

In order to measure exposure, *Billboard* surveys the playlist of leading radio stations. The survey includes approximately 240 stations that are weighted by audience reach (i.e., being the number-one record on a 50,000-watt station in New York City is worth more than being number one at a 5,000-watt station in a rural area). Note that another mass medium, radio, plays an important part in the feedback mechanism for sound recording. In addition, radio stations with a music format rely on the *Billboard* charts to determine what records they should play. Thus sound recording functions as a feedback mechanism for radio. This reciprocity is another example of a symbiotic relationship between media (see Chapter 1).

When all the sales and exposure data have been collected, *Billboard* combines the two measures and winds up with a final index number for each album or single release. These rankings are then translated into the Hot 100 pop singles or soul recordings or some other list, depending upon what chart is being prepared.

Figure 20.5, page 484, reproduces one of *Billboard's* charts. It contains several pieces of information: the record's standing for the current week and the week before; number of weeks on the chart; title of song and the artist; the producer, writer, and label number (important information for ordering a record); and, if necessary, the distributing label. *Billboard* publishes a chart for almost all formats of popular music. For example, each issue will contain popularity rankings for not only pop singles but also jazz albums, Latin albums, country albums, country singles, classical albums, middle-of-the-road singles, soul albums, and soul singles, and a chart that lists hit records all over the world. For example, in late 1988, "Tattoo," by Akina Nakamori, topped the charts in Japan while "Yeke Yeke," by Mory Kante, was a big hit in West Germany and Michael Jackson's "Dirty Diana" was number one in the Netherlands.

FEEDBACK: TELEVISION AND FILM

Feedback mechanisms in television resemble those used in radio, while feedback systems in the film industry are similar to those used in sound recording.

Television Viewer Responses

In television, audience-generated feedback typically takes the form of telephone calls and letters to the station's management. Since TV stations tend to be more visible

FOR WEEK ENDING MARCH 11, 1989

Billboard **HOT 100**® **SINGLES**™

"When you play it, Say it!"

©Copyright 1989, Billboard Publications, Inc. No part of this publication may be reproduced, stored in any retrieval system, or transmitted, in any form or by any means, electronic, mechanical, photocopying, recording, or otherwise, without the prior written permission of the publisher.

Compiled from a national sample of retail store and one-stop sales reports and radio playlists.

THIS WEEK	LAST WEEK	2 WKS AGO	WKS. ON CHART	TITLE / PRODUCER (SONGWRITER)	ARTIST / LABEL & NUMBER/DISTRIBUTING LABEL
1	1	2	8	★★ NO. 1 ★★ 2 weeks at No. One LOST IN YOUR EYES D.GIBSON (D.GIBSON)	◆ DEBBIE GIBSON (C) ATLANTIC 7-88970
2	4	9	10	THE LIVING YEARS C.NEIL,M.RUTHERFORD (M.RUTHERFORD, B.A.ROBERTSON)	◆ MIKE + THE MECHANICS (C) ATLANTIC 7-88964
3	5	7	17	YOU GOT IT (THE RIGHT STUFF) M.STARR,M.JONZUN (M.STARR)	◆ NEW KIDS ON THE BLOCK (T) (C) COLUMBIA 38-08092
4	8	12	10	RONI L.A.,BABYFACE (BABYFACE)	◆ BOBBY BROWN (T) (C) MCA 53463
5	10	14	9	PARADISE CITY M.CLINK (GUNS N' ROSES)	◆ GUNS N' ROSES (C) GEFFEN 7-27570
6	9	11	12	SURRENDER TO ME (FROM "TEQUILA SUNRISE") R.ZITO (R.VANNELLI, R.MARX)	ANN WILSON & ROBIN ZANDER (C) CAPITOL 44288
7	12	17	10	GIRL YOU KNOW IT'S TRUE F.FARIAN (PETTAWAY, SPENCER, LYLES, HOLLAMAN, ADEYEMO)	◆ MILLI VANILLI (T) (C) ARISTA 1-9781
8	2	4	19	THE LOVER IN ME L.A.,BABYFACE (BABYFACE, L.A.REID, D.SIMMONS)	◆ SHEENA EASTON (T) (C) MCA 53416
9	13	18	14	MY HEART CAN'T TELL YOU NO R.STEWART,A.TAYLOR,B.EDWARDS (S.CLIMIE, D.MORGAN)	◆ ROD STEWART (C) WARNER BROS. 7-27729
10	3	1	15	STRAIGHT UP ● E.WOLFF,K.COHEN (E.WOLFF)	◆ PAULA ABDUL (T) (C) VIRGIN 7-99256
11	17	26	6	ETERNAL FLAME D.SIGERSON (S.HOFFS, B.STEINBERG, T.KELLY)	◆ BANGLES (C) COLUMBIA 38-68533
12	16	19	9	DON'T TELL ME LIES B.SARGEANT (D.GLASPER, M.LILLINGTON)	◆ BREATHE (T) (C) A&M 1267
13	25	31	5	THE LOOK C.OFWERMAN (GESSLE)	◆ ROXETTE (C) EMI 50190
14	7	8	16	WHAT I AM P.MORAN (E.BRICKELL, K.WINTHROW)	◆ EDIE BRICKELL & NEW BOHEMIANS (C) GEFFEN 7-27696
15	18	22	12	I BEG YOUR PARDON B.HARRIS (B.HARRIS)	KON KAN (T) (C) ATLANTIC 7-88969
16	21	24	8	YOU'RE NOT ALONE R.NEVISON (J.SCOTT)	◆ CHICAGO (C) (CD) REPRISE 7-27757
17	6	3	15	WILD THING ▲2 M.ROSS,M.DIKE (M.YOUNG, T.SMITH, M.DIKE, M.ROSS)	◆ TONE LOC (T) (C) (M) DELICIOUS VINYL 102/ISLAND
18	20	25	10	DREAMIN' D.ROBINSON (L.MONTEGOMARY, G.PASCHAL)	◆ VANESSA WILLIAMS (C) WING 871 078-7/POLYGRAM
19	26	30	7	WALK THE DINOSAUR D.WAS,D.WAS (D.WAS, D.WAS, R.JACOBS)	◆ WAS (NOT WAS) (T) (C) CHRYSALIS 43331
20	23	27	8	JUST BECAUSE M.POWELL (M.O'HARA, S.MCKINNEY, A.BROWN)	◆ ANITA BAKER (C) (CD) ELEKTRA 7-69327
21	30	39	7	★★★POWER PICK/SALES★★★ SHE DRIVES ME CRAZY DAVID Z.,FINE YOUNG CANNIBALS (D.STEELE, R.GIFT)	◆ FINE YOUNG CANNIBALS (T) (C) I.R.S. 53483/MCA
22	28	32	8	STAND S.LITT,R.E.M. (BERRY, BUCK, MILLS, STIPE)	◆ R.E.M. (C) (CD) WARNER BROS. 7-27688
23	11	6	13	SHE WANTS TO DANCE WITH ME R.ASTLEY,P.HARDING,I.CURNOW (R.ASTLEY)	◆ RICK ASTLEY (T) (C) RCA 8838
24	14	15	14	A LITTLE RESPECT S.HAGUE (V.CLARKE, A.BELL)	◆ ERASURE (T) (C) SIRE 7-27738/REPRISE
25	29	33	8	YOU GOT IT J.LYNNE (J.LYNNE, R.ORBISON, T.PETTY)	◆ ROY ORBISON (C) VIRGIN 7-99245
26	27	29	9	THE LOVE IN YOUR EYES R.ZITO,E.MONEY (D.P.BRYANT, A.GERVITZ, S.DUBIN)	◆ EDDIE MONEY (C) COLUMBIA 38-68532
27	32	37	7	SUPERWOMAN L.A.,BABYFACE (L.A.REID, BABYFACE, D.SIMMONS)	◆ KARYN WHITE (C) WARNER BROS. 7-27773
28	31	35	12	MORE THAN YOU KNOW M.JAY (MARTIKA, M.JAY, M.MORROW)	◆ MARTIKA (T) (C) COLUMBIA 38-08103
29	35	38	7	CRYIN' D.COLE,R.NEIGHER (G.TRIPP, J.PARIS)	◆ VIXEN (C) EMI 50167
30	15	5	16	BORN TO BE MY BABY B.FAIRBAIRN (J.BON JOVI, R.SAMBORA, D.CHILD)	◆ BON JOVI (C) (CD) MERCURY 872 156-7/POLYGRAM
31	37	46	4	YOUR MAMA DON'T DANCE T.WERMAN (K.LOGGINS, J.MESSINA)	◆ POISON (C) (CD) ENIGMA 44293/CAPITOL
32	24	16	23	WHEN I'M WITH YOU S.HEYDON (A.D.LANNI)	SHERIFF (C) CAPITOL 44302
33	19	13	14	DIAL MY HEART L.A.,BABYFACE (L.A.REID, BABYFACE, D.SIMMONS)	◆ THE BOYS (T) (C) MOTOWN 53301
34	22	10	16	WALKING AWAY F.MAHER (P.ROBB)	◆ INFORMATION SOCIETY (T) (C) TOMMY BOY 7-27736/REPRISE
35	40	43	7	SHE WON'T TALK TO ME L.VANDROSS,M.MILLER (L.VANDROSS, H.EAVES III)	◆ LUTHER VANDROSS (T) (C) EPIC 34-08513/E.P.A.
36	41	44	7	FEELS SO GOOD VAN HALEN,D.LANDEE (EDDIE, ALEX, SAMMY, MIKE)	◆ VAN HALEN (C) WARNER BROS. 7-27565
37	50	67	3	HEAVEN HELP ME G.MICHAEL (D.ESTUS, G.MICHAEL)	◆ DEON ESTUS (C) MIKA 871 538-7/POLYGRAM
38	44	52	5	SECOND CHANCE R.MILLS (J.CARLISI, M.CARL, C.CURTIS)	THIRTY EIGHT SPECIAL (C) A&M 1273
39	45	50	8	ORINOCO FLOW (SAIL AWAY) N.RYAN (ENYA, R.RYAN)	◆ ENYA (T) (C) GEFFEN 7-27633
40	48	60	4	ROOM TO MOVE S.BARRI,T.PELUSO (S.CLIMIE, R.FISHER, D.MORGAN)	◆ ANIMOTION (T) (C) POLYDOR 871 418-7/POLYGRAM
41	34	23	19	WHEN THE CHILDREN CRY M.WAGENER (V.BRATTA, M.TRAMP)	◆ WHITE LION (C) ATLANTIC 7-89015
42	46	54	6	THINKING OF YOU C.RODGERS,A.MARIN (R.DESALVO, W.COSMO, B.STEELE)	◆ SA-FIRE (T) (C) CUTTING 872 502-7/POLYGRAM
43	33	20	18	I WANNA HAVE SOME FUN FULL FORCE (FULL FORCE)	◆ SAMANTHA FOX (T) (C) JIVE 1154/RCA
44	51	56	5	CAN YOU STAND THE RAIN J.JAM,T.LEWIS (J.HARRIS III, T.LEWIS)	◆ NEW EDITION (T) (C) MCA 53464
45	54	57	8	SINCERELY YOURS S.PECK (R.PAGAN, J.MALLOY)	◆ SWEET SENSATION (WITH ROMEO J.D.) (T) (C) ATCO 7-99246
46	61	—	2	ROCKET R.LANGE (CLARK, COLLEN, ELLIOTT, R.LANGE, SAVAGE)	◆ DEF LEPPARD (C) (CD) MERCURY 872 614-7/POLYGRAM
47	60	—	2	FUNKY COLD MEDINA M.ROSS,M.DIKE (M.YOUNG, M.ROSS, M.DIKE)	◆ TONE LOC (T) (C) DELICIOUS VINYL 104/ISLAND
48	49	55	6	24/7 DINO (DINO)	◆ DINO (T) (C) 4TH & B'WAY 7471/ISLAND
49	36	40	8	THE LAST MILE A.JOHNS,T.KEIFER,E.BRITTINGHAM (T.KEIFER)	◆ CINDERELLA (C) (CD) MERCURY 872 148-7/POLYGRAM
50	47	51	6	WE'VE SAVED THE BEST FOR LAST P.BUNETTA,R.CHUDACOFF (L.PARDINI, D.MATKOSKY, P.GORDON)	◆ KENNY G (C) ARISTA 1-9785
51	82	—	2	★★★POWER PICK/AIRPLAY★★★ I'LL BE THERE FOR YOU B.FAIRBAIRN (J.BON JOVI, R.SAMBORA)	BON JOVI (C) (CD) MERCURY 872 564-7/POLYGRAM
52	52	53	7	BRING DOWN THE MOON A.MARDIN (G.MERRILL, S.RUBICAM)	◆ BOY MEETS GIRL (C) RCA 8807
53	39	34	19	ALL THIS TIME G.E.TOBIN (T.JAMES, S.MCCLINTOCK)	◆ TIFFANY (C) MCA 53371
54	56	66	4	ONE METALLICA,F.RASMUSSEN (HETFIELD, ULRICH)	◆ METALLICA (C) (CD) ELEKTRA 7-69329
55	42	36	22	THE WAY YOU LOVE ME L.A.,BABYFACE (BABYFACE, L.A.REID, D.SIMMONS)	◆ KARYN WHITE (T) (C) WARNER BROS. 7-27773
56	62	80	4	I WANNA BE THE ONE STEVIE B. (STEVIE B)	STEVIE B (T) (C) (M) LMR 74003
57	38	21	13	ANGEL OF HARLEM J.IOVINE (BONO, U2)	◆ U2 (T) (C) (CD) ISLAND 7-99254/ATLANTIC
58	67	85	3	BIRTHDAY SUIT R.LAWRENCE (R.LAWRENCE, D.PITCHFORD)	JOHNNY KEMP (T) (C) COLUMBIA 38-68569
59	NEW▶		1	★★★HOT SHOT DEBUT★★★ AFTER ALL (LOVE THEME FROM "CHANCES ARE") P.ASHER (T.SNOW, D.PITCHFORD)	CHER & PETER CETERA (C) GEFFEN 7-27529
60	65	68	5	A SHOULDER TO CRY ON A.MARDIN,J.MARDIN (T.PAGE)	TOMMY PAGE (C) SIRE 7-27645/WARNER BROS.
61	70	84	3	RADIO ROMANCE G.TOBIN (J.DUARTE, M.PAUL)	◆ TIFFANY (C) MCA 53623
62	69	81	3	DRIVEN OUT W.WITTMAN (C.CURNIN)	◆ THE FIXX (C) RCA 8837
63	72	77	3	IT'S ONLY LOVE S.LEVINE (J.CAMERON, V.CAMERON)	◆ SIMPLY RED (T) (C) (CD) ELEKTRA 7-69317
64	73	78	3	SEVENTEEN B.HILL (K.WINGER, R.BEACH, B.HILL)	◆ WINGER (C) ATLANTIC 7-88958
65	77	97	3	TRIBUTE (RIGHT ON) P.WINGFIELD (THE PASADENAS, P.WINGFIELD)	◆ THE PASADENAS (T) (C) COLUMBIA 38-68575
66	63	63	5	END OF THE LINE O.WILBURY,N.WILBURY (G.HARRISON, J.LYNNE, B.DYLAN, T.PETTY, R.ORBISON)	◆ TRAVELING WILBURYS (C) WILBURY 7-27637/WARNER BROS.
67	43	28	12	ALL SHE WANTS IS DURAN DURAN,J.ELIAS,D.ABRAHAM (J.TAYLOR, N.RHODES, S.LEBON)	◆ DURAN DURAN (T) (C) CAPITOL 44287
68	NEW▶		1	FOREVER YOUR GIRL O.LEIBER (O.LEIBER)	PAULA ABDUL (C) VIRGIN 7-99230
69	53	45	21	MY PREROGATIVE ● G.GRIFFIN (G.GRIFFIN, B.BROWN)	◆ BOBBY BROWN (T) (C) MCA 53383
70	86	—	2	IKO IKO (FROM "RAIN MAN") B.TENCH (J.JONES, S.JONES, M.JONES, J.THOMAS, HAWKINS, J.JOHNSON)	THE BELLE STARS (C) CAPITOL 44343
71	76	89	15	WHERE ARE YOU NOW? B.KELLY,J.G.HLUDZIK (J.HARNEN, R.CONGDON)	JIMMY HARNEN WITH SYNCH (C) WTG 31-68625
72	66	65	6	FADING AWAY B.ROSENBERG (B.ROSENBERG)	◆ WILL TO POWER (T) (C) EPIC 34-68543/E.P.A.
73	55	41	19	DON'T RUSH ME R.WAKE (A.FORBES, J.FRANZEL)	◆ TAYLOR DAYNE (T) (C) ARISTA 1-9722
74	81	—	2	CLOSE MY EYES FOREVER M.CHAPMAN (L.FORD, O.OSBOURNE)	◆ LITA FORD (DUET WITH OZZY OSBOURNE) (C) RCA 8899
75	59	49	20	EVERY ROSE HAS ITS THORN ● T.WERMAN (B.DALL, C.C.DEVILLE, B.MICHAELS, R.ROCKETT)	◆ POISON (C) (CD) ENIGMA 44203/CAPITOL
76	75	79	4	NEVER HAD A LOT TO LOSE R.ZITO (R.ZANDER, T.PETERSSON)	◆ CHEAP TRICK (C) EPIC 34-68563/E.P.A.
77	NEW▶		1	CULT OF PERSONALITY E.STASIUM (V.REID, W.CALHOUN, C.GLOVER, N.SKILLINGS)	◆ LIVING COLOUR (C) EPIC 34-68611/E.P.A.
78	58	59	7	INTO YOU G.COLE (CAMPSIE, G.MCFARLANE, G.COLE)	◆ GIANT STEPS (T) (C) A&M 1256
79	64	47	16	HOLDING ON S.WINWOOD,T.LORD-ALGE (S.WINWOOD, W.JENNINGS)	◆ STEVE WINWOOD (T) (C) (CD) VIRGIN 7-99261
80	80	88	4	HALLELUIAH MAN G.KATZ (J.GRANT)	◆ LOVE AND MONEY (C) MERCURY 870 596-7/POLYGRAM
81	71	69	6	GOT IT MADE N.BOLAS,CROSBY,STILLS,NASH & YOUNG (S.STILLS, N.YOUNG)	CROSBY, STILLS, NASH & YOUNG (C) ATLANTIC 7-88966
82	57	42	17	ARMAGEDDON IT R.J.LANGE (CLARK, COLLEN, ELLIOTT, R.LANGE, SAVAGE)	◆ DEF LEPPARD (C) MERCURY 870 692-7/POLYGRAM
83	88	93	3	THIS TIME N.MARTINELLI (SINGLETON)	◆ KIARA (DUET WITH SHANICE WILSON) (C) ARISTA 1-9772
84	90	—	2	GOOD LIFE K.SAUNDERSON (K.SAUNDERSON, P.GRAY, R.HOLMAN)	◆ INNER CITY (T) (C) VIRGIN 7-99236
85	95	—	2	LET THE RIVER RUN (THEME FROM "WORKING GIRL") C.SIMON,R.MOUNSEY (C.SIMON)	◆ CARLY SIMON (C) ARISTA 1-9793
86	92	94	3	I CAN'T FACE THE FACT N.MUNDY (GOMEZ, N.MUNDY, FOSTER)	GINA GO-GO (T) CAPITOL 44233
87	97	—	2	WIND BENEATH MY WINGS (FROM "BEACHES") A.MARDIN (L.HENLEY, J.SILBAR)	◆ BETTE MIDLER (C) ATLANTIC 7-88972
88	79	72	13	DOCTORIN' THE TARDIS THE TIMELORDS (R.GRAINER, G.GLITTER, THE TIMELORDS)	◆ THE TIMELORDS (T) (C) (M) (CD) TVT 4025
89	NEW▶		1	RUN TO PARADISE P.BLYTON,B.MCGEE,CHOIRBOYS (M.GABLE, B.CARR)	◆ CHOIRBOYS (C) WTG 31-68564
90	68	48	17	TWO HEARTS P.COLLINS,L.DOZIER (P.COLLINS, L.DOZIER)	◆ PHIL COLLINS (C) ATLANTIC 7-88980
91	83	62	21	I REMEMBER HOLDING YOU D.COLE,J.PASQUALE (J.PASQUALE)	◆ BOYS CLUB (C) MCA 53430
92	89	76	6	TELL HER R.ZITO (B.RUSSELL)	◆ KENNY LOGGINS (C) COLUMBIA 38-68531
93	78	73	28	KOKOMO (FROM THE "COCKTAIL" SOUNDTRACK) ▲ T.MELCHER (M.LOVE, T.MELCHER, J.PHILLIPS, S.MACKENZIE)	◆ THE BEACH BOYS (C) ELEKTRA 7-69385
94	91	91	3	FALLING OUT OF LOVE D.KORTCHMAR (I.NEVILLE)	◆ IVAN NEVILLE (C) POLYDOR 871 484-7/POLYGRAM
95	NEW▶		1	DEAR GOD M.URE (M.URE)	◆ MIDGE URE (C) CHRYSALIS 43319
96	93	71	12	THE GREAT COMMANDMENT CAMOUFLAGE (H.MAILE, M.MEYN, O.KREYSSIG)	◆ CAMOUFLAGE (T) (C) ATLANTIC 7-89031
97	85	75	8	TEARS RUN RINGS M.ALMOND,LA MAGIA (M.ALMOND)	◆ MARC ALMOND (T) (C) CAPITOL 44240
98	84	70	20	LITTLE LIAR D.CHILD,K.LAGUNA (J.JETT, D.CHILD)	◆ JOAN JETT AND THE BLACKHEARTS (C) BLACKHEART 4-08095/E.P.A.
99	87	58	14	SHAKE FOR THE SHEIK C.KIMSEY (THE ESCAPE CLUB)	◆ THE ESCAPE CLUB (T) (C) ATLANTIC 7-88983
100	74	61	8	GIVE ME THE KEYS (AND I'LL DRIVE YOU CRAZY) HUEY LEWIS & THE NEWS (GIBSON, H.LEWIS, LEWIS)	◆ HUEY LEWIS & THE NEWS (C) CHRYSALIS 43335

◯ Products with the greatest airplay and sales gains this week. ◆ Videoclip availability. ● Recording Industry Assn. Of America (RIAA) certification for sales of 1 million units. ▲ RIAA certification for sales of 2 million units. Catalog no. is for 7-inch vinyl single. *Asterisk indicates catalog no. is for 12-inch vinyl single; 7-inch unavailable. (C) Cassette single availability. (M) Cassette maxi-single availability. (T) 12-inch vinyl single availability. (CD) Compact disk single availability.

92 BILLBOARD MARCH 11, 1989

FIGURE 20.5 *Excerpt from* Billboard's *Hot 100 chart. (© 1989 by Billboard Publications Inc. Compiled by Billboard Research Department and reprinted with permission.)*

Watching the Charts

Billboard began charting the popular music industry way back in 1913 when it started publishing the most popular songs in vaudeville and the best-selling sheet music. In 1940, the magazine began running a weekly chart of best-selling records. A few years later the magazine started listing the top five albums. Currently, *Billboard* carries about two dozen different charts that tabulate the popularity of every style of American music.

The charts are to music fans what baseball statistics are to baseball fans. Recently a number of books have appeared that tabulate virtually everything anybody would want to know about American pop music. *Top Pop Singles,* *1955–1986,* for example, lists every act to have a record in *Billboard*'s Top 100 chart. In the appendix are such fascinating tidbits as the number of records that Elvis Presley had on the charts (149!) and the number of Beatles records that reached number one (20). Further research reveals that only four songs have stayed at number one for at least ten weeks: "Don't Be Cruel"/"Hound Dog," "Singin' the Blues," "Physical," and "You Light Up My Life." What song spent more weeks on the Hot 100 than any other? Soft Cell's 1982 smash, "Tainted Love," lasted forty-three weeks.

and reach a larger audience than most radio stations, they generally attract a larger volume of mail and calls. Television networks also draw a great deal of mail; one estimate places NBC's audience mail at between 50,000 and 75,000 letters yearly. Many of these, however, are generated by letter-writing campaigns organized by special-interest groups. Another significant portion of audience letters to the networks comes from people protesting the cancellation of their favorite show. Cancellations can spark massive volumes of mail, as evidenced by the 150,000 or so angry letters that NBC received when it canceled "The Monkees" in 1968 or the 85,000 letters received by ABC when "The Lawrence Welk Show" was dropped in 1971.

Because of the delayed nature of feedback in the industry, letters and calls generally have little impact. By the time the viewer protests get to the network, the show has long been canceled and the cast has scattered to other jobs. There are times, however, when audience reaction can influence network behavior. Such an event occurred in the 1970s when ABC was planning to air the situation comedy "Soap." Advance word about the program's "adult" themes and content prompted several church groups to protest the planned scheduling of the show. In response, the network toned down the program's content and protests evaporated. More recently Viewers for Quality Television, a citizens' group that tries to keep worthwhile TV shows on the air, was instrumental in CBS's decision to renew such programs as "Cagney and Lacey" and "Designing Women." In 1988, they were unsuccessfully campaigning to save "A Year in the Life."

Even feedback from one person can make a difference. In 1989, a woman from Detroit, offended by Fox's "Married with Children," wrote letters to the companies who advertised on the program. Two firms removed their ads and Fox promised to monitor the show's content more closely.

At the local level, many television stations set aside segments of the newscast for reading viewer letters over the air. Other stations may have a call-in program entitled something like "Let Me Speak to the Manager" in which audience members are encouraged to express their views. Certain cable television systems have set aside one or two channels, called public-access channels, whereby viewers can appear on television, usually either free or at a nominal cost, and state their opinions on a topic of their choice. There are limitations, however, on these forms of audience-generated feedback. Since stations have a limited time set aside for reading viewer letters, only a few can be presented over the air. Not all stations have programs where viewers are encouraged to call. Relatively few cable systems have access channels, and in those systems that do, few people seem to understand their purpose and fewer still watch the channels. Consequently, at the local level, feedback opportunities in television are somewhat limited. Television broadcasters, however, generally pay very close attention to the feedback they do receive and tend to treat it seriously.

Since television stations are licensed by the FCC, they are also subject to audience-filed petitions to deny renewal or transfer of a license. In fact, some television stations have been involved in well-publicized cases. To mention just two, in 1971 Triangle Publications Company proposed to sell several broadcast properties, including five television stations, to Capital Cities Broadcasting Corporation. This sale was held up when a citizens' group petitioned for denial of the transfer on the grounds that the sale was not in the public interest. The petition was finally removed when Capital Cities negotiated an agreement with the citizens' group whereby the new owner agreed to pay $1 million for development of minority programs in three of the cities affected by the transfer. In return, the citizens' group agreed to drop its petition. In 1978, a similar situation occurred in San Jose, California, when a citizens' group agreed to withdraw its petition to deny the sale of a television station in return for a $192,000 donation from the new owner to start a community media center. Obviously, this form of audience-generated feedback has raised concern among broadcast executives. Stations faced with petitions to deny have accumulated substantial expenses in responding to this extreme form of negative feedback; sometimes these expenses total more than $100,000. Similar to the situation in radio, the emphasis on broadcasting deregulation has made it more difficult for groups to effectively pursue petitions to deny.

Measuring TV Viewing

The late eighties have seen tremendous changes in the way TV audience viewing data are collected. These changes have sparked both controversy and confusion. This section will first examine how the ratings for network TV shows are compiled and then examine how ratings are gathered for local stations.

Peoplemeters For about thirty years the **A.C. Nielsen Company,** the biggest market research company in the world, held a monopoly on the measurement of network programs. To compile its Nielsen Television Index (NTI), the company used what was known as the passive meter system. A computerlike device attached to the sets of about 1700 families compiled household viewing data. These meters measured only whether the set was on and the channel it was tuned to. They could not determine who, if anyone, was watching the program. Detailed demographic information was obtained from another sample of households whose members filled out diaries. These data were merged with the results from the passive meters. Many in the TV industry, particularly those representing "superstations" and cable channels, such as CNN and MTV, were dissatisfied with this arrangement since they felt their services were undermeasured. Then, in 1987, a British firm, Audits of Great Britain,

The Peoplemeter is an alternative to diaries and automatic devices that record the channel to which a TV is tuned. The Nielsen Peoplemeter records and stores individual viewing data on each household member, providing detailed information on the audience for a given program. (Courtesy, Nielsen Media Research)

Inc. (AGB), entered the field using a new device, called a **Peoplemeter.** Nielsen countered by developing its own Peoplemeter. Both companies introduced their service during the 1987–1988 season, and a new era in audience measurement was born.

Peoplemeters offer what is known as ''single-source'' data. Demographic data are obtained from each member of a sample household and each member is then assigned a number. Then, while they are watching TV, each family member is supposed to punch that number on a hand-held device that resembles a remote-control unit. In addition to the hand-held device, a ''people monitor,'' a box about the size of a clock radio, is placed on top of every set in the house to display the buttons that have been pushed on the hand-held unit. Some Peoplemeters have a red light that flashes every fifteen minutes to remind viewers to press the appropriate button to reconfirm that they are still viewing.

The data are collected from the people monitors each night. The research company's computer simply ''calls'' the monitor and offloads the information. Peoplemeters can be used to tabulate all viewing: network, syndicated, and cable. Some meters were even equipped to tabulate VCR playbacks.

Both AGB and Nielsen selected their Peoplemeter households by first sampling geographic regions and then randomly selecting households from within those regions. Nielsen, for example, drew its first sample from more than 770 U.S. counties. Families who agreed to participate received a modest compensation. Nielsen and AGB both launched their service with a sample of 2000 households. AGB planned to increase its sample to 5000; Nielsen announced it would aim for an ultimate sample of 4000 and that each sample would be replaced every two years. Both companies reported that usable data are received from about 90 percent of the meters.

The Peoplemeter service was sold to ad agencies, syndication companies, cable channels, and the networks. The price was not cheap. Each network paid about $3 million to $5 million a year for the Peoplemeter data.

Peoplemeters provide fast and detailed data. For example, Nielsen offered a Peoplemeter Daily Report delivered electronically from its mainframe computer to clients' personal computers. In addition, the Nielsen Pocketpiece (see Figure 20.6), the traditional ratings report, would be issued weekly instead of biweekly with increased information about viewer demographics. AGB promised comparable services.

FIGURE 20.6 *Excerpt from Nielsen's NTI report.* (The Pocketpiece, Nielsen Television Index, National TV Ratings. *Copyright © 1988 Nielsen Media Research. Used by permission.*)

A-4 *Nielsen* NATIONAL TV AUDIENCE ESTIMATES   EVE. TUE. SEP. 6, 1988

TIME	7:00	7:15	7:30	7:45	8:00	8:15	8:30	8:45	9:00	9:15	9:30	9:45	10:00	10:15	10:30	10:45	
HUT	51.7	52.7	53.6	55.8	55.9	58.4	60.4	61.9	61.2	61.3	60.9	61.0	58.9	57.7	55.9	53.4	

ABC TV — WHO'S THE BOSS? (R) — FULL HOUSE-TUE. (R) — MOONLIGHTING (R)(PAE) — THIRTYSOMETHING (R)

AVERAGE AUDIENCE (Hhlds (000) & %) {		14,550		14,740		9,850				8,590						
		16.1		16.3		10.9	11.1 *		10.7 *	9.5	9.7 *		9.3 *			
SHARE AUDIENCE %		28		27		18	18 *		18 *	17	17 *		17 *			
AVG. AUD. BY 1/4 HR %		15.0	17.2	15.9	16.7	11.4	10.8	10.3	11.1	9.8	9.5	9.3	9.3			

CBS TV — CBS SUMMER PLAYHOUSE(R) TICKETS, PLEASE — EVERYTHING'S RELATIVE — CBS TUESDAY MOVIE WOMEN OF VALOR (R)(PAE)

AVERAGE AUDIENCE (Hhlds (000) & %) {		2,980		2,710		12,110										
		3.3		3.0		13.4	11.2 *		12.3 *		15.0 *		15.1 *			
SHARE AUDIENCE %		6		5		23	18 *		20 *		26 *		28 *			
AVG. AUD. BY 1/4 HR %		3.4	3.2	2.9	3.1	10.7	11.8	12.1	12.6	14.8	15.1	15.6	14.5			

NBC TV — MATLOCK (R) — IN THE HEAT OF THE NIGHT (R) — NBC NEWS SPECIAL IT'S NOT EASY BEIN' TEEN

AVERAGE AUDIENCE (Hhlds (000) & %) {		13,290				11,480				8,410						
		14.7	13.7 *		15.6 *	12.7	12.8 *		12.6 *	9.3	9.5 *		9.2 *			
SHARE AUDIENCE %		25	24 *		25 *	21	21 *		21 *	17	16 *		17 *			
AVG. AUD. BY 1/4 HR %		13.1	14.4	15.7	15.5	12.6	12.9	12.8	12.4	9.6	9.4	9.1	9.2			

INDEPENDENTS (INCL. SUPERSTATIONS)

AVERAGE AUDIENCE	13.1		12.4		12.2		13.1		14.2		14.5		15.1		13.1	
SHARE AUDIENCE %	25		23		21		21		23		24		26		24	

SUPERSTATIONS

AVERAGE AUDIENCE	2.6		3.5		3.7		4.2		4.6		4.9		4.8		4.2	
SHARE AUDIENCE %	5		6		6		7		8		8		8		8	

PBS

AVERAGE AUDIENCE	1.6		2.4		2.8		3.1		2.7		2.9		2.1		1.8	
SHARE AUDIENCE %	3		4		5		5		4		5		4		3	

CABLE ORIG.

AVERAGE AUDIENCE	4.8		5.6		6.1		7.0		8.7		7.8		6.9		6.0	
SHARE AUDIENCE %	9		10		11		11		14		13		12		11	

PAY SERVICES

AVERAGE AUDIENCE	3.0		2.9		2.8		3.3		3.6		3.6		3.1		3.2	
SHARE AUDIENCE %	6		5		5		5		6		6		5		6	

U.S. TV HOUSEHOLDS: 90,400,000

For explanation of symbols, See page B.

A-5

Unfortunately, the transition to Peoplemeters has not been smooth. The first problem became apparent when ratings for shows measured by the Peoplemeter were generally found to be lower than those determined by traditional methods. For example, the audience for "Moonlighting" as measured by Peoplemeters was almost 10 percent below its rating when measured by diary and passive meter. Ratings for "60 Minutes" fell by 18 percent. This translates into trouble between the networks and the ad agencies who buy time on these shows. Many agencies tried to wring price cuts from the nets based on the lower Peoplemeter numbers. A drop of a couple of ratings points might translate into a loss of thousands of dollars per show for the networks.

To make matters more confusing, during the first year Peoplemeters were used, the numbers provided by AGB and Nielsen showed noticeable differences. "Growing Pains" got an 18.1 rating according to Nielsen's Peoplemeters but AGB gave it only 16.0. "Who's the Boss?" was 10 percent lower as measured by AGB. Advertisers had a hard time figuring who was more accurate. Moreover, viewing for kids' programs showed even greater declines. Experts suggested that children were not able or were unwilling to use the Peoplemeters properly. Executives at the ratings companies argued that these discrepancies should disappear when their samples were increased and the bugs worked out of the system.

As the 1988–1989 TV season approached, the situation became even more complicated. AGB announced it was in financial difficulty and could not continue its operation unless all three major networks subscribed to its service (although many ad agencies bought the AGB numbers, CBS was the only net to sign up). ABC and NBC had yet to decide if they would buy AGB's ratings as well as Nielsen's. Ultimately, AGB announced it was suspending its American operation.

If that wasn't enough, Arbitron announced plans to begin its own Peoplemeter service. Arbitron's service would include a new wrinkle. Its sample households would not only be measured by Peoplemeter, but household members would also run a scanning wand over the Universal Product Code on all products purchased at drug stores and supermarkets. Subscribers to Arbitron's service would be given viewing data and product consumption information, a combination that most advertisers would find extremely valuable.

Before suspending operations in 1988, the R.D. Percy Company installed about 1000 Peoplemeters in the metro New York market and used them not only to rate programs but also to measure viewership of commercials. Results showed that ratings for TV commercials were about 20 percent lower than that of the programs. To put it another way, about one in five viewers either leaves the room or changes channels when the commercials come on. This finding stirred up a debate over whether advertising charges should be based on the ratings of the commercial or of the program. Obviously, if fees were based on commercial ratings, advertisers would argue that they should pay significantly less.

Finally, Nielsen is testing a passive meter which determines whether anybody is in front of the set by using an image recognition sensor that would scan and store an individual's facial features in a computer. Each time the set is turned on, the sensor would match the faces in the room with those stored in its memory.

All in all, it looks as though life in the Peoplemeter era will be complicated.

Local-Market TV Ratings. Ratings of local-market TV stations still depend on the traditional diary and passive meter techniques. Nonetheless, it is only a matter of time before the Peoplemeter invades the local market (it's already being used in some bigger markets). Thus the following discussion describes the situation circa 1989.

Two companies provide feedback on audience viewing behavior to the TV industry. One is Arbitron, the same company described in the section on radio, and the other is the A.C. Nielsen Company. Arbitron surveys more than 210 local television markets every year, while Nielsen surveys around 220. Both companies use the diary technique to collect viewing data, and both use essentially the same procedures in selecting sample households. In simplified form, the method used by both companies is this. A computer selects phone numbers at random from a listing of all telephone directories in the area. The households selected into the sample are then contacted by letter and by telephone and are asked to keep a diary record of their television viewing.

Households that agree to participate receive one diary for every working TV set in the household. The diary provides a space for entering the viewing of the head of the household as well as any other family members or visitors who happen to be watching television. Participants are asked to record their viewing every quarter-hour. In addition, the respondents are asked to record the sex and age of all those who are watching. At the back of the diary are questions concerning family size, the city where the household is located, and whether the family subscribes to a cable television system. Diaries are kept for seven days, after which they are returned to the ratings company. Both Arbitron and Nielsen report that they are able to use approximately 50–55 percent of the diaries that they send out.

Once the diaries are received, they are checked for accuracy, and diaries from households with more than one set are edited in order to provide an estimate of unduplicated viewing for a household. The handwritten information in the diaries is then keystroked into a form that can be processed by computers. In a few weeks the data are tabulated, and the ratings books, as they are called, are ready to be mailed to subscribing organizations.

In more than fifteen large markets, including New York, Los Angeles, and Chicago, both Nielsen and Arbitron maintain a separate sample of households that are hooked up to passive meters. Viewing information from this sample is compiled overnight and sent to subscribers early the next morning. These local meter data are augmented by information from diaries.

Television Ratings

Television viewing data are reported for TV in essentially the same way as they are for radio except that the unit of analysis is now expressed in terms of households (or people) viewing TV rather than listening to radio. To illustrate, the following formula is used to calculate the **rating** for a TV program in a local market:

$$\text{Rating} = \frac{\text{number of households watching a program}}{\text{number of TV HH}},$$

where TV HH equals the number of households in a given market equipped with television.

Similarly, the **share of the audience** is found by using the following formula:

$$\text{Share of Audience} = \frac{\text{number of households watching a program}}{\text{number of HUT}},$$

where HUT equals the number of households using (watching) television at a particular time.

The information reported in the Nielsen and Arbitron ratings books is essentially similar. Figure 20.7, page 492, reproduces a sample page from a local Arbitron ratings book. As can be seen, Arbitron reports shares, ratings, and an estimate of the number of people in the audience in various demographic categories for different areas in the market.

Four times every year (February, May, July, and November), both Arbitron and Nielsen conduct a "sweep" period during which every local television market in the entire country is measured. Local stations rely on these ratings to set their advertising rates. Naturally enough, affiliated stations, anxious for the highest ratings possible, pressure the networks for special programming that will attract large audiences. All three networks generally go along with the affiliates' desires. As a result, blockbuster movies and specials are scheduled in competing time slots, leaving many viewers to wonder why all the good programs on TV always come at once. For example, consider what happened during the May 1988 sweeps. On May 1 and May 2, ABC ran its much-publicized miniseries "The Richest Man in the World: The Story of Aristotle Onassis." CBS countered with the final episode of its "Magnum P.I." series. On May 22, NBC ran "The Incredible Hulk Returns" against ABC's controversial "Baby M" docudrama. Also that week NBC ran "Bob Hope's Birthday and 50th Anniversary with NBC" special and an expensive science fiction miniseries, "Something Is Out There."

Determining the Accuracy of Ratings

Because the numbers in the ratings books are the basis for spending vast amounts of money, it is important that they be as accurate and reliable as possible. The organization that is responsible for ratings precision is the Electronic Media Ratings Council (EMRC). During the early 1960s, in the wake of the quiz show and payola scandals, Congress took a close look at the broadcasting industry. In response to one congressional committee's criticism of audience-measurement techniques, advertising and broadcasting leaders founded the EMRC. (It was originally called the Broadcast Ratings Council.) The task of the EMRC is basically threefold. It monitors, audits, and accredits broadcast measurement services. The council monitors performance of ratings companies by making sure that reported results meet the minimum standards of performance set up by the EMRC. Audits are performed on a continuing basis. During an audit, the EMRC checks the sample design, data processing, and computer programs and even double-checks the calculations of some ratings to ensure accuracy. If the ratings company passes the audit, it is accredited and is allowed to display the EMRC's seal of approval on its ratings reports.

Despite the EMRC's work, broadcast ratings are still subject to widespread criticism. One common complaint, voiced by many who evidently do not understand the statistical theory that underlies sampling, is directed at Neilsen's national survey. How can a sample of only 4000 homes, these critics ask, accurately reflect the viewing of 90 million television households? In actuality, this sample size will generate tolerably accurate results within a specified margin of error (see boxed material, pages 494–495). Other criticisms, however, deserve closer attention.

First, it is possible that the type of person who agrees to participate may have viewing habits different from those of the viewer who declines to participate. Second, in the case of both Arbitron and Nielsen reports (based on about 55 percent of the diaries sent out), it is possible that "returners" behave differently from "nonreturn-

Time Period Estimates

STATION BREAK AVERAGES

	ADI RTG				PERSONS		WOMEN							MEN					TNS	CHILD		TIME — TSA IN 000's				
DAY AND TIME **STATION PROGRAM**	TN 12-17	CHILD 2-11	CHILD 6-11	TV HH	18+	12-34	18+	18-34	18-49	25-49	25-54	WKG WOM	18+	18-34	18-49	25-49	25-54	12-17	2-11	6-11	ADI TV HH RTG	MET TV HH RTG	TV HH	WOM 18+	MEN 18+
col #	36	37	38	39	42	41	45	46	47	48	49	50	51	52	53	54	55	56	57	58	5	8	39	45	51
RELATIVE STD-ERR 25% THRESHOLDS (1σ) 50%	12 3	12 3	15 4	12 3	19 4	20 5	14 3	16 4	14 3	13 3	13 3	14 3	15 3	19 5	15 3	13 3	13 3	17 4	32 8	25 6	2 –	4 1	12 3	14 3	15 3

FRIDAY

8:00P- 8:30P

Station Program	TN17	C2-11	C6-11	TVHH	P18+	P12-34	W18+	W18-34	W18-49	W25-49	W25-54	WKG	M18+	M18-34	M18-49	M25-49	M25-54	TNS	C2-11	C6-11	ADI	MET	TVHH	WOM	MEN
WBTV BEAUTY-BEAST	7	6	8	127	189	63	113	32	67	57	67	47	75	17	46	41	46	14	26	21	15	14	120	106	72
WSOC WEBSTER-S	4	5	5	49	67	20	48	11	23	17	21	19	19	2	8	6	9	7	15	10					
OLYMPICS-PT	6	6	8	118	207	97	119	46	77	69	71	50	87	42	62	55	55	10	15	13					
--4 WK AVG--	5	5	6	84	137	58	84	28	50	43	46	35	53	22	35	31	32	8	15	12	11	13	79	73	54
WHKY TWN WRST		1	1	1	1	1	1	1	1	1	1								2						
FRI MOVIE																									
--4 WK AVG--			1	1	1	1	1	1	1	1	1		1		1	1			2						
WCCB 8 CLOCK MOVE	2	1		33	54	17	26	6	13	11	12	8	29	8	15	11	11		1	1					
WPCQ MAIN EVENT				55	68	27	34		16		19		35		22		22	2	6	1	5	5	38	34	24
DISNEY KNGDM				24	56	8	16		3		3		40		19		11								
DISNEYS DTV				43	52	46	40		32		14		13		13		11								
FRI NT SRPRS				38	57	33	35		27		23		22		19		11								
--4 WK AVG--	5	4	5	40	58	29	31	12	19	14	15	15	27	9	18	14	14	8	14	9	6	7	41	34	28
WJZY HAWAII 5-0	4			24	38	15	20	4	12	10	10	9	18	5	8	3	3	6	1	1	4	5	29	21	22
WNSC PTV				1	1		1		1	1	1	1	1		1										
WTVI PTV				4	6		3		1	1	1		3										2	2	1
WUNG PTV				4	6		3		1	1	1		3		1	1	1						3	2	2
H/P/T	31	30	30	318	490	183	282	83	165	139	154	115	209	61	124	102	109	38	63	45	54	54	312	272	203

8:30P- 9:00P

Station Program	TN17	C2-11	C6-11	TVHH	P18+	P12-34	W18+	W18-34	W18-49	W25-49	W25-54	WKG	M18+	M18-34	M18-49	M25-49	M25-54	TNS	C2-11	C6-11	ADI	MET	TVHH	WOM	MEN
WBTV BEAUTY-BEAST	7	7	9	128	189	65	114	33	70	59	67	48	76	18	48	43	49	14	28	23	16	15	128	114	76
WSOC MR BELVEDERE	5	4	5	43	62	20	43	9	22	15	20	22	19	4	12	10	10	8	10	8					
OLYMPICS-PT	6	6	8	121	213	99	122	47	77	70	72	52	91	41	63	58	58	10	15	13					
--4 WK AVG--	6	5	6	82	138	60	83	28	49	42	46	37	55	23	37	34	34	9	12	11	12	13	83	84	55
WHKY TWN WRST		1	1	1	1	1	1	1	1	1	1								2						
FRI MOVIE																									
--4 WK AVG--			1	1	1	1	1	1	1	1	1								2						
WCCB 8 CLOCK MOVE	2	2		30	49	17	22	6	11	9	10		27	8	14	10	10	3	7	1	4	4	31	23	27
WPCQ MAIN EVENT				62	86	37	41		23		26	8	45		33		33								
DISNEY KNGDM				26	66	14	21		8		6		45		23		11								
DISNEYS DTV				51	62	56	44		37		19		17		17		17								
FRI NT SRPRS				40	59	36	37		29		25		22		19		11								
--4 WK AVG--	5	5	6	45	68	36	36	16	24	18	19	19	32	11	23	18	18	8	17	12	6	8	42	32	29
WJZY HAWAII 5-0	4			24	38	13	21	3	13	11	11	10	17	4	7	3	4	6	1	1	3	4	24	21	18
WNSC PTV				1	1		1		1	1	1		1		1								1	1	
WTVI PTV				5	7		4		1	1	1		3										1	1	1
WUNG PTV				4	6		2						3		1	1	1						4	3	3
H/P/T	33	29	30	320	497	192	284	87	169	141	155	123	214	64	131	110	118	40	66	49	57	56	318	283	212

9:00P- 9:30P

Station Program	TN17	C2-11	C6-11	TVHH	P18+	P12-34	W18+	W18-34	W18-49	W25-49	W25-54	WKG	M18+	M18-34	M18-49	M25-49	M25-54	TNS	C2-11	C6-11	ADI	MET	TVHH	WOM	MEN
WBTV DALLAS	7	4	4	193	308	96	190	46	93	85	98	78	118	37	69	58	67	13	11	6	20	20	160	151	96
WSOC THE THORNS	2	3	3	15	32	12	20	8	15	9	9	14	12	2	9	7	7	2	9	5					
OLYMPICS-PT	6	6	7	108	181	79	96	34	61	54	61	40	86	34	59	53	53	10	16	13					
--4 WK AVG--	4	4	5	61	107	45	58	21	38	31	32	27	49	18	34	30	30	6	12	9	10	12	71	70	51
WHKY WRLDWDE WRST	1	1	1	4	5	2	3				2	2	2	1	1	1	1	6	1	2					
FRI MOVIE				4					3		3		3		3		3								
--4 WK AVG--	1	1	1	4	5	2	3		1		2	1	2	1	2	1	2	1	1	1					
WCCB 8 CLOCK MOVE	1	2	2	26	42	14	19	5	11	11	11	1	23	6	14	10	10	2	2	1	3	3	28	20	25
WPCQ MIAMI VICE	5	3	3	44	72	50	42	24	33	23	24	21	30	18	28	23	23	8	7	3	4	6	45	40	32
WJZY 9 OCLOCK MOV	1	2	1	33	43	12	17	5	12	11	11	9	26	6	16	13	13	1	5	2	4	5	29	19	21
WNSC PTV				1	1		1		1	1	1	1											1	1	1
WTVI PTV				4	6		4		2	2	2		2		1	1	1						4	4	2
WUNG PTV					1										1								2		2
H/P/T	29	25	25	366	585	219	334	101	191	165	181	142	251	86	165	138	147	31	45	25	59	58	342	308	231

9:30P-10:00P

Station Program	TN17	C2-11	C6-11	TVHH	P18+	P12-34	W18+	W18-34	W18-49	W25-49	W25-54	WKG	M18+	M18-34	M18-49	M25-49	M25-54	TNS	C2-11	C6-11	ADI	MET	TVHH	WOM	MEN
WBTV DALLAS	9	4	3	189	304	98	188	46	93	85	99	77	116	37	69	57	67	14	10	5	24	24	191	189	118
WSOC SLEDGE HAMMR	1	4	4	20	27	4	15	1	10	10	11	7	11	2	8	5	7	1	11	7					
OLYMPICS-PT	7	6	8	108	179	79	91	32	61	54	55	38	88	36	63	57	57	11	17	14					
--4 WK AVG--	4	5	6	64	103	42	53	17	35	32	33	22	50	19	35	31	32	6	14	10	9	10	62	55	49
WHKY WRLDWDE WRST			1	4	3		2				1	1	2						1						
FRI MOVIE				4	3		3		3		3		2												
--4 WK AVG--				4	3		3		1		2	1	1						1						
WCCB 8 CLOCK MOVE	1	2	2	26	42	13	19	5	11	11	11	1	23	6	14	10	10	2	7	1	3	3	26	19	23
WPCQ MIAMI VICE	4	2	2	43	70	50	39	25	32	23	23	19	31	19	29	23	23	6	7	4	6	6	43	40	30
WJZY 9 OCLOCK MOV		1	1	34	42	11	17	5	11	11	11	8	26	6	16	14	14		4	2	4	5	33	16	25
WNSC PTV				1	1		1		1	1	1		1										1	1	
WTVI PTV				3	5		4		1	1	1	1	1		1	1	1						1	4	1
WUNG PTV					1																	1		5	1
H/P/T	29	22	23	363	571	214	323	98	185	164	181	134	249	87	164	136	147	28	43	25	60	58	363	327	249

10:00P-10:30P

Station Program	TN17	C2-11	C6-11	TVHH	P18+	P12-34	W18+	W18-34	W18-49	W25-49	W25-54	WKG	M18+	M18-34	M18-49	M25-49	M25-54	TNS	C2-11	C6-11	ADI	MET	TVHH	WOM	MEN
WBTV FALCON CREST	7	2	1	137	213	71	135	32	70	62	73	56	78	27	45	35	42	12	5	2	21	21	163	161	96
WSOC 20/20	1	4	5	54	82	14	48	8	30	27	32	25	34	4	24	24	27	2	12	8					
OLYMPICS-PT	6	5	9	115	181	85	96	38	65	58	62	43	85	37	64	58	58	10	15	15					
--4 WK AVG--	4	5	7	84	132	50	72	25	48	42	47	34	60	21	44	41	42	6	13	11	11	13	75	63	55
WHKY UNIFOUR TNGT				1	2		1				1		1									2	2		1
WCCB M DILLON				8	13	1	7	1	1	1	2	1	5												
8 CLOCK MOVE	1	2	3	35	42	13	20	7	11	8	10	11	22	4	11	9	11	2	7	5					
--4 WK AVG--	1	1	1	22	28	7	14	4	6	5	6	6	14	2	5	5	5	1	4	2	3	3	23	15	18
WPCQ UNSLVD MYSTR				35	56	22	27		12		12		29		20		20								
SONNY SPOON	4	1		25	48	34	32	17	27	10	11	7	16	7	13	11	11	10	3						
--4 WK AVG--	4	1	1	28	50	31	31	15	23	11	12	7	19	8	15	13	13	8	3	1	5	5	35	35	26
WJZY 9 OCLOCK MOV		1	1	34	41	12	16	5	11	10	11	7	25	7	16	13	13		4	2	4	5	34	16	26
WNSC PTV				2	1		2	1	1	1	1		1		1										
WTVI PTV				2	2	1	2	1	1	1	1												2	2	
WUNG PTV					1																				
H/P/T	25	14	16	307	469	172	271	80	159	131	150	110	197	65	125	107	115	27	29	18	54	54	334	294	222

| col # | 36 | 37 | 38 | 39 | 42 | 41 | 45 | 46 | 47 | 48 | 49 | 50 | 51 | 52 | 53 | 54 | 55 | 56 | 57 | 58 | 5 | 8 | 39 | 45 | 51 |

FEBRUARY 1988 TIME PERIOD AVERAGES   64   FRIDAY   CHARLOTTE

Daily

FIGURE 20.7 *Sample of an Arbitron TV ratings book.* (Arbitron Ratings—Television. Copyright © 1988 Arbitron Ratings Company. Reprinted by permission.)

ers.'' Third, people who know that their viewing is being measured may change their behavior. A family might watch more news and public-affairs programs than usual in order to appear sophisticated in the eyes of the rating company. Fourth, both ratings companies admit that they have a problem measuring the viewing of certain groups. Minorities, particularly blacks and Hispanics, may be underrepresented in the ratings companies' samples. Lastly, the stations that are being measured can distort the measurement process by engaging in contests and special promotions or by running unusual or sensational programs in an attempt to ''hype'' the ratings. This activity is frowned on by the ratings companies, which usually append a warning label to their ratings books that identifies any unusual promotional activity during the ratings period. The distinction between hype and legitimate programming, however, is somewhat fuzzy. Clearly, the ratings aren't perfect. Nonetheless, despite all their flaws, they present useful information at an affordable price to advertisers and to the television industry. As long as the United States has a commercial broadcasting system, some form of the ratings will always be around.

Questionnaires, Concept Testing, and Pilot Testing

In addition to ratings, there are still other forms of media-originated feedback in the TV industry. The TV networks gather three special types of feedback from the audience to help them predict what television shows will be popular with viewers. The first kind of research consists of questionnaires that attempt to measure audience tastes, opinions, and beliefs. Perhaps as many as 100,000 people per year are questioned in person or over the phone as the networks try to identify what situations and topics might be acceptable for programs.

A second form is called **concept testing.** In concept testing, a one- or two-paragraph description of an idea for a new series is presented to a sample of viewers, who are asked for their reactions. Here's a hypothetical example.

"First and Ten"

Sandi and Marcia are two young women enrolled in law school at Southern Methodist University in Dallas, Texas. During the fall season, they must juggle their studies with their jobs as cheerleaders for the Dallas Cowboys. Sometimes this is tough—such as the time Sandi's law books were accidentally locked up in the football team's locker room and she tried to retrieve them at the same time the team came in from practice. Or the time when Marcia was asked to represent the team's star player in tough contract negotiations with the team's owner.

Would you:

_____ definitely watch this series
_____ don't know if I'd watch or not
_____ definitely not watch this series

Show ideas that do well in concept testing have an increased chance of getting on the air.

The third form is **pilot testing.** (A pilot is the first show of a proposed series.) Pilot testing consists of placing a group of viewers in a special test theater and showing them an entire program. The audience usually sits in chairs equipped with dials or buttons that are used to indicate the degree to which audience members like or dislike what is shown. For example, the audience might be told to press a green

Sampling and Precision

Many people find it hard to believe that a sample of approximately 4000 homes can adequately represent the viewing of 90 million households. How can a sample that includes only 0.0044 percent of all homes be accurate? Some people might concede that a sample of 4000 from a city of 50,000 might be adequate but surely not for a population of 90 million. This line of reasoning seems to make intuitive sense, but it's off base.

To illustrate why, we'll have to make a brief excursion into what statisticians call "sampling theory." First, two definitions. A **population** is the whole collection of households or persons or whatever it is we're interested in. Thus for the A. C. Nielsen Company, the 90 million U.S. homes with TV sets constitute the population. A **sample** is a segment of the population that is taken to represent the population. Nielsen's 4000 randomly selected households would constitute a sample. Now for an example. Pretend that we had a big urn (a statistician's favorite piece of furniture) filled with 10,000 Ping-Pong balls (the population). Pretend further that 3000 of the Ping-Pong balls (30 percent) were red and 7000 were white. Now let's select 100 Ping-Pong balls at random from the urn (the sample). Clearly, it would be a rare event if we were to draw 100 red Ping-Pong balls (such an outcome is possible but highly, highly unlikely). Similarly it would be unlikely that all 100 would turn out to be white. Moreover, we would not expect our sample to contain *exactly* the same percentage of red and white Ping-Pong balls as the population, that is, 30 red and 70 white. The odds are that we would get a result fairly close to 30 percent, the actual population figure, but we would probably be off by a little bit. As a matter of fact, if we used statistical formulas of probability we could calculate that the odds would be 20 to 1 that the percentage of red Ping-Pong balls in our sample would be somewhere between 21 and 39 percent, a spread of 18 percentage points.

Now let's take a *really* big urn and fill it with 10 million Ping-Pong balls, 30 percent of which are red and 70 percent of which are white, and draw another sample of 100. Again, we would not expect to get 100 red or 100 white in our sample. Nor would we expect to get exactly 30 red and 70 white. Using the same statistical formulas of probability that we used in the above sample, we would find that the odds would still be 20 to 1 that we would draw somewhere between 21 and 39 percent red Ping-Pong balls—a spread of 18 percentage points and exactly the same as our previous example. The size of the population has nothing to do with the precision (the spread of percentage points) of our results. Assuming that the red–white split stays the same, it's irrelevant if the urn contains 10,000 or 10 million or 90 million Ping-Pong balls.

What does have an impact on precision? The size of the *sample*. If we took a sample of 400 Ping-Pong balls, the odds would be 20 to 1 that we would get somewhere between 25.5 and 34.5 percent red, a spread of 9 percentage points. If we sampled 1600, the odds would be 20 to 1 that we would get between approximately 27.7 and 32.3 percent red, a spread of only 4½ percentage points. The larger the sample, the smaller the spread (statisticians call this spread **sampling error**). To reiterate, it is the sample size, not the population size, that will determine sampling error. Thus a sample of 4000 randomly chosen from the population of Los Angeles will have the same degree of sampling error as a sample of 4000 drawn randomly from the population of the entire world. (The problem, of course, is that the time, energy, and cost of drawing a random sample would increase as the population increases.)

Now let's replace Ping-Pong balls with households. The red Ping-Pong balls become homes watching a particular show and the white Ping-Pong balls turn into homes that are not viewing. Using Nielsen's sample size of 4000 and assuming that for a single week 30 percent of the homes in the sample are viewing (the red Ping-Pong balls), we find that the odds are 20 to 1 that the true value in the population lies between 28.6 and 31.4 percent, a spread of 2.8 points. (A note of caution here. This example is based on a single week's viewing. In actuality, Nielsen may average viewing reports for more than one week—a procedure that reduces the spread or sampling error.) By sampling more people, it would be possible for Nielsen to report more precise results. But increased sample size means increased costs, which would make the ratings more expensive. Consequently, the ad agencies, networks, and production companies that buy the ratings books have settled for this sample size as one that strikes an acceptable balance between precision and cost.

Finally, if after reading this section you are still not convinced of the validity of sampling theory, then make sure you inform your doctor of this fact the next time you go for a blood test.

button when they see something on screen that they like and a red button when they see something they dislike. Networks sometimes do pilot testing themselves or hire private firms to do it for them.

In addition, a company called Marketing Evaluations conducts surveys of program and performer popularity (see boxed material). Viewers in a national panel are asked if they are familiar with a certain program or performer and if that program or performer is one of their favorites. The "TvQ score" is the percentage of people familiar with a show or star who indicate that the star or program is one of their favorites. TvQ data have been available since the 1950s and have been influential in many programming decisions. Shows such as "All in the Family," "ChiPs," and "Hill Street Blues" were saved from early cancellation in part because they had high TvQ scores.

Cartoon Q

Marketing Evaluations conducts a Cartoon Q study in which viewers are asked to identify their favorite animated characters appearing in commercials. The 1986 results, in the order of preference:

1. The California Raisins

2. Pillsbury Doughboy

3. Snuggle (the fuzzy bear from Lever Brothers)

4. The Noid (Domino's Pizza)

5. Snap, Crackle, and Pop (Kellogg's)

6. Tony the Tiger (Kellogg's)

7. The Nestle's Quik Rabbit

8. Charlie the Tuna (Starkist)

9. The Keebler Elves

10. A tie between Ronald McDonald and Sprout (Pillsbury Green Giant)

Film Industry Audience Responses

Audience-generated feedback in the film industry is virtually nonexistent. Motion picture stars do receive fan mail, but people seldom send letters to a director or to a film studio. Feedback that does occur is primarily aimed at local theater owners, and it is questionable whether this information ever gets back to the producer or distributor. Although it is true that film critics provide some qualitative feedback, their opinions are typically less important than box-office figures. As with the sound-recording industry, the critical form of feedback is economic: the amount of money taken in at the box office.

Compiling Box-Office Receipts

Media-originated feedback in the movie industry revolves around the box-office figures compiled and reported in the trade publication *Variety.* Each week, *Variety* reports the top-grossing films across the United States. An example of this listing is reproduced in Fig. 20.8.

To compile these data, *Variety*, in cooperation with the Standard Data Corporation, surveys approximately 1600 theaters located in twenty-two major urban areas across the country. The theaters in this sample usually account for about one-fourth of the total box-office gross in the United States. Most of the column headings in *Variety*'s chart are self-explanatory. Each film's title is listed, followed by the company that is handling distribution. Box-office gross for the listed week and for the previous week are then reported and given a rank ordering. The next four columns show the number and type of theaters showing the film for the listed week and the average revenue per screen. The weeks-on-chart column is followed by the total earnings of the film to date in *Variety*'s sample cities. In order to estimate the film's total earnings in all markets, *Variety* suggests multiplying this column by three or by four. (It varies, depending on the particular release pattern and the appeal of a film. Some movies will die in small towns and do well in urban areas, while a film like *Smokey and the Bandit* will bomb at New York's Radio City Music Hall and yet wind up as Universal Picture's number-two all-time moneymaker.) Note that this chart reports only a film's gross earnings; it does not show how much, if any, profit a film has made.

The economic feedback contained in *Variety* is extremely important in the movie industry. One or two blockbuster films can improve the financial position of an entire company. Directors who turn out a moneymaker are usually assured of more films to direct (usually with a larger production budget). In addition, a film successful at the box office is apt to inspire one or more sequels and several imitators.

Market Research

Audience research has become more influential in the movie business because of two events. The first was the entrance of the Coca-Cola Company into the industry through its acquisition of Columbia Pictures. Coke applied its market research skills to the movie business, and many other companies followed suit. A second reason was the embarrassing failure of the 1980 film *Heaven's Gate.* Budgeted at more than $40 million, the film proved to be a colossal flop when it was first released (one critic said it was about as exciting as a three-and-a-half-hour tour of your living room). In an effort to cut down on such financial disasters, many motion picture studios turned toward market research. At most studios the first step is concept testing to find promising plot lines. The next step is an analysis of the script.

NATIONAL SAMPLE 20 TOP GROSSING FILMS

Film	DISTR	CURRENT SAMPLE $	RANK	PREV. WEEK SAMPLE $	RANK	CITIES	FIRST RUN	SHOW CASE	TOTAL SCREENS	AVG. $ PER SCREEN	WEEKS ON CHART	SAMPLE TOTAL TO DATE $
The 'Burbs	U	2,878,135	1			16	3	249	252	11,421	1	2,878,135
Rain Man	UA	2,044,681	2	1,597,487	2	18	2	236	238	8,591	10	30,921,728
The Fly II	FOX	1,630,561	3	2,550,563	1	17	2	235	237	6,880	2	4,121,780
Cousins	PAR	1,618,095	4	1,535,813	3	18	1	197	198	8,172	2	3,163,410
Bill & Ted's Adventure	ORI	1,612,263	5			16	1	173	174	9,265	-	1,612,263
True Believer	COL	1,394,008	6			16	1	185	186	7,494	-	1,394,008
Working Girl	FOX	1,310,819	7	1,133,617	6	17	5	170	175	7,490	9	18,024,948
The Mighty Quinn	MGM	1,148,857	8			9	2	109	111	10,350	1	1,148,857
Three Fugitives	BV	1,132,278	9	1,355,840	4	18	4	179	183	6,187	4	5,952,350
Beaches	BV	1,071,105	10	1,118,586	7	18	5	166	171	6,263	9	9,616,458
Dangerous Liaisons	WB	1,056,111	11	903,645	9	18	6	85	91	11,605	9	6,149,888
Tap	TST	943,073	12	1,171,113	5	16	3	139	142	6,641	2	2,123,578
Mississippi Burning	ORI	809,975	13	647,618	12	16	6	133	139	5,827	11	8,659,920
Twins	U	475,571	14	665,238	11	16	2	107	109	4,363	11	24,629,270
Her Alibi	WB	456,542	15	966,360	8	16	3	104	107	4,266	3	2,801,152
The Accidental Tourist	WB	361,455	16	445,478	13	15	6	57	63	5,737	9	9,685,422
I'm Gonna Git You Sucka	UA	297,985	17	222,817	16	10	4	39	43	6,929	8	4,738,997
Who's Harry Crumb?	TST	226,583	18	740,062	10	15	4	89	93	2,436	3	2,210,720
Lawrence Of Arabia	COL	205,000	19	130,000	18	3	3		3	68,333	21	2,428,481
Women On The Verge	ORC	170,900	20	162,511	17	12	9	7	16	10,681	15	2,183,534
ALL OTHERS		868,468		1,514,758			79	150	229	3,792		13,224,895,033
GRAND TOTAL		21,712,465		16,861,506			151	2809	2960	7,335		13,369,339,932

HOW TO INTERPRET THE CHART

Approximately 2,500-3,000 screens are sampled in each reporting period, thereby representing 10-12% of the nation's theaters. The b.o. grosses are from a sample and do not purport to be overall domestic market boxoffice for any given film; separate news articles and/or corporate announcements in the case of major film successes provide total market b.o. Due to differing release patterns, the "Average Per Screen" column often can be more meaningful than aggregate b.o. dollar totals for "This Week." Weekly and cumulative sample b.o. totals include all films reported, although only the 20 highest-ranking titles are listed. "Weeks on chart" refers to top 50.

For additional explanatory and qualifying material, send self-addressed/stamped envelope to: Chart, c/o Variety, 475 Park Ave. S., New York, N.Y. 10016.

Listed on this page are, for the period indicated, the highest-grossing films measured by the Variety sample of 17-20 major and medium metropolitan domestic market areas.

Compiled by Standard Data Corp., N.Y.

FIGURE 20.8 *Excerpt from* Variety's *report on the fifty top-grossing films. (Reprinted by permission from* Variety.)

Silent Night, Deadly Night

Audience-generated feedback sometimes can be very effective in the motion picture industry as demonstrated by the furor surrounding the 1984 Tri-Star movie *Silent Night, Deadly Night*. The picture was about a maniac who disguised himself as Santa Claus and went about carving up his victims. When TV ads for the movie showing a man in a Santa suit swinging an ax at an unlucky victim started appearing around Christmas time, parents across the nation were aghast. The idea of kindly old St. Nick portrayed as a slasher/ stalker was evidently too much for them to handle.

When the film opened in New York, picketers stood outside the theater and sang Christmas carols. Tri-Star quickly realized it had overstepped the bounds of propriety and pulled the picture out of distribution less than a week after it opened.

One organization, the Emotional Response Index System Company (ERIS), claims that it can forecast whether a movie will be successful before it is even completed. ERIS analyzes a film's shooting script to see if it contains key appeals that audiences usually look for in movies. Based on a sampling of thousands of people, ERIS has concluded that audiences look primarily for the qualities of money, affection, status, and security in films. If the script appears strong along these dimensions, ERIS claims that it will have a good chance of success.

Once the studio has a rough cut of the finished film, **focus group** sessions are held. A focus group is a small sample (usually about ten to fifteen people) of the target audience, which is asked detailed questions about what they liked or didn't like. With this information, the studio can add or drop a scene, modify the ending, change the musical score, or make other alterations. (The original ending of *Fatal Attraction* was changed because of audience reaction to the rough cut.) Once these changes are completed the movie is released for a sneak preview. Audience members fill out preview cards that summarize their reactions to the film, its characters, and its stars. It is possible for the director to make limited changes in the film in response to this feedback, but it is usually too late to make wholesale changes. Consequently, the preview cards are used mainly for fine tuning. Once the movie opens, the studios hire independent research firms to interview members of the audience as they leave the theater. The results of this survey tell the studios if they have a promising or a disappointing film on their hands and allows them to adjust their advertising and marketing plans.

SUGGESTIONS FOR FURTHER READING

Further information about the concepts in this chapter can be found in the books listed below.

THE ARBITRON COMPANY, *Inside the Arbitron Television Report*, 1977.

BEVILLE, HUGH, *Audience Ratings: Radio, Television, Cable*, Hillsdale, N.J.: Lawrence Erlbaum, 1988

FLETCHER, ALAN, AND THOMAS BOWERS, *Fundamentals of Advertising Research*, Columbus, Ohio: Grid Publishing Company, 1979.

MEYER, PHILIP, *The Newspaper Survival Book*, Bloomington: Indiana University Press, 1985.

A.C. NIELSEN COMPANY, *What the Ratings Really Mean*, Chicago: A.C. Nielsen, 1964.

WIMMER, ROGER, AND JOSEPH DOMINICK, *Mass Media Research: An Introduction,* 2nd ed., Belmont, Calif.: Wadsworth, 1986.

Part Seven

The Social Impact of Mass Communication

Chapter 21

Effects of Mass Communication on Knowledge and Attitudes

Anyone who watches even a moderate amount of television would probably agree that the world of TV is a fairly violent place. Whereas in the following chapter we will examine the potential link between the portrayal of media violence and aggressive behavior, in this chapter we will concentrate on the impact of mass communication on people's knowledge, perceptions, and attitudes. In particular, we will focus on the extent to which a regular diet of TV mayhem can affect an individual's tolerance of aggression in real-life situations.

To begin, let us look at the results of three studies conducted by a team of psychologists and reported in the Autumn 1975 issue of the *Journal of Communication*. In the first study, forty-four third- and fourth-graders were taken individually by an experimenter to a "new trailer" parked on the school ground. Each child was told that the trailer was used by a kindergarten teacher and his students from a neighboring school and was then given a tour of the trailer's playroom where toys and games were kept. The experimenter made a point of telling each child that the trailer also contained a TV camera that took pictures of the entire room.

After the tour had ended, half of the children were taken to an adjacent gameroom, where they were shown a violent western film. The rest of the children didn't see any film. Next, the experimenter told the child that he (the experimenter) had a problem: He had promised a friend, a kindergarten teacher who was scheduled to work with young children in the trailer playroom, that he would watch the children for his friend over the TV monitor. The experimenter then clicked on the set in the gameroom and showed the child the scene from the empty playroom next door. However, he explained, he had to go to the principal's office for a while and was afraid that the children might arrive while he was gone. The experimenter then asked the child to watch the TV set and keep track of the kindergarten children if they should arrive while he was away. Each child was instructed to come and get the experimenter if the kindergarten children got into any kind of trouble. As he left the room, the adult told the child to begin viewing the monitor.

What the children actually saw on the monitor was a videotape constructed for this experiment. After two minutes, the tape showed an adult and two young children

CHAPTER 21 EFFECTS OF MASS COMMUNICATION ON KNOWLEDGE AND ATTITUDES 503

(a boy and a girl) entering the empty room. These two children played quietly for about a minute with a set of building blocks after the adult had left. Then the boy knocked over the structure the girl had built. This act was followed by yelling, pushing, crying, and shoving. Violence between the two escalated until it appeared that the TV camera in the next room had been destroyed. The researchers, of course, were interested in seeing how long the children observing the fight would let it continue before summoning the experimenter. As it turned out, the children who had viewed the violent film waited longer before seeking help than did the children who had seen no film.

A second and a third study were then conducted along the same lines. In the first instance, one group of children watched an aggressive excerpt from a TV detective program, and another group saw an excerpt from an exciting sports event. The results confirmed the findings of the first study: Children who saw the aggressive program were slower to report the alleged fight than were the children who had not been exposed to media violence. The third study was identical to the second, except that older children (fifth-graders) were tested. Like the children in the first two studies, the fifth-graders who had watched the detective program were slower to seek help once the fight began. Although these studies cannot be called conclusive, they do provide preliminary evidence that short-term exposure to televised violence may affect some children's attitudes by increasing their tolerance of violence.

These three studies represent only a tiny sample of the experiments and surveys performed in an effort to evaluate the impact of the mass media on the way people think about and view the world. Sometimes the dividing line between attitudes and behaviors is fuzzy. In many instances, we can only infer that an attitude or perception exists by observing relevant behavior. Thus many of the research studies cited may involve the measurement of *both* behavior and attitudes. Of course, we cannot hope to cover all research on this topic in a single chapter. Therefore, we will examine six topics that seem to best represent those issues that have generated the most research interest:

1. the role of the media in socialization

2. cultivation analysis

3. the impact of TV advertising on children

4. the diffusion of information

5. agenda setting

6. media exposure and cognitive skills

THE MEDIA AND SOCIALIZATION

In Chapter 2, we defined socialization as the ways in which an individual comes to adopt the behavior and values of a group, and we briefly discussed the implications of "media socialization." In Chapter 22, we will consider the socializing impact of the media in connection with the acquisition and performance of certain behaviors, most notably, antisocial and prosocial acts. In this chapter we will concentrate on the role of the media in a more subtle area—the socialization of the individual in regard to certain knowledge, attitudes, and beliefs.

Before we begin, we should point out that television is the medium with the greatest potential for transmitting information and beliefs from one group to another.

It is particularly influential in the socialization of children. Television is found in almost every American home; it requires only minimal skills and its visual nature makes it particularly appealing to youngsters. (In fact, some studies have reported a form of TV watching in children who are only a year old.) Finally, because television attracts large numbers of children, its audience of young people numbers in the millions. For all these reasons, our primary emphasis will be the socializing impact of television on children (the area that has generated the most research interest).

Socialization is a complex process, extending over a number of years and involving various people and organizations. These people or organizations are called **agents of socialization,** and they all contribute in some degree to the socialization process. Figure 21.1 represents a simplified diagram of some of the more common agencies.

As the figure demonstrates, parents, siblings, school friends, personal experience, and the media are all potential sources of socialization. From each of these sources, the child receives information and learns attitudes and behaviors through formal instruction (being told what to do), through direct experience, or through the observation of the actions of others. This last form of education, known as **observational learning,** can take place when a child observes either someone in real life or a fictional character portrayed by the media.

In many situations, the media's contribution to socialization will be slight. Other primary agents with greater influence might be parents ("Eat your spinach. It's good for you."), friends ("Don't be a tattletale."), or direct experience ("I'd

FIGURE 21.1 *Agencies of socialization.*

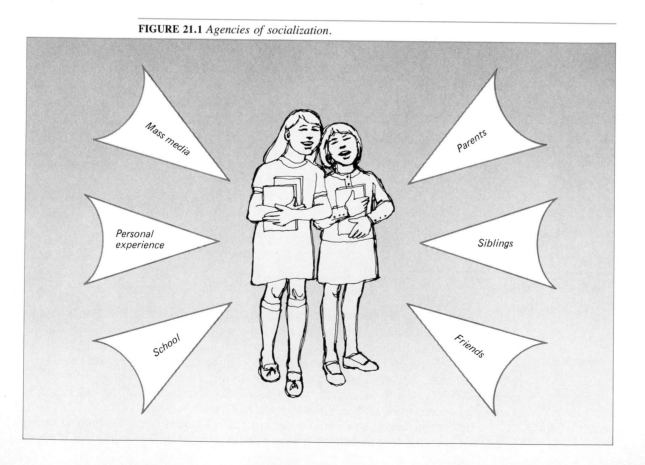

better not take my sister's things, because the last time I did she hit me in the mouth."). On the other hand, the media may play an important role in socialization when it comes to certain topics. Let us now examine evidence pinpointing some of these areas.

The Media as a Primary Source of Information

Learning is an important part of the socialization process, and children acquire information from various sources. There is increasing evidence that the media serve as important sources of information for a wide range of topics, and one such topic concerns politics and public affairs. To illustrate, a survey of sixth- and seventh-graders found that 80 percent named a mass medium as the source of most information about the president and vice president, 60 percent named a mass medium as the primary source of information about Congress, and half named a mass medium as chief information source about the Supreme Court. Similar results were obtained in a study done in the late 1970s concerning junior high school students and their sources of information about political figures and government institutions. About 80 percent named television as their principal source of information about the federal government and the president.

Other research has shown that the media, primarily TV, served as a primary information source about the Watergate scandal, government activity, foreign cultures, and war and peace. This phenomenon is not limited to political and public affairs information. There is reason to believe that media presentations, including those in entertainment programs, are important sources for information on topics such as occupations, crime, law enforcement, alcohol and drug usage, the environment, and minorities.

Shaping Attitudes, Perceptions, and Beliefs

The mass media also play an important role in the transmission of attitudes, perceptions, and beliefs. Several writers have suggested that under certain conditions, the media (especially TV) may become important socialization agencies in determining the attitudes of young people. To be specific, TV will be an influential force when the following factors are operative:

1. The same ideas, people, or behaviors recur consistently from program to program; that is, they are presented in a stereotyped manner.

2. A child is heavily exposed to TV content.

3. A child has limited interaction with parents and other socializing agents and lacks an alternative set of beliefs to serve as a standard against which to assess media portrayals.

All of this means that under certain conditions TV will be an influential force in shaping what children think about certain topics. Complicated though the task is, some researchers have identified some of the conditions, the topics, and the children to which the above theory applies. Moreover, they have specified some of the effects that may result when television does the socializing.

Creating Stereotypes. In studying media socialization, it is helpful to identify consistent themes or stereotypes present in media content. For instance, consider how television programs typically portray law enforcement and crime. Programs about crime and law enforcement are a staple of prime-time television; research has indicated that between 20 and 35 percent of all program time consists of shows dealing with cops and robbers. The popularity of this format means that the large percentage of law enforcement characters portrayed on TV does not accurately reflect the actual percentage employed in this capacity in real life. Similarly, when a suspect is brought to trial in a TV program, that trial is almost always conducted before a jury (as any "L.A. Law" fan will attest), even though judges decide the majority of cases in real life. Furthermore, on television, at least, crime doesn't pay. One study found that some 90 percent of crimes were solved; real-life law enforcement agencies are not nearly as effective.

Television also overrepresents violent crimes such as murder, rape, and armed robbery. One study found that violent crime accounted for about 60 percent of all TV crimes in one week of programming. To give some perspective to this figure, only 10 percent of crimes are violent in the real world. Lastly, television emphasizes certain aspects of the legal system (ask a young fan of any police show to name an arrested suspect's rights), while ignoring others (ask that same young fan what happens at an arraignment or about the functions of a grand jury).

Further, a study of TV ads in the early 1980s found that elderly Americans were underrepresented. Less than 10 percent of the commercials portrayed a character over sixty. Of the older characters who did appear, only 1 percent were females over sixty, highly inconsistent with the actual demographics of the U.S. population. Another study examined the portrayal of the elderly in magazine ads from 1960 to 1980 and found a similar pattern. Only 4 percent of the women in the ads were judged to be over forty (in the U.S. population almost 60 percent of women are forty or older).

It is important to note that although the mass media (particularly television) may influence the shaping of stereotypical images, the media also have the power to change such stereotypes. For example, in one study examining children's perceptions of sex roles, children were shown commercials specially made for "Zing" fruit drink. One set of commercials depicted women in conventional female occupations such as model, file clerk, and telephone operator. A second set of commercials portrayed women in traditional male jobs such as butcher, welder, and druggist. Girls who saw the women in male-dominated jobs were more likely to aspire to these occupations than were girls who saw women in the traditional roles. Some stereotypes, however, were particularly hard to extinguish. In a study done in the late 1980s, children saw a tape portraying the visit of a young child to the office of Dr. Mary and Nurse David. When asked shortly after viewing to describe the tape, a large number of boys reported the tape featured Dr. David and Nurse Mary.

In summary, there appears to be evidence that the TV world often presents images that are at odds with reality. In addition to the field of crime and law enforcement, stereotyping has also characterized sex role portrayals, the depiction of occupations, methods of problem solving, portrayals of scientists, and depiction of mental illness.

The Effects of Heavy Viewing. It seems probable that youngsters who are heavy TV viewers should display a pattern of beliefs and perceptions consistent with media portrayals. The earliest research in this area, completed in the 1930s, found that frequent viewing of crime and gangster movies could change attitudes on topics such as capital punishment and prison reform. More recently, other researchers have noted a connection between heavy viewing of violent TV programs and favorable attitudes toward the use of violence in real life. Further, children who were heavy viewers of cops-and-robbers TV programs were more likely to believe that police were more successful in apprehending criminals than were children who were not fans of these shows. This socialization effect is not confined to American children. A study in Great Britain indicated that five- and six-year-olds who were heavily exposed to news of the violence in Northern Ireland were more likely to perceive the world as a violent place in which to live than were children who were not so exposed.

In other areas, several studies have linked high levels of television viewing with attitudes favoring traditional sex roles. In other words, children who were heavily exposed to television were more likely to feel, among other things, that men would make better doctors and that women would make better nurses or that raising children was a job for women rather than men.

Socialization by TV can also have positive effects. For example, a television program such as "Sesame Street" can help children develop skills and knowledge that will help them in school. "Sesame Street" is probably the most researched program ever to appear on TV. Findings have indicated that children who watched this program scored higher on tests measuring knowledge of numbers, letters, relationships, and vocabulary—concepts that the series was designed to teach. Similar research indicates that a related program, "The Electric Company" has also been successful in teaching specific reading skills to youngsters. In addition, there is evidence that "Sesame Street" has also promoted attitudes associated with academic success (such as favorable feelings about school) that were not explicitly mentioned in the show. Finally, "Sesame Street" has been shown to affect general prosocial attitudes that are not directly concerned with school. Children who watched scenes in which white and minority children played together showed more tolerance in their

"Sesame Street" is one of the most praised programs ever to appear on TV. Regular viewing of the series seems to promote math and vocabulary skills. (Courtesy of Children's Television Workshop)

"Sesame Street": Success and Criticism

"Sesame Street" is probably the most successful educational television program ever produced. After its debut in 1969, the show was showered with praise from critics, parents, teachers, and children. Initial research projects indicated that the program was accomplishing its educational goals. However, even something as universally acclaimed as "Sesame Street" did not succeed without generating some criticism.

Seven years after its inception, "Sesame Street" had established itself as an international favorite. The program was viewed regularly in more than forty countries around the world, and Big Bird, Cookie Monster, and Oscar had become household words. Children in Latin America watched "Plaza Sesamo"; in Germany, "Sesamstrasse"; and in Holland, "Sesamstraat."

With international prominence came international problems. The Spanish-language version, "Plaza Sesamo," was faced with the difficult task of producing a program that would adequately reflect the diverse subcultures of 22 million Latin American preschoolers. For example, in English there is one form for the second person: *you*. In Spanish, however, there are two choices: the formal *usted* or the more informal *tu;* other South American countries use *vos* and *che*. The rules concerning which form to use differ from region to region. The program ignored the language variations in favor of a standardized approach. Further, although Latin America has many varieties of folk music, the first series of "Plaza Sesamo" contained only one Latin American

selection per program; other selections consisted of American rock. Soon critics of the program emerged, charging that "Plaza Sesamo" was submerging local culture and substituting a standardized American-influenced culture in its place.

Another criticism that emerged closer to home complained that "Sesame Street" was teaching too well. One of the program's original goals was to aid the intellectual growth of disadvantaged children, and the show was clearly meeting this goal. However, advantaged children were also watching "Sesame Street" and learning from it, sometimes at a faster pace than their disadvantaged counterparts. As a result, critics noted that "Sesame Street" had done little to narrow the gap between the two groups and, in fact, might even have widened it, thus placing poor children at even more of a competitive disadvantage. Other educators criticized the program's fast-paced format, which contrasted dramatically with the slower-paced classroom environment of local school systems. Such a frenetic format, these educators claimed, might contribute to hyperactivity and other behavioral problems in the classroom.

In recent years "Sesame Street" has tried to address these criticisms. International versions of the show have striven to incorporate greater cultural awareness. In the United States, efforts have been made to narrow the learning gap between advantaged and disadvantaged children, and teachers have been shown how to integrate the program into the classroom to minimize behavior problems.

racial attitudes than did children who had not viewed the scenes. Similarly, the TV series "Freestyle," "Villa Allegre," and "Big Blue Marble" aired on public television, were attempts to create programs that would alter stereotypes about sex roles and ethnic groups. When coupled with in-class discussions, viewing of these series led to a reduction in ethnic stereotyping and a broader acceptance of the different sexes in various occupations. "Square One," a more recent series from the creators of "Sesame Street," has been found to help students develop math skills.

To be fair, we must again stress that this type of research *assumes,* but does not necessarily *prove,* that the mass media play a significant part in creating the attitudes held by these youngsters. Surveys can only highlight associations. It is very possible, for example, that young people who hold traditional sex-role concepts may be more inclined to watch television. Although some experimental evidence points to the media as the cause of certain attitudes, we cannot entirely rule out other interpretations. Nevertheless, it is likely that the link between media exposure and certain attitudes demonstrates reciprocal causation. What this means is best shown by an example. Watching violent TV shows might cause a youngster to hold favorable attitudes toward aggression. These favorable attitudes might then prompt him or her to watch more violent TV, which, in turn, might encourage more aggressive attitudes, and so on. At the risk of some redundancy, the two factors might be said to be mutually causing one another.

The Absence of Alternative Solutions. Although research evidence is less consistent in this area than in others, it appears that, for some young people under some circumstances, television can affect attitudes about matters for which the environment fails to provide first-hand experience or alternative sources of information. To be specific, one survey that examined the potential impact of TV on dating behavior found that teenagers were more likely to turn to TV for guidance when they had limited real-life experience with dating. Another study, conducted in the late 1960s, asked three groups of youngsters—low-income black, low-income white, and middle-income white teenagers—how much they believed that life, as pictured on TV, resembled real life. Low-income black teenagers, the group least likely to have contact with white middle-class society (the world most portrayed on TV), held the greatest degree of belief. Middle-income white teenagers, the group most likely to have direct experience with white middle-class society, showed the most disbelief.

To provide one more example, a survey among teenagers designed to examine the relationship between viewing violent TV shows and attitudes toward the use of aggression in real life, found that the association between these two factors was strongest in homes where the parents had not communicated an explicit set of attitudes about violence to their children. In those homes where parents had established an antiviolence set of values, the relationship between the viewing of violence and favorable attitudes toward aggression was much lower. Apparently, the socializing impact of the family overrode the influence of TV.

Finally, in a more recent study, it was noted that foreign students who depended most on television for their information about Americans had stereotyped beliefs about Americans. Chinese students who depended primarily on TV for most of their information and who had little interpersonal contact with Americans rated them as more pleasure seeking and materialistic (two characteristics consistent with TV's portrayal of Americans) than did students who relied more on other sources.

Before closing, we should point out that where media influence is indirect, it is also more difficult to pinpoint. This is particularly true in situations where the media operate simultaneously with other agencies of socialization and where interpersonal channels may outweigh media channels in forming attitudes and opinions. In the area of politics, for instance, the media probably supply youngsters with information and viewpoints that are subsequently commented on by parents and friends. Political beliefs and attitudes evolve out of this double context. In such cases, the socializing impact of parents and other interpersonal sources is more important than that of the media. One study dealing with attitudes toward police found that although children spent a great deal of time watching TV cop shows,

Television and Childhood's End

As the text suggests, the mass media, especially television, play an important role in the socialization of children. But is it possible that television is also changing the experience of childhood itself? Professor Joshua Meyrowitz of the University of New Hampshire, for one, thinks that it is. In fact, he argues in his book *No Sense of Place* that television is subtly putting an end to what we used to call "childhood." Here, in condensed form, is what Professor Meyrowitz suggests.

Back in the nineteenth and early twentieth centuries, children were looked upon as innocent and weak creatures who had to be shielded from the harsher realities of life. Children were dressed differently from adults; they had their own games; there were words and topics that were taboo for children or for adults in conversations around children. The school system consisted of rigid grades that defined what children of certain age should or should not know.

Recently, however, all of that seems to be changing. It is no longer unusual to see kids dressed in designer jeans and three-piece suits and other outfits that mimic adult clothing. At the other end of the spectrum, adults now dress in Superman T-shirts and sneakers and wear Mickey Mouse watches—grownup versions of play clothes. The distinction between children's play and adult play has also been obscured. Adults now zip around on rollerskates and skateboards and attend summer camps. The new "toys" made possible by electronic technology—computer and video games—can be and are being played by both adults and kids. Further, the list of taboo topics unfit for children to know has shrunk and, more importantly, children are learning previously taboo topics at younger and younger ages. Formal programs of sex and drug education, for example, are hampered because young people frequently enter them having considerable experience with the topics and with their opinions already formed. The changing nature of childhood is readily apparent in mass entertainment. The Shirley Temple films of the 1930s have given way to the Molly Ringwald films of the 1980s.

What has TV had to do with this changing nature of childhood? Professor Meyrowitz contends that TV has changed the pattern and sequence of access to social information. When a society moves from dependence on one medium as a primary information source to another, there are shifts in the ease with which certain information becomes available. For example, in the early part of the century, print was a primary means of communicating social information. Young children had to master complex reading skills before they were able to have access to information in print. Thus young children without the necessary symbolic skills were automatically forbidden access to information contained in books, newspapers, and magazines. Moreover, printed information could be directed at children of different ages simply by varying the complexity of the message.

Television, however, is completely different. It takes little skill to watch television, and the information it provides is available to all who watch it. Thus second-graders, ninth-graders, and adults are all simultaneously exposed to programs about junkies, prostitutes, crooked cops, adulterous parents, and unscrupulous politicians. In fact, with TV, shielding children from such information is extremely difficult. An adult book might be hidden in a drawer or stored on a high shelf, but the TV set is available to everybody. More than half the households in the United States have more than one TV, and many of these sets are located in children's rooms. Even the advisories placed at the beginning of some programs ("This show deals with adult themes and situations. Parental discretion is advised.") can have a boomerang effect by increasing the child's interest in what follows.

Additionally, in a print culture, children were given an "onstage" view of adults. Traditional children's books presented idealized and stereotyped versions of adult behavior.

Politicians acted nobly; parents knew what was best; the teacher was always right. In a television culture, children are shown a "backstage" view. Newscasts, situation comedies, and dramatic programs show children crooked politicians, depressed parents, and incompetent teachers long before they get the idealized view. Children also learn that adults play roles. They act one way in front of children and another way when children are not present. This fact also reduces the traditional distance between children and adults.

In short, the information presented on TV immediately thrusts children into the adult world. It is no longer possible to go through the leisurely process of socialization by stages that typified print culture. As Professor Meyrowitz sums up: "In the shared environment of television, children and adults know a great deal about each other's behavior and social knowledge—too much, in fact, for them to play the traditional complementary roles of innocence vs. omnipotence."

friends and family were the important socializing agents. The point is this: The media play a significant role in socialization. Sometimes this role is easy to detect; sometimes it is indirect and harder to see; at still other times, it is apparently slight. Clearly, numerous factors are influential in determining how a child comes to perceive the world. The media (and television, in particular), however, seem to have become important factors in the socialization process.

CULTIVATION ANALYSIS

Directly related to socialization is an area of research called **cultivation analysis.** Developed by George Gerbner and his colleagues at the University of Pennsylvania, cultivation analysis suggests that heavy TV viewing "cultivates" perceptions of reality consistent with the view of the world presented in television programs. This notion has already been suggested in our discussion of socialization effects. With cultivation analysis, however, Gerbner has expanded his focus to include the possible effects of media content on adults as well as on children. Additionally, cultivation analysis concentrates on the long-term effects of exposure rather than the short-term impact on attitudes and opinions. Gerbner and his associates have been performing cultivation analyses for several years, using large and in some instances national samples of respondents. The results suggest that television may have a subtle effect on the way many of us look at the world.

Methodology

The first stage in cultivation analysis is a careful study of television content in order to identify predominant themes and messages. Since 1967, Gerbner and his colleagues have been meticulously analyzing sample weeks of prime-time and daytime television programming. Not surprisingly, television portrays a rather idiosyncratic world that is unlike reality along many dimensions. To mention a few examples, television's world is usually populated by a preponderance of males. In fact, in an average season, about two-thirds to three-quarters of all leading characters are men. Moreover, in portraying occupations, television overemphasizes the professions and, as previously mentioned, overrepresents the proportion of workers engaged in law enforcement and the detection of crime. Lastly, the TV world is a violent one—around 70 to 80 percent of all programs usually contain at least one instance of violence.

Step two examines what, if anything, viewers absorb from heavy exposure to the world of television. Respondents are presented with questions concerning social reality and are asked to check one of two possible answers. One of these answers (the "TV answer") is more in line with the way things are portrayed on television; the other (the "real-world answer") more closely resembles situations in actual life. An example might help to demonstrate what we are talking about:

What percentage of all males who have jobs work in law enforcement and crime detection?

Is it

_____ 1 percent or _____ 10 percent?

On television, about 12 percent of all male characters hold such jobs. Thus 10 percent would be the "TV answer." In reality, about 1 percent are employed in law enforcement; thus 1 percent is the "real-world answer." The responses of a large sample of heavy TV viewers are then compared with those of light TV viewers. If heavy viewers show a definite tendency to choose TV answers, we would have evidence that a cultivation effect was occurring.

Research Findings

Is there evidence to suggest such an effect? At the risk of oversimplifying, it appears that most findings suggest that among some people TV is cultivating distorted perceptions of the real world. To illustrate, in one survey done among approximately 450 New Jersey schoolchildren, 73 percent of heavy viewers compared to 62 percent of light viewers gave the TV answer to a question asking them to estimate the number of people involved in violence in a typical week. This same survey discovered that youngsters who were heavy viewers were more fearful about walking alone at night in a city. They overestimated the number of people who commit serious crimes, how often police find it necessary to use force, and how frequently police have to shoot at fleeing suspects. These results are in line with the expected predictions of cultivation analysis.

In addition, results from a national survey of adult viewers indicate that cultivation is not limited to children. In this survey, heavy television viewers evidently felt that TV violence and crime presented an accurate depiction of reality, since they also were more fearful of walking alone at night and were more likely to have bought a dog recently or to have put locks on windows and doors than were light TV viewers. Although the differences in findings between heavy and light viewers were not large in the absolute sense, they were almost certainly not due to chance. Even more intriguing was the finding that heavy TV viewers were more likely to keep a gun in order to protect themselves than were light viewers.

Research has shown that content other than crime and violence might also demonstrate a cultivation effect. One study of college students conducted in 1981 found that heavy soap opera viewers were more likely than light viewers to overestimate the number of real-life married people who had affairs or who had been divorced and the number of women who had abortions (common occurrences in the soap opera world).

Although the results of cultivation-analysis studies are evocative and fascinating, conclusions are clouded by two problems. First, it is difficult to determine cause and effect. Does heavy TV viewing cause people to be fearful of walking alone at night or does being fearful cause them to stay home and watch more TV? Since the problem of causation is one that cannot adequately be addressed through the use of only survey data, it is necessary to examine the results of laboratory experiments for added information. In the case of cultivation analysis experiments are difficult to conduct since, by its very nature, cultivation analysis is concerned with long-term effects of exposure to consistent television portrayals.

One experiment that attempted to address the issue of cause and effect manipulated television viewing among college students to create heavy- and light-viewing groups. After six weeks of structured viewing, heavy viewers, who had been exposed to large doses of action-adventure programs, were more fearful and anxious about life in the real world than were light viewers. This result supported the cultivation hypothesis.

Another experiment used specially constructed TV programs to look for a cultivation effect. One group of experimental subjects saw a program in which justice triumphed (the good guy shot the bad guy). A second group saw a version in which injustice won out (the bad guy shot the good guy). In addition, a third group saw a documentary about crime, while a control group watched an episode of ''The Love Boat.'' It was hypothesized that cultivation of greater anxiety and a perception of increased crime in the world should be greatest among those who saw the version depicting injustice (the bad guy triumphed and was free to strike again). The actual results were not clear-cut. As predicted, subjects who saw the version depicting injustice were more anxious than those in the other conditions. When asked about their perceptions of the frequency of crime, subjects in both the injustice condition and the documentary condition showed a tendency to overestimate its frequency compared to other groups. When the subjects were questioned again three days later, however, the difference had dissipated. Taken together, these two experiments suggest that the cultivation effect is more complicated than previously thought. Both the type of content that is viewed and the time factor apparently influence its potency.

The second problem concerns the fact that heavy and light TV viewers differ in ways other than their TV viewing habits. Consequently, factors other than TV watching might affect the differences in perceptions and attitudes between heavy and light viewers. Analyzing this problem is somewhat difficult. When certain factors that appear relevant to the cause-and-effect relationship (such as age, sex, and education) are statistically controlled, one factor at a time, the association between TV watching and perceptions is evident, but somewhat weakened. When two or more factors are controlled simultaneously (e.g., examining the relationship between TV viewing and anxiety, while simultaneously controlling for effects of both sex and age), some overall relationships disappear. We cannot conclude, however, that a relationship does not exist. In fact, recent research indicates certain subgroups will show a cultivation effect while others won't.

Gerbner and his associates, for example, have detected a phenomenon they have labeled **mainstreaming,** whereby differences apparently due to cultural and social factors tend to diminish among heavy TV viewers. They have also found evidence for what they call **resonance,** a situation in which the respondent's real-life experiences are congruent with those of the television world, thereby leading to a greater cultivation effect.

The recent emphasis in cultivation studies has been on specifying the conditions that are most likely to encourage or hinder cultivation. Although results are not as clear-cut as we might like, cultivation appears to depend on the motivation for viewing. Individuals who watch TV simply to pass time or because it becomes a habit appear to be more affected than people whose viewing is planned and motivated. Moreover, cultivation appears to be enhanced when the viewer perceives the content of entertainment shows to be realistic. Audience members who look with skepticism on the accuracy of TV shows seem less likely to display the cultivation effect. Finally, some studies have noted cultivation seems to work best when audience members have only indirect or distant contact with the topic. Interestingly enough, this finding seems to run counter to the resonance notion.

To sum up and perhaps oversimplify, it is probably fair to say that although not all mass communication scholars are totally convinced by the reasoning underlying cultivation analysis, a growing body of evidence suggests that the cultivation effect is indeed real for many people. Nonetheless, it's obvious that a lot of research still needs to be done before the cultivation process is completely understood.

CHILDREN AND TELEVISION ADVERTISING

If you've ever watched Saturday morning television, you are probably familiar with Tony the Tiger, Captain Crunch, Count Chocula, Ronald McDonald, and Snap, Crackle, and Pop. This is not surprising because by the time you graduated from high school, you had already seen about 350,000 TV commercials. A typical child will see about 20,000 commercials every year, mostly for toys, cereals, candies, and fast-food restaurants. The effects of this massive exposure to TV persuasion became a topic of concern during the 1970s as the citizens' group Action for Children's Television brought this issue to the attention of the Federal Communications Commission (FCC) and the Federal Trade Commission (FTC). By the early part of the 1980s, most people had accepted the notion that children constitute a special audience and deserve special consideration from television advertisers. It has been argued that children constitute a special audience because of the following reasons:

1. Children are a vulnerable audience and should not be exploited by TV advertising.

2. Children, especially younger children, might be deceived by TV techniques that make products appear more desirable than they really are.

3. The long-term effects of exposure of TV ads might have a negative effect on a child's socialization as a future consumer.

Using this threefold division, we will examine some of the many research studies that have investigated the effects of TV advertising on children.

A Vulnerable Audience?

Adults have little problem in distinguishing commercials from regular television programs, and they realize that the purpose of a commercial is to promote some idea, product, or service. But what about children? Can they recognize a commercial and understand its purpose? Research suggests that this ability is related to age. Younger children (five to eight years old) were able to identify commercials, but they had difficulty in separating ads from the rest of the program and had little idea as to the purpose behind them. When asked to differentiate between a TV program and a TV commercial, these youngsters typically responded that commercials were "shorter" or "funnier" than the programs that contained them. These same children did not perceive that commercials were designed to sell things to people. Additionally, it was discovered that ads that used program characters and program hosts to sell the product further confused the distinction between program and ad. They were more persuasive with youngsters, probably because of the trust and identification children place in these characters.

Older children (nine to twelve years old) were better able to differentiate the ads from the rest of the program and had little trouble in distinguishing between the purpose of an ad and a program. A typical response from a child in this age group was that "programs entertain" and "commercials try to sell things." These older children were also less susceptible to the selling efforts of hosts and program characters in ads.

Partly as a result of these findings, the FCC, in a 1974 inquiry into advertising aimed at children, concluded that some device was needed to clearly separate commercials from programs. Shortly thereafter, broadcasters started using a separation device. This separation device was five to ten seconds long and contained the words "We will return after these messages" and "We now return to (name of program)." Experiments in this area have shown that program separators are ineffective with young children (five and younger). The separators worked better with older children, who were better able to distinguish the difference between programs and commercials if separators were included. Although young children have trouble differentiating an ad from programming even with separators, it is apparent that the broadcasting industry has acknowledged the special nature of the child audience.

Effects of Special Selling Techniques

When you were much younger, some of you may have had an experience like the following. On Saturday morning, while watching your favorite cartoon show, you may have seen an ad for a toy, perhaps a plastic model truck called "Toughie." In the ad, the truck, with headlights flashing and horn blowing, was shown dumping a load of sand in the middle of a miniature construction site, surrounded by miniature construction workers. The truck was then shown in close-up, practically dwarfing the young child in the background. Excited, you told your parents that "Toughie" was the one thing you wanted most for Christmas. When Christmas arrived and you were lucky enough to find Toughie under the tree, you might have been disillusioned to find that the actual truck was much smaller than it had appeared on TV. The headlights didn't flash and the horn didn't blow because batteries weren't included with the truck. There was no sand, no miniature construction site, and no tiny construction workers. Somehow, it wasn't the same toy that you remembered.

Then again, you might have seen an ad for "Cuddly Carol," a perfectly lovable doll dressed in three or four different outfits, who presided over a miniature tea party furnished with a complete tea set, while an announcer told you that "Cuddly Carol" was the best doll around. If you were fortunate enough to receive "Cuddly Carol," you might have discovered that whenever you tried to stand her up, "Cuddly" had an irritating tendency to fall flat on her face. Further, the several outfits shown on TV were not included, and the miniature tea set was nowhere to be found. Somehow, "Cuddly Carol" looked a lot better on TV.

It's obvious that toys and other products designed for children can be made to look more appealing through the use of special camera angles, lenses, advertising copy, sound effects, animation, and special lighting techniques. The ability of

The effects of television on young viewers is one of the most thoroughly researched areas in mass communication. (Frostie/Woodfin Camp and Associates, Inc.)

children to distinguish the illusion created by these techniques from the real object has been an area of continuing interest among policymakers and mass communication researchers. Recently, in response to tighter industry guidelines, commercials directed toward children have included disclaimers, messages such as "Some assembly required," or "Batteries not included," or "Accessories sold separately," which are read by an announcer and/or flashed on the screen. Some critics have argued that these disclaimers are not understood by children, and several research studies have examined this area. This section will provide a brief summary of what is known about this issue.

Turning first to the effects of special TV production techniques, we find that there has been relatively little research addressed to this topic. Studies of ads broadcast during children's programs have indicated that animation occurs in about 40 percent of all commercials and in about 80 percent of cereal commercials. Additionally, special visual effects are used to enhance the appearance of the product in about 15-20 percent of children's commercials. Product close-ups occurred in about 40 percent of all ads and were particularly likely to show up in ads for toys. One study indicated that children aged five to eight had trouble interpreting the meaning of a close-up or a zoom that magnified the object. Young children who saw a candy bar in a medium shot followed by a close-up of the candy bar or a zoom into a close-up of the candy bar thought the object itself had gotten larger.

The effects on children of the use of special selling techniques are unclear. One study showed children a particular television commercial that exaggerated the virtues of the product it was promoting, a simple child's game. Young boys who saw only the TV ad were willing to pay a higher price for the game than were boys who saw the actual toy. Interestingly, girls did not show this tendency. In another experiment, a group of children were shown a commercial that purposefully exaggerated the appeal of a building-block game. Other children saw a similar commercial that was more modest in its depiction of the toy. Those children who saw the exaggerated version had greater expectations about the game and were evidently disappointed when the real item failed to live up to its promised potential.

Other research has examined the effects of product disclaimers appearing in ads. A disclaimer such as ''Batteries not included'' was remembered by far more children when it was both mentioned by the announcer and superimposed on the screen than when it was only shown on the screen. Further, the wording of product disclaimers has been shown to be an important factor in their effectiveness. In one experiment, two toy commercials were shown to two groups of six- and eight-year-olds. One used the standard disclaimer, ''Some assembly required''; the other contained a simplified disclaimer, ''You have to put it together.'' Results indicated that children who were exposed to the standard ''Some assembly required'' had no better understanding that the toy must be put together than did children who saw the ad without any disclaimer. In other words, the standard line did nothing to improve comprehension. On the other hand, children who heard the simplified version were far more likely to realize that assembly was necessary. In another study, it was found that a disclaimer stating that a certain cereal was only ''part of a balanced breakfast'' had little apparent impact on young viewers. Most of the four- to eight-year-olds who saw the commercial didn't know what a ''balanced breakfast'' was.

In light of the above research, the television and advertising industries have acknowledged the potential of television production techniques to influence children's perceptions of TV commercials. Industry guidelines for toy products now state that audio and video techniques should not misrepresent the appearance and performance of toys and that disclaimers should be used when batteries are needed, when the product must be assembled by the consumer, or when accessory items shown in the ad are not included in the price of the advertised product. The research we've mentioned above also suggests that perhaps these guidelines should be amended to cover the actual language used in the disclaimer.

Children's Ads and Consumer Socialization

Consumer socialization includes all those processes by which children learn behaviors and attitudes relevant to their future behavior as consumers. Like socialization in general, consumer socialization is accomplished by several agents—parents, the school, direct experience, and, more pertinent to our discussion, television advertising. It is obvious to any parent that television commercials teach children the names of certain products, slogans, and jingles and even make celebrities of young performers in commercials (the ''cereal that Mikey likes'' made Mikey a TV star). In more general terms, the question addressed by many researchers in this area concerns the ultimate contribution that TV advertising makes to consumer socialization. This is not an easy question to answer. Many members of the advertising industry argue that advertising, particularly TV advertising, aids children's general understanding of the American free-enterprise system and helps them learn about products and purchasing skills. On the other hand, critics of advertising for children charge that TV ads help foster materialism in children and promote generally unhealthy social attitudes.

Although relevant research evidence is not clear-cut, primarily because concepts such as consumer skills and materialism are hard to define, certain generalizations can be made. We do know that as a child gets older the influence of parents as a consumer-socialization force decreases and the influence of the peer group increases.

Mass media influences appear to be small but are constant with age. Unfortunately, there have been no long-term studies demonstrating a link between childhood socialization experiences and subsequent adult consumer behavior. There is evidence, however, that certain effects do occur, at least among five- to twelve-year-olds. One phenomenon that has been observed several times is that as children get older, they begin to distrust commercials and even become cynical about them. In one survey, children of different ages were asked if they believed that commercials always told the truth. About 35 percent of the five- to seven-year-olds said yes, compared with about 15 percent of the eight- to ten-year-olds and only 5 percent of the eleven- to twelve-year-olds. Another study that asked the same question in a slightly different way found that the percentage of youngsters who trusted commercials declined from 65 percent to only 7 percent by the fifth grade. Why do children come to mistrust TV commercials? One reason seems to be that as children get older they find out that products do not live up to the expectations that commercials give. Coupled with this disillusionment is a growing awareness of the actual motives behind commercials. "They're tricky and try to get you to buy things" and "They just want to make money" are some reasons given by youngsters for their mistrust.

Developing Consumer Skills. A second area of research has investigated the contribution of TV ads to the development of children's consumer skills. Consumer skills might consist of abilities such as comparing prices, finding out how well a product

The typical child sees up to 20,000 commercials in a year, many for popular games and toys, then heads straight for the toy store. The impact of television advertising and its role in the consumer socialization of children have been closely studied. (Tom Kelly)

will perform, checking several sources of information about a product, and so on. One survey found that although consumer skills increased with age, in most instances exposure to TV commercials seemed to be unrelated to this increase. In those few situations in which viewing of commercials was associated with consumer skills, the association produced negative results. In effect, children who were exposed to many TV ads actually had lower levels of skills than children not so heavily exposed. Other studies have also turned up little evidence of a relationship between viewing ads and consumer skills. In general, then, we might conclude that there is little reason to accept the argument that being an intelligent and skillful consumer is a function of exposure to media advertising. To be fair, however, we should point out that the inability to prove an association might be due to the difficulty in accurately measuring consumer skills. More research in the area is needed before a definitive conclusion can be drawn.

Advertising and Materialism. A third area of socialization and advertising concerns materialism—that is, preoccupation with possessions and wealth. Research has turned up a link between positive attitudes toward commercials and endorsement of materialistic attitudes. For example, adolescents who favorably regarded television ads also thought that money and physical possessions were necessary for happiness. This finding, however, again does not conclusively determine cause and effect. It may be that people who are already materialistic are predisposed to like TV ads.

In one experiment that tried to pin down the direction of causation, young children were divided into two groups. One group watched TV commercials promoting a particular toy; the other group did not. The children were then shown pictures of two boys: One was empty-handed and described as "nice"; the other was holding the toy shown in the commercials and was described as "not nice." The children were then asked which of the boys they would like to play with. In the group that didn't see the commercial 70 percent chose the empty-handed "nice boy," compared with only 35 percent of the group that saw the TV ads. Most of this latter group chose the "not-nice" boy with the toy, thereby suggesting that TV commercials had increased the importance of the material possession. This and similar studies are interesting because they suggest a possible cause–effect relationship between ads and materialism; however, the issue deserves more study before a final verdict can be pronounced.

Advertising and the Parent–Child Relationships. The last area of socialization we will consider is the effect of television advertising on the relationship between parents and children. Does television advertising turn children into miniature salespersons who pressure parents into buying a product? Advertisers evidently agree that commercials can influence children into pressuring their parents to buy certain products. In fact, industry guidelines discourage such advertising, stating that children shall not be directed to purchase or ask a parent to buy a product or service for them. Consequently, if you watch children's TV, you will probably not hear someone say, "Kids, get your parents to buy you the hot-action Whirlybirds Fun Kit!" or words to that effect. Advertisers, however, can encourage children to request things from their parents by more subtle means. This is the area that has caused most concern.

Much of the research surrounding this topic has centered upon three questions:

1. Does exposure to television commercials prompt children to make purchase requests of their parents?

2. Do parents grant or deny these requests?

3. Does conflict between parent and child result if the parent denies the purchase request?

To begin, we know that the occurrence of requests to purchase a product is related to many factors other than television viewing. As a child gets older, requests to parents typically decline. Moreover, youngsters are more likely to request products that they frequently consume (candy, fast food, breakfast cereal) or use (toys). In addition to these factors, however, viewing of television commercials has its own independent impact. Surveys indicate that children who are heavy television viewers (and, as a result, see many commercials) are more likely to request advertised toys and games than are children who do not watch TV as often. Saturday morning TV viewing apparently relates to purchase requests for food products; the more TV, the more frequent the requests. In one particular survey, children were asked how often they requested their parents to buy toys for them that they had seen advertised on TV. Forty percent of the children who were heavy TV viewers reported making "a lot" of these requests, compared with only 16 percent of light TV watchers. The same pattern was found in requests for cereals after seeing their ads on TV. Among heavy viewers, 41 percent reported a lot of requests to their parents for a specific cereal, contrasted with only 24 percent of the light viewers. The results of another survey suggested that advertising for non–child-oriented products also encouraged requests from children for the product. One investigation on the impact of over-the-counter medicine advertising found an association between exposure to ads and requests to parents for such medicine.

How do parents handle these requests? If the request concerns a product that is consumed or used primarily by the child, parents generally give in. Parents of middle-class children disclosed in a survey that they yielded to their children's requests 87 percent of the time for cereals, 63 percent for snack foods, 54 percent for toys, and 42 percent for candy, compared with only 16 percent for shampoo and 7 percent for pet food. Another study that actually observed parents and children in a shopping situation uncovered the same pattern, although the percentages of parental yielding were somewhat different. To generalize, parents seem to give in to about two-thirds of their children's requests for child-oriented products.

But what happens when parents say no to TV-inspired requests for cereal, candy, and toys? Sometimes arguments and anger result. One survey noted that one-sixth of the children whose requests for toys were denied argued with their parents. One-fifth said they usually became angry. Fortunately, such conflicts were generally short-lived. In a study involving in-store observations of request denials, researchers reported that episodes of children's angry and unhappy reactions (sometimes expressed by loud crying) passed quickly and were evidently soon forgotten.

Before we close, it might be valuable to examine the results of an experiment that attempted to analyze what happens when TV-inspired requests for a toy are turned down. In this study, one group of children viewed a TV program containing commercials for a particularly appealing toy. A second group of children viewed the same program minus commercials. After the program was over, all children were shown two photographs. One showed a boy happily embracing his father; the other showed the boy sullenly walking away from him. The children were then asked what they thought a young boy whose father didn't buy him the toy would do. Would he still play with his father as shown in the first photo, or would he avoid his father as shown in the second? Sixty percent of the children who did not see the

Studying the Effects of TV Commercials

How do scientists determine if viewing TV commercials has an impact on children's purchase requests? Below is a summary of a typical study that appeared in a 1976 issue of *Child Development*. Two psychologists, Joann Galst and Mary Alice White, tested forty-one children aged five through eleven. First, in order to determine the degree of attention these children paid to TV commercials, a TV set was installed in an empty classroom and each child was given a chance to watch a popular TV show (complete with commercials). There was a catch, however. If the child wanted to view the program, he or she had to press a button that brought four seconds of the program onto the screen. When the child failed to press the button, the screen temporarily went dark. By analyzing the patterns of button pushing, the investigators could identify those children who evidently liked commercials and paid attention to them (they pressed the button during the ads) and those children who paid little attention (they did not keep pushing the button).

The children's purchase requests were measured by having one researcher accompany each child and his or her parent to the supermarket during their next shopping trip. Pretending to be shopping herself, the researcher followed parent and child around the store and noted each time the child requested an item (by asking for it, putting it in the shopping cart, pointing at it, or by asking for it when given a choice by the parent). On the average,

these children made fifteen purchase requests during the shopping trip.

The next step was to determine if there was a relationship between purchase requests and the amount of attention paid to TV commercials and to hours of commercial TV viewed at home. During the study, Galst and White had asked the children's parents to fill out questionnaires reporting how many hours their children spent watching commercial TV at home. Statistical analysis revealed that those children who paid more attention to commercials (the frequent button pushers in the laboratory study) were more likely to make more purchase attempts. Moreover, the same findings occurred when home commercial TV viewing was considered—those children who were heavy viewers made more purchase requests. Further analysis revealed that cereals and candy—two of the most frequently advertised products on TV—were the items requested most often.

Galst and White summed up their study by stating:

> While correlations do not imply causality, still it is hard to escape the suggestion that children who may be more "tuned in" to TV commercials may be developing an attitude toward consumerism and product acquisition from commercial television. . .
>
> Thus, television, a medium which could be a powerful educational tool to inform children of good health and nutrition, is instead at present a vehicle for unhealthy persuasion.

---

ads said the boy would still play with his father; only 40 percent among the group that saw the ads thought so. Although far from conclusive, this one experiment suggests that TV ads for toys can lead to requests for those toys and that denial of those requests may prompt negative feelings in the child toward the parent.

The mid-1980s saw the emergence of a new area of controversy regarding advertising's influence on young people. This time the problem centered on the effects of alcohol advertising on adolescents. Several surveys discovered that young people who were heavily exposed to this type of advertising were more likely to consume alcohol or state that they would probably start drinking in the future. A

Senate subcommittee considering imposing a ban on alcohol advertising on radio and television heard lengthy testimony in this area. Ultimately, it was decided that instead of legislation, the broadcasting industry would present a series of public-service announcements warning against the abuse of alcohol.

In summary, we have seen in this brief review that some criticisms voiced by public-interest groups such as Action for Children's Television appear to be supported by research. Some children, especially younger ones, have trouble understanding the basic intent of advertising. As a child matures, repeated exposure to commercials evidently results in disillusionment and cynicism about the merits of advertising. Additionally, family conflicts may result if children respond to the ad with purchase requests directed toward their parents. As is probably obvious by now, this whole topic raises questions of regulation. It is to be hoped that the construction of a public policy dealing with the general issue of advertising for children is a task that organizations such as the Federal Trade Commission and the Federal Communications Commission will accomplish in the near future.

THE DIFFUSION OF NEWS AND INFORMATION

One effect of mass media that is so obvious it is almost overlooked is the ability of the media to disseminate information rapidly to a large group of people. Before the emergence of a mass communication system, it took a long time for news and information to reach large numbers of people. As noted in Chapter 2, it took nearly two months for news of the signing of the Treaty of Ghent, which officially ended the War of 1812, to reach America. Ironically, the American victory at the battle of New Orleans occurred two weeks after the treaty had been signed but five weeks

Prince Andrew's marriage to Sarah Ferguson was seen by a global television audience of 300 million. Because of modern technological developments, like satellites, the rate of diffusion for such news items is much faster than at any previous time in history. (Topham/ The Image Works)

before news of the end of the war was received in the United States. Had there been a mass communication system in place in 1815, the course of world history might have been much different.

Mass media researchers have carefully studied how mass communication channels function in the distribution of news and information. This area of study has been labeled **news diffusion** and is defined as the dissemination (spread) of information in a society across time. Three main stages of the diffusion process have been identified. The first stage is called the **newsbreak** and consists of the time it takes for reporters to transmit the essential facts of a story back to a media organization, which, in turn, publishes or broadcasts the news. The second is called the **dissemination stage** and consists of the period during which the news is spreading through the audience and during which the facts are becoming known to the members of some community or society. The last stage, called **saturation,** occurs when most of the population has heard the story and it no longer can be classified as breaking news. For our purposes, we will define saturation as occurring when approximately 90 percent of the population has heard the news.

An example may serve to illustrate these three stages better. When President John Kennedy was assassinated in November of 1963, the event took place at approximately 1:30 P.M. (Eastern Standard Time). The first news bulletins announcing the event were broadcast about four to five minutes later. Thus the newsbreak for this story was only four to five minutes long. At this point the dissemination stage began. As would be expected, news of this magnitude spread quickly, with about two-thirds of the audience having heard the facts within half an hour. The saturation stage was reached only one hour after the event.

The Kennedy assassination, however, was not a typical news event. Most news stories do not diffuse as quickly. Studies of more common news events have been fairly consistent in their description of the diffusion process. For these events, the speed of dissemination is a function of the news value of the event. Extremely important events will reach the saturation stage in a matter of a few hours. Important events—those that receive bulletin treatment in radio and television and banner headlines in the newspaper—will typically reach saturation six to twelve hours after the newsbreak. Events of intermediate importance usually require twenty-four to thirty-six hours to reach 90 percent of the population. Less important events may take two or three days to reach saturation, if at all.

If we were to graph the cumulative percentage of people who know about an event and the elapsed time after the event, we would find that diffusion curves for news events of differing importance would have certain similarities. The curves would take roughly an S-shape, indicating a rapid initial spread of information that eventually tapers off with the passing of time. Figure 21.2, page 524, illustrates typical diffusion curves for events of three different levels of newsworthiness.

Of course, the particulars of diffusion will vary according to the type of story that is being reported. The dissemination of news for an anticipated event is much faster (and the resulting diffusion curve much steeper) than is the case with an unanticipated story. In some instances, the story might be anticipated and covered live by the media (as is the case with a presidential inauguration or press conference), and the time between the newsbreak and the dissemination stage will be zero.

Moreover, the source of first exposure for a news story will, with some exceptions, be one of the mass media. In most cases, radio or television will serve as the first source of information for approximately 50–70 percent of the population. The remainder will learn about a news story from one of the print media or through interpersonal channels. This same general diffusion pattern occurred in the spread

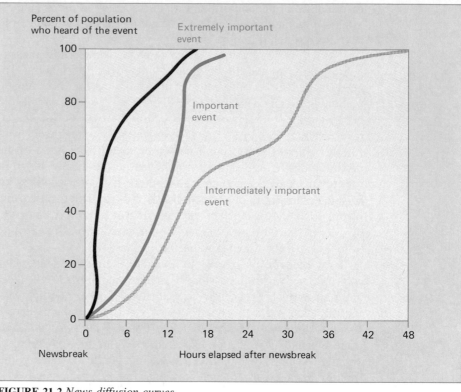

FIGURE 21.2 *News diffusion curves.*

of news about the attempted assassination of Ronald Reagan and the shooting of Pope John Paul II.

The role of interpersonal channels in supplementing news diffusion has been studied in some detail. Generally speaking, there are apparently two types of events for which interpersonal communication is often the first source of information: (1) those events that are so important that everybody is interested in them; and (2) those events of such minor importance that only a few people are interested in them. (As for news events of intermediate importance, interpersonal communication serves as the first source of information for only about 3–5 percent of the population.) Consider what occurred when Kennedy was shot: About one out of every two people (50 percent) who heard the news heard it first from another person, either in person or over the phone. The interpersonal channel was also the most important in finding out about the shooting of Ronald Reagan. About 45 percent heard about the event from other people. Similarly, events of relatively minor importance—local stories that might be of interest to only a few people—are also more likely to be passed along via interpersonal channels. One survey found that 10–11 percent of the population first heard about such relatively low newsworthy events from other people, about twice the usual percentage.

AGENDA SETTING

One influence of mass media that has turned up in many studies of mass communication is called the **agenda-setting effect.** (An agenda is a list of things to be considered or acted upon.) When we say that the media have an impact on agenda setting we mean that they have the ability to choose and emphasize certain topics, thereby causing the public to perceive these issues as important. Or, to paraphrase Bernard Cohen in his book *The Press and Foreign Policy,* the media may not always be successful in telling people what to think, but they are usually successful in telling people what to think about.

Agenda-setting studies typically concern themselves with information media: news magazines, newspapers, television, and radio. Although some studies have examined the role of news magazines, far more attention has been paid to newspapers and television in agenda-setting research. The few studies that have examined radio have found that this medium has little effect on agenda setting. Further, much of the research on agenda setting has been carried out during political campaigns. There are two reasons for this. First, messages generated by political campaigns are usually designed to set agendas (politicians call this tactic emphasizing the issues). Second, political campaigns have a clear-cut beginning and end, thus making the time period for study unambiguous.

Public concern about the situation in South Africa was heightened by the televising of demonstrations. In fact, the South African government was so concerned about the effects of this coverage on international opinion that it banned reporters from taking pictures of scenes of violence. Here women participate in a placard demonstration. (Wendy Schwegmann/Reuters-Bettmann Newsphotos)

To illustrate a typical agenda-setting study, one investigation of the 1968 presidential election asked a sample of voters to rank-order what they believed to be the key issues of the campaign. While this was going on, researchers examined news magazines, newspapers, and television newscasts, and a ranking of campaign issues was prepared according to the time and space the media devoted to each issue. When the media's ranking was compared to the voters' ranking, there was a strikingly high degree of correspondence. In other words, the voters perceived as important those issues that the media judged important, as evidenced by the amount of coverage they received. Similar studies of more recent elections have found similar results. Although such studies strongly suggest a relationship between personal agendas and media agendas, they do not address the question of causation, an issue that we have encountered before. Although it can be assumed that the media's agenda influences the public's agenda, it is also possible that the public's agenda actually influences that of the media.

Additional research upholds the theory that at times the media have formed the public's perceptions. The Watergate episode illustrates this pattern of influence. At first, the story received limited coverage, primarily in newspapers; then it was featured more prominently in magazines and network television newscasts. However, public concern did not match media coverage until the TV networks began live coverage of congressional hearings. Subsequently, the Watergate issue began to assume increased importance among the general public. Interestingly enough, the same phenomena did not occur during the Iran–Contra affair.

To complicate matters, additional studies indicate that there are other situations in which the direction of cause and effect is unclear—or will even depend on the medium under consideration. At least two studies report that newspapers exert a greater agenda-setting effect than does television. In fact, one survey found that during a political campaign television appeared to alter its coverage to conform to voter interest, while newspapers appeared to shape the voters' agendas. Other research studies have attempted to clarify the differences between the influence of newspapers and television on agenda setting. Interestingly enough, newspapers seemed to become more influential as researchers examined more detailed and differentiated levels of an agenda for a particular topic. For example, one team of researchers postulated that there were at least three different levels of agenda setting: Level one consisted of broad issues such as crime; level two consisted of various subissues such as gun control or mandatory jail sentences; level three consisted of specific information about these subissues such as arguments for or against gun control. The findings of the study revealed that newspapers had more influence on agenda setting at all levels than did television, but were especially important at levels two and three. A person's experience with a certain news topic will also influence the agenda-setting effect. Stories about inflation, a topic that most consumers experience directly, will have little impact on the public's perception of the importance of this issue. On the other hand, coverage of foreign affairs, where most people lack direct experience, has been found to have a considerable agenda-setting effect.

The occurrence of the agenda-setting effect also depends on other factors, namely, a person's interest in the information, age, education, and political involvement, to name a few. In general, however, we can conclude that the mass media, newspapers and magazines in particular, do have an impact on their audience's perception of certain topics and issues. Sometimes, although not always, television will be less influential than newspapers, probably because of the different characteristics of the two media.

Are You a TV Addict?

There are numerous references to the addictive nature of TV in popular literature: "Turned On, Tuned In, Strung Out" in *High Times*; "Are You a Secret TV Addict?" in *Vogue*; "Turned On but Tuned Out" in *Redbook*; Marie Winn's *The Plug-In Drug*. Is it possible to be addicted to TV the same way some people are addicted to drugs?

A doctoral dissertation by Robin Smith attempted to construct a scale that would measure possible TV addiction. Some of the items follow. (Score yourself 4 if you answer "always"; 3 for "frequently"; 2 for "sometimes"; and 1 for "never.")

1. I feel depressed when I can't watch TV.

2. I lose track of the time while I'm watching TV.

3. I can't walk away from the TV once it is on.

4. When I'm watching TV I feel like I can't stop.

5. I feel nervous when I can't watch TV.

6. I can't think of anything to do on the weekend or the holidays.

7. I'll watch anything that's on TV.

Total your score. If it's above 14, you scored above the average TV watcher.

Professor Smith's research leading to the development of this scale indicated that if there were TV addicts out there, they were hard to find. None of the 491 people surveyed scored high enough to be considered an addict. Smith concluded that the popular conception of TV as a drug was invalid.

TELEVISION AND COGNITIVE SKILLS

Television has been charged with producing a generation of couch potatoes who simply vegetate in front of the tube, showing little sign of intellectual life. What does the research tell us? This section will briefly examine the connections between TV viewing, IQ, and school achievement.

At first glance, the relationship between TV viewing and IQ seems simple enough. Heavy viewers tend to have slightly lower IQs. On closer examination, however, age seems to be a complicating factor. A couple of surveys showed that in children up to the age of ten or eleven, heavy viewing was associated with a higher IQ. Older children showed the opposite pattern. After about age twelve, the familiar negative relationship showed up. (It may be that the general level of TV programming is geared to the level of a bright ten- or eleven-year-old. As these kids get older, they tend to outgrow their attraction to TV.) Note that these data do not establish that TV *causes* a lower IQ. It may be that youngsters with a low IQ are drawn to the undemanding world of TV for entertainment.

The relationship between TV viewing and school achievement became a hot news item in the 1970s and 1980s because of the steep drop of SAT scores. Some critics blamed much of this decline on TV viewing. The research findings in this area suggest that there is a slight negative relationship between school grades and

TV viewing. In one study that statistically controlled for IQ, heavy TV viewers tended to score lower on tests of vocabulary and language achievement than did light viewers, but math achievement scores were not linked to amount of TV viewing. Another study noted that the type of TV content was important. Youngsters who watched a lot of news and educational programs did better than kids who watched lots of action-adventure shows.

Studies of the relationship between reading achievement and TV viewing are hard to summarize. Most have found a slight negative relationship between entertainment viewing and reading skills, but this relationship was influenced by such factors as IQ, social class, age, and parental attitudes toward reading. In short, TV is certainly not the biggest culprit behind the slide in SAT scores. Its impact is relatively light. By the same token, the hours that youngsters invest in watching TV don't seem to pay off in better academic skills.

SUGGESTIONS FOR FURTHER READING

The books listed below are valuable sources for additional information on the topics discussed in this chapter.

ADLER, RICHARD, GERALD LESSER, LAURENCE KRASNY MERINGOFF, THOMAS S. ROBERTSON, JOHN R. ROSSITER, AND SCOTT WARD, *The Effects of Television Advertising on Children,* Lexington, Mass.: D. C. Heath, 1980.

BARCUS, EARL, *Images of Life on Children's Television,* New York: Praeger, 1983.

COMSTOCK, GEORGE, *Television in America,* Beverly Hills, Calif.: Sage, 1980.

COMSTOCK, GEORGE, STEVEN CHAFFEE, NATAN KATZMAN, MAX McCOMBS, AND DONALD ROBERTS, *Television and Human Behavior,* New York: Columbia University Press, 1978.

DENTON, ROBERT, AND GARY WOODWARD, *Political Communication in America,* New York: Praeger, 1985.

GRABER, DORIS, *Mass Media and American Politics,* Washington, D.C.: Congressional Quarterly Press, 1989.

GREENBERG, BRADLEY, AND EDWIN PARKER, *The Kennedy Assassination and the American Public,* Stanford, Calif.: Stanford University Press, 1965.

JEFFRES, LEO, *Mass Media: Processes and Effects,* Prospect Height, Ill.: Waveland Press, 1986.

LIEBERT, ROBERT M., JOHN NEALE, AND EMILY DAVIDSON, *The Early Window: Effects of Television on Children and Youth,* New York: Pergamon Press, 1988.

McCOMBS, MAXWELL, AND LEE BECKER, *Using Mass Communication Theory,* Englewood Cliffs, N.J.: Prentice-Hall, 1979.

PALMER, EDWARD, AND AIMEE DORR, *Children and the Faces of Television,* New York: Academic Press, 1980.

TAN, ALEXIS, *Mass Communication Theories and Research,* New York: Wiley, 1985.

Chapter 22

The Effects of Mass Communication on Behavior

E manuel Priola was a hard worker. He would spend many long hours at his West Orange, New Jersey, bar, sometimes not closing until well after midnight. But on this particular autumn evening in 1938, he did an extraordinary thing—he closed up early. Hustling the dozen or so customers out the door, Emanuel Priola rushed home to save his wife and children from the Martians who were invading New York. Luckily for Mr. Priola (and, for that matter, the rest of the world), the Martians hadn't landed. He had just been fooled by a CBS radio dramatization of H.G. Wells' "War of the Worlds."

The Air Lines Pilots Association knew it was a bad idea. Shortly before Christmas in 1966, NBC was planning to broadcast a made-for-TV movie, written by Rod Serling, called *The Doomsday Flight*. In the film, a man hides a bomb that is rigged to an altimeter aboard an airliner. If the plane drops below a certain altitude, the bomb will explode. While the plane is airborne, the man calls the airline and offers to disclose the location of the bomb in exchange for a large sum of money. The Pilots Association was afraid that such a film would prompt some unstable individuals to imitate what they had seen. The pilots were right. Even before the telecast was over, one bomb threat based on the idea in the film was telephoned to an airline. In the days following the broadcast, twelve more similar threats were received. (Ignoring the above, Australian TV broadcast the same film in 1971. The effects were the same. In fact, Qantas Airlines paid out half a million dollars in ransom to a person who called in to report a bomb on one of their planes heading for Hong Kong.)

The manager of the Esplanade Triplex Theater in Oakland, California, was uneasy. Paramount Pictures had chosen February 1979, to release one of its newest pictures, *The Warriors*. The film was about gang warfare in New York City, and the manager had noticed that it had attracted a rather unusual crowd to his California theater. Many in the crowd looked as though they belonged to gangs themselves. The audience was unusually rowdy during the screening of the film, but there were no major incidents and the manager began to breathe a little more easily as the crowd slowly filtered out into the lobby after the film was over. Suddenly, before anybody could tell what was happening, a knife fight, much like the one portrayed in the film, broke out between two rival gangs. Before the manager could stop it, an eighteen-year-old boy was fatally stabbed.

In the early part of 1988, it seemed as though history was about to repeat itself. A new movie, *Colors*—directed by Dennis Hopper and starring Sean Penn—was scheduled to open in southern California. Like *The Warriors,* the movie was about gang warfare but this time the setting was Los Angeles. To make matters worse, L.A. was in the midst of an epidemic of gang violence—nearly 90 people had been killed since the year began. Mindful of their experience with *The Warriors,* the authorities were ready. When *Colors* opened in L.A., police officers were stationed at theaters in areas where there had been gang activity. The massive police presence was effective. There were no major incidents of violence, although two theaters did report that rival gangs got into shoving matches after watching the film.

These four incidents, drawn from four different decades, highlight the dramatic power that mass media possess—the power to affect a person's behavior. Typically, of course, the media are not this influential. Not everyone who listened to "War of the Worlds" fled for the hills, and not everyone who saw *The Doomsday Flight* phoned in a bomb threat. Nonetheless, the mass media have the potential to influence audience behavior, and throughout the years there has been an expression of social concern over the extent of this impact.

As we have seen, some of this concern has been reflected in formal and informal controls over the media. For example, the Supreme Court has recognized that children are a special audience that need protection from exposure to potentially harmful material, such as pornography (see Chapter 17). Additionally, television networks recognize that there may be harmful effects for some people in viewing some program content. Consequently, the networks have standards and guidelines that attempt to minimize any negative impact (see Chapter 18). Moreover, the media are a powerful force in shaping a society's culture. This chapter will focus on what is known about the media's impact on actual behavior. Our goal is to present a basic overview of the effects of media on how people behave.

INVESTIGATING MASS COMMUNICATION EFFECTS

There are many ways to investigate what is or is not an effect of mass communication. Some individuals claim that personal observation is the best way of establishing proof. Others rely on expert opinions and evaluations; still others point to common sense when they wish to support their views. All of these methods have their place, and each can be quite valid. Nonetheless, in an area as complicated as this, many feel that the best sources of information are those derived from scientific study of the media's impact on individuals. Consequently, most of this chapter will consist of a discussion and summary of these studies. You should keep in mind that when it comes to gathering information about media effects, scientists have typically used two main methods:

1. The **survey** is carried out in the real world and usually consists of a large group of individuals who answer questions put to them via a questionnaire. Although the survey is usually not sufficient proof of cause and effect, it does help to establish associations between various factors. A special kind of survey, a **panel study,** allows researchers to be more confident about attributing patterns of cause and effect in survey data. The panel study collects data from the same people at two or more different points in time. As a result, it is possible, for example, using sophisticated techniques that control

the effects of other variables, to see if viewing televised violence at an early age is related to aggressive behavior at a later date. Panel studies are expensive and take a long time to complete.

2. The **experiment** is performed in a laboratory and usually consists of the controlled manipulation of a single factor to determine its impact on another factor. A special kind of experiment, a **field experiment,** is conducted in a real-life setting. Field experiments are more realistic than laboratory experiments but they are also harder to control. Experiments are useful because they help establish causality.

MEDIA EFFECTS ON BEHAVIOR: A CAPSULE HISTORY

It was early motion pictures that first inspired questions about the impact of the entertainment media on society. After all, children would sit for hours in a darkened theater, away from parental supervision, and watch films produced by the inhabitants of Sin City (more precisely, Hollywood). During the late 1920s and early 1930s, the "gangster" film became quite popular. (Some of these films still show up on late-night TV. Try to watch one if the opportunity arises to see what all the shouting was about.) People were lining up to see movies such as *Me, Gangster* (1928), *Little Caesar* (1930), and *The Public Enemy* (1931). It wasn't long before concerned parents and civic groups began to question the impact of these films on their children.

Consequently, in 1929 the first full-scale investigation into the effects of the entertainment film was begun. The study (actually, there were twelve studies in all) was sponsored by the prestigious Payne Fund. Experiments and surveys were carried out to address such questions as: How do the mores of the movies compare with the mores of America? Do films directly or indirectly affect the conduct of children? Are films related to delinquency and crime? Although these studies did not conclusively prove that movies caused delinquency, their findings brought a tremendous amount of pressure to bear on the government and on the industry to take action. As a result, the production code of the Motion Pictures Producers and Distributors of America, a powerful industry group, was strengthened to make sure that films did not portray gangsters in a favorable light.

Growing Public Concern

The potentially harmful effects of gangster and action-adventure radio programs were again the subject of limited research attention during the 1930s. The area that aroused the most research interest, however, was the political impact of the mass media, especially that of radio. Franklin Roosevelt had used radio effectively during his first two terms in office. In Louisiana, Huey Long also used radio addresses to increase his political influence. Many people feared that a skilled political demagogue might use the new radio medium to shape popular opinion to his advantage. As a result, large-scale studies of the voting process were conducted during the 1940 presidential campaign to gauge the extent of media influence. After an interruption caused by World War II, the 1948 election was similarly studied by sociologists and political scientists. Somewhat surprisingly, these researchers found that the media had little direct effect on political decision making. Instead, personal influence was more important, and individuals called "opinion leaders" were thought to be quite

Franklin D. Roosevelt effectively used radio as a political communication tool during his ''fireside chats'' with the nation. The increasing importance of radio as a political force prompted several large-scale studies during the 1940s. (The Bettmann Archive)

important in transmitting political information (recall the discussion of the multistep flow in Chapter 19).

The explosive growth of television in the early 1950s refocused research attention on media impact on young people. Families with children were among the first to acquire TV sets, and children tended to watch a lot of television. Some of the cartoon programs and slapstick comedies that were the staples of early television contained a good deal of violence. Parents were worried that, as had been the case with movies, their children would imitate and adopt some of the violent behaviors they were watching. This concern was translated to the national level when in 1952 Senator Estes Kefauver held hearings into the causes of juvenile delinquency. Part of the hearings examined the effect of violent portrayals on television and in comic books. When this same committee held hearings again during 1954–1955, it concluded that violent programming in large doses could be potentially harmful to children.

The growing importance of television was also evident in the increased attention given to it by scientists concerned with the effects of mass communication. In the late 1950s and early 1960s three important books discussing the impact of the media, and of TV in particular, were published. Two were somewhat similar in approach. The first of these, *Television and the Child,* appeared in 1958 and discussed the results of interviews with several thousand English youngsters. In this English study, the researchers found that television had an impact on children's values and their perceptions of the world. Three American scientists—Schramm, Lyle, and Parker—

reported the results of surveys conducted in ten American cities in their book *Television in the Lives of Our Children* (1961). In many ways their reported findings were similar to those of their British counterparts. The American researchers noted that as children grew older, those with lower IQ scores watched more television than did those with higher IQ scores. They also noted that children who had unsatisfactory social relationships reported heavier viewing. These researchers further reported that although there was no indication that television causes delinquency or violent behavior in most normal children, certain children might be susceptible. In short, Schramm and his colleagues emphasized that the intellectual and emotional characteristics of children were important factors in determining TV's influence.

The third book, *The Effects of Mass Communication* (1960), was written by a sociologist, Joseph Klapper. Its main thesis stressed the social and psychological factors that would "mediate" the direct effects of the mass media. Klapper argued that because of these mediating factors, the media would operate far more frequently to reinforce a person's behaviors, attitudes, and values than they would to change them. Based on his research, Klapper concluded that although the mass media do not necessarily cause viewers to become more apathetic, passive, or aggressive, they might reinforce tendencies already present in the viewers. (Taken together, these three books marked the emergence of the effects of mass communication as an area of scientific research and served to highlight many areas of concern that were to encourage more research. We will have more to say about many of these topics later in this chapter.)

During the 1960s, there was considerable concern over the impact of the mass media, as evidenced by Senate subcommittee hearings on juvenile delinquency conducted in 1961 and again in 1964. The report of this subcommittee warned that violent television content might cause antisocial behavior among young people. The concern was reinforced by the assassinations and civil disorders of the middle sixties, and in 1967 President Lyndon Johnson appointed the National Commission on the Causes and Prevention of Violence. The commission reiterated the need for more significant research in the area and concluded that a "constant diet of violent behavior on television had an adverse effect on human character and attitudes." In addition, the commission studied the role of the news media in creating and aggravating civil disorders by their very presence on the scene.

At about this same time, another national commission was preparing a report on a totally different topic. Because of less stringent laws governing pornographic and obscene materials, "adult-oriented" films, books, and magazines were becoming more prevalent. The National Commission on Obscenity and Pornography was established to examine the potentially negative effects of this material. When it released its report in 1970, it urged, among other things, that all laws prohibiting the distribution of pornographic materials be repealed.

The 1970s: Concern over TV Violence

The big story of 1970, however, concerned the impact of television violence. Through the efforts of Senator John Pastore, the Office of the Surgeon General (the same office that had earlier released a report on the health hazards of smoking) was given a million dollars to sponsor a program of original research to "establish scientifically insofar as possible what harmful effects, if any, television programs have on our children." A scientific advisory committee, composed of distinguished scientists, was to be set up to conduct the research program. Unfortunately, controversy soon developed over the way committee members were selected. (The television networks were allowed to veto potential committee members whom they felt would be "biased" in their outlooks.)

Ultimately, research was completed and the report released in 1972. Consisting of a summary written by the advisory committee and five technical volumes encompassing twenty-three separate research reports and more than forty separate technical papers, the project was the single most concerted research effort directed at determining the effects of violent media content on the audience. More controversy met the release of this report. Several researchers who had contributed technical reports to the series felt that the summary volume, written by the advisory committee (which consisted of two employees in the research departments of NBC and CBS, respectively, and several others who had done consulting work for the networks), did not accurately summarize the results. Not surprisingly, criticism also surrounded the reporting of the research results in the popular press. Newspaper and television reports were based on the summary volume rather than on the technical reports. Critics charged that the summary volume was a "whitewash" that minimized the negative effects of viewing televised violence.

It was unfortunate that so much controversy obscured the findings of this research effort, which was a valuable project, reporting significant results about the effects of televised violence. Using both the survey and the experimental techniques, researchers had concluded that exposure to televised violence could increase the probability of antisocial behavior over both the short and long term. In addition, the researchers announced evidence of a causal link between viewing TV violence and antisocial behavior. This was the first time such a statement had been made by a body of distinguished researchers. Reinforcement for this causal link came a few years later from a study done in England by William Belson. Belson's survey, which examined more than 1500 London youngsters, reported data demonstrating that watching violence on television apparently prompted the commission of serious aggressive acts. In 1982, a follow-up study to the Surgeon General's report confirmed the findings of the original and stated in stronger terms the link between viewing televised violence and antisocial behavior.

In the early 1980s, a considerable amount of attention was given to studying the media's impact on what was called **prosocial behavior** (simply a catchall term that researchers assign to behaviors that are judged to be desirable or worthwhile under the circumstances). The popularity of this topic had declined by the mid-1980s, possibly because of the difficulty in defining precisely what was meant by the concept and the difficulty in finding links between viewing prosocial behavior on TV and real-life prosocial actions.

In the middle 1980s, a great deal of research attention was devoted to investigating the behavioral effects of the new technologies. Several studies examined who first acquired VCRs, teletext, cable, or home computers. Other research analyzed how the new technologies were used by consumers and how much time was spent with each. Still other researchers tried to determine what impact the new media were having on society. In the area of political communication, two topics attracted research attention. The first had to do with the impact of televised debates between presidential and vice-presidential candidates on voting behavior. The second had to do with the effects of exit polling and early projections of winners on the outcomes of elections. (Both of these topics are discussed further below.) In the late 1980s, sparked by the publication of a new federal report on the topic, a considerable amount of attention and controversy were focused on the effects of aggressive and nonaggressive pornography. The results of this research (summarized later in this chapter) were at the center of a scientific and political debate.

To summarize,

1. As of 1989, the bulk of media research has been concerned with potentially antisocial effects of the mass media on their audiences.

2. Research questions deemed important by the federal government have received the major share of research attention (in part because the federal government can make money for research available).

3. Most research into the effects of mass communication on behavior has focused on children and adolescents.

4. Since the 1960s, studies concerning the impact of television have been the most numerous.

We will now examine more closely some of the topics mentioned in this summary. We begin by considering the topic that has generated the most research attention: the effects of TV violence.

THE IMPACT OF TELEVISED VIOLENCE

Does television viewing prompt violent or other antisocial behaviors on the part of the viewer? As we have just seen, this question has been debated for the better part of three decades. It is a complicated issue, and the absolute answer has not yet been found. Nonetheless, enough evidence has been gathered so that we can begin to point to some preliminary conclusions. In order to arrive at these conclusions it will be necessary to examine research data from surveys and from experiments.

Survey Results

The following represent abbreviated and modified questionnaire items taken from surveys designed to analyze violent TV viewing and aggressive behavior.

About how often do you watch the following TV programs:

	Almost Always	Often	Sometimes	Never
"Hunter"	_____	_____	_____	_____
"Cheers"	_____	_____	_____	_____
"Midnight Caller"	_____	_____	_____	_____
"The Cosby Show"	_____	_____	_____	_____
"Miami Vice"	_____	_____	_____	_____
"The Equalizer"	_____	_____	_____	_____
	_____	_____	_____	_____

Next, what would you do if these things happened to you?

1. Pretend somebody you know takes something from you and won't give it back. What would you do?

_____ Hit the other person and take my property back

_____ Call the police

_____ Ask the person to return it

_____ Nothing

2. Pretend somebody is telling lies about you. What would you do?

_____ Hit the person and make the person stop

_____ Ask the person to stop telling lies

_____ Nothing

As you can see, with measures like the above (assuming, of course, a questionnaire that was much longer), it would be possible to index a person's viewing of programs that generally contain violence. It would also be possible to measure that same person's tendency to report his or her willingness to use violence in everyday situations. If violent TV viewing does affect behavior, we would expect to find some relationship between reported heavy viewing of violence and an individual's own self-report of aggressive tendencies. If we do not find such a link, we might assume that exposure to media violence has no impact on subsequent aggressive tendencies. If, however, we do find a connection, we might conclude that media violence could actually cause aggression. We could not be sure, however, because survey data alone are not sufficient to establish a cause-and-effect relationship. (It might be possible, for example, that aggressive tendencies actually cause people to view violent TV shows, or that some third factor, related to both viewing TV violence and aggression, is the real cause.) We must also keep in mind that there are different ways of measuring exposure to TV violence and aggressive tendencies. In fact, as we shall see, some of the inconsistencies found in survey research might be due to variations in the way that exposure to violence is measured.

Early surveys revealed no significant relationship between general television viewing and aggressive actions. The British surveys reported in *Television and the Child* found no differences in aggressive tendencies among young children who had access to TV sets and those who didn't. Schramm and his co-workers found the same in a survey done among Canadian youths. These researchers also found no differences on scales designed to measure antisocial aggression between young people classified as heavy viewers and others labeled as light viewers. Overall exposure to television, however, is perhaps not the same as overall exposure to *television violence,* a factor that might account for the lack of a relationship.

The Surgeon General's report discusses other surveys that used somewhat different measures of exposure to TV violence. At least two studies in which young people were asked to name their favorite TV programs found a connection between aggression and the number of violent programs named, but at least two other surveys using similar techniques failed to uncover any such association. More recent research suggests why such inconsistencies may have occurred. It appears that classifying individuals on the basis of selecting four or five favorite programs may not be an accurate measure of the total amount of TV violence that they see. Interestingly, most surveys that measure viewing of TV violence by measuring all programs usually watched in a specified time period (the abbreviated form of that particular measurement technique is illustrated in the example preceding this section) have consistently demonstrated a positive relationship between such viewing and measures of aggressiveness. This relationship persists when the effects of other factors (such as sex, school performance, and social class) are statistically controlled.

Viewed as a whole, these studies and other surveys compiled over the years are difficult to sum up. Perhaps the most concise generalization about the results of survey research is one that appears in a recent summary of television research findings. After carefully analyzing all survey results, the authors of this summary state: ". . . we conclude that the evidence to date indicates that there is a significant correlation between the viewing of violent television programs and aggressive behavior in day-to-day life."

Nevertheless, as already mentioned, a relationship is not necessarily evidence of cause and effect. Remember, however, that the special survey technique known as a panel study gives us a little more confidence in making cause-and-effect statements based on survey data. Since panel studies cost a lot and sometimes take years to complete, not many exist. Further, the results from those that are available are not as clear as we might like them to be. One panel study was included in the 1972 Surgeon General's report on television and social behavior. Although its methods might have been stronger, it found evidence that viewing violent TV shows at an early age was a cause of aggression in later life.

Additional survey evidence appeared in 1982 with the publication of *Television and Aggression: A Panel Study*. This book reported the results of a three-year research project sponsored by the NBC television network. Data on aggression, TV viewing, and a large number of sociological variables were collected on six different occasions from children in two Midwestern cities. Eventually, about 1200 boys in grades two through six participated in the main survey. Exposure to TV violence was measured by giving each child a program checklist. Aggression was measured by asking each boy to nominate peers who "hit and punch other people" or "hurt others by pushing or shoving."

Lengthy and detailed analysis of the data suggested that there was no relationship between violent TV viewing and subsequent aggressive behavior. Later, other researchers were given the opportunity to reanalyze the NBC data. One reexamination did find some partial evidence of a causal relationship between TV violence and aggression, but its impact was tiny. In sum, if a causal relationship was present in the NBC data, it was extremely weak and hard to find.

In 1986, an international team of scientists reported the results of panel studies done in five countries: the United States, Finland, Australia, Israel, and Poland. The U.S. study and the Polish study found that early TV viewing was significantly related to later aggression. The Finnish study reached a similar conclusion for boys but found no similar relationship for girls. In Israel, viewing TV violence seemed to be a cause of subsequent aggression among boys and girls who lived in urban areas but not for those who lived in the country. The panel study done in Australia was not able to find a causal relationship. Despite these differences, the five panels were consistent in at least two findings. First, the relationship between the viewing of violence and aggression tended to be somewhat weak. Second, there was a pattern of circularity in causation. Viewing violent TV caused some children to become more aggressive. Being aggressive, in turn, caused some children to watch more violent TV.

Children test their wits and reflexes with the popular Nintendo interactive video game. Critics have voiced concern over such toys, suggesting that they encourage aggressive behavior and promote long hours in front of the TV screen. (Tom Kelly)

What are we to make of all these panel studies? On the whole, they seem to suggest that there is a mutual causal connection between watching TV violence and performing aggressive acts. This connection, however, is small and influenced by individual and cultural factors.

Perhaps at this point we should turn to the results of laboratory studies to aid us further in forming a conclusion about what causes what. In the lab, time order is strictly controlled and possible third factors can be ruled out (because the random assignment of people to experimental conditions would cancel out any extraneous influences). If experimental studies confirm survey results, we could feel more confident about drawing a correlation between viewing violence on television and aggressive acts in everyday behavior.

Experimental Results

Imagine the following. It is a cold winter night. As part of the requirements of Psychology 100, a course in which you are enrolled, you are required to serve as a subject in three hours of research. Tonight is your night to fulfill part of your obligation. Thus you find yourself trudging across campus to the Psychology Building. Upon arriving, you join several dozen other students in a large auditorium. Before long an individual enters the room, introduces himself as Professor so-and-so, and tells you that you are about to begin your first experiment of the evening.

Professor so-and-so has a new IQ test that he is trying to develop and needs your cooperation. The test booklet is passed out and you are told to begin. As soon as you start the test, you realize that it is unlike any IQ test you have ever seen before. There are questions about advanced calculus, early Greek architecture, and organic chemistry, which you have no idea how to answer. In a few minutes, Professor so-and-so starts making sarcastic comments: "You'll never finish college if this simple test takes you so long"; "It looks as if this group will certainly flunk out"; "High school students have finished this test by now." Finally, with an air of exasperation, the professor says, "There's no hope for you. Hand in the papers. Since most of you won't be in school after this semester's grades, let me say good-bye to you now." With that, the professor storms out of the room.

A few minutes go by and then another individual enters the room and calls out two lists of names. Each group is assigned to another room down the hall. When you report to your assigned room, you find another professor already there. She tells you that this is the second experiment you will participate in tonight. It is a study to see how much people remember from films. You are going to be shown a brief excerpt from a film, and then you will be asked questions about it. The lights go out, and all of a sudden you are watching an eight-minute fight scene from a Kirk Douglas film called *The Champion*. In the movie, Douglas, playing a boxer, gets the stuffing beaten out of him as he competes for the championship. (Unknown to you, that other group of students is also seeing a film. At the same time you're watching Douglas get battered, they're viewing a totally different scene from *Canal Boats in Venice*.) When the film ends, you are asked several memory questions about its content.

You are then directed to yet another room. Once in this cubicle, you are told that the third and last experiment is to begin. You are seated in front of a rather strange looking machine with a dial that can be moved from a setting of one to eleven. You also notice a button and a light connected to something behind the machine. The researcher explains that you are to be part of an experiment designed to investigate memory. In another room, but wired up to this same machine, is a student who is learning a word-association test. Every time this other student makes a mistake, you are to punish him by giving him a shock. The dial on your panel determines the intensity of the shock; when you press the button, it will be administered. You can choose any level you like; you can hold the button down as long as you like. The experimenter then gives you a level-two shock to show you what it feels like. You jump and wonder why you didn't take botany instead of psych. Your thoughts are interrupted, however, when the little light on the panel flashes on. The other student has made a mistake. It's your job to administer punishment. Your hand reaches for the dial. . . .

The Catharsis vs. Stimulation Debate

The above is an abstracted, simplified, and condensed version of the prototype experimental design used in several key studies to investigate the impact of media violence. The idea behind this experiment is to test two rival theories about the effects of watching violence. The first theory is thousands of years old; it is called the **catharsis theory** and can be traced back to Aristotle. This theory holds that viewing scenes of aggression can actually purge the viewer's own aggressive feelings. Thus a person who sees a violent television program or movie might end up less likely to commit violence. The other theory, called the **stimulation theory,** argues just the opposite. It suggests that seeing scenes of violence will actually stimulate an individual to behave more violently afterward.

As you may realize, in the above hypothetical experiment everybody was first insulted and presumably angered (this part of the experiment gave you some hostility to be purged); one group saw a violent film while the other saw a nonviolent film. Both groups were then given a turn at the punishment machine. If catharsis is right, then the group that saw *The Champion* should give less intense shocks; if stimulation is correct, then *The Champion* group should give more intense shocks.

The catharsis vs. stimulation debate was one of the earliest to surface in the study of mass media's effects. One early study seemed to point to catharsis, but a series of studies carried out by psychologist Leonard Berkowitz and his colleagues at the University of Wisconsin found strong support for the stimulation hypothesis. Since that time, the bulk of the evidence seems consistent: Watching media violence tends to stimulate aggressive behavior on the part of the viewer. There is little evidence for catharsis.

Bandura's Experiment

The catharsis vs. stimulation question was only one of several topics that sparked early experimental work in the investigation of the effects of the media. Another controversy arose over the possibility that TV and movies were serving as a school for violence. Would children imitate violent behavior they had just observed in films or TV programs in their own real-life play behaviors? A series of experiments

A series of still photographs of the famous study by Bandura, Ross, and Ross (1961). In this experiment children watched adults act aggressively toward a BoBo doll. When allowed to play in the same room, these same children imitated the behavior of the adult models. (Courtesy of Albert Bandura)

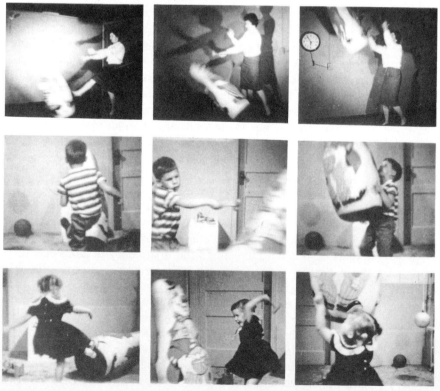

Imitating TV

Bandura's laboratory experiments showed that young children can learn violent behaviors from TV. An article in the December 28, 1985, edition of *TV Guide* demonstrated that this phenomenon was not confined to the lab. A family court judge in New York City banned two teenage brothers from watching pro wrestling matches on TV. Why? The two boys had been imitating what they saw and had injured each other with body slams and choke holds.

conducted by psychologist Albert Bandura and his colleagues during the 1960s indicated that, in fact, films and TV might teach aggressive behaviors.

Preschool children were shown films in which a model reacted violently to a large rubber doll (called a Bobo doll). When children were placed in a play situation similar to the one they had just observed, they mimicked the behaviors they had just seen, performing far more aggressively toward the unfortunate Bobo doll than did children who had not seen the film. It was further determined that children would behave more aggressively if they were rewarded for doing so or if they saw the model in the film rewarded. Of course, as you are probably aware, there is a big difference between hitting an inanimate doll and hitting a human being. To account for this, more recent studies have substituted a human being dressed as a clown for the faithful Bobo doll. Although more children were willing to hit the rubber doll, a large number also physically assaulted the human clown. This reaction did not occur among children who had not seen the violent film.

Complicating Factors

Of course, there are many complicating factors that might influence the results of such experiments. To begin with, many of these studies used specially made films and videotapes. In laboratory situations, the experimental "program" may not be able to duplicate the impact of real-life TV or films. In those films and tapes produced especially for laboratory use, the violence is concentrated in a short period; there is usually a clear connection between the violence and its motivations and consequences. Contemporary films or TV shows are not this direct, and violence is usually embedded in a larger story line. Punishment for violence may not occur until the end of the program. Motives may be mixed or unclear.

Further, it is likely that a person's age, sex, social class, and prior level of aggression will influence the ultimate effect of viewing televised violence. Boys, for example, tend to be more affected by TV violence than girls. Children who come from homes where there are no explicit guidelines condemning violence also seem to be more strongly affected. Evidence concerning age and social class is not as clear-cut. It also appears that a similarity between the setting and circumstances surrounding televised violence and the situation in which a person finds himself or herself immediately after viewing is an important factor. The more alike the two settings, the more aggressively the person is likely to behave. (Recall the example of *The Warriors* mentioned in the beginning of this chapter. Also, see boxed material.)

Finally, the presence or absence of others and their reactions directly influence aggression. If children were watching an aggressive film in the company of an adult who made positive comments about the media violence, they acted more aggressively than children who viewed with a silent adult. Conversely, children who heard the on-screen aggression condemned committed fewer aggressive acts. It has also been shown that children who view violence in pairs act more aggressively than children who are alone.

Field Experiments

Recall that field experiments are experiments that take place in a natural setting. People are studied in their typical environment, where they probably react more naturally than they do in the lab. On the other hand, field experiments are subject to the contaminating influences of outside events.

The results of field experiments are not entirely consistent but they do suggest some preliminary conclusions. At least two field experiments done in the early 1970s revealed no link between TV and aggression. On the other hand, five field experiments have yielded data consonant with the survey and lab data. Their main conclusion is that people who watched a steady diet of violent programs tended to exhibit more antisocial or aggressive behavior.

One of the more elaborate field experiments involved identifying a Canadian town that was surrounded by mountains and unable to receive a TV signal until 1974. Two similar towns were selected for comparison—one could get only Canadian TV while the other could get Canadian and U.S. channels. The research team gathered data from all three towns in 1974 and again two years later. Children in the town that just got U.S. TV showed an increase in their rate of aggressive acts that was more than three times higher than that of children living in the other two towns. Taken as a whole, although the results from the field experiments are not as striking as they might be, they tend to support the notion that violent TV viewing fosters aggressive behavior.

Let us now try to summarize the results of these surveys and experiments. Although no single survey or experiment can provide a conclusive answer about the effects of media violence and although every single study can be criticized for certain shortcomings, there appears to be a thread of consistency running throughout these studies. Surveys and panel studies have indicated that there is a relationship between viewing violent programs and aggressive behavior. Lab and field experiments also have shown that watching violence increases the possibility of behaving aggressively. Taken as a whole, these results encourage a tentative acceptance of the proposition that watching violence on television increases aggressiveness on the part of at least some viewers. This conclusion, however, should be qualified.

Viewing TV violence is only one of many factors that might prompt a person to behave aggressively and, in relative terms, its influence is not particularly strong. But is a weak relationship an inconsequential relationship? Much of the recent debate about TV violence has centered on this question. In statistical terms, researchers gauge the strength of any relationship by the amount of variability in one measure that is accounted for by the other. For example, height and weight are two factors that are related. If I know how tall you are, I can make a better guess about your weight than if I didn't know your height. I may not get your weight exactly right, but at least I'll be closer to the correct figure. Consequently, height "explains" some of the variability associated with weight. If two factors are perfectly related, one explains 100 percent of the variability of the other. If two factors are strongly related, one might account for 60–70 percent of the variability of the other. If two factors are not related, for example, weight and IQ, one would explain 0 percent of the

Triggering Violence: Appropriate Targets

After an individual has seen a violent film or TV program, his or her aggressive tendencies might remain in low gear unless something in the postviewing environment sets them off. It is possible, for example, that a person who has witnessed scenes of a brutal fight in a movie might not exhibit any aggression immediately afterwards unless that person encounters something or someone that has some association with the filmed fight.

In a series of intriguing experiments, Dr. Leonard Berkowitz and his associates at the University of Wisconsin studied one circumstance that seems important in triggering violent behavior: the similarity between the victim of the screen violence and the potential target of the viewer's aggression. In one experiment, similar in design to the simplified experiment reported in the text, college students were insulted by a confederate of the experimenter who was posing as another subject. The confederate was introduced to one group of subjects as a ''speech major'' and yet to another group as a ''college boxer.'' The insulted subjects were then shown either a violent film of a boxing match (the fight sequence from *The Champion* in which star Kirk Douglas gets beaten up) or a nonviolent film. Afterwards, all participants were given a chance to administer electric shocks to the confederate (the one who had earlier insulted them) as part of an alleged learning experiment. What group gave the larger number of shocks? The group that had seen the boxing film and that had been insulted by the ''college boxer.''

In a follow-up study, Berkowitz linked the film's victim and the potential target by giving them the same name. Again, two films were used—the boxing film starring *Kirk* Douglas and another nonviolent but exciting film of a track race. One group of subjects was insulted by a confederate called ''Bob.'' Another group of subjects was insulted by a confederate named ''Kirk,'' the same name as that of the victim in the movie, a ''coincidence'' that was pointed out by the experimenter. Each group then saw either a violent or nonviolent film and was given a chance to administer electric shocks to the person who had recently insulted them. What group gave the most shocks? As you might have already surmised, the group that saw the boxing film and that had been insulted by ''Kirk.''

We can conclude from the above experiments that one important condition for the triggering of violent behavior is the availability of an appropriate target who resembles the victim in the media portrayal of violence.

variability of the other. As far as TV violence and aggression are concerned, exposure to TV violence typically explains from about 2–9 percent of the variability of aggression. In other words, about 91–98 percent of the variability in aggression is due to something else. Given these figures, is the impact of TV violence really that important in a practical sense?

The answer to this question is more political and philosophical than scientific, but research does provide some benchmarks for comparison. In psychology, the relationship between undergoing psychotherapy and being ''cured'' of your mental ailment is only slightly stronger than that between TV violence and aggression. Psychotherapy explains about 10 percent of the variability in cure rates. In relative terms, however, this means that psychotherapy increases the success rate from 34 percent to 66 percent of patients, hardly an outcome to be labeled inconsequential. Moreover, the effect size for TV violence's impact on antisocial behavior is only slightly less than that of the effect size between viewing ''Sesame Street'' and readiness for school. "Sesame Street," of course, was regarded as a great success. Furthermore, the Food and Drug Administration has released for general use several drugs whose therapeutic effect was about as great or even less than the size of the effect between TV violence and aggression. Thus, although the size of the effect is not great, it is not too different from effects in other areas that we treat as socially and practically meaningful. Even though the effect might be small, it is not necessarily trivial.

ENCOURAGING PROSOCIAL BEHAVIOR

Most of the early research into the effects of mass communication dealt with the negative or antisocial effects of the media. Increasing violence in society and rising crime rates were important social issues that attracted attention. Toward the end of the 1960s, however, sparked perhaps by the success of public television's "Sesame Street," researchers realized that many positive behaviors could be promoted by television programs. (These behaviors are generally referred to by the umbrella term of **prosocial behavior** and can include actions such as sharing, cooperating, self-control, and helping.) For the sake of simplicity, we will divide our discussion into three parts; each part will examine one specific area of prosocial behavior that has received research attention.

Therapeutic Effects

If film and television can have adverse effects on some people, it is possible that they might also encourage positive attitudes, such as courage, in children. Early studies demonstrated that these media could help children overcome psychological childhood phobias. For example, many children are afraid of dogs (caninophobia). In an early experiment, some fearful children viewed films of children playing with dogs while other fearful youngsters saw a different film. Subsequent to the film viewing, the youngsters exposed to the film portraying the play of youngsters and dogs were more willing to pet and play with dogs than the other group. There is even evidence that exposure to specially made TV programs can help overcome a very potent fear in young children—fear of going to the dentist (dentophobia). In this particular experiment, a film showed an eight-year-old boy climbing fearlessly into the dentist's chair while a nervous four-year-old looked on. As the film progressed, the younger child became more courageous until, when her turn came, she climbed fearlessly into the chair to be treated. This particular film was then shown to phobic youngsters. After viewing it, these same youngsters were far more likely to visit the dentist than were other fearful children who had not seen the film. Lastly, experiments done in a nursery school indicated that withdrawn children became more outgoing after watching films depicting appropriate nursery-school behavior. This is a rather dramatic finding when we consider that ordinarily such behavior change would have occurred only after rather intensive psychological therapy.

Developing Self-Control

Laboratory experiments have also shown that films and TV programs can affect a young child's self-control. These studies typically use a brief television program to depict a particular aspect of self-control. This program is shown to one group of children, while other groups see a different program or perhaps no program at all.

To illustrate, one study was designed to examine children's resistance to temptation. Five-year-olds were brought into a room containing several attractive toys and a dictionary. The boys were told they could not play with the toys but could look at the dictionary (not exactly a five-year-old's idea of fun). These boys were then divided into three groups. One group saw no film; a second group saw a film in which a boy played with these toys and was even joined by his mother (this was called the "model-rewarded" condition). In yet a third condition, youngsters saw a film in which a boy played with the toys but was scolded for doing so when his mother entered the room (this was the "model-punished" condition). Each boy was then left alone in the room, and hidden observers measured how much time each spent playing with the forbidden toys and how long it took to disobey. As you might expect, those boys who saw the model-punished film resisted temptation for a longer period of time and spent less time playing with the toys. (As it turned out, most boys who had seen the model-punished version didn't even attempt to play with the forbidden toys; also, as you might expect, the boys who saw the model-rewarded film played with the toys the longest.)

Cooperation, Sharing, and Helping

Experiments that have investigated sharing behavior usually use the same basic approach as described above in the self-control experiments. In this instance, however, children watch a film depicting a model playing a game and receiving a prize for winning (usually money). A film model then donates part of his or her winnings to charity. The child then wins at the same game and is also given the option to donate some money to charity. In general, the many experiments in this area indicate that observing a generous model prompts young people to behave more generously. Other experiments have shown that children are willing to imitate cooperative behavior that they have seen portrayed in a television program. One study showed children a segment of "The Waltons" in which cooperation was depicted. These children were more willing to help one another in a subsequent game-playing situation than were those who did not view that particular episode.

Survey Data

In comparison with the survey research examining antisocial behavior, there is little comparable survey research analyzing prosocial behavior. Apparently, the research effort in this area has just begun. Some data exist, however. Research on the CBS series "Fat Albert and the Cosby Kids" revealed that about 90 percent of approximately 700 children were able to express at least one prosocial theme from episodes of the series. Other research indicated that children who watched "Sesame Street" were able to identify accurately the cooperation messages contained in that program. Thus it appears that the prosocial messages are at least perceived. Do these messages influence the day-to-day behavior as measured in real life? One large-scale survey found little relationship between viewing prosocial programs and performing prosocial acts in school, when all other variables were statistically controlled.

Judging from this study, we can say that it is apparent that the relationship between viewing and prosocial behavior is much weaker than that between viewing and aggressive behavior. Closer examination indicates why this should be the case. Violent behaviors as portrayed on TV and in films are blatant, easy to see, and physical; prosocial behaviors are subtle, sometimes complicated, and largely verbal actions. Because children learn better from simple, direct, and active presentations,

The innovative Saturday morning children's program "Pee-wee's Playhouse" features an offbeat star and inanimate objects that move and speak. Its unique appeal and positive images have made it a popular program among older viewers as well as children. (Michael McLean & Associates)

aggressive behaviors may be more easily learned from media content. Further, it is possible that since most children are taught early in life that they should be friendly, helpful, and cooperative, media content may only reinforce what children already know. On the other hand, aggressive behavior is usually punished at home and at school, and frequent viewing of it on TV might serve to overcome children's inhibitions against performing this discouraged behavior. It appears that much more research evidence is necessary in this area before the total impact of the media on prosocial behavior is known. Unfortunately, at present only a few researchers are studying this topic and results are accumulating slowly.

To summarize:

1. When presented in a controlled environment, film and television can promote the learning of prosocial attitudes and behaviors, particularly among young people.

2. In everyday situations, the impact of prosocial TV programs and films is much harder to detect.

OTHER BEHAVIORAL EFFECTS

Political Behavior

The effect of the mass media on political behavior is a complicated one. It first came into prominence in 1940 when sociologists and political scientists feared that a

Smiles and the Presidency

Can a newscaster's smile influence your vote for president? This was the intriguing question asked by Brian Mullen and his colleagues. Briefly, here's what they did.

Twelve hours of network newscasts were videotaped. Segments in which the anchorperson referred to one of the major 1984 presidential candidates (Reagan or Mondale) were edited to a separate tape. With the audio turned down, subjects were then asked to judge the facial expression of the anchorperson to see if any one exhibited positive or negative expressions toward the candidates. Tom Brokaw and Dan Rather exhibited no apparent bias toward either candidate, but subjects judged that ABC's Peter Jennings exhibited a strong positive bias toward Reagan, apparently displaying a subtle smile when he referred to him.

Could Jennings' smile have influenced the way people voted? The researchers surveyed about 140 people who were frequent viewers of the networks' newscasts. The proportion of people who watched NBC and CBS who voted for Reagan was compared with the proportion of ABC viewers who voted for him. If the smile was having an impact, more ABC viewers should have voted for Reagan. The results: 75 percent of the ABC viewers voted for Reagan compared with 63 percent of the CBS and NBC viewers, a result that was statistically significant.

You can find the full study reported in *Journal of Personality and Social Psychology* (1986), Vol. 51, pp. 291–295.

particularly skilled demagogue might use the media to achieve political power. These early studies found surprisingly little impact due solely to the influence of mass communication; interpersonal sources were found to be more powerful. Interest in the unique effects of the media was rekindled by the 1960 Kennedy–Nixon debates and by the subsequent emergence of a group of political consultants who served as media imagemakers. (You might read Joe McGinniss' book *The Selling of the President 1968* for a vivid account of the activities of these consultants.)

Trying to summarize the many studies that have been conducted about the influences of the media on politics would require far more space than we have available. Consequently, we will restrict our discussion to the more central findings. Keep in mind that throughout our review our focus will be on the political *behavior* of the individual as it has been affected by the media. Chapter 21 summarized the impact of the media on a person's political knowledge, attitudes, and perceptions. At the core of our current discussion will be an examination of the individual's most important political behavior, the ultimate payoff in any political campaign, namely, voting behavior.

Studies of Voter Turnout. Voter turnout in presidential elections generally increased from 1924 to 1960 (if we discount the war years). From that time, however, the trend has been reversed, and fewer people have voted in presidential elections. Have the media had an impact in this area? The data are not conclusive, and many people have different viewpoints. At least one political scientist has argued that part of the increased voter turnout from 1930 to 1940 was due to the impact of radio. As this new medium reached those who were less educated and less politically involved and beyond the reach of printed media, it apparently stimulated greater interest in politics and increased the tendency to vote. The parallel emergence of TV did not have such an impact, although many argued that the visual dimension of TV would make the political process more vivid and so further increase participation. But turnout has decreased, starting with the 1964 election (interestingly enough, this was the first election in which the first "TV generation" would be eligible to vote). A current explanation for this drop holds that the unique characteristics of TV news are in part responsible. TV news, it is argued, presents the news in such a way that it is hard to avoid messages about the opposition. Seeing an opponent making a good case for his or her position will rarely convert a voter, but it might make that voter less sure of his or her own views and more confused. As a result, these voters might simply tune out and become less interested in politics and voting.

Data from presidential elections from 1960 to 1976 indicate that the frequency of reading a newspaper was strongly related to voter turnout, but radio and television exposure were not. These data suggest that the recent decline in newspaper reading among those of voting age might be part of the cause of the low turnout rather than the alleged confusion that might result from viewing TV news. Obviously, the relationship between media exposure and turnout is complicated, and it is likely that the future will bring more evidence to help us better understand the situation.

One area of voter turnout that has been studied in some depth is the effect of exit polls. An **exit poll** is conducted on election day at a polling place among voters who have just cast their ballots. These polls enable the TV networks to project winners early in the day, before the polls have closed. Although common sense suggests that people won't turn out to vote if they think their vote is meaningless or if their candidate has already been declared a loser, the research suggests the impact

Exit polls, conducted among voters who have just cast their ballots, enable TV networks to project winners before the polls close. The impact of such early projections is a subject of debate; surveys suggest that media coverage is a factor in decreasing voter turnout. (Billy Barnes)

of exit polling is much more complicated. First, the closeness of the race is important. If exit polls simply confirm a landslide predicted by preelection surveys, their impact might be different from that of exit polls which confirm a close race or show that preelection surveys were wrong. The most recent evidence suggests that exit polls are most influential when they change perceptions about the closeness of a race. Second, only those potential voters who have yet to vote and who hear an election being called can be affected. People who haven't voted by the time a call is made are usually not very interested in politics and are not likely to be exposed to election calls. Third, in some states the polls may close shortly after a call is made, whereas in other states the polls may be open much longer. Finally, a lot of extraneous factors, such as bad weather, early concession speeches, and close local races will also affect turnout.

Taking all these complications into account, the consensus of research in this area suggests that in an election where exit polls predict a clear winner in a race that had previously been thought close, election calls based on exit polling decrease voter turnout about 1–5 percent if the polls are open more than an hour after the call. In other situations, any effect will be hard to find. Of course, if Congress passes a uniform poll closing bill or if the networks decide informally to refrain from calls until everybody has voted, the issue will become academic.

Effects of the Mass Media on Voter Choice. When it comes to choosing a candidate to vote for, the mass media function along with many other factors, both social and psychological, to affect a person's choice. Still, some tentative generalizations can be made. First of all, it would appear that conversion (changing your vote from Republican to Democrat, for example) is unlikely to occur because of media exposure. Conversion seldom occurs because it is difficult for the media to persuade someone whose mind is already made up to change to an opposing view and because it appears that most people (roughly two-thirds) have already made up their minds before the political campaign begins. Far more common are two effects that have a direct bearing on voter choice: **reinforcement** and **crystallization.** Reinforcement means the strengthening or support of existing attitudes and opinions. Crystallization means the sharpening and elaboration of vaguely held attitudes or predispositions. One key factor that would influence whether reinforcement or crystallization occurs is a person's partisan leanings. If a person approaches a campaign undecided or neutral, then crystallization is likely to occur. If the person has already made up his or her mind, then reinforcement will probably take place.

In recent national elections there has been an increase in ticket-splitting (supporting one party's candidate for president and another's for governor, for example). This phenomenon may be due to crystallization, which in turn results from exposure to mass media. The flow of information during the campaign evidently crystallizes a vague voting intention that these individuals may have and, in many instances, these choices do not square with party loyalty. On the other hand, when partisan voters are exposed to the media, reinforcement is likely. A study of the 1948 election found that people who chose their candidate early were more likely to expose themselves to media content that supported their chosen candidate and reinforced their initial view. Further, results from at least six studies of the 1960 debates showed that people who had already made their vote choice declared their candidate to be the winner far more often than the opponent.

These findings do not necessarily mean that the media are not influential. A key factor in winning any election is to keep the party faithful loyal (reinforcement) and to persuade enough of the undecideds to vote for your side (crystallization) in order to win. Thus even though widespread conversion is not usually seen, the media are still influential. Even more important, the media may have significant indirect influence on the electorate. By serving as important sources of political news, by structuring "political reality," and by creating an image of candidates and issues, the media may have a potent effect on a person's attitudes about the political system. Furthermore, our discussion has been mainly concerned with the effects of the media in national elections. Local elections present a somewhat different picture. Most research evidence indicates that the media, especially local newspapers, might be highly influential in affecting voter choice in a city, county, or district election.

The Debates. A basic knowledge of the effects of mass media on politics would not be complete without an examination of the presidential debates of 1960, 1976, 1980, 1984, and 1988. Thirty-one different studies were done on the Nixon–Kennedy debates to gauge their impact. As mentioned above, reinforcement of voter choice seemed to be the main effect since many had already made up their minds prior to the debate. There was also evidence of crystallization in that independent voters became more favorable to one or the other candidate throughout the course of the debates. Significantly, more independents shifted to Kennedy. All in all, the number of voters actually influenced appeared rather small. The 1960 election, however, was decided by a tenth of a percentage point. Thus even a relatively small effect in

A televised presidential debate between George Bush and Michael Dukakis. Numerous studies are conducted following televised debates to determine the impact on viewers and the likelihood that the candidates' performances will convince viewers to change their votes. (Pamela Price/Picture Group)

terms of numbers might have an enormous social impact. The 1976 Carter–Ford debates showed a more pronounced media effect. Consistent viewers of the debates put more weight on differences over issues in determining their vote. This group was also the group that showed a greater tendency to change their vote choice. Declines in party loyalty and identification made reinforcement a less likely effect and suggested an even more important role for the media.

Because of the last minute scheduling of the 1980 presidential debate between Jimmy Carter and Ronald Reagan, few detailed studies evaluating its impact were conducted. Public opinion polls taken after the election showed that Reagan benefited most, picking up the previously undecided vote by a two-to-one margin. The two debates between Ronald Reagan and Walter Mondale in the 1984 campaign were studied more extensively. Surveys showed that Mondale did better in the first debate, with even Reagan supporters conceding that he performed better than their candidate. The polls showed that Reagan scored a narrow victory in the second debate. In any event, the debates had apparently little effect in determining the final outcome. Reagan had a lopsided lead all through the campaign, which was translated into a landslide victory on election day. If anything the 1984 debates again demonstrated the reinforcement effect. After the debates, about 85 percent of the moderate Mondale supporters and 75 percent of the moderate Reagan supporters made their final decision to vote for their candidate.

Television and the Political Behavior of Politicians. On a general level, it is clear that the emergence of television has affected the political behavior of politicians and political campaigns. A comparison of pre-TV practices with those occurring after TV's adoption reveals the following:

1. Nominating conventions are now planned with television in mind. They are designed not so much to select a candidate as to make a favorable impression on public opinion.

2. Television has increased the cost of campaigning.

3. Television has become the medium around which most campaigns are organized.

4. Campaign staffs now typically include one or more television consultants whose job it is to advise the candidate on his or her television image.

Effects of Obscenity and Pornography

Research into the effects of obscene and pornographic material is not as advanced as it is in the other areas we have examined. The most concerted effort in this area was conducted by the Commission on Obscenity and Pornography, which sponsored a three-year study of the impact of such material. The writing of this commission's report was immersed in many political considerations, and the commission was unable to issue a unanimous statement. Nonetheless, the major research findings are of interest. The commission found that the most frequent users of pornography were middle-class and middle-aged males. It found no evidence to indicate that viewing pornography was related to antisocial or deviant behavior and attitudes. Further, the commission even stated that pornographic material served a positive function in some healthy sexual relationships. The majority of this commission went so far as to make the politically unpopular recommendation that all laws prohibiting the sale of this

The image of convicted mass murderer Ted Bundy on a TV monitor at Florida State Prison during an exclusive final interview before his execution. In the interview, Bundy claimed that his violent sexual fantasies were a result of his exposure to pornographic material. (Pete Cosgrove/UPI Bettmann Newsphotos)

material to adults should be repealed. The Nixon administration repudiated the recommendations of this body in 1970, and since that time this report has been largely ignored.

During the next decade, however, pornography became more abundant and more extreme. In addition, the results of new research cast doubt on the conclusions of the earlier commission. Consequently, a new National Commission on Pornography was appointed in 1984 and released its report in 1986. Surrounded by political considerations, the new commission concluded that pornography, particularly violent pornography, was harmful and that its distribution should be curtailed. More recent studies have found that sexual arousal might be linked to subsequent aggressive behavior if other outlets for release are not available. Other research has indicated that the responses of males and females to this content are becoming more alike.

In addition, several studies done in the mid-1980s found a disturbing link between exposure to pornography and feelings of callousness toward women. In one experiment, college students were divided into three groups. One group saw thirty-six erotic films over a six-week period. A second saw eighteen erotic and eighteen nonerotic films over the same period, while a control group saw thirty-six nonerotic films. After the viewing period was over, all groups were questioned concerning their attitudes toward pornography, rape, and women in general. The group that received the heaviest dose of pornography was less likely to think that pornography was offensive, had less compassion for women as rape victims, and were less supportive of women's rights than were the other groups. In a similar study, males viewed five movies showing both erotic and violent behavior toward females. The subjects were questioned about their perceptions of violence after viewing just one film and again after viewing all five. The results indicated that after seeing all five films the subjects had fewer negative reactions to the films and perceived them as less violent and less degrading to women, suggesting a desensitization effect of this material.

The most recent debate in this area is over the relative effects of violent versus nonviolent pornography. Several studies have noted a link between exposure to films that were both violent and pornographic and feelings of sexual callousness toward women. But is it the violence or the pornography that is the cause? At least one study has found the same result after viewing nonviolent pornography but others have failed to replicate this finding. More research is needed to clarify the effects of this content.

COVERAGE OF CIVIL DISORDERS AND TERRORISM

During the 1960s, it was widely feared that the reporting of urban violence, especially on-the-scene reports by TV and radio reporters, was responsible for a **contagion effect,** that is, reports of violence sparked new incidents of violence. To study this and other questions concerning the urban disorders, the National Advisory Commission on Civil Disorders was formed. Regarding the relationship of media coverage to violence, the commission concluded that, on the whole, the media made an effort to present a balanced and factual account of the disorder. This conclusion was reached after an extensive study of all media content in cities hit by unrest. The commission found that only a small portion of news coverage (about 5 percent) showed mob action or looting; far more time was devoted to nonviolent scenes. However, further study of the participants in the disorders in Detroit in 1967 produced some additional considerations. This survey revealed that about three out of four participants had seen riots on TV before the Detroit incidents and that about 50 percent remembered seeing property destroyed. Thus, although only a small proportion of total coverage might be regarded as inflammatory, the impact of this coverage might be out of proportion to its actual magnitude.

The commission was unable to reach a firm conclusion about the effects of media presence on prompting further violence. It was evident, however, that marked vans, cameras, microphones, tape recorders, and lights all attracted attention during a disturbance. Recognizing this, many media organizations established guidelines to minimize the impact of their presence.

Fortunately, the wide-scale urban disorders of the 1960s have not reappeared. New concerns, however, have surfaced. One of the major problems has to do with the coverage of acts of terrorism—kidnaping, hostage taking, hijacking, bombing, and so on—and the effects of this coverage. Many authorities claim that massive media coverage of acts of terrorism also has a contagion effect, promoting even more terrorism. In 1974, while the House Committee on the Judiciary was debating impeachment charges, a telephone bomb threat was received, which emptied the room. The networks dutifully reported what had happened. In the next few days, no less than seven bomb threats were phoned in.

This issue was back in the news again in 1985 when terrorists hijacked an airplane and held thirty-nine passengers hostage at the Beirut airport. Critics charged that during this incident television became ''terrorvision,'' playing into the hands of the terrorists and limiting the options available to the government. Before it was

Covering Terrorism: Guidelines from CBS News

In April 1977, Hanafi Muslims took over three buildings in Washington, D.C., and held 134 people hostage. After the leader of the Muslims read a list of his demands on the local 6 o'clock news show, CBS News issued guidelines to its reporters concerning how these events should be covered. These guidelines were under review after the 1985 hijacking of a TWA airplane. The sections below have been excerpted from those guidelines:

Because the facts and circumstances of each case vary, there can be no specific self-executing rules for the handling of terrorist/hostage stories. CBS News will continue to apply the normal tests of news judgment and if, as so often they are, these stories are newsworthy, we must continue to give them coverage despite the dangers of ''contagion.'' . . . Nevertheless, in providing for such coverage there must be thoughtful, conscientious care and restraint. Obviously, the story should not be sensationalized beyond the actual fact of its being sensational. We should exercise particular care in how we treat the terrorist/kidnapper.

The guidelines also go into specific detail:

1. An essential component of the story is the demands of the terrorist/kidnapper and we must report those demands. . . .

2. Except in the most compelling circumstances, and then only with the approval of the President of CBS News, or in his absence, the Senior Vice President of News, there should be no live coverage of the terrorist/kidnapper since we may fall into the trap of providing an unedited platform for him. . . .

3. News personnel should be mindful of the probable need by the authorities who are dealing with the terrorist for communication by telephone and hence should endeavor to ascertain, wherever feasible, whether our own use of such lines would be likely to interfere with the authorities' communications.

4. Responsible CBS News representatives should endeavor to contact experts dealing with the hostage situation to determine whether they have any guidance on such questions as phraseology to be avoided, what kinds of questions or reports might tend to exacerbate the situation, etc. . . .

5. Local authorities should also be given the name or names of CBS personnel whom they can contact should they need further guidance or wish to deal with such delicate questions as a newsman's call to the terrorists or other matters which might interfere with authorities dealing with the terrorists.

6. Guidelines affecting our coverage of civil disturbances are also applicable here, especially those which relate to avoiding the use of inflammatory catchwords or phrases, the reporting of rumors, etc. As in the case of policy dealing with civil disturbances, in dealing with a hostage story reporters should obey all police instructions but report immediately to their superiors any such instructions that seem to be intended to manage or suppress the news.

Courtesy of CBS News.

over, the hostages and their families became media celebrities and gaining the release of the hostages was a struggle to free people who were almost like friends (remember the discussion of parasocial relationships in Chapter 2). After the episode was resolved, the networks once again were forced to examine their policies on covering such events. Some suggestions that surfaced included forbidding interviews with terrorists or hostages, downplaying the crisis atmosphere that might surround such a story, and refraining from overcoverage of the hostages' families. In sum, the difficulties in covering such a story are formidable, and news-gathering organizations are still considering how best to balance their need to inform the audience about what is happening with the needs of the government and the safety of the hostages themselves.

Covering terrorism is a continuing problem for the media. TV networks carry press conferences featuring hostages and their kidnappers or hostages who have returned to the United States, such as this coverage of Father Jenko's safe return from Lebanon. Critics argue that this improves the bargaining power of the terrorists and transforms a political issue into a personal one. (Tom Kelly)

SUGGESTIONS FOR FURTHER READING

The books and articles listed below represent good sources of further information.

BAKER, R. K., AND S. J. BALL, eds., *Violence and the Media. A Staff Report to the National Commission on the Causes and Prevention of Violence,* Washington, D.C.: Government Printing Office, 1969.

BRYANT, JENNINGS, AND DOLF ZILLMANN, *Perspectives on Media Effects,* Hillsdale, N.J.: Lawrence Erlbaum, 1986.

CATER, DOUGLASS, AND STEPHEN STRICKLAND, *TV Violence and the Child,* Beverly Hills, Calif.: Sage Publications, 1975.

COMSTOCK, GEORGE, "The Evidence on Television Violence," Santa Monica, Calif.: RAND Paper Series, October 1976.

COMSTOCK, GEORGE, STEVEN CHAFFEE, NATAN KATZMAN, MAXWELL McCOMBS, AND DONALD ROBERTS, *Television and Human Behavior,* New York: Columbia University Press, 1978.

DAILY, CHARLES U., ed., *The Media and the Cities,* Chicago: University of Chicago Press, 1968.

DE SOLA POOL, ITHIEL, "Why Don't People Vote?" *TV Guide,* October 14, 1976, p. 6.

GREENBERG, BRADLEY, AND BRENDA DERVIN, eds., *Mass Communication and the Urban Poor,* New York: Praeger, 1970.

HUESMANN, L. ROWELL, AND LEONARD ERON, eds., *Television and the Aggressive Child,* Hillsdale, N.J.: Lawrence Erlbaum, 1986.

JOSLYN, RICHARD, *Mass Media and Elections,* Reading, Mass.: Addison-Wesley, 1984.

KLAPPER, JOSEPH, *The Effects of Mass Communication,* New York: The Free Press, 1960.

LIEBERT, ROBERT M., JOHN M. NEALE, AND EMILY DAVIDSON, *The Early Window: Effects of Television on Children and Youth,* 3rd ed., New York: Pergamon Press, 1988.

LOWERY, SHEARON, AND MELVIN DEFLEUR, *Milestones in Mass Communication Research,* New York: Longman, 1983.

McCOMBS, MAXWELL E., "Mass Communication in Political Campaigns: Information, Gratification and Persuasion," in KLINE, F. G., AND PHILIP TICHENOR, eds., *Current Perspectives in Mass Communication Research,* Beverly Hills, Calif.: Sage Publications, 1972.

SPRAFKIN, JOYCE, AND ELI RUBINSTEIN, "Children's Television Viewing Habits and Prosocial Behavior: A Field Correlational Study," *Journal of Broadcasting,* Vol. 23:3 (Summer 1979), pp. 265–276.

U.S. GOVERNMENT, *Report of the National Advisory Commission on Civil Disorders,* New York: Bantam, 1968.

———, *Television and Social Behavior, Reports and Papers* (5 volumes), Washington, D.C.: Department of Health, Education and Welfare, 1972.

WEISS, WALTER, "Effects of the Mass Media of Communication," in LINDZEY, G., AND E. ARONSON, eds., *The Handbook of Social Psychology, Vol. 5: Applied Social Psychology,* Reading, Mass.: Addison-Wesley, 1969, p. 77–195.

WILLIAMS, TANNIS, ed., *The Impact of Television,* New York: Academic Press, 1986.

WINICK, CHARLES, ed., *Deviance and Mass Media,* Beverly Hills, Calif.: Sage Publications, 1978.

Part Eight

Mass Communication and the Future

Chapter 23

Mass Media in the Future: Progress Report on the Communication Revolution

Throughout history, new media have continually appeared. Sometimes, they survived, like radio and TV. Other times, they didn't catch on and became historical oddities, like the 1950s picturephone. Nonetheless, in 1981, when most of the first edition of this book was written, the world was poised on the brink of what was termed a communications revolution. New media and new forms of media delivery were being developed, and many thought they would have drastic impact on our daily lives. It was predicted by some that two-way television would be the wave of the future. People would shop at home, bank at home, and maybe even skip commuting and work at home through their TV sets. Direct broadcasting by satellite (DBS) would mean a nation equipped with small, rooftop dishes that would pluck original programming from powerful satellites orbiting above. Electronic publishing would supplant the traditional newsprint and ink paper. Low-power TV stations would mean that every community would have its own station. Cable systems would provide us with 108 channels of specialized programming. Videocassette recorders would open up new markets for films. AM stereo and digital recording would likewise break new ground. Well, almost ten years later, it's obvious that the communications revolution has run into resistance from social and economic forces. This is not to say that the new communication technologies have not had an impact. They have. The media of today are significantly different from the media of ten years ago. Perhaps "revolution" is not quite the right word to describe the impact of the new media. Maybe "evolution" is a better choice since the changes will take time to appear and their effects may not be seen for generations. Nonetheless, they'll get here.

This chapter will briefly review some of the innovations that have already influenced the media's evolution, look at those yet to catch on, and scan the horizon for new developments that promise to alter the future of the media.

Technicians at NBC studios fine-tuning new robotic cameras that the network will soon begin using to broadcast its newscasts, including "NBC Nightly News" with Tom Brokaw. (David Rentas/New York Post Photo)

PUBLISHING INDUSTRY: NEWSPAPERS, MAGAZINES, AND BOOKS

As we mentioned in earlier chapters, the computer has had enormous impact in publishing. Video-display terminals have replaced the traditional typewriter; manuscripts can be electronically edited; and whole pages can be laid out with computer assistance. Electronic pagination is expected to save the industry about $2.5 billion in the next decade. Satellites now transmit whole pages of copy to outlying printing plants where the actual paper is put together. And ADSAT sends advertising copy to member newspapers.

Currently under development are systems that allow the editor to have complete control of the newspaper content—changing makeup, digital photography (a computer-assisted method of displaying photos on the printed page), which allows electronic cropping of photos, and headline construction. This new system means that the current method of photocomposition, page paste-up, photographing the page, and then making plates can be simplified with all the information going straight to the computer and having the plates made directly from electronically stored information. Ink jet printers, which "paint" each letter with microscopic drops of ink, will allow papers to be printed more quickly, and it is hoped, more cheaply.

New ways of assembling newspapers will make them more similar to magazines and will allow them to become even more specialized. As mentioned in Chapter 5, magazines print demographic editions, which are designed for a particular group of readers. The development of new insertion and assembly equipment will enable papers to insert special sections and supplements into the paper at about the same speed that the paper is printed. To illustrate the reason behind this idea, consider the business section of the typical paper. Surveys indicate that only one-third of the audience reads this section, and as far as the other two-thirds of the audience is concerned, the business section could be eliminated from the paper, and it would not be sorely missed. It would seem to make sense, then, from a marketing viewpoint, to supply the business pages only to those who actually want them. Similarly, the sports section might be inserted only in those copies of the paper going to readers who are interested in sports. The use of high-speed assembly equipment lets a newspaper tailor each copy for the individual subscriber. To illustrate, a subscriber would pay a basic fee for the core of the paper but would be required to pay extra for any customized inserts that he or she wished to read. The paper might offer as many as a dozen special inserts including "Food," "Business," "Society," "Sports," and "Entertainment." Each reader's choices would be recorded and stored in a central computer. Specific quantities of each combination would be printed, address labels attached, and the copy delivered to the subscriber's doorstep. This technique would ultimately be more efficient in its use of paper and allow advertisers to buy space in a section that would reach a well-defined reader group. Manufacturers of business products would advertise in the business section and be reasonably certain that their messages would go only to those interested in their products.

The future of teletext and videotex (see Chapter 7) is hard to predict. Most media companies have backed away from further developing these services. Many experts think that videotex and teletext will be used to compile large data bases and will ultimately serve a small, specialized audience such as the financial or scientific community. Another scenario suggests that telephone companies will become the leader in this area and use it to store their directories and other specialized data. In 1988, the FCC issued a preliminary opinion, subject to review, that would allow the various phone companies to provide such services, a necessary first step.

Another printed medium likely to be around quite a while is the magazine. A safe prediction is that many new and special magazines will appear and that some of these will survive and others won't. New businesses, hobbies, and leisure-time activities will produce new magazines. Market research will spur the inception of others as publishers try to reduce some of the risks involved in starting new publications. Since market research aims at attracting a relatively affluent, relatively young, college-educated crowd, many future magazines will reflect the interests of this group, especially topics concerned with life-styles, self-improvement, and self-fulfillment. There are limits, of course, to the degree of specialization that can be achieved without overspecializing the magazine out of the market. Some critics have suggested, only somewhat jokingly, that in the future we'll have magazines like *Sweatsox and Leash,* a magazine for joggers who own poodles, and *Smashed Scissors,* the magazine for barbers and hairdressers who have also been run over by a bus. Clearly, specialization can be taken too far.

Other technological advances promise to improve the magazine's production process, making color photos easier to reproduce and more colorful to the eye. Editorial copy will be transmitted by satellite, enabling publishers to speed up printing and delivery.

Likewise, we can probably expect more specialization from the book publishing industry. The continuing trend in job specialization will probably prompt growth in the professional and educational areas. In addition, the market for children's and juvenile books appears to be a growth area as many publishers realize that this age group can be wooed away from the TV screen. Further, several children's books are now being marketed in combination with related videocassettes. The cross-media symbiosis that is apparent in other areas will probably become more important in book publishing as well.

Finally, many reference books—dictionaries, encyclopedias, almanacs, first aid guides, and the like—might be transferred to compact disc. A video compact disc player would display the information requested.

RADIO AND SOUND RECORDING

Radio has already demonstrated its capacity to survive technological change and will probably continue to do so in the near future. Unlike the print media, radio faces no technological upheaval comparable to the creation of the electronic newspaper. In fact, major changes in the radio industry will likely occur more in the format area than in the hardware area. To be sure, radio will undergo some mechanical developments. On the one hand, many portable sets will become smaller: Some will eventually become so flattened that they will resemble credit cards, while others will be miniaturized to the point where they can be worn around the wrist or clipped to the ear like an earring. On the other hand, some sets will become bigger and will be designed so that they will be barely portable enough to be carried around in public places.

The coming of stereophonic sound to AM radio has yet to stop that service's audience-erosion problem. One of the problems apparently delaying the widespread acceptance of AM stereo is technological. There are currently two noncompatible systems battling it out in the marketplace. Current radio sets cannot pick up either system. To hear AM stereo, you have to buy a specially made receiver. Radio receiving set manufacturers, as well as consumers are taking a wait-and-see attitude before investing heavily in AM stereo. Hundreds of stations across the country are now broadcasting in AM stereo, but consumer awareness and interest is so low that many stations don't even promote it. In any case, AM stereo has not been the savior of the beleaguered AM band that many thought. Perhaps once the technical battles are solved, AM stereo might have more of an impact.

Digital audio tape (DAT; see Chapter 8) will figure prominently in the future of radio and sound recording. DAT is the next step after the CD. It allows a person to play back and record audio with the same quality now possible only in a compact disc. Big electronics companies like Sony, which is pioneering DAT in Japan, are eager for DAT to penetrate the American market. American record companies are afraid that DAT recording will cause a rash of pirated tapes that will hurt industry profits. (Sony, which recently bought CBS Records, is in the interesting position of having one of its divisions favor DAT and the other oppose it.)

Are the record companies' fears justified? A lesson from history may be helpful here. When audio cassettes were first introduced, the record companies claimed that the ease of home taping would ruin their industry. They argued that people would simply make copies of a friend's cassettes and not buy the original. This obviously happens, but the record companies are still turning profits. Only 3 percent of all audio cassette sales are accounted for by blank tapes; the rest are prerecorded. It's likely that the same thing will happen with DAT. In any case, the demand for DAT will probably be so great that it will be difficult to keep off the market for long.

The government will also figure prominently in radio's future. The current FCC has authorized the construction of more than a thousand new radio stations. Competition will be even more keen in the future.

HOME COMPUTERS

Home computers are the newest addition to machine-assisted communication. A computer equipped with a modem allows the user to send electronic mail to other computer owners, paste messages on electronic bulletin boards, shop, bank, or make airline reservations at home, tap into various data bases, or communicate with other computer users in a sort of electronic CB. From 1980 to about 1984, sales of home computers soared, and many predicted that they would revolutionize our communication habits and our life-styles. Then, in 1985, the bottom fell out. IBM announced it was no longer making its PCjr, Apple closed four factories in a week, Coleco pulled the plug on its Adam computer, and Commodore had $450 million of unsold computers. The home market did not look as promising as it once did (sales of computers designed for business use continued to do well). A lot of people apparently bought computers because they thought it was the thing to do and then discovered that computers didn't provide enough benefits to become an integral part of their lives. Another part of the problem was the high price tags that went with the home systems and the fact that many weren't "user friendly" and required a lot of work to learn. Once the first wave of customers (called TAFs—technologically advanced families—by the industry) bought computers, the machines became harder to sell. As of 1988, computers were in 15 percent of U.S. households, but surveys showed that the number who planned to buy a computer in the near future was dropping. It appears that any drastic reshaping of our life-style because of the home computer is still somewhat in the future.

Whoops! Mispredicting the Future

The many people who made fevered predictions about the burgeoning communications revolution of the early 1980s and then, much to their dismay, discovered that their predictions didn't actually pan out needn't feel so bad. Many other expert predictions didn't come about either. Consider:

Thomas Edison totally misread the future of the phonograph. He thought it could be used as a sort of telephone answering machine or a device for recording the last words of prominent persons before they died.

A Massachusetts newspaper predicted that the telephone would be primarily used to transmit music and news.

When the telegraph was first perfected, people thought the new device would make the whole world into one neighborhood and become "a sublime force for preserving morality."

A prominent magazine, flushed with the potential of radio, predicted that radio's biggest use would be person-to-person communication. It also predicted several other bizarre uses for radio, including radio-powered roller skates.

(Of course, if a person waits long enough, sometimes even a wayward prediction comes true. A recent invention, called cellular radio, now uses radio technology to create a system of mobile telephones to be used in person-to-person communication. So far, however, there's been no word of radio-powered roller-skates.)

The big problem facing the home computer industry is the same confronted by the radio, film, and sound-recording industries years before. What is the home computer good for? Most available programs are for business uses, home education, or games. What is lacking is one compelling application that appeals to everyone. As one analyst stated: "Before the home computer becomes *the* appliance of the . . . 1990s, it has to make living easier, less expensive or allow people to do something they couldn't do before." Of course, someday, someone (maybe you) will solve that problem and revolutionize the industry . . . and become quite rich and famous in the process.

THE FUTURE OF MOTION PICTURES AND BROADCASTING

Although the demise of the motion picture industry has been predicted several times, somehow or other it has always managed to survive. Hollywood is likely to stay in business in the near future, but there will be major changes in film production, distribution, and exhibition. In the production sector computer-assisted graphics have revolutionized the special-effects area. Further, the distinction between film and television will become blurry as video technology begins to replace more and more material that used to be confined to film. For example, in one new system employing high-definition television, scenes that would ordinarily be shot on film are shot on videotape. The tape can be played back immediately, thus eliminating the time it takes for film processing. A computer-assisted editing system makes the tape as easy to edit as film. Further, a greater variety of special effects are possible with video, and they can be done less expensively. This system will ultimately save the motion picture industry money since there are no costs for film developing and processing. Finally, by using a laser scanner, the finished videotape is transferred to thirty-five- or seventy-millimeter film, and the film is then shipped to theaters where it can be shown over conventional projectors. Eventually, even this last conversion to film may be eliminated, once high-resolution TV systems that project either videotape or live signals received via satellite have been installed in motion picture theaters.

As we saw in Chapter 12, the biggest change prompted by the new technologies in the motion picture industry has been the new distribution channels made possible by videocassettes. Movies on cassette have already become an important source of income for the industry and pay-per-view promises to become an important revenue source. The symbiosis between motion pictures and TV will become even closer in the years to come.

What impact will the coming of videocassettes have on motion picture exhibitors? If people can see movies less expensively in their homes, will anybody still go to the motion picture theater? The answer is yes, some people will still go to the movies. Remember that in Chapter 19 we pointed out that for many people moviegoing was more of a social experience than a media experience. Going to the movies will continue to be an important dating activity for teens who seek to avoid the confines and supervision of the house and for other young adults seeking relatively low-cost recreation. It is quite probable that movie theater owners will start to stress the social aspect of moviegoing. Single seats may be replaced by couches; movie theaters may be merged with restaurants, bars, and even nightclubs. Live entertainment might precede the film (sort of a throwback to vaudeville). Since the moviegoing audience will continue to be composed primarily of young people, motion picture theaters might become part of an entertainment complex geared to this age group with skating rinks, electronic games, and miniature golf.

Other theater owners may attempt to attract a somewhat older crowd. New ultra-swank theaters with plush seats, improved soundproofing, and concession stands stocked with Perrier, croissants, and frozen yogurt are already springing up in Southern California.

Other changes that will also affect the exhibition segment of the industry will be innovations in the way films are screened. Sound systems will become more sophisticated. Quadraphonic or quintaphonic systems seem well suited for movie sound and will be especially appropriate for sound tracks recorded by means of the digital method. Although the age of experimentation with giant screens and multiple screens may be over, some theaters will probably attempt new projection methods. One possibility that has already been tested involves putting the spectators in steep balconies and projecting a film simultaneously on two screens, one lying on the floor and the other standing vertically. Another arrangement puts the audience on a device resembling a merry-go-round and turns them toward different screens at different times. A third idea is the interactive movie, in which audience members are given a small device on which they vote for a particular plot option and the film proceeds accordingly. (The problem with this technique is that a large amount of film has to be shot to cover all the possible permutations and combinations.) Some of these ideas might catch on, but it is probable that the traditional motion picture screen will persist into the immediate future.

NEW TELEVISION TECHNOLOGIES: WINNERS AND LOSERS

The one medium that was supposed to be most affected by new communication technologies was television. At least six innovations came on the scene in 1980–1981 and were expected to change completely the face of conventional television broadcasting. Now, with the benefit of hindsight, it's apparent that four of these six (subscription TV, low-power TV, direct broadcasting by satellite, and two-way cable) have so far failed to live up to expectations, one showed mixed results (new cable programming channels) and one (VCRs) exceeded predictions (Fig. 23.1). We will first examine those four innovations that have yet to fulfill their predicted potential.

Subscription television (STV) is a system whereby conventional TV stations broadcast commercial-free programming (usually movies) for a monthly fee to subscribers equipped with a special decoder. STV was on the way up in 1980, and it was predicted that by 1985 STV would be in about thirty-five markets with annual revenues of more than $1 billion. As it turned out, 1985 was the year when most companies were getting out of the business. After hitting a peak of about a million and a half subscribers in 1982, the medium went into a tailspin. Unable to cope with the competition from cable, most STV systems went under. At the start of 1986, there were fewer than 300,000 subscribers. STV, which looked promising just a few years ago, wound up costing a lot of companies a good deal of money.

When the FCC first suggested the institution of a system of low-power TV (LPTV) in 1980, it set off a frenzied scramble for channels. Hundreds of individuals and companies applied for literally thousands of channels, creating a paper logjam that the FCC is still trying to clear. This backup has resulted in LPTV licenses being issued in drops and driblets at an agonizingly slow pace. The FCC decided to issue the first LPTV permits in markets where no competing applications were received. These were usually in sparsely populated areas. These new stations lacked the ''critical mass'' of audience necessary to attract programming services and regional and national advertisers. Consequently, low-power TV became identified with low-

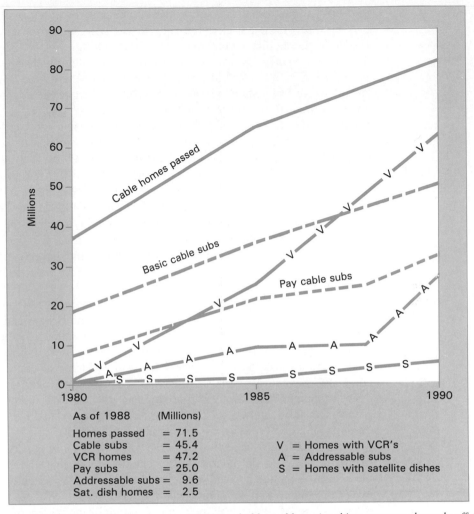

As of 1988   (Millions)

Homes passed	= 71.5
Cable subs	= 45.4
VCR homes	= 47.2
Pay subs	= 25.0
Addressable subs =	9.6
Sat. dish homes	= 2.5

V = Homes with VCR's
A = Addressable subs
S = Homes with satellite dishes

FIGURE 23.1 *In 1989, 63 percent of TV households could receive thirty or more channels off the air.*

budget TV and discouraged many investors from the area. In addition, the economics associated with the first LPTV stations worked against the new medium. The start-up costs of putting a TV station on the air (including low-power stations) are high, and most new LPTV stations lacked an audience big enough to attract local advertisers. In addition, many lacked the money necessary to stay in business through the expensive formative years and went under. Others simply became remote transmitters, rebroadcasting the signals of nearby full-power stations. As of 1988, there were about 390 LPTV stations in operation, and about half of these were simply relaying the signals of other stations.

Of course, this situation may change. The FCC has instituted a lottery system for deciding among equally qualified applicants for the same LPTV market. When LPTV stations are in operation in densely populated urban areas, such as New York and Los Angeles, the economic picture may improve. It will be a while, however, before this occurs. As it stands now, LPTV has yet to achieve the optimistic forecasts that greeted its inception.

DBS (direct broadcasting by satellite) differs from the service that people now pick up through their backyard dishes in that DBS is not meant for retransmission. People with satellite dishes are really intercepting signals meant for some other distribution agency. True DBS is designed to go directly to viewers' homes. DBS once looked to be a formidable competitor for conventional broadcasters. From a satellite or two in a stationary orbit 22,300 miles above the equator, a DBS operator could theoretically broadcast multiple programming services to every home in the country that was equipped with the small, inexpensive rooftop DBS receiver (Fig. 23.2). Frightened by this prospect, conventional broadcasters tried to block the development of DBS in the courts and before the FCC. As it turned out, they needn't have worried. DBS is currently struggling to stay alive. The biggest problem DBS ran into was a financial one. DBS needs enormous amounts of capital, maybe hundreds of millions of dollars, to start in business. So far, investors have not been willing to pour this money into the industry, primarily because they see little financial return. The initial audience size would be too small for the system to rely on advertising revenue. Consequently, consumers would have to pay for the service. One DBS company offered six channels for about $25 per month, much more than what a cable company charges.

As of 1988, there was only one company planning a DBS service; its schedule would consist exclusively of religious programs. The British and the Japanese were experimenting with a DBS system but were also running into the price obstacle. If costs for DBS decrease, it has the potential to be the most important TV distribution system. As it stands now, however, DBS is in a state of suspended animation. Some companies have tested the DBS waters, and most have wound up soaked in red ink. After dropping $140 million in five years, the Comsat Corporation, one of the pioneers in DBS, closed its DBS operation. United States Communications, Inc., dropped about $50 million experimenting with DBS.

The fourth new technology that has yet to live up to expectations is interactive or two-way TV. In the interactive system, the subscriber can send signals back to the central computer located at the head end of the cable company. The premiere two-way system in this country is the QUBE system in Columbus, Ohio. QUBE offered a variety of services including shopping at home, interactive game and talk shows, and home security.

The QUBE system demonstrated the state of the art in interactive cable TV and helped Warner Amex win franchises in several other major cities. These other cities were also hooked into the QUBE system. After a while, however, the novelty effect wore off, and QUBE subscribers became somewhat jaded. The system was never able to pay for itself. In January 1984, in an attempt to cut costs, Warner Amex announced cutbacks in its QUBE service. In November of the same year, the company sold its QUBE system in Pittsburgh. The new owner, also trying to cut costs, eliminated the interactive system entirely and substituted pay-per-view movies. In addition, Warner Amex was permitted to postpone (perhaps indefinitely) its promise to equip the city of Milwaukee with two-way cable. Other cities allowed other cable companies to defer their plans for interactive cable. Warner Amex sold off another cable system with planned two-way capability. The new owners were not eager to introduce the costly system and asked that the cities involved not insist on two-way cable.

In sum, the QUBE system was hailed by many as the prototype of life-style changes and the advent of a new era in communications. However, although the QUBE system showed the cable industry the potential of the two-way technology, it never did demonstrate how that technology could be used to make money. Until

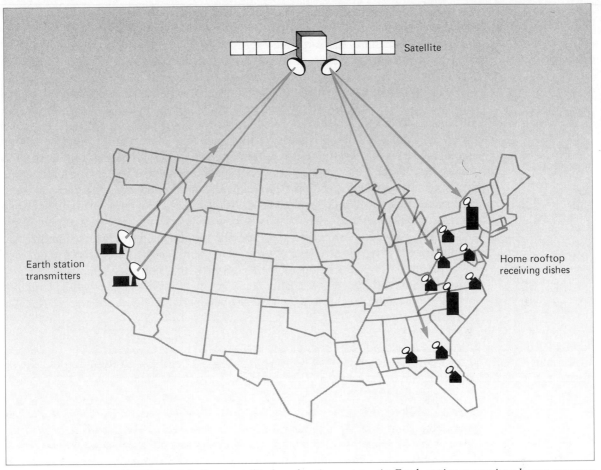

FIGURE 23.2 *A direct satellite broadcasting system: An Earth station transmitter beams program material to a satellite that, in turn, amplifies the signal and retransmits it to a terrestrial system or an individual receiver.*

two-way capability is able to support itself, many of its predicted benefits will not materialize.

New cable TV programming networks have certainly had a significant impact on mass communication but so far the so-called television of abundance, with a cornucopia of cable services cascading down from satellites to systems all over the country, has not come to pass. An economic shake-up hit the industry in the mid-1980s and many new services quickly went out of business. CBS Cable, the Satellite News Channel, The Entertainment Channel, and Ted Turner's Cable Music Channel were early casualties. Some services that were on the drawing boards never made it to the air. Clearly, these new services have expanded viewer choice and have taken away some of the audience from the three TV networks.

The consensus in the cable industry is that no more than twenty or so "basic" services—supported by advertising and carriage fees—and a few pay services will make it. Experts predict that some additional services will fall by the wayside the next few years and are not optimistic about the chances of any new service making the grade. In short, the new cable services have permanently changed the face of conventional TV, but the change was not as drastic as forecast.

The one medium that surprised everybody and caught on far more quickly and had more of an impact than anybody suspected was the VCR. When VCRs first came on the scene, many in the industry dismissed them as appliances that would only appeal to the real "hardware fanatics" in the audience. One industry executive said it would take at least twenty years before enough people had VCRs to make a difference. As it turned out, in the VCR's first decade, it penetrated American homes faster than did color TV. In fact, VCRs caught on more rapidly than any other appliance except TV itself. VCRs are now in more American homes than cable TV. As we have seen, its impact has significantly changed TV viewing and movie watching. Timeshifting (recording programs off the air and replaying them at more convenient times) expanded the audience for network programs, particularly soap operas, and for cable movies. A whole new industry, renting prerecorded films, drastically changed the marketing picture for motion pictures. Many families are buying inexpensive video cameras to go with portable VCRs to shoot their own home movies. New units that combine a camera with a built-in VCR, called "Camcorders," were selling well. A smaller tape size, eight millimeters in width, promised to make these units even more lightweight and portable. In short, the VCR has a promising future.

ON THE HORIZON: DIGITAL TV, FLAT SCREENS, HDTV, TELECONFERENCING, AND TELECOMMUTING

If audio can be transformed into digital form, why not video? In fact, TV stations have been using digital equipment for a number of years. What will be new in the 1990s is the introduction of digital home receivers and VCRs. Digital receivers will do a number of wondrous things. For instance, they'll be able to monitor the quality of the picture tube and compensate for signs of wear. Digital sets will also provide for picture-in-picture (PIP) display. PIP allows the viewer to watch one channel while simultaneously monitoring others. If that's not enough, digital TV provides for freeze frames and zooms. Some companies have already introduced digital VCRs.

Several companies are also developing flat-screen TVs. Conventional TVs are bulky and take up a lot of space. As the name suggests, flat-screen TVs would hang from the wall, like a painting. One method makes use of a liquid crystal display (LCD), similar to that now used in digital watches. The problem is that the largest set manufactured so far has only a seven-inch screen. Building a bigger screen hurts the picture's resolution and brightness. A more promising system using field-emission vacuum technology was demonstrated in 1988.

Another significant development in television that will be on the scene shortly is **High-Definition TV (HDTV).** Currently, the television signal carried on all home receiving sets consists of 525 lines of resolution. HDTV technology will replace those 525 lines with approximately 1100 lines. The immediate result of this increase will be better picture quality and visual clarity unmatched by today's conventional TV. In fact, many people who have seen high-definition TV in operation compare its picture quality with that of thirty-five millimeter motion picture film. In addition, HDTV is more compatible with wide-screen TV projection systems (such as the one marketed by Advent) and has the capacity of carrying stereophonic sound.

The only real delay to the introduction of an HDTV system is administrative. The engineers of the world have yet to come up with a common technical transmis-

High definition television (HDTV) employs new technology that produces pictures of such clarity they rival the quality of 35-mm motion picture film. At the left, is an image broadcast via conventional television, which is much fuzzier than the same image broadcast via an HDTV system (right). (Jay Brousseau)

sion standard. As of 1988, the leading system was one developed by the Japanese that calls for 1125 picture lines and widens the screen width-to-height ratio from the current 4:3 to 5:3. The catch is that HDTV signals take up more spectrum space than conventional signals. This extra bandwidth can't be handled by regular TV sets so, as it stands now, viewers would have to buy a new TV set to receive it. Originally HDTV needed about five times the normal bandwidth of the present system, but engineers have now managed to get the signal size down to about two or one and a half times the current size. This still presents problems for conventional broadcasters who don't have that extra space handy, but it's not a barrier for VCRs or cable systems. Hence it's likely that the first product on the market that includes the new HDTV sets will be HDTV VCRs. The other option is to use a DBS system to distribute HDTV. In fact, the Japanese have announced plans for such a system to begin in the 1990s.

The first HDTV sets would probably sell for about $2000–$3000. Consumer reaction to this price will play a big role in determining the future of HDTV. One survey taken at an experimental showing of HDTV indicated that more than 80 percent of the 300 people surveyed were willing to pay 50 percent more than the list price of a conventional TV set in order to receive HDTV pictures. Whether or not customers are willing to shell out $2000 remains to be seen.

Teleconferencing substitutes telecommunications for transportation. Large corporations spend more than $100 million every year on business travel, and the cost of travel is constantly increasing. As a result, many organizations investigated alternatives to travel. One promising substitute was the **teleconference,** a system by which individuals in different cities could interact by means of television. At its most sophisticated level, here's how a teleconference would work. Let's assume that individuals in three different cities are involved. Each conference site is equipped

TV Wars

High-Definition TV (HDTV) means more than just better looking pictures. It also means $145 *billion* market in the next twenty years, which could generate more than 100,000 new jobs. These high stakes have prompted an all-out struggle among consumer electronics manufacturers in Japan, Europe, and the United States to see who will dominate this market. As of early 1989, the United States was not winning.

The Japanese are starting their MUSE HDTV system in 1990. They have formally asked the International Radio Consultative Committee (IRCC, the body that decides technical matters in international radio and television) to name the MUSE system as the world standard for HDTV. The electronics companies of Western Europe, concerned that this request would mean a Japanese monopoly over future TV set manufacturing, convinced the IRCC not to make a decision until after 1990. Then they quickly organized a consortium to compete with the Japanese, and after a crash research and development program that cost more than $200 million, Phillips NV, leader of the effort, announced its MAC HDTV system. Neither system, however, is compatible with American TV sets.

In the race for HDTV, the United States started off at a disadvantage since only one manufacturing company, Zenith, is still American-owned. The rest are owned either by Japanese or European companies. Nonetheless, American research centers, under pressure from the FCC to meet a September 1988 deadline for proposing new TV systems, came up with proposals for ATV (advanced TV). ATV is not as good as HDTV, but it is compatible with existing American sets.

The eventual U.S. and world standards are yet to be decided. That will probably happen after 1991. If the United States wins, it will mean that the current $15 billion trade deficit in consumer electronics products would be erased. If the United States loses, the trade gap gets a lot worse.

with two-way video and audio equipment. Signals are sent by microwave using communications satellites. Thus, the people in location one can make a presentation over TV complete with graphs and visual aids to the people in the other two locations. In turn, the participants in the other cities can ask questions of the people who made the presentation. Personnel in a central control room direct the conference. They decide what scene to show on the TV monitors and what audio signals are to be transmitted.

Teleconferencing was enjoying a boom as the eighties closed. There were more than 12,000 satellite receiving sites at corporations and other organizations. Big hotel chains like Hilton and Holiday Inn had their own private networks for video meetings. Big companies are optimistic about this technology. In 1985, the Compaq Computer Corporation used a videoconference to introduce two new models to dealers in the United States, Canada, and Europe by means of an elaborate setup using three different communication satellites. About 3000 people saw the finished product—at a cost of more than a quarter of a million dollars, a tidy sum but less than it would have cost to bring all the participants to Compaq's base in Texas. It appears that the long-term prospect for the teleconference is excellent.

Telecommuting is another example of substituting communication for travel. The majority of the labor force in the United States has jobs concerned with transmitting or manipulating information. A lot of this work involves computer terminals and word processors. With the proper communication links, a lot of this work could be done at home, saving employees the expense and trouble of commuting to work.

Telecommuting systems have three basic parts: (1) a central computer that distributes the work to be done and receives the finished product; (2) a computer terminal where the person actually performs the work to be done; and (3) a communication link, usually over phone lines, that connects the terminal to the central computer. The most appropriate work for telecommuting involves computer programming, data analysis, and word processing. The most common kind of remote work stations are quite simple: a computer, a printer, and some file cabinets located in a study, bedroom, or kitchen. A more flexible alternative is the portable work station. Thanks to light weight, lap-sized computers, an employee can move from place to place, hooking up with the central computer only when it's necessary to transmit work or to receive further assignments.

As it currently stands, about 500 U.S. companies have some type of telecommuting program employing about 600,000 telecommuters. Consider some specifics. Blue Cross and Blue Shield of South Carolina has installed personal computers in the homes of its data entry clerks, who earn from four to ten cents per line for their work. The Grumman Corporation has about forty engineers working at a satellite office in Florida. They telecommute to Grumman's New York office because the company couldn't persuade them to relocate there.

The field has grown so fast that there's now a monthly newsletter, *Telecommuting Review,* devoted to it. As the technology improves and more workers and companies discover the benefits, some experts predict that by the year 2000 at least 15 million people will be telecommuters.

It's easy to see the potential of telecommuting and teleconferencing for higher education. For better or worse, much of the instruction that takes place in college uses the lecture method—a technique that has shown little change since medieval times. There is nothing inherently wrong with the lecture method, but there is no compelling reason why lecturer and lecturees have to assemble in the same place to get the thing done. Instead of traipsing across campus in a rainstorm to get to a dreary lecture hall filled with 150 other bodies where you take your seat in front of someone with a chronic sinus problem, it would be far easier for students (and professors) to do the whole thing over interactive TV. At the appointed hour, a student could tumble out of bed, switch on the TV, and there, in living color, would be the professor talking about today's topic. As the session went on, the professor could call up films, tapes, TV graphics, and other visual devices far superior to chalkboards and overhead projectors. If a student had a question, he or she would merely press a button on the keypad, and the instructor's console would light up, thus alerting him or her that a student had raised a question. The student then would ask the question by switching on a small microphone on top of the TV screen. The professor would hear the question and could then answer it. Would you need to take notes with such a system? You could, but it might make more sense to make a videotape of the whole session for later review. Many feel that the above arrangement would be a big improvement over the present system.

THE FAR FUTURE

The laser has already been widely used in medicine, engineering, and data transmission. In the field of mass communication, the area of laser application with the most promise appears to be **holography.** Briefly defined, holography is three-di-

---

What Will They Think of Next?

Scientists working with the Media Lab at the Massachusetts Institute of Technology are investigating the following:

- Holographic X-rays that let surgeons peek around bones and other organs before operating.

- A computerized synthetic performer that plays the piano in perfect synch with one to five live musicians.

- Interactive videodiscs that create "video travelogues" and "movie maps" of major U.S. tourist sites.

- Fiber optic cables that deliver movies directly to the home via phone lines, allowing the consumer to see every movie ever made on demand.

- Electronic cameras that store snapshots on microchips, eliminating film.

- Holographic projection systems that display sporting events in miniature on the living room floor.

---

mensional (3-D) lensless photography done with laser light. In the following section, we will briefly explore the promise and current problems of holography.

Lasers and Coherent Light

The theory of holography was developed during the late 1940s by Dennis Gabor, a Hungarian physicist. Gabor discovered that if interference patterns created by coherent light waves reflecting from an object were captured on a photosensitive material, they could be reconstructed to form a three-dimensional image. Familiar sources of light such as the sun and electric light bulbs emit light irregularly. As a result, the light waves have different frequencies and travel in different directions. Coherent light, on the other hand, is made up of light waves of the same wavelength, emitted in a coordinated way so that they move "in step" much like soldiers in a close-order drill. Gabor tried using a mercury arc lamp, but although the results demonstrated the validity of his theory, they were not impressive.

An actual demonstration of holography had to be postponed until someone created a reliable source of coherent light. By 1962, someone had created such a source the laser. A laser emits a constant stream of light waves at a uniform frequency. This beam of radiated light is very intense and it is coherent; since it is almost perfectly parallel, it does not spread out or diffuse as it travels. If you pointed a flashlight at the moon, the light waves would eventually reach the moon but would be so scattered that it would be hard to detect their arrival. A pencil-thin beam of laser light, however, would arrive at the moon in essentially the same form as that in which it left the Earth—the beam would be about the same thickness (Fig. 23.3).

With the invention of the laser, physicists could now conclusively demonstrate Gabor's theory of holography. In 1962, two scientists at the University of Michigan, Emmitt Leith and Jaris Upatnieks, put Gabor's theory to the test by using a laser as the light source for creating 3-D images. Their experiments confirmed that Gabor's theory was correct. In 1971, Dennis Gabor received the Nobel Prize in physics for his theory of holography.

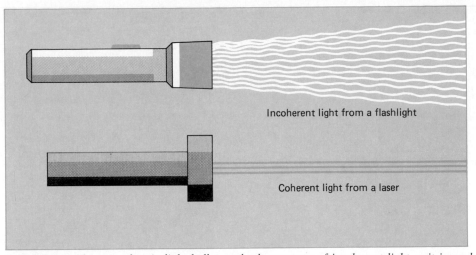

Incoherent light from a flashlight

Coherent light from a laser

FIGURE 23.3 *The sun, electric light bulbs, and other sources of incoherent light emit irregular light waves of different frequencies that spread out in different directions. Laser, or coherent light, however, is composed of light waves of the same length, moving ''in step'' with one another. The intense beam produced is almost parallel and diffuses only slightly, even after traveling considerable distances.*

Holograms

The three-dimensional image created by holography is called a **hologram.** It is important to recognize that a hologram is not the same kind of three-dimensional image created by viewing two slightly different images through polarized or colored glasses (the method used for 3-D movies and TV commercials). You do not need glasses to see a hologram. The image is truly three-dimensional and can be viewed from different positions and different angles. You can even see around or behind objects. In fact, objects in the foreground of the image will eclipse objects in the background as your position changes. In short, the hologram is an accurate three-dimensional representation of the scene it records.

A hologram generates a three-dimensional image by rebuilding the original light waves that are reflected from an object. The simplest method of creating a hologram involves splitting a laser beam into two parts. One beam, the reference beam, bounces off a mirror directly onto a photographic plate; the other, the object beam, reflects off the object or scene being photographed. The photographic plate is located so that it will be struck where the two beams meet and form an interference pattern composed of light waves from one source mingling with light waves from the other. A similar effect occurs when two stones are dropped into a pool of water and the two concentric rings of ripples converge. This interference pattern, captured in the photographic emulsion, is the hologram.

To view a hologram, a person looks directly at the highly sensitive photographic plate while it is illuminated with laser light (or in some cases, ordinary white light). The photographic film or plate becomes a ''window,'' and the three-dimensional object appears to float in space either behind or in front of the window, depending on the technique used to create the hologram. The three-dimensional illusion occurs because the observer perceives the waves as coming from the actual object rather than from the hologram. Figure 23.4, page 574, is a simplified version of how a hologram is created.

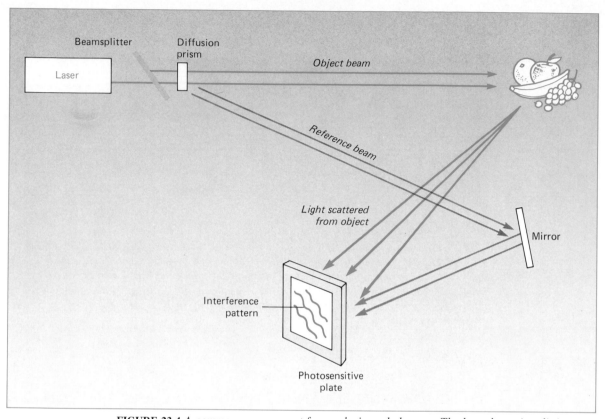

FIGURE 23.4 *A common arrangement for producing a hologram: The laser beam is split into two parts. One, the reference beam, is reflected from a mirror so as to strike a photographic plate. The other, the object beam, reflects off the object being photographed. The hologram is produced by the interference pattern formed where these two beams meet and are recorded on the photographic emulsion.*

There is a certain amount of shock associated with one's initial viewing of a hologram, for the sight of an image popping off the photographic plate toward the viewer is somewhat disconcerting. (The feeling may resemble what moviegoers of the 1880s felt when they first saw moving pictures.) The natural urge is to reach out and touch the object hanging there in space. Naturally, a person's hand passes right through the image since the object isn't really there but exists only in the person's optical system and brain.

During the 1970s, the United States underwent a surge of interest in holography. RCA, General Electric, and IBM, among others, spent large sums on holographic research. McDonnell Douglas Corporation created a life-sized holographic portrait of Dennis Gabor, Tiffany used holograms in its window display, and Salvador Dali dabbled in holographic art. The 1970s saw the birth of holographic motion pictures that could be viewed by using ordinary white light. Although these early films were short and crude-looking, they convincingly showed that holographic motion pictures were possible. (If you saw *Star Wars*, you saw a rendition of a holographic motion picture when R2D2 replayed Princess Leia's message. What you saw was a two-dimensional representation of what a hologram would look like. It was not an actual

Holography is a very promising application of laser technology. Here a technician examines a laser-etched hologram of a bald eagle printed on sheets of foil, each containing 25,000 three-dimensional images. The eagle was used on the cover of National Geographic, *the first magazine to use a hologram on its cover. (AP/Wide World Photos)*

hologram.) Advertisers were also interested in holograms, and publishers of medical books began binding holograms of various organs and tissues into their texts.

The increased interest in holography also uncovered some major technical problems that will have to be overcome before holography can become a true mass medium. First, it is difficult to make holographic movies that can be shown to large audiences; ''projecting'' a hologram poses special problems. Second, no one has yet invented a way to match a soundtrack to holographic film. Third, a hologram that yields true-to-life colors is still awaiting development—most current holograms are tinged with yellow, red, or green. Finally, holograms are still extremely expensive to produce.

Some progress toward solving these problems was being made in the 1980s. A group of Russian scientists was developing a specially constructed, seven-foot-wide holographic screen that could display holographic motion pictures to an audience of about 400 persons. A New York company developed a way to increase the size of the viewing window and magnify the image size so that the viewer would see the 3-D image floating several feet in front of the frame. Figure 23.5, page 576, represents what this arrangement would look like. (Unfortunately, a two-dimensional book page can't do justice to a three-dimensional hologram, so Fig. 23.5 is an artist's conception of what this system might look like.)

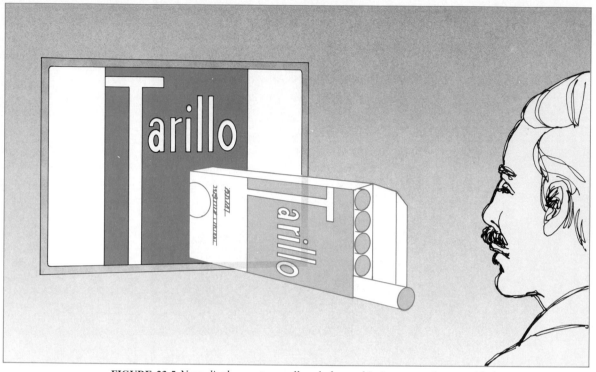

FIGURE 23.5 *New display systems allow holographic images to be magnified ten or more times life size without loss of their three-dimensional characteristics. The 3-D image appears to hang in midair several feet in front of the viewing window.*

Holography has made other advances in the 1980s. It is now routinely used by many industries to test stress loads on such things as airplane and automobile parts. Holograms can now be mass produced, and credit card companies are placing holograms on their plastic cards to guard against counterfeits. There are now holographic greeting cards. Holograms of scenes from *ET* were placed in bags of Reese's Pieces candy as a promotional device. *National Geographic* became the first magazine to put a hologram on its cover. (The magazine sold an additional 400,000 copies of that issue.)

Thanks to the development of a pulse laser, holographic portraits can now be done in a fraction of a second. Astronomer Carl Sagan, Gloria Steinem, Chicago Bears' coach Mike Ditka, and David Byrnc (a Talking Head whose portrait was a floating head) are just some of the many celebrities who have posed for the 3-D portrait. (The price is not cheap. One Illinois company charges $950 for a five-by-seven inch picture.)

And Zebra Books, which specializes in steamy historical romance novels, has begun to put holographic stickers on the cover of paperbacks to catch consumers' attention. Distribution of Zebra Books has gone up 200 percent.

Holography When Perfected

Holography in the late 1980s is about at the same point that motion pictures were at in the 1880s or television in the 1930s. Significant problems have to be solved, but there appears to be no essential reason why holograms cannot be made into whatever form we desire. Skeptics might say that holography is an interesting phenomenon that will remain merely a curiosity and that it will never amount to much. (Other skeptics made the same comments about early radio, TV, and movies.) It will take time, but holography appears on its way to becoming an important mass communication medium.

When perfected, the first application of holography will be as a substitute for motion pictures. New theaters will have to be developed since a holographic film will not take place on a flat plane but will occur out toward the audience. The "holofilm" theaters will probably be horseshoe shaped, with a viewing area thrusting out into the spectators' seats. Of course, all the conventional aesthetics of the flat screen will no longer work for 3-D movies, and a new set will have to be worked out for this art form. After holographic motion pictures, the next step will be holographic TV or perhaps laservision (LV?). Home architecture will have to accommodate 3-D viewing, and a whole wall of a room in a house will be converted into a holographic viewing window. Family members will sit along the walls to watch the action, which will appear to occur in the middle of the room. If a person wants to peer around the edge of the scene, he or she will simply get up and walk to the far corner to see what can be seen. For example, suppose you were watching the twenty-first–century version of "The Tonight Show" and wondered what things were kept on the table behind the guest's chair. You could get up, walk to the edge of the screen, and look in back of the chair and see for yourself (provided the optical system was sophisticated enough).

In its early stages, holographic TV will be expensive to produce. This means that it will have to attract large audiences in order to be commercially successful either as an advertiser-supported or pay medium. Consequently, the content of "holovision" will be general in its appeal, and the mass audience, now in a state of fragmentation, may be resurrected by holographic TV.

What lies farther down the road with holography? Now we are dealing with sheer speculation—but sometimes sheer speculation has an interesting tendency to come true. One plan calls for affixing a tiny electrical charge to the surface of the holographic image as it is suspended in space. When a person's hand touches the surface of the hologram, the tiny electrical charges will stimulate the nerve endings of the fingers and the person will be fooled into thinking that he or she is touching something solid. Holography would then be extended into another sense realm, and the distinction between image and reality would be obscured. The perceptual problems this would create would be staggering since it would be difficult to distinguish your real friends from their holograms.

CAREERS IN THE FUTURE

What are the implications of all this change for young people who plan media careers? In the first place, expect to be retrained several times in your career. Newspaper reporters, for example, had to set aside their typewriters and learn how to operate video-display terminals.

Television reporters had to learn to work with portable ENG equipment. Employees in the sound-recording industry are now coping with the change from analog to digital recording. The emerging technologies guarantee that your education will continue on the job.

Second, students should learn to be flexible. New communication media mean expanding employment opportunities. For instance, in the past a person interested in reporting for the print media had two basic choices: newspapers or magazines. Today, there are job possibilities in videotex, teletext, on-line computer data bases, and specialized information services. A young person interested in TV production is no longer limited to broadcast television stations and networks. Opportunities exist in cable systems, cable networks, private corporations, and specialized production companies. In sum, young people need to be able to evolve as their profession develops, be responsive to trends, and at the same time maintain the principles of their profession even in the midst of all this change.

THE FARTHER FUTURE

After holograms, what next? Now we are in the realm of science fiction, but it's still worth thinking about. Aldous Huxley, in *Brave New World,* suggested the "feelies," a system in which viewers of a motion picture were hooked up with electrodes and had the appropriate brain center stimulated electrically so that they would "feel" what they were seeing on screen. Science fiction writer Ray Bradbury, in his short story "The Veldt," suggests a system of audience-participation media in which viewers suddenly find themselves transported through the screen and actually become part of the media world, interacting with the media characters. (In Bradbury's story the media world becomes a little too real, and some audience members don't survive their "trip.") Others have suggested a media implant—a tiny receiving and sending station implanted surgically at birth behind the mastoid bone and hooked into the brain and the central nervous system. The implant becomes our own personal telephone, radio, and, if hooked into the brain's optic center, television set. Some writers have even suggested that the brain be wired so that information and entertainment could be pumped directly into the cerebral cortex, totally bypassing eyes, ears, and other sense organs. All of these ideas are certainly a far cry from sitting in a movie theater munching popcorn.

In any event, perhaps the best way we might close this chapter is to quote scientist and science fiction writer Arthur C. Clarke. Someone once asked Clarke what kind of communication systems we will likely have in the future. Replied Clarke, "Whatever kinds we can think of."

SUGGESTIONS FOR FURTHER READING

The sources listed below contain additional information on the future of mass media.

BERNER, JEFF, *The Holography Book,* New York: Avon, 1980.
CLARKE, ARTHUR C., *Voices from the Sky,* New York: Pyramid, 1965.
GROSS, LYNNE SCHAFER, *The New Television Technologies,* Dubuque, Iowa: William C. Brown, 1986.
KASPER, JOSEPH, *The Hologram Book,* Englewood Cliffs, N.J.: Prentice-Hall, 1985.
"The Media Decade," *Next,* February 1981, pp. 27–63.
RICE, RONALD, *The New Media,* Beverly Hills, Calif.: Sage Publications, 1984.
SINGLETON, LOY, *Telecommunications in the Information Age,* Cambridge, Mass.: Ballinger, 1986.
SMITH, ANTHONY, *Goodbye Gutenberg,* New York: Oxford University Press, 1980.
YOUNGBLOOD, GENE, *Expanded Cinema,* New York: E. P. Dutton, 1970.

Glossary

A.C. Nielsen Company. The world's largest market research firm, best known for network TV ratings.

Acculturation. In a media context, the tendency of reporters or other media professionals to adopt the ideas and attitudes of the groups they cover or with which they have a great deal of contact.

Agenda-Setting Effect. The influence of the mass media created by emphasizing certain topics, thus causing people to perceive these same issues as important.

Agents of Socialization. The various people or organizations that contribute to the socialization of an individual.

AM. Amplitude modulation of radio waves.

Arbitron. The professional research organization that measures radio and TV audiences.

Audience Flow. Scheduling TV programs so that the audience attracted to one show naturally carries over to the following show.

Audience-Generated Feedback. Feedback that occurs when one or more audience members attempt to communicate their opinions or points of view to a mass medium.

Audit Bureau of Circulations (ABC). An organization formed by advertisers and publishers in 1914 to establish ground rules for counting circulation data.

Authoritarian Theory. The prevailing belief that a ruling elite should guide the intellectually inferior masses.

Backmasking. Technique used to hide a message in a record or tape so that it can be heard only by playing it backward.

Barter Deal. In TV syndication, the program syndicator keeps most of the available commercial minutes to sell in the syndicated program.

Billboard. The sound-recording industry trade publication that tabulates record popularity.

Block Booking. A policy of major film studios that required theater owners to show several of a studio's low-quality films before they could receive the same studio's top-quality films.

Brownlines. Sample copies of the final edition of a magazine.

Business to Business Advertising. Advertising directed not at the general public but at other businesses.

Campaign. In advertising, a large number of ads that stress the same theme and appear over a specified length of time.

Carriage Fee. In cable TV, a fee per subscriber paid by the local cable company to cable programming services.

Cash Plus Barter Deal. In TV syndication, a station pays cash to a syndication company and gives up some commercial minutes to the company to sell nationally.

Catharsis. A release of pent-up emotion or energy occurring as a function of viewing certain art forms, such as theater or music.

Catharsis Theory. A theory that suggests that viewing aggression will purge the viewer's aggressive feelings.

CATV. Cable television system introduced in the 1950s in order to extend conventional television signals to fringe areas.

Cease-and-Desist Order. A Federal Trade Commission order notifying an advertiser that a certain practice violates the law. Failure to comply with a cease-and-desist order can result in fines being levied against the advertiser.

Channel. The pathway by which a message travels from sender to receiver.

Churn. In cable TV, the tendency of subscribers to cancel shortly after signing up for cable services.

Circulation. The total number of copies of a publication delivered to newsstands, vending machines, or subscribers.

Clock Hour. Radio format that specifies every element of the program.

Cold Type. A process in which the elements of a newspaper page are pasted down and photographed; the finished product is then transferred onto a plate for the printing press.

Commercial Television System. Local stations whose income is derived from selling time on their facilities to advertisers.

Communications Act of 1934. Act of Congress creating the Federal Communications Commission.

Compact Disc (CD). A sound system using laser technology that reproduces audio quality very precisely.

Comprehensive Layout. The finished model of a print ad.

Concept Testing. A type of media-organized feedback in which a one- or two-paragraph description for a new series is presented to a sample of viewers for their reactions.

Consent Order. Federal Trade Commission order in which the advertiser agrees to halt a certain advertising practice.

Consumer Advertising. Advertising directed at the general public.

Contagion Effect. In a media context, the theory that reports of violence can instigate new violence.

Controlled Circulation. A type of circulation in which publications are sent free or distributed to a select readership, such as airline passengers or motel guests.

Conversational Currency. Topic material presented by the media that provides a common ground for social conversations.

Copy. Headlines and message in an ad.

Corantos. Sheets of foreign and commercial news that originated in Holland around 1620 and were the forerunners of newspapers.

Corporation for Public Broadcasting (CPB). The network office of the Public Broadcasting Service.

Counter programming. Airing a program designed to appeal to a different segment of the audience than those on competing stations.

Creative Boutique. Advertising organization that specializes in the creative side of advertising.

Credibility. The trust that the audience holds for media that perform surveillance functions.

Crystallization. The sharpening and elaboration of a vaguely held attitude or predisposition.

Cultivation Analysis. An area of research that examines whether television and other media encourage perceptions of reality that are more consistent with media portrayals than with actuality.

Cycle. In all-news radio, the amount of time that elapses before the program order is repeated.

Decoding. The activity in the communication process by which physical messages are translated into a form that has eventual meaning for the receiver.

Demo. A demonstration tape used to sell a musical performer.

Demography. The study of audience characteristics such as age, sex, and socioeconomic status.

Developmental Journalism. Type of journalism practiced by many Third World countries that stresses national goals and economic development.

Digital Audio Tape (DAT). High-quality audio tape that uses digital audio technology to achieve fidelity comparable to that of a compact disc.

Direct Broadcasting by Satellite (DBS). A system in which a home TV set receives a signal directly from an orbiting satellite.

Dissemination Stage. In a news diffusion study, the period of time during which news spreads through a particular society.

Distribution System. The actual cables that deliver the signals to CATV subscribers.

Diurnals. Seventeenth-century daily publication of domestic and local events.

Double Feature. Practice started by theaters in the 1930s of showing two feature films on the same bill.

Dummy. A plan or blueprint for upcoming magazine issues that shows the contents in their proper order.

Duopoly Rule. Federal Communications Commission provision that prohibits ownership of more than one AM, one FM, or one TV station in a single community.

Dysfunction. Consequences that are undesirable from the point of view of the welfare of society.

Editorial Policies. Guidelines followed by a media organization with regard to certain public issues or political positions.

Electronic News Gathering (ENG). Producing and airing field reports using small, lightweight portable TV equipment.

Elite Audience Stage. A stage of audience evolution in which the audience for the medium is relatively small and represents the more educated and refined segments of society.

Encoding. The activity in the communication process by which thoughts and ideas from the source are translated into a form that may be perceived by the senses.

Equal Opportunities Rule. Part of the Communications Act of 1934. Section 315 allows bona fide candidates for public office to gain access to a broadcast medium during political campaigns.

Exit Poll. Survey technique in which voters are asked whom they voted for as soon as they leave the polling booth. Used to make computer projections of election winners.

Experiment. A research technique that stresses controlled conditions and manipulates variables.

Fair Use. Under copyright law, people can use copies of the protected work for legitimate purposes.

Federal Communications Commission. A regulatory agency, composed of five individuals appointed by the president, whose responsibilities include broadcast and wire regulation.

Feedback. The responses of the receiver that shape and alter subsequent messages from the source.

Field Experiment. An experiment that is conducted in a natural setting as opposed to a laboratory.

First Amendment. The first amendment of the Bill of Rights, stating that Congress shall make no law . . . abridging the freedom of speech, or of the press.

First Sale Doctrine. Motion picture companies make a profit on only the first sale of a videocassette. The studios make no additional money from cassette rentals.

Flexographic Printing. A printing technique that cuts paper waste and makes ink less likely to rub off on a reader's hand.

FM. Frequency modulation of radio waves.

Focus Group. A group of ten to fifteen people led by a moderator that discusses predetermined topics.

Format. Consistent programming designed to appeal to a certain segment of the audience.

Format Wheel. A pie chart of an hour divided into segments representing different program elements.

Four-Walling. A practice that allows the distributor to rent a theater at a specified fee for a predetermined length of time and to keep all box-office receipts.

Franchise. An exclusive right to operate a business in a given territory.

Freedom of Information Act. Law that states that every federal executive branch agency must publish instructions on what methods a member of the public should follow to get information.

Full-Service Agency. An ad agency that handles all phases of advertising for its clients.

Functional Approach. A methodology that holds something is best understood by examining how it is used.

Gag Rules. Judicial orders that restrict trial participants from giving information to the media or that actually restrain media coverage of events that occur in court.

Galleys. Sheets of paper used to display typeset copy.

Gatekeeper. Any person (or group) who controls what media material eventually reaches the public.

Gramophone. A ''talking machine'' patented in 1887 by Emile Berliner that utilized a disc instead of a cylinder.

Graphophone. A recording device similar to the phonograph, but utilizing a wax cylinder rather than tinfoil.

Grazing. Method of TV watching in which a viewer rapidly scans all the available channels using a remote-control device.

Head End. The antenna and related equipment of the CATV system that receives and processes distant television signals so that they may be sent to subscribers' homes.

Heavy-Metal Sound. Counterculture musical trend of the 1960s–1970s, characterized by a vaguely threatening style and heavy utilization of amplification and electronic equipment.

Hertz (Hz). The basic unit of frequency. Named after German physicist Heinrich Hertz.

Hicklin Rule. A longstanding obscenity standard based upon whether a book or other item contains isolated passages that might deprave or corrupt the mind of the most susceptible person.

High-Definition Television (HDTV). High-resolution television system that uses over a thousand scanning lines as compared with traditional 525-line system.

Hologram. The three-dimensional image created by holography.

Holography. Three-dimensional lensless photography by means of a laser beam.

House Drop. The section of the CATV cable that connects the feeder cable to the subscriber's TV set.

Hypodermic Needle Approach. A sociological view that regarded the mass communication audience as a collection of isolated individuals who responded in essentially the same way to a message presented via the media.

Independents. Radio or TV stations unaffiliated with any network.

Injunction. A court order that requires an individual to do something or to stop doing something.

Instrumental Surveillance. A media function that occurs when the media transmit information that is useful and helpful in everyday life.

Interactive Audience Stage. A stage of audience evolution in which the individual audience member has some selective control over what he or she chooses to see or hear.

Interactive Cable System. An arrangement whereby signals can be sent from the head end to the home and also from the home to the head end. Also known as two-way TV.

Interpersonal Communication. A method of communication in which one person (or group) interacts with another person (or group) without the aid of a mechanical device.

Jazz. A form of popular music that emerged during the Roaring Twenties era and was noted for its spontaneity and disdain of convention.

Jazz Journalism. Journalism of the Roaring Twenties era that was characterized by a lively style and a richly illustrated tabloid format.

Joint Operating Agreement (JOA). In order to preserve editorial competition, two newspapers merge their business and printing operations but maintain separate newsrooms.

Joint Venture. Method of movie financing where several companies pool resources to finance films.

Kenaf. A shrub whose pulp is being tested as a replacement for paper.

Kinetoscope. The first practical motion picture camera and viewing device developed by William Dickson in 1889.

Libel. Written defamation that tends to injure a person's reputation or good name or that diminishes the esteem, respect, or goodwill due a person.

Libel per Quod. Written material that becomes libelous under certain circumstances.

Libel per Se. Falsely written accusations (such as labeling a person a ''thief'' or a ''swindler'') that automatically constitute libel.

Libertarian Theory. The assumption that all human beings are rational decision makers and that governments exist to serve the individual.

Limited Partnership. Method of movie financing in which a number of investors put up a specified amount of money for a film.

Linkage. The ability of the mass media to join different elements of society that are not directly connected by interpersonal channels.

Linotype Machine. A machine for molding lines of type from hot metal.

Low-Power Television (LPTV). A TV station that broadcasts with lower power than the normal broadcast station and that has a coverage area of twelve to fifteen miles in radius.

Machine-Assisted Interpersonal Communication. A method of communication involving one or more persons and a mechanical device (or devices) with one or more receivers. Possibly separated by time and space.

Macroanalysis. A sociological perspective that considers the functions performed by a system (i.e., mass media) for the entire society.

Magazine. In colonial times, literally storehouses of material gathered from books, pamphlets, and newspapers and bound together under one cover.

Mainstreaming. In cultivation analysis, the tendency of differences apparently due to cultural and social factors to disappear among heavy TV viewers.

Management by Objectives (MBO). Management technique that sets observable, measurable goals for an organization to achieve.

Mass Audience Stage. A stage of audience evolution in which the potential audience consists of the entire population, with all segments of society likely to be represented.

Mass Communication. The process by which a complex organization, with the aid of one or more machines, produces and transmits public messages that are directed at large, heterogeneous, and scattered audiences.

Mass Media. The channels of mass communication.

Mechanicals. Completed paste-ups (of magazine pages) ready to be taken to the camera room.

Media Buying Service. Organization that specializes in buying media time for advertisers.

Media-Originated Feedback. Feedback consisting of information about the audience that media industries go out of their way to gather.

Mediamark (MRI). Company that measures magazine readership.

Message. The actual physical product in the communication process that the source encodes.

Microanalysis. A sociological perspective that considers the functions performed by a system (i.e., mass media) for the individual.

Mix-Down. The process of reducing multiple recording tracks down to a two-track stereo master.

Motion Picture Patents Company (MPPC). An organization formed by the nine leading film and film equipment manufacturers in 1908 for the purpose of controlling the motion picture industry.

MPAA Rating System. The G-PG-PG-13-R-X rating system for movies administered by the Motion Picture Association of America.

Muckrakers. Term coined by Theodore Roosevelt to describe the reform movement undertaken by leading magazines in the 1890s. Corrupt practices of business and government were exposed to the general public by crusading members of the press.

Multiple System Operator (MSO). A cable company that owns more than one cable system.

Multistep Flow Model. A classic theory suggesting that the persuasive effects of mass media alone will be unlikely to change audience opinions on important issues because the media's influence is filtered through a social network of opinion leaders.

National Advertiser. Advertiser who sells a product all across the country.

Network. An organization composed of interconnecting broadcasting stations that cuts costs by airing the same programs.

Newsbreak Stage. The time it takes for reporters to transmit the essential facts of a story back to a media organization, which in turn publishes or broadcasts the news.

News Diffusion. The spread of information through a society over time.

Newshole. The amount of space available each day in a newspaper for news.

Nickelodeon. A popular name for the many penny arcades and amusement centers that emerged around the beginning of the twentieth century and specialized in recordings and film.

90–10 Split. Common method of dividing motion picture box office revenue. After the exhibitor subtracts operating expenses, the distributor takes 90 percent of what's left and the exhibitor keeps 10 percent.

Noise. In communication, anything that interferes with the delivery of a message.

Noncommercial Television System. Those stations whose income is derived from sources other than the sale of advertising time.

Nonduplication Rule. FCC rule passed in 1965, stating that an AM–FM combination may not duplicate its AM content on its FM channel for more than 50 percent of the time.

O and Os. VHF broadcasting stations owned and operated by each of the three commercial networks.

Observational Learning. A form of education in which individuals learn by observing the actions of others.

Offset Plate. In the newspaper printing process, a plate is made by placing a photographic negative between glass and a sheet of photosensitive metal and exposing the plate to light.

Offset Printing. A process that transfers an image of a newspaper page captured on a photosensitive plate to a rubberized blanket and then to the surface of paper.

Oligopoly. An economic situation in which a few mutually interdependent firms dominate the market.

Ombudsperson. An individual in a media organization assigned to handle complaints from audience members.

One-stops. Individuals who sell records to retail stores and juke box operators who are not in a position to buy directly from the record company.

Operating Policies. Guidelines that cover the everyday problems and situations that crop up during the operation of a media organization.

Option Contract. An exclusive right to put into effect an agreement for rights or services over a fixed period of time.

Page Proof. A page-size piece of paper with all the elements—type, photos, and illustrations—positioned in their proper places.

Paid Circulation. A type of circulation in which the reader must purchase a magazine through a subscription or at a newsstand.

Panel Study. A research method in which data are collected from the same individuals at different points in time.

Parasocial Relationship. A situation whereby audience members develop a sense of kinship or friendship with media personalities.

Pass-Along Audience. That portion of a magazine's total audience composed of individuals who pick up copies of a magazine while at the doctor's office, at work, traveling, etc.

Payola. Bribes of gifts and money paid to DJs by record companies in order to gain favorable airplay for their releases.

Pay per View (PPV). A system that allows cable TV subscribers to pay a one-time fee to view one specific program or movie.

Penny Press. Term that describes the mass-appeal press of the early nineteenth century.

Peoplemeter. A mechanical device used to measure TV viewing that electronically records individual TV watching data.

Percentage Split. Method by which exhibitor and distributor divide the box office receipts of a motion picture.

Persistence of Vision. Quality of the human eye that enables it to retain an image for a split second after the image has actually disappeared.

Phi Phenomenon. Tendency of the human perceptual system to perceive continuous motion between two stationary points of light that blink on and off. Basis for the illusion of motion in motion pictures.

Phonograph. A ''talking machine'' developed by Thomas Edison in the late 1870s. The hand-cranked device preserved sound on a tinfoil-wrapped cylinder.

Photocomposition Machine. High-speed, computerized device that translates electronic impulses into images and words.

Pickup. A technique of financing a motion picture.

Pilot. The first episode of a projected television series.

Pilot Testing. A process that involves showing a sample audience an entire episode of a show and recording their reactions.

Policy Book. At radio and TV stations, a book that spells out philosophy and standards of operation and identifies what practices are encouraged or discouraged.

Political Press. A polarization of the press into factions advocating specific political views; reached its extreme around 1800–1820.

Portfolio. A collection of one's personal work.

Positioning. In advertising, stressing the unique selling point of a product or service to differentiate it from the competition.

Press Council. An independent agency whose job it is to monitor the day-to-day performance of the media.

Press-Radio War. A series of confrontations between newspaper publishers and radio station owners caused by economic competition in the 1930s.

Primary Audience. That portion of a magazine's total audience made up of subscribers or those who buy it at the newsstand.

Prime-Time Access Rule. Rule adopted in 1970 intended to expand program diversity by barring network programs from the 7:30-8:00 P.M. (E.S.T.) time slot.

Prior Restraint. An attempt by the government to censor the press by restraining it from publishing or broadcasting material.

Programming. In radio and TV, deciding what programs to produce and where to place them in the schedule.

Property. A creative idea submitted to a film producer.

Prosocial Behavior. A general term used by researchers to describe behaviors that are judged to be desirable or worthwhile under the circumstances.

Public Broadcasting Act of 1967. Congressional act that established the Public Broadcasting System.

Publicity. Placing stories in the mass media.

Rack Jobbers. Individuals who service record racks located in variety and large department stores by choosing the records to be sold in each location.

Radio Act of 1927. Congressional act establishing the Federal Radio Commission, a regulatory body that would issue broadcasting licenses and organize operating times and frequencies.

Rating. The ratio of listeners to a particular station to all people in the market.

Receiver. The target of the message in the communication process.

Reinforcement. Support of existing attitudes and opinions by certain messages.

Resonance. In cultivation analysis, the situation in which a respondent's life experiences are reinforced by what is seen on TV, thus reinforcing the effect of TV content.

Retail (Local) Advertiser. Business that has customers only in one trading area.

Rough Layout. Early version of a print ad.

Satellite News Gathering (SNG). Using specially equipped vans and trucks to transmit live stories from any location via satellite.

Saturation Stage. In news diffusion, the stage at which most of the population has learned of an event and the story is no longer classified as news.

Sedition Act. Act of Congress passed in the late 1790s that made it a crime to write anything ''false, scandalous or malicious'' about the U.S. government or Congress; it was used to curb press criticism of government policies.

Sell-through Market. In home video, movies on cassettes that are meant to be bought by consumers rather than being rented from a video store.

Share of the Audience. The ratio of listeners to a particular station to the total number of listeners in the market.

Shield Laws. Legislation that defines the rights of a reporter to protect sources.

Simmons Market Research Bureau (SMRB). The organization that offers the most comprehensive feedback about magazine readership.

Slander. Spoken defamation. (In many states, if a defamatory statement is broadcast, it is considered to be libel, even though technically the words are not written. Libel is considered more harmful and usually carries more serious penalties.)

Sliding Scale. An arrangement whereby as the box-office revenue for a motion picture increases, so does the amount of money that the exhibitor must pay the distributor.

Social Responsibility Theory. The belief that the press has a responsibility to preserve democracy by properly informing the public and by responding to society's needs.

Social Utility Function. In psychological terms, the social integrative needs that spring from an individual's compulsion to affiliate with family, friends, and others in our society.

Socialization. The ways in which an individual comes to adopt the behavior and values of a group.

Source. The originator of a thought or idea subsequently transmitted to others in the communication process.

Specialized Audience Stage. A stage of audience evolution that is typified by fragmented, special-interest audience groups.

Status Conferral. A process by which media attention bestows a degree of prominence on certain issues or individuals.

Stimulation Theory. A theory that suggests viewing violence will actually stimulate an individual to behave more violently.

Storage Instantaneous Audimeter (SIA). A small device hooked to a television set that allows rapid computer retrieval of viewing information.

Storyboard. A series of drawings depicting the key scenes in an ad.

Straight Cash Deal. In TV syndication, a station pays a fee to a syndicator and retains the right to sell all the commercial spots in the program.

Strategic Planning. Management technique that sets long-range goals.

Subscription TV (STV). System in which conventional TV stations broadcast commercial-free programming to subscriber households equipped with a decoder.

Surveillance. The news and information function of the mass media.

Survey. A technique of gathering data that typically uses a questionnaire.

Symbiotic Relationships. In mass media, relationships of mutual benefit between industries; for example, television and film, radio and the record industry.

Tabloid. Heavily illustrated publication usually half the size of a normal newspaper page.

Tactical Planning. Management technique that sets short range goals.

Target Audience. In advertising, the segment of the population for whom the product or service has an appeal.

Telecommuting. Using computers, modems, and phone lines to transmit information and data from the home to the office instead of commuting.

Teleconference. System in which individuals in different cities interact via TV.

Teletext. Electronic news delivery system in which the viewer uses a computer to select information from a broad spectrum of electronic pages that can be viewed on a TV screen.

Tie-in. Releasing a message in one medium to coincide with some other media content. For example, books released along with motion pictures, record albums along with TV shows, etc.

Timeshifting. Recording programs off the air and playing them back when more convenient.

12-12-12 Rule. FCC regulation which permits an organization or individual to own twelve AM, twelve FM, and twelve TV stations.

UHF. The ultra-high frequency band of the electromagnetic spectrum. Channels 14-69 on the TV set.

Underground Press. A type of specialized reporting that emerged in the mid- to late 1960s, with emphasis on politically liberal news and opinion and cultural topics such as music, art, and film.

Uses-and-Gratifications Model. A model proposing that audience members have certain needs or drives that are satisfied by using both nonmedia and media sources.

Variety. The entertainment industry trade publication.

VHF. The very high frequency band of the electromagnetic spectrum. Channels 2-13 on the TV set.

Video-Display Terminal (VDT). An electronic display keyboard widely used for the composition and printing of news copy. It is capable of storing typed information that can later be called out on the viewing screen for further design and editing.

Videotex. Electronic news delivery system in which the viewer interacts with the computer in selecting the exact content choice desired.

Vitascope. An early motion picture projector developed by Thomas Edison.

Warning (Beware) Surveillance. A media function that occurs when the media inform the public of short-term, long-term, or chronic threats.

Yellow Journalism. Period of sensationalized journalism during the 1890s noted for its emphasis on sex, murder, popularized medicine, pseudoscience, self-promotion, and human-interest stories.

Zoned Edition. Newspaper that has special sections for specific geographic areas.

Index